Treasures in Isaiah

Good News in "The Gospel Prophet"

By

Ellet J. Waggoner

TEACH Services, Inc.
www.TEACHServices.com

Copyright © 2004 TEACH Services, Inc.
ISBN-13: 9781479615964
Library of Congress Control Number: 2002113818

Published originally in England as articles or editorials in the magazine, *The Present Truth.* Original British Spelling retained.

Published by
TEACH Services, Inc.
www.TEACHServices.com

Table of Contents

PREFACE

Thousands around the world are awaking to discover long-buried treasures of theological truth in the writings of Ellet J. Waggoner (1855-1916). A physician who early left a lucrative career in medicine to devote his life to the ministry, his heart was in love with the gospel as being very Good News. Paul had written, "I am not ashamed of the gospel of Christ, for it is the power of God unto salvation to everyone who believes" (Rom. 1:16). Waggoner also loved sharing with others the "unsearchable riches of Christ." He found them in Isaiah, as well as in the New Testament.

One afternoon young Waggoner caught a rare vision of the meaning of the cross of Christ. He resolved ever after to study the Bible with the sacrifice of the Son of God as its central truth. Building on the foundation of Martin Luther's grasp of justification by faith in Romans as "the clearest gospel of all," Waggoner came to see truths in Scripture that were fresh and beautiful to his contemporaries. They are also that to us today! Those who knew him best saw in him a "Christian gentleman" as well as a profound theologian.

In the autumn of 1888 he was invited to present before a conference of pastors, evangelists, and church leaders his remarkable studies on the New Covenant. These studies, now famous in history, electrified his church and its leadership and have become to many today a source of inspiration in Bible study and ministry. They believe that Waggoner was gifted in developing further Luther's understanding of righteousness by faith as a necessary preparation for a people who will be ready when Christ returns.

In presenting in book form Waggoner's studies in Isaiah, the publishers rejoice to offer a rare treasure to eager readers everywhere. Remembering that we are not to expect perfection in any one man's work (only in Christ!), thoughtful and discerning readers will discover herein almost innumerable gems that will make Isaiah glow with new light.

Carol Kawamoto

CHAPTER 1

THE GOSPEL OF ISAIAH

SMITING AND HEALING

Isaiah 1:1–9

1.   The vision of Isaiah the son of Amoz, which he saw concerning Judah and Jerusalem; in the days of Uzziah, Jotham, Ahaz, Hezekiah, kings of Judah: –

2.   Hear, O ye heavens; and give ear, O earth, For it is Jehovah that speaketh. I have nourished children, and brought them up; and even they have revolted from Me.

3.   The ox knoweth his possessor; and the ass the crib of his lord; but Israel knoweth not Me: neither doth My people consider.

4.   Ah sinful nation! A people laden with iniquity! A race of evil doers! children degenerate! They have forsaken Jehovah; they have rejected with disdain the Holy One of Israel; they are estranged from Him; they have turned their back upon Him.

5.   On what part will ye smite again, will ye add correction? The whole head is sick, and the whole heart faint;

6.   From the sole of the foot area to the head, there is no soundness therein; it is wound, and bruise, and putrefying sore; it hath not been pressed, neither hath it been bound; neither hath it been softened with ointment.

7.   Your country is desolate, your cities are burnt with fire; your land, before your eyes strangers devour it; and it is become desolate, as if destroyed by an inundation.

8.   And the daughter of Zion is left, as a shed in a vineyard; as a lodge in a garden of cucumbers, as a city taken by a siege.

9.   Had not Jehovah God of Hosts left us a remnant, we had soon become as Sodom; we had been like unto Gomorrah.

Inasmuch as everybody has the Bible in the so-called "Authorized Version," and can refer to it at pleasure, and very many have the Revised also, it has been thought best in the present study to give the readers the benefit of another translation. The one chosen has been that of Bishop Lowth, which is without doubt, as a whole, the best English translation of the prophecy of Isaiah. Accordingly we shall print the text of this, as above, and shall in the notes give the student the benefit of any other translations that serve to make any portion of the text more striking. This statement of the case will serve for the regular reader, so that it will not need to be repeated.

Let every one who proposes to derive lasting benefit from these studies of the Gospel according to Isaiah give heed to the following counsel: First of all study the text carefully. How? Read it again and again, taking special pains to find out exactly what it says. Note the dependence of every verse and sentence upon that which precedes. Nobody in the world can tell you anything that is true concerning the text, that is not found in the text itself; and if you give heed, you can tell what the Lord says as well as anybody; for He uses the language of the common people. The notes that follow are only designed to fix your attention more sharply on what is contained in the text, and so help you to retain it by associating it with other familiar portions of Scripture. You will see that nothing is introduced that is not contained in the text of the lesson, and will thus learn how rich is the Word of God.

"Hear, O heavens, and give ear, O earth." Why? Because the Lord hath spoken. When the Lord speaks, it is the time for every one in heaven and earth to keep silence. "The Lord is in His holy temple; let all the earth keep silence before Him." Hab. 2:20. "Job answered the Lord and said, Behold, I am vile; what shall I answer Thee? I will lay my hand upon my mouth. Once have I spoken; but I will not answer; yea, twice; but I will proceed no further." Job 40:3–5.

The importance of keeping still when the Lord speaks cannot be too strongly emphasized. When one of the great men of earth speaks on a subject of which he is supposed to be master, most people have the good sense to give attention, esteeming it a privilege to be permitted to hear; and even though they do not fully agree with all he says, they are modest about expressing their opinion; but few have any scruples about answering back when the Lord speaks. Almost everybody considers himself competent to be a critic of the Bible. But if we would always keep silence before the Lord, not even in our inmost hearts uttering a word, but allowing God to give us His thoughts, we should find not only life but sound wisdom as well; for the word of God is life, and "the Lord giveth wisdom; out of His mouth cometh knowledge and understanding." Prov. 2:6.

But there is a special force in calling upon the heavens and the earth as witnesses when the rebellion of men is mentioned; for they have never transgressed God's will. The earth is obedient to the voice of God, and has been ever since He said, "Let the earth bring forth grass." "For ever, O Lord, Thy word is settled in heaven. Thy faithfulness is unto all generations; thou hast established the earth, and it abideth. They abide this day according to Thine ordinances: for all things are Thy servants." Ps. 119:89–91. See Jer. 2:12, 13 and Deut. 32:1–3 for other instances where the Lord calls upon the heavens and the earth to witness the apostasy of the people.

Notice the contrast brought to view in verses 2 and 3. In the original the contrast is very marked, – children as against dumb brutes. "Children have I made great and exalted, and even they have rebelled against Me." So much for *children*, while the ox and the ass recognize their master. The ox and the ass give more respect to their possessor than children to their Father. What a striking contrast.

Whom do the ox and the ass recognize as their lord and master? The answer is easy; it is the one who feeds them. The ass knows the crib of his lord. He knows where he finds his sustenance. And the beasts show their recognition of their owner by bending their necks to the burden which the master lays upon them. They give service to the one from whom they receive their support.

Does some one say that this does not require very much discernment on the part of the beasts? Then what shall be said of the children whom God has nourished? If the recognition of a master is so simple a thing that even a beast is not considered as specially worthy of credit for submitting to the hand that feeds him, what language can express the stupidity of men who do not know the

Lord "who giveth us richly all things to enjoy?" even "life, and breath, and all things." Remember that man was made to be the lord of the brute, and as such is designed to be infinitely above the brute in knowledge. What excuse can be made for him then, when he is ignorant of that which the slowest witted of beasts know perfectly well?

To know God is the easiest thing in the world. If it were not, there would be some who would have excuse for not knowing Him. But all are "without excuse," for everything reveals Him. One does not need to be a philosopher, in order to know God. All that is required is that one have as much knowledge as an ox or an ass, to recognize the simplest facts. Continually to recognize the One who feeds us, is all that is needful to make one a Christian. One does not need to theorize; the Gospel is not a theory, but a fact. Simply to believe things that are, is all that is wanted. "He that cometh to God must believe that He is." And then evidence that He is, is seen in the gift of our daily bread.

Everybody can easily see that he does not feed himself. The ox and the ass know that. All our living comes from without ourselves, and we do not make it. Now in order that no one can have any chance to cavil, and say, "How can I know the name of the one who does provide this food?" we may say, "All that you are required to do is recognize the Creator." Worship the One who made "heaven and earth, and the sea, and the fountains of waters." When we do this, it will be easy to see that the One who gives us life has a right to the management of that life, and our duty is done. "Ask now the beasts, and they shall teach thee." Job. 12:7.

Some one may be inclined to say that the portion of Scripture allotted to this lesson is not very comforting, since it is all reproof. Well, it is true that the necessities of the case have forced us to take only a broken fragment of the message, but it is not without comfort, even if it is reproof. It is a reproof addressed to children, and the Lord says, "My son, despise not the chastening of the Lord; neither be weary of His correction; for whom the Lord loveth He chasteneth; even as a father the son in whom he delighteth." Prov. 3:11,12. The Holy Spirit, whose special office is that of Comforter, is first of all a Reprover of sin. John 16:7,8. "The commandment is a lamp, and the law is light; and reproofs of instruction are the way of life." Prov. 6:23.

"Ah sinful nation, a people laden with iniquity." Shall we cringe and cower before the Lord because He addresses us in that manner? – Not by any means; for we hear the call of the Saviour: "Come unto Me, all ye that labour, and are heavy laden; and I will give you rest. Take My yoke upon you, and learn of Me; for I am meek and lowly in heart; and ye shall find rest unto your souls." Matt. 11:28,29.

"Take My yoke upon you," says the Lord. Certainly. The ox and the ass submit to the yoke of the one who feeds them; why should not we? And they bear heavy burdens for their masters; but our Master calls us to come to Him, that He may relieve us of our burdens. We are "laden with iniquity." Why? – Because we have departed from Him. His yoke is easy, and His burden is light. Only when we "have gone away backward" do we find hard labour and heavy burdens. What a blessed service it is, that gives rest from labour!

"Why will ye be still stricken, that ye revolt more and more?" When the ox and the ass are rebellious and refuse to bear the burden placed upon them by their lord, or when they turn aside out of the way, what do they bring upon themselves? The rod of correction, of course. Even so it is with us, when we depart from the way. But bear in mind that the strokes that come are not given arbitrarily. Departing from the way of life is in itself death. So the offence brings its own punishment. "For that they hated knowledge, and did not choose the fear of the Lord: they would none of My counsel: they despised all My reproof. Therefore they shall eat of the fruit of their own way, and be filled with their own devices. For the turning away of the simple shall slay them, and the prosperity of fools shall destroy them." Prov. 1:29–32. They that sin are treasuring up unto themselves wrath against the day of wrath. Rom. 2:5. "His mischief shall return unto his own head, and his violent dealing shall come down upon his own pate." Ps. 7:16.

"From the sole of the foot even unto the head there is no sound-ness" in the body because of the sin that has been committed; but "wounds, and bruises, and putrefying sores." That is the result of refusing to hear the words of the Lord, which "are life unto those that find them, and health to all their flesh." Prov. 4:20–22. Nothing is more sure than that there is the closest connection between sin and disease. Disease is only the working of death; and death came into the world with sin. Rom. 5:12. But for sin, there would be no disease in the world. "Faith cometh by hearing, and hearing by the Word of God." Rom. 10:17. And "the just shall live by faith." That is, men can live by the words of the Lord. It is a fact that we have no life except that which the Lord gives us. This everybody must admit. And it is also a fact that the Lord's life is perfect and eternal. There is no life but the life of the Lord, therefore the life which the Lord gives us is a perfect life. Then is it not, to say the least, as easy for the Lord to give us perfect health as to have us suffering from all manner of disease? Certainly, and far easier; for the Lord cannot give us any other life than that which is perfect. Why then do we suffer disease? – Simply because we "have all gone out of the way," and have departed from the Lord. We have rejected His words, which are Spirit and life. It is not the Lord who sends us disease, but disease comes as the result of rejecting or neglecting the word of the Lord. "My people are destroyed for lack of knowledge." Hosea 4:6.

Read Ps. 38:1–8 to find a parallel to Isa. 1:4–6. Notice how often in the Bible disease of body is named as a result of departing from the Lord. When men shall have wholly rejected the Spirit and Word of the Lord, the first manifestation of it will be a plague of "a noisome and grievous sore" upon them. And the plague that appears in the body of a man, will be only the working out of "the plague of his own heart."

Read Luke 7:50 and 8:48, noting the margin of the Revision. There we see that Jesus used the same words to the one whose sins He forgave as to the one whom He healed of a grievous disease. "Thy faith hath saved thee," is the same as "Thy faith hath made thee whole." Salvation is simply the work of making whole. When Jesus on the Sabbath day healed the lame man at the pool of Bethseda, He made him "every wit whole." John 10:21–23. Afterward when He found the man in the temple, He said to him, "Behold, thou art made whole: sin no more, lest a worse thing come upon thee." John 5:14. This shows us (1) that the man's disease had been the result of personal sin; and (2) that Jesus in healing his disease had saved him from the sin, even as He did the paralytic. See Matt. 9:2–6. "Bless the Lord, O my soul, and forget not all His benefits; who forgiveth all thine iniquities; who healeth all thy disease." Ps. 103:2,3.

"From the sole of the foot even unto the head there is no soundness in it." That is our condition apart from the Lord. But when the lame man at the gate Beautiful was healed by the name of Jesus of Nazareth, Peter said to the people who gathered round, "His name through faith in His name hath made this man strong, whom ye see and know; yea, the faith which is by Him hath given him this *perfect* soundness in the presence of you all." Acts 3:16. That man was not only healed in body, but saved as to his soul, for all the prophets gave witness "that through His name whomsoever believeth in Him shall receive remission of sins." Acts 10:48. Moreover when Peter talked of the case the next day before the judges, he declared that the man stood there whole in the name of Jesus of Nazareth, in whom alone there is salvation, thus identifying the healing of the body with salvation.

One thing more we must not omit in the consideration of this lesson. Note the horrible condition brought to view in Isa. 1:5,6. Remember that disease is but the outward physical manifestation of sin. It is not always the result of our own personal sin, but that makes no difference: if we are not responsible for it, we may be sure that God will save us from it, since He saves us from the result of our rebellion. The fact which we wish to keep in mind is that disease is but the working of death, which is the fruit of sin. Now a body that is full of wounds, and bruises, and putrefying sores is not by any means a pleasant object to look at. It is, indeed, most disgusting. Now remember that, no matter how fair one's person may be to the sight of man, if the heart is corrupt that person looks to God just as he would to us if covered with loathsome ulcers. "The Lord seeth not as man seeth; for man looketh on the outward appearance, but the Lord looketh on the heart." 1 Sam. 16:7.

Remember also that this fearful condition of body is the result of departing from the Lord and lading with iniquity. Then read the blessed Gospel according to Isaiah: "Surely He hath borne our griefs and carried our sorrows;" (Compare Matt. 8:16,17) "but He was wounded for our transgressions, He was bruised for our iniquities; the chastisement of our peace was upon Him; and with His stripes we are healed. All we like sheep have gone astray; we have turned every one to his own way; and the Lord hath laid on Him the iniquity of us all." Isa. 53:4–6. If we are laden with iniquity, and covered with sores and bruises, we but share the lot of the Lord. We put it that way, although the fact is that He shares our lot. He takes our burden of sin and our sicknesses. What for? In order that we may be freed from it all. His sores heal our sores. How so? Because His sores are our sores. What? Are the sores that He has my sores? Yes, certainly. Why, then I do not have them any more. No; they are all upon Him. Let Him keep them, for "He will swallow up death in victory." Wonderful Physician, who heals our diseases by His own; but so it is, and so let it be.

CHAPTER 2

THE GREAT CASE AT LAW

(Isaiah 1:10–20, Lowth's Translation)

10. "Hear the word of Jehovah, O ye princes of Sodom! Give ear to the law of our God, ye people of Gomorrah!

11. What have I to do with the multitude of your sacrifices? saith Jehovah; I am cloyed with the burnt-offerings of rams, and the fat of fed beasts; and in the blood of bullocks, and of lambs, and of goats, I have no delight.

12. When you come to appear before Me, who hath required this at your hands?

13. Tread My courts no more; bring no more a vain oblation; incense! It is an abomination unto Me. The new moon, and the Sabbath, and the assembly proclaimed, I cannot endure; the fast, and the day of restraint.

14. Your mouths and your solemnities, My soul hateth; they are a burthen upon Me; I am weary of bearing them.

15. When ye spread forth your hands, I will hide Mine eyes from you; even when ye multiply prayer, I will not hear; for your hands are full of blood.

16. Wash ye, make ye clean; remove ye far away the evil of your doings from before Mine eyes;

17. Cease to do evil; learn to do well; seek judgment; amend that which is corrupted; do justice to the fatherless; defend the cause of the widow.

18. Come on now, and let us plead together, saith Jehovah; though your sins be as scarlet, they shall be as white as snow; though they be red like crimson, they shall be like wool.

19. If ye shall be willing and obedient, ye shall feed on the good of the land;

20. But if ye refuse, and be rebellious, ye shall be food for the sword of the enemy; for the mouth of Jehovah hath pronounced it."

Whoever would get the full benefit of these verses must not fail to read them in connection with the verses that precede, which were quoted in the last week's lesson. In studying these it will be necessary to make frequent reference to those.

The Remnant

"Except the Lord of hosts had left unto us a very small remnant, we should have been as Sodom, and we should have been like unto Gomorrah." They were utterly destroyed. But "though the number of Israel be as the sand of the sea, a remnant shall be saved." Romans 9:27. Because it is written, "Behold, I will send you Elijah the prophet before the coming of the great and terrible day of the Lord; and he shall turn the heart of the fathers to the children, and the heart of the children to the fathers, lest I come and smite the earth with a curse," or, as the words really signify, "lest I come and smite the earth with utter destruction." Mal. 4:5–6. Thus we see that this prophecy of Isaiah, which we are studying, has special reference to the last days. The remnant is the last, and the words describe the condition just before the coming of the Lord, when iniquity will abound, and the love of many will wax cold (Matt. 24:12), when faith will be so scarce in the earth that one must enquire for it (Luke 18:8), and when even the professed church will be very like the heathen. Compare 2 Tim. 3:1–5 and Rom. 1:28–32. So full of wickedness does the church become, that the Lord addresses it as Sodom and Gomorrah. Isa. 1:10. Let the reader pay special heed to this fact, for it is not cited for the purpose of accusation, but of emphasizing the mercy of God, of which we come to speak.

Vain Worship

Compare Isa. 1:11–15 with Amos 5:21–24. Although we are exhorted not to forsake the assembling of ourselves together, religion does not by any means consist in going to meetings. There are times when all religious services are an abomination to the Lord. Singing is called noise, and prayer is disgusting to Him. Yet let no one think that this means that there is ever a time when the Lord refuses to listen to a sinner's plea for pardon, on the ground that he is too sinful to be forgiven. Far from it; this portion of Scripture which we are studying teaches us exactly the opposite. But the Lord cannot be deceived with honeyed phrases that mean nothing. Flattery does not tickle His ear. The double-minded man – not the man who does not know his own mind, but the one who wants the evil even while asking the good – receives nothing from the Lord. Hypocrisy is detestable. The self-righteous Pharisees, whose lives were outwardly models of propriety, but who were hypocrites, were objects of the Lord's most scathing rebukes, while He most tenderly drew to Himself the publicans and harlots, whose lives were one mass of guilt, but who sincerely longed for something better.

Useless Prayers

"When ye spread forth your hands, I will hide Mine eyes from you; yea, when ye make many prayers, I will not hear." What a terrible statement that is! Yet it need not discourage a single soul. Not one who asks pardon of the Lord will ever be turned away. The Lord calls all to come, and He says, "Him that cometh to Me I will in no wise cast out." "Whosoever will, let him take the water of life freely." But the Lord does not like to look upon blood, that is, upon bloody deeds; and when men stretch out their bloody hands to Him, offering Him wickedness as if it were righteousness, He cannot but turn away His eyes. That is not real praying, but simply the making of prayers. To "say a prayer" is vastly different from praying. One man may say a prayer that somebody else has prepared for him, and put into his mouth, or which he himself has devised and learned so that he can repeat it from memory, but that is not praying. Nobody in the world is so ignorant that he does not know how to pray acceptably to the Lord. The man who depends upon somebody else to make a prayer for him, would not be praying if he should repeat it a thousand times a day. Prayer is simply the asking for what one wants. Prayer to God must of course be the asking for goodness, since He has nothing else to give. Now if a person wants a thing, he knows that he wants it, and then it is as simple a thing to ask for it, as it is for a child to ask for a piece of bread when it is hungry. No one who is hungry needs to have somebody tell him how to ask for something to eat; even so whoever hungers and thirsts after righteousness knows how to ask for it successfully better than anybody can tell him. No true parent ever refuses to give his child food when it is hungry; but there is not a mother in the world who would not very often let a child's request for food go unheeded if it were in the habit of coming to her many times a day, regardless of whether it were hungry or not, and formally reciting to her a request for something to eat. She would regard the condition of its stomach, rather than its words.

Verse 12 is thus rendered in the Danish and Swedish: "When ye come to be seen before My face, who has required this of you, that ye should trample upon My courts?" The last part of the thirteenth verse is by these and other versions rendered, "I cannot endure unrighteousness and a festival." Thus does the Lord make emphatic His desire for sincerity. The man who would cover his sins with a cloak of piety, multiplying religious forms in order to divert attention from his wicked deeds is loathsome to the Lord, while the vilest sinner who desires freedom from his wicked ways, is the object of the Lord's tenderest love.

Sacrifices of Righteousness

"Bring no more vain oblations." Vanity is emptiness. A vain oblation is an offering which contains nothing. Here we learn that the Lord has no delight in empty forms and ceremonies. In the true worship of God there is no place for the doing of a thing merely to represent something else. God desires the thing itself. When David had committed a grievous sin, he knew that an offering would not please the Lord. "Thou desirest not sacrifice; else would I give it; Thou delightest not in burnt offering." "To obey is better than sacrifice." When a man has sinned, God does not wish him to come before Him with something as a substitute for righteousness, but with righteousness itself. "Offer the sacrifices of righteousness, and put your trust in the Lord." Ps. 4:5. Put your trust in the Lord, who provides the righteousness which we need, so that none need come before Him empty. "Then shalt Thou be pleased with the sacrifices of righteousness."

Wash and be Clean

To whom is this said? – To those who are as bad as they can be. To a people laden with iniquity, a seed of evil doers, children that are corrupters. It is spoken to those who are so full of the loathsome leprosy of sin, that from the sole of the foot even to the head there is nothing in them but wounds, and bruises, and putrefying sores. Even such may be "as white as snow."

Of the reality of this cleansing we have ample evidence in the Scriptures. Naaman the Syrian was a leper. He went to the prophet Elisha, who, as the servant of the Lord, spoke the word of the Lord to him, saying, "Go and wash in Jordan seven times, and thy flesh shall come again to thee, and thou shalt be clean." 2 Kings 5:10. He said, in short, just what we have in the text we are studying, "Wash, and be clean." 2 Kings 5:13. And Naaman, after a little sulking, did as he was commanded, "and his flesh came again as the flesh of a little child, and he was clean." Verse 14. Was it the water of the Jordan that effected the cure? Was it true that the water of the Jordan was so much better than the waters of the rivers of Damascus? – Certainly not; that which cleansed him was the word of the Lord, which he listened to. The prophet did not tell him to cleanse himself, nor did he expect him to, but he gave him the word of the Lord, and that made the leper clean. In that case we see the cleansing power of the word of the Lord.

But the case is not yet complete. There came a man "full of leprosy" and said to Jesus, "Lord, if Thou wilt, Thou canst make me clean." Jesus instantly said, "I will; be thou clean. And immediately his leprosy was cleansed." Matt. 8:2–3. The same thing was done for this man that was done for Naaman, only in this case no visible means was used. If we had only the story of Naaman, then we might think that the water was what did the cleansing; and if we had only the case of the man who came to Jesus, then we should lose the impressive lesson taught in the first instance. But the two taken together teach us that the Lord cleanses us by "a water bath in the word," for so Eph. 5:26 is properly translated in many versions.

"Now are ye clean through the word which I have spoken unto you." John 15:3.

We are full of the uncleanness of sin, and the Lord says to us, just as He did to the man full of the uncleanness of leprosy, "Be clean." Did the Lord expect that the leper was to go away and cure himself? – Certainly not; He knew that it was impossible. What had the man to do? – Only to accept the word of the Lord. In his case the faith was already present, while the proud officer Naaman was required to give evidence that he did accept the word in humility; but both were cleansed in exactly the same way – by the word of the Lord. The word of the Lord is healing medicine. The words of the Lord "are life unto those that find them, and medicine to all their flesh." Prov. 4:22, margin.

"His commandment is life everlasting." John 12:50. God said, "Let the earth bring forth grass;" "and it was so." He said "Be light;" and instantly light was. Jesus said to the leper, "Be clean;" and immediately he was clean. So He says to us, "Wash you; make you clean;" and if we are not too proud to accept the word, we are instantly clean. It matters not how sinful we are; the greater our need, the greater our recommendation to the mercy of the Lord. He pardons our iniquity just because it is great. Ps. 25:11.

A Case in Court

"Come now, and let us reason together, saith the Lord." Isa. 1:18. Pay particular attention to this verse as it is given in the translation at the head of this study: "Come on now, and let us plead together, saith Jehovah." This is the language of the courts, and is in harmony with the German, Swedish, and Danish translations, which have it, "Come now, and let us go into court together, saith the Lord." This is a strictly literal rendering of the Hebrew. The expression is the same as in Job 23:7, where we have unmistakably a court scene. Read verses 3–7. In no place in the Bible is the Hebrew word that occurs here used in the sense that is ordinarily conveyed by the word "reason," and in no other place than this is it so rendered in our version. It occurs in Gen. 31:37, "Set it here before my brethren and thy brethren, that they may judge betwixt us both," where the idea of a decision of a case at law is clearly indicated.

The idea that a trial in court is in progress is indicated in the very first verse of the prophecy: "Hear, O heavens, and give ear, O earth." The call is for "Silence in the court;" for a great case is on, which involves the whole universe. This thought, introduced in the very beginning of the prophecy of Isaiah is very prominent throughout, and we shall have frequent occasion to refer to it, so that it is worthwhile to give it a little special study now. When we have once grasped the thought, we shall see that it appears throughout the whole Bible.

Two texts set the whole matter briefly before us. In Psalm 51:4 we read "Against Thee, Thee only, have I sinned, and done this evil in Thy sight; that Thou mightest be justified when Thou speakest, and be clear when Thou judgest." Turn now to Rom. 3:4, where we have this verse quoted thus: "Let God be true, but every man a liar; as it is written, that Thou mightest be justified in Thy sayings, and mightest overcome when Thou art judged." In the first instance we have God as the Judge, and in the second we have Him as the one judged, yet winning His case. The same Spirit that inspired the words in the first place, also inspired the quotation, so that both expressions must mean the same thing. Therefore we learn that when God judges the world, He is at the same time judged. That is to say, the Judgment is simply the summing up of a case that has been pending since sin entered the universe of God. God has been declared to be unjust, not only by Satan, but by every one who has committed sin. "All have sinned, and come short of the glory of God." Therefore every one who justifies himself, thereby declares that God is wrong; and whoever refuses to acknowledge himself to be a sinner, thereby justifies himself. But every man is unlike God. Therefore if men were right, that would prove God to be in the wrong. Everybody who refuses to confess his sins, by that very refusal charges God with being unjust. And the same thing is done by those who acknowledge themselves to be sinners, but who doubt God's willingness to forgive.

It is evident that if God could be convicted of one act of injustice, He could not judge the world. In order that rebellion shall be put down for ever, never more to have any possibility of arising, every creature in the universe must see and acknowledge the righteousness of God. Few of the inhabitants of this world do that now; but the Judgment is to make it plain. The great Judgment is not for the purpose of enabling God to judge of the character of men, but to cause all men to see the true character of God. Men are now taking sides for and against Him. The time will come when every secret thing will be brought to light. Then all will see that God has always been true and good. Every knee will bow, and every tongue will confess. But it will be too late for those who have waited until then; they have taken sides against the Lord, and when He wins His case, they necessarily lose. On the other hand, those who now put themselves on the side of the Lord, declaring that His way is right, which means that theirs is wrong, and who maintain their loyalty to Him against opposition, and even when they cannot explain some of His acts, will of course share in His triumph. The details of this great case, the matter of witnesses, etc., will come in later on in our study; what we wish to keep before our minds is that the great question at issue is the character of God. He has infinitely more at stake than any man can possibly have.

This is our strong consolation. God's righteousness is revealed in the forgiveness of sin. "If we confess our sins, He is faithful and just to forgive us our sins, and to cleanse us from all unrighteous-ness." 1 John 1:9. Whoever declares that God will not forgive sins, no matter whose, charges Him with being unjust. He forgives by His righteousness, His justice, and when we confess our sins, we become partakers of His righteousness. This assures our standing in the Judgment. Now God challenges us to try the case in court, and calls upon heaven and earth to act as jury, to see if there is a single case of acknowledged sin that He does not forgive. "Though your sins be as scarlet, they shall be white as snow; though they be red like crimson, they shall be like wool." This is His case. He stakes His life upon that. That is the thing upon which He bases His claim to righteousness, and His right to judge the world. If God is willing to risk His case upon that claim, cannot we? Our life stands with His if we do. We'll trust Him, believing that His character will stand every test. Indeed, that is the only sensible thing to do; for if it were possible that we could prove Him unjust, we should gain nothing, since that would mean the end of His Government, so with that would go our lives and the life of all creatures. So we see that it is the height of folly to try to pick flaws in God's character. It is like a man trying to saw off the limb upon which he is sitting over an abyss. But no fault can be found in God. "There is no unrighteousness in Him." "Trust ye in the Lord for ever; for in the Lord Jehovah is everlasting strength."

This call to come and be forgiven is to those who are as bad as they can possibly be. Every sin has produced its sore, and the result is that there is not a sound spot in the whole body. There is not a spot on which a stroke of correction could be laid, if sin were to be increased. To such ones He calls, in order that all may have hope, and may come with confidence. With what boldness we may come! How it enlarges our view of the Gospel, and lifts the whole subject to a plane infinitely beyond the mere selfish inquiry, Is it possible for me to be saved? It is God's case, not ours. He must forgive, or lose His life; for He gave His life for the express purpose of cleansing sins, and if He should not do it the life would be thrown away. Let us then come boldly to the throne of grace, fully assured that we shall obtain mercy, and find grace to help in time of need.

CHAPTER 3

REGENERATION OF DESTRUCTION

(Isaiah 1:21–31, Lowth's Translation)

21. "How is the faithful city become a harlot! She that was full of judgment, righteousness dwelled in her; but now murderers!

22. Thy silver is become dross; thy wine is mixed with water.

23. Thy princes are rebellious, associates of robbers; every one of them loveth a gift, and seeketh rewards; to the fatherless they administer not justice; and the cause of the widow cometh not before them.

24. Wherefore saith the Lord Jehovah, God of Hosts, the Mighty One of Israel; Aha! I will be eased with Mine adversaries; I will be avenged of Mine enemies.

25. And I will bring again Mine hand over thee, and I will purge in the furnace thy dross; and I will remove all thine alloy.

26. And I will restore thy judges, as at the first; and thy counsellors, as at the beginning; and after this thy name shall be called The city of righteousness, the faithful metropolis.

27. Sion shall be redeemed in judgment and her captives in righteousness;

28. But destruction shall fall at once on the revolters and sinners; and they that forsake Jehovah shall be consumed.

29. For ye shall be ashamed of the ilexes, which ye have desired; and ye shall blush for the gardens which ye have chosen;

30. When ye shall be as an ilex, whose leaves are blasted; and as a garden, wherein is no water.

31. And the strong shall become tow, and his work a spark of fire; and they shall both burn together, and none shall quench them."

Study the two sections of the first chapter, which we have already studied, in connection with this one, and see how the whole chapter overflows with rich, Gospel truth. There is no half-way dealing; the condition of the people addressed is the worst possible, and the salvation offered is full and complete.

One caution should be given here, which it will be well to observe in all Bible study. It is this: Don't waste time over what you do not understand. You will never learn anything by arguing and questioning and speculating over obscure or difficult texts. Some may think that this is strange; but it is true. No man can by searching find out God. He must reveal Himself, and He will do it as fast as we are able to see Him. The Bible must make itself clear. So we must always arrive at the meaning of that which is hidden, through that which at once reveals itself to our gaze. Never guess; never speculate. We *believe*, not argue nor theorize, our way to an understanding of God's Word. Meditate upon, but do not talk about, what you do not understand. So in the study of this chapter, and this book, do not take precious time from the consideration of clearly-revealed Gospel truths, for empty wondering and guesses as to the meaning of something that is obscure. It is all good, but you can profit only by what you understand. There are truths enough that lie near the surface of the prophecy of Isaiah to keep us employed for many months. When we have gathered up these, we shall find that many of the things that were before concealed were simply the second layer, and are brought to light by taking up the first.

The Blessing of Conviction

Verses 4–7 should always be read in connection with verses 16–18. Perhaps no portion of Scripture is quoted oftener than verse 18, "Though your sins be as scarlet, they shall be as white as snow; though they be red like crimson, they shall be as wool;" yet emphatic and comprehensive as it is, much of the force of it is lost because the fact is not considered that these words are addressed to the very same people that are described in verses 4–7 as so full of the sores of sin that there is not room for any more. What a blessed thing it is that the Lord so strongly sets forth the heinousness of our sins! If He did not set our case before us in its very worst phase, we might think that the offer of salvation did not reach us; but when He expressly makes it known that His salvation is for people who are as bad as they possibly can be, there is no room for doubt or discouragement.

The Cause of Destruction

Read verses 6–9, and think how accurately they describe the condition of men and of the earth after probation has closed, and the plagues of God's wrath are poured out. Compare them with Rev. 16:1–2; Zeph. 1:2–18; Joel 1:15–20. Mind, the statement is not made that Isa. 1:6–9 is a description of the time of trouble, but that the condition described is very similar. Now the closing of probation does not make any change in the characters of men. The character of the wicked will not be different after that time from what it has been before. He that is unjust and filthy remains so, that is all. Rev. 22:11. The only difference is that at the close of probation their choice of evil is irrevocably fixed. That is what makes their probation end – they will no longer listen to the Gospel. They could be saved if they were willing to be saved. "If ye be willing," etc. So we see that men who are as bad as the wickedest men who will be destroyed when the Lord comes, may be saved. The reason, and the only reason, why any will be lost, is not that they are too wicked to be forgiven and saved, but that they do not wish to be saved. It is not the guilt of sin, but the love of sin, that shuts men out of the Kingdom; for if men will cease to love sin, the guilt of it, however deep, will be taken away.

A Question of Eating

If ye be willing and obedient, ye shall eat the good of the land; but if ye refuse and rebel, ye shall be eaten by the sword. The force of this is weakened in our version by the rendering "devour" in the second instance, although the word is the same in both verses. Eat or be eaten. Eat what? – "Eat ye that which is good." And what is good? – "O taste and see that the Lord is good." "Jesus said unto them, I am the Bread of Life; he that cometh to Me shall never hunger; and he that believeth on Me shall never thirst." "For My flesh is true meat, and My blood is true drink." John 6:35,55. "Except ye eat the flesh of the Son of man, and drink His blood, ye have no life in you." If one eats only the body of Christ, he eats to life; but whoever eats that which is not the body of Christ (and it can be eaten only by faith), that which he eats consumes him, instead of building him up. He is devoured by that which he feeds upon. "He that doubteth is damned if he eat because he eateth not of faith; for whatsoever is not of faith is sin." Rom. 14:23. Here is the alternative: Eat the flesh of Christ, and abide for ever; or eat that which is not bread, and be consumed by it.

Degeneration and Regeneration

Verses 21–23 present a picture of degeneration. Adultery is the one word that covers the whole. Everything has become adulterated. Faithfulness and purity have been crowded out. The one sin that God's people commit is adultery. The Lord is the husband of his people. Jer. 3:14; 31:32; Rom. 7:4; 2 Cor. 11:2; Eph. 5:31–32. His people are one flesh in Him. Departure from Him to any degree is adultery; so that whatever sin anyone commits, it is adultery – the allowing of another to take the place that should be filled with Christ. This adulteration – the substitution of the false for the true may go on until the faithful city becomes a harlot, and that which once was pure metal, only dross.

But there is a remedy for all this. "God hath not cast off His people which He foreknew." Nay, "for the Lord will not cast off for ever." Lam. 3:31. Never will He turn any away. "If we believe not, yet He abideth faithful." 2 Tim. 2:13. So He says: "Return thou backsliding Israel, saith the Lord; and I will not cause Mine anger to fall upon you; for I am merciful, saith the Lord, and I will not keep anger for ever. Only acknowledge thine iniquity, that thou hast transgressed against the Lord thy God, and hast scattered thy ways to the strangers under every green tree, and ye have not obeyed My voice, saith the Lord." Jer. 3:12–13. Only confess the sin, and it is forgiven, purged, for "Zion shall be redeemed with judgment, and her converts with righteousness." "My God shall supply all your need, according to His riches in glory." Phil. 4:19. The Lord regenerates us by supplying that which we lack. His own righteousness and faithfulness are given to redeem us from sin.

Practical Piety

Notice that one of the gravest charges against the wicked is that "they judge not the fatherless, neither doth the cause of the widow come unto them." Also in the exhortation to put away evil, the only things specified under the head of well-doing are, "relieve the oppressed, judge the fatherless, plead for the widow." Christianity is not a mere sentiment or emotion; it consists in deeds. Not that by any amount of deeds we can earn the favour of God, but that these good deeds are the manifestation of the life of Christ within. He "went about doing good, and healing all that were oppressed of the devil; for God was with Him." Acts 10:38. Kindness is the characteristic of God, for "God is love." "Every one that loveth, is born of God, and knoweth God." 1 John 4:7. And remember that it is not sermons about doing good, but the actual *doing*, that constitutes Christianity.

Complete Restoration

When God made man in the beginning, he, as well as everything else, was "very good." Christ is the Beginning, and all who are in Him find restoration. The adulteration will be removed, and the fine gold will be restored. We are "made full" in Him. "Thy hands have made me and fashioned me." Ps. 119:73. We have greatly degenerated from the original model; but God has promised to bring His hand upon us again, so that we may be new creatures, bearing again the impress of God.

Utter Destruction

Just as surely as there will be complete restoration, will there be utter destruction. Indeed, the promise of the restoration of the original perfection necessarily includes the destruction of those who cling to the evil. Mercy rejected means wrath. It cannot be otherwise. So none should presume upon the mercy of God, to continue in sin, that grace may abound. The greater the mercy offered, the greater the disaster that follows its rejection. Thus it is that men will suffer the wrath of God, whose "mercy endureth for ever."

The destruction of the wicked is simply the natural fruit of their own ways. There is nothing forced or arbitrary about it. "

Whatsoever a man soweth, that shall he also reap." When the plagues begin to appear at the close of probation, in the form of grievous sores in the bodies of men, it is only the breaking out of the corruption within. When men eat and drink death, – and they do this when they do not feed on Christ, the life, – it is but natural that the poison should permeate them, until they become bodies of death. And the fact that the first plague for sin is disease, emphasizes the fact that righteousness is health. The keeping of God's law means physical health as well as moral purity.

See how strongly the destruction of the wicked is put in verses 30–31. "Ye shall be as an oak whose leaf fadeth, and as a garden that hath no water." Such a condition is but a preparation for fire. But that is not all. "The strong shall become tow, and his work a spark of fire." Every one knows how inflammable a substance tow is; let fire come near it, and it is gone in a flash. Now think of tow which generates fire? – What hope of salvation is there for it? – Absolutely none. The wicked prepare their own destruction; their own works consume them. The destruction is certain, and God is clear; for bear in mind that this is only the fate of those that forsake the Lord. They only will be consumed. Whoever hearkens to the Lord "shall dwell safely, and shall be quiet from fear of evil." Prov. 1:33.

CHAPTER 4

THE GOSPEL OF ISAIAH

It has already been pointed out that the Gospel as given through the prophet Isaiah was for the people who lived in the time of the promise, a time when the work of the Gospel could be closed up and the King of glory come, if the people would only receive the message. So it is emphatically a message for the present time when "the great day of the Lord is near, it is near, and hasteth greatly." It is also clear that in this first chapter of Isaiah a complete view of the Gospel work is presented, reaching to the full restoration through judgment and righteousness, in the experience of those who accept it, or the destruction of those who reject it, and thus "forsake the Lord." So the work to be done just before the Lord comes will be set forth in this chapter, and the people who are doing the closing work will be carrying out the principles which are here laid down. Let us therefore study some of these principles.

A Question of Food

The Lord calls upon heaven and earth to listen while He presents His case concerning His children. He says that He has nourished them, but they have turned against Him. Even the beasts of burden recognize their owner and expect to serve those who feed them, but His children do not so. It is no mere accident that the food question is mentioned here. It was through yielding to the temptation of Satan over this very question that sin came into the world in the first place. It was over this same matter that the children of Israel murmured in the wilderness. "And they tempted God in their hearts by asking meat for their lust. Yea, they spake against God; they said, Can God furnish a table in the wilderness?" Ps. 78:18–19. Satan attempted to overthrow Jesus in the wilderness on this same question. Matt. 4:3–4. We may therefore be sure that in the closing work of the Gospel God's people will be tested to show that the victory which was gained over this question by Jesus has been fully appropriated through faith by His followers. Study anew the question of healthful living, of eating what the Lord has given for food with a constant recognition of what He gives in such food, and see that it is not a matter of chance that it is now coming into such prominence. Observe that the closing message must deal with this matter. Compare Rev. 14:6–7 with Acts 14:15–17 and 17:24–25, and note what is involved in the recognition of God as the Creator. Read 1 Cor. 10:1–11; those things "are written for our admonition," because the same test will be experienced by those "upon whom the ends of the world are come."

The Snare of Ritualism

From verses 10–15 we learn that in the very time of the promise the professed people of God were depending upon the forms of worship to commend them to God while their lives were full of evil. This is but one phase of the same old effort to put self in the place of God. The Lord's rebuke upon such mockery is intended to save the people from depending upon that which will fail them when the test comes. Read Jer. 17:5–8. There is nothing arbitrary in these statements. The simple consequences of man's own choice are presented. Every offering, every form of service, in which the righteousness of Christ is lacking, is a vain oblation, and empty form. It is no more acceptable than was the offering of Cain. But these principles must be emphasized in the closing work. The falling away and the mystery of iniquity reach their climax in the final struggle of the great controversy when the professed church and the world have united against God and His truth. "Babylon is fallen, is fallen." The warning *against* the worship of the beast and his image (Rev. 14:9–10) is just as much a part of the closing message as is the instruction to worship God. It is again the time of the promise, and so now we see a professed religion of forms and ceremonies substituted for the reality of the life that cleanses from sin. But this is not a question simply of some church. It is a matter of individual experience, and the only safeguard against it is in an individual acceptance of the life of God in Christ: "Receive ye the Holy Ghost."

Christian Help Work

The spirit of the Gospel is to help the poor and the unfortunate. This is shown in the whole work of Christ for us. Those who are "wretched, and miserable, and poor, and blind, and naked" are the very ones whom He came to help. He came to a fatherless family to be "the Everlasting Father" to them, the second Adam. He "gave Himself for us." The spirit of Satan and of the world is selfish, to think only of oneself. In the closing days this spirit will be most fully revealed by those who have refused the blessings of the Gospel, and this will open the way and create a demand as it were for helping those who are thus brought into distress. So in the closing work of the Gospel, just before the people of God are to hear the invitation, "Come ye blessed of My Father, inherit the kingdom," they will call "the poor, the maimed, the lame, the blind," to share with them in things temporal and things spiritual. And so the instruction to "relieve the oppressed, judge the fatherless, plead for the widow" will be carried out by those who are giving the last message of mercy, and by this work it will be shown that it is a message of mercy. Note that the definition of religion given in James 1:27 shows that it is not an abstract quality, but a principle which manifests itself in life, and determines our relationship to the unfortunate. That the poor, who are really the children of God, can do Christian Help Work is shown from the fact that Jesus helped others, although He had not where to lay His head. And giving from their scanty funds was so common that this came to the mind of the disciples as the probable reason why Judas left them on the night of the betrayal. John 13:27–29. Peter had no money, but he bestowed an inestimable gift upon the lame man. Acts 3. God makes believers sufficient to be ministers of His own life. 1 Cor. 3:4–6.

A GOSPEL EPITOME

In our study of the first chapter of Isaiah, it has been necessary to divide into three lessons what is really one connected lesson, and so it will be profitable to consider the whole chapter together. As the whole text has already been printed, as translated by Lowth, we shall for the sake of space omit it here and refer the reader to the three preceding numbers of this paper, or to his Bible, or better still to his own knowledge of the chapter from previous study.

Of course the only thing to be studied in the Scripture is the Gospel of Christ the Saviour, the Gospel of abundant life (John 10:10), imparted to us through our faith (John 20:30–31). But the character of God is inseparable from the power of His life, and so the Gospel is the Gospel of His character, freely given to man in the gift of His Son Jesus, "the Lord our Righteousness." And the need of such a Gospel arises from the fact of man's unlikeness to God, even though originally made in His image, for all now lack His glory (character) through sin (Rom. 3:23); and so the picture is complete only when we see man's lost and pitiable condition through his rebellion against God the Father, his utter inability to save himself by his own works, God's power and willingness to save even the vilest, and the results of accepting or rejecting this offered salvation. Such a complete picture is presented in the first chapter of Isaiah.

The Lord's own description of the condition of every man who has departed from Him is given in verses 4–6, and what a pitiable condition is here presented! There is absolutely no soundness, nothing from which goodness can ever be developed. It is a case entirely without hope, unless a restoring power can be found outside of itself. The cause of this distressing experience is found in verse 2. It is rebellion; and the rebellion of children against a father who has nourished and brought them up. And here it is shown that man, who was created in the image of God, to have dominion "over the cattle," has through his sin lost his place of power and become more brutish than the beast of the field. For children treat their Father with less consideration than the ox and the ass treat their owner. Thus has the head become the tail, and thus is God's glory trailed in the very dust before the face of all the universe.

And how clearly it appears that this course of rebellion against God has brought in its train the most terrible misery to man and a destroying curse upon the earth. Wounds, bruises, and sores cover the man from head to foot, while his country is desolate, his cities are burned, and strangers devour his land. The foes within and the foes without have both gained a complete victory over him, and were it not for the wonderful mercy of the long-suffering, though powerful "Lord of hosts," powerful to save, not even a remnant could be saved from such depths of woe. How wondrously are the mercy and the saving grace of God revealed in His own statement of the consequences of man's rebellion! How tender and strong is the love which comes to the rescue of the lost one whose condition is so repulsive! But "God is love," and man's need is his strongest plea, and the life which heals and saves is freely given by the Great Physician "who gave Himself for our sins."

The deceitfulness of sin and the perversity of the human heart are revealed in the way in which the Lord's provision to save us from sin is turned, by the suggestion of Satan, into an excuse for continuing in sin with the utmost complacency. Repentance for sin and faith in the efficacy of His blood (life) who has "appeared to put away sin by the sacrifice of Himself," shown by offerings made with "a broken and a contrite heart," which thus become "the sacrifices of righteousness," will bring pardon and cleansing from the sin, which means salvation from sinning. But a multitude of sacrifices, which are mere "vain oblations," and many prayers made with outstretched hands which are "full of blood," are simply sin added to sin under the guise of religion, as are all our efforts at saving ourselves apart from the grace of Christ. This is only to add to the burden which we have already brought upon the Lord's life, and so He becomes "weary to hear them." Thus is again emphasized how great is our need of Divine deliverance, as it appears that even the forms of worship provided by the Lord Himself become an expression of deeper degradation when attempted by us as works of righteousness. Satan, who desired power for selfish purposes, God's power without His character, often seeks to satisfy our sense of need by a multiplication of forms without the life, which when present will find expression for itself. Where sin abounded, there grace did much more abound, but not that we should continue in sin. God's salvation is *from* sin, not *in* sin. The blood upon the hands shows the need, not of making any pharisaical prayers, but of applying to the heart the blood that cleanseth from all sin.

And so we come to the central thought of the chapter, God's willingness and ability to cleanse from the deepest stains of sin. But this He does by virtue of what He Himself is, by the power of His own character. And so in every commandment of His, which the saved sinner knows as "life everlasting," He is simply offering to us the assurance of His own character through His "exceeding great and precious promises." For when He tells us to "relieve the oppressed, judge the fatherless, plead the cause of the widow," He is holding out to us the gift of His own life, that life finds expression in doing the same things for us. For is it not His delight to let the oppressed go free? And "a father of the fatherless, and a judge of the widows, is God in His holy habitation." All that God is He desires to share with His children, and the most wonderful thing about the inheritance is that we may become "heirs of God" Himself, temples for His own indwelling. And although the temple has become defiled, yea even "a den of thieves," yet "shall the sanctuary be cleansed." Hear the Lord's Word: "I am merciful, saith the Lord, and will not keep anger for ever. Only acknowledge thine iniquity." "If we confess our sins, He is faithful and just to forgive us our sins, and to cleanse us from all unrighteousness."

> "Father, I have wandered from Thee,
> Often has my heart gone astray;
> Crimson do my sins seems to me –
> Water cannot wash them away.
> Jesus, to that fountain of Thine,
> Leaning on Thy promise I go;
> Cleanse me by Thy washing divine,
> And I shall be whiter than snow."

And so complete is the cleansing and the restoration that even though the faithful city had become an harlot, and its princes rebellious and the companions of thieves, wholly given up to the work of the thief (John 10:10), yet shall it again be called "The city of righteousness, the faithful city." Thus are we encouraged to believe that there is forgiveness with the Lord that He may be feared, and that there is help for every one of us. He redeems by His own righteousness, a free gift to be received through faith. There is no sin so heinous from which we may not be justified by faith, that faith which works by love, the only faith there is. The unpardonable sin is the sin which refuses to be pardoned. "Therefore being justified by faith, we have peace with God through our Lord Jesus Christ." "There is therefore now no condemnation to them which are in Christ Jesus, who walk not after the flesh but after the Spirit. For the law of the Spirit of life in Christ Jesus hath made me free from the law of sin and death." This is the glorious result of accepting the Gospel of life, the Gospel of the gift of God's own character through faith in Christ!

And now the chapter closes by stating the inevitable result of refusing this same Gospel of life. "They that forsake the Lord shall be consumed." "He that believeth on the Son hath everlasting life: and he that believeth not the Son shall not see life; but the wrath of God abideth on him." "He that hath the Son hath life; and he that hath not the Son of God hath not life." "An oak whose leaf fadeth," and "a garden that hath no water" are the types of the man who refuses the water of life. "Blessed is the man that trusteth in the Lord, and whose hope the Lord is. For he shall be as a tree planted by the waters. ... Her leaf shall be green." "The ungodly are not so." And so the dry oak and the parched garden are ready for the great conflagration when "the earth also and the works that are therein shall be burned up." But this is "the day of the Lord," when He "will come as a thief in the night." And so this chapter takes us from the first cause of sin, through its most loathsome manifestation, through the offers of Divine mercy, to the sure results of the acceptance or the rejection of the Gospel of God's own life through Christ. And thus is the Gospel preached unto us as well as unto them.

CHAPTER 5

GOD ALONE IS GREAT

(Isaiah 2:6–22, Lowth's translation)

6. Verily Thou hast abandoned Thy people, the house of Jacob; because they are filled with diviners from the East, and with soothsayers like the Philistines; and they multiply a spurious brood of strange children.

7. And his land is filled with silver and gold; and there is no end to his treasures; and his land is filled with horses; neither is there any end to his chariots.

8. And his land is filled with idols; he boweth himself down to the work of his hands, to that which his fingers have made;

9. Therefore shall the mean man be bowed down, and the mighty man shall be humbled; and thou wilt not forgive them.

10. Go into the rock, and hide thyself in the dust; from the fear of Jehovah, and from the glory of His majesty, when He ariseth to strike the world with terror.

11. The lofty eyes of men shall be humbled; the height of mortals shall bow down; and Jehovah alone shall be exalted in that day.

12. For the day of Jehovah God of hosts is against everything that is great and lofty; and against everything that is lofty, and it shall be humbled.

13. Even against all the cedars of Lebanon, the high and the exalted; and against all the oaks of Bashan;

14. And against all the mountains, the high ones; and against all the hills, the exalted ones;

15. And against every tower, high raised; and against every mount; strongly fortified.

16. And against all the ships of Tarshish; and against every lovely work of art.

17. And the pride of man shall bow down; and the height of mortals shall be humbled; and Jehovah alone shall be exalted in that day;

18. And the idols shall totally disappear,

19. And they shall go into caverns of rocks, and into holes of the dust; from the fear of Jehovah and from the glory of His majesty, when He ariseth to strike the earth with terror.

20. In that day shall a man cast away his idols of silver, and his idols of gold, which they have made to worship, to the moles and to the bats;

21. To go into the caves of the rocks, and into the clefts of the craggy rocks; from the fear of Jehovah, and from the glory of His majesty, when He ariseth to strike the earth with terror.

22. Trust ye no more in man, whose breath is in his nostrils, for of what account is he to be made?

In verse 6 there is nothing in the original text to indicate with what the people are filled from the East. The text, literally rendered, reads, "because they are filled from the East." This is indicated in the Revised Version, as well as in our common version. That with which they are filled is not limited to diviners or any other one thing. The idea is that whatever the people have comes from the East. The expression that is used, however, is the ordinary Hebrew idiom to express comparison, so that it might be read, "because they are filled more than the East," which is still more emphatic. In the East idolatry has been practiced the longest of any place on earth.

"They are soothsayers, like the Philistines." The Philistines were people of Canaan, whom God commanded to be cast out for their abominations, among which was witchcraft – pretended communication with the dead. The word rendered "soothsayer" is from the word meaning "cloud," indicating that those who practice that art act secretly, under cover.

"They please themselves with the children of strangers." Literally, "they strike hands with the children of strangers." The people of Israel were forbidden to make any league with the people of the land. They were to be separate from all the people on earth.

Ex. 33:16. They were not to be reckoned among the nations, nor to be like them. Num. 23:9. They were to depend on the Lord alone for defense, consequently they did not need any alliance with other people, however numerous. God's people must not enter into any covenant, except with Him. To form any alliance in partnership, or to be in any way whatever entangled or identified in interests with other people, is to be false to God. It is those who are "rich and increased with goods" (Rev. 3:16–17), who are spewed out of the Lord's mouth. "He hath filled the hungry with good things; and the rich He hath sent empty away." Luke 1:53.

Note the place whence real fullness comes. In Christ all fullness dwells (Col. 1:19), and we are "made full" in Him. Col. 2:10, R.V. He says, "Open thy mouth wide, and I will fill it." Ps. 81:10. But when the fullness that people have is not from Him, it is really nothing but emptiness; they are puffed up, not filled.

"Their land is also full of idols; they worship the work of their own hands, that which their own fingers have made." What a terrible fall from the high place for which God created man. "Thou hast made him but little lower than God, and crownedst him with glory and honour. Thou madest him to have dominion over the works of Thy hands; Thou hast put all things under his feet." Ps. 8:5–6, R.V. Yet "What is Man?" At his best state he is altogether vanity; of himself he is nothing at all; but with God dwelling in him in all His fullness, He is lord of the works of God's hands. And from this high estate men have fallen so low as to worship – acknowledge themselves inferior to – the works of their own hands. From having dominion over the work of God's fingers, they abase themselves before the works of their own fingers! Could fall ever be greater? That is what idolatry is.

But all idolaters do not set up images of wood or stone or some metal in a temple, and fall down before them. It is not necessary that one should do obeisance to a carved image in order to be an idolater. All that is necessary to constitute one an idolater is that he worship his own works. Now people worship that in which they put their trust for salvation. Whoever therefore depends upon anything that he has done, as a means of salvation, is an idolater. Then have you never seen idolaters? Do you not know any? Would you need to go out of your own house to find one? Notice that just before the statement that their land is full of idols, we read: "Their land also is full of silver and gold, neither is there any end of their treasures." Is there any land to which that would apply more truly than to this? Does it make any difference whether the silver and gold that men worship be made into an image, or simply bear the stamp of the Government? There is no land on earth that is not full of idols. Then let us say these words to the Lord: "Take away iniquity, and receive us graciously. Asshur shall not save us; we will not ride upon horses; neither will we say any more to the work of our hands, Ye are our gods; for in Thee the fatherless findeth mercy." Of all who thus acknowledge their sin, God says: "I will heal their backsliding: I will love them freely." Hosea 14:2–4.

God is no respecter of persons; therefore "the mean man" – the man of low degree – and "the mighty man" – the hero in the world's estimation – shall alike be bowed down and humbled, if they persist in exalting themselves above God. "For the day of the Lord of hosts shall be upon every one that is proud and lofty, and upon every one that is lifted up; and he shall be brought low." "The lofty looks of man shall be humbled, and the haughtiness of men shall be bowed down, and the Lord alone shall be exalted in that day." The Judgment will reveal everything just as it is, and then it will be seen that God alone is great. None of the men of the earth who claim to be great will be able to make their claim good in that day.

That will be a terrible day. "The kings of the earth, and the great men, and the chief captains, and the mighty men, and every bondman, and every freeman" (Rev. 6:15) "shall cast his idols of silver, and his idols of gold, which they made each one for himself to worship, to the moles and to the bats; to go into the clefts of the rocks, and into the tops of the ragged rocks, for fear of the Lord, and for the glory of His majesty, when He ariseth to shake terribly the earth," and shall say to the mountains and rocks, "Fall on us, and hide us from the face of Him that sitteth on the throne, and from the wrath of the Lamb; for the great day of His wrath is come; and who shall be able to stand?" Yet to behold that same face will be the reward and the highest delight of those who have been humble before God. Ps. 17:15; Rev. 22:4.

The Gospel is now seeking to prepare men for that great and terrible day. "For the weapons of our warfare are not carnal, but mighty through God to the pulling down of strongholds; casting down imaginations, and every high thing that exalteth itself against the knowledge of God, and bringing into captivity every thought to the obedience of Christ." 2 Cor. 10:4–5. The Gospel does the very thing that the great day of God does, only it is better to submit to the process now, willingly, than to wait till then. God only is "high and lifted up." He has not exalted Himself at the expense of others, as men do; but He cannot be other than He is. The Creator is by the very nature of things infinitely greater than all created things. Only by His greatness can anything exist; and whoever gladly recognizes and acknowledges that greatness, is by it exalted. When men exalt themselves, everything is reversed and in disorder. It is necessary that God's rightful place in the universe should be recognized; otherwise confusion would always reign. The Gospel is working to this end, and the great day of the Lord will complete the work, by the destruction of those whose high pretensions have made them ignore God. They will simply be left to the full trial of their claims, and as a consequence will "be as the morning cloud, and as the early dew that passeth away, as the chaff that is driven with the whirl-wind, and as the smoke out of the chimney." Hosea 13:3. When put to the test of trying to exist separate from God, they will be "found wanting." Like the idols which they have made, they will simply "pass away," because when the support of God, which they have despised and rejected, is withdrawn, there is nothing left.

The conclusion of the matter is, "Cease ye from man, whose breath is in his nostrils; for wherein is he to be accounted of?" "Cursed be the man that trusteth in man, and maketh flesh his arm, and whose heart departeth from the Lord." Jer. 17:5. This is not a curse put upon those who trust in man, – in themselves, – as a punishment. It is not at all because they have offended the dignity of God: God is not a man, that He should feel offended because His rank is not recognized; He is meek and lowly in heart. The curse is simply a statement of fact. Suppose a man suspends himself over the bottomless pit, on nothing; what else but his utter destruction can result? Man is nothing, and whoever trusts in man, even in himself, must inevitably come to nothing. The Judgment will do nothing more than reveal things as they are, and leave every man to the result of his own choice, and God will be clear from the blood of the wicked who are destroyed. Recall Isa. 1:31.

The lesson that we should not fail to learn, is the power of the Gospel. Its power is equal to the power manifested in the great and terrible day of the Lord. God's power to save – to make something for eternity out of men who are nothing – is the mighty power that will shake the heavens and the earth. When the Lord comes, it is to save His people. The prophet Habakkuk saw a vision of God going forth for the salvation of His people, and "His glory covered the heavens, and the earth was full of His praise, and His brightness was as the light; He had bright beams coming out of His side; and there was the hiding of His power. Before Him went the pestilence, and burning coals went forth at His feet. He stood, and measured the earth; He beheld, and drove asunder the nations; and the everlasting mountains were scattered, and perpetual hills did bow … the sun and moon stood still in their habitation." All that power is even now exerted to save people, and will save them, if they but trust it. Only two things are necessary for anybody to know, namely, that man is nothing, and God is everything. He who has learned this, has eternity with all its riches and wisdom in his grasp.

CHAPTER 6

SAVED AND SENT

(Isaiah 6, Lowth's Translation)

In the year in which King Uzziah died, I saw Jehovah sitting on a throne high and lofty; and the train of His robe filled the temple. Above Him stood the seraphim; each of them had six wings; with two of them he covereth his face, with two of them he covereth his feet, and two of them he useth in flying. And they cried alternately, and said: –

Holy, holy, holy, Jehovah God of Hosts!

The whole earth is filled with His glory.

And the pillars of the vestibule were shaken with the voice of their cry; and the temple was filled with smoke. And I said, Alas for me! I am struck dumb; for I am a man of polluted lips; and in the midst of a people of unclean lips do I dwell; for mine eyes have seen the King, Jehovah God of Hosts. And one of the seraphim came flying unto me; and in his hand was a burning coal, which he had taken with the tongs from off the altar. And he touched my mouth, and said: –

Lo! this hath touched thy lips;

Thine iniquity is removed, and thy sin is expiated.

And I heard the voice of Jehovah, saying, Whom shall I send; and who will go for us? And I said, Behold, Here am I; send me. And he said: –

Go, and say thou to this people:

Hear ye indeed, but understand not;

See ye indeed, but perceive not;

Make gross the heart of this people;

Make their ears dull, and close up their eyes;

Lest they see with their eyes, and hear with their ears,

And understand with their hearts, and be converted; and I should heal them.

And I said: How long, Jehovah? And He said: –
Until cities be laid waste, so that there be no inhabitant;
And the land be left utterly desolate.
Until Jehovah remove man far away;
And there be many a deserted woman in the midst of the land.
And though there be a tenth part remaining in it;
Even this shall undergo a repeated destruction;
Yet, as the ilex, and the oak, though cut down, hath its stock remaining,
A holy seed shall be the stock of the nation.

"I saw Jehovah." Compare John 12:37–41 with verses 9 and 10 of this chapter, and it will be seen that it was Christ whom Isaiah saw in His glory. From this we learn something of the wondrous glory of our Redeemer, and what He gave up for the sake of saving us. He is the effulgence of the Father's glory, and the express image of His person. Heb. 1:1–2. The glory which He had with the Father before the world began is His now (John 17:5), and He gives it to us, for we shall be "glorified together." Rom. 8:17.

"His train filled the temple." The word rendered "train" is the same that in Jer. 13:22,26, and other places is translated "skirts," and in Ex. 28:33–34; 39:24–26, is translated "hem." The hem or skirt of His garment filled the temple.

What is this garment? Here is the answer: "O Lord my God, Thou art very great; Thou art clothed with honour and majesty. Who coverest Thyself with light as with a garment; who stretchest out the heavens like a curtain." Ps. 104:1–2. The light and glory of the Lord is His clothing; His train, that filled the temple, was His glory.

"The whole earth is full of Thy glory." That is, the garment with which the Lord covers Himself is the fullness of the earth. Not only the temple in heaven, but the whole earth is filled with the hem of His garment. Now remember that when Jesus was here in the flesh, all that was needed for the healing of a poor, afflicted woman was that she should "touch the hem of His garment." So wherever we are, we are in reach of the hem of the garment which brings life and health and salvation.

> "The healing of the seamless dress
> Is by our beds of pain;
> We touch Him in life's throng and press,
> And we are whole again."

"The fullness of the whole earth is His glory." This, as may be seen from the margin of the Revision, is the literal rendering of the Hebrew. Wherever in the earth we see fullness, revealing itself in the multiplied forms of life, it is the glory of the Lord. Remembering now that in even the hem of His garment there is healing, what can this teach us except that God expects all to be healed, to be whole – holy. He has provided liberally to this end. All that is needed is that we come into conscious touch with Him by intelligent faith. Jesus Christ came that we might have life, and that we might have it in abundance. John 10:10. The life is the light of men. If we would but see the life, as it is all about us, and allow ourselves to be controlled by it, sickness would become a thing of the past, for eternal freshness is the characteristic of the life. To speak plainly, if we recognize that what are called "the laws of nature" are but the manifestations of the life of God, and let these laws rule in us, we shall find the life of Jesus manifested even in "our mortal flesh," and that will mean victory over disease as well as over sin.

"Above it stood the seraphim." Or, "above Him stood the seraphim." The Hebrew does not distinguish between masculine and neuter. In this case it amounts to the same thing, for above the throne would be above the Lord. The word "seraphim" means "burning ones." The difference, if any, between them and cherubim, is not revealed; but we read in Ezekiel 28:14 about the "anointed cherub that covereth;" and on the cover to the ark in the tabernacle of Moses were figures of cherubim overshadowing the glory of the Lord.

Each seraph covered his face with two of his wings, as unable or unworthy to look directly upon God. Yet the redeemed saints "shall see His face." Rev. 22:4. Oh, marvelous privilege accorded to the sons of Adam! to be on such terms of intimacy with the God of hosts as is not permitted even to the highest of the unfallen angels. And to show the special favour, granted to humble followers of Christ even now, He says, "in heaven their angels do always behold the face of My Father which is in heaven." Matt. 18:10. This shows that there is a difference, and that the angels who are specially commissioned to guard the faithful of earth, have access to the Father to a degree that others do not. "Let us therefore come boldly unto the throne of grace." "One thing have I desired of the Lord; that will I seek after; that I may dwell in the house of the Lord all the days of my life; to behold the beauty of the Lord, and to enquire in His temple." Ps. 27:4.

"Woe is me; for I am undone, cut off, struck dumb; because I, a man of unclean lips, have seen the King, the Lord of hosts." It was the sight of the Lord that made Isaiah conscious of his own imperfection. Job said, "Now mine eye seeth Thee, wherefore I abhor myself." Job 42:5–6. The sight of the Lord makes known the presence of sin, and either removes the sin, or destroys the sinner, according to the circumstances under which He is seen.

"This hath touched thy lips; and thine iniquity is taken away, and thy sin purged." It is fire from the altar, which, when cast on the earth, works destruction. The same fire that cleanses those who confess their sins, consumes those who cling to them. The saints of God, having been tried in the fire, as gold, and having had all the alloy of sin purged away by it, can dwell amid everlasting burnings which will consume the wicked like chaff. Read Mal. 3:2–3; Isa. 33:14–15.

Mark how quickly Isaiah's sins were removed. All he did was to acknowledge that he was a sinner. As soon as he said, "I am a man of unclean lips," the angel touched him with the coal from God's altar, saying, "Thine iniquity is taken away." "If we confess our sins, He is faithful and just to forgive us our sins, and to cleanse us from all unrighteousness." Only acknowledge your sin, and you may know that it is gone. Some sincere souls say: "I have confessed all the sins I know of, and I am resolved not to stop until I have discovered every sin in my character, and have confessed it; so that I may be forgiven." Why, you could not nearly enumerate all your sins in a lifetime. They are more than can be numbered. Isaiah did the whole thing at once: "I am a man of unclean lips," which meant that he was unclean in heart. The publican said: "God be merciful to me, a sinner," and went to his house justified. Be assured that if you acknowledge yourself to be a sinner, you are forgiven.

God saves men only for service. The object of our cleansing is not merely that we may escape destruction, but that we may be messengers of salvation. As soon as the Lord had cleansed Isaiah from sin, He called out, "Whom shall I send, and who will go for us?" It was a general question, yet intended especially for the ears of Isaiah. And the prophet heard, and immediately responded, "Here am I; send me." God reconciles us to Himself by Christ, and puts the word of reconciliation in us, that we, in the place of Christ, may be agents for reconciling others. 2 Cor. 5:18–20. He says, "Come!" and then to all who heed the call, He says, "Go!"

The Lord has said that there will be but few saved. So He fortified Isaiah against discouragement, by letting him know at the outset what the result of his message would be. He was to carry a message whose effect would be to harden hearts, and make people blind and deaf to the truth.

Look at John 12:37, and you will see what sort of a message it is that hardens men's hearts. "Though He had done so many miracles before them, yet they believed not on Him." Yet the miracles were done and recorded solely for the purpose of enabling people to believe on Jesus, and to obtain life through His name. John 20:30–31. And some did believe. Thus we see that it is the tender mercy of God that hardens men. "Let favour be shown to the wicked, yet will he not learn uprightness." Isa. 26:10. But God is clear. How can any soul hold God responsible for his unbelief, when it was the goodness of God, which leads men to repentance, that hardened him?

How long is this commission to Isaiah to be in force? – Until the end of the world. "Until the cities be wasted without inhabitant, and the houses without man, and the land be utterly desolate." But Isaiah is long since dead. True, but the message is still to be given; for remember that the Lord made His call general, and not particularly to Isaiah. "Who will go for us?" He is waiting for agents, and is anxious to use every one who will allow his sin to be purged. We are to be "ready to every good work" (Titus 3:1), and this readiness is gained through the cleansing power of God. God will use the instrument that is ready at hand when His work is to be done. This chapter emphasizes what was set forth in the article, "The Time of the Promise," at the beginning of this study in Isaiah, namely, that Isaiah's prophecy was especially for the last days. We do not need to make any interpretation, but simply take it as applying now. Although it was so long ago, the people who then heard his words were in the same condition and circumstances that the people of these days are. They did not profit by the message. Let us therefore give the more earnest heed to the things which we have heard, and fear lest, a promise having been left us, any of us should come short of it, and fall after the same example of unbelief.

Although destruction be determined upon all the land, a remnant shall be saved. "As a terebinth, and as an oak, whose stock remaineth, when they are felled; so the holy seed is the stock thereof." The holy seed, the humble believers in Christ, are the seed that prevent the earth from total and irretrievable ruin. As a tree will sprout and grow again, although cut down, so although the earth be made desolate, the few men who are left – the righteous ones – will be the sprout that will spring up and cause the whole earth to be renewed. "Israel shall blossom, and bud, and fill the face of the world with fruit." Isa. 27:6.

CHAPTER 7

GOD OUR ONLY REFUGE AND STRENGTH

(Isaiah 8:9–22, Lowth's Translation)

9. Know ye this, O ye peoples, and be struck with consternation; and give ear to it, all ye of distant lands: gird yourselves, and be dismayed; gird yourselves and be dismayed.

10. Take counsel together, and it shall come to naught; speak the word, and it shall not stand; for God is with us.

11. For thus said Jehovah unto me, as taking me by the hand He instructed me, that I should not walk in the way of this people, saying;

12. Say ye not, It is holy, of everything of which this people shall say, It is holy: and fear ye not the object of their fear, neither be ye terrified.

13. Jehovah God of Hosts, sanctify ye Him; and let Him be your fear, and let Him be your dread.

14. And He shall be unto you a sanctuary; but a stone of stumbling, and a rock of offence, to the two houses of Israel; a trap and a snare to the inhabitants of Jerusalem.

15. And many among them shall stumble, and shall fall, and be broken; and shall be ensnared, and caught.

16. Bind up the testimony, seal the law among My disciples,

17. I will therefore wait for Jehovah, He who hideth His face from the house of Jacob; yet will I look for Him.

18. Behold, I, and the children, whom Jehovah hath given unto Me; for signs and for wonders in Israel, from Jehovah God of Hosts, who dwelleth in the mountain of Sion.

19. And when they shall say unto you: Seek unto the necromancers and the wizards; to them that speak inwardly, and that mutter; should not a people seek unto their God? Should they seek, instead of the living, unto the dead?

20. Unto the command, and unto the testimony, let them seek; if they will not speak according to this word, in which there is no obscurity,

21. Every one of them shall pass through the land distressed and famished; and when he shall be famished, and angry with himself, he shall curse his king and his god.

22. And he shall cast his eyes upwards, and look down to the earth; and lo! distress and darkness! Gloom, tribulation, and accumulated darkness!

In studying this lesson, let each one use diligently both the King James and the Revised Versions, in connection with the translation that is given here. There is quite a variation in the wording, but to the thoughtful student this will be a help instead of a cause of confusion. The different renderings, when carefully and thoughtfully compared, will only serve to give a broader view of the message of God. Different verbal renderings mean, not contradiction, but fullness.

The reading of verse 9 in the common version, or in the Revision, is clearer and more in harmony with the text than that given by Lowth. The thought, as will be seen by comparison, is the same as that in the second Psalm. We can readily see how the rendering, "Make an uproar" is consistent with, "Associate yourselves." A crowd is likely to make an uproar. "The heathen rage." Notice that the people are not commanded to associate themselves together, or to make an uproar. This will be seen from the context. Even though they associate themselves, and rage against the Lord and His people, they "shall be broken in pieces." It is "a vain thing" that the heathen imagine, when they set themselves against the Lord, and against His Anointed, saying, "Let us break their bands asunder, and cast away their cords from us." Instead of breaking, they will be broken.

"There is no power but of God; the powers that be are ordained of God." Rom. 13:1. This being the case, it is evident that no one can withstand God. "Our God is in the heavens. He hath done whatsoever He hath pleased." Ps. 115:3. He rules over the kingdoms of the heathen, and in His hand is power and might, so that none is able to withstand Him. 2 Chron. 20:6. Therefore "fight ye not against the Lord God of your fathers; for ye shall not prosper." 2 Chron. 13:12. God cannot be overthrown by His own power turned against Him.

This is the comfort of the people of God in times of persecution. Verse 10 reads in the French of Segond, "Form projects, and they shall come to nothing; give orders, and they shall be without effect; for God is with us." "If God be for us, who can be against us?" Rom. 8:31. God is King of kings. He makes His servant His firstborn, "higher than the kings of the earth." Ps. 89:27. Read verses 17–27. This is spoken to the seed of David. Christ was born of the seed of David according to the flesh, but as His flesh is ours, we share His exaltation. He has been raised to sit at the right hand of God in the heavenly places, "far above all principality and power and might and dominion," and we are raised to sit with Him. Eph. 1:20–21; 2:1–6. "He raiseth up the poor out of the dust, and lifteth the needy out of the dunghill; that He may set him with princes, even with the princes of His people, and to make them inherit the throne of glory." Psalms 113:7–8; 1 Sam. 2:8.

God's people, therefore, have nothing to fear from man, or from any combination of men. If they are indeed His, they have a position higher than that of any earthly king. All nations may be arrayed against them, but they can accomplish no more against those who dwell in the secret place of the Most High than they can against the Almighty Himself. Read Psalms 118:6–17. It is true that earthly rulers may put some of God's people to death, even as they crucified Christ, but even so they cannot prevail against them. Christ conquered when He went into the grave. One man who knows the Lord (and the only way we can know Him is to have Him dwelling in us), is stronger than all nations combined. His authority is greater than theirs. This is the fact; unfortunately there are so many Christians who do not know their rightful place.

The fact that God's people have a place higher than the kings of the earth does not make them defiant. They are not to use their authority against men nor governments, but to help. Indeed, as soon as they assume a defiant, dictatorial attitude, they lose their power. Their strength is the strength of meekness. God clothes His people with His own kingly authority, in order that they may properly represent Him as ambassadors. Paul, brought before the Roman governors, preached the Gospel to them; and the man in chains caused the man on the throne to tremble.

People confederate for the purpose of maintaining or executing some project which they think is right. So the translation which we are following has in verse 12, "it is holy." We shall get the sense, however, better, if we follow the common or the Revised rendering, "a confederacy," or "a conspiracy." God would not have His people become bound up in any worldly compact. Ancient Israel were forbidden to make any league with the inhabitants of the land. Even so now they are not to be members of any human organization whatever. The church of Christ, of which He is the direct Head, provides for every want. Benevolent associations, so-called, are not needed by Christians, for the church is that. A little reflection will enable anybody to see that these associations are selfish, and so opposed to the Gospel of Christ.

It is not because God would have His people exclusive, that He tells them to make no league with the people of earth, and not to unite with any worldly society whatever for protection or help. No; it is because He would have them save the world. When His people unite with the world in any organization or society for mutual help or protection, they thereby disparage Him, who is the only real help. They give the world the impression that the church of Christ, nay, Christ Himself, does not afford sufficient protection and help. They put themselves in the position of dependents upon men, instead of occupying the position of benefactors, which God designs that they should hold. They are to give to the world, even to kings, and not to receive from them. A true child of God, poor and unknown, is better able to offer protection to an earthly ruler, than the Government is to protect him. This being so, how much more does it apply to all smaller combinations of men.

In ancient times anyone who acknowledged God could join His people. Even so it is now. The church is God's kingdom. All may come into it, who are willing to have Christ reign over and in them. And God's people, instead of being exclusive, must mingle with the people of the world, even going out into the highways and the lanes to find them, to do them good, and to invite them to come and share the blessings of God's house. But how dishonouring to the God whom they profess to serve, when they, finding that danger threatens, seek protection from those whom they are sent to deliver. There are many societies organized for the purpose of helping men temporally and spiritually, – of improving their physical and moral condition, – and they all do more or less good; but that is no reason why the Christian should join them. He must not oppose them, but let them do all the good they can; but he must know that he, as a member of Christ's body, has a field of operation, and a power for good, infinitely greater than they have, so that to join them would narrow his efforts. The glorious Gospel is the sovereign remedy for all human ills; therefore lift the standard high, and do not let it be confused with anything else.

"Sanctify the Lord of Hosts Himself; and let Him be your fear, and let Him be your dread. And He shall be for a sanctuary." Compare I Peter 3:14–15: "If ye suffer for righteousness' sake, happy are ye; and be not afraid of their terror, neither be troubled; but sanctify the Lord God in your hearts, and be ready always to give an answer to every man that asketh you a reason of the hope that is in you with meekness and fear." The only place of safety for any man is the secret place of the Most High. But we abide in God only when He abides in us. When God is set in the soul-temple as supreme; He Himself is the Sanctuary of the soul. Then the man has a hope of which he can give a good account. It is a living hope.

"Let Him be your fear, and let Him be your dread." But God is a kind and compassionate Father, as much more tender with His children than any earthly father is with his children as He is greater than man. Earthly fathers *have* love for their children, but "God *is* love." What a blessed position to be in, when the only thing in the universe to be afraid of is God, who is love. He loves men, even sinners, but hates sin. He is terrible to nothing but sin. When He is our fear, the result is the destruction of sin. The only dread we need to have, with respect to God, is the dread if displeasing Him; and when we fear to displease Him, so much that we will trust Him, and yield to His ways, He will give us the testimony that we please Him.

"Behold, I and the children whom God hath given me are for signs and for wonders in Israel from the Lord of Hosts." Who says this? – Read Heb. 2:9–13, and it will at once be seen that Christ is the speaker here. Then we may take courage to go back and read verse 17 of our lesson: "I will wait upon the Lord, that hideth His face from the house of Jacob, and I will look for Him." Has God hidden His face from us? So He did from Christ, yet Christ saw Him again. Not long ago one said to me, "God has forsaken me." Very well, said I, that is just what Christ said. "Ah, but," said the other, "God had not cast Him off." Indeed He had not; and since all that He suffered was for you, and in your place, you may be just as sure that He has not cast you off. No matter how much God seems to hide His face, if we go through the dark experience with Christ, we may be confident. Of all overcomers it is said, "They shall see His face."

But what about the signs and wonders? That is the most glorious prospect. It presents the most marvelous possibilities before believers in God. "I and the children whom the Lord hath given Me, are for signs and wonders," says Christ. That is, we ourselves are classed in with Christ. It is not merely that we are to *do* signs and wonders, but we are to *be* them. All the marvels of "the Man Christ Jesus" are to be reproduced in all who are men in Christ. The world is to wonder at Christians just as much as it did at Christ, and for the same reason.

"The Jews require a sign, and the Greeks seek after wisdom; but we preach Christ crucified, unto the Jews a stumbling block, and unto the Greeks foolishness; but unto them which are called, both Jews and Greeks, Christ the power of God, and the wisdom of God." I Cor. 1:22–24. Here we have the same stumbling block as in our lesson. Thank God that the stumblingblock is the sanctuary to believers. The stumblingblock is the sign; it is Christ crucified. You will remember that Christ said the Jews should have no other sign than His crucifixion. See Matt. 16:4. He gave them the most wondrous sign that could be given, and they stumbled at it. God's people are to present the same sign to the world. When the death and resurrection of Christ are fully manifest in their lives, they themselves will be signs greater than any miracle that they could perform. Let the sign, then, the sign of the cross, shine out.

The remaining verses in this chapter were quoted for the sake of the connection, but will be left for special study till next week.

CHAPTER 8

THE POWER AND GLORY OF THE KINGDOM

(Isaiah 8:19–23, Isaiah 9:1–6, Lowth's Translation)

19. And when they shall say unto you: Seek unto the necromancers and the wizards; to them that speak inwardly, and that mutter: should not a people seek unto their God? Should not they seek, instead of the living, unto the dead?

20. Unto the command, and unto the testimony, let them seek; if they will not speak according to this word, in which there is no obscurity,

21. Every one of them shall pass through the land distressed and famished; and when he shall be famished, and angry with himself, he shall curse his king and his god.

22. And he shall cast his eyes upwards, and look down to the earth, and lo! distress and darkness! Gloom, tribulation, and accumulated darkness!

23. But there shall not hereafter be darkness in the land which was distressed, in the former time He debased the land of Zebulon, and the land of Naphthali; But in the latter time He hath made it glorious; even the way of the sea, beyond Jordan, Galilee of the Gentiles.

1. The people that walked in darkness have seen a great light; they that dwelled in the land of the shadow of death, unto them hath the light shined.

2. Thou hast multiplied the nation, thou hast increased their joy; they rejoice before Thee as with the joy of harvest; as they rejoice who divide the spoil.

3. For the yoke of his burden, the staff laid on his shoulder, the rod of his oppressor, hast Thou broken, as in the day of Midian.

4. For the graves of the armed warrior in the conflict, and the garment rolled in much blood, shall be for a burning, even for a fuel of fire.

5. For unto us a Child is born; unto us a Son is given; and the Government shall be upon His shoulder; and His name shall be called Wonderful, Counsellor, the Mighty God, the Father of the everlasting age, the Prince of peace.

6. Of the increase of His Government and peace there shall be no end, upon the throne of David, and upon his kingdom, to fix it, and to establish it, with judgment and with justice, henceforth and for ever; the zeal of Jehovah God of Hosts will do this.

It will be noticed that in Lowth's translation, which is here printed, the chapter division is not the same as in our common version. The eighth chapter is given twenty-three verses, so that what we ordinarily call the seventh verse of the ninth chapter is here the sixth. Some other versions follow this division, which is according to that in the Hebrew Bible. But both amount to the same thing however, since it is clearly to be seen that there is no break in the subject, and in the prophecy as originally written there was no division whatever into chapters and verses. The scripture is just the same whether it be called eighth or ninth chapter, and attention is here called to the fact of the difference in numbering the verses, so that none may be confused.

"When they shall say unto you, Seek ...unto wizards." The meaning of the word "wizard" is "one who knows." The Hebrew word rendered "wizard" is merely a form of the verb "to know." Of course people would not be exhorted to seek to them who did not profess to know. But if they know, why not seek to them? Because they do not know. Their knowledge is foolishness. They "speak inwardly;" their knowledge is of themselves, and not from God. It is not the wisdom that comes from above. God "frustrateth the tokens of liars, and maketh diviners mad;" He "turneth wise men backward, and maketh their knowledge foolishness." Isa. 44:25.

"The Lord giveth wisdom, out of His mouth cometh knowledge and understanding." Prov. 2:6. In Christ are "hid all the treasurers of wisdom and knowledge." Col. 2:3. The place to go for wisdom is to the Fountain Head, and not to any man, even though he got his wisdom from God. God gives to *all* liberally. Much less should we go to those who speak from themselves. For remember that wisdom is a gift from God. Truth is *revealed*, not searched out by human shrewdness. No man knows the place where light dwelleth, but light springs forth, and we see it. Even so with truth, which is light, we get it merely by looking – looking to God and His Word. The man who thinks that he can "originate thought," will find out at the last that his supposed thought was emptiness. Only the thoughts of God shall stand.

But if we should not seek wisdom from living men, not even from ourselves, how utterly foolish to go to the dead for wisdom. "The dead know not anything." Eccl. 9:5. "Put not your trust in princes, nor in the son of man, in whom there is no help. His breath goeth forth, he returneth to his earth; in that very day his thoughts perish." Ps. 146:3–4. We pity the folly of poor heathen who ask wisdom from a piece of wood or stone; but what shall be said of the foolishness of men calling themselves enlightened Christians, who go to the dead for knowledge? What an insult to God!

"To the law and to the testimony." Because "the testimony of the Lord is sure, making wise the simple. The statutes of the Lord are right, rejoicing the heart; the commandment of the Lord is pure, enlightening the eyes." Ps. 19:7–8. "Thou through Thy commandments hast made me wiser than mine enemies." Ps. 119:98. "The fear of the Lord, that is wisdom; and to depart from evil is understanding." Job. 28:28. The Lord gives wisdom, but not apart from Himself in Christ. He cannot separate any of His attributes from Himself. All things are in Christ, and He gives us all things in giving us Christ. Nothing is inherent in man; but whatever good thing there is in any man is the working of God in Him. Christ is "the wisdom of God and the power of God," and He is that to us who believe. God is not niggardly with His gifts. He "giveth to all liberally." So it is better for a man to acknowledge the truth, that he knows nothing, because then he has for use all the wisdom of God. "Let no man deceive himself. If any man among you seemeth to be wise in this world, let him become a fool, that he may be wise." 1 Cor. 3:18.

Even as God cannot separate His attributes from Himself, for in that case He would cease to be God, so He cannot separate them from each other, "for the Lord our God is one Lord." Therefore wisdom and righteousness go together. Christ is "made unto us wisdom, and righteousness, and sanctification, and redemption." 1 Cor. 1:30. If we seek the kingdom of God, and His righteousness, all necessary things, including wisdom, will be added. "If any man willeth to do His will, He shall know." John 7:17. The way of wisdom is therefore the way of the cross, which saves from sin. "The preaching of the cross is to them that perish foolishness; but unto us which are saved, it is the power of God;" and this power is the direct antithesis of foolishness. All that any man has to do is to live a life of faith in God's Word, thus pleasing God, and this will bring him into such close companionship with the Source of all wisdom that he cannot fail to know things that are hidden from the wise men of the earth. How much better to seek wisdom from a living God than from a mortal man.

Whatever reading of verse 20 we follow, we find the same thing. "To the law and to the testimony; if they speak not according to this word, it is because there is no light in them." God's word is light, and those who reject that word have no light, and so must walk in darkness. Or we may take it as given in the Revision, "If they speak not according to this word, surely there is no morning for them." How can there be, if they reject the only source of light – God's Word? Or we may take the rendering of our text, "If they will not speak according to this word, in which there is no obscurity, every one of them shall pass through the land distressed and famished," and shall find only darkness. All the readings agree in the one thing, that God's Word is light, and that apart from it there is only darkness. And it is true food also; so that those who reject it must go hungry.

By comparing versus 1 and 2 of chapter 9 with Matt. 4:12–16, we see that it is a direct prophecy concerning Christ. There was formerly great darkness in the land, but now "hath He made it glorious." Though darkness cover the earth, and gross darkness the people, the glory of the Lord shall lighten the gloom; for He is the Light of the world, and the Light shineth in darkness, and the darkness has not overcome it. "The people that walked in darkness have seen a great light; they that dwell in the land of the shadow of death upon them hath the light shined." The light of Christ pierces even the darkness of the grave, for He went there; and even the grave was not able to quench the light of His life. His life – the light – triumphed over the darkness of the tomb.

The Revised Version renders verse 3 (verse 2 according to Lowth) just as we have it in our text: "Thou hast multiplied the nation, Thou hast increased the joy." The connection shows that this is better than, "Thou hast *not* increased the joy;" for immediately we read, "They joy before Thee according to the joy in harvest, and as men rejoice when they divide the spoil." The question at once arises, "How can there be so marked a difference, even a direct contradiction, in the two translations?" The answer is at hand: In the Hebrew the word "not," and the phrase "to him" are almost identical, and are pronounced exactly the same. Look now in the margin of verse 3, in King James' version, and you will see the words "to him" given as an alternative. The nation has been multiplied by Christ, and thereby the joy to Him has been increased.

We read of Christ that, having been made an offering for sin, "He shall see His seed, He shall prolong His days, and the pleasure of the Lord shall prosper in His hand," "and He shall divide the spoil with the strong." Isa. 53:10–12. Christ is the Seed, but, having died, He bears much fruit, so that the nation is increased. This is His joy, and His people share it with Him. It is the joy of harvest, because in the harvest – the end of the world – all His people will be gathered into the kingdom to shine forth as the sun. Matt. 13:38–43. It will be the rejoicing of them that divide spoil, because He then opens the graves, and takes away from "him that had the power of death, that is the devil" (Heb. 2:14), millions whom he has shut up in his prison house, the grave, claiming them as his own. The joy that is increased to Jesus in the multiplying of the nation, is shared by all His saints, because He gives them a share in His redeeming work, and thus says to them, "Enter thou into the joy of thy Lord."

"Thou hast broken the yoke of his burden, and the staff of his shoulder, the rod of his oppressor." For Jesus took part in flesh and blood "that He might destroy" not death merely, but "him that had the power of death, that is the devil." "Having spoiled principalities and powers, He made a show of them openly, triumphing over them in Himself." Col. 2:15; margin. Satan is the oppressor, who binds heavy burdens on men. He has laden men with iniquity, but the bands have been broken, and liberty is proclaimed to all the captives. To all who are in prison the Lord says, "Go forth," and they can do it if they wish, for in the face of that command Satan has no power to hinder.

"For all the armour of the armed man in the tumult, and the garments rolled in blood, shall even be for burning, for fuel of fire." Yes, the Lord "maketh wars to cease unto the end of the earth; He breaketh the bow, and cutteth the spear in sunder; He burneth the chariot in the fire." Ps. 46:9. War is of the devil, the destroyer. Christ redeems by destroying the destroyer, and so all the instruments of destruction will be destroyed. And the power by which at the last great battle all who destroy and all their weapons of destruction shall be destroyed, is the power by which today the yoke of Satan's oppression is broken for every believer.

"For unto us a child is born, unto us a Son is given." Who is He? – "The Son of man." He is born unto *us*. The message that came to the shepherds of Bethlehem on the night of Christ's birth, is spoken equally to us, "Unto you is born this day in the city of David a Saviour, which is Christ the Lord." Luke 2:11. He is our Saviour, our Christ, our Son. He belongs to us, and so all that He has is ours. With Him God freely gives us all things.

The Government is upon His shoulder; the kingdom is His. Therefore we shall reign with Him; for He who is born to us is also "the Everlasting Father." In Him we have obtained an inheritance. "For if by one man's offence death reigned by one; much more they which receive abundance of grace and of the gift of righteousness shall reign in life by One, Jesus Christ." Rom. 5:17. Never forget that as Christ is raised to the throne of God, "far above all principality and power and might and dominion," and we are made to sit together with Him in heavenly places (Eph. 1:20–21; 2:1–6), we have thus with Him power "over all the power of the enemy"

(Luke 10:19); so that in Christ we may assert our freedom from every bondage. Since Christ has given us power over "the prince of this world," "the spirit that now worketh in the children of disobedience," how can we have any fear of what wicked men may do to us. God can restrain the wrath of man, and that which He allows to manifest itself, He makes to praise Him.

His name is Counsellor. He is "wonderful in counsel and excellent in working." Isa. 28:29. He is a host in Himself, so that the "multitude of counselors," in which there is safety, is found in Him. We read so often in the Bible of people who went to seek counsel of the Lord, and they were not disappointed. Why not do the same thing now, since God is the same? of them who walk not in the counsel of the ungodly, but delight in the law of the Lord, it is said that all that they do shall prosper. The Lord Himself is pledged to execute any action that He counsels, so that in Him we find not only advice as to what to do, but the thing itself done. He who is the wisdom of God, is of God made unto us wisdom and right doing.

"Of the increase of His Government and peace there shall be no end, ... the zeal of the Lord of hosts will perform this." Christ does not ask any help of man to establish His kingdom. "The Lord God shall give unto Him the throne of His Father David." Luke 1:32. All that man has to do is to submit to His reign. We have not to enact laws and prepare the kingdom for Him, and then conduct Him to it; the kingdom is His, for God has anointed Him King in Zion, and He will put all His enemies under His feet. It is not by strife, not by force, not by human effort, but by the peaceful power of God in individual hearts, that the kingdom is made ready for the King. Then leave others alone, and "let the peace of God rule in your hearts."

CHAPTER 9

STRENGTH OUT OF WEAKNESS

(Isaiah 11:1–9, Lowth's Translation)

1. But there shall spring forth a rod from the trunk of Jesse; and a scion from his roots shall become fruitful.

2. And the Spirit of Jehovah shall rest upon Him; the Spirit of wisdom, and understanding; the Spirit of counsel and strength; the Spirit of the knowledge, and the fear of Jehovah.

3. And He shall be of quick discernment in the fear of Jehovah: so that not according to the sight of His eyes shall He judge; nor according to the hearing of His ears shall He reprove.

4. But with righteousness shall He judge the poor; and with equity shall He work conviction in the meek of the earth. And He shall smite the earth with a blast of His mouth, and with the breath of His lips shall He slay the wicked one.

5. And righteousness shall be the girdle of His loins; and faithfulness the cincture of His reins.

6. Then shall the wolf take up his abode with the lamb; and the leopard shall lie down with the kid; and the calf and the young lion, and the fatling shall come together; and a little child shall lead them.

7. And the heifer and the she-bear shall feed together, together shall their young ones lie down; and the lion shall eat straw like the ox.

8. And the suckling shall play on the hole of the aspic, and upon the den of the basilisk shall the weaned child lay his hand.

9. They shall not hurt, nor destroy, in all My holy mountain; for the earth shall be full of the knowledge of Jehovah, as the waters that cover the depths of the sea.

It will be seen that this chapter is a continuation of something begun in the preceding chapter. Read verses 33 and 34 of chapter 10, and you will see that a general destruction is foretold. "Behold Jehovah shall lop the flourishing branch with a dreadful crash; and the high of stature shall be cut down, and the lofty shall be brought low; and He shall hew the thickets of the forest with iron, and Lebanon shall fall by a mighty hand." But, although there shall be this cutting off of the mighty trees of the forest, "there shall spring forth a rod out of the stem of Jesse, and a scion from his roots shall be fruitful. And the Spirit of Jehovah shall rest upon Him," so that He shall do great things.

"There shall spring forth a rod." The Hebrew word here rendered "rod" occurs in but one other place in the Bible, namely, Prov. 14:3: "In the mouth of the foolish is a rod of pride." A rod, a stick, only a stick, yet of more value than all the trees of the forest because of the Spirit of Jehovah resting upon Him. This also is for our learning and comfort. Did you never feel that you were but a useless stick? Never mind; it is with a stick, a rod such as one might cut as a useless thing, that God will judge the world. "I can of Mine own self to do nothing." "I am a worm, and no man; a reproach of man, and despised of the people." This is what Christ said of Himself. No man can possibly feel himself more helpless and useless. But it is not what we are, but what God is, that determines what shall be done. He is. That is enough. "He that cometh to God must believe that He is."

"Yes, but I am so" –

Stop! It is not you are, but *He is*. If you come to God believing that He is, you will not straightway begin to say of yourself, "I am."

"But hear me out. I was only going to say that I am nothing at all."

Of course you are not; that is embraced in the statement that He is. As long as He is, you don't need to be. Let Him be what He is, – everything, – and then you will find your happiness in the fact that you are nothing. But don't forget that the only proper way for you to declare that you are nothing is to acknowledge that God, and God only, *is*.

The Spirit of Jehovah shall abide upon Him. The same Spirit is given to us, that He may abide with us for ever. He will be to us all that He was to Jesus, for He is "the eternal Spirit." The spirit of man is the life of man, since "the body without the spirit is dead." So the Spirit of God is the life of God. "The Spirit is life because of righteousness." When the Spirit of Jehovah rests upon one, that one has the power of the life of Jehovah, – "the power of an endless life." What can be done by that one then (Mind, it is not what that one can do, but what can be done through him. See Acts 2:22), is measured only by God's own purpose for him. When the life of Jehovah animates a person, it matters not how insignificant he is, – he is then the instrument of Almighty power. When God breathed His life into a lump of earth, the clod became a man having dominion over all the earth.

How diversified are the manifestations of the Spirit! Here are set forth at least six of "the seven Spirits of God." The Spirit of God is pre-eminently wisdom and power for eyes are a synonym for perception, and horns indicate power; and the slain Lamb in the midst of the throne has "seven horns and seven eyes, which are the seven Spirits of God sent forth into all the earth." Rev. 5:6. Why are they sent forth into all the earth? Is it to spy upon people! – By no means; they are sent forth to be our wisdom; for Christ is to us "the power of God, and the wisdom of God."

"The Spirit of wisdom and understanding; the Spirit of counsel and might." Wisdom is practical, not theoretical; it is real, and not simply a conception. The wisdom of God does not exhaust itself in formulas and statements. That which God in His wisdom counsels, He does. The counsel of peace is between the Father and the Son, and Christ our peace has come making peace for us. "He layeth up sound wisdom for the righteous." Prov. 2:7. This word, "wisdom," and also in Job 12:16, "with Him is strength and wisdom," are the same as the words "substance" and "working" in the following texts: "Thou dissolvest my *substance*." (Job 30:22), and "the Lord of hosts ... wonderful in counsel, and excellent in *working*." Isa. 28:29. There is in His wisdom the performance of the thing. "He hath made the earth by His power, He hath established the world by His wisdom, and hath stretched out the heavens by His discretion."

Jer. 10:12. This is the wisdom that God gives us. It is the wisdom that succeeds. It is not the wisdom of man, which plans, and then tries the plans to see if they will work; God's plans always work. His plan works itself. Why need any man fail? He cannot, if he accepts the free gift of God. The wisdom of God and the power of God must overcome everything; and they are ours in Christ. Of the man who walks in the counsel of God, it is said that "whatsoever he doeth shall prosper." Ps. 1:1–3.

"And shall make Him of quick understanding in the fear of the Lord." The two words "quick understanding" are from a single Hebrew word, the verb meaning "to smell." It is the verb from which comes the Hebrew word for wind, air, spirit. It is the same word that is rendered "smell" in Gen. 8:21, "the Lord *smelled* a sweet savour," in Ps. 115:6, "noses have they, but they smell not," and in other places. So we may read this verse, "The Spirit of the Lord shall cause Him to smell the fear of the Lord." But one smells by breathing, drawing in the air. So we have the most literal rendering by Segond, "Il respirera la crainte de l'Eernel," – He shall breathe the fear of the Lord. That is to say, the fear of the Lord is His life, He breathes it in with every breath. And since it is only because of our breath that we are able to have any pleasure, and breathing is itself a delight, we can see in the text the rendering also of the Revised Version, "His delight shall be in the fear of the Lord."

Remember that Jesus is the representative Man. The one here referred to is from "the stem of Jesse." Christ was made of the seed of David according to the flesh. Rom. 1:3–4. Therefore it is "the Man Christ Jesus" upon whom this spirit of understanding rests. Therefore in Him the same gift is ours. Every one whose delight is in the law of the Lord, shall have prosperity in everything; and the Spirit of God is given in order that we may have our delight in the fear of the Lord. If in the air that we breathe we recognize God's own Spirit of life, life itself will be a greater pleasure than ever before, and the delight of our life will be the presence of the Lord. So it was with Jesus.

Can the breath of God make a man good? – Most certainly. Christ breathed upon the disciples, and said, "Receive ye the Holy Ghost." John 20:22. In the beginning God made man of the dust of the ground. The man was perfect in form, but there was no life in him. As a man he was good for nothing. Then God breathed into his nostrils the breath of life, and man became a living soul – a "very good" man. As soon as God had made the man perfect by breathing into him, He saw everything that He had made, and, behold, "it was very good." But that could not have been said of man before the breath of God was put into him. Therefore it was the breath of God that made man good – very good. But it was the breath of life – the life of God in Christ – that made Him good, and it is by that that we are saved. See Rom. 5:10. As freely as the air, is the Holy Spirit given to us, and He comes to us in the very gift of the air. God gives us air, breathing it moment by moment into our lungs, in order that we may live. But He expects us to live righteously, and He gives us the means whereby to live righteously, for the life which He gives to all men is His own life, and His life is righteousness. If we but recognize the Lord as He is, we should breathe in righteousness with every breath. The Spirit of God would be our life, so that we should be wholly spiritual. See Rom. 8:9–10. The Spirit would be our wisdom and our power. We should know the will of God, because God would do our thinking in us, thus working to *will*; and we should do His will, because He would at the same time work to *do* of His good pleasure. There are infinite possibilities before the man who accepts the Spirit of God as his life. What eye hath not seen, nor ear heard, and what the mind of man has never conceived, God hath revealed unto us by His Holy Spirit.

He shall not judge according to appearance nor according to hearsay. But that is just the way men judge, and the only way they judge. Note the contrast: "He shall not judge after the sight of His eyes, nor reprove after the hearing of His ears; but with righteousness shall He judge." That is to say, He judges with righteousness because He does not judge after sight nor hearing. Therefore to judge after the sight of one's eyes, and after the hearing of one's ears, is to judge unrighteously. But since this is the only way by which judgment in the world is rendered, it follows that there is not on earth any such thing as righteous judgment. A well-known London magistrate said to a man who came to his court seeking justice: "You must know that law and justice are two entirely different things; you can get the law here, but not justice." This is so, not because there are no men yet in the world who have right desires, but because the best human judgment must be faulty. It is absolutely impossible that there should be a perfectly just human government.

"With righteousness shall He judge." He Himself is righteousness; His life is righteousness. He judges with righteousness because He judges by Himself. It is personal experience with Him. He has passed through every possible phase of human experience. Although in Him was never any sin, He was made to be sin for us, and as a sinner He experienced the punishment due to sin. "The chastisement of our peace was upon Him." Now He was made to be sin for us, in order "that we might be made the righteousness of God in Him;" therefore when this purpose is fulfilled in us, we do not come into judgment at all (see John 5:24); but if not, then we experience the punishment that inevitably follows the rejection of His life. When in the judgment it appears that God's perfect, eternal life has been given to all men, each soul will pronounce sentence on himself, and declare that God is just. No one can say that it is unfair in God to give us exactly what He gave His only begotten Son.

With the breath of His lips shall He slay the wicked one. Compare 2 Thess. 2:8. "Our God is a consuming fire." His life is constantly working to consume evil, – all that tends to death, – else we could not live. The life of God in the sunlight, the air, and the water, is continually at work to purify the earth. Waste products are consumed. This shows us how God's Spirit is working for our cleansing. But if, in spite of the goodness of God, we cling to evil, so that we ourselves are evil, then at the last that life which is given us for our support, and which works for our good by consuming that which is corrupt will necessarily consume us as plague-spots on the earth. So the slaying of the wicked at the last day is by the life of God, and is in keeping with the working of God to preserve life. The working of the life will result in the destruction of death, by destroying every cause of death.

Then shall the wolf dwell with the lamb, and the leopard lie down with the kid; the cow and the bear, and their young ones, shall feed and lie down together; so gentle will these beasts be that a child can lead them at pleasure; and the now venomous beasts will be the harmless playmate of the prattling babe: "they shall not hurt nor destroy," because the whole earth will then be full of the knowledge of the Lord; and "the wisdom that is from above is first pure, then peaceable, gentle, and easy to be entreated, full of mercy and good fruits." James 3:17.

See what a change is to take place in the nature of the now ferocious beasts; but do not suppose that this involves any new plan; it is only the restoration of that condition of things which existed at the beginning. God never made one beast to prey upon another. In the beginning, when God gave to man his diet of fruits and grains, He said, "And to every beast of the earth, and to every fowl of the air, and to everything that creepeth upon the earth, wherein there is life, I have given every green herb for meat; and it was so." Gen. 1:30. The wolf, the leopard, and the lion, were therefore vegetarians in the beginning, just as the ox is.

God is the Good Shepherd, who feeds His flock, watching over it for its own good, and giving His life that the sheep of His pasture may have life. He does not tend His flock in order that He may live off them. Satan is the roaring lion going about seeking whom he may devour. From him man has learned to destroy life in order that he may live, and by so doing has shortened his own life; for destruction can never produce life, any more than the wrath of man can work the righteousness of God. And when man, creation's lord, began to develop the Satanic instinct of preying on animals that were placed under him for protection and care, they also themselves developed the same traits, the strong devouring, instead of shielding, the weaker. Thus the earth became so full of violence that God was compelled to cleanse it by a flood of water. Now after so long a time is the condition that existed in those days returning (Matt. 24:37), so that God will be compelled to cleanse the earth again by a flood of fire. "Then judgment shall dwell in the wilderness, and righteousness remain in the fruitful field, and the work of righteousness shall be peace; and the effect of righteousness quietness and assurance for ever;" and God's "people shall dwell in a peaceable habitation, and in sure dwellings, and in quiet resting places." Isa. 32:16–18.

From all this it is easy to see that in the new earth, which will simply be the earth as it was first made for the abode of man, there will be no flesh-eating among men. Slaughter-houses will be unknown. No streams of blood will flow, and no beast will groan out its life to satiate the fiendish instincts of its cruel master. Man will then rejoice to live as God designed that he should. Life will be sustained by life, and not by death, and so life will be perfect.

There is probably no one who will dispute this. The most ravenous devourer of flesh would not think, if he should stop to think, of slaying and eating in the abode of God, when "the tabernacle of God is with men, and He will dwell with them." Rev. 21:3. But cannot all see in this a reason for now leaving off the use of flesh as food, and adopting in its stead the abundant bill of fare which God gave man? This time is given us in which to prepare for the future world. We must now begin to live the life that is to continue to eternity. No man would think that he should continue to indulge hatred and envy, expecting God to change his character to love and peace at His coming; then why should anyone think that any other habit is to be continued, which will not exist in the perfect state?

Some one may urge that the beasts still prey upon one another, and that the nature of animals will not be changed until the coming of the Lord. True; and that very thing contains a reason why men should correct their habits. Men are not beasts, but are made with moral natures, so that they may be associates of God. If man were not endowed with a free will, which allies him to God, then he would have no responsibility, and would depend on God to effect all changes in him, without his co-operation; but as it is, man must perfect holiness in the fear of God. What a humiliating thing for any man to admit that he is waiting for God to effect changes in his character, just as He does in the beasts. God's kingdom is to come, and His will be done in earth as it is in heaven, by the yielding of individuals at this present time to the perfect will of God. Let the peace of God rule in your hearts.

CHAPTER 10

THE LORD MY BANNER

(Isaiah 11:10–16, Lowth's Translation)

10. And it shall come to pass in that day, the root of Jesse, which standeth for an ensign to the peoples, unto Him shall the nations repair, and His resting-place shall be glorious.

11. And it shall come to pass in that day, Jehovah shall again the second time put forth His hand. To recover the remnant of His people that remaineth, from Assyria, and from Egypt, and from Pathros, and from Cush, and from Elam; and from Shimar, and from Hamath, and from the western regions.

12. And He shall lift up a signal to the nations; and He shall gather the outcasts of Israel, and the dispersed of Judah shall He collect, from the four extremities of the earth.

13. And the jealousy of Ephraim shall cease; and the enmity of Judah shall be no more; Ephraim shall not be jealous of Judah; and Judah shall not be at enmity with Ephraim.

14. But they shall invade the borders of the Philistines westward; together shall they spoil the children of the East; on Edom and Moab shall they lay their hand; and the sons of Ammon shall obey them.

15. And Jehovah shall smite with a drought the tongue of the Egyptian sea; and He shall shake His hand over the river with His vehement wind; and He shall strike it into seven streams, and make them pass over it dry-shod.

16. And there shall be a highway for the remnant of His people, which shall remain from Assyria; as it was unto Israel, in the day when he came up from the land of Egypt.

The first glance at this text composing this lesson will show the student that he must go back in order to get the connection. "It shall come to pass in that day." In what day? – Evidently in the day when the rod springs forth out of the stem of Jesse. Let the whole of the eleventh chapter of Isaiah be studied in connection, and it will be seen that it covers the entire period from the first advent of Christ till His second coming and the restoration of all things. The chapter is, however, divided into two sections. The first nine verses cover this entire period, and then, beginning with verse 10 the same period is covered again, with some additional details.

Compare verse 10 with John 12:32: "I, if I be lifted up from the earth, will draw all men unto Me." So the verse before us says that the nations shall repair to "the root of Jesse, which standeth for an ensign to the peoples." The Lord is the banner, and it is "Christ and Him crucified" that constitutes this ensign, round which the people are to gather.

It is written, "Cursed is every one that hangeth on a tree." Gal. 3:13. The cross was the sign of ignominy and reproach. It was the most humiliating death that could be imposed on anybody. Yet this very ignominious death is Christ's glory. By the cross, which was supposed by the men of His time to be the miserable end of an adventurer, Jesus was elevated to the right hand of the Majesty in the heavens. The badge of disgrace was the crown of glory. "God forbid that I should glory, save in the cross of our Lord Jesus Christ." Gal. 6:14.

What is the lesson in this for us? – Just this, that there is the brightest hope for the lowest and most despised of mankind. The banner round which God proposes to gather "the outcasts of Israel" is the Christ crucified, that is, Christ despised and rejected of men. If He took His stand in some exalted place, in a halo of glory, and from there called the poor outcasts to Him, they might well hesitate; but when the very rallying place is the lowest point of degradation, there can be no doubt that "whosoever will" may come. The way is adapted to the lowest and weakest; it must necessarily be in order that none be shut out; but where the lowest and weakest can come in, the highest and strongest cannot possibly be excluded. They can easily humble themselves and come down, if they will; but the others could not possibly lift themselves up.

The Jews thought that they were inflicting the most crushing defeat on Christ, – that they were degrading Him to the uttermost, –

whereas they were really lifting Him up. He was lifted up from the earth, even to the height of heaven. The way to heaven lies by the cross. This world consists of pride and self-exaltation, – "the lust of the flesh, the lust of the eyes, and the pride of life," – so that the cross does in reality lift one up and away from this earth.

"His rest shall be glorious." The cross gives rest. Jesus calls, "Come unto Me, all ye that labour, and are heavy laden, and I will give you rest." Matt. 11:28. The rest is Sabbath rest, – the rest which God took when He had finished the six days' work of creation. The cross creates: "if any man be in Christ, he is a new creature" or, "there is a new creation," The cross restores what was lost in the fall. The fall deprived man of the glory of God; the cross restores it. The cross creates anew, doing the same work that God did in the beginning. The cross represents a perfect work completed – for on it Jesus said, "It is finished." Now finished work means rest; it can mean nothing else, therefore the cross of Christ must give rest to all who come to it.

Moreover, since redemption is identical with creation, – *is* creation, – restoring that which was lost, it is evident that the rest which it brings is identical with the rest which followed the finished work of creation in the beginning. In the cross of Christ we find the Sabbath, the rest, of the Lord. See how people have reversed God's order. They find in God's Sabbath only a cross; to rest on the seventh day of the week, "according to the commandment" when the majority of men make it the busiest day of the week, seems to them too great a cross to be borne. Well, if that is the way they look at it, they will find no rest in it. But let them come to the cross of Christ, accepting it without any reservation. Let them not take a part of it, rejecting another portion, but let them take the cross with the whole life of Jesus; then they will find perfect rest – God's Sabbath. And then it will be a joy to indicate the perfect rest which Christ gives, by resting from their labours on the day which He has given as the memorial, the sign of His power to redeem.

"It shall come to pass in that day that the Lord shall set His hand again the second time to recover the remnant of His people." This will not be a small affair, but will be gathering "from the four corners of the earth." And since it is "the remnant" that are to be gathered, it is evident that this work is the last thing that will be done in connection with the people of God. This is the closing work of the Gospel. It is by the Gospel that God's Israel – overcomers – are to be gathered. On this matter of the setting of God's hand "the second time" to gather His people, read the first article entitled "The Time of the Promise," which appeared on the first page of PRESENT TRUTH for December 29, 1898, in connection with the first of these lessons in Isaiah.

The last verses of this chapter indicate the power that is to accompany the closing work of the Gospel. "There shall be an highway ... like as it was to Israel in the day that he came up out of the land of Egypt." Read the account of God's wonderful leading then. It was not by any human strength, but by the strength of Almighty God, that the deliverance was effected. Think of the marvelous miracles in Egypt, and the dividing of the Red Sea. Yet while all this was but the manifestation of God's own power it was all accomplished through a human agent. He led His people like a flock by the hand of Moses and Aaron. Ps. 77:20. It was always by the stretching out of the rod in the hand of Moses, that these signs were wrought. Now just that power must be manifested in the preaching of the Gospel before the Lord comes. The power that divided the Red Sea must and will be seen in the work when the Sabbath – the sign of Jehovah's creative power – is given its rightful place among God's people. God's rest will be seen to be glorious, and by it the earth will be filled with the knowledge of the glory of the Lord.

CHAPTER 11

THE NEW SONG

(Isaiah 12:1–6, Lowth's Translation)

1. "And in that day thou shalt say: I will give thanks unto Thee, O Jehovah; for though Thou has been angry with me, Thine anger is turned away, and Thou hast comforted me.

2. Behold, God is my salvation; I will trust, and will not be afraid: for my strength, and my song, is Jehovah; and He is become my salvation.

3. And when ye shall draw waters with joy from the fountains of salvation, in that day ye shall say:

4. Give ye thanks to Jehovah; call upon His name; make known among the peoples His mighty deeds; record ye, how highly His name is exalted.

5. Sing ye Jehovah; for He hath wrought a stupendous work; this is made manifest in all the earth.

6. Cry aloud, and shout for joy, O inhabitress of Sion; for great in the midst of thee is the Holy One of Israel."

This is a most wonderful chapter, and everybody ought to study it so thoroughly that the words will be for ever impressed on the mind. Such passages as this, full of comfort and encouragement, should be perfectly familiar to every person. They should not be studied mechanically as a school-boy studies his spelling lesson, so that they can be repeated parrot-like, but intelligently and thought-fully. It will not take long to fix the chapter so thoroughly in the mind that the words will come naturally in their proper order. When this has been done, we can study the Bible at any odd moment, and can feed on the living Word, which is always fresh.

It will be noticed that this chapter is a continuation of chapter 11. "In that day." In what day? – Why, in the day when the root of Jesse stands for an ensign to the peoples; when the Lord sets His hand the second time to gather the remnant of his people – the outcasts of

Israel. In short, *now*, for "Now is the accepted time; now is the day of salvation." It is not in the future, immortal state that this song is to be taken up and learned. Now is the time for men to say, "Jehovah is my strength and my song; He also is become my salvation;" "I will trust, and not be afraid."

Take notice that this song is identical with that sung by Moses after the crossing of the Red Sea. Compare Ex. 15:2. When the redeemed stand on Mount Zion, they will sing "the song of Moses the servant of God, the song of the Lamb" (Rev. 15:2–3), and it will be this very song; but they will have learned it before they get there. Moses was yet in the wilderness when he sang his song of triumph. There was no water in the desert where the children of Israel were when they joined in the chorus. But it was right for them to sing it. The trouble was that they stopped singing, and that stopped their progress; for "the redeemed of the Lord shall return, and come with singing unto Zion; and everlasting joy shall be on their head." Isaiah 51:11. The "new song" of the redeemed is that which they have learned on earth, inspired by the love of God, which, though everlasting, is always new. The "new commandment" is the old commandment that was from the beginning. When God brings a man up out of the horrible pit, and the miry clay, He puts a new song in his mouth. Ps. 40:1–3. So,

> "When in scenes of glory,
> I sing the new, new song,
> 'Twill be the old, old story
> That I have loved so long."

"Behold, God is my salvation; I will trust, and not be afraid." Why not? How could one fear, knowing God Himself to be his salvation? It is not merely that God saves, but He Himself is salvation. Having Him, we have salvation, and are not merely looking forward to it, and hoping for it. He is our salvation, – from what? – From everything that we need to be saved from. "I sought the Lord, and He heard me, and delivered me from all my fears." Psalms 34:4. That is the best of all. God not only saves us from death, but from the fear of death. Heb. 2:14–15. Many things that we fear, exist only in our imagination; but the trouble is just as great to us as though the danger were real; our fears are as oppressive. Now God saves us from all these fears. God says, "Be not afraid of sudden fear, neither of the desolation of the wicked, when it cometh. For the Lord shall be thy confidence, and shall keep thy foot from being taken." "Whoso hearkeneth unto Me shall dwell safely, and shall be quiet from fear of evil." Prov. 3:25–26; 1:33.

"There is no fear in love; but perfect love casteth out fear; because fear hath torment. He that feareth is not made perfect in love." I John 4:18. Remember that God is near at hand "in all things that we call upon Him for." Deut. 4:7. "He giveth to all life, and breath, and all things." "In Him we live, and move, and have our being." Acts 17:25,28. And He is Almighty; there is none able to withstand Him. 2 Chron. 20:6. "Our God is in the heavens; He hath done whatsoever He hath pleased." Ps. 115:3. And His thoughts towards us are thoughts of peace, and not of evil, to give us an expected end. Jer. 29:11. Is it not clear, therefore, that every fear, no matter what kind of a fear it is, nor what it is that we are afraid of, is evidence of distrust? We either distrust His care or His power. If we are afraid, that shows that we do not believe that God is at hand, or else we do not believe that He cares for us, or else we do not believe that He is able to save us. Give this sober thought; think how often you have been afraid, and how often you are seized and controlled by fear; and then decide whether you do really love and trust the Lord.

"God is our refuge and strength; a very present help in trouble. Therefore will not we fear, though the earth be removed, and though the mountains be carried into the midst of the sea. Though the waters thereof roar and be troubled, though the mountains shake with the swelling thereof." Ps. 46:1–2. Some one will say, "No; I don't expect to be afraid in the last great day; I shall then be confident in the Lord." Why will you be more confident in the Lord then than now? Will He at that time be more trustworthy than now? Do you not know that if you do not get acquainted with the Lord, and learn to trust Him now, you will not trust Him then? Jesus is coming to take vengeance on them that know not God. 2 Thess. 1:7–8. Now all those who know the name of the Lord put their trust in Him. Ps. 9:10. Therefore those who are saved when the Lord comes will be found trusting.

"But there are so many little things that startle me, and make me nervous; I am not afraid of great things; I know the Lord will protect me then; but I can't expect Him to keep me from nervousness at sudden noises, or from being timid and afraid to speak a word in meeting, or from being anxious at sea, or for those who are on it." Why not? Do you not see that this is a virtual shutting out of God from all the ordinary affairs of life? He is a God nigh at hand as well as afar off. Jer. 23:23. He who does that which is greatest, is abundantly able to do that which is least. Fear in little things is evidence of distrust in God, just as much as fear in great things. It shows that we do not believe that God is very near, or that He is great enough to look after details. The true child of God, who is living a life of constant trust in Him, need not, cannot, be afraid of anything in the world. He who is not afraid of God, cannot be afraid of anything; for nothing is so great as He.

"The Lord is my light and my salvation; whom shall I fear? The Lord is the strength of my life; of whom shall I be afraid?" Psalm 27:1. He is "the confidence of all the ends of the earth, and of them that are afar off upon the sea." Psalms 65:5. "The eternal God is thy refuge, and underneath are the everlasting arms." Deut. 33:27. "He that dwelleth in the secret place of the Most High shall abide under the shadow of the Almighty. I will say of the Lord, He is my refuge and my fortress; my God; in Him will I trust. Surely He shall deliver thee from the snare of the fowler, and from the noisome pestilence. He shall cover thee with His feathers, and under His wings shalt thou trust; His truth shall be thy shield and buckler. Thou shalt not be afraid for the terror by night; nor for the arrow that flieth by day; nor for the pestilence that walketh in darkness; nor for the destruction that wasteth at noonday." Psalms 41:1–5.

This perfect confidence is the result of acquaintance with the Lord. Because one has learned to trust the Lord in all things, proving that nothing is too small for His attention, he can trust Him in the great trial. "In returning and rest shall ye be saved; in quietness and confidence shall be your strength." Isa. 30:15. When the perfect love casts out all fear, then perfect rest must remain. This is the rest that remains to the people of God. It is the perfect keeping of the Sabbath. It is this blessed rest that the Sabbath of the Lord makes known. "The seventh day is the Sabbath of the Lord thy God:" but the keeping of the Sabbath is not by any means met by resting from manual labour on the last day of the week. The ceasing from our work on that day is but the sign of our perfect rest in God – of the committing of our souls to God in well-doing, as unto a faithful Creator. I Peter 4:19. But perfect rest must be constant; to trust one day and be anxious and fearful the next, is not to rest in God. So in the message of the Sabbath of the Lord, which is the message that prepares for His coming, we find that revelation of God as Creator and Lord, that will keep us from ever being afraid again. What a glorious message!

"My strength and my song is Jehovah; and He is become my salvation." Just see what one gets in return for acknowledging that he has no strength: he gets the Lord for his strength. All the strength of the Lord is his. Thus he is "strengthened with all might, according to his glorious power." Col. 1:11. This is far better than the utmost that anyone could hope for, even at the highest estimate of his own strength.

"With joy shall ye draw waters from the wells of salvation." When? – Now; whenever you are thirsty for salvation. Jesus cried: "If any man thirst, let him come to Me, and drink." John 7:37. "Let him that is athirst, come. And whosoever will, let him take of the water of life freely." Rev. 22:17. God is "the fountain of living waters." Jer. 2:13. "In Him we live;" therefore we are continually drawing water from the wells of salvation, whether we know it or not. Recognize the fact, and the drinking of the water of life will be a joy.

"Make known among the peoples His mighty deeds." This is the proper occupation of all men. Nobody has any right to talk to another soul about his own weakness. Our sole business is to speak of the glory of God's kingdom, and to talk of His power; "to make known to the sons of men His mighty acts, and the glorious majesty of His kingdom." Ps. 145:12. Say unto the cities of Judah, "Behold your God!" We don't, as a general thing, need to tell people very much about our own weakness and insignificance; they usually have a fair knowledge of that without our taking special pains to point it out. It does them no good, and it increases our own discouragement, when we talk of our own weakness. But when we speak of the power of Jehovah, we have an endless theme, and one which strengthens and encourages both speaker and hearer.

"Cry out and shout, thou inhabitant of Zion; for great is the Holy One of Israel in the midst of thee." "There is a river, the streams whereof shall make glad the city of God, the holy place of the tabernacles of the Most High; God is in the midst of her; she shall not be moved." Psalms 46:4–5. The presence of God in Zion renders it immovable; so the presence of God in the midst of His people assures their safety. God's presence recognized in a man makes him "steadfast, unmovable, always abounding in the work of the Lord." I Cor. 15:58. Why shout? because you are so great? – No; because God is so great, and He dwells in us. "Greater is He that is in you than he that is in the world." 1 John 4:4. "What shall we say then to these things? If God be for us, who can be against us?" "I am persuaded, that neither death, nor life, nor angels, nor principalities, nor powers, nor things present, nor things to come, nor height, nor depth, nor any other creature, shall be able to separate us from the love of God, which is in Christ Jesus our Lord."

CHAPTER 12

THE JUDGMENT UPON BABYLON

(Isaiah 13:1–22, Lowth's Translation)

2. Upon a lofty mountain erect the standard; exalt the voice; beckon with the hand; that they may enter the gates of princes.

3. I have given a charge to my enrolled warriors; I have even called My strong ones to execute My wrath; those that exult in My greatness.

4. A sound of a multitude in the mountains, as of a great people; a sound of the tumult of kingdoms, of nations gathered together! Jehovah, God of hosts, mustereth the host for the battle.

5. They come from a distant land, from the end of the heavens; Jehovah, and the instruments of His wrath, to destroy the whole land.

6. Howl ye, for the day of Jehovah is at hand; as a destruction from the Almighty shall it come.

7. Therefore shall all hands be slackened; and every heart of mortal shall melt; and they shall be terrified;

8. Torments and pangs shall seize them; as a woman in travail, they shall be pained; they shall look upon one another with astonishment; their countenances shall be like flames of fire.

9. Behold, the day of Jehovah cometh, inexorable; even indignation, and burning wrath; to make the land a desolation. And her sinners He shall destroy from out of her.

10. Yea, the stars of heaven, and the constellations thereof, shall not send forth their light; the sun is darkened at his going forth, and the moon shall not cause her light to shine.

11. And I will visit the world for its evil; and the wicked for their iniquity; and I will put an end to the arrogance of the proud; and I will bring down the haughtiness of the terrible.

12. I will make a mortal more precious than fine gold. Yea, a man than the rich ore of Ophir.

13. Wherefore I will make the heavens tremble; and the earth shall be shaken out of her place; in the indignation of Jehovah God of Hosts; and in the day of His burning anger.

14. And the remnant shall be as a roe chased; and as sheep when there is none to gather them together; they shall look every one towards his own people; and they shall flee every one to his own land.

15. Every one that is overtaken shall be thrust through and all that are collected in a body shall fall by the sword.

16. And their infants shall be dashed before their eyes; their houses shall be plundered, and their wives ravished.

17. Behold, I raise up against them the Medes, who shall hold silver of no account; and as for gold, they shall not delight in it.

18. Their bows shall dash the young men; and on the fruit of the womb they shall have no mercy. Their eye shall have no pity even on the children.

19. And Babylon shall become, she that was the beauty of kingdoms, the glory of the pride of the Chaldeans, as the overthrow of Sodom and Gomorrah by the hand of God.

20. It shall not be inhabited for ever; nor shall it be dwelt in from generation to generation; neither shall the Arabian pitch his tent there, neither shall the shepherds make their fold there.

21. But there shall the wild beasts of the desert lodge; and howling monsters shall fill their houses; and there shall the daughters of the ostrich dwell; and there shall the satyrs hold their revels.

22. And wolves shall howl to one another in their palaces; and dragons in their voluptuous pavilions; and her time is near to come; and her day shall not be prolonged.

This is "the oracle concerning Babylon which was revealed to Isaiah the son of Amos." Isa. 13:1. The lesson may seem to be very long, but the principal point that needs consideration is, What is

Babylon? When this point is understood, the chapter as a whole is very simple, for it consists simply in plain statements concerning the fate of Babylon; and therefore we could not well consider it except as a whole.

The origin of Babylon is given in the eleventh chapter of Genesis. After the flood the people came to a plain in the land of Shinar, and said to one another, "Let us build a city and a tower whose top may reach unto heaven, and let us make us a name lest we be scattered abroad upon the face of the whole earth." The Lord saw what they "imagined to do," and confounded their language so that they could not continue to build. Thus that which they thought to avoid came upon them: They were scattered abroad. The name of the city which they began to build was called "Babel," which means "confusion," because their language as well as their lofty ideas was confounded. Since Babel, or Babylon, means confusion, it is evident that the term is not limited to a particular spot or city, but that wherever there is confusion there is Babylon.

"Where envy and strife is, there is confusion, and every evil work." James 3:16. "The Lord knoweth the thoughts of the wise that they are vain." I Cor. 3:20. He therefore provided the spiritual weapons that are "mighty through God to the pulling down of strongholds, casting down imaginations, and every high thing that exalteth itself against the knowledge of God, and bringing into captivity every thought to the obedience of Christ." 2 Cor. 10:4–5. God's way is perfect, because His thoughts are perfect and they alone endure to all generations. Only the mind of God can think right thoughts, even as God alone can do righteous acts. "There is no power but of God." Man has no more power in himself to think than he has in himself to live and to move. Just as every attempt of man to act for himself results in erratic movements, so every attempt of man to think in opposition to God must come to nothing; that is, will be utterly confounded. We see, therefore, that Babylon exists as extensively and as long as there is opposition to God.

As long as the ancient city of Babylon stood, it was the embodiment of boastful exaltation against God. The fourth chapter of Daniel sets forth this spirit. In Isaiah 47:8 we read of Babylon, that she said, "I am, and none else beside me." This spirit has character-ized every nation since the day when Belshazzar's blasphemous boastings were cut short by the destruction of his kingdom by the Medes.

Babylon was a universal kingdom. Dan. 2:37–38. The kingdom as a name, ceased with the death of Belshazzar and the capture of the city by the Medes; but in reality it has existed to the present day. That this is so is evident from the chapter before us, for it tells of judgments upon Babylon, yet these are evidently none other than the final judgments upon the whole earth. Thus we read that the Lord "mustereth the hosts of the battle from the end of heaven, and the weapons of His indignation to destroy the whole land." Verses 4–5. "Behold the day of the Lord cometh, cruel, both with wrath and fierce anger to lay the land desolate, and He shall destroy the sinners out of it." The Lord says that at the time of this judgment of Babylon, He will punish the world for their evil and the wicked for their iniquity, and will cause the arrogancy of the proud to cease and will lay low the haughtiness of the terrible. He will shake the heavens, and the earth shall be removed out of her place in the wrath of the Lord of hosts and in the day of His fierce anger. Compare this with the second chapter of Isaiah, where we have the account of the judgments of God upon every high tower and every fenced wall when the loftiness of men shall be bowed down and the monuments of men shall be made low and the Lord alone shall be exalted.

By comparing Isa. 47:8–9, with Rev. 18:7–8, we see that the prophet John, a century after Christ, used exactly the same language concerning Babylon that is used by the prophet Isaiah seven hundred years before Christ. This shows that the fulfillment of the prophecy of Isaiah was yet in the future in the days of John, yet the city that was built in the plain of Shinar had been leveled to the ground long before. We do not need to resort to the idea that one was literal Babylon and the other spiritual or figurative Babylon, for the language of John refers to just as literal a city as does that of Isaiah; but we do see that Babylon was not by any means confined to the city of brick and stone that was embellished by Nebuchadnezzar, nor to the people known as Babylonians. It still exists and its destruction will be the final judgment upon the earth when sin and sinners shall be destroyed out of it, and rebellion against God be made to cease for evermore.

The question may arise, if this threatened judgment upon Babylon, Isa. 13, refers to the final judgment upon the wicked, how is it that the Medes are referred to as taking part in this retribution? The answer is very simple. It is because judgment upon Babylon began twenty-five hundred years ago, when the Medes captured the city and destroyed Belshazzar in the height of his insolent pride. The desolation of that proud and wicked city is a proof that everything that exalts itself against God shall be destroyed.

With these facts in mind, this chapter is very simple. With a knowledge of what Babylon is, not only this, but a great portion of the prophecies of Isaiah, Jeremiah, and Ezekiel is made plain. God calls His people to come out of Babylon where they have been to a large extent ever since. They were carried captive because of their haughty rebellion against God. Every one whose soul is lifted up is in Babylon. A man can come out and be free at any time by allowing the mind of the Spirit of God to take the place of his carnal mind, which is enmity against God. Now is the time to hasten from Babylon; for "Her time is near to come, and her day shall not be prolonged."

CHAPTER 13

ISRAEL'S DELIVERANCE

(Isaiah 14:1–12, Lowth's Translation)

1. For Jehovah will have compassion on Jacob, and will yet choose Israel. And He shall give them rest upon their own land; and the stranger shall be joined unto them, and shall cleave unto the house of Jacob.

2. And the nations shall take them, and bring them into their own place; and the house of Israel shall possess them in the land of Jehovah, as servants and as handmaids; and they shall take them captive, whose captives they were; and they shall rule over their oppressors.

3. And it shall come to pass in that day, that Jehovah shall give thee rest from thine affliction, and from thy disquiet, and from the hard servitude that was laid upon thee; and thou shall pronounce this parable upon the king of Babylon; and shalt say: –

4. How hath the oppressor ceased! the exactress of gold ceased!

5. Jehovah hath broken the staff of the wicked, the sceptre of the rulers.

6. He that smote the nations in wrath, with a stroke unremitted; he that ruled the nations in anger, is persecuted, and none hindereth.

7. The whole earth is at rest, is quiet; they burst forth into a joyful shout;

8. Even the fir trees rejoice over thee, the cedars of Libanus: since thou art fallen, no feller hath come up against us.

9. Hades from beneath is moved because of thee, to meet thee at thy coming; he rouseth for thee the mighty dead, all the great chiefs of the earth; he maketh to rise up from their thrones, all the kings of the nations.

10. All of them shall accost thee, and shall say unto thee: Art thou, even thou too, become weak as we? Art thou made like unto us?

11. Is then thy pride brought down to the grave; the sound of thy sprightly instruments? Is the vermin become thy couch, and the earthworm thy covering?

12. How art thou fallen from heaven, O Lucifer, son of the morning!

It would be well if every one who is following these studies in Isaiah could keep with him for constant reference the article entitled, "The Time of the Promise," which accompanied the first lesson. Each succeeding lesson would impress the truth there summarized more and more on the mind, until a glance at any part of the book of Isaiah would enable the student to see that it refers to the last days of this world's history.

Consider the condition of Israel in the time when this prophecy was written. They were not in captivity, but were dwelling in the land of Canaan, under their own king. We do not know at just what date this was written, but we know that it was not later than 700 B.C. Isaiah prophesied during the reign of Uzziah, Jotham, Ahaz, and Hezekiah, beginning at the close of the reigns of Uzziah. See Isa. 1:1 and 6:1–9. Jotham and Ahaz each reigned sixteen years, and Hezekiah twenty-nine years. 2 Chron. 27:1; 28:1; and 29:1. It was in the fourteenth year of Hezekiah's reign that Isaiah had a special message for him, announcing his death, and later his restoration. We know this because at that time fifteen years were added to the king's life. 2 Kings 21:6. The prophet had therefore been prophesying at least forty-six years, and this was 713 B.C. He did not prophesy after Hezekiah's death, even if he did so long as that, since if he had it would have been mentioned in Isa. 1:1. But even if he continued till the death of Hezekiah, his work was all at least 700 before Christ, for Hezekiah died in 698 B.C.

Now this little study of date is not a technical matter. It is a thing of vital importance. From it we see that this prophecy of Isaiah concerning the choosing of Israel, and bringing them to their own place, giving them rest in their own land, was uttered nearly a hundred years before they were carried away to Babylon. At the time the promise was spoken, the kingdom was enjoying prosperity, and the Israelites were dwelling safely in the land of Canaan; yet God promised that they should yet have rest in their own land. This is very significant.

A similar thing is found in the history of David. See 2 Sam. 7:1–10. There we learn that when David, at the height of his power, the Lord having given him rest from all his enemies, proposed to build a house for the Lord, he received a great promise from God, a part of which was this: "Moreover I will appoint a place for My people Israel, and will plant them, that they may dwell in a place of their own, and move no more; neither shall the children of wickedness afflict them any more as beforetime." These things show plainly that the present land of Canaan, even though as fruitful as in the days of Joshua, is not good enough for an inheritance for God's people. David confessed that he was only a stranger and a sojourner in the land, and that was when the kingdom was at its greatest. 1 Chron. 29:15. He considered himself as much a sojourner as were Abraham, Isaac, and Jacob. Only when sinners are destroyed out of the land, so that the children of wickedness cannot afflict any more, do the meek inherit the earth, and delight themselves in the abundance of peace. Ps. 37:9–11.

"Of whom a man is overcome, of the same is he brought in bondage." 2 Peter 2:19. "Every one that committeth sin is the bondservant of sin." John 8:34, R.V. "His own iniquities shall take the wicked himself, and he shall be holden with the cords of his sins." Prov. 5:22. No man can be in bondage if he is not overcome by sin. Daniel was in Babylon for more than seventy years, but he was never in bondage. He would not yield to sin, and so instead of being a servant, he became ruler of the realm. His three companions were likewise free. So free were they, even in Babylon, that when they were bound with cords, and cast into a burning furnace, because of their loyalty to God, the fire that was designed for their destruction, merely burned the bonds, and allowed them to walk at liberty. They were "free indeed," for the Son Himself made them free. See Dan. 3:13–25. Thus we see that only sin can make one a captive in Babylon, and Satan is the author of sin; therefore when we read the promise that God's people shall take captive those by whom they were formerly taken captive, and shall rule over their oppressors, we know that it means victory over all their sins, and over all the power of the devil. It is the fulfillment of the oath which God swore to our father Abraham "that He would grant unto us, that we being delivered out of the hand of our enemies might serve Him without fear, in holiness and righteousness before Him all the days of our life." Luke 1:73–75.

This victory is ours now, for "This is the victory that hath overcome the world, even our faith." 1 John 5:4. But there will come a time when Satan himself shall be bound, so that he can "deceive the nations no more." Rev. 20:1–3. Then not only a part but all of God's people, gathered out of all the lands, will burst forth into singing: "How hath the oppressor ceased! the golden city ceased! The Lord hath broken the staff of the wicked, and the sceptre of the rulers. He who smote the people in wrath with a continual stroke, he that ruled the nations in anger, is persecuted, and none hindereth." The promise is that they who seek after our soul, and devise our hurt, shall be turned back and brought to confusion; they shall "be as chaff before the wind," and the angel of the Lord shall chase them; their way shall be dark and slippery, and the angel of the Lord shall persecute them." Ps. 35:4–6. The song of the redeemed upon Mount Zion must be learned here, for the redeemed of the Lord shall return and come with singing unto Zion. Isa. 51:11. It will be a new song that they sing; but it is now, in this present age, that the Lord lifts us out of the horrible pit, and the miry clay, and sets our feet on the Rock, and establishes our goings, and puts a new song in our mouths. Ps. 40:1–3.

This song of redemption is sung over deliverance from the power of the king of Babylon. Can there be any question as to who this king is? – It is the one who smites the nations in wrath with a continual stroke. When he is laid low, "the whole earth is at rest, and is quiet." It is none other than the adversary, the devil, who goes about in the whole earth, to destroy the inhabitants thereof. Even he is to be brought low, although at one time he was "Lucifer, son of the morning," but is "fallen from heaven." No chapter shows this identity between the real king of Babylon, and Satan, more fully than this one. Let this fact be fully grasped and held; let it be understood that the book of Isaiah was written for the last days, and that it applies specially to us, and the entire prophecy becomes simple, and may be read with pleasure and profit.

"The prince of the power of the air, the spirit that now worketh in the children of disobedience" (Eph. 2:2) is Satan, "the god of this world." 2 Cor. 4:3–4. As he has gained the place which rightly belongs to God, in the hearts of men, it naturally follows that he rules in the nations that forget God. In ancient times there were no nations on earth but unqualified heathen. Devil-worship was the worship of heathendom, and Satan was the real ruler in every kingdom. Now the leading nations of earth are professedly Christian, yet every one is openly and decidedly at variance with the teaching of Christ. The precepts of God are defied, and those who will follow them and teach others to do so, are punished. Consequently Satan, the author of confusion, because the originator of envy and strife, – the king of Babylon, – still reigns, and oppresses many, even of the people of God. But "thanks be to God, who giveth us the victory through our Lord Jesus Christ." God has visited the nations, to take out of them a people for His name, every one who overcomes will be given power over the nations. Rev. 2:26–27. But the necessary qualification for ruling the nations is the ruling of one's own spirit, and this can be done only through Christ, who has been given "power over all flesh," and in whom we are made complete.

CHAPTER 14

SELFISH AMBITION AND ITS FALL

(Isaiah 14:12–27, Lowth's Translation)

12. How art thou fallen from heaven, O Lucifer, son of the morning! Art cut down to the earth, thou that didst subdue the nations!

13. Yet thou didst say in thy heart, I will ascend the heavens; above the stars of God, I will exalt my throne; and I will sit upon the mount of the Divine Presence on the sides of the North;

14. I will ascend above the heights of the clouds; I will be like the Most High.

15. But thou shalt be brought down to the grave, to the sides of the pit.

16. Those that see thee shall look attentively at thee; they shall well consider thee: Is this the man that made the earth to tremble; that shook the kingdoms?

17. That made the world like a desert: that destroyed the cities? That never dismissed his captives to their own home?

18. All the kings of the nations, all of them, lie down in glory, each in his own sepulchre;

19. But thou art cast out of the grave, as the tree abominated; clothed with the slain, with the pierced by the sword, with them that go down to the stones of the pit; as a trodden carcass.

20. Thou shalt not be joined unto them in burial; because thou hast destroyed thy country, thou hast slain thy people; the seed of evil-doers shall never be renowned.

21. Prepare ye slaughter for his children, for the iniquity of their fathers; lest they rise, and possess the earth; and fill the face of the earth with cities.

22. For arise against them, saith Jehovah God of Hosts; And I will cut off from Babylon the name, and the remnant; and the son, and the son's son, saith Jehovah.

23. And I will make it an inheritance for the porcupine, and pools of water; and I will plunge it in the miry gulf of destruction, saith Jehovah God of Hosts.

24. Jehovah God of Hosts hath sworn, saying, Surely as I have devised, so shall it be; and as I have purposed, that thing shall stand:

25. To crush the Assyrian in My land, and to trample him on My mountains. Then shall his yoke depart from off them; and his burden shall be removed from off their shoulder.

26. This is the decree which is determined on the whole earth; and this is the hand which is stretched out over all the nations;

27. For Jehovah God of Hosts hath decreed; and who shall disannul it? And it is His hand that is stretched out; and who shall turn it back?

Those who are making a special study of the book of Isaiah should pay special attention to the text, for *there* is where they will get their knowledge. Light comes from the Word. Read the portion of Scripture that composes the lesson many times carefully, giving thought to each statement, comparing everything with what precedes and what follows. The notes that are given in the paper, in connection with the lesson text, are simply designed to fasten your attention more closely upon it.

In studying this lesson, begin with the thirteenth chapter, and read through the fourteenth. It would be well also to read the second chapter again. Recall what has been said concerning the time of the promise, and the purpose of the book of Isaiah, and remember also the meaning of Babylon. Even without these things before us, but more especially with them, we cannot fail to see that the judgment upon Babylon means the destruction of "all the proud" and "all that do wickedly" (Mal. 4:1) at the last day. This lesson is therefore specially important now.

Lucifer means "light-bearer." The margin gives "day star," and other renderings are the same. He is also called the "son of the morning." A glorious being he certainly was, but now fallen from heaven through overweening ambition. There can be no question but that he is the mightiest of "the angels that sinned" and so "kept not their first estate," who are now "reserved in everlasting chains under darkness unto the Judgment of the great day." 2 Peter 2:4; Jude 6. It is Satan, no longer the bearer of light, but the prince of darkness, the chief of "the rulers of the darkness of this world." Eph. 6:11–12. But though fallen from his state of light and glory, he still remembers enough of it to be able to transform himself into an angel of light. 2 Cor. 11:14–15. Therefore we need to be on our guard lest we be deceived. Even when we are walking most in the light, he will try to steal in as a part of that light, and thus lead us astray while we think we are still in the right way. But we have one safeguard, namely, "the sword of the Spirit, which is the Word of God," the word of truth. Eph. 6:17; John 17:17. He who "abode not in the truth," and who is "a liar, and the father of it" (John 8:44), cannot endure the word of truth. Keep fast hold of that, and the devil will flee. See James 4:7; 1 Peter 5:8–9.

"Pride goeth before destruction, and an haughty spirit before a fall." Prov. 16:18. "For the day of the Lord of hosts shall be upon every one that is proud and lofty, and upon every one that is lifted up; and he shall be brought low." Isa. 2:12. This is because righteousness must prevail, and only God can rule in righteousness, and He is of a lowly spirit. "Behold his soul which is lifted up is not upright in him; but the just shall live by his faith." Hab. 2:4. When righteousness, which is meekness, prevails, then pride and ambition must be destroyed.

God says, "Be ye holy, for I am holy." "Be ye therefore perfect, even as your Father which is in heaven is perfect." Lucifer said, "I will be like the Most High." Wherein then was Lucifer wrong? – Simply in this, that he took the wrong way to be like God. He thought that by exalting himself he could be like God, whereas self-exaltation makes one most unlike Him. Whoever lifts himself up will not find God, for God calls on all to humble themselves to walk with Him. Micah 6:8, margin. "He hath put down the mighty from their seats, and exalted them of low degree." Luke 1:52. "He that humbleth himself shall be exalted." God "raised up the poor out of the dust, and lifteth up the beggar from the dung-hill, to set them among princes, and to make them inherit the throne of glory." 1 Sam. 2:8.

In contrast with Lucifer who tried to exalt himself to occupy God's place, we have the case of Christ, "who, being in the form of God, thought it not robbery to be equal with God; but made Himself of no reputation, and took upon Him the form of a servant, and was made in the likeness of men; and being found in fashion as a man, He humbled Himself and became obedient unto death, even the death of the cross. Wherefore God also hath highly exalted Him, and given Him a name which is above every name; that at the name of Jesus ever knee should bow, of things in heaven, and things in earth, and things under the earth; and that every tongue should confess that Jesus Christ is Lord, to the glory of God the Father." Phil. 2:6–11.

Self-righteousness is therefore unrighteousness. He who thinks to make himself righteous, – he who thinks that he has goodness in himself, – is guilty of the same sin that Lucifer was, and is moved by the same spirit. It is the spirit of the man of sin "who opposeth and exalteth himself above all that is called God, or that is worshipped; so that he as God sitteth in the temple of God, showing himself that he is God," or, setting himself forth as God. 2 Thess. 2:3–4. Whoever justifies himself, and refuses to receive the reproofs of instruction, which are the way of life (Prov. 6:23), is a part of the man of sin. The one who is always anxious to make himself out to be right, who becomes irritated when corrected, and who is always ready with a plausible excuse for everything that he does, shows himself to be one with Lucifer, and in danger of sharing his destruction. Let us learn this lesson indeed. Let us learn of Christ, who is meek and lowly in heart, "who did no sin, neither was guile found in his mouth;" yet "when He was reviled, reviled not again; when He suffered, He threatened not; but committed Himself to Him that judgeth righteously." 1 Peter 2:22–23.

"I will sit also upon the mount of the congregation in the sides of the north." Literally, "in the uttermost north." Everybody knows that the farther north he goes, the higher the north star appears. From this each can learn that if he stood at the north pole, north would be directly overhead. North, therefore, is up. God is "the Most High," and therefore He dwells "in the uttermost north." His dwelling-place is "the high and holy place." Isa. 57:15. "Great is the Lord, and greatly to be praised in the city of our God, in the mountain of His holiness. Beautiful for situation, the joy of the whole earth, is mount Zion, on the sides of the north [literally, "the uttermost north"], the city of the great King. God is known in her palaces for a refuge." Ps. 48:1–3.

"Promotion cometh neither from the east, nor from the west, nor from the south. But God is the Judge; He putteth down one, and setteth up another." Ps. 75:6–7. Promotion comes not from the east, the west, nor the south; therefore it must come from the north; and since God alone is Judge, to lift up and to put down, it follows that He dwells in the north. There alone is where promotion comes from. Therefore when Lucifer thought to occupy the north, he meditated an impossibility, for he could not get there without being drawn up by the Lord of hosts.

There is a mystery about the north. This is true even of this earth. There is an attraction there. The Hebrew word rendered "north" signifies secret, hidden. What is this attraction – this drawing power? It is God. Every manifestation of force is but the working of God. Christ said of His crucifixion, "I, if I be lifted up, will draw all men unto me." John 12:32. By the cross of shame and humiliation He was lifted up to the right hand of God, – up to "the uttermost north." The power therefore by which God draws all things, by which the worlds are kept in their places, is the power of the cross. All creation, the whole universe, preaches the cross. Every manifestation of attractive energy tells us of the power of the cross to save us from sin. The way to the Highest is the way of the cross. If we humble ourselves to the death of the cross, we may even now dwell in the "secret place of the Most High," and "abide under the shadow of the Almighty." For "the secret of the Lord is with them that fear Him."

"How art thou cut down to the ground, which didst weaken the nations!" Righteousness is strength; sin is weakness. Satan, the adversary, once Lucifer, the light-bearer, brought sin into the world, and all sinned. By sin man lost his dominion. It was not arbitrarily taken from him, but he could not hold it any longer. He lost his power to rule. He could not rule himself, and so could rule nothing. Then "when we were yet without strength, in due time Christ died for the ungodly." Rom. 5:6. Satan weakens us, but it is our glorious privilege to "be strong in the Lord, and in the power of His might." Eph. 6:10. Christ, the meek and lowly One, is given to us, and He is "the power of God." He has conquered, and in Him we have "power and authority over all devils." Luke 9:1. One of the most blessed of all the words of comfort is the assurance that by faith we may be "made strong" "out of weakness." Heb. 11:34.

"Thou art cast out of thy grave like an abominable branch." Christ is the true Vine. He says of the Father, "Every branch in Me that beareth not fruit, He taketh away." "If a man abide not in Me, he is cast forth as a branch, and is withered; and men gather them, and cast them into the fire, and they are burned." John 15:1–6. Christ is the tree of life, because He is "the wisdom of God" (1 Cor. 1:24), and wisdom is "a tree of life to them that lay hold upon her." Prov. 3:18. He is the life. John 14:6. There is no life except in Him. He is also the Way – the way to God. John 14:5–6; Heb. 10:19–20. Only by Him can anyone approach God. John 14:6; Eph. 2:13,18. Lucifer would not accept this way; he "abode not in the Truth," and so he was "cut down to the ground," cast out like an abominable branch. This is a warning to us, to abide in the Vine. It is so easy to do this, for we have but to let ourselves rest. Only in trying to lift ourselves up, do we wear ourselves out.

Remember the origin of Babylon (Gen. 11) and the character of its rulers. It was the spirit of Lucifer, – envy of any who occupied a superior position, and a determination to be above them. But "where envying and strife is, there is confusion and every evil work." James 3:16. That is why Satan is full of all evil, and why the whole world, inspired with the same spirit is corrupt. But this is why the destruction of Babylon involves the whole earth. "For I will rise up against them, saith the Lord of hosts, and cut off from Babylon the name, and remnant, and son, and nephew, saith the Lord. I will also make it a possession for the bittern and pools of water; and I will sweep it with the besom of destruction, saith the Lord of hosts. The Lord of hosts hath sworn, saying, Surely as I have thought, so shall it come to pass; and as I have purposed, so shall it stand; that I will break the Assyrian in My land and upon My mountains tread him under foot; then shall his yoke depart from off them, and his burden depart from off their shoulders. *This is the purpose that is purposed upon the whole earth;* and this is the hand that is stretched out upon all the nations."

How shall we escape in this time of destruction? "God is our refuge and strength, a very present help in trouble. Therefore will not we fear, though the earth be removed, and though the mountains be carried into the midst of the sea." Ps. 46:1–2. God, who dwells in "the high and holy place," dwells also with him that is of a contrite and humble spirit. Isa. 57:15. The high and holy place is therefore the place of humility. So then "he that dwelleth in the secret place of the Most High [the place of lowliness and meekness] shall abide under the shadow of the Almighty." "He shall cover thee with His feathers, and under His wings shalt thou trust; His truth shall be thy shield and buckler. Thou shalt not be afraid for the terror by night; nor for the arrow that flieth by day; nor for the pestilence that walketh in darkness; nor for the destruction that wasteth at noonday. A thousand shall fall at thy side, and ten thousand at thy right hand; but it shall not come nigh thee. Only with thine eyes shalt thou behold and see the reward of the wicked. Because thou hast made the Lord, which is my refuge, even the Most High, thy habitation; there shall no evil befall thee, neither shall any plague come nigh thy dwelling."

CHAPTER 15

THE DEVOURING CURSE

(Isaiah 24:1–23, Lowth's Translation)

1. Behold, Jehovah emptieth the land, and maketh it waste; He even turneth it upside down, and scattereth abroad the inhabitants.

2. And it shall be, as with the people, so with the priest; as with the servant, so with his master; as with the handmaid, so with her mistress; as with the buyer, so with the seller; as with the borrower, so with the lender; as with the usurer, so with the giver of usury.

3. The land shall be utterly emptied, and utterly spoiled; for Jehovah hath spoken this word.

4. The land mourneth, it withereth; the world languisheth, it withereth; the lofty people of the land do languish.

5. The land is even polluted under her inhabitants: for they have transgressed the law, they have changed the decree:

6. They have broken the everlasting covenant. Therefore hath a curse devoured the land; because they are guilty that dwell in her. Therefore are the inhabitants of the land destroyed; and few are the mortals that are left in her.

7. The new wine mourneth; the vine languisheth; all, that were glad of heart, sigh.

8. The joyful sound of the tabour ceaseth; the noise of exultation is no more; the joyful sound of the harp ceaseth;

9. With songs they shall no more drink wine; the palm-wine shall be bitter to them that drink it.

10. The city is broken down; it is desolate; every house is obstructed, so that no one can enter.

11. There is a cry in the streets for wine; all gladness is passed away; the joy of the whole land is banished.

12. Desolation is left in the city; and with a great multitude the gate is battered down.

13. Yea, thus shall it be in the very centre of the land, in the midst of the people; as the shaking of the olive; as the gleaning when the vintage is finished.

14. But these shall lift up their voice, they shall sing; the waters shall resound with the exaltation of Jehovah.

15. Wherefore in the distant coasts, glorify ye Jehovah; in the distant coasts of the sea, the name of Jehovah, the God of Israel.

16. From the uttermost part of the land we have heard songs. Glory to the righteous! But I said, Alas, my wretchedness, my wretchedness! Woe is me! the plunderers plunder; yea the plunderers still continue their cruel depredations.

17. The terror, the pit, and the snare, are upon thee, O inhabitant of the land:

18. And it shall be, that whoso fleeth from the terror, he shall fall into the pit; and whoso escapeth from the pit, he shall be taken in the snare; for the floodgates from on high are opened; and the foundations of the earth tremble.

19. The land is grievously shaken; the land is utterly shattered to pieces; the land is violently shattered out of its place:

20. The land reeleth to and fro like a drunkard; and moveth this way and that, like a lodge for a night; for her iniquity lieth heavy upon her, and she shall fall, and rise no more.

21. And it shall come to pass that day, Jehovah shall summon on high the host that is on high, and on earth the kings of the earth; and they shall be gathered together, as in a bundle for the pit;

22. And shall be closely imprisoned in the prison; and after many days, account shall be taken of them.

23. And the moon shall be confounded, and the sun shall be ashamed; for Jehovah God of Hosts shall reign on Mount Zion, and in Jerusalem; and before His ancients shall He be glorified.

The reading of this chapter makes more deep the impression that the book of Isaiah is emphatically a book for the last days. To the prophets of old it was revealed "that not unto themselves, but unto us they did minister the things, which are reported unto you by them that have preached the Gospel unto you with the Holy Ghost sent down from heaven." 1 Peter 1:12. This chapter tells us not only what shall take place in the last days, but also the cause of it. Study the chapter through as a whole, and note that it is a unit, presenting only one thing.

Note that which is to come upon the earth; it is to become empty, turned upside down, "devoured by the curse," "clean dissolved," is to reel to and fro like a drunkard, and be removed like a cottage. These are very strong expressions; they mean nothing less than utter destruction at the coming of the Lord.

The terms languish, fade away, indicating weakness, sickness, are frequent in this chapter. The verb in the expression "turneth it upside down," means "beset with pain." So in verse 4, "the world *languisheth*," we have the fact that the earth becomes sick. It is getting old and feeble, hence it staggers and totters, instead of going steadily.

Why does this take place? Verse 5 tells. It is "because they have transgressed the laws, changed the ordinance, broken the everlasting covenant." In the beginning man was given dominion over the earth; not simply over the beasts and birds, and the fishes, and over every creeping thing that creeps upon the face of the earth, but over the earth itself. Gen. 1:26. Now when the governor cannot control himself, when he transgresses the laws, and makes them void, what can result but that all that is under him should be out of order? The earth sympathizes with its lord. Man having lost his dominion, the earth runs wild. The curse eats up the earth, not because God arbitrarily sends it, but because man's disobedience to the laws which he should keep and execute, brings the curse.

"Few men left." Thank God, He sends His messenger before His face, to turn the hearts of the children to the fathers, and the fathers to the children, so that He need not come and smite the earth with utter destruction. See Mal. 4:5–6. When the Lord has "removed men far away," and there is a "great forsaking in the midst of the land," yet "the holy seed shall be the substance thereof." Isa. 6:12–13. Who will be one of the few? "Whosoever will" may come.

Compare verses 21–22 with Rev. 20:4–6. At the coming of the Lord all the wicked who are then alive will be destroyed by the brightness of His coming. 2 Thess. 2:8. They cannot endure the sight. A thousand years the earth will lie desolate, while God's people, caught up at Christ's coming, both living and dead made immortal (1 Cor. 15:51.54; 1 Thess. 4:13–18) will be with the Lord. At the end of the thousand years the wicked who have been gathered together as prisoners are gathered in the pit, shall be visited. Then will their iniquity be visited upon them, and the earth will be purified, and "the first dominion" will return. Micah 4:8. "Then the Lord of hosts shall reign in Mount Zion and before His ancients gloriously."

Note verse 20: "The earth shall reel to and fro like a drunkard," and the transgression thereof shall be heavy upon it. Here we see plainly that it is the weight of sin, that causes the earth to be removed, even as it does men.

"The earth is clean dissolved." Verse 19. Compare this with 2 Peter 3:11. Read the whole of this latter chapter, and it will be seen even more clearly that the coming of the Lord is under consideration in the prophecy of Isaiah. But although all these things shall be dissolved at that time, "nevertheless we, according to His promise, look for new heavens, and a new earth, wherein dwelleth righteousness."

Do not lose sight of the fact that in that day "the Lord shall punish the host of the high ones on high." Verse 21. Compare this with Eph. 6:12, margin, "wicked spirits in high places." Compare the last part of the second chapter of Isaiah. The day of the Lord is against every thing that is proud and lofty. Let us, then, in order that we may escape, hide ourselves in Him who is meek and lowly in heart, that the storm may pass over our heads, so that we shall be among those who glorify God from the ends of the earth, and "sing for the majesty of the Lord." Verses 13–15.

CHAPTER 16

DELIVERANCE OF GOD'S PEOPLE

(Isaiah 25:1–9, Lowth's Translation)

1. O Jehovah, Thou art my God; I will exalt Thee; I will praise Thy name; for Thou hast effected wonderful things; counsels of old time, promises immutably true.

2. For Thou hast made the city an heap; the strongly fortified citadel a ruin; the palace of the proud ones, that it should be no more a city; that it should never be built up again.

3. Therefore shall the fierce people glorify Thee; the city of the formidable nations shall fear Thee.

4. For Thou hast been a defense to the poor; a defense to the needy in his distress; a refuge from the storm, a shadow from the heat; when the blast of the formidable rages like a winter storm.

5. As the heat in a parched land, the tumult of the proud shalt Thou bring low; as the heat by a thick cloud, the triumph of the formidable shall be humbled.

6. And Jehovah God of Hosts shall make for all the peoples, in this mountain, a feast of delicacies, a feast of old wines; of delicacies exquisitely rich, of old wines perfectly refined.

7. And on this mountain shall He destroy the covering that covered the face of all the peoples; and the veil that was spread over all the nations.

8. He shall utterly destroy death for ever; and the Lord Jehovah shall wipe away the tear from off all faces; and the reproach of His people shall He remove from off the whole earth; for Jehovah hath spoken it.

9. In that day shall they say, behold, this is our God; we have trusted in Him, and He hath saved us; this is Jehovah; we have trusted in Him; we will rejoice, and triumph, in His salvation.

"O Lord, Thou art my God." Whoever says this understandingly, from the heart, has everything. Nothing can make him discontented; nothing can cause him to worry; nothing can make him afraid. Read Ex. 34:6–7, to find out what the Lord is, and also 1 Chron. 29:11–12, and Ps. 95:3–5, to learn His power, and then think what an infinite treasure every one has who can say, "O Lord, Thou art my God."

Jehovah is not merely the Being whom we worship, to whom we bow down in reverence as One infinitely above us, but He is ours. He belongs to us, as truly as we belong to Him. "The Lord is the portion of mine inheritance and of my cup." Ps. 16:5. To as many as receive Christ "gave He power to become the sons of God, even to them that believe on His name." John 1:12. By believing we become sons of God, "and if children, then heirs; heirs of God, and joint-heirs with Jesus Christ." Rom. 8:17. Through faith we become partakers of the nature of God, just as Christ is one with Him. He is ours to the extent that everything that He has, and everything that He is, belongs to us. We have Him.

It was this knowledge that gave Jehoshaphat and all Israel the victory over a vastly superior force, even before the battle had begun, and when everything seemed against them. They were in an extremity, and there was no earthly prospect that they could escape. Then Jehoshaphat stood in the midst of the congregation of Israel, and said, "O Lord God of our fathers, art not Thou God in heaven? and rulest not Thou over all the kingdoms of the heathen? and in Thine hand is there not power and might, so that none is able to withstand Thee?" 2 Chron. 20:6. The fact that God is in heaven, shows that He is over all, and does whatever pleases Him. Ps. 115:3. Nothing is hard for Him, and no enemy can withstand Him. Therefore when in addition to this Jehoshaphat could say, "Art not Thou our God?" he had the victory already; for since God was his, all who came against him came also against the Lord; and their overthrow was assured. Accordingly when this prayer of faith had been uttered, the assurance came, "Be not afraid nor dismayed by reason of this great multitude; for the battle is not yours, but God's." "Ye shall not need to fight in this battle; set yourselves, stand ye still, and see the salvation of the Lord with you." 2 Chron. 20:15,17. To God belongs victory; "His right hand, and His holy arm, hath gotten Him the victory." Ps. 98:1. When by faith we claim Him as ours, then we prove that faith is the victory that hath overcome the world.

"Thou hast done wonderful things." His name is Wonderful (Isa. 9:6), so that it is His nature to do wonderful things. He does nothing that is not wonderful. The age of miracles is the age of God. "Who is so great a God as our God? Thou art the God that doest wonders; Thou hast declared Thy strength among the people." Ps. 77:13–14. "Many, O Lord my God, are Thy wonderful works which Thou hast done, and Thy thoughts which are to us-ward; they cannot be reckoned up in order unto Thee; if I would declare and speak of them, they are more than can be numbered." Ps. 40:5. Therefore let us "sing unto the Lord a new song; for He hath done marvelous things." Ps. 98:1. "I will speak of the glorious honour of Thy majesty, and of Thy wondrous works." Ps. 145:5. Here is something to talk about. "All Thy works shall praise Thee, O Lord; and Thy saints shall bless Thee. They shall speak of the glory of Thy kingdom, and talk of Thy power." Verses 10–11. If men would do this all the time, such a thing as discouragement or fear would be unknown.

"Thy counsels of old are faithfulness and truth." Both of these words, "faithfulness" and "truth," are from the one root which we have Anglicized as "amen." The word means firmness, steadfastness, solidity, immovability. So we might read, "Thy counsels of old are amen and amen," or, as Lowth has it, "immutably true." Jesus Christ is "the Amen, the faithful and true witness." Rev. 3:14. His name also is Counsellor. Isa. 9:6. So "all the promises of God in Him are yea, and in Him Amen." 2 Cor. 1:20.

All the promises of God center in the one great promise, the promise of Christ's coming. He is not slack concerning His promise, even though unbelieving men may think He is. 2 Peter 3:3–4,9. This has been the purpose of God since the world began, and He "worketh all things after the counsel of His own will." Eph. 1:11. His promises are "immutably true." His faithfulness is established "in the very heavens" (Ps. 89:2), so that as true as the heavens is the promise of Christ's coming. Always true to their appointed times are the heavenly bodies; those who observe their movements, and keep note, know that they will keep their appointments to the very second; even so will it be with Christ's coming in glory to judgment and salvation.

"God is our refuge and strength, a very present help in trouble." Ps. 46:1. The children of men take refuge under the shadow of His wing. Ps. 36:7. "Because thou hast made the Lord, which is my refuge, even the Most High, thy habitation; there shall no evil befall thee, neither shall any plague come nigh thy dwelling." Ps. 91:9–10. The Lord is everything that anybody requires. He is "a refuge from the storm," and "a shadow from the heat," yet He is a sun, even "a consuming fire" (Heb. 12:29), and He "hath His way in the whirlwind and in the storm." Nahum 1:3. From Him we get light and heat, and also shade. That is, in Him we find evenness of temperature. But those who do not put their trust in Him will be in darkness, and at the same time consumed by the heat. "Blessed are all they that put their trust in Him."

The Lord of hosts will make unto all people a feast of fat things, a feast of wines on the lees, of fat things full of marrow, that is, all sorts of delicacies. He provides the table for all, and whoever will may come and eat, "without money and without price." "Thou preparest a table before me in the presence of mine enemies; Thou anointest my head with oil; my cup runneth over." Ps. 23:5. Even though the enemy may be coming on in full strength, raging and boasting, and threatening dire calamity, we can quietly sit down and eat. The Lord invites us to His feast, and even when He comes to us as our guest, He provides the food.

"In this mountain." That is, in Mount Zion. See last verse of the preceding chapter. That is God's dwelling-place (Ps. 2:6, 48:1–2), and it is there that He has prepared the feast of salvation for all people.

The covering that is cast over all people, and the veil spread over all nations, is to be taken away in Mount Zion. Over all the earth and over all minds and all lives, rests the shadow of the curse. "Christ hath redeemed us from the curse of the law, being made a curse for us." Gal. 3:13. It is through the blood of the new covenant, – the everlasting covenant, – that remission of sins is found. But the god of this world has blinded the minds of all that believe not (2 Cor. 4:4), and this veil of unbelief keeps the glory of the cross, which swallows up the curse, from shining in. Nevertheless when the heart turns to the Lord, the veil is taken away. The true light now shineth, and whoever will may see light in His light. Even though the majority will not believe, but persist in walking in darkness, the time is coming when even they shall see that God's way is perfect, and shall be compelled by force of evidence to acknowledge that He is just. The covering which has concealed God's gracious working will be removed in the Judgment, and God will stand clear. It will then be too late, however, for any to receive benefit from the light that will shine, since they have rejected light when they might have walked in it.

This veil, the curse, which is even now taken off from all who truly believe, is to be for ever removed from the earth. The very earth itself is to be delivered from the bondage of corruption into the glory of the liberty of the sons of God. For "He will swallow up death in victory; and the Lord God will wipe away tears from off all faces; and the rebuke of His people shall He take away from off all the earth." Tears will be wiped away, because the cause of tears – sin and death – will be removed. Compare Rev. 21:1–5 for further evidence that in the prophecy of Isaiah we have in detail the things that are only briefly mentioned in the New Testament.

"He will swallow up death in victory." Literally, "He will swallow up death in *eternity*," or for ever. In 1 Cor. 15:54 we have this same thing quoted, and there the Greek has it plainly, "victory," while in the Hebrew of Isa. 25:8 it is just as plainly "eternity." Does this indicate a contradiction, or any lack of harmony in the two texts? – Not the slightest; it simply shows that the two words mean the same thing. Victory, in order to be really victory, must be eternal. A seeming victory, which does not last, is not victory at all. When God gives us the victory through our Lord Jesus Christ, it is for eternity, for "whatsoever God doeth, it shall be for ever." Eccl. 3:14.

But the final victory over death is only the present victory over sin, which is the sting of death. The power by which the righteous will be raised from their graves, immortal, is identical with the power by which in their lifetime they were raised above the power of sin. That is the power of Christ's resurrection. It was not possible for death to hold Him (Acts 2:24), because guile was not found in His mouth. I Peter 2:22. John, in prophetic vision saw the Lamb standing on Mount Zion, "and with Him an hundred and forty-four thousand, having His Father's name written in their foreheads." "And in their mouth was found no guile; for they are without fault before the throne of God." Rev. 14:1–5. So we see that there will be found a people over whom death will have no more power than it had over the Lord Jesus. We know that He could not die except by His own will, because He was sinless. In like manner those who "keep the commandments of God, and the faith of Jesus" (Rev. 14:12) will be superior to death. No man, not even Satan, can take their life from them, and hence they will be translated. Their translation without seeing death is not due to the accident of their being on earth when Christ comes, but to their life of perfect righteousness by faith. There is nothing accidental about it; it is the natural working out of the life of Christ. At any time in the past God's people might have been translated, if at any time it could have been said of them, "Here are they that keep the commandments of God and the faith of Jesus."

Men are saved only by the righteousness of God in Jesus Christ. It is not abstract righteousness, but the righteousness of Christ's real life "unto all and upon all them that believe; for there is no difference" (Rom. 3:22), that saves us. The instant any man, however sinful he may be, believes on the Lord Jesus, and confesses Him, he is counted righteous. God declares him righteous, and that makes him righteous. If he should die that very hour, as was the case with the thief on the cross, he would be saved, and would appear in heaven as though he had never sinned. Thousands will appear in the kingdom of God without fault, who never in their lifetime knew all the commandments of God, nor all that is involved in the faith of Jesus. Consequently not all the righteousness of the law has been exhibited in their lives. They have unconsciously been living in violation of some precepts of the law, but from all these secret, hidden faults they have been cleansed. But these have learned the lesson of submission to God, and were willing to serve Him. They can be taken to heaven, therefore, they will make no break in its harmony, for the instant they see the fullness of God's righteousness they will embrace it with joy.

But if all the righteous were saved in this way there would be an opportunity for the accuser of the brethren, who accuses them before God day and night (Rev. 12:10), to say that it is impossible for God to make men absolutely perfect in this world; that He is obliged to take them to heaven, and get them out of the reach of Satan's temptations, in order to make them perfectly righteous. To be sure, he can be confronted with the case of Christ, who lived an absolutely perfect life, in spite of all Satan's temptations; but he would evade the force of that by saying, as men, and even Christian men, do now, that Christ was different from other men. Therefore, in order to show that Christ was here in this world with no advantages over other men, and that what God did by Him, He is able to do for all, to exalt the power of God, to show that Christ has power over all flesh, and effectually to stop the mouths of all gainsayers, God will not send Jesus the second time until He can point to a people who, like Jesus, are absolutely without fault, and who, surrounded by sin, and subject to Satan's onslaughts, live entirely above the power of sin and death. They will be complete possessors of the victory that hath overcome the world. Thus will not only the mouths of all the wicked be stopped, but there will be given the perfect witness of God's power to salvation, which will draw many in the last days from the world to God.

It is eternity – eternal life – that swallows up death. Absolutely perfect faith means perfect knowledge of God's Word, because "faith cometh by hearing, and hearing by the Word of God." Rom. 10:17. "The just shall live by faith," so that perfect faith means perfect life, – the life of Jesus manifest in our mortal flesh. When this is experienced, the individual will be delivered from all diseases, even though in weak, mortal flesh, with disease attacking him, just the same as he will be delivered from all sin, even while beset and in heaviness by manifold temptations. Thus will Christ and those whom God gives Him be for signs and wonders. They will walk unscathed in the midst of raging pestilence, just as the three Hebrews did in the burning, fiery furnace, because "the form of the fourth" is with them. And this will be not only in the time when the plagues of the unmingled wrath of God are falling on the reprobate, but before men have made their final decision, so that the witness will tell for the salvation of many. It is just as easy for God to make a man perfectly whole now, and to keep him so, as it is to keep him alive at all; for it is the one life that does all.

In that day shall they say "Behold, this is our God, we have trusted in Him, and He hath saved us." Not merely, "He will save us," but, "He hath saved us." A present, complete salvation is the assurance of future salvation. All that is necessary for anybody to be able to say is, "The Lord has saved me, and He saves me now." Keep trusting, and the salvation will continue. Those who have become acquainted with the Lord, will know Him when He comes. The Lord Himself will come, and He will not be a stranger. "We will rejoice, and triumph in His salvation," because we have trusted in Him, and have proved the power of that salvation. But the power of the salvation now is worth rejoicing over just as much as it will be at the coming of the Lord. Therefore "rejoice in the Lord alway; and again I say, rejoice" (Phil. 4:4), because it is with rejoicing that the redeemed of the Lord come to Zion, the mountain of God.

CHAPTER 17

TRUST AND PROTECTION

(Isaiah 26:1–14, Lowth's Translation)

1. In that day shall this song be sung: – In the land of Judah we have a strong city; salvation shall He establish for walls and bulwarks.

2. Open ye the gates, and let the righteous nation enter:

3. Contrast in the truth, stayed in mind: thou shalt preserve them in perpetual peace, because they have trusted in Thee.

4. Trust ye in Jehovah for ever; for in Jehovah is never-failing protection.

5. For He hath humbled those that dwell on high; the lofty city, He hath brought her down; He hath brought her down to the ground; He hath leveled her with the dust.

6. The foot shall trample upon her; the foot of the poor, the steps of the needy.

7. The way of the righteous is perfectly straight; Thou most exactly levelest the path of the righteous.

8. Even in the way of Thy laws, O Jehovah, we have placed our confidence in Thy name; and in the remembrance of Thee is the desire of our soul.

9. With my soul have I desired Thee in the night; yea, with my inmost spirit in the morn have I sought Thee. For when Thy judgments are in the earth, the inhabitants of the world learn righteousness.

10. Though mercy be shown to the wicked, yet will he not learn righteousness; in the very land of rectitude he will deal perversely; and will not regard the majesty of Jehovah.

11. Jehovah, Thy hand is lifted up, yet will they not see: but they shall see, with confusion, Thy zeal for Thy people; yea, the fire shall burn up Thine adversaries.

12. Jehovah, Thou wilt ordain for us peace; for even all our mighty deeds Thou hast performed for us.

13. O Jehovah, our God! Other lords exclusive of Thee have had dominion over us: Thee only, and Thy name, henceforth will we celebrate.

14. They are dead, they shall not live; they are deceased tyrants, they shall not rise. Therefore hast Thou visited and destroyed them; and all memorials of them Thou hast abolished.

Note the difference in punctuation in the first verse of Lowth's translation, as compared with the ordinary version. There is no difference in the sense, but Lowth's rendering makes it a little more emphatic. Not only is the song sung in the land of Judah, but the city is there. This is of course implied in the common rendering? The city is therefore Jerusalem made new – New Jerusalem, which cometh down out of heaven from God. Rev. 3:12; 21:2. It is a city built up entirely new, and will occupy the very place where the present city stands, only it will be very much more extended. See John 14:1–2; Zech. 14:1–9; Lowth's rendering of Isa. 26:15 also indicates this: "Thou hast added to the nation; Thou art glorified; Thou hast extended far all the borders of the land."

This is the city for which the patriarchs of old looked. Heb. 10:10,14–16. Its builder and maker is God; and its foundations are described in Rev. 21:18–21. Coming down, as it does, in the land of Canaan, the land that was promised to Abraham and his seed for an inheritance, the promise of God is fulfilled to the very letter. To apply the prophecies concerning the building up of Jerusalem to any work done by men, and in this present state, is a gross perversion of the Scriptures, and a depreciation of the promises of the Gospel. Only God Himself can fulfill His own promises, and only He can build a city suitable for the habitation of His redeemed ones.

It will be a "strong city." Its defense will be salvation. It will be so strong that it will be able to withstand a siege by Satan and all his hosts, including all the armies of wicked men who have trained under Satan's banner. See Rev. 20:7–9. Some one will exclaim, "Of course no enemy in the universe could take the city of God, the New

Jerusalem! It would be absurd for anyone to try." Very true; yet that city will be no safer than are God's people now; for it will be kept only by the very same power that now keeps those who trust in the Lord. The humblest and most insignificant person on earth, who trusts the Lord, is just as safe as will be the hosts of the redeemed in the New Jerusalem. The wicked far outnumber the righteous, and the mighty host marching against the city of the saved would strike terror to their hearts, if they had not individually learned the power of Christ's salvation. The Gospel is the power of God to salvation, to every one that believeth, and that is the power that will be the confidence of the redeemed in the Holy City when it is besieged by Satan's hosts.

The righteous nation is the nation that keeps the truth. Jesus said, "He that hath My commandments, and keepeth them, he it is that loveth Me." John 14:21. God has committed His truth to men, even to wicked men, to see what they will do with it. If they repress it then the wrath of God is justly revealed from heaven against them. Rom. 1:18. But if they keep it, letting it have free course in them, then it will preserve them from all evil. The truth of God is the shield of His people. Ps. 91:4.

God is the God of peace (Heb. 13:20; 1 Thess. 5:3), therefore all who put their trust in Him are necessarily kept in perfect peace. The peace and protection that are given are not a reward for trusting, but are the necessary consequence of that trust; "for in Jehovah is never failing protection." "In the Lord Jehovah is an everlasting Rock," or "the Rock of Ages." Revised Version.

There is nothing in this world that troubles people more than pride. And pride is what the Lord has promised to bring down. Pride is an abomination to the Lord. This fact, instead of alarming us, should be a cause of rejoicing, for it means deliverance from our worst enemy. Note in the chapters of Isaiah, which we have already studied, how much is said about bringing down that which is proud and lofty. "He hath humbled those that dwell on high; the lofty city, He hath brought her down." But before that time comes, He delivers His people from pride, and therefore from the destruction that follows it. Read the promise in Ps. 31:19–21; "Oh how great is Thy goodness, which Thou hast laid up for them that fear Thee; which Thou hast wrought for them that trust in Thee before the sons of men! Thou shalt hide them in the secret of Thy presence from the pride of man; Thou shalt keep them secretly in a pavilion from the strife of tongues. Blessed be the Lord: for He hath showed me His marvelous loving kindness in a strong city." Note that it is "from the pride of man" that God promised to keep those who trust in Him. Then of course He keeps us from our own pride, and that is the only pride from which we are in any danger.

What a blessed assurance is contained in verse 7. The text that we have quoted is very much more close to the original than is our common version, yet there is a very precious suggestion in this latter. Mark the expression, "Thou, Most Upright, dost weigh the path of the just." The word rendered "weigh," means to ponder, think upon. Compare Ps. 1:6. The Lord makes the way of His people the object of special solicitude; He makes it straight and plain, and that is why they are upright. He is no respecter of persons, and therefore He takes the same care of all people; but the wicked will not walk in the way marked out for them. All anybody has to do, to be righteous, is to walk in the way of the Lord. Ps. 119:1–2.

"The Lord is good to all; and His tender mercies are over all His works." Ps. 145:9. He encompasses the wicked with the same mercy that He does the righteous. The whole earth is surrounded with an atmosphere of grace and mercy, which the inhabitants breathe in as they do the air, so that nothing is lacking for the salvation of any person. Therefore if any are destroyed, it is only because they reject the mercy of the Lord. The only thing that any lost soul will have to bring against the Lord will be that He dealt mercifully with him. "He hath not dealt with us after our sins; nor rewarded us according to our iniquities." Surely God will be clear when He judges, since those who are lost have been hardened only by His mercy. See the case of Pharaoh, and note how it was the forbearance and mercy of the Lord that hardened his heart. He regarded the kindness of the Lord as weakness, and presumed on it. Ex. 8:15,31–32; 9:34–35.

"Lord, Thou wilt ordain peace for us; for Thou also hast wrought all our works in us." Verse 12. "It is God which worketh in you both to will and to do of His good pleasure." Phil. 2:13. He is striving to work in all, but many will not allow Him to have His own way with them, and He will not force any, since He works only by love. It is the pride of men, their unwillingness to acknowledge that they are not their own masters, that keeps them from yielding to God. Whoever is willing to admit that he is nothing, and is not able to do anything, not even to make a single movement of himself, but will acknowledge God in all his ways, will find that God works in him, making his way perfect. What a blessed thing it is to be able to see, from the working of God in the things round about us, how able He is to do all our works in us, and to do marvelous things. In the things that are made, the everlasting power and Divinity of God are clearly seen. Rom. 1:20. The least thing that He does is great, and shows His almighty power. They are all unconsciously passive in His hands, and so His will is wrought in them. Because their yielding is involuntary, there is no morality in the fulfillment of God's will in them; but when we voluntarily yield as completely as the inanimate things do involuntarily, then does God make our way even as His own, and gives to us the credit of having done that which only His omnipotence could accomplish. Read Ps. 90:16–17.

Other lords besides Jehovah have had dominion over us. Who is there that has not been guilty of idolatry? "Thou shalt have no other gods before Me," is not an arbitrary commandment, but a blessed promise to all who will put their trust in the Lord. God rules only by love and gentleness, but other lords exercise dominion over us, compelling us to serve them. Being delivered from the bondage of corruption, we say to the Lord, "Thee only, and Thy name, henceforth will we celebrate."

"They are dead, they shall not live; they are deceased tyrants, they shall not rise." There is no God but Jehovah. All the gods of the heathen are nothing. "They must needs be borne, because they cannot go. Be not afraid of them; for they cannot do evil, neither also is it in them to do good." "But the Lord is the true God, He is the living God, and an everlasting King." Jer. 10:5,10. A man is like that which he serves. Hence he who serves a dumb, dead idol is himself destitute of life. "They that make them are like unto them, so is every one that trusteth in them." Ps. 115:8. When we trusted in the works of our own hands, we were lifeless – dead in trespasses and sins; but having been made alive in Christ, we reign with Him, instead of being lorded over. Not only will all false gods perish, but the very memory of them will be destroyed. The memorial of God, on the other hand, endures for ever. Ps. 135:13.

CHAPTER 18

GOD'S CARE FOR HIS PEOPLE

(Isaiah 26:19–21, Isaiah 27:1–6, Lowth's Translation)

19. Thy dead shall live; my deceased, they shall rise: awake, and sing, ye that dwell in the dust! For thy dew is as the dew of the dawn; but the earth shall cast forth, as an abortion, the deceased tyrants.

20. Come, O My people; retire into thy secret apartments; and shut thy door after thee; hide thyself for a little while, for a moment; until the indignation shall have passed away.

21. For behold, Jehovah issueth forth from His place, to punish for his iniquity the inhabitant of the earth; and the earth shall disclose the blood that is upon her; and shall no longer cover her slain.

1. In that day shall Jehovah punish with His sword, His well-tempered, and great, and strong sword. Leviathan the rigid serpent, and Leviathan the winding serpent; and shall slay the monster that is in the sea.

2. In that day, to the beloved Vineyard, sing ye a responsive song.

J.3. It is I, Jehovah, that preserve her; I will water her every moment; I will take care of her by night; and by day I will keep guard over her.

V.4. I have no wall for my defense; O that I had a defense of the thorn and the briar! Against them should I march in battle. I should burn them up together.

J.5. Ah, let her rather take hold of My protection.

V. Let them make peace with me! Peace let Him make with me!

J.6. They that come from the root of Jacob shall flourish, Israel shall bud forth; and they shall fill the face of the world with fruit.

The student will notice the initials "J" and "V" before a few of the verses in the beginning. These stand for Jehovah and Voice, respectively, indicating a colloquy between the Lord and His people, which the translator supposes to be transcribed in the first part of the chapter. They are no part of the text, but simply express the translator's idea of it. The student will compare this rendering with that in his Bible, and take the suggestion for what he considers it worth.

Promise of the Resurrection

"Thy dead shall live; My deceased, they shall arise." This is much plainer and more forcible than as it is rendered in our common version. There it is made to appear as though it were simply the prophet saying that his dead body shall arise; but the fact is that it is God who is speaking of His own dead, – of those who die in the Lord. Israel has been mourning, and God comforts her with the assurance that her dead shall live, for He claims her deceased ones as His own; and he that believeth in God, "though he were dead, and yet shall he live."

Joy in Dust

"Awake and sing, ye that dwell in the dust!" Out of the dust the Lord God formed man in the beginning, and set him over the works of His hands. God took the dust to make a king, and a king that should bear rule over things in heaven as well as on earth. This is the assurance to us that "He taketh up the poor out of the dust, and lifteth up the beggar from the dunghill, to set them among princes, and to make them inherit the throne of glory." 1 Sam. 2:8. A heart broken and crumbled into dust (contrite), the Lord does not despise, because He knows the possibilities in dust. Indeed, that is the only material out of which a perfect man can be made. Therefore when man has in his pride and self-exaltation departed out of the way, and has fallen, God turns him again to dust, and says, "Come again, ye children of men." Conversion is the pledge of the resurrection, for it is but the working of resurrection power. God's people can rejoice over the grave, for since they have been created from the dust, and made to sit with Christ in the heavenly places, they know that death cannot separate them from the love of God which is in Christ Jesus their Lord.

The Dew of the Morning

There is not so much difference as there might seem at first glance between the rendering, "Thy dew is as the dew of herbs," and "Thy dew is as the dew of the dawn," which is found in other versions besides that of Lowth; for the dew of herbs is the dew that falls in the morning. The French of Segond has it, "a vivifying dew," which is very pertinent. The Hebrew expression is thus given in one lexicon, "a light-reflecting dew." How expressive this is of the joy and freshness of the resurrection, when God's people reflect the light of life.

But why is it that the dew of God's people is as the dew of the morning? the answer is found in Ps. 133. It is because they have brotherly kindness and unity, which is "the dew of Hermon, and as the dew that descended upon the mountains of Zion; for there the Lord commanded the blessing, even life for evermore."

The Enemies Cast Out

The reader will notice that instead of, "the earth shall cast out the dead," Lowth renders it, "the earth shall cast out, as an abortion, the deceased tyrants." If you examine the margin of the Revision, you will see that the word in the Hebrew is "Rephaim," which is the name of one of the wicked nations that the Lord promised to cast out of the land of Canaan, before the children of Abraham. See Gen. 14:5; 15:20. So here we find an intimation of the fact that the resurrection is the time when the promise to Abraham shall be fulfilled.

The Avenger of Blood

"Behold, the Lord cometh out of His place to punish the inhabitants of the earth for their iniquity; the earth also shall disclose her blood, and shall no more cover her slain." All the righteous blood that has been shed on earth, from that of Abel, cries to God for vengeance. Ever since nations have legalized murder if only committed by wholesale, it has been thought only a light thing to cause the death of men. Worldly men are so bent on carrying out their schemes, that they think nothing of it if a few just men are destroyed in the process. The slain sink out of sight, the earth covers them up, and drinks up their blood, and the oppressors think that the transaction is ended. Not so; soon will the earth give up her dead, and will no more be an unwilling accomplice in bloody deeds.

Safety for God's People

It will be a terrible time when God comes out of His place to punish the inhabitants of the earth for their iniquity. The earth shall be "utterly broken down," and "clean dissolved." The prophet Habakkuk had a vision of that day, when God "drove asunder the nations; and the everlasting mountains were scattered, the perpetual hills did bow." "Before Him went the pestilence, and burning coals went forth at His feet." "The sun and moon stood still in their habitation; at the light of Thine arrows they went, and at the shining of Thy glittering spear. Thou didst march through the land in indignation, Thou didst thresh the heathen in anger." When the prophet saw the "great and terrible day of the Lord," he trembled; his lips quivered, and his very bones seemed to become rotten, and he desired for himself that he might rest in the day of trouble. Read Hab. 3. So God has promised that in the time of trouble such as never was since there was a nation, His people shall be delivered. Dan. 12:1. He says, "Come, My people, enter thou into thy chambers, and shut thy doors about thee; hide thyself as it were for a little moment, until the indignation be overpast." The ninety-first Psalm tells where they will hide. There they will be during the thousand years that intervene between the first and second resurrections (Rev. 20), and during the time when the fire of God's wrath consumes the wicked; but they will be no more safe then than during the seven last plagues, when they are here on the earth, in the midst of the destruction. All the time "the Lord will be the hope of His people, and the strength of the children of Israel." Joel 3:9–16.

God's Vineyard

"A vineyard of red wine." Let it not be forgotten that "the new wine is found in the cluster," and that "a blessing is in it." Isa. 65:8. The best wine is that which is procured by pressing the grape direct into the cup. See Gen. 40:10–11. Such wine it was that the Saviour furnished by a miracle for the wedding guests at Cana, which the governor of the feast pronounced the best. But the vineyard of the Lord is His people. Isa. 5:1–7. The miracle at Cana shows how the Lord's servants are to bear fruit to His glory. The servants obeyed the words of the Lord to the letter. They are nameless, and very little thought is given to them; yet they acted a most important part in the miracle. It was done by them. The vessels stood empty, and Jesus said, "Fill the water pots with water." This the servants did without any objection, although it must have seemed to them an unnecessary act. Then said Jesus, "Draw out now, and bear unto the governor of the feast." This was seemingly a more foolish command than the other, and one likely to cost the servants their position; for they might have reasoned: "It is not water, but wine, that is wanted; if we carry this water to the governor of the feast, he will think that we are insulting him, and we shall not only make ourselves the laughing-stock of the guests, but shall be discharged for unseemly action." Let it be remembered that it was water that was in the pots, and that it was water that the Lord told the servants to draw out and carry to the governor. They did as they were commanded, and some time in the process, we do not know at what point, the water became wine. Through the servants as agents of the Lord, the transformation was effected.

Thus would the Lord show us how we are to be branches of the true Vine. It is the branches that bear the fruit, yet they do not bear it of themselves. They are simply the channels for transmitting the water from the root to the clusters. They do not make the wine, but are servants used in the performance of the miracle. Those servants in Cana acted the part of branches in a vineyard. The Lord did by them what He ordinarily does by the branches of the grape vine. If we, like them, do whatever He says to us, we shall also be fruit bearing branches of the living Vine.

God's Care for His Vineyard

"I the Lord do keep it; I will water it every moment; lest any hurt it., I will keep it night and day." This agrees with what we have just learned. If we abide in His Word, He will water us continually, so that we may be fruitful. Read Ps. 1:1–3. A vineyard that is gently watered night and day, cannot but be a flourishing one. And not a moment does God forget His charge. "He that keepeth thee will not slumber. Behold, He that keepeth Israel shall neither slumber nor sleep. The Lord is thy keeper; the Lord is thy shade upon thy right hand. The sun shall not smite thee by day, nor the moon by night." Ps. 121:3–6. This is a most pertinent and cheering promise; for in the day when the Lord "with His great and strong sword" shall punish "that crooked serpent," which is the dragon and Satan (Rev. 12:9; 20:2), the sun will have power to scorch men with fire. Rev. 16:8–9; Joel 1:19–20. But during all the time when the fire of God's rejected grace shall be consuming the wicked, "there shall be a tabernacle for a shadow in the daytime from the heat, and for a place of refuge, and for a covert from storm and rain." Isa. 4:6. Yet the safety of the people of God in that day will be by nothing else than by the very same loving protection that is given them now day by day.

The Consummation

"Israel shall blossom and bud, and fill the face of the world with fruit." This will be the completion of the work of the Gospel, the last proclamation of which is, "Fear God, and give glory to Him; for the hour of His judgment is come; and worship Him that made heaven, and earth, and the sea, and the fountains of waters." Rev. 14:7. It is by our bearing fruit, that God is glorified. John 15:8. When Israel fills the face of the world with fruit, then will the earth be filled with the knowledge of the glory of the Lord. And this will be accomplished by recognizing and honouring God as the Creator, the One by whose direct care and attention all the processes of nature are effected; "For as the earth bringeth forth her bud, and as the garden causeth the things that are sown in it to spring forth; so the Lord God will cause righteousness and praise to spring forth before all the nations."

CHAPTER 19

THE CROWN OF SHAME AND THE CROWN OF GLORY

(Isaiah 28:1–13, Lowth's Translation)

1. Woe to the proud crown of the drunkards of Ephraim, and to the fading flower of their glorious beauty! To those that are at the head of the rich valley, that are stupefied with wine!

2. Behold the mighty one, the exceeding strong one! Like a storm of hail, like a destructive tempest; like a rapid flood of mighty waters pouring down; He shall dash them to the ground with his hand.

3. They shall be trodden under foot, the proud crowns of the drunkards of Ephraim:

4. And the fading flower of their glorious beauty, which is at the head of the rich valley, shall be as the early fruit before the summer; which whoso seeth, he plucketh it immediately; and it is no sooner in his hand, than he swalloweth it.

5. In that day shall Jehovah God of Hosts become a beauteous crown, and a glorious diadem, to the remnant of His people:

6. And a spirit of judgment, to them that sit in judgment; and strength to them, that repel the war to the gate (of the enemy).

7. But even these have erred through wine, and through strong drink they have reeled; the priest and the prophet have erred through strong drink; they are overwhelmed with wine; they have reeled through strong drink: they have erred in vision, they have stumbled in judgment.

8. For all their tables are full of vomit; of filthiness, so that no place is free.

9. "Whom (say they) would He teach knowledge; and to whom would He impart instruction?" To such as are weaned from the milk, as are kept back from the breast?

10. "For it is command upon command; command upon command; "Line upon line; line upon line; "A little here, and a little there."

11. Yea verily, with a stammering lip and a strange tongue, He shall speak unto this people.

12. For when He said unto them: This is the true rest; give ye rest unto the weary; and this is the refreshment; they would not hear.

13. Therefore shall the word of Jehovah be indeed unto them, command upon command, command upon command; line upon line, line upon line; a little here, and a little there; that they may go on, and fall backward; and be broken, and snared, and caught,

There are several different renderings of the first verses of this chapter. The student will see that the first verse differs somewhat in Lowth's translation from what it is in the common version. The Revised Version, however, seems to be more consistent than any other, in that it keeps one subject throughout. In this it is the proud crown of the drunkards of Ephraim, which is the fading flower of his glorious beauty, and which stands at the head of the fat valley. In the others it would seem that the woe is pronounced against the crown of pride, and against the drunkards of Ephraim, as well.

There is, in fact, however, no difference, for since the crown of pride which stands at the head of the fat valley is undoubtedly the city of Samaria, it follows that the drunkards of Ephraim suffer in the woe pronounced against her.

Let no one think, because this prophecy specifies Ephraim and the city of Samaria, which long since ceased to have any importance as a city, that it is merely local, and all in the past. Look ahead in the chapter, and read in verse 22, and it will be seen that the destruction threatened against Ephraim is "the consumption" "determined upon the whole earth."

Remember that the earth was given to man in the beginning. It was to be the possession of a perfect people. Therefore when God brought His people out of Egypt, and gave them the lands of the heathen, "that they might keep His statutes," it was in fulfillment of the promise to Abraham, that he and his seed should possess the earth. Rom. 4:13. All of God's dealing with his people, no matter how localized, had reference to the one great promise. This was the thing that God always had in view. "The Lord is not slack concerning His promise." At any time up to the captivity of Judah, the people might have had the fulfillment of the promise, in the resurrection; and whenever God tells of judgments that shall come upon them because of their disobedience, it involves the whole earth. When God punishes those who have been His people, because they have become like the heathen, it follows that He will at the same time punish the heathen themselves.

Keeping those principles always in mind, we may read this prophecy as applying to us, that is, to the professed people of God in this day, no matter what their name. The glory of those who lift up themselves in pride shall be as a fading flower. "For all flesh is grass, and all the goodliness thereof is as the flower of the field; the grass withereth, the flower fadeth; because the Spirit of the Lord bloweth upon it; surely the people is grass. The grass withereth, the flower fadeth; but the word of our God shall stand for ever." Isa. 40:6–8.

"And the fading flower of their glorious beauty, which is at the head of the rich valley, shall be as the early fruit before the summer; which whoso seeth, he plucketh it immediately; and it is no sooner in his hand, than he swalloweth it." So quickly will be the destruction of those who exalt themselves against God, and boast of their own security. "The day of the Lord so cometh as a thief in the night. For when they shall say, Peace and safety, then sudden destruction cometh upon them, as travail upon a woman with child; and they shall not escape." 1 Thess. 5:2–3.

What a glorious prospect is held out in verses 5–6. When the crown of pride shall be trodden underfoot, and the glorious beauty of the transgressors shall be a fading flower, "in that day shall the Lord of hosts be for a crown of glory, and for a diadem of beauty, unto the residue of His people, and for a Spirit of judgment to him that sitteth in judgment, and for strength to them that turn the battle to the gate." The residue is the remnant, and the remnant shall be saved. God is from everlasting to everlasting; therefore those who have Him for their crown of glory, have a crown "which fadeth not away." The heavens and the earth shall wax old like a garment, but He remains the same, and His years do not fail.

Since God is to be the crown of glory to His people in the day of destruction to all in which haughty men boast, it is plain that in God alone should men trust and make their boast now. "Let not the wise man glory in his wisdom, neither let the mighty man glory in his might, let not the rich man glory in his riches; but let him that glorieth glory in this, that he understandeth and knoweth Me, that I am the Lord which exercise loving-kindness, judgment, and righteousness, in the earth; for in these things do I delight, saith the Lord." Jer. 9:23–24. "The Lord knoweth the thoughts of the wise, that they are vain. Therefore let no man glory in men." 1 Cor. 3:20–21. "God has chosen the foolish things of the world to confound the wise; and God hath chosen the weak things of the world to confound the things which are mighty; and base things of the world and things which are despised, hath God chosen, yea, and things which are not, to bring to naught things that are; that no flesh should glory in His presence. But of Him are ye in Christ Jesus, who of God is made unto us wisdom, and righteousness, and sanctification, and redemption; that, according as it is written, He that glorieth, let him glory in the Lord."

The Lord is to be the crown of glory to His people. He Himself is to be the only ornament that His people will wear. Their adorning must be "the hidden man of the heart, in that which is not corruptible, even the ornament of a meek and quiet spirit, which is in the sight of God of great price."1 Peter 3:4. This crown of glory will not be appreciated by the world. Indeed, the world may scoff at those who wear it, even as they did at Christ Himself. "The world knoweth us not, because it knew Him not." 1 John 3:1. When Christ was on earth He had "no form nor comeliness;" and when men saw Him there was no beauty in Him that would cause them to desire Him; therefore they hid their faces from Him, and esteemed Him smitten of God. Isa. 53:2–3. Yet He had glory that could be seen by those who had eyes for it, even "the glory as of the only begotten of the Father," but it was the glory of grace and truth. John 1:14. When the Lord comes, those who have this beauty, – the beauty of holiness, – will shine forth as the sun. Matt. 13:43. Those who will now show such appreciation of the beauty of the Lord that they will be content with it, and not put a slight upon it by seeking to supplement it with the adorning of the world, even though they be considered plain, have the assurance that through all eternity they will be as beautiful as the heavens.

The time is coming when "the saints shall judge the world," and angels as well. 1 Cor. 6:2–3. They will surely need the very best judgment then; therefore the Lord of hosts will be "for a spirit of judgment to him that sitteth in judgment." It will be no human judgment that will be exercised in that day, but the judgment of the Lord Himself, working in men. But the fact that this perfect judgment is to be exercised by the saints in glory is set forth as the reason why they should not now act foolishly. God will now be judgment to those who trust Him, as well as in the day of final judgment. Just as it will be His Spirit that speaks in His children when they are called upon to answer for the hope that is in them (Matt. 10:20), so will He now be wisdom and judgment for them in all the affairs of life. See Isa. 54:13; Ps. 1:1–3; Col. 1:9–10. But let it be remembered that this spirit of judgment is but the manifestation of the spirit of meekness with which God's people are adorned. "The meek will He guide in judgment; and the meek will He teach His way." Ps. 25:9. Is it not better to acknowledge that we have no wisdom at all, and to have the wisdom of God, which is perfect, than to boast of our independence, and be left to act foolishly? In other words, Is it not much better to act wisely, and give God the credit, than to act foolishly, and take all the credit to ourselves?

God says that the priest and the prophet, as well as the people, have erred through wine, and are out of the way through strong drink, and that therefore "they stumble in judgment." This is too true in the most literal sense, for it is a sad fact that very many professed Christians, including many who call themselves ministers of the Lord, are often filled with wine in which is excess, rather than with the Spirit. But there is a wine, against the use of which no temperance society that has ever yet been formed has ever protested, and that is the wine of Babylon, the wine of worldly pride. See Rev. 14:8; 18:3. It is very easy for Christians to become intoxicated with the prospect of worldly fame and applause, and thus to depart from the simplicity of the faith. Proud Babylon, the Church of Rome, whose religion is outward pomp and worldly prosperity and political power, is but the aggregate of the working of the spirit of worldliness in individuals. Beware of this form of drunkenness, lest you be where "there is no place clean." Isa. 28:8. Compare Rev. 18:2.

Those who are drunken with the wine of their own pride, and who, trusting in their own wisdom, scorn to be directed by the plain and simple Word of God, – "the sincere milk of the Word," – say contemptuously, "Whom will He teach knowledge? and whom will He make to understand the message? them that are weaned from the milk, and drawn from the breasts? For it is precept upon precept, precept upon precept; line upon line, line upon line; here a little, and there a little." Vain in their imaginations, and puffed up with the pride of their own opinions, thinking themselves competent to sit in judgment upon the Bible, men resent being taught like little children. Yet in no other way can they enter into the kingdom of heaven. Matt. 18:3. Men of the world, "professing themselves to be wise," choose to reason things out, to work up complex "systems" of belief; children, however, learn by accepting simple statements of fact. The child grows in knowledge merely by believing, and consequently it grows rapidly. At no other period in a person's life does he learn so much and so rapidly as in the first three or four years, when he takes everything by faith. Afterwards, as he gradually "comes to years of understanding," that is, as he thinks that he must manufacture wisdom, instead of receiving it as a gift from God, his progress is much slower. But God designs that His children shall always remain little children, so that their progress in wisdom may be as great in later years as in the beginning. So He will continue to teach by giving precept upon precept, precept upon precept; line upon line, line upon line; here a little, and there a little. Constant repetition of simple truths which, although simple, contain infinity, is the way to acquire "the wisdom which is from above."

But how about the statement that this sort of teaching is to be given to the people, "that they might go and fall backward, and be broken, and snared, and taken?" Ah, that is the same thing for which Jesus gave thanks, saying, "I thank Thee, O Father, Lord of heaven and earth, because Thou hast hid these things from the wise and prudent, and hast revealed them unto babes." Matt. 11:25. Men go with heads lifted up so high, looking so far off for wisdom, that they stumble over simple truth lying at their feet. Is it not a thing to be thankful for, that the only way the Lord makes the way of life hard for anybody is by making it easy? How can any of the wise men of earth, who stumble and fall over the teaching of the Lord, accuse Him of injustice in His dealing with them, when that which He set forth before them was so simple that a babe could understand it? To say that the way of life was too hard for them, would be to deny all their pretensions to wisdom, and to confess that they did not know as much as the babes. No; there is no excuse. The only reason why any err from the truth is that they will not hear. God not only offers them rest and peace, but says, "This is the rest wherewith ye may cause the weary to rest; and this is the refreshing;" but they refuse to hear. He would make them fellow-workers with Himself, but they will not. Let us not refuse to learn the lesson. "See that ye refuse not Him that speaketh."

CHAPTER 20

THE SURE FOUNDATION

(Isaiah 28:14–18, Lowth's Translation)

14. Hear ye the word of Jehovah, ye scoffers; ye of this people in Jerusalem, who utter sententious speeches:

15. Who say, we have entered into a covenant with death; and with the grave we have made a treaty: the overflowing plague, when it passeth through shall not reach us: for we have made falsehood our refuge; and under deceit we have hidden ourselves.

16. Wherefore thus said the Lord Jehovah: Behold, I lay in Sion for a foundation a stone, an approved stone; a corner-stone, precious, immovably fixed: he, that trusteth in Him, shall not be confounded.

17. And I will mete out judgment by the rule; and the strict justice by the plummet: and the hail shall sweep away the refuge of falsehood; and the hiding-place the waters shall overwhelm.

18. And your covenant with death shall be broken; and your treaty with the grave shall not stand: when the overflowing plague passeth through, by it shall ye be beaten down.

Let the student read carefully again the first portion of this chapter, together with the twenty-second verse, and remember that the instruction and warnings given are for us no less than for the people in Isaiah's time. The word of the Lord is living, and is addressed to us just as directly as though we heard the tones of the prophet's voice.

The word of the Lord is here to those who are proud in their own conceit; who know so much in their own estimation that they are not willing to be taught. Scorning to be thought so ignorant as to need the simple precepts of the Scriptures, "precept upon precept, precept upon precept; line upon line, line upon line; here a little and there a little," they fail to learn anything. The case of those of whom the Apostle Paul speaks in Rom. 1:22 is not peculiar to them. Whenever men profess themselves to be wise, they become fools; therefore, "if any man among you seemeth to be wise in this world, let him become a fool that he may be wise. For the wisdom of this world is foolishness with God." 1 Cor. 3:18–19.

The foolishness of those who profess themselves to be wise is seen from what they put their trust in for safety. They say, "We have made a covenant with death, and with hell are we at agreement. When the overflowing scourge shall pass through, it shall not come unto us, for we have made lies our refuge, and under falsehood have we hid ourselves." Isa. 28:15. They have thought to anticipate God, and to head off punishment that He would bring. They have bribed death to protect them; but death and hell are poor protectors. Falsehood and lies cannot save. The only place of protection that death has is the grave. To be at agreement with hell, is deliberately to go to perdition. It is the kid fleeing to the tiger for protection from the bear.

"No lie is of the truth." Whoever, therefore, rejects truth chooses falsehood. There are many people who pride themselves upon their honesty, that are nevertheless hiding themselves under falsehood. They might not themselves tell deliberate lies, but truth is a unit, and whoever deliberately rejects any truth that comes to him, thereby rejects all truth. That portion of truth which he elects to retain, he changes into a lie. Rom. 1:25. Satan works "with all power and signs and lying wonders, and with all deceivableness of unrighteousness in them that perish, because they received not the love of the truth, that they might be saved." 2 Thess. 2:9–10. And all who receive not the love of the truth will certainly perish, because it alone is a shield and buckler. See Ps. 91:4.

Truth cannot be built up by a falsehood. Truth and falsehood have no connection. Truth is *that which is*, therefore truth is life. This is seen in the words of Christ, "I am the way, the truth, and the life." John 14:6. And since truth is life, falsehood is death. So to make lies one's refuge, hoping by them to escape death, is like a man cutting his own throat to save his neck from the halter. Those who err from the truth, trusting in death to save them, have said, "When the overflowing scourge shall pass through it shall not come unto us." "Therefore thus saith the Lord God, Behold I lay in Zion for a foundation a stone, a tried stone, a precious corner stone, a sure foundation. He that believeth shall not make haste: judgment also will I lay to the line, and righteousness to the plummet, and the hail shall sweep away the refuge of lies, and the waters shall overflow the hiding-place." "And your covenant with death shall be disannulled and your agreement with hell shall not stand; when the overflowing scourge shall pass through, then ye shall be trodden down by it."

This sure foundation is truth, for Christ is the truth. John 14:6. And He is the only foundation (1 Cor. 3:11) that will stand. Whatever is not in harmony with that will be swept away, for even death itself shall be destroyed.

A foundation is that upon which one builds. In the Hebrew the word "to believe" is from a root which also has a specification, to build, to establish. In 2 Chron. 20:20, "Believe in the Lord, so shall ye be established," the words "believe" and "be established" are from the same Hebrew word, and the sentence might be rendered, "Build upon the Lord your God, so shall ye be built up." Abraham built upon God when he believed in God.

Christ is the sure foundation. He is also the Word, the living Word. He is the truth, and His word is truth. Whoever, therefore, builds upon His word, builds upon the rock, and when the rains descend, and the floods come, and the winds blow and beat upon that house, it does not fall. Matt. 7:25–26. But whoever does not build upon His words, – that is to say, whoever does not let those words control him, and manifest themselves in his life, – builds upon the sand; and when the tide rises, and the rain descends, and the winds blow and beat upon that house, it will fall, and its destruction will be great. The rock will stand, because it is "the Rock of Ages." "In the Lord Jehovah is the Rock of Ages." Isa. 26:4. Whoever builds upon God shall not be ashamed (Rom. 9:33) nor confounded. I Peter 2:6. As the text says, "He shall not make haste." He will not need to run when the storm comes, because he is already in a place of safety. "He that dwelleth in the secret place of the Most High, shall abide under the shadow of the Almighty." "I will say of the Lord, He is my refuge, my fortress; my God; in Him will I trust."

This stone which God lays in Zion for a foundation is a "tried stone." "God was in Christ, reconciling the world unto Himself." God placed His character in Christ. He had pledged Himself to the redemption of the world, and sent Christ to do the work. He made a promise to Abraham, and to his seed, and confirmed it with an oath, that we might have a strong consolation, who have fled for refuge to lay hold upon the hope set before us, which hope we have as an anchor of the soul, both sure and steadfast, and which entereth into that within the veil, whither the forerunner is for us entered, even Jesus. Heb. 6:13–20. Thus we learn that God swore by Himself that He would forgive the sins of all who sought forgiveness through Christ. Jesus Christ is the manifestation of God. If Christ had failed or become discouraged because of the difficulties of His task, God's oath would have been broken; but if God's oath would have been broken, God's own life would have been forfeited; and since He is the Creator and upholder of all things, everything would have ceased to be. Now we can see how well tried is the foundation upon which we are asked to build. God placed Himself and the weight of the entire universe upon it, and it stood the test. Therefore, we can rest upon it in confidence. It is a precious stone to those who believe.

The Word will be the only standard in the Judgment. The Word is righteousness, and righteousness will be the plumb line. The whole building must square with this foundation. Nothing must project over the edge; that is, nothing must go beyond the Word. Whatever is outside of the Word of God, will be swept away with the overflowing scourge. The hail shall sweep away the refuge of lies. Read Job 38:22–23; Rev. 16:21.

This tried stone which is laid for a foundation is a living stone. 1 Peter 2:4. Whoever comes in contact with it is made alive. Living things grow, and so in Christ "All the building fitly framed together groweth unto an holy temple in the Lord." We read, "As ye have therefore received Christ Jesus the Lord, so walk ye in Him, rooted and built up in Him, and stablished in the faith." Col. 2:6–7. Thus we see that the house built upon Christ and His Word, is not like an ordinary house built by men, which simply stands upon its foundation, but it is a living house, built upon a living foundation, of which it becomes a part, so that the house and the foundation are as firmly joined together, and as much a part of each other; as the tree and its roots. Therefore, there is no danger that the house will be swept off from the foundation, and the foundation be left standing. Every one who stands on God's Word and lives by it, will stand as long as God lives, and will be as immovable as He.

From the last lesson, in the first part of this chapter, we learn that those to whom the Lord is speaking, reject the simple instruction of His Word, and therefore they stumble and fall. They profess themselves to be wise, yet they stumble at that which is revealed to babes. Even so it is in their relation to this sure foundation, which the Lord lays, and upon which men are to build and be safe. While it is a foundation and a sanctuary, it is also a "stone of stumbling." Isa. 8:14. "As it is written, Behold I lay in Sion a stumbling stone and rock of offense, and whosoever believeth on Him shall not be ashamed." Rom. 9:33. Here the two passages of Isaiah are brought together, and we learn that the same Lord who is the foundation which builds up those who build upon it, and makes them a sanctuary, is at the same time a stumbling stone. If men will not place their feet upon that which is made for them to stand upon, then they stumble over it. So the very thing which is salvation to those that believe, is destruction to those who do not believe. See 1 Peter 2:6–8. This being the case, there is no possible chance left for anybody to accuse God of injustice. When that which causes some people's destruction is nothing other than the salvation which God provides for all men, God is surely clear when He judges.

CHAPTER 21

THE RIGHTEOUS JUDGMENT OF GOD

(Isaiah 28:18–29, Lowth's Translation)

18. Your covenant with death shall be broken, and your treaty with the grave shall not stand: when the overflowing plague passeth through, by it shall ye be beaten down.

19. As soon as it passeth through, shall it seize you; yea, morning after morning shall it pass through, by day and by night; and even the report alone shall cause terror.

20. For the bed is too short, for one to stretch himself out at length; and the covering is too narrow, for one to gather himself up under it.

21. For as in Mount Peratsim, Jehovah will arise; as in the valley of Gibeon, shall He be moved with anger; that He may execute His work, His strange work; and effect His operation, His unusual operation.

22. And now, give yourselves up to scoffing no more, lest your chastisements become more severe: for a full and decisive decree have I heard, from the Lord Jehovah God of Hosts, on the whole land.

23. Listen ye, and hear My voice; attend, and hearken unto My words.

24. Doth the husbandman plough every day that he may sow, opening and breaking the clods of the field?

25. When he hath made even the face thereof, doth not he then scatter the dill, and cast abroad the cummin; and sow the wheat in due measure; and the barley, and rye, hath its appointed limit?

26. For his God rightly instructeth him; He furnished him with knowledge.

27. The dill is not beaten out with the corn-drag; nor is the wheel of the wain made to turn upon the cumin: but the dill is beaten out with the staff;

28. And the cummin with the flail: but the bread-corn with the threshing-wain. But not for ever will he continue thus to thresh it, nor to vex it with the wheel of his wain; nor to bruise it with the hoofs of his cattle.

29. This also proceedeth from Jehovah God of Hosts: He showeth Himself wonderful in counsel, great in operation.

The first five verses of the portion here given have already been considered, but we give them again in order to preserve the connection. Not only they, but all the preceding verses should be read in connection with this lesson. Remember that the Bible does not consist of isolated texts, but each writer has a message from the Lord. One can no more get the sense of the Scriptures by taking a verse here and another there, than we can get the meaning of a letter that we receive, by reading a sentence in the middle of it, then another near the beginning, and then another at the close. We must read it through from beginning to end, and then whenever we wish to refer to some particular sentence in it, we must take it in connection with the rest. We must at the same time we quote it, remember what has preceded, and what follows. Even so must we deal with the message which the Lord sends us by His prophets.

Those who recall not only the first part of this chapter, but the preceding chapters will know that the general subject is the judgments of God. The last days, and the very last judgments of God upon this earth, are very vividly brought to view. But let it never be forgotten that the idea is salvation rather than destruction. God comes to save His people. Too many always connect the Judgment with thoughts of revenge, as though God had in mind nothing except to destroy somebody. Let all remember that God is a Shepherd, and that His sole solicitude is for His flock. When He comes to deliver His sheep from the mouth of the lion, who would devour them, He is moved by feelings of the deepest love and compassion. The last judgment is only a wonderful manifestation of God's everlasting love for His people. Read again Isa. 27:3–4: "I the Lord do keep it; I will water it every moment; lest any hurt it, I will keep it night and day. Fury is not in me." God is love just as much when He destroys the wicked, who would destroy His people, as when He gives His life for the world. In the execution of His greatest judgments, "His mercy endureth for ever." See Ps. 136:10–24.

Great as is God's power to destroy, so great is His power to redeem. The destruction of the wicked is only one part of the great work of redemption. This is shown in the death of Christ. Christ died for the world of sinners. He was made to be sin for us, and therefore He suffered the penalty for sin. He was made to be sin for us, in order that we might be made the righteousness of God in Him, and even so He suffered as a sinner, in order that guilty sinners might be saved from wrath through Him. In giving His only Son to die for sinners, and giving Himself in His Son, God showed us not only the inevitable fate of sinners but also how much He longed not to see a single sinner punished. He has no pleasure in the death of any. See Eze. 33:11. The wicked who will be destroyed at the last day, will only be taking by themselves that which they would not share with Christ. The cross of Christ appears in everything. So in the description of future judgments, God is making known to us some of the sufferings of Christ for sinners, that we may know how great is His power now to redeem those who fly to Him for refuge.

Thus we may understand that when God arises to Judgment, and is "wroth as in the valley of Gibeon" (See Josh. 10:10–11), where He smote the enemies of His people, and "slew them with a great slaughter," and "chased them," and "cast down great stones from heaven upon them," (Compare Rev. 16:21), it is for Him a "strange work." The angels were awed into silence, and the heavens grew black with astonishment, when God showed His marvelous love for man by giving His Son to die. Such a way of showing love, not for friends, but for enemies, could be conceived and understood only by the heart of God. Even yet the angels desire to understand it. See 1 Peter 1:10–12. Since no man nor angel can comprehend the love of God that is manifested in the death of Christ for sinners, let no one childishly accuse God of injustice and cruelty when he reads of the judgments that are to fall upon the hoards of those who reject the redemption that is in Christ Jesus.

Terrible things will come, too. "Even the report alone shall cause terror." The prophet Habakkuk saw in vision the time when the Lord went forth for the salvation of His people, threshing the heathen by the power that was hidden in His glorious, wounded side (Hab. 3:4, margin, 12–13), and he said, "I heard and my belly trembled, my lips quivered at the voice, rottenness entered into my bones, and I trembled in my place; that I should rest in the day of trouble, when it cometh up against the people which invadeth Him in troops." Verse 16, R.V. So Jesus, describing to His disciples the terrors of that day, said, "There shall be signs in the sun and moon and stars; and upon the earth distress of nations, in perplexity for the roaring of the sea and of the billows; men expiring for fear, and for expectation of the things which are coming on the world; for the powers of the heavens shall be shaken." Luke 21:25–26, R.V.

"In that day a man shall cast his idols of silver, and his idols of gold, which they made each one for himself to worship, to the moles and to the bats; to go into the clefts of the rocks, and into the tops of the ragged rocks, for fear of the Lord, and for the glory of His majesty, when He ariseth to shake terribly the earth." Isa. 2:20–21. All the men of this earth, both great and small, will flee to hide themselves, and will say to the mountains and rocks, "Fall on us, and hide us from the face of Him that sitteth on the throne, and from the wrath of the Lamb; for the great day of His wrath is come; and who shall be able to stand?" Rev. 6:15–17. But there will be no place for hiding; "for the bed is too short for one to stretch himself out at length; and the covering is too narrow for one to gather himself up under it." This is a striking figure, which all can under-stand. Who has not at some time suffered with cold because of scanty bed-clothing? Try as you would, you could not get protec-tion. Such an experience the Lord uses to illustrate the vain efforts of those who would escape His righteous judgments. There will be no place of concealment, for God will then "bring to light the hidden things of darkness." 1 Cor. 4:5.

Here is an exhortation that comes to all: "Now therefore be ye not mockers, lest your bands be made strong: for I have heard from the Lord of hosts a consumption, even determined upon the whole earth." Even as the Gospel is "to all people," so all people are interested in the account of these judgments. They come not upon one particular locality, but upon the whole earth. Compare with this the second Psalm, "Why do the heathen rage, and the people imagine a vain thing? The kings of the earth set themselves, and the rulers take counsel together, against the Lord, and against His Anointed, saying, Let us break their bands asunder, and cast away their cords from us." They will enter into an alliance with death and the grave against the Lord; but the Lord will laugh at their vain efforts. The Son, whom they despise, will "break them with a rod of iron," and will "dash them in pieces like a potter's vessel." So the exhortation comes, " Be wise now therefore, O ye kings; be instructed, ye judges of the earth." If not, the bands which they vainly think to break and cast off, will be made tighter; but if they will but submit themselves to the yoke of the Lord, then they will find the bands tokens of liberty, since they are bands of love.

Last of all in this chapter which we are studying, we have a lesson from the seasons, and the work which comes with each. Just as in the service of the Jewish tabernacle the whole work of the Gospel was set forth in figure each year, even so it is now, and has been from the beginning, in nature. Seed-time and harvest are yearly reminders to all men of the work of God for men, – of the Gospel and its consummation. Everybody is familiar with the growth of grain, and the harvest, so we have need only to read the last five verses of Isa. 28 to have material for many lessons.

The husbandman does not plough all the time, neither is he all the time sowing. When he has broken up the earth, and harrowed it, making the surface smooth, then he scatters the various kinds of grain. Each kind of grain has its appointed time, and is sown in its season. "For this God doth instruct him to discretion and doth teach him." Yes, the wisdom which men have to till the soil comes from God alone. There is nothing that men know, that they have not learned from God. Whatever men know well, when priding themselves upon their skill and dexterity in doing it, let them remember that God knows how to do it infinitely better, and can still teach them more. Righteousness comes by faith. But righteousness is right doing. That is, the man who lives by faith will do whatever he has to do much better than the one who is not a Christian. If men have not always seen it so, then it is to the shame of the professed Christians; they have not lived up to their profession. Since faith makes a man righteous, a right doer, then it follows that faith – true and intelligent faith – will make a man a better farmer, a better carpenter, a better workman in any line. God is "wonderful in counsel; and excellent in working," and those who trust in Him fully will find it manifest in themselves.

But this is only by the way, important as it is. It is a side lesson. The special thing to be learned from this reference to agriculture is that God works consistently, and adapts His means to the ends He has in view. The farmer does not thresh all kinds of grain with the same instrument. The machine that is used for threshing corn, would utterly destroy some more delicate kinds of seeds. So God adapts His judgments to the individual. There is only one standard in the Judgment, namely, the law of God, – the perfect life of the Lord, – but each person will be judged only by the amount of the light and knowledge of the law he has had. "For as many as have sinned without law shall also perish without law; and as many as have sinned in the law shall be judged by the law; in the day when God shall judge the secrets of men by Jesus Christ according to my Gospel." Rom. 2:12,16. "For not the hearers of the law are just before God, but the doers of the law shall be justified. For when the Gentiles, which have not the law, do by nature the things contained in the law, these, having not the law, are a law unto themselves; which show the work of the law written in their hearts, their conscience also bearing witness, and their thoughts the meanwhile accusing or else excusing one another." Verses 13–15. In the Judgment, the man who has never seen the Bible, and who has had no knowledge of God, other than that which is revealed in the book of nature, will not be held accountable for the same light that the one is who has lived all his life amid the greatest Gospel privileges. It will then be seen, however, that there is no one who has not had an opportunity to hear the Gospel, and who has not both heard and seen it. "Have they not heard? Yea, verily, their sound went into all the earth, and their words unto the ends of the world." Rom. 10:18. "The wrath of God is revealed from heaven against all ungodliness and unrighteousness of men, who hold down the truth in unrighteousness; because that which may be known of God is manifest in them." All are without excuse, because ever since the creation of the world the everlasting power and Divinity of God are clearly seen in the things which He has made. Rom. 1:18–20.

The seed-time is the giving of the news of salvation. "The seed is the Word of God" (Luke 8:11), and Christ is the Word. John 1:1–14. "Except a corn of wheat fall into the ground and die, it abideth alone; but if it die, it bringeth forth much fruit." John 12:24. Christ is the Seed (Gal. 3:16), and He died and was buried to bring many sons unto glory. Every springing seed speaks, to all who will hear of the power of the resurrection, and so of the power of God to salvation.

"The harvest is the end of the world." Matt. 13:39. John says, "And I looked, and behold a white cloud, and upon the cloud one sat like unto the Son of man, having on His head a golden crown, and in His hand a sharp sickle. And another angel came out of the temple, crying with a loud voice to Him that sat on the cloud, Thrust in thy sickle, and reap; for the time is come for thee to reap; for the harvest of the earth is ripe. And He that sat on the cloud thrust in His sickle on the earth; and the earth was reaped." Rev. 14:14–16. This is when "He cometh with clouds; and every eye shall see Him, and they also that pierced Him; and all kindreds of the earth shall wail because of Him." Rev. 1:7. Thus we see again that the things spoken of in our lesson are no light thing concerning only a few Jews hundreds of years ago. They are matters of present and universal importance.

"But not for ever will He continue thus to thresh it, nor to vex it with the wheel of His wain; nor to bruise it with the hoofs of His cattle." "The Lord is merciful and gracious, slow to anger, and plenteous in mercy. He will not always chide; neither will He keep His anger for ever." Ps. 103:8–9. "For yet a very little while, and the indignation shall cease, and Mine anger in their destruction." Isa.

10:25. It is a strange thing for God to execute punishment upon His creatures; therefore He will not keep for ever before His eyes, and the eyes of the universe, the spectacle of people tormented in flames. Men may make a covenant with death and the grave, thinking thus to escape the righteous judgments of God; but that will avail nothing, for both death and the grave shall be utterly consumed in the lake of fire (Rev. 20:14), so that "yet a little while, and the wicked shall not be; yea, thou shalt diligently consider his place, and it shall not be." Ps. 37:10. The wicked are chaff, stubble, and noxious weeds. "Therefore as the fire devoureth the stubble, and the flame consumeth the chaff, so their root shall be as rottenness, and their blossom shall go up as dust; because they have cast away the law of the Lord of hosts, and despised the word of the Holy One of Israel." Isa. 5:24. "The day cometh, that shall burn as an oven; and all the proud, yea, and all that do wickedly, shall be stubble; and the day that cometh shall burn them up, saith the Lord of hosts, that it shall leave them neither root nor branch." Mal. 4:1. As the tares are gathered and burned in the fire, "so shall it be in the end of this world. The Son of man shall send forth His angels, and they shall gather out of His kingdom all things that offend, and them which do iniquity; and shall cast them into the furnace of fire; there shall be wailing and gnashing of teeth. Then shall the righteous shine forth as the sun in the kingdom of their Father. Who hath ears to hear, let him hear." Matt. 13:40–43.

CHAPTER 22

THE CAUSE OF IGNORANCE

(Isaiah 29:1–14, Lowth's Translation)

1. Woe to Ariel, to Ariel, the city which David besieged! Add year to year; let the feasts go round in their course.

2. Yet will I bring distress upon Ariel; and there shall be continual mourning and sorrow. And it shall be unto Me as the hearth of the great altar.

3. And I will encamp against thee, like David; and I will lay siege against thee with a mound; and I will erect towers against thee.

4. And thou shalt be brought low; thou shalt speak as from beneath the earth; and from out of the dust thou shalt utter a feeble speech; and thy voice shall come out of the ground like that of a necromancer; and thy words from out of the dust shall give a small, shrill sound.

5. But the multitude of the proud shall be like the small dust; and like the flitting chaff the multitude of the terrible; yea, the effect shall be momentary, in an instant.

6. From Jehovah God of Hosts there shall be a sudden visitation, with thunder, and earthquake, and a mighty voice; with storm, and tempest, and flame of devouring fire.

7. And like as a dream, a vision of the night, so shall it be with the multitude of all the nations, that fight against Ariel; and all their armies, and their towers, and those that distress her.

8. As when a hungry man dreameth; and lo! he seemeth to eat; but he awaketh, and his appetite is still unsatisfied; and as a thirsty man dreameth, and lo! he seemeth to drink; but he awaketh and he is still faint, and his appetite still craving; so shall it be with the multitude of all the nations, which have set themselves in array against Mount Sion.

9. They are struck with amazement, they stand astonished; they stare with a look of stupid surprise; they are drunken, but not with wine; they stagger, but not with strong drink.

10. For Jehovah hath poured upon you a spirit of profound sleep; and hath closed up your eyes; the prophets, and the rulers; the seers hath He blindfolded.

11. So that all the vision is to you, as the words of a book sealed up; which if one delivers to a man, that knoweth letters, saying, Read this, I pray thee; he answereth, I cannot read it; for it is sealed up.

12. Or should the book be given to one that knoweth not letters, saying, Read this, I pray thee; he answereth, I know not letters.

13. Wherefore Jehovah hath said: Forasmuch as this people draweth near with their mouth, and honoureth Me with their lips, while their heart is far from Me; and vain is their fear of Me, teaching the commandments of men;

14. Therefore behold, I will again deal with this people, in a manner so wonderful and astonishing; that the wisdom of the wise shall perish, and the prudence of the prudent shall disappear.

What is Ariel? That it is a city, is plainly stated. What city? In the translation which we are using, it is stated to be the city which David besieged, which is not very definite, since David besieged more than one city. In the Revised Version we have the better rendering, "the city where David encamped," and when we put by the side of this the rendering of the common version, "the city where David dwelt," we have no difficulty in understanding that Jerusalem is the city referred to in the prophecy.

In the twenty-eighth chapter we have the case of Samaria set forth, and now in this chapter Jerusalem is dealt with; but in both it is the whole world that is involved.

The word "Ariel" means "lion of God." A few moments' study of the passages in which this word occurs may be of interest. Aside from this chapter, we find it in 2 Sam. 23:20, and the parallel passage in 1 Chron. 11:22, where it is stated that Benaiah "slew two lion-like men of Moab." The Revision shows us that the words "men of" are added by the translator. Literally it is "two Ariel of Moab," which is not a translation, and which to us does not mean anything. Translated it would read, "two lions of God of Moab." Now when we remember that the phrase "to God" is often used to express the superlative degree as to size, fairness, etc., (See Ps. 36:6; Acts 7:20, with the margin of both cases), we understand that Benaiah slew two very great lions of Moab.

Again the word occurs in Eze. 43:15–16, where it is rendered "altar." The marginal rendering is in one case "mountain of God," and in the other, "lion of God." This we can understand when we remember that the temple, the essential part of which was the altar, was on the summit of Mount Zion, and that Mount Zion and the temple stood for Jerusalem.

Jerusalem stands as the center of the worship of the true God, and therefore all the judgments that come upon Jerusalem because of the corruption of the worship of Jehovah will surely come wherever that worship has been perverted. It should also be noted, in reading the text, that instead of "Woe to Ariel!" we may read, "Ho, Ariel!" as in the Revision and in the margin of our common version. So combining the various renderings, we may arrive at this: "Ho, Ariel, Ariel, the city where David dwelt! add ye year to year; let the feasts be observed in their courses, and the sacrifices be offered, yet will I bring distress upon Ariel, and there shall be mourning." That is to say, ceremonies and festivals, no matter how numerous nor how strictly observed, will never ward off judgments, nor take the place of personal righteousness of character. Compare this with verses 13–14. It is the same lesson that is set forth in the first chapter of Isaiah, and one which cannot be repeated too often in this generation.

The reader will notice that Lowth's rendering of the first part of verse 3, is widely different from that in the common version or the revision. Lowth has it, "I will encamp against thee, like David," while the others have it, "I will camp against thee round about." The difference comes in this way: The Hebrew word for "circle" differs from the Hebrew of "David" only in the last letter, and those two letters are so nearly alike that one is easily mistaken for the other, and some ancient manuscripts have it David. It is really a matter of no importance, and attention is called to it only that we may see that little differences of that kind do not affect the meaning. If we read, "I will encamp against thee, like David," it is the same as though we read, "I will camp against thee round about," for that is the way David did.

We can now read the verses and see the picture which they present. Jerusalem, although very scrupulous in the observance of all the forms and ceremonies of the law, and of many of which the law knew nothing, yet disregarding the weighty matters of the law, namely, judgment, mercy, faith, was besieged by the Assyrians, afterward by the Babylonians, and still later by the Romans, and laid low. These nations, heathen and wicked as they were, were the agents of God, so that God Himself could say that He was encamping against the city. And those judgments upon Jerusalem of old were only a foretaste of the final destruction which shall come upon all who choose to follow their own way rather than God's way. Compare verse 6 with 1 Thess. 4:15–16; 5:3; Rev. 6:12–17; and Rev. 11:18–19.

"And thy voice shall be, as of one that hath a familiar spirit, out of the ground." When Saul consulted a woman with a familiar spirit, the answer came out of the ground. See 1 Sam. 28:7–13. Evil comes from beneath; all that is good comes from above. "Every good gift and every perfect gift is from above." James 1:17. Christ said to the wicked Jews: "Ye are from beneath; I am from above; ye are of this world; I am not of this world." John 8:23. "He that cometh from above is above all; he that is of the earth is earthly, and speaketh of the earth; He that cometh from heaven is above all." John 3:31. The evil spirit speaks from the earth; Christ speaks from heaven. Heb. 12:25. Jerusalem is to be visited with thunder, and with earthquake, and great noise, and storm and tempest, and the flame of the devouring fire (Verse 6), and its destruction is to be sudden. When they shall say, Peace and Safety, then sudden destruction cometh. 1 Thess. 5:3. The multitude of the proud shall be as chaff that passeth away. "For, behold, the day cometh that shall burn as an oven; and all the proud, yea, and all that do wickedly, shall be stubble; and the day that cometh shall burn them up, saith the Lord of hosts, that it shall leave them neither root nor branch." Mal. 4:1. The time when this judgment shall be executed upon Jerusalem is very evident.

"And the multitude of all the nations that fight against Ariel, even all that fight against her and her munition, and that distress her, shall be as a dream of a night vision." The fact that men are instruments in the hands of God to execute judgments, does not necessarily prove that what they do is righteous. They are unconscious and unwilling instruments. They are intent upon carrying out their own purposes, but God overrules all in such a way that His purposes are accomplished. See the case of the selling of Joseph by his brethren. They were moved by envy and hate (Gen. 37:17–28; Acts 7:9), nevertheless it was God's purpose that was carried out in the deed. Gen. 45:7–8; Ps. 105:17–18: So it is when God allows unfaithful servants to fall into the hands of their enemies. What they suffer is but a part of God's judgment upon them, yet the men who execute this judgment are prompted only by their evil passions, and must themselves receive punishment for the judgments that they inflict.

One can readily see how Jerusalem will be the center of contention among the nations. Among all professed Christian nations the Turk is regarded as something to be got rid of. Professed ministers of the Gospel have been for years crying out for vengeance to be executed upon the Turks, and berating the heads of Government for their slowness to begin the war of extermination. The Turkish Empire would long since have ceased to be a part of Europe, if the other Governments could have been agreed as to who should be its successor. In process of time it will be driven out, and when the Turkish Empire is limited to Asia, Jerusalem will be the natural capital of it, inasmuch as it is the principal city in many respects. But since even now the cry has gone out for the Turk to be driven off the face of the earth, so much the more will it go forth then. So that it will be at Jerusalem that the armies of the nations will chiefly be assembled when the Lord appears in flaming fire taking vengeance on them that know not God, and that obey not the Gospel.

When the Lord appears in the clouds, all the wicked will be destroyed by the brightness of His coming. 2 Thess. 2:8. This will be but the beginning of their destruction. At the appearing of Christ, all the righteous dead will be raised incorruptible, and will be taken to be with the Lord. 1 Thess. 4:16–17; 1 Cor. 15:51–52. But the rest of the dead, the wicked, will not live again until the end of a thousand years, during which the righteous will be sitting in judgment with Christ, in heaven. Rev. 20:5–6. "And when the thousand years are expired, Satan shall be loosed out of his prison, and shall go out to deceive the nations which are in the four quarters of the earth, Gog and Magog, to gather them together to battle; the number of whom is as the sand of the sea. And they went up on the breadth of the earth, and compassed the camp of the saints about, and the beloved city; and fire came down from God out of heaven, and devoured them." Rev. 20:7–9. They go up with the intent to capture the city; but, lo, the city against which they now come is the New Jerusalem. Jerusalem has undergone a transformation while they have been asleep; and against this new city they are powerless.

When the psalmist went into the sanctuary of God, he under-stood the end of the wicked. He said, "Surely Thou didst set them in slippery places; Thou castedst them down into destruction. How are they brought into desolation, as in a moment! they are utterly consumed with terrors. As a dream when one awaketh; so, O Lord, Thou shalt despise their image." Ps. 73:17–20. So the multitude of those who come up to fight against Jerusalem shall be "as a dream of a night vision." They are to be "punished with everlasting destruction," and the fire with which they will be consumed is "eternal fire," yet they are "suddenly consumed, as in a moment." Their destruction is the more speedy simply because the fire is eternal, even the consuming fire of God's own glory. No matter how long a time is occupied in the act of consuming them, compared with the eternity to follow it is but a moment. "So shall the multitude of all the nations be that fight against Zion."

Men who receive not the love of the truth, that they might be saved, have no alternative but strong delusion, that they should believe a lie. 2 Thess. 2:10–12. The greater the light which God sends, the greater will be the darkness if it is rejected. Thus it is that the Lord pours out the spirit of deep sleep, and closes the eyes of the prophets and rulers. Verse 10. The rendering of this verse in the Revised Version is very striking and suggestive: "For the Lord hath poured out upon you the spirit of deep sleep, and hath closed your eyes, the prophets; and your heads, the seers, hath he covered." The prophets and the seers are the eyes and heads of the people; when therefore these are drunken the whole body must necessarily stumble and fall.

A vision is a thing seen. To give a vision is to make something plain. Think then in what a condition of dullness people are, to whom a vision is as a sealed book, or like an open book handed to one who cannot read. In verses 11–12, we have a picture of a time of gross ignorance. What can be the cause of it? The Lord Himself tells us. The wisdom of the wise perishes, and the understanding of the prudent man is hid, because the people draw near the Lord with their mouth, while their heart is far from Him, and their fear toward Him is taught by the commandment of men. Here is something for serious consideration.

Compare the reading of verse 13 in the Revised Version: "Their fear of Me is a commandment of men which hath been taught them," or, as the margin has it, "learned by rote." There is no thought or reason in it, but they have been told certain things to do, and have learned them parrot-like, and do them mechanically. Ignorance, and not simply ignorance, but the inability to comprehend, is the inevitable consequence of such a course; for when men do not use the gifts that God has bestowed on them, those talents are sure to fall into decay. God has given all men minds which are to be used to their utmost limit, and that can take place only when He is allowed to use them; but when some men allow other men to serve as minds for them, they of course have no use for one of their own, and so it is removed. Only the commandments of men may be learned by rote. Men may attempt to learn the commandments of God in that way, but it is impossible. God's commandments are a living force, and wherever they are, there must be activity.

Commandments of men are not to be regarded. Of course this refers to matters pertaining to God. There is no man in the world so good that his word is to be regarded as of any authority in things pertaining to God. If it is his word, it is of no more value than the wind. But if he speaks the word of God, then the word will be with power, and will have the stamp of authority. No man is authorized by the Lord to speak his own words to the people, and whoever does so is a false teacher, seeking only his own profit. "He whom God hath sent speaketh the words of God." John 3:34. "To the law, and to the testimony; if they speak not according to this word, there is no light in them." Isa. 8:20.

When the wisdom of the wise men perishes, and the understanding of the prudent men is hid, what will become of the poor people who trust in the wisdom of men? They will evidently fall into the ditch, together with their blind leaders. "Cursed be the man that trusteth in man, and maketh flesh his arm, and whose heart departeth from the Lord. For he shall be like the heath in the desert, and shall not see when good cometh." Jer. 17:5–6.

What then is a poor, ignorant man to do? His course is plain; he is to go to the Lord for wisdom; "for the Lord giveth wisdom; out of His mouth cometh knowledge and understanding." Prov. 2:6. If anyone, no matter how poor, lack wisdom, "let him ask of God, who giveth to all men liberally, and upbraideth not; and it shall be given him." James 1:5. "Through Thy precepts I get understanding." Ps. 119:104. "I have more understanding than all my teachers; for Thy testimonies are my meditation." Verse 99. God has not made any one class of men the depositories of wisdom. "If any man willeth to do His will, he shall know." The Book is open, and it is plain; let each one read it for himself, and whatever he finds there let him adopt, without waiting to inquire of some man. The most ignorant may become wise, simply by giving heed to the Word of God; while the wisest men become fools when they turn away from that Word.

Some will say, "We have no time to study the Word of God, and to become acquainted with it." That is indeed strange. It is like the captain of a ship who is so busy navigating his vessel that he has no time to consult the chart and compass, or to take observations. It is like a man who has no time for eating. Men live only by the word of God; therefore the study of the word is the only thing they have time for. Time is given to men for the sole purpose of enabling them to gain eternity. Yet how few will believe it. They will act as though this short life were all, and as though it depended on them to secure it; whereas this life is given by God, and is but the ante-room to the life eternal. Who will be wise? let him seek first of all the kingdom of God, and His righteousness, and infinite wisdom and riches will be his.

CHAPTER 23

TOO DEEP FOR JEHOVAH

(Isaiah 29:13–24, Lowth's Translation)

13. Wherefore Jehovah hath said: Forasmuch as this people draweth near with their mouth, and honoureth Me with their lips, while their heart is far from Me; and vain is their fear of Me, teaching the commandments of men;

14. Therefore behold, I will again deal with this people, in a manner so wonderful and astonishing; that the wisdom of the wise shall perish, and the prudence of the prudent shall disappear.

15. Woe unto them, that are too deep for Jehovah in forming secret designs; whose deeds are in the dark; and who say, who is there, that seeth us; and who shall know us?

16. Perverse as ye are! shall the potter be esteemed as the clay? Shall the work say of the workman, He hath not made me? And shall the thing formed say of the former of it, He hath no understanding?

17. Shall it not be but a very short space, ere Lebanon become like Carmel, and Carmel appear like a desert?

18. Then shall the deaf hear the words of the Book, and the eyes of the blind, covered before with clouds and darkness, shall see.

19. The meek shall increase their joy in Jehovah: and the needy shall exult in the Holy One of Israel.

20. For the terrible one faileth, the scoffer is no more; and all that were vigilant in iniquity are utterly cut off.

21. Who bewildered the poor man in speaking; and laid snares for him, that pleaded in the gate; and with falsehood subverted the righteous.

22. Therefore thus saith Jehovah the God of the house of Jacob, He who redeemed Abraham; Jacob shall no more be ashamed; his face shall no more be covered with confusion!

23. For when his children shall see the works of My hands, among themselves shall they sanctify My name; they shall sanctify the Holy One of Jacob, and tremble before the God of Israel.

24. Those that were led away with the spirit of error, shall gain knowledge; and the malignant shall attend to instruction.

The chief thing necessary in order to an understanding of the prophecy of Isaiah, is to keep in mind the fact that it all applies to the very last days. It was indeed a present, personal, practical message to those who lived when Isaiah was writing, but it has a still greater application to us since we are nearer the time of its fulfillment than they were. We are, however, no nearer than they might have been if they had believed the message. If in our study we watch for the expressions which plainly indicate the application of the prophecy to the end of time, we shall have much less difficulty in reading with profit.

There is no profit in hypocrisy. Those who honour God only with their lips, while their hearts are far from Him, will soon lose what little of reality they have to begin with. Whatever is not used, degenerates, and ultimately goes to decay.

In our common version, as well as in the Revision, we read in verse 13, that the people "have removed their hearts" far from the Lord. The Norwegian has it, "They hold their hearts from Me." Compare this with the first chapter of Romans, where we read of those who hold down the truth in righteousness, and note in both places that the same result follows.

We very often hear of one who has "learned a thing by heart." That is the only way men can learn the things of God. But that does not mean learning them by rote, like a parrot. It means that the Scriptures must be translated into the life – must become a part of one's being. Because men have removed their hearts from the Lord, their understanding wanes and vanishes. The only difficulty there is in understanding the Word of God, is of the heart, and not of the head. It is because of the unwillingness to have the life conformed to the law of the Lord, that men find difficulty in understanding the

Bible. "If any man willeth to do His will, he shall know of the doctrine."

Because men have been content with the wisdom of this world, and have despised the wisdom that comes from God only, because they have taken the commandments of men instead of the commandments of God, the Lord will work in a way so wonderful that the wisdom of the wise shall fail; it will perish and disappear. That means simply that He will do such wonders that they will be compelled to stand in open-mouthed astonishment. Their science will be utterly inadequate to account for His working. But mind that this inability comes because they have trusted in human wisdom. That indicates that if they had trusted the Lord, and had allowed Him to instruct them, they would understand His working. Why not? Those who faithfully learn the simple lessons that the Lord gives them, may well go on to deeper things. The Holy Spirit is given us in order that we may know the things that are freely given us of God. I Cor. 2:12. But God give us all things. Acts 17:25. Therefore the Holy Spirit will teach us all things, even "the deep things of God." But without the Spirit of God, no one can really know anything as he ought to know it. Do not forget that God does not arbitrarily deprive anybody of wisdom. No, He continues to give more light and knowledge, so that all may understand, and men lose their understanding solely because they have refused to let God teach them as children.

A woe is pronounced upon those who think to hide their deeds from the Lord. What a terrible disappointment it must be for men who have imagined that they were "too deep for Jehovah" to find out that "all things are naked and opened unto the eyes of Him with whom we have to do." Heb. 4:13. "If I say, Surely the darkness shall cover me; even the night shall be light about me. Yea, the darkness hideth not from Thee; but the night shineth even as the day; the darkness and the light are both alike to Thee." Ps. 139:11–12. For a time it seems as if everything were well concealed. But "every man's work shall be made manifest; for the day shall declare it." When the Lord comes, He will "bring to light the hidden things of darkness, and will make manifest the counsels of the hearts." 1 Cor. 4:5. In the Judgment it will be as though every evil deed that has been done in secret had been performed in open daylight before all men. Ah, but many things that are done under cover of darkness would not be done if all men could see them; then let us remember that the light is always shining, and let us walk as children of the light. It is not wise to try to have any secrets from the Lord. Whatever secrets we have, let us share them with the Lord.

"O what perversity!" That is what we have in many versions in place of "turning things upside down," in verse 16. The same idea is in Lowth's translation. Perverse means the same as turning upside down. This saying by those who think to hide their deeds from the Lord, "Who seeth us?" is a turning of things upside down. It is as though God were inferior to man. It is as though the clay were greater than the potter. "Shall the work say of the workman, He made me not? or shall the thing framed say of him that framed it, He hath no understanding?" There is nothing about the clay that the potter does not know; the carpenter understands all about the wood with which his works, and therefore understands to the full that which he has made; even so, and infinitely more, does God know the secrets of every man, and not only all that he does, but all that it is possible for him to do.

"Is it not yet a very little while, and Lebanon shall be turned into a fruitful field, and the fruitful field shall be esteemed a forest?" God can in very deed turn things upside down, but when He does so, it is only the putting of things right. Things that men have perverted shall not be allowed to remain in that condition. See in chapter 24 how and when God turns the earth upside down.

In that day, the deaf shall hear the words of the book, and the eyes of the blind shall see out of obscurity, and out of darkness. Now the learned say that they cannot read the words of the book, but then even the blind shall read, and the deaf shall hear it. And the result will be that the meek shall increase their joy in the Lord, and the poor among men shall rejoice in the Holy One of Israel. The face of the covering that has been cast over all people, and the veil that is cast over all nations shall then be removed, and all will be able to see things just as they are. Now many are held in bondage, the bondage of the fear of men who are over them. Parents coerce children, husbands tyrannize over wives, and many who occupy the place of ministers of the Gospel lord it over God's heritage. There are many who, through their very fear of God are held in bondage, because they mistakenly suppose that those who thus hold them are in the place of God to them. The very spirit which would make them obedient to the will of God, if they rightly understood it, hold them subject to those who have gained the mastery over them. But the time is surely coming when the terrible one shall be brought to naught; and even before the time comes that the scorner is no more and the vigilant in iniquity are utterly cut off, their influence will be so destroyed that all the honest ones whom they have held in bondage shall be set at liberty.

On verse 21 the Revised Version is better than the others. It reads, "That make a man an offender in a cause, and lay a snare for him that reproveth in a cause, and turn aside the just with a thing of naught." Compare James 5:1–7. "Ye have condemned and killed the just, and he doth not resist you." Snares will be laid for the men whom God has set to reprove the world for sin, the innocent will be made out to be offenders, and the just will be condemned without evidence. Thus it has been since sin entered the world, even so was Christ declared guilty, and so it will be until the Lord takes all power to Himself and reigns. At that time the house of Jacob, God's people, shall not be afraid nor ashamed. No more will their faces grow pale with fear of the oppressor.

Verse 24 contains a great comfort for the faithful workers in the cause of God, who often feel, as they look at their work, "I have laboured in vain, I have spent my strength for naught, and in vain." The promise is, "They also that erred in spirit shall come to understanding, and they that murmured shall learn doctrine." In the days following Pentecost thousands who had been led into error came to the knowledge of the truth. Many who had cried out, "Crucify Him," yea, and a great company even of the priests, some of whom had been the betrayers and murderers of Christ, were obedient to the faith. Acts 6:7. But "better is the end of a thing than the beginning thereof." If the early rain yielded such abundant fruits, much more will the latter rain bring forth. Let the children of God expect great things of Him, and great things will be done by Him who is wonderful in counsel, and excellent in working.

CHAPTER 24

WORLDLY ALLIANCE A FAILURE

(Isaiah 30:1–15, Lowth's Translation)

1. "Woe unto the rebellious children, saith Jehovah; who form counsels, but not from Me; who ratify covenants, but not by My Spirit: that they may add sin to sin.

2. Who set forward to go down to Egypt; but have not enquired at My mouth: to strengthen themselves with the strength of Pharaoh; and to trust in the shadow of Egypt.

3. But the strength of Pharaoh shall be your shame; and your trust in the shadow of Egypt your confusion.

4. Their princes were at Tsoan; and their ambassadors arrived at Hanes;

5. They were all ashamed of a people that profited them not; who were of no help, and of no profit; but proved even a shame, and a reproach unto them.

6. The burden of the beasts traveling southward, through a land of distress and difficulty. Whence come forth the lioness, and the fierce lion; the viper, and the flying fiery serpent; they carry on the shoulders of the young cattle their wealth; and on the bunch of the camel their treasures: to a people that will not profit them.

7. For Egypt is a mere vapour; in vain shall they help; wherefore have I called her, Rahab the inactive.

8. Go now, write it before them on a tablet; and record it in letters upon a book; that it may be for future times; for a testimony for ever.

9. For there is a rebellious people, lying children; children who choose not to hear the law of Jehovah:

10. Who say to the seers, See not; and to the prophets, Prophesy not right things; speak unto us smooth things, prophesy deceits.

11. Turn aside from the way; decline from the straight path; remove from our sight the Holy One of Israel:

12. Wherefore thus saith the Holy One of Israel: because ye have rejected this word; and have trusted in obliquity, and perversion; and have leaned entirely upon it:

13. Therefore shall this offense be unto you like a breach threatening ruin; a swelling in a high wall; whose destruction cometh suddenly, in an instant.

14. It shall be broken, as when one breaketh a potter's vessel; so that there shall not be found a shard among its fragments, to take up fire from the hearth, or to dip up water from the cistern.

15. Verily thus saith the Lord Jehovah, the Holy One of Israel; By turning from your ways, and by abiding quiet, ye shall be saved; In silence, and in pious confidence, shall be your strength; but ye would not hearken."

One of the earliest things taught by the prophet Isaiah is that the name of the Mighty God, – the Everlasting Father, the Prince of Peace, on whose shoulder the Government rests, and in whom alone there is stability and everlasting dominion, – is Wonderful, Counsellor. Isa. 9:6–7. He only is "wonderful in counsel, and excellent in working." Isa. 28:29. Therefore it is easy to understand the woe pronounced upon those who do indeed take counsel, but not of the Lord. It is not an arbitrary curse captiously uttered, as though the Lord were angry because He has been slighted, but the simple statement of the inevitable result to those who despise the counsel of the Lord. There is no real counsel except from Him.

The text itself gives us the picture of the circumstances that called it forth. The Israelites, threatened by the Assyrians, were seeking help from Egypt, their ancient house of bondage. The Egyptians had evidently promised them assistance, which the prophet assured them would never be rendered. This is seemingly the sum of the transaction, but the case was not an ordinary one, and it has lessons for God's people to the end of time.

In the first place, we must consider what Egypt really is. We will not take time and space here to go into it in detail, but we find a key in Rev. 11:8, where we read that the dead bodies of God's "two witnesses," who are slain for the true testimony that they give, shall lie in the street of "that great city, which spiritually is called Sodom and Egypt, where also our Lord was crucified." Now it was "this present evil world" that crucified Christ, because "it knew Him not." See 1 John 3:1; 1 Cor. 2:7–8; John 16:1–3. The cross of Jesus is that by which we are crucified unto the world, and since we are to be crucified with Him, it is that by which He was crucified unto the world. Gal. 6:14; 2:20. By it we are delivered from this present evil world. Gal. 1:4. We may therefore set it down as a fact that Egypt represents the world, as opposed to Christ.

Christ as a little child went down into Egypt, that the saying might be fulfilled. "Out of Egypt have I called my Son." Matt. 2:15. Israel was brought out of Egypt in order that they might keep God's commandments. Ps. 105:43–45. All the children of God, therefore, – all Christians, must come out of Egypt; so long as they remain in Egypt they cannot render God the service due Him, for Egypt is "the house of bondage." Ex. 20:1–3. The recognition of God as the one, true God, to the exclusion of all false gods, means coming out of Egypt.

Think what a marvelous change had taken place when the children of Israel could think of making the alliance with Egypt, and could deliberately seek help against their enemies, from the people who had made them "serve with rigour," and had "made their lives bitter with hard bondage." Ex. 1:13–14, "All the service, wherein they made them serve, was with rigour." "And the children of Israel sighed by reason of the bondage, and they cried" (Ex. 2:23), for the Egyptians "evil entreated" them, "so they cast out their young children, to the end they might not live." Acts 7:19. Yet to this same people the Israelites were now turning for assistance in their time of need. What a change time had wrought.

What and in whom was this change? Had the Egyptians become converted? Did they now acknowledge and worship the true God? Not at all. They were heathens the same as of old, and were as much opposed to God as their fathers ever were. They had crucified Christ in the days of Moses, for Moses esteemed it great riches to share "the reproach of Christ," and that reproach is the cross. See Heb. 13:12–13; Ps. 69:7,9,20–21. What then did it mean when the people of Israel turned to Egypt for deliverance? – It meant that they had forsaken God, the Rock of their salvation. The change was in the Israelites, not in the Egyptians. What blindness was there manifested! to go to the house of bondage to find deliverance!

Listen to the talk of some of the "progressive" leaders of the people on those days: "Why shouldn't we make an alliance with the Egyptians, for mutual help? Why should we always keep in memory the ancient differences? The Egyptians are very good fellows, when you come to know them; in fact, they are not so very much different from us. The world has made much progress in the last thousand years, and we ought to be liberal-minded enough to make some concessions to it. It's all very fine to talk about trusting in the Lord, but it isn't practical; "God helps those who help themselves," and common sense should teach us that our only hope of existence as a people is in joining our forces with the Egyptians. On some things we will "agree to disagree," and so we shall gain influence with them at the same time that they afford us material aid." Ah yes, we have all heard them talk.

What says the Lord? "The strength of Pharaoh shall be your shame; and your trust in the shadow of Egypt your confusion." "For Egypt is a mere vapour; in vain shall they help; wherefore have I called her, Rahab the inactive." The help of the world is in vain, for, "the world passeth away, and the lust thereof." 1 John 2:17. "But he that doeth the will of God abideth for ever." "It is better to trust in the Lord, than to put confidence in princes."

Notice the various readings of the 7 verse. The common version has it, "Their strength is to sit still." That expresses the idea very well, but we need to know the meaning of the word "Rahab," in order to appreciate the text. In Job 9:23, the word occurs, and is rendered "*proud* helpers;" and in Job 26:12 it occurs in the sentence rendered, "He smiteth through the *proud*." In two or three other places in the Bible it is to be found, as in Ps. 89:10, and Isa. 51:9, but always as something hateful to God. The idea, it is plain to be seen, is that of proud boasting. "Rahab" is connected with Babylon, in Ps.

87:4, and we know that Babylon originated in pride, and boasting was its ruin. So Egypt is called the people which make great promises and boasts, but do nothing. So their strength of which they boast, is nothing but emptiness. Recall the history of Pharaoh's haughty opposition to God in the days of Moses, and think how empty it was, and you will understand the force of this text, and will also better see the folly of Israel's going to the Egyptians for help. They say, and do not.

Going back to the first verse, we notice that where our version has "cover with a covering," Lowth has it, "ratify covenants." The margin of our Bibles has, however, "weave a web," or "make a league." In some versions it is rendered, "pour out a drink offering," which was a common way of ratifying a league, and which is perpetuated to this day in the custom which many have of pledging friendship with a glass of wine. The covenant which the Israelites were making with the Egyptians was designed as a covering, a protection; but the trouble was, it was not the covering of the Spirit of God. It was a flimsy web that they were weaving.

Why was it wrong for Israel to make a covenant with the Egyptians or with any other people? – Because such a covenant would have been a rejection of God, who had chosen them as His special people. He had made a covenant with them, to be their God, and to take them for His people. It was not because these people were better than others, that they were called God's people, but because they bore the name "Israel," and gloried in it. "Israel" means "a prince of God," a Christian, for all followers of Christ are kings and priests of God. Rev. 1:6. Whenever a people bear that name, – no matter what the form, whether *Christian* or Israelite, – they thereby proclaim that Jehovah is their God and their protector; for such to make any alliance with the world is to be untrue to God, for "the friendship of the world is enmity with God. Whosoever therefore will be a friend of the world is the enemy of God." James 4:4.

The children of Israel were expressly warned, on going into the land of Canaan, not to make any league with the inhabitants of the land. God's plan for them was this: "The people shall dwell alone, and shall not be reckoned among the nations" Num 23:9. Yet this did not mean that they should be exclusive and misanthropic. On the contrary, they were to be exponents of God's unselfishness and loving kindness to mankind. Any people might join them, and share the blessings God had for them, but in so doing these other peoples were to give up their distinct nationality, and become simply Christians; for in Christ "there is neither Greek nor Jew, circumcision nor uncircumcision, barbarian, Scythian, bond nor free; but Christ is all and in all." Col. 3:11. Christians are a peculiar people, a nation with an invisible Ruler. They have everything to give "to all people," but no other people have anything to give them. For them therefore to make any alliance whatever with the world, is to deny their King and their profession. It is the same as saying that they do not receive all they need from the Lord, and to put the world in His place. It is to weaken the force of the Gospel to those other people, by conveying the idea that to be a citizen of any earthly country is as good or the same as being a Christian.

All that is said in this chapter applies to us as much as to the people who lived when it was written, because it was written "for a testimony for ever." The rebellious people are those who do not choose to hear the law of Jehovah; they are not willing to hear the law. Jehovah is the rightful King of all the earth; all who do not regard His law are rebels and outlaws, no matter though they rank as kings on earth. For Israel to make an alliance with Egypt, – for the professed Church of Christ to enter into any sort of alliance with the world, – is to declare that "the rudiments of the world" are as good as the law of God. God's law is *the* only law for all mankind; whatever is contrary to that law is rebellion and idolatry.

But the church has taken upon itself to make laws, calling them God's laws. "After their own lusts" have men "heaped to themselves teachers, having itching ears," and have turned aside from the truth unto fables. 2 Tim. 4:3–4. They "say to the seers, See not; and to the prophets, Prophesy not right things; speak unto us smooth things, prophesy deceits." Men choose their own teachers – those who will say the things that they like to hear – and then will quote the sayings of those teachers as authority, in opposition to the law of God. This is identical with the course of the heathen, who makes his own god, and then says, "Deliver me, for thou art my god." Yet these professed people of God will not believe that what the Bible says of the heathen applies to them.

What will be the result of all this? – Because men reject the word of the Lord, even the "Holy one of Israel;" sudden destruction shall come upon them, and they shall not escape; they shall be broken in pieces like a potter's vessel, and their destruction will be complete. Compare verses 12–14 with 1 Thess. 5:3 and Ps. 2. They who put their trust in men will come to nothing, while "they that trust in the Lord shall be as Mount Zion, which cannot be removed, but abideth for ever." Ps. 125:1.

"For thus saith the Lord God, the Holy One of Israel: In returning and rest shall ye be saved; in quietness and confidence shall be your strength." This, coming in the connection that it does, shows that the Lord affords practical, material aid. The Israelites were in great danger: the Assyrians were threatening their destruction; according to all human calculations they needed just such help as the Egyptians could afford, – men and horses and munitions of war. But God said, "No; they will be your ruin; your strength is in quietly trusting in Me, in returning to Me, and in absolute rest on My word, you will find complete deliverance. They did not believe Him, and people do not believe it now.

We know as a fact that they preferred to trust in men, whom they could see, rather than in God, whom they could not see, and that the Assyrians took them captive. Why should we not learn the lesson? It is for each individual, as well as for the whole church. It is recorded for the purpose of teaching the church that its strength lies in strict adherence to the Word of God, and in departing from the world. Conformity to the world, whether for the avowed purpose of winning worldlings to the church, or to induce the world to lend the church material aid, is ruin. The world can do nothing for the church, except to corrupt it, but it cannot do that as long as the church trusts in God alone.

But the individual lesson is the one that concerns us most; for if the individuals are faithful, the church must be right. Each person has troubles of various kinds; in the Lord alone is there help.

"Commit thy way unto the Lord; trust also in Him; and He shall bring it to pass." Ps. 37:5. We all know the ways of the world: Self-assertion, insisting on one's rights, bitterness, revenge; everybody who does not know the Lord, shows how he acts when he is in difficulty, when he is tempted, and when people irritate or injure him, and everybody who does know the Lord, can remember how he once did and how he is still tempted to do. Well, that is the way not to do; that is the way of the world; that is going down into Egypt for help – to the house of bondage for freedom. It is all in vain. "God is our refuge and strength; a very present help in trouble." There is infinite strength in quietly giving up one's self, and resting in the Lord. "Trust ye in the Lord for ever, for in the Lord Jehovah is everlasting strength."

CHAPTER 25

WAITING TO BE GRACIOUS

(Isaiah 30:15–33, Lowth's Translation)

15. Verily thus saith the Lord Jehovah, the Holy One of Israel; by turning from your ways, and by abiding quiet, ye shall be saved; in silence, and in pious confidence, shall be your strength; but ye would not hearken.

16. And ye said: Nay, but on horses will we flee; therefore shall ye be put to flight; and on swift coursers will we ride; therefore shall they be swift, that pursue you.

17. One thousand, at the rebuke of one; at the rebuke of five, ten thousand of you shall flee; till ye be left as a standard on the summit of a mountain; and as a beacon on a high hill.

18. Yet for this shall Jehovah wait to show favour unto you; even for this shall He expect in silence, that He may have mercy upon you: (For Jehovah is a God of Judgment; blessed are all they that trust in Him)!

19. When a holy people shall dwell in Sion; when in Jerusalem thou shalt implore Him with weeping: at the voice of thy cry He shall be abundantly gracious unto thee; no sooner shall He hear, than He shall answer thee.

20. Though Jehovah hath given you the bread of distress, and the water of affliction; yet the timely rain shall no more be restrained; but thine eyes shall behold the timely rain.

21. And thine ears shall hear the word prompting thee behind, saying, This is the way; walk ye in it; turn not aside, to the right, or to the left.

22 And ye shall treat as defiled the covering of your idols of silver; and the clothing of your molten images of gold; thou shalt cast them away like a polluted garment; thou shalt say unto them, Be gone from me.

23. And He shall give rain for thy seed, with which thou shalt sow the ground; and bread of the produce of the ground; and it shall be abundant and plenteous. Then shall thy cattle feed in large pasture;

24. And the oxen, and the young asses, that till the ground, shall eat well-fermented maslin, winnowed with the van and the sieve.

25. And on every lofty mountain, and on every high hill, shall be disparting rills, and streams of water, in the day of the great slaughter, when the mighty fall.

26. And the light of the moon shall be as the light of the meridian sun; and the light of the meridian sun shall be seven-fold: in the day when Jehovah shall bind up the breach of His people; and shall heal the wound, which His stroke hath inflicted.

27. Lo, the name of Jehovah cometh from afar; His wrath burneth, and the flame rageth violently; His lips are filled with indignation; and His tongue is as a consuming fire.

28. His Spirit is like a torrent overflowing; it shall reach to the middle of the neck; He cometh to toss the nations with the van of perdition; and there shall be a bridle, to lead them astray, in the jaws of the people.

29. Ye shall utter a song, as in the night when the feast is solemnly proclaimed; with joy of heart, as when one marcheth to the sound of the pipe; to go to the mountain of Jehovah, to the Rock of Israel.

30. And Jehovah shall cause His glorious voice to be heard, and the lighting down of His arm to be seen; with wrath indignant, and a flame of consuming fire; with a violent storm, and rushing showers, and hailstones.

31. By the voice of Jehovah shall the Assyrian be beaten down; he, that was ready to smite with his staff.

32. And it shall be, that wherever shall pass the rod of correction, which Jehovah shall lay heavily upon him; it shall be accomplished with tabrets and harps; and with fierce battles shall He fight against them.

33. For Tophet is ordained of old; even the same for the king is prepared; He hath made it deep; He hath made it large; a fiery pyre, and abundance of fuel; and the breath of Jehovah, like a stream of sulphur shall kindle it.

Although the selection of Scripture for study is rather long, we need not become confused by it. Do not expect to understand every expression in it at first. There are very few parts of the Bible where we cannot find things that are hard to be understood, even when the general matter is very plain. In all such cases work in the line of least resistance. Do not spend time working backwards; that is, do not begin at the end and try to work to the beginning. In studying the Scriptures, always seize first upon that which is evident at first sight, such as simple promises. These will lead you gently along to the understanding of that which is not so obvious. Remember that the cross of Christ is the revelation of God to man, and that therefore it is through the promises that we are to understand all His sayings and dealings. Our previous study of Isaiah has shown us that it applies to us as well as to the men who lived when it was written; therefore we must study it for our own personal benefit. If in any lesson we perceive one truth that is new to us, or one new setting of truth, which will lighten our pathway, and make it easier for us to lay hold of Divine strength and to overcome, we are doing well. Sometimes we shall be able to find many such things.

Strength in Quietness

For the sake of the connection we take in one verse that was in the preceding lesson. The fifteenth verse should be so firmly fixed in the mind of every one that it can never be forgotten. "In returning and rest shall ye be saved; in quietness and confidence shall be your strength." Resting in the Lord! What strength it affords. All power is then exerted in our behalf. "The Lord is my portion, saith my soul; therefore will I hope in Him. The Lord is good unto them that wait for Him, to the soul that seeketh Him. It is good that a man should both hope and quietly wait for the salvation of the Lord." Lam. 3:24–26.

"But ye were not willing." That was the case with Israel of old, and it is largely the case now. We show our heathenism by our unwillingness to trust the Lord. By fearing to trust the Lord, and thinking that in this case we must use our own skill to help us out of the difficulty, we show that we regard ourselves as gods, greater than the God of heaven.

"But ye said, No, for we will flee upon horses; therefore shall ye flee." A horse is swift, and promises well as a means of escape from danger. For those who trust Him, God prepares a table in the presence of their enemies (Ps. 23:5), where they can quietly sit down and eat while the enemy rages and spends its strength in vain: but people mostly become frightened at the roaring of the adversary, and fly from their place of protection. They think that there is greater safety in flight than in trusting the Lord. What is the consequence? – "Therefore shall ye be put to flight." Certainly; that is what we have planned for; and if we are put to flight, there will surely be some one pursuing, and they that pursue will be swift. We plan for defeat instead of victory.

Notice the contrast between those who trust the Lord and those who try to "fight their own battles." God's promise to Israel was that if they trusted in Him, and kept His commandments, one man should chase a thousand, and two should put ten thousand to flight. See Deut. 32:30; Josh. 23:10. But what a change takes place when God is forsaken. Then "one thousand shall flee at the rebuke of one;" and at the rebuke of five ten thousand shall flee. The case is exactly reversed. Mind that it needs only a threat to make them flee when they do not trust in the Lord. "The wicked flee when no man pursueth; but the righteous are bold as a lion." Prov. 28:1.

Everlasting, Unselfish Love

And now comes a most unexpected and gracious promise. It is unexpected, because it is so entirely unlike human nature, and therefore it is all the more gracious. After recounting the stubbornness of the people, how they have said, "Cause the Holy One of Israel to cease from among us," and have refused to rely on Him, choosing rather their own way, the Lord says, "Therefore will the Lord wait, that He may be gracious unto you, and therefore will He be exalted, that He may have mercy upon you; for the Lord is a God of judgment; blessed are all they that wait for Him." Why will the Lord wait to be gracious? – Because the people have been rebellious. The meaning of the word rendered "wait," is "to long for," "to desire;" and the statement is that although the people have rejected Him, there is nothing He is more anxious for than to do them a kindness. "The Lord hath appeared of old unto me, saying, Yea, I have loved thee with an everlasting love, therefore with loving kindness have I drawn thee." Jer. 31:3. Was there ever a more perfect example of unselfish love? "Greater love hath no man than this, that a man lay down his life for his friends." "But God commendeth His love toward us, in that, while we were yet sinners, Christ died for us." Rom. 5:8. Human love is selfish; people love for the pleasure that they derive from the object of their affection, and usually cease to love when they are slighted or neglected. With God it is entirely different. He loves, in order that He may give pleasure to the objects of His affections, and He finds His pleasure in the happiness which His love imparts to the loved ones. Hatred and abuse only call out greater manifestations of His everlasting, unchangeable love. Where sin abounds, grace does much more abound. He knows the mortal disease from which sinners are suffering, and He longs with all His infinite soul to deliver them from it. Was anything ever more wondrously gracious!

"Oh, hope of every contrite heart!
Oh, joy of all the meek!
To those who fall, how kind Thou art!
How good to those who seek!

"And those who find Thee, find a bliss
Nor tongue nor pen can show;
The love of Jesus, what it is,
None but His loved ones know."

If we grasp this one truth it will be a most profitable lesson for us. To know the love of Jesus, which is but the manifestation of the love of God, is to know the wisdom of eternity. But let us remember that to know it means to make a practical application of it. We must accept it in order to know it. And acceptance of the love of God does not mean mere selfish enjoyment of its blessings. There is no selfishness in the love of God, and therefore nobody can selfishly enjoy it. The acceptance of it drives out selfishness. If we indeed receive the love of God, then the hatefulness of others, instead of making us cold and hard towards them, will but increase our desire to do them kindness. You say that that is not natural, and that no man can do it. No, it is not natural, but it is spiritual; and it is not possible for any human nature to manifest such love; the only way it can be done is by having the love of God shed abroad in our hearts; and this is done by the Holy Spirit, that is so freely given to all who are willing to receive. Shall we not learn this lesson of Divine love?

Judgment and Mercy

Why does the Lord show such marvelous loving kindness and mercy? – Because "the Lord is a God of judgment." You thought that justice and judgment meant punishment? Oh no, not necessarily. Justice and judgment are the foundation of God's throne, and His throne is a throne of grace. God is just in that He is the justifier of them that believe in Jesus. Rom. 3:26. That is a declaration of His righteousness, for God rests His claim to righteousness on the fact that He is faithful to forgive sins, and to cleanse from all unrighteousness. 1 John 1:9.

"He will be very gracious unto thee at the voice of thy cry." The Lord is looking for opportunities to do good. "He delighteth in mercy." Micah 7:19. He is hearkening to hear what His people will say to Him. Mal. 3:16. "No sooner shall He hear, than He shall answer thee." He bends down to earth, anxiously waiting to hear some cry. So intently does He listen that not only does He hear the faintest whisper, but the first impulse to call upon Him reaches His heart. He knows the thoughts and intents of the heart, and responds to them. He is not like the unjust judge, who must be importuned and besieged before he would grant the righteous request. See Luke 18:1–8. God is a God of judgment, and is not unjust; therefore He hears and avenges speedily. Surely we have every encouragement that could possibly be given, to call on the Lord, that we may obtain mercy, and find grace to help in time of need.

This chapter abounds in gracious promises. Although we have had affliction as the necessary result of our own waywardness, yet our teachers shall not be removed from us, but our eyes shall see them. The Lord will not leave us to wander in ignorance of the way, but our ears shall hear a word behind us, saying, "This is the way; walk ye in it." How strange it is that we are so apt to think that timely warning and instruction are a hardship instead of a blessing! "It is not in man that walketh to direct his step," therefore we do well to pray, "O Lord correct me, but with judgment." Jer. 10:23–24.

Refreshing Teachers

In verse 20 we have an excellent illustration of the blessings of various translations of the Bible, instead of only one. All the languages of earth are only fragments of the perfect language of heaven. The blight of the curse is upon everything, so that even if we had all the languages combined we should still have only an imperfect reproduction of the original language. God's thoughts are not as our thoughts, but are very deep, and higher than the heavens. Is it then impossible for us to understand the Word of God, because we have only one of the many imperfect languages at our command? – No, not by any means. It would be impossible for us to understand it, even though we were master of them all, if we were left to our own wisdom; but the Holy Spirit is given us, in order that we may know the things that are freely given us of God. I Cor. 2:12. Nevertheless we are to make use of every means that God has placed in our reach, and among these is a knowledge of various languages, or the use of various translations into the one tongue that we understand. So in this instance we learn much from the fact that whereas in one translation we have the word "teachers," in another we have the word "rain" for the same thing.

There is no contradiction in this, no lack of harmony; for the fact is that the Hebrew word is correctly rendered both "teacher" and "rain." This is not because of the poverty of the language, but rather because of its richness, each word being so comprehensive. There is a lesson to be learned from it: a teacher is to be one who refreshes his pupils, as the rain refreshes the earth. There is no teacher like God (Job 36:22), for He is the fountain of living waters (Jer. 2:13), "a place of broad rivers and streams" (Isa. 33:21), and is "as the dew unto Israel." Hosea 14:5. God pours showers upon him that is thirsty, and on the dry ground floods, even His Holy Spirit, which is the water of life. Isa. 44:3; John 7:37–39. Therefore those who believe shall send forth streams of living water. Christ, the greatest of teachers, knows how to refresh the weary with a word. "Give ear, O ye heavens, and I will speak; and hear, O earth, the words of My mouth. My doctrine shall drop as the rain, My speech shall distil as the dew, as the small rain upon the tender herb, and as the showers upon the grass; because I will publish the name of the Lord; ascribe ye greatness unto our God." Deut. 32:1–3.

The Life-Giving, Consuming Breath

Gracious are the promises of God, and everlasting and infinite is His love; yet that does not mean that wickedness will be allowed to continue for ever. "Though hand join in hand, the wicked shall not be unpunished." Those who persist in doing evil according to the hardness of their own impenitent hearts, are but treasuring up to themselves wrath against the day of wrath and revelation of the righteous judgment of God, who will render to every man according to his works. Rom. 2:4–6. But in the visitation of punishment, there is no change in God. He is still the same God of love. "His mercy endureth for ever." The destruction of the wicked is only the natural, inevitable result of the rejection of the infinite love of Him whose favour is life. Take notice that it is the breath of God that kindles the fires of Gehenna. "He shall smite the earth with the rod of His mouth, and with the breath of His lips shall He slay the wicked," yet "righteousness shall be the girdle of His loins, and faithfulness the girdle of His reins." Isa. 11:4–5. That breath which destroys the wicked, is the breath of life, – the very same breath which is now given to all mankind, wicked as well as righteous, and without which there would be no life on earth. How then can it be that it will finally consume the wicked? – Simply because they will not accept it for what it is. Not recognizing God in the air that they breathe, they do not allow it to do the work for them which God designs, namely, to remove all iniquity from them. The breath of God is at work every moment in all the earth, consuming impurity, and making it possible for men to live. Every where and all the time God is showing us for what purpose breath is given: it is to purify and cleanse, and give life. Then when men identify themselves with vileness and sin, it is inevitable that they should be consumed by that which would be their life, if they were willing. "Our God is a consuming fire." The very same fire that purifies the gold burns up the dross. Everything therefore depends upon how we stand related to God. Shall we receive Him as our life indeed, by allowing Him to redeem us from all iniquity, or shall He be to us the devouring fire? "Blessed are all they that put their trust in Him."

A Literal Place of Punishment

Tophet was a part of the valley of the son of Hinnom, near Jerusalem, where the abominations of the heathen had been practiced, and where the Jews also practiced them when they apostatized. It was here that they made their children to pass through fire. See 2 Kings 23:10; Jer. 7:31. It was thus regarded as an accursed spot, and was the place for burning up the refuse matter of the city. From this comes the word "Gehenna" in Mark 9:45,47, and elsewhere. See margin of R.V. The word simply means, "valley of Hinnom." When Jesus spoke of it as the place where the wicked should receive their punishment, the Jews would well understand that it meant utter destruction – the place where the unrighteous should be stubble, and should be burnt up "root and branch." Mal. 4:1. And it was not a mere figure of speech, either, for it is in that very place that the wicked will be gathered when the fire comes down from God out of heaven, and devours them. Rev. 20:9. God does not speak at random, but means what He says.

CHAPTER 26

THE REIGN OF RIGHTEOUSNESS

(Isaiah 32:1–20, Lowth's Translation)

1. Behold, a King shall reign in righteousness; and princes shall rule with equity.

2. And the Man shall be as a covert from the storm, as a refuge from the flood; as canals of waters in a dry place; as the shadow of a great rock in the land fainting with heat:

3. And Him, the eyes of those that see shall regard; and the ears of those that hear shall hearken.

4. Even the heart of the rash shall consider, and acquire knowledge; and the stammering tongue shall speak readily and plainly.

5. The fool shall no longer be called honourable; and the niggard shall no more be called liberal;

6. For the fool will still utter folly; and his heart will devise iniquity; practicing hypocrisy, and speaking wrongfully against Jehovah; to exhaust the soul of the hungry, and to deprive the thirsty of drink.

7. As for the niggard, his instruments are evil; he plotteth mischievous devices; to entangle the humble with lying words; and to defeat the assertions of the poor in judgment.

8. But the generous will devise generous things; and he by his generous purposes shall be established.

9. O ye women, that sit at ease, arise, hear My voice! O ye daughters, that dwell in security, give ear unto My speech!

10. Years upon years shall ye be disquieted, O ye careless women: for the vintage hath failed, the gathering of the fruits shall not come.

11. Tremble, O ye that are at ease; be ye disquieted, O ye careless ones! Strip ye, make ye bare; and gird ye sackcloth

12. Upon your loins, upon your breasts: mourn ye, for the pleasant field, for the fruitful vine.

13. Over the land of My people the thorn and the brier shall come up; yea, over all the joyous houses, over the exulting city.

14. For the palace is deserted, the populous city is left desolate; Ophel and the watch-tower shall for a long time be a den, a joy of wild asses, a pasture for the flocks;

15. Till the Spirit from on high be poured out upon us; and the wilderness become a fruitful field; and the fruitful field be esteemed a forest;

16. The judgment shall dwell in the wilderness; and in the fruitful field shall reside righteousness.

17. And the work of righteousness shall be peace; and the effect of righteousness perpetual quiet and security.

18. And My people shall dwell in a peaceful mansion, and in habitations secure, and in resting places undisturbed.

19. But the hail shall fall, and the forest be brought down; and the city shall be laid level with the plain.

20. Blessed are ye who sow your seed in every well-watered place; who send forth the foot of the ox and the ass.

"Behold, a King shall rein in righteousness." What need to ask who this King is, who reigns in righteousness? Jesus Christ? He it is of whom the Lord says: "I will raise unto David a righteous Branch, and a King shall reign and prosper, and shall execute judgment and justice in the earth. In His days Judah shall be saved, and Israel shall dwell safely; and this is His name whereby He shall be called, THE LORD OUR RIGHTEOUSNESS." Jer. 23:5–6.

He is supreme, but He reigns not alone, for it has pleased Him that others shall share His high state. He is King of kings and Lord of lords. With Him "princes shall rule in judgment;" for the Father hath bestowed this love upon us, that we should also be called the sons of God, even as He Himself is. 1 John 3:1–2. "Now are we the Sons of God," "and if children, then heirs; heirs of God, and joint-heirs with Christ. Rom. 8:17. "He hath loved us, and washed us from our sins in His own blood, and hath made us kings and priests unto God and His Father." Rev. 1:5–6. Yea, He hath made us alive from our death in trespasses and sins, and hath raised us up, and made us to sit together with Him in the heavenly places, at the right hand of God. Eph. 1:20–21; 2:1–6. "He raiseth up the poor out of the dust, and lifteth up the beggar from the dunghill, to set them among princes," "even with the princes of His people," "and to make them inherit the throne of glory." 1 Sam. 2:7–8; Ps. 113:7–8.

"And a man shall be as an hiding place from the wind, and a covert from the tempest; as rivers of water in a dry place, as the shadow of a great rock in a weary land." The Danish, Norwegian, Swedish, and French versions have it, *"Every man* shall be as an hiding place," etc. Lowth, as we see, has it, "The Man." This would make it refer especially to Christ, to whom it unquestionably has chief application; but all the renderings are correct, since He is pleased to make us whatever He is. Every one whom Christ makes kings and princes and priests will be such only by virtue of His nature; and therefore they will share with Him the joy and honour of His salvation, not merely of being saved, but of saving others.

What a glorious prospect is this! Poor, fallen men, way-worn, famished, fainting, fallen, and helpless are themselves to be so transformed by the refreshing that they receive from the Fountain of life and the Rock of their salvation, that they will be to others in like condition as an hiding place from the stormy wind, as rivers of water in a dry place, and as the shadow of a great rock in a weary land. Yes, "Jesus is a Rock in a weary land," but He has left representatives here on earth, to carry out His work, and to be in His stead to men. What is more refreshing than streams of water in a dry, hot day? and this is the place that every child of God is privileged to occupy, for whosoever believeth in the Son, "out of his belly shall flow rivers of living water." John 7:38. Think also of the shadow of a great rock in a fainting land. How wonderfully cool it is! It not only excludes the rays of the sun, but imparts a refreshing coolness. Just such help is every Christian intended to be to some fainting souls in this world. For understand that these promises are not confined to the future. Even now Christ reigns in righteousness, and now we are the sons of God, and therefore princes. When should it apply if not at a time when there are souls fainting and weary?

"Princes shall rule in judgment." Yea, for the heaven-inspired, and therefore to-be-answered, prayer for us is that our love should "abound yet more and more in knowledge and in all judgment," or discernment. Phil. 1:9. Also the promise is that we shall "be filled with the knowledge of His will in all wisdom and spiritual understanding." Col. 1:9. The fact that the saints are to judge the world and angels, is given as a reason why they ought to be able to exercise good judgment now in all the affairs of life. 1 Cor. 6:2–3. And well it may be; for this is the time of preparation for the duties of the world to come. This good judgment, the knowledge of what is right and fitting to be done on all occasions, does not come by any magic, but by giving good heed to the words of the Lord; "for the Lord giveth wisdom; out of His mouth cometh knowledge and understanding." Prov. 2:1–6. "Behold, the fear of the Lord, that is wisdom; and to depart from evil is understanding." Job 28:28.

Sight, hearing, speech, and understanding are the gifts of righteousness. See verses 3–4. And more, it is the princes who rule in judgment with the King of righteousness, who are to be instrumental in giving sight to the people, and making the hasty to understand knowledge. Only the difference of one letter changes "to him" to "not," in the Hebrew, and Lowth is undoubtedly correct in saying that this change has been made. True, the eyes of them that see shall not be dim, and it will be because they will regard Him who is the light. They will see Him in those whom He has enlightened.

"The vile person shall no more be called liberal." From 1 Sam. 25:25 we learn that Nabal means foolish; and that is the word that is used here in the Hebrew; so that it is correctly rendered "fool," as Lowth gives it. And who is the fool? He is the one who does not regard the Lord, who acts as if there were no God. See Ps. 14:1. Since the fear of the Lord is wisdom, it follows what folly is unrighteousness. The fool is the one who bears false witness against God, and thereby tends to weaken the faith of men, – to make the hungry and thirsty after righteousness still more empty.

In this connection it will be well to read what the Lord says by the prophet Ezekiel. Read chapter 13:17–23. Some have with lies made the heart of the righteous sad, and have strengthened the hands of the wicked, that he should not depart from his wicked way, by promising him life. They say, either by their actions or by their words, that it will be well with the wicked, and that no matter what a man does he will live to all eternity. Thus they put no difference between him that serveth the Lord and him that serveth Him not.

In verses 13–14 we have a description of the effects of the curse. Jerusalem is specially referred to, but the application is to all the earth. Because of man's sin, the earth was cursed. This was not an arbitrary curse, but God merely stated the inevitable consequence of Adam's sin. When he who was set to be master and lord of the earth fell, it could not be otherwise than that his dominion should go to waste. The field of the drunkard and the sluggard will bring forth thorns and thistles. This curse we see now, but it will increase rapidly as the end approaches, and "evil men and seducers shall wax worse and worse, deceiving and being deceived." 2 Tim. 3:13. At the last, the earth will be utterly desolate and waste, even as it was in the beginning before the Spirit of God moved upon the face of the waters. See Gen. 1:2 and Isa. 24:1.

The same Spirit that in the beginning brought order out of chaos, will effect the complete restoration after sin has completed its work of ruin. The Spirit of righteousness will undo the work of sin. When the Spirit be poured upon us from on high, "then will the wilderness become a fruitful field." "When judgment shall dwell in the wilderness, and righteousness remain in the fruitful field." Although violence shall fill the earth, even as in the days that were before the flood (see Gen. 6:11; Matt. 24:37), yet "the work of righteousness shall be peace, and the effect of righteousness quietness and assurance for ever." And since righteousness is to dwell in the earth simply because there will be righteous men, made so by the Spirit of God, it follows that this restoration of all things, and the bringing back of the reign of peace is effected through men. God is the great Author of all things, but He works through men who fear Him, and yield themselves to Him as instruments of righteousness. "Since by man came death, by man came also the resurrection of the dead." 1

Cor. 15:21. In like manner, since by man came the curse, by man comes also the blessing; since by man came the desolation, by man comes also the restoration. In every good work does the Lord associate His people with Himself, and He gives to them the glory. He gives them the glory, and they give it to Him.

"But the hail shall fall." Terrible commotions will accompany the work of restoration. Not without a struggle will sin be rooted out of the earth. There shall be voices, and thunders, and a great earthquake, "such as was not since men were upon the earth, so mighty an earthquake and so great," and there shall fall upon men great hail out of heaven, "every stone about the weight of a talent." Rev. 16:17–21. Yet even at this time the people will "dwell in a peaceable habitation, and in sure dwellings, and in quiet resting places." During the time of trouble the saints of God on this earth will be as safe as they will afterwards be in heaven, for that is even now their dwelling place. See Ps. 91:1–16, 46:1–5.

Verse 20 is based upon the manner of sowing rice, which grows upon wet soil, and is sowed even while the water covers the ground. Then the oxen and the horses are driven upon it, and by them the seed is trampled into the ground. Thus most literally is bread cast upon the waters, to be received with increase after many days. Blessed are they who have confidence enough in the Lord to sow the seed of righteousness, even the living Word of God, at morning and at evening, although the prospect is most forbidding. Sow beside all waters, and the harvest will reveal, instead of a watery waste, a land smiling with ripened grain, the fruit of righteousness.

CHAPTER 27

DWELLING WITH CONSUMING FIRE

(Isaiah 33:2–16, Lowth's Translation)

2. O Jehovah, have mercy on us; we have trusted in Thee; be Thou our strength every morning; even our salvation in the time of distress.

3. From Thy terrible voice the peoples fled; when Thou dist raise Thyself up, the nations were dispersed.

4. But your spoil shall be gathered as the locust gathereth; as the caterpillar runneth to and fro, so shall they run and seize it.

5. Jehovah is exalted; yea, He dwelleth on high; He hath filled Sion with judgment and justice.

6. And wisdom and knowledge shall be the stability of thy times, the possession of continued salvation; the fear of Jehovah, this shall be thy treasure.

7. Behold, the mighty men raise a grievous cry; the messengers of peace weep bitterly.

8. The highways are desolate; the traveler ceaseth; he hath broken the covenant; he hath rejected the offered cities; of men he maketh no account.

9. The land mourneth, it languisheth; Libanus is put to shame, it withereth; Sharon is become like the desert; and Bashan and Carmel are stripped of their beauty.

10. Now will I arise, saith Jehovah; now will I lift up Myself on high; now will I be exalted.

11. Ye shall conceive chaff; ye shall bring forth stubble; and My Spirit, like fire, shall consume you.

12. And peoples shall be burned, as the lime is burned; as the thorns are cut up, and consumed in the fire.

13. Hear, O ye that are afar off, My doings; and acknowledge, O ye that are near, My power.

14. The sinners are struck with dread; terror hath seized the hypocrites; who among us can abide this consuming fire? who among us can abide these continued burnings?

15. He who walketh in perfect righteousness, and speaketh right things; who detesteth the lucre of oppression; who shaketh his hands from bribery; who stoppeth his ears to the proposal of blood; who shutteth his eyes against the appearance of evil.

16. His dwelling shall be in the high places; the strongholds of the rocks shall be his lofty fortress; his bread shall be duly furnished; his waters shall not fail.

Mercy to the Trusting

The prayer with which this lesson opens is not a vain one, for we are assured, "He that trusteth in the Lord, mercy shall compass him about." Even in sinful man, the very fact of being trusted makes one kindly disposed; we cannot help being drawn to one who manifests confidence in us; it put us, as it were, on our honour. What then shall be said of God, whose nature is love, and who delights in mercy! He also cannot do otherwise than do kindness to them that trust Him.

Every Morning New

This mercy endureth for ever, and is unlimited. We may draw on it at will. We are continually recipients of it, for "it is of the Lord's mercies that we are not consumed;" "they are new every morning." Lam. 3:22–23. Yet we ourselves determine to a great extent how much of it we will enjoy. We often claim but little, although the amount that we may enjoy is limited only by our willingness to receive. Here is a prayer inspired by the Holy Spirit. "Let Thy mercy, O Lord, be upon us, according as we hope in Thee." Ps. 33:22. "The eye of the Lord is upon them that fear Him, upon them that hope in His mercy." Verse 18. Whatever the Spirit of the Lord tells us to ask for, we may be sure will be granted, for when "we know not what we should pray for as we ought," the Spirit comes to our aid. Rom. 8:26. Do you want unbounded mercy? then trust in the Lord without reservation.

The Mercy of the Dayspring

"Trust ye in the Lord for ever, for in the Lord Jehovah is everlasting strength." Yea, for the mercy of the Lord is strength. "As the heaven is high above the earth, so powerful is His mercy toward them that fear Him." Ps. 103:11. So as the Lord's mercies are new every morning, He is our strength every morning. Now "through the tender mercy of our God, whereby the dayspring from on high hath visited us." He gives the knowledge of salvation unto His people "by the remission of their sins." Luke 1:77–78. Therefore every morning's dawn is an assurance to us that God is merciful to our unrighteousness. As the light springs forth from the east, it should be a reminder to us of "the dayspring from on high." The beams of the morning sun are to remind us of "the Sun of righteousness," who arises with healing in His wings. Mal. 4:2. So every morning God in His endless mercy gives us the assurance of forgiveness of sin, and of overcoming grace. "Truly the light is sweet, and a pleasant thing it is for the eyes to behold the sun." Eccl. 11:7.

The Lord Our Arm

The word rendered "strength," in verse 2, is literally "arm." So the inspired prayer is, "Be Thou our arm every morning." What a wonderful promise! for every inspired prayer is a promise of God. God's mercies are new every morning, and His mercy is strength; but He does more than merely to strengthen our arm: He Himself promises to become our arm. Truly, "they that wait on the Lord shall renew their strength." "It is God that worketh in you, both to will and to do of His good pleasure." Phil. 2:13. God has "a mighty arm;" His hand is strong (Ps. 89:13); but think of the courage with which one could go forth to his work in the morning, who knew that God was not only at his right hand, but was indeed his arm. Well, this is only saying in another way what we learned in Isa. 12:2: "The Lord Jehovah is my strength and my song; He also is become my salvation.

It will not be difficult for us to see how literally true this is, if we but stop to consider the conditions of our life. God is our life, and the length of our days. Deut. 30:20. We have no life in ourselves;

everything comes from above. We eat the Word of God, even the very life of Christ, in the grains and fruits. Thus all the strength that anybody has is the strength of God; for He alone has power. He is the Almighty. All power in heaven and earth is Christ's. Our lack of strength, therefore, is due to our failure to live by faith in God – to eat and drink the flesh and blood of Christ by faith. The prayer, "Be Thou our arm every morning," should be prayed every morning, and that would mean that we propose to live only by the Word of God, as, like the manna, it comes to us fresh every morning. Thus our every-day life becomes to us the pledge of eternal salvation. "While there's life there's hope," because life itself is hope.

Wisdom is a Defense

"Wisdom and knowledge shall be the stability of thy times." Knowledge is indeed power, provided it is right knowledge. Wisdom is certainly power, for Christ, the wisdom of God, is the power of God. 1 Cor. 1:24. "Wisdom is a defense, and money is a defense; but the excellency [the advantage] of knowledge is that wisdom giveth life to them that have it." Eccl. 7:12. How much stability does wisdom give? – Consider the heavens and the earth, the works of God, and you will see; for "He hath established the world by His wisdom, and hath stretched out the heavens by His discretion." Jer. 10:12. The last message, the last proclamation of the Gospel, calls upon men with a loud voice to give glory to God, "and worship Him that made heaven, and earth, and the sea, and the fountains of waters." Rev. 14:7. We are to recognize God in His works, to trust the power and the wisdom that are manifested in the tiniest flower or the smallest insect, as well as in the shining orbs of the sky. The knowledge of God is wisdom and strength and riches. Jer. 9:23–24. That wisdom which made and upholds them will also sustain us, if we trust it.

> "That hand which bears creation up,
> Shall guard His children well."

A Vital Question

"Who among us shall dwell with the devouring fire? Who among us shall dwell with everlasting burnings?" One would naturally say that such a thing is impossible; but the Lord says that some can and will do it. Who are they? It is the one who walks in righteousness, even "the righteousness which is of God, by faith" (Phil. 3:9), who speaks right things, who will have nothing to do with anything gained by fraud, who cannot be bribed, and who will not hear of bloody deeds, or look upon evil. Such an one can live in eternal fire, and be at ease amid the devouring flame.

No Future for the Wicked

Take particular notice that only the righteous can dwell with everlasting, devouring fire. The wicked will suffer the vengeance of eternal fire, – they will be cast into the fire that never shall be quenched, – but they cannot abide there; the fire will consume them as chaff. "As thorns cut up shall they be burned in the fire." There is therefore no eternity for the wicked. "The transgressors shall be destroyed together; the end [literally, "the future time"] of the wicked shall be cut off." Ps. 37:8. So to the oft-repeated question, "Where will you spend eternity?" there can be but one answer. Those who spend it anywhere will spend it in the presence of God, dwelling in Him and His light; those who do not live in His righteousness, dwelling in the secret place of the Most High, will spend eternity nowhere. "They shall be as though they had not been." Obadiah 16. "For yet a little while, and the wicked shall not be; yea, thou shalt diligently consider his place, and it shall not be." Ps. 38:10. "For, behold, the day cometh, that shall burn as an oven; and the proud, yea, and all that do wickedly, shall be stubble; and the day that cometh shall burn them up, saith the Lord of hosts, that it shall leave them neither root nor branch." Mal. 4:1. Yet the righteous will dwell in that same fire in safety, and will bask in its grateful warmth throughout eternity.

The Fire of God's Presence

By comparing Isa. 33:14–16 with Ps. 15:1–5, it will be seen that the people who dwell with the devouring fire and the everlasting burnings, are the same people that "ascend into the hill of the Lord," and abide in His tabernacle. Thus it must be that the everlasting, devouring fire is in the tabernacle, the secret place, of God. That is

175

exactly the case. Let us collect a few texts of Scripture that show this.

Verse 11 of this chapter, according to Lowth's reading, says, "My Spirit, like fire, shall consume you." This agrees with Isa. 11:4, "He shall smite the earth with the rod of His mouth, and with the breath of His lips shall He slay the wicked," and 2 Thess. 2:8, which says that the Lord shall consume "that wicked" "with the Spirit of His mouth."

"Our God is a consuming fire." Heb. 12:29. He descended on Mount Sinai in fire (Ex. 19:18), and spoke to the people "out of the midst of the fire." Deut. 4:12; verse 22. "From His right hand went a fiery law for them." Deut. 33:2.

The Lord "sitteth between [or upon] the cherubim." Ps. 99:1. When He drove Adam and Eve out of the garden of Eden, "He placed at the east of the garden of Eden cherubim and a flaming sword, which turned every way, to keep the way of the tree of life." Gen. 3:24. This was the indication of His own presence; to this place Adam and his family came to worship, and from here Cain went out from the presence of the Lord.

The Lord reigns in righteousness, and "a fire goeth before Him, and burneth up His enemies round about," and the hills melt like wax at the presence of the Lord. Ps. 97:1–5. So when Christ comes, it is "in flaming fire taking vengeance on them that know not God, and that obey not the Gospel of our Lord Jesus Christ." 2 Thess. 1:8. So at the last, when the wicked are all gathered together to do battle against God and His people, fire comes down from God out of heaven, and devours them. Rev. 20:8–9. In Isa. 30:33 we have read that "the breath of the Lord, like a stream of brimstone" kindles Tophet.

God covers Himself with light as with a garment (Ps. 54:2), and dwells in light that no man can approach unto. 1 Tim. 6:16. When Isaiah saw the Lord, sitting on His throne, "the house was filled with smoke" (Isa. 6:4.), indicating the presence of fire; and this is still further indicated by the fact that the beings that stand above His throne are the "Seraphim," that is, "the burning ones." Remember also that God went before Israel, to guide them, in a pillar of fire by night and a pillar of cloud by day.

In this Presence, amid this fire, the saints of God will dwell throughout eternity, but in order that they may do this, they must here become accustomed to the glory of God, of which the whole earth is full. By beholding it they become changed into the same image "from glory to glory," even by the Spirit of the Lord. 2 Cor. 3:18. The presence of the Lord consumes everything that is evil, and so their dwelling with God in this time fits them for His unveiled glory. The sunlight, which destroys disease germs, is a daily proof to us of the fact that the glory of God consumes evil. But those who refuse to recognize God as He is now revealed, will not be able to abide the day of His coming, and will be consumed.

So it is indeed eternal fire that consumes the wicked, but it is not fire specially created for that purpose, nor does the fact that it is eternal prove that those who suffer from it will live eternally, but just the opposite. All, both saints and sinners, will be in the midst of it, so that all will be treated alike, and God cannot be accused of injustice; but the nature of the individual will determine how the fire will affect him. Only those who have become transformed into the likeness of God, who have His life as their life, so that they are partakers of the Divine nature, sharers of the glory, will be able to come through the fire unscathed, and, in fact, to continue dwelling in it. They are of the same nature as the devouring flame, and hence can dwell in it and not be consumed. All others will perish. The mercy of God endures for ever, and that which perpetuates the existence of those who become assimilated to it, ends the existence of the rebellious. How pertinent, therefore, the message, "Fear God, and give glory to Him, for the hour of His judgment is come."

CHAPTER 28

THE KING IN HIS BEAUTY

(Isa. 33:17–24, Lowth's Translation)

17. Thine eyes shall see the King in His beauty; they shall see thine own land far extended.

18. Thine heart shall reflect on the past terror: where is now the accomptant? where the weigher of tribute? where is he that numbered the towers?

19. Thou shalt see no more that barbarous people; the people of the deep speech, which thou couldst not hear; and of a stammering tongue, which thou couldst not understand.

20. Thou shalt see Sion, the city of our solemn feasts; thine eyes shall behold Jerusalem, the quiet habitation, the tabernacle unshaken; whose stakes shall not be plucked up for ever, and whose chords none shall be broken.

21. But the glorious name of Jehovah shall be unto us a place of confluent streams, of broad rivers; which no oared ship shall pass, neither shall any mighty vessel go through.

22. For Jehovah is our Judge; Jehovah is our Lawgiver; Jehovah is our King; He shall save us.

23. Thy sails are loose; they cannot make them fast; thy mast is not firm; they cannot spread the ensign. Then shall a copious spoil be divided; even the lame shall seize the prey.

24. Neither shall the inhabitant say, I am disabled with sickness; the people that dwell therein is freed from the punishment of their iniquity.

Before studying this lesson, do not fail to read again the first portion of the chapter, and recall the lesson we there learned. The people here addressed are those who are able to dwell with the devouring fire, and amid everlasting burnings. Only those who have been tried as by fire, and have stood the test, so that they can dwell in the fire, can behold Him who is Light itself, and who has His fire in Zion, and His furnace in Jerusalem. (See Isa. 31:9.)

The picture here presented is beyond question that of the new earth, after the fire from the Lord has consumed sin and sinners; when only those are left, who can dwell with the consuming fire. It is the time when in all the earth "there shall be no more curse; but the throne of God and of the Lamb shall be in it; and His servants shall serve Him; and they shall see His face.." Rev. 22:3–4. They shall see the King in His beauty, and they shall also see the land stretching far to northward and eastward and southward and westward, as God promised to Abraham. Gen. 13:14–17.

"And they shall see His face." "Thine eyes shall see the King in His beauty." What is the beauty of the King, that to look upon it should fill up the measure of all happiness and bliss? Let us give it a little study, for when we know it, and can recognize it, we shall find the joy of life, even in this sin-cursed earth, marvelously increased.

That the Lord is beautiful, the verse before us states. The prophet Zechariah, seeing in vision the Lord saving His people like a flock, was moved to exclaim, "How great is His goodness, and how great is His beauty!" Zech. 9:16–17. His goodness and His beauty are linked together, for His beauty is the beauty of holiness. Now the goodness of God is infinite; it is the only goodness that there is in the universe; therefore the beauty of the Lord must be infinite. No tongue can possibly describe it; it must be seen to be appreciated, and seen not for a moment merely, but throughout eternity.

"Strength and beauty are in His sanctuary." Ps. 96:6. Zion itself, His dwelling place, is "the perfection of beauty." Ps. 50:2. Even one of His creatures, the covering cherub that fell, is declared to have been "full of wisdom and perfect in beauty." Eze. 28:12–14. What then must the Creator be?

David "the sweet psalmist of Israel," the one by whom the Spirit of the Lord spake (2 Sam. 23:1–2), spoke of the things touching the King, and he said, "Thou art fairer than the children of men; grace is poured into Thy lips." Ps. 45:1–2. To the psalmist wonderful revelations of Divine things had been vouchsafed, and so great was his appreciation of the beauty of the Lord that he said, "One thing have I desired of the Lord, that will I seek after; that I may dwell in the house of the Lord all the days of my life, to behold the beauty of the Lord, and to enquire in His temple." Ps. 27:5. To see the beauty of the Lord was his sole desire, and that is to be the reward of the righteous.

"The heavens declare the glory of God." Ps. 19:1. They tell of His glory by revealing it in their shining; for He has set His glory "upon the heavens." Ps. 8:1, R.V. Remember that everything exists only by the power of the life of God. All things were created by the Word of God, and the Word is life. "In Him all things consist." Col. 1:17. "We are His offspring" (Acts 17:28), but we are not the only products of His Being. The mountains and hills were "brought forth" by Him who from everlasting to everlasting is God. Ps. 90:1–2. All are familiar with the term, "brought forth," so that it is scarcely necessary to say that in the Hebrew the word is plainly "born," and several translations have the text, "before the mountains were born."

The everlasting power and Divinity of God are clearly seen in the things that are made. Rom. 1:20. The Father impresses His image on His offspring. So "He hath made everything beautiful in its time." Eccl. 3:11. "He that planted the ear, shall He not hear? He that formed the eye, shall He not see? He that chastiseth the heathen, shall not He correct? He that teacheth man knowledge, shall not He know?" Ps. 94:9–10. In like manner we may continue, "He that hath clothed the heavens and the earth with beauty, and hath made all things beautiful, shall not He be beautiful?"

All these things show us that the beauty that we see in created things is but the reflection or the reproduction of the beauty of the Creator. Just as there is no goodness but from the Lord, so there is no beauty except that which comes from Him. Take all the varied tints of all the beautiful flowers on earth (remember that, beautiful as they are, they are under the curse, and are but the shadow of what they were in the beginning, and of what they will be in the restoration), and add to these the richness of the meadows and the forest, and to this still the glory of the rainbow, and the dazzling splendour of the clouds kissed by the setting sun; let the telescope reveal to your admiring gaze a few of the star-clusters that shine with light of every colour, and remember that when the most powerful telescope and the art of the photographer have revealed to us the presence of countless millions of suns that are invisible to the naked eye, awing us with glimpses of measureless space, "these are but the outskirts of His ways," and a very small whisper of His power. Job 26:14. Therefore all these things reveal to us only a very small portion of the beauty of the face of the Lord. Think of all the beauty in earth and sea and the heavens, even the heaven of heavens, concentrated into one single Presence, and you have the measureless measure of the beauty of the Lord. And all this wondrous beauty the saints of God will be privileged to gaze upon, and they will be made able to endure the sight! Truly, the face of God will be enough to satisfy anyone. No wonder the psalmist exclaimed, "As for me, I shall behold Thy face in righteousness; I shall be satisfied, when I awake, with Thy likeness." Ps. 17:15.

What is the practical benefit of this study? Is it merely to inspire in us a desire to see that glorious sight, and thus stir us up to righteousness? Partly, but that is not by any means all. The chief thing is to let us know the possibilities set before us even in this life, as expressed in the inspired prayer, "Let the beauty of the Lord our God be upon us." Ps. 90:17. If we but allow our hearts to be the sanctuary of the living God, then He that dwells between the cherubim will "shine forth." Ps. 80:1. "Arise, shine; for thy light is come, and the glory of the Lord is risen upon thee. For, behold, the darkness shall cover the earth, and gross darkness the people; but the Lord shall arise upon thee, and His glory shall be seen upon thee." Isa. 60:1–2. The beauty of the Lord is the beauty of holiness, and just as He has laid up great goodness for them that trust in Him before the sons of men (Ps. 31:19), so does He impart to them His beauty. The world will not recognize it, for they did not desire the beauty of the Lord when they saw Him; their standard of beauty is not the Lord's standard; nevertheless the beauty is present whenever righteousness is present; and it is beauty that will never fade. That is the true test of beauty. By beholding the glory of God in the face of Jesus Christ, we become changed into the same image, even in this life, and are thus prepared for the full revelation of the beauty of the world to come, when the righteous shall shine forth as the sun.

Even now may we behold the beauty of the Lord, if our eyes are but anointed by the Spirit. In all His works, we may see the shining of His face. "Blessed is the people that know the joyful sound; they shall walk, O Lord, in the light of Thy countenance." Ps. 89:15. So we may ever dwell in the house of the Lord; and ever behold the shining of His glorious face. "Blessed are they that dwell in Thy house; they will be still praising Thee." Likewise in eternity, the saints, although privileged to roam throughout the entire universe, will always know themselves to be in the Presence of the King, everywhere beholding the beauty of His face. With this truth ever in our minds, we may realize to the full all that is contained in the expression "living near to the Lord."

Verses 18–20 make still more plain the fact that the time of which we are now studying is that after the wicked who have surrounded the camp of the saints, and the Beloved City, have been devoured by the fire from heaven. Rev. 20:9. "Thine heart shall reflect on the past terror," but only to magnify the wondrous power and mercy of the Lord. Where now are those who counted the towers, and who in the madness of wickedness had devoted the holy city to destruction? No more shall they be seen, for they are as though they had not been. Jerusalem, instead of falling a prey to them, as they had planned, will be seen as "the quiet habitation, the tabernacle unshaken, whose stakes shall not be plucked up for ever, and of whose chords none shall be broken."

"But there the glorious Lord will be unto us a place of broad rivers and streams." Is this literally true? – Most certainly; for God is "the Fountain of living waters." Jer. 2:13. From Himself flows the river of water of life – His own life flowing forth for the everlasting refreshment of His people. But this is true now for those who have eyes to see spiritual things, and who know the reality of them. It is from the river of God that this earth is watered. Ps. 65:9. It is full of water, even to overflowing, and never runs dry. The rain that falls from heaven to enrich the earth, is from that river. Consequently the streams of water on this earth are but branches of the same river. In the flowing streams and the waves of the sea we may see the life of God; then will it be no more a mere figure of speech that our peace shall be as a river, and our righteousness as the waves of the sea. Dwelling in the house of the Lord, we shall constantly see His face, and drink of the river of His pleasure.

Jehovah is our Judge, our King, and our Lawgiver, and He is this by right, because He will save us. Only He who can save has the right to give laws, and only to Him should we hearken. Our daily prayer is, "Thy kingdom come, Thy will be done in earth, as it is in heaven." That means that we should now regard the Lord as our King just the same as though we were now in heaven. He is the only rightful King; our part is to recognize His right to rule over us.

"And the inhabitants shall not say, I am sick," or, as Lowth has it, "I am disabled with sickness." That will be a glorious change from this present state. "God shall wipe away all tears from their eyes; and there shall be no more death, neither sorrow nor crying, neither shall there be any more pain; for the former things are passed away." Rev. 21:4.

Why will there be no more sickness in that land? – The reason is given in the text: "The people that dwell therein shall be forgiven their iniquity." God, who forgives all iniquities also heals all diseases, and the healing is because of the forgiveness – a consequence of it. Few people realize the fullness of the blessing of forgiveness, and that is the reason so many Christians say that there is a much higher state in the Christian life than that of justification. They think that to live in the consciousness of sins forgiven is but a trifle compared with the blessings that God has for those who fully trust Him. But to live in the constant knowledge of sins forgiven is the highest possible for any creature. It is to live in fellowship with God. 1 John 1:7. Our sins are forgiven by the substitution of the righteousness of Christ, which means that it is by God's giving us His life instead of ours. That means a complete transformation.

"The blood of Jesus Christ His Son cleanseth us from all sin." The life of Christ, the stream from the throne of God, constantly flowing through us, and being our sole source of life, takes sin away. But when the Lord gives us His life, He gives us the whole of it. He gives us Himself, and He is not divided. Therefore He gives us His health as well as His righteousness. It is just as easy for the Lord to make a man perfectly whole as to forgive his sins, for it is all done by the same life. Indeed, if we but knew the extent of the gift of the righteousness which takes away sin, we should always take with it the healing of our bodies; it is ours, if we will but receive it.

Why is it that so many people who know the Lord as the One who forgives all their iniquities do not experience the blessings of health? – Simply because they do not understand and comply with the conditions. They know that "if we confess our sins, He is faithful and just to forgive us our sins, and to cleanse us from all unrighteousness," and so they confess their sins, and do not expect to continue them. They would not expect to be forgiven if they were not willing to cease from sinning. Well now, why not be as reasonable with regard to health? There are conditions of life and health. No one would expect the Lord to keep him from being burned, if he persisted in going into the fire. Even so we need not expect the Lord to keep us in health if we continually disregard the laws of health, any more than we should expect forgiveness if we ignored the ten commandments. God has given us food, drink, air, rest, and clothing, to keep us in health. If we eat and drink only the things that He has indicated as good for us, and in proper measure, allow our lungs the utmost quantity of the purest air, and do not contaminate it with vile tobacco poison, and if we have the right relation between labour and rest, then, trusting in the Lord, we may expect strength sufficient for all our duties, so that even in this life we need not say, "I am disabled with sickness." This is practical godliness, which is profitable for this life as well as for that which is to come.

CHAPTER 29

THE EARTH DESOLATED

(Isa. 34:1–17, Lowth's Translation)

1. Draw near, O ye nations, and hearken; and attend unto Me, O ye peoples! let the earth hear, and all the fullness thereof; the world, and all that spring from it.

2. For the wrath of Jehovah is kindled against all the nations; and His anger against all the orders thereof: he hath devoted them; He hath given them up to the slaughter.

3. And their slain shall be cast out; and from their carcasses their stink shall ascend; and the mountains shall melt down with their blood.

4. And all the host of heaven shall waste away; and the heavens shall be rolled up like a scroll; and all their host shall wither; as the withered leaf falleth from the vine, and as the blighted leaf from the fig tree.

5. For My sword is made bare in the heavens; behold, on edom it shall descend; and on the people justly by Me devoted to destruction.

6. The sword of Jehovah is glutted with blood; it is pampered with fat; with the blood of lambs, and of goats; with the fat of reins of rams; for Jehovah celebrates a sacrifice in Bozrah, and a great slaughter in the land of Edom.

7. And the wild goats shall fall down with them; and the bullocks, together with the bulls; and their own land shall be drunken with their blood, and their dust shall be enriched with fat.

8. For it is the day of vengeance to Jehovah; the year of recompense to the defender of the cause of Zion.

9. And her torrents shall be turned into pitch, and her dust into sulphur; and her whole land shall become burning pitch,

10. By night or by day it shall not be extinguished; for ever shall her smoke ascend; from generation to generation she shall lie desert; to everlasting ages no man shall pass through her;

11. But the pelican and the porcupine shall inherit her; and the owl and the raven shall inhabit there; and He shall stretch over her the line of devastation, and the plummet of emptiness over her scorched plains.

12. No more shall they boast the renown of the kingdom; and all her princes shall utterly fail.

13. And in her palaces shall spring up thorns; the nettle and the bramble in her fortresses; and she shall become an habitation for dragons, a court for the daughters of the ostrich.

14. And the jackals and the mountain-cats shall meet one another; and the satyr shall call to his fellow; there also the screech-owl shall pitch; and shall find for herself a place of rest.

15. There shall the night-raven make her nest, and lay her eggs; and she shall hatch them, and gather her young under her shadow; there also shall the vultures be gathered together; every one of them shall join her mate.

16. Consult ye the book of Jehovah, and read: not one of these shall be missed; not a female shall lack her mate; for the mouth of Jehovah hath given the command! and His Spirit itself hath gathered them.

17. And He hath cast the lot for them; and His hand meted out the portion by line; they shall possess the land for a perpetual inheritance; from generation to generation shall they dwell therein.

The subject of this chapter is very easy to discern, and is manifestly that indicated in the title. The whole chapter is devoted to the one subject, so that it is easy of comprehension.

Here is a proclamation of something that concerns the whole earth. All the earth, and all the nations on it are called to hear what the Lord has to say. It is nothing less than the proclamation of the wrath of God against all the nations. The most cursory reading of the chapter must convince anybody that the things here set forth are not limited to any one section of the earth, nor to any one people.

There is a strange idea very prevalent among readers of the Bible, and in religious circles, namely, that in ancient times God confined His attentions specially to one people – the Jews; that He was shut up to them, and cared little or nothing for any other people. How anybody who reads the Bible could get such an idea is most strange. This chapter alone is enough to show the contrary; it is addressed to all the nations of the earth. The prophet is commissioned to preach to all mankind, and so understands his mission.

Think how much of the book of Isaiah is directly addressed to other people than the Jews. Chapters fifteen to twenty-three are entirely devoted to other nations, who are directly appealed to by name. Moab, Tyre, Egypt, Assyria, and all the great nations are addressed one by one. And then other chapters mention the whole earth, showing that the events with which the prophet had to deal were not local. Indeed, the book begins with an appeal to the whole earth, and to heaven as well.

From the earliest times God has showed Himself the God of the Gentiles as well as of the Jews. There were no Jews at all until more than two centuries of the world's history had passed, yet in all that time God had had faithful men, a proof that He was revealing Himself to whom-soever would accept Him. The Jews themselves originated from a man taken from the midst of heathendom. People in these days seem to think that they must perpetuate the blindness of people of other days. Because the Jews in their national conceit imagined that the Lord did not care for any other people than themselves, most Bible readers have thought that it must have been so. But the fact was very evident from the beginning, to any person who would use his eyes and reason, that God is no respecter of persons, but that "in every nation he that feareth Him and worketh righteousness is accepted with Him." The book of Isaiah, as indeed the books of all the other prophets, was addressed to the nations at large as well as to the Jews. And it concerns all the nations on earth today.

If one follows the book of Revelation in connection with Isaiah, it will be very apparent that the prophet John had no new message given him for the people. The Apostle Peter testifies that the message given to the ancient prophets was the same that the apostles had to give. 1 Peter 1:10–12. Compare for instance verse 4 of this chapter with Rev. 6:12–14. In many cases the words in Revelation are but a repetition of those used by the earlier prophet. That does not show that he was a mere borrower of other men's message, but that the Holy Spirit had the same message to give by the two men. Both had a message for the last days.

A few facts gleaned from various parts of the Bible will help us to read this chapter more understandingly. First, we must remember that when the Lord comes the second time it is for the consummation of the salvation of His people, and this is effected by the destruction of the wicked, who will be on the point of exterminating them. For "evil men and seducers shall wax worse and worse, deceiving and being deceived." 2 Tim. 3:13. This statement immediately following the one that "all that will live godly in Christ Jesus shall suffer persecution," shows that at the last day the people of God will be in more bitter persecution than at any other time in the world's history. Before the flood the earth was filled with violence, and at the coming of the Lord it is to be in the same condition as then. Gen. 6:11–12; Matt. 24:37.

Remember also that both righteous and wicked live together on this earth until the end of the world (Matt. 13:24–30, 36–43), and that there is no secret coming of the Lord, but that when He comes it will be openly, so that all can see Him, and the pomp and awful majesty will be such that none can help giving heed. See Rev. 1:7; Acts 1:11; Matt. 24:23–27; 1 Thess. 4:16–17. At that time the wicked who still remain alive after the plagues that have come on the earth, will be destroyed by the brightness of Christ's coming, and the righteous, both dead and living, will be caught up, immortal, to be ever with the Lord. 1 Thess. 4:16–18; 2 Thess. 2:8. This is the first resurrection. "Blessed and holy is he that hath part in the first resurrection; on such the second death hath no power, but they shall be priests of God and of Christ, and shall reign with Him a thousand years." Rev. 20:6.

But the rest of the dead, that is, the wicked, will not live again until the thousand years are finished. At the end of that time they will be raised, and will be deceived by Satan into thinking that they can capture the Holy City, the New Jerusalem, which has come down from God out of heaven, and while surrounding it will be destroyed. Rev. 20:5–9. This is in brief the outline of events in connection with the coming of the Lord, as set forth in the Scriptures.

During this thousand years, in which the saints are reigning with Christ in heaven, sitting in judgment on the earth and on fallen angels, the earth will be a desolate waste, as set forth in the chapter before us. In the twentieth chapter of Revelation we read of "the bottomless pit." Now the word there used in the Greek corresponds exactly with the Hebrew word in the first chapter of Genesis, where we are told that in the beginning the earth was without form, and void. It was chaos. The Septuagint has exactly the same word: the Spirit of God moved upon the face of the *abyss*. In the eleventh verse of this chapter of Isaiah, we have, in "the line of *confusion*, and the stones of *emptiness*," the exact words that occur in Gen. 1:2. So we find that during the thousand years the earth will be desolate, uninhabited by man, and unfit for human habitation. This is the time described in this chapter. In the thirteenth chapter the condition is set forth, in the account of the judgment upon Babylon.

This condition of things is said to last for ever and ever; yet the very next chapter describes a condition of Eden beauty on this earth. In 2 Peter 3:10–13 we read of the destruction of the earth in the day of the Lord, yet we are assured that there shall be, "according to His promise," "new heavens and a new earth." So we learn that the duration of that which is spoken of as being for ever and ever, depends on the nature of the thing spoken of. When God is the subject, or the saints whom He has made immortal, then we know that there is never any end; but when it is something that is contaminated by sin, then we know that there will be a limit to its continuance. "Sodom and Gomorrah, and the cities round about them in like manner, giving themselves over to fornication, and going after strange flesh, are set forth for an example, suffering the vengeance of eternal fire" (Jude 7), yet the places where they once stood are now a desolate plain.

One special lesson must be indicated before we leave the chapter. Notice how the vilest and most loathsome creatures are described as inhabiting the desolate earth. They hold sway over it while it is destitute of men. This is the natural end of the first sin, and of all that have succeeded. In the beginning man was given complete dominion over the earth, and over everything on it. That dominion was the rule of righteousness. But man sinned, and the dominion and the glory departed from him. More and more has he been losing his control over the earth and its creatures. Instead of governing the lower orders of animals, he is exterminating them as fast as possible. Wherever man goes, destruction marks his course. Finally, when sin has come to the full, and has ripened to the harvest, the condition that existed at the first will be utterly reversed, and only vile and hateful creatures – scavengers – will rule where once man had sway. All this terrible fall is involved in every sin. This is what the rule of man brings the earth to. Then will be seen in its fullness, or rather, in its emptiness, the result of man's having his own way. Shall we not be warned in time, and submit ourselves to the rule of the One who has power to govern with stability?

CHAPTER 30

THE EARTH RESTORED

(Isa. 35:1–10, Lowth's Translation)

1. The desert and the waste shall be glad; and the wilderness shall rejoice, and flourish;

2. Like the rose shall it beautifully flourish; and the well-watered plain of Jordan shall also rejoice; the glory of Lebanon shall be given unto it, the beauty of Carmel and Sharon: these shall behold the glory of Jehovah, the majesty of our God.

3. Strengthen ye the feeble hands, confirm ye the tottering knees.

4. Say to the faint-hearted: be ye strong; fear ye not, behold your God! Vengeance will come; the retribution of God; He Himself will come, and will deliver you.

5. Then shall be unclosed the eyes of the blind; and the ears of the deaf shall be opened:

6. Then shall the lame bound like the hart, and the tongue of the dumb shall sing: for in the wilderness shall burst forth waters, and torrents in the desert:

7. And the glowing sand shall become a pool, and the thirsty soil bubbling springs: and in the haunt of dragons shall spring forth the grass, with the reed, and the bulrush.

8. And a highway shall be there; and it shall be called the way of holiness; no unclean person shall pass through it; but He Himself shall be with them, walking in the way, and the foolish shall not err therein.

9. No lion shall be there; nor shall the tyrant of the beasts come up thither: neither shall he be found there; but the redeemed shall walk in it.

10. Yea, the ransomed of Jehovah shall return: they shall come to Sion with triumph; and perpetual gladness shall crown their heads. Joy and gladness shall they obtain; and sorrow and sighing shall flee away.

"The thing that hath been, it is that which shall be." Eccl. 1:9. This is most emphatically true of the things that God has made. For "I know that, whatsoever God doeth, it shall be for ever; nothing can be put to it, nor anything taken from it." Eccl. 3:15. When God made the world, and all things beautiful, "He created it not in vain." The fact that God made the earth perfect, is proof that it will be perfect. Not one of God's plans can ever fail. To man's short sight it may seem as though everything had failed; but God has eternity for His own, and can afford to be misunderstood and yet to wait. A few years, or a few thousand years are not a finger's breadth compared with eternity. So although sin brings complete desolation upon the earth, the end of sin, which is destruction, will be self-destruction; and death, the last enemy, having been swallowed up in victory, the earth will be renewed, and "the desert shall rejoice and blossom as the rose."

"It shall blossom abundantly, and rejoice even with joy and singing; the glory of Lebanon shall be given unto it, the excellency of Carmel and Sharon; they shall see the glory of the Lord, and the excellency of our God." The places once most fertile are now most desolate. The earth is waxing old like a garment; but like an old garment, it is soon to be changed, and then it will reflect to perfection the excellency and beauty of Jehovah. We have learned something of the beauty of the Lord; that wondrous beauty will yet be seen even in the most desolate and barren portions of this earth. Is it not a glorious prospect? What assurance have we of this? Is not the assurance of God's Word sufficient? But we have ample demonstration of it in the fact that man, who was made to rule over a perfect earth, and was therefore himself made perfect, but who fell, and thereby caused the desolation of the earth, is himself by the Word of God made a new creature even now in this present time.

When the king is restored to his kingly state, is that not proof that he will have back his dominion?

In view of this, what is said? – "Strengthen ye the weak hands, and confirm the feeble knees. Say to them that are of a fearful heart, Be strong, Fear not." When does this apply? Is it in the time spoken of in the first two verses? – Most certainly not; for in the earth renewed there will be no occasion to say to anybody, "Fear not!" The people shall then "dwell in a peaceable habitation, and in sure dwellings, and in quiet resting places." No; now is the time when the assurance of what God will certainly do for even this sin-cursed earth must be set before the faint-hearted, to encourage them. The "blessed hope" is "the glorious appearing of the great God and our Saviour Jesus Christ." Titus 2:13. "He will come and save you."

What else should be said to them that are of a fearful heart? – This: "Behold your God!" Where? – Everywhere. "Do not I fill heaven and earth? saith the Lord." Jer. 23:24. When Christ appears in the clouds of heaven there will be no fearful ones among His people. That will be the moment of the joy of deliverance. No one will then need to say, "Behold your God!" for "every eye shall see Him." "And it shall be said in that day, Lo, this is our God; we have waited for Him, and He will save us: This is the Lord, we have waited for Him, we will be glad and rejoice in His salvation." Isa. 25:9. Therefore this exclamation, "Behold your God!" is to be uttered now in the ears of all the fainting ones of earth.

"That which may be known of God is manifested in them; for God manifested it unto them. For the invisible things of Him since the creation of the world are clearly seen, being perceived through the things that are made, even His everlasting power and Divinity." Rom. 1:19–20. He upholds all things by the Word of His power. Heb. 1:3. To be able to see God in all the things that exist, to know that He has not forsaken the earth, is enough to put courage into any man. What means it that He is here? – Nothing less than that He claims all things as His own, and is determined to stay by them. Though they be marred, and the Divine image may be almost effaced, yet He does not become disheartened or disgusted with them, but will by His presence restore them as at the first. If He did not claim them as His own, and did not intend to make them again worthy of Himself, He would not remain in them; the fact that He tarries even amid the curse, is sufficient proof that He means salvation; and what He purposes He will surely perform. Therefore behold your God in the lowest and meanest created thing, that you may know that He has not forsaken man, His crowning work. Be of good courage; He will come and save you.

"Then the eyes of the blind shall be opened, and the ears of the deaf shall be unstopped. Then shall the lame man leap as an hart, and the tongue of the dumb sing." When shall all this be? Well, it will certainly be when the Lord comes to save His people, for then the dead themselves will be raised incorruptible, and the living will be changed in a moment, in the twinkling of an eye, to immortality. 1 Cor. 15:51–53; 1 Thess. 4:16–17. At that time there will surely not be a saint of God with any blemish either of soul or body. Christ will have "a glorious church, not having spot, or wrinkle, or any such thing." Eph. 5:27. But we are warranted in believing that a restoration will take place even before the appearing of the Lord, not indeed to immortality, but to soundness of mortal bodies. When Jesus comes "every eye shall see Him." But there is even stronger evidence than this. Christ's presence here on earth brought healing to all that were diseased in any way. The proof of the Divinity of His ministry was this, that "the blind receive their sight, and the lame walk, and the deaf hear, the dead are raised up, and the poor have the Gospel preached unto them." Matt 11:3–5. Now there was never a time in the world when there was more need of convincing proof of the genuineness of the Gospel than now. When Satan works with "all power and signs and lying wonders, and with all deceivableness of unrighteousness" (2 Thess. 2:9–10), as he sees the end near, God will not leave Himself without witness among men, but will also work with many miracles and wonders and signs. The Christ who once walked among men, revealing the Father, will be reproduced in all His people, so that no particle of evidence will be lacking. So as He then healed all who were sick and blind and lame, wherever

He went, we may be sure the same thing will be done again, when all His people learn to behold Him still among them and in them.

"In the wilderness shall waters break out, and streams in the desert." That will be fulfilled when the wilderness and the solitary place are made new, and the desert blossoms as the rose; but we may expect to see it fulfilled even before the coming of the Lord. When Israel went out from Egypt, water was brought from the flinty rock for them in the desert. God "turned the rock into standing water, the flint into a fountain of waters." Ps. 114:8. When God sets His hand again the second time to deliver His people, "there shall be an highway for the remnant of His people, which shall be left, from Assyria; like as it was to Israel in the day that he came up out of the land of Egypt." Isa. 11:16. Therefore we may expect to see the same wonders, and even greater ones, repeated. "Behold, the days come, saith The Lord, that they shall no more say, the Lord liveth, which brought up the children of Israel out of the land of Egypt; but, The Lord liveth, which brought up and which led the seed of the house of Israel out of the north country, and from all countries whither I had driven them; and they shall dwell in their own land." Jer. 23:7–8. The wonders of the last days will entirely eclipse the miracles of the exodus from Egypt.

"An highway shall be there." Where? Without doubt in the new earth, in the holy city; but we should miss the joy of the Scripture if we put it all off till the future. Christ is the way, the way of holiness, and the way is plain. "The way ye know." Anyone can find it; it is revealed unto babes; and the most simple cannot make any mistake in it. "The redeemed shall walk there."

Even now "God hath visited and redeemed His people." Therefore now the redeemed must have a place in which to walk. And they shall walk in the way, and they "shall return, and come to Zion with songs and everlasting joy upon their heads." Mark that it is with singing that they come into Zion. They do not wait until they get there to sing; they sing now. It is because they sing that they get there. Read 2 Chron. 20:1–30, and note verses 21 and 22. It was when Israel began to sing and to praise the Lord, that they gained the victory. Then let the desert resound and be made glad with singing.

> "Let those refuse to sing
> Who never knew our God;
> But children of the heavenly King
> Must speak their joys abroad."

This they must do, because they "are come unto Mount Zion, and unto the city of the living God, the heavenly Jerusalem, and to an innumerable company of angels, to the general assembly and church of the firstborn, which are written in heaven, and to God the Judge of all, and to the spirits of just men made perfect, and to Jesus the Mediator of the new covenant, and to the blood of sprinkling, which speaketh better things than that of Abel," and

> "The hill of Zion yields
> A thousand sacred sweets,
> Before we reach the heavenly fields,
> Or walk the golden streets."

CHAPTER 31

A PRAYER FOR HEALING ANSWERED

(Isa. 38:1–8, 21–22, Lowth's Translation)

1. At that time Hezekiah was seized with a mortal sickness; and Isaiah the prophet, the son of Amos, came unto him, and said unto him: Thus saith Jehovah: Give orders concerning thy affairs to thy family;

2. For thou must die; thou shalt no longer live. Then Hezekiah turned his face to the wall, and

3. Made his supplication to Jehovah. And he said: I beseech Thee, O Jehovah, remember now how I have endeavoured to walk before Thee in truth, and with a perfect heart; and have done that which is good in Thine eyes. And Hezekiah wept, and lamented grievously.

4. Now [before Isaiah was gone out into the middle court] the word of Jehovah came unto him, saying: Go [back], and say unto Hezekiah,

5. Thus saith Jehovah, the God of David thy father: I have heard thy supplication; I have seen thy tears. Behold I will heal thee; and thou shalt go up into the house of Jehovah.

6. And I will add unto thy days fifteen years. And I will deliver thee, and this city, from the hand of the king of Assyria;

22. And I will protect this city. And [Hezekiah said: By what sign shall I know that I shall go up into the house of Jehovah?

7. And Isaiah said:] This shall be the sign from Jehovah, that Jehovah will bring to effect this word which He hath spoken.

8. Behold I will bring back the shadow of the degrees, by which the sun is gone down on the degrees of Ahaz, ten degrees backward. And the sun returned backward ten degrees, on the degrees by which it had gone down.

21. And Isaiah said: Let them take a lump of figs; and they bruised them, and applied them to the boil; and he recovered.

In studying this lesson, reference should be made to the record in 2 Kings 20:1–11. It will be noticed that the Lowth's Translation, which we have reprinted here, two sections are inserted in brackets in the fourth and fifth verses, from the corresponding verses of the account in 2 Kings. Also, in order that the record of the event may be complete in one lesson, verses 21–22 are brought into the narrative in the regular course, instead of being left, as in our common version, at the close of Hezekiah's song of thanksgiving. Let the student diligently compare this reading with that in his Bible. There is no alteration, but only a bringing of the different parts of the narrative into one.

"At that time." At what time? For an answer read chapter 36 and 37. The lesson itself (verse 6) indicates that it was at the time that the king of Assyria was besieging Jerusalem. Read also the accounts in 2 Kings 18 and 19, and 2 Chron. 32.

The first thing that claims our attention in this study is the kindness of God in giving Hezekiah timely warning of his approaching death. For what reason Hezekiah was to die at that time, is not stated, and we have no business to conjecture. It would do no good if we should. Of one thing we may be sure, and that is that it was not because Hezekiah was a bad man. The record concerning his reign is that "he did that which was right in the sight of the Lord, according to all that David his father had done." 2 Chron. 29:2. He "wrought that which was good and right and truth before the Lord his God. And in every work that he began in the service of the house of God, and in the law, and in the commandments, to seek his God, he did it with all his heart, and prospered." 2 Chron. 31:20–21. No king has ever had a better testimony given him than that.

One of the most common things when a kind, benevolent, and good person dies, is to hear people say, "What had he done, that he should be taken away? if it had only been such and such an one, I could understand it, for he would never have been missed; but to take away so useful a member of society, – it is inexplicable." Or sometimes a parent says, when a devoted and pious child is taken, "What have we done, that she should be taken from us?" Just as though God never thought of anything but devising some means of punishing people, and trying to make them miserable! Just as though it would be a mark of greater mercy on the part of God if He should allow all the unprepared ones to die, leaving behind only those who are ready either for life or death! God has "no pleasure in the death of him that dieth." Eze. 18:32. "The righteous perisheth, and no man layeth it to heart; and merciful men are taken away, none considering that the righteous is taken away from the evil to come." Isa. 57:1. The death of a good man, indispensable as he may seem to be, is often the greatest mercy that could befall both him and those who are left behind. Indeed, we may be sure that whatever takes place, the mercy of God endures for ever. "Though He cause grief, yet will He have compassion according to the multitude of His mercies. For He doth not afflict willingly nor grieve the children of men." Lam. 3:32–33.

Death a Costly Thing

Let no one, however, think that it is a light matter to the Lord that any person, whether good or bad, dies. Death is not in God's plan for men. He is the living God, and the God of life. He is the Father of all, and from Him all parental love comes. There is no fatherly love on earth that is not simply a little fragment of the love of God for all men. Then let any father think of his own sorrow at the death of a loved child, and he will have an exceedingly faint idea of the sorrow that moves the heart of God when one of His children dies. See Jesus shedding tears at the grave of Lazarus, even when He knew that in a few minutes He would call His friend back to life. Read the one hundred and sixteenth Psalm. Note especially the fifteenth verse: "Precious in the sight of the Lord is the death of His saints." That word "precious" is from the same word that is often rendered "costly," and it always has that meaning, as anyone will know, who considers its origin. So we should read the verse as it appears in several versions, "Costly in the sight of the Lord is the death of His saints." It costs the Lord more than the human mind can compute, for Him to allow one of His saints to die, even though it be necessary. Death is an expensive thing to the Lord. It costs Him many a heartache. It is a personal loss to Him; He feels it, because every creature is a part of Himself. "We are His offspring," and "in Him we live, and move, and have our being." Acts 17:28. But more, it is a loss to Him in the great work that He has to do in the earth. It is a common thing for men to say that God could get along without any of us, as though He were so self-contained and so self-satisfied and so far above all human feelings that nothing can move Him; when the fact is that everything moves Him. God has given the earth to man, and has never recalled the gift. Through man He has purposed to rule the world, and although we in our selfishness may not be able to understand it, it is a fact that God cannot get along without man. He showed this in that He gave His life for us. He could not live without man. He desires man to be His constant companion. It is for that purpose that He created man. Therefore we may be sure that it was not with a light heart that God said to Hezekiah, "Thou shalt die, and not live."

Death an Enemy

Hezekiah did not wish to die; the thought of it was most painful to him. "Hezekiah wept sore." Was it because he felt that he had been a bad man, and therefore dreaded to meet His God? – No; for he had so little consciousness of guilt that he could recount to the Lord the integrity in which he had walked before Him. If dying means, as the theologians tell us, to be with the Lord, why should Hezekiah have felt so sorrowful at the thought of dying? – Ah, he knew better. There is no man in his senses that would not rather live than die. The tears that people shed over the dead, even while they try to make themselves believe that death is a friend, show that it is impossible for anybody to believe that lie. Every funeral train and every tear are testimonies to the effect that death is an enemy, and not a friend. Death speaks of the devil, the adversary of mankind. The righteous hath hope in his death, simply because he has the assurance through Christ that death shall be destroyed, and he be delivered from its grasp. Death is always and everywhere a thing for tears, and not for joy.

"No" as an Answer to Prayer

The Lord heard Hezekiah's prayer, and allowed him to live a little longer. Yes, "He heard his prayer." How natural it is for us to say that, when we have prayed for something, and have got it. But suppose we do not get it, what then? – Then we shake our heads mournfully, and say, "The Lord didn't see fit to hear us." Just as if there were ever anything that God did not hear. People in their selfishness generally have the idea that the universe is run for their own individual benefit, regardless of anybody else, and each one thinks that his own wishes should be attended to in every detail, and at once, no matter how many others may be distressed by it. So if God does not say "Yes" to every request of theirs, they feel that they have been greatly abused, and even insulted, because, say they, "I prayed to the Lord, and He did not answer me." Haven't they ever heard that "No" is as much an answer as "Yes" is? And has not God as good a right to say "No" once in a while as any earthly parent has, who knows several things that his child does not know? Many a child has lived long enough to find out that the answer "No," to a request for some much-longed-for thing, which seemed to him almost like a death blow, was the greatest blessing that could have been given him. It is always so when God says it, for He gives everything that is good, and He gives nothing that is not good.

Hezekiah Gained Nothing

But Hezekiah received "Yes" as an answer to His prayer. We will not say that he received "a favourable answer." He got what he asked for, although it was directly contrary to what God had said he should have. Did he really get it, though? "Certainly he did," you say. Let us see. What did he ask for? – He asked for a reversal of the decree that had gone forth, that he should die, and not live. "And he did live," you say. How long? – Fifteen years. That is not very long, and when that time had elapsed, what then? – Why, then he died. Yes, that was what God had said concerning him. He had to die just the same as if it had happened fifteen years before; death is just the same one time as another. But how much better off was Hezekiah after the close of that fifteen years than he was at the beginning? What had he gained by trying to overthrow the word of God? Ah, God works all things after the counsel of His own will; His word will be fulfilled sooner or later, and it is well for mankind that it is so.

Hezekiah's Healing a Public Calamity

Whatever Hezekiah may have gained personally in his own feelings by the result of his prayer, it is certain that the people lost by it. We do not hear very much of Hezekiah after that incident. He appears only once, and then in a circumstance that is not greatly to his credit. But we know that in that fifteen years Manasseh was born, for Manasseh was only twelve years old when he succeeded him at his death. Read a little about him: "Manasseh was twelve years old when he began his reign, and he reigned fifty and five years in Jerusalem; and he did that which was evil in the sight of the Lord, like unto the abominations of the heathen, whom the Lord had cast out from before the children of Israel. For he built again the high places which Hezekiah his father had broken down, and he reared up altars for Baalim, ... and he caused his children to pass through the fire in the valley of the son of Hinnom; also he observed times, and used enchantments, and used witchcraft, and dealt with a familiar spirit, and with wizards; he wrought much evil in the sight of the Lord, to provoke Him to anger. ... So Manasseh made Judah and the inhabitants of Jerusalem to err, and to do worse than the heathen, whom the Lord had destroyed before the children of Israel." 2 Chron. 33:1-9. "Moreover Manasseh shed innocent blood very much, till he had filled Jerusalem from one end to another; beside his sin wherewith he made Judah to sin, in doing that which was evil in the sight of the Lord." 2 Kings 21:16. Surely the people of Israel had no reason to be very jubilant over the result of Hezekiah's prayer.

Right and Wrong Praying

When we look at what followed, it seems quite evident that it would have been better if Hezekiah had kept still and allowed things to take the course pointed out by the Lord. "What! Isn't it always right to pray to the Lord for what we want, especially for life and health?" Yes; provided we pray in accordance with the will of God. That is always the rule. We must allow that God knows best. He sees the end from the beginning; and when God tells a man that he is to die, and sends a special messenger, a holy prophet, to bear the message, the very best thing for that man, and for everybody else, is that he should die. There is "a time to be born, and a time to die" (Eccl. 3:1–2), and knowing how much the death of one of His children costs the Lord, we may be sure that the time for a man to die is when God says so.

"Shall we then not dare ask the Lord for a continuance of life?" Why not? We have not received any message from the Lord, telling us that we are to die, and not live. On the contrary we are told, "Is any among you afflicted? let him pray. Is any merry? let him sing psalms. Is any sick among you? let him call for the elders of the church; and let them pray over him, anointing him with oil in the name of the Lord; and the prayer of faith shall save the sick, and the Lord shall raise him up; and if he have committed sin, they shall be forgiven him." James 5:13–15. That is for us, unless we have received some direct intimation from the Lord that we are to be an exception. But let us remember that it is the prayer of faith, that saves the sick, and that "faith cometh by hearing, and hearing by the Word of God." Rom. 10:17. Then we must not ask for anything contrary to the Word of God, and we must know the Word of God as personally addressed to us.

The Use of Remedies

"And Isaiah said, Let them take a lump of figs; and they bruised them, and applied them to the boil; and he recovered." Some one will say, "Why, Hezekiah was healed by natural means, after all; it was a strange and unusual remedy, to be sure, but it was a remedy, nevertheless." Well, what of it? "Oh, when the Lord heals, He does not use remedies." Ah, how did you learn that? Does not the Lord use instruments for the performance of His will? He uses things that are, and even things that are not, for the accomplishment of His purpose. Do not imagine that a thing is any the less a work of God, because He has done it through some agency, human or otherwise. Know this, that there was never a person healed of any disease in this world except by the Lord, and that He always uses some means, visible or invisible. The means is none the less real, if it is invisible. Do not get the idea that when you see a thing done, and see the thing that doest, it is not from the Lord; and that the miracle occurs only when you cannot see anything but the result. The words of the Lord are medicine, whether they are in visible form, or are invisible. Prov. 4:20–22, margin. It is His Word that He sends to heal the afflicted. Ps. 107:20.

Remedies are always in place when people are sick, and are always perfectly consistent with fervent prayer for their recovery, even with the course that is set forth in the fifth chapter of James. But remember that they must be only the Lord's remedies. They must be remedies which are the embodiment of the living Word of God. They must not be things which contain death, and are themselves but the agencies of death. God heals by imparting life, not by giving death. "Men ought always to pray," but that does not mean that they should sit still and do nothing. We ought to pray for our daily bread; but the command to do that comes from the same source as the command that "if any would not work, neither should he eat." 2 Thess. 3:10. When we have done an honest day's work, and have received food as the reward, we are to thank God for the gift just as much as if the ravens had been sent to feed us while we sat by the brook. It is from His hands just the same. And so we are always to pray for the recovery of the sick, and at the same time to make use of every means that God has made known to us as serviceable. This does not include poisonous drugs, for they are not life-bearers, but death agents. And then if, after applying the means that God Himself indicated, the patient recovers, we are to thank the Lord just as heartily for the performance of a miracle of healing as if we had heard Him speak with an audible voice, and tell the disease to depart. The Lord is the Great Physician, and there is not a medical man in the world that cannot learn things from Him that will astonish him.

A Sign From the Lord

The Lord gave Hezekiah a sign by which he might know that he should recover. We notice by reading 2 Kings 20:8–10 that Hezekiah was very particular as to the sign. He did not want any doubt about it. So the shadow on the dial was made to go backward ten degrees. Wonderful! Yes; but no more so than the healing of Hezekiah. Nay, it was no more wonderful than is the daily going forward of the shadow. Everything is wonderful, for in everything the eternal power and Divinity of God are manifest. We have known professed Christian men who had the audacity to attempt to explain the miracle of the going backward of the shadow on the dial, as well as the standing still of the sun in the days of Joshua. Some people think that they are in duty bound to seem to know as much as the Lord; but all will at the last be obliged to admit that the Lord knows many things that we do not. We would not minimize the going backward of the shadow, or the standing still of the sun, but would magnify the miracles that are taking place every day, and which are unnoticed because of their frequency. The fact that the sun keeps its place in the heavens, and that all the heavenly bodies move in their courses so exactly that men who watch them closely can tell to a second when to expect them at any particular point, is a stupendous miracle. God placed them in the heavens "for signs," as well as "for seasons, and days, and years." Gen. 1:14. They are signs to all men that the power and mercy of the Lord are everlasting. They are signs of the faithfulness of God, which is established in the very heavens. When we see the shadow moving forward we may be as sure of the fulfillment of the Word of God to us as Hezekiah was when he saw it going backward. No word of God can fail, and every sunbeam is proof of it. God has not left Himself without witness, and we are not obliged to ask for something special in our case. All we have to do is to look round us.

CHAPTER 32

HEZEKIAH'S TRIBUTE OF THANKSGIVING

(Isa. 38:9–20, Lowth's Translation)

9. The writing of Hezekiah King of Judah, when he had been sick, and was recovered from his sickness:

10. I said, when my days were just going to be cut off, I shall pass through the gates of the grave; I am deprived of the residue of my years!

11. I said, I shall no more see Jehovah in the land of the living! I shall no longer behold man, with the inhabitants of the world!

12. My habitation is taken away, and is removed from me, like a shepherd's tent; my life is cut off, as by the weaver; He will sever me from the loom; in the course of the day Thou wilt finish my web.

13. I roared until the morning, like the lion; so did He break to pieces all my bones.

14. Like the swallow, like the crane did I twitter; I made a moaning like the dove. Mine eyes fail with looking upward; O Lord, contend Thou for me; be Thou my surety.

15. What shall I say? He hath given me a promise, and He hath performed it. Through the rest of my years will I reflect on this bitterness of my soul.

16. For this cause shall it be declared, O Jehovah, concerning Thee, that Thou hast revived my spirit; That thou hast restored my health, and prolonged my life.

17. Behold my anguish is changed into ease! Thou hast rescued my soul from perdition; yea, Thou hast cast behind Thy back all my sins.

18. Verily the grave shall not give thanks unto Thee; death shall not praise Thee! They that go down into the pit shall not await Thy truth;

19. The living, the living, he shall praise Thee, as I do this day; the father to the children shall make known Thy faithfulness.

20. Jehovah was present to save me; therefore will we sing our songs to the harp, all the days of our life, in the house of Jehovah.

In this writing we learn why it was that Hezekiah was so much troubled when he learned that he must die. It was because it did not mean an entrance into a larger life with greater possibilities, as some would have us believe. Death is not life, in any sense of the word. The message to Hezekiah was, "Thou shalt die, and not live." If death had meant life under far better conditions than are possible on this earth, then we may be sure that Hezekiah, who all his life had "walked before the Lord," would not have had any objection to it. But he knew better. When the word came to him, he said, "I am deprived of the residue of my years." It was not that he was going to live in another place, under somewhat changed circumstances, much as one will go to a distant country; – a man does not weep sore over that, even if the country be not quite so good as the one he is leaving; – Hezekiah wept because he was not going to live anywhere any more.

"I said, I shall not see the Lord, even the Lord, in the land of the living; I shall behold man no more with the inhabitants of the world." But this could not be if at death Hezekiah were going to be with the Lord. He had learned to see the Lord in His works and ways, but now this delight was to be cut off. He could no longer behold God or man. The same thought was expressed by David, when he had been delivered from death. He said, "I will walk before the Lord in the land of the living." Ps. 116:9. It is a fact that "God hath given to us eternal life," so that the life that we now live, if it be by faith, is but the beginning of that which we shall live in the world to come. The future life will be but a continuation of this, so that while we live, whether in this world or that which is to come, we may walk before the Lord. At this present time we may walk in the light of His countenance (Ps. 89:15–16), and in the new earth His servants "shall see His face" (Rev. 22:4); but "in death there is no remembrance" of the Lord (Ps. 6:5); only by the resurrection, at the coming of Christ, can the righteous dead "ever be with the Lord." 1 Thess. 4:16–17.

In verse 12 Lowth has it, "My habitation is taken away," while our common version has it, "Mine age is departed." The Revised Version has the same, with "habitation" in the margin as an alternative reading. The Hebrew allows both renderings, and both are in reality the same, since so long as a man lives he must live somewhere. When a man's life is taken away, his habitation is taken away; and if there is absolutely no place for him to live, it is because he has no life any more. Most vivid expressions are used to indicate the great change that death brings. "My life is cut off, as by the weaver; He will sever me from the loom; in the course of the day Thou wilt finish my web." Life is likened to a web in the loom, the threads of which are composed of moments; Hezekiah's web was about to be cut off from the loom incomplete. An end was to be made of him. This explains the reason of his great sadness at the thought of death. It does not, however, excuse Hezekiah's lack of resignation to the message of the Lord. Death is an enemy, and always hateful, and the fact that God Himself allows one of His servants to suffer it, does not in the least make it any more attractive; but the fact that the Lord Himself does allow His servants to die, and that even in death they do not suffer anything that He has not suffered, should make them resigned, and even happy, in the face of it. "The righteous hath hope in his death." Christ, who died, is alive for evermore, and has the keys of death and the grave, so that, although Satan has the power of death, he can hold no one except at the pleasure of the Lord. The grave can no more hold a child of God beyond God's will than it could hold Jesus after the third day. Therefore although the grave is indeed a hateful, terrible place, no one whose life is hid with Christ in God need fear it.

"Thou hast in love to my soul delivered it from the pit of corruption; for Thou hast cast all my sins behind Thy back." What kind of place is the grave? – It is "the pit of corruption." That is where people go at death. The patriarch Job said, "If I wait, the grave is mine house; I have made my bed in darkness. I have said to corruption, Thou art my father; to the worm, Thou art my mother, and my sister." Job. 17:13–14. The land of darkness, and the shadow of death, is "a land of darkness, as darkness itself; and of the shadow of death, without any order, and where the light is as darkness." Job 10:21–22. Yet the Christian, who knows the Lord, to whom the darkness and the light are both alike, may fear no evil, even in the valley of the shadow of death.

We must not think that Hezekiah's prayer for deliverance from the grave was wholly selfish. No; the reason why he wished to live, and not go into the grave, is thus told by him to the Lord, "For the grave cannot praise Thee, death cannot celebrate Thee; they that go down into the pit cannot hope for Thy truth." "The dead praise not the Lord, neither any that go down into silence." Ps. 115:17. The psalmist also said, "I cried to Thee, O Lord; and unto the Lord I made my supplication. What profit is there in my blood, when I go down to the pit? Shall the dust praise Thee? shall it declare Thy truth?" Ps. 30:8–9. Thus we see that it is not wrong to ask the Lord to keep us from the grave: much of the Psalms, which are given for our guide in the matter of prayer and praise, is composed of this very petition. Again we read, "Mine eye mourneth because of mine affliction; Lord, I have called daily upon Thee, I have stretched out my hands unto Thee? Wilt Thou show wonders unto the dead? shall the dead arise and praise Thee? Selah. Shall Thy loving kindness be declared in the grave? or Thy faithfulness in destruction? Shall Thy wonders be known in the dark? and Thy righteousness in the land of forgetfulness?" Ps. 88:9–12. From this we get the facts as to the nature of the grave, and the conditions there. Who that has ever looked into an open grave cannot appreciate the description?

"The living, the living he shall praise Thee, as I do this day." In this there is something more than a point of doctrine for us. Notice in all the scriptures that have been quoted, that the inability to praise the Lord in the grave is the reason why these faithful servants of the Lord wished to be delivered from it. The matter of praising the Lord makes all the real difference between death and life. The man who does not praise the Lord is as dead. Idols of silver and gold, the work of men's hands, which are in every respect the farthest removed from any likeness to the God that is in the heavens working all things after the counsel of His own will, are thus described: "They have mouths, but they speak not; eyes have they, but they see not; they have ears, but they hear not; noses have they, but they smell not; they have hands, but they handle not; feet have they, but they walk not; neither speak they through their throat. They that make them are like unto them; so is every one that trusteth in them." Ps. 115:3–8. That is to say, that every one who does not trust in the Lord is like a dead piece of metal. The man who sees nothing in the world for which to praise the Lord, does not see anything, for all His works praise Him (Ps. 145:10), and is the same as though he had no eyes. And he who does not speak to the praise of God is as though he had no mouth at all; and if his feet and hands do not move in the service of the Lord, then he is as though he had no life. "Dead in trespasses and sins." The same Psalm that tells about the deadness of idols and of those who trust in them, tells us that "the dead praise not the Lord." See a man that does not praise the Lord; – he is dead, and needs to be made alive. As surely as a man is alive he will praise the Lord. "Let everything that hath breath praise the Lord." Ps. 150:6.

One thing more must not be overlooked in reading this tribute of thanksgiving. Hezekiah said to the Lord, "Thou hast in love to my soul delivered it from the pit of corruption; for Thou hast cast all my sins behind Thy back." Sin and death are inseparable. "By one man sin entered into the world, and death by sin; and so death passed upon all men, for that all have sinned." Rom. 5:12. God redeems our life from destruction, and heals all our diseases, because it is He that forgives all our iniquities. Ps. 103:3–4. In the directions for prayer for the sick, given by the Apostle James it is said that "the prayer of faith shall save the sick, and the Lord shall raise him up; and if he have committed sins, they shall be forgiven him." James 5:15. Not that we are to understand by this that everybody who dies is a sinner: far from it; "the righteous is taken away from the evil to come" (Isa. 57:1), and a blessing is pronounced upon those who die in the Lord. Rev. 14:13. Yet if it were not for sin, there would be no death. We have inherited mortal bodies, and they are allowed to go into the grave; but it is the power by which sins are forgiven, and the very forgiveness itself, that insures our resurrection from the dead. There will be a people, however, in the last days, just before the unveiled revelation of the glory of Christ in the heavens, who will represent Christ so completely that death will have no power over them, and they will be translated to heaven without seeing death. "We shall not all sleep, but we shall all be changed." 1 Cor. 15:51. Therefore "Blessed is the man whose transgression is forgiven, whose sin is covered. Blessed is the man unto whom the Lord imputeth not iniquity, and in whose spirit there is no guile."

CHAPTER 33

GOING TO BABYLON

(Isa. 39, Lowth's Translation)

At that time Merodach Baladan, the son of Baladan king of Babylon, sent letters, and ambassadors, and a present to Hezekiah; for he had heard that he had been sick, and was recovered. And Hezekiah was rejoiced at their arrival; and he showed them his magazines, the silver, and the gold, and the spices, and the precious ointment, and his whole arsenal, and all that was contained in his treasures; there was nothing in his house, and in all his dominion, that Hezekiah did not show them.

And Isaiah the prophet came unto King Hezekiah, and said unto him: What say these men? and from whence came they unto thee? And Hezekiah said: They are come to me from a distant country, from Babylon. And he said: What have they seen in thy house? And Hezekiah said: They have seen everything in my house: there is nothing in my treasures, which I have not shown them. And Isaiah said unto Hezekiah: Hear thou the word of Jehovah God of hosts. Behold, the day shall come, when all that is in thy house, and that thy fathers have treasured up unto this day, shall be carried away to Babylon; there shall not anything be left, saith Jehovah. And of thy sons which shall issue from thee, which thou shalt beget, shall they take; and they shall be eunuchs in the palace of the king of Babylon. And Hezekiah said unto Isaiah: Gracious is the word of Jehovah, which thou hast delivered! For, added he, there shall be peace, according to His faithful promise, in my days.

And Hezekiah had exceeding much riches and honour; and he made himself treasuries for silver, and for gold, and for precious stones, and for spices, and for shields, and for all manner of pleasant jewels; storehouses also for the increase of corn, and wine, and oil; and stalls for all manner of beasts, and

cotes for flocks. **Moreover he provided him cities, and possessions of flocks and herds in abundance; for God had given him
substance very much. This same Hezekiah also stopped the
upper watercourse of Gihon, and brought it straight down to
the west side of the city of David. And Hezekiah prospered in all
his works. Howbeit in the business of the ambassadors of the
princes of Babylon, who sent unto him to enquire of the wonder
that was done in the land, God left him, to try him, that he might
know all that was in his heart. 2 Chron. 32:27–31.**

Exhibitions of Self

This lesson is very short, and very simple, yet it is one of the most
important in the whole Bible. Everybody stands in need of it. The
tendency to "show off" seems to be inherent in human nature, and it
is most assiduously cultivated. The baby in its mother's arms must
exhibit its infantile attainments to every visitor, besides a hundred
times a day to its admiring friends, until the child as soon as it begins
to think, very naturally concludes that whatever he does must be of
exceptional merit and interest, simply because it is he that does it. At
home he must show off his accomplishments, in order that the
parents may be complimented on having so wonderful a child. At
school he must be put on exhibition for the benefit of the school and
the teacher; and in Sabbath School he is used for the same purpose.
No wonder that so many continue through life to exhibit themselves
on their own account.

The good housewife gratifies her pride, and awakens the envy of
her neighbors, by showing them all her stores of household goods;
and the merchant and the farmer do the same. It is true that one may
very often show another some of his possessions, in order to help
that other one, – to give him some ideas as to how to get something
for himself, or simply to bring some freshness and change into the
life of one whose range is very limited. That is all right; but every
one who reads this will know that very often there is in the exhibition of one's attainments or possession merely the gratification of
pride, and the desire to receive compliments, to excite astonishment, and to be the subject of conversation.

See My Zeal for the Lord

It is this same spirit that leads religious societies and churches to publish many of the statistics that are continually being given to the world. So much of a business has this become that in many instances men are kept constantly employed to make note of every step of progress, or of supposed progress, so that no time may be lost on any occasion in impressing visitors with the amount of work done, the liberality of the donations, and the vast sums expended in buildings, etc. All this is done of course "for the good of the cause," in forgetfulness of the fact that since even "a man's life consisteth not in the abundance of the things which he possesseth" (Luke 12:15), much less does the cause of God consist in material wealth. It is not what a man *has*, but what he *is*, that God looks at; even so progress in the Lord's work is not indicated by numbers of professed converts, by large amounts of money contributed, or by huge piles of buildings in which church work is done, but in soul-growth, which can be measured by the Lord alone. Its praise is not of men, but of God. None of us are aware of how much emulation there is in our work for the Lord. We may not always say in so many words, with Jehu, "Come with me, and see my zeal for the Lord" (2 Kings 10:16), but the feeling is present, nevertheless. Where there are hundreds who are willing to engage in even the most disagreeable work, provided it comes before the eyes of the public, there are very few who are willing to work for the Lord unknown, except by Him, and with none to recognize and applaud. In fact, we must all plead guilty to more or less selfishness in our work for the Master, who is unselfishness itself.

The Babylonish Spirit

Now all this is evidence that God's people have not yet got free from Babylon. It was at least a striking coincidence that it was to the ambassadors from Babylon that Hezekiah made this exhibition of his wealth and grandeur; for that was the very spirit of Babylon. Nebuchadnezzar had received from the Lord "a kingdom, power, and strength, and glory." Dan. 2:37. It was He who made Babylon "the glory of kingdoms, the beauty of the Chaldess' excellency." Isa. 13:19. But he did not in humility of heart give God the glory, but as he walked in his palace he said, "Is not this great Babylon, that I have built for the house of the kingdom by the might of my power, and for the honour of my majesty?" Dan. 4:29–30. This is the spirit of Babylon, derived from Lucifer, the real king of Babylon, who thought only of exalting himself, and gave not God the glory. Isa. 14:13–14. Since the possessor of the treasures that were shown to the messengers from Babylon had the Babylonish spirit, it was very fitting that they should be taken to Babylon. They belonged in Babylon as much as in Jerusalem. They were in reality Babylonish possessions, although gathered by the kings of Israel. But Hezekiah did not know this at the time.

A Lost Opportunity

What a wonderful opportunity Hezekiah had to teach those Babylonian ambassadors the truth of God. They had heard that he had been sick, and had recovered, and they knew of the great wonder in the heavens, the sign of God's healing power, and they came to enquire about it and at the same time congratulate Hezekiah. What better preparation of the way could anyone ask than that to make known the saving power of God? It was for that very purpose that God had put it into their hearts to come. But instead of improving the time by telling them of the God that made the heavens and the earth, and making Him known as the sole Healer of the souls and bodies of men, Hezekiah magnified himself in their eyes, by showing them his own treasures. What a mistake he made!

But we must not condemn Hezekiah; our part is simply to note the facts, that we may see ourselves in his picture. Do not get the idea that there was conscious self-exaltation in Hezekiah's act. The treasures were not his own personal property, but belonged to the kingdom. He had not gathered them all himself, but they had been accumulated through many prosperous reigns. It was not his personal wealth that he was showing to the ambassadors from Babylon, but he was impressing them with the greatness of the Jewish kingdom, to the throne of which he had been called. In this exhibition of the royal treasures, Hezekiah was trying to advance the cause of God among the heathen; for "when Israel went out of

Egypt, the house of Jacob from a people of strange language, Judah was His sanctuary, and Israel His dominion." Ps. 114:1–2. We may be sure that Hezekiah thought he was impressing those heathen ambassadors with a sense of the greatness of God's cause and people, and preparing the way for the Babylonian people to be favourably impressed with the truth. He did not know that he was preparing the way for the captivity of Israel.

Robbing God of the Glory

Hezekiah's course has been repeated thousands of times to this day. Christians who would not boast of their own possessions, take great pride in telling what "our church" has done, how much it has contributed, and how great facilities it has for carrying on the work of the Lord. They forget that the only impression that can possibly be made on the world is that the men who have been engaged in this work are shrewd business men; for the world is full of instances of poor boys who have amassed great property, without any thought of Christianity. It is true that it is God who gives men the power to get wealth; but the possession of property is not by any means an evidence that God is pleased with a person or a society, or that He has any special connection with them over other people. If it were, then it would show that God's favour is specially with the world, for more property is in the hands of the world than in the church. Babylon had greater riches than Jerusalem had, so that while the ambassadors might be impressed with the progress of the Israelites, they really could only think that their gods were greater than the God of the Jews. But there were none of their gods that could heal diseases or forgive sins, and in telling of that, Hezekiah might have led the proud heathen to worship in spirit and in truth.

But why should God say that for this error on the part of Hezekiah all the people and treasures of Israel should be taken to Babylon? Ah, there was nothing arbitrary in this; it was a necessity, and the natural consequence of the king's act. God had sent the ambassadors to Jerusalem to learn the truth, and since they did not get it, He had to send His people to Babylon to teach it to them there. This was the necessary consequence of Hezekiah's act. That the cupidity of the ambassadors should be aroused at the sight of the treasures, was a most natural thing. When the king of Babylon afterwards took it into his head to besiege Jerusalem, he knew what he was after. The treasurers in which Hezekiah had taken so much pride, "honest pride," rejoicing to think that he was connected with so great a people, were scattered, and the treasure-houses destroyed, but the truth of God remained the same. That in which men can boast will all pass away, and God will make it plain to His own people as well as to the whole world, that His truth does not depend upon, and cannot be measured by, anything that men can make or gather together. It is not by might nor by power, but by the Spirit of God, that His work is to be accomplished, and therefore no display of wealth or power, but only the manifestation of the Holy Spirit, can draw men to Him and His truth.

Hezekiah was a good man, one who sincerely loved the Lord. God was with him, and prospered him. God loved him, and He loved him none the less when he fell into the error concerning the visit of the ambassadors. But God left him to himself for a while, "that he might know what was in his heart." And it was written for our learning, that we might know what is in our hearts; for the hearts of all men are alike, and what is in one is in all. "The heart is deceitful above all things, and desperately wicked; who can know it?" Jer. 17:9. Pride of every kind is in the hearts of all men; when they turn to the Lord, then it is apt to exhibit itself in other forms. God has left this case on record for us, that we, knowing that it is in our hearts, may allow Him to cleanse us from it. May He deliver us all from Babylon and the Babylonish spirit, and fill us with His own Spirit, the Spirit of meekness.

CHAPTER 34

THE LAST LOUD GOSPEL CRY

(Isaiah 40:1–11)

1. Comfort ye, comfort ye My people, saith your God;

2. Speak ye to the heart of Jerusalem, and cry unto her, that her warfare is accomplished, that her iniquity is pardoned; for she hath received at the Lord's hand double for all her sins.

3. A voice crieth: In the wilderness prepare ye the way of Jehovah! Make straight in the desert a highway for our God!

4. Every valley shall be exalted, and every mountain and hill shall be made low; and the crooked shall be made straight, and the rough places a smooth plain;

5. And the glory of Jehovah shall be revealed; and all flesh shall see together the salvation of our God; for the mouth of Jehovah hath spoken it.

6. A voice sayeth, Cry! and I said, What shall I cry? All flesh is grass, and all its glory like the flower of the field;

7. The grass withereth, the flower fadeth, because the breath of Jehovah bloweth upon it; surely the people is grass.

8. The grass withereth, the flower fadeth; but the Word of our God shall stand for ever.

9. Get thee up upon a high mountain, O thou that tellest glad tidings to Sion. Exalt thy voice with strength, O thou that bringest glad tidings to Jerusalem. Lift it up; be not afraid; say to the cities of Judah, Behold your God!

10. Behold, the Lord Jehovah shall come as a Mighty One, and His arm shall prevail for Him. Behold, His reward is with Him, and His work before Him.

11. Like a shepherd shall He feed His flock; in His arm shall He gather up the lambs, and He shall bear them in His bosom; the nursing ewes shall He gently lead.

In these first eleven verses of the fortieth chapter of Isaiah we have not followed any one translation, but have combined several, in order to present the best and most vivid rendering; for the passage is a very vivid one. The student can compare the variations with his own Bible. Nothing is given that is not strictly literal.

Although we have printed eleven verses at this time, we shall not try to cover them in this lesson. All we propose to do in this lesson is to give an outline, so that we may be perfectly sure of the nature of the message, and the time to which it applies, and may know to whom it is addressed, and who is to give it. We therefore request all who may be using these lessons in Sabbath Schools to confine themselves at this time to these things; for the details of the verses will be considered in subsequent lessons.

Not a single reader of the Bible will have any difficulty in connecting this message with the work of John the Baptist, for the connection is plainly made in the Bible. John came preaching "the baptism of repentance for the remission of sins; as it is written in the book of the words of Esaias the prophet, saying, The voice of one crying in the wilderness, Prepare ye the way of the Lord, make His paths straight. Every valley shall be filled, and every mountain and hill shall be brought low; and the crooked shall be made straight, and the rough ways shall be made smooth; and all flesh shall see the salvation of God." Luke 3:3–6. Our lesson therefore has direct reference to the work of John the Baptist.

What was the work committed to him? – To prepare the way of the Lord. "Many of the children of Israel shall he turn to the Lord their God. And he shall go before Him in the spirit and power of Elias, to turn the hearts of the fathers to the children, and the disobedient to the wisdom of the just; to make ready a people prepared for the Lord." Luke 1:16–17. Thus spoke the angel Gabriel. John's father, filled with the Holy Ghost, spoke these words to him. "Thou child shalt be called the prophet of the Highest; for thou shalt go before the face of the Lord to prepare His ways; to give knowledge of salvation unto His people by the remission of their sins, through the tender mercy of our God; whereby the dayspring from on high hath visited us, to give light to them that sit in darkness and in the shadow of death, to guide our feet into the way of peace." Luke 1:76–79.

If anything were needed to convince any reader that we have the Gospel in Isaiah, we have it here. It is that Gospel which preaches the baptism of repentance for the remission of sins, and makes known salvation through this remission; it brings men from the darkness of death to the light of life, guides their feet in the way of peace and righteousness, and prepares them for the coming of the Lord. And that is just the Gospel for this time.

Then it would seem as though the work of John the Baptist did not end with his death. Most certainly it did not; and the scripture before us teaches us that it did not. Indeed, it was only begun when he died. Most people have obtained the idea that John's work was simply to prepare the way for and announce the coming of Jesus as a Preacher and Teacher in Galilee and Judea; but it was much more than this. The same portion of scriptures which tells us of his work, to prepare the way of the Lord, says, "Behold, the Lord God will come with strong hand, and His arm shall rule for Him: behold, His reward is with Him, and His work before Him." Now compare this with Rev. 22:12, where Christ says, "Behold I come quickly; and My reward is with Me, to give every man according as his work shall be," and we cannot fail to see that the work of John the Baptist reaches to the second coming of Christ in glory; "for the Son of man shall come in the glory of His Father with His angels; and then shall He reward every man according to his works." Matt. 16:27.

Notice that this message is to be given with a loud voice. The voice that cries is to be lifted up with strength, and the crier is to get up upon a high mountain, in order that the sound may reach to the furthest possible extent. Now read Rev. 14:6–7: "And I saw another angel fly in the midst of heaven, having the everlasting Gospel to preach unto them that dwell on the earth, and to every nation and kindred, and tongue, and people, saying with a loud voice, Fear God, and give glory to Him; for the hour of His judgment is come; and worship Him that made heaven, and earth, and the sea, and the fountains of waters." This message, as might be expected from its nature, is followed by the coming of the Son of man in the clouds of heaven to reap the harvest of the earth, which is the end of the world. Rev. 14:14–16; Matt. 13:39.

Every message of importance must be earnestly proclaimed. One cries with a loud voice in order to make many people hear; and this message preparing the way for the coming of the Lord is to be proclaimed so extensively that all the world shall hear. The Gospel of the kingdom is "for all people," and is to be "preached in all the world, for a witness unto all nations; and then shall the end come." Matt. 24:14; Luke 2:10. But the nearer one comes to the end, the louder must the message be proclaimed. If you saw a man approaching a precipice, you would cry out, to warn him of his danger. If he did not pay any attention, you would cry louder; and the nearer he approached, unconscious of his danger, the louder you would cry. Even so the nearer we come to the end of the world, which will be the destruction of those who are not looking for it, the louder and more clear must the Gospel message announcing it ring forth. So the scripture which we are studying has a more direct application to the people of this time than to any other people that ever lived. It is emphatically present truth.

Who shall give this message? – "Let him that heareth say, Come!" Rev. 22:17. Remember that John the Baptist was but a voice. "The Word of God came unto John the son of Zacharias in the wilderness." Luke 3:2. John was called "the prophet of the Highest." A prophet is one who speaks for another. Compare Ex. 4:14–16 and 7:1. A prophet of God is therefore the mouthpiece of God, proclaiming the Word of God. Every one to whom the Word of the Lord comes is to sound it forth, that people may be saved from their sins, and be ready for the second coming of Christ.

From this it follows that the last message of the Gospel is pre-eminently a prophetic message. It is given by the power of the Spirit of God, which is the Spirit of prophecy. God's people are "a kingdom of priests," and the holy wish for them is that all the Lord's people might be prophets, and that "the Lord would put His Spirit upon them." Num. 11:26–29. Those who proclaim the Gospel and the coming of the Lord, must do so with authority as the oracles of God.

221

But there must be the most perfect unity, and there will be when the true message is given; for it is nothing but the unchangeable Word of God that is to be given. The voice is God's; the people furnish only the mouth; so that although there be tens of thousands of mouths, only one voice is heard. In the days of the coming of the Lord the admonition of the Apostle Paul will be perfectly heeded: "Now I beseech you, brethren, by the name of our Lord Jesus Christ, that ye all speak the same thing, and that there be no divisions among you; but that ye be perfectly joined together in the same mind and in the same judgment." 1 Cor. 1:10. "Thy watchmen shall lift up the voice; with the voice together shall they sing; for they shall see eye to eye, when the Lord shall bring again Zion." Isa. 52:8.

Let us now sum up what we have learned from this first part of the fortieth chapter of Isaiah. 1. It is the message of John the Baptist. 2. It is the Gospel of the kingdom, the Gospel of salvation. 3. It prepares the way for the coming of the Lord, even for His coming in glory, that is, to the end of the world. 4. This part of the scripture has special reference to the last days, because then the imminence of the coming of the Lord makes a loud cry especially imperative. 5. It consists simply of the preaching of the Word of God. 6. It is to be proclaimed by every one who hears it, if he will. 7. There are many mouths concerned in the proclamation, but only one voice. 8. The Spirit of prophecy is in it, and it goes with power.

Finally, let it be noted that the whole of the remaining portion of the book of Isaiah is but the continuation of this message. Therefore as we proceed in our study let us not forget the setting of any portion of the text. There is no part of Scripture more important at this time than this book, and none that can more thoroughly furnish the student to good works, and fit him for the presence of the King in His beauty.

CHAPTER 35

THE COMFORT OF THE GOSPEL

Isa. 40:1–2: "Comfort ye, comfort ye My people, saith your God. Speak ye comfortably to Jerusalem, and cry unto her, that her warfare is accomplished, that her iniquity is pardoned; for she hath received at the Lord's hand double for all her sins."

I John 2:1–2, R.V., margin: "My little children, these things I write unto you, that ye may not sin. And if any man sin, we have a Comforter with the Father, Jesus Christ the Righteous: and He is the propitiation for our sins; and not for ours only, but also for the sins of the whole world."

John 14:16–18: "I will pray the Father, and He shall give you another Comforter, that He may abide with you for ever; even the Spirit of truth; whom the world cannot receive, because it seeth Him not, neither knoweth Him; but ye know Him; for He dwelleth with you, and shall be in you. I will not leave you comfortless; I will come to you."

John 14:26: "The Comforter, which is the Holy Ghost, whom the Father will send in my name, He shall teach you all things, and bring all things to your remembrance, whatsoever I have said unto you."

John 16:7–8: "It is expedient for you that I go away; for if I go not away, the Comforter will not come unto you; but if I depart, I will send Him unto you. And when He is come, He will reprove the world of sin, and of righteousness, and of Judgment."

2 Cor. 1:3–5: "Blessed be the God and Father of our Lord Jesus Christ, the Father of mercies and God of all comfort; who comforteth us in all our affliction, that we may be able to comfort them that are in any affliction, through the comfort wherewith we ourselves are comforted of God. For as the

sufferings of Christ abound unto us, even so our comfort also aboundeth through Christ."

WARFARE ENDED

John 16:33: "These things I have spoken unto you, that in Me ye might have peace. In the world ye shall have tribulation; but be of good cheer: I have overcome the world."

Eph. 6:11–13: "Put on the whole armour of God, that ye may be able to stand against the wiles of the devil. For we wrestle not against flesh and blood, but against principalities, against powers, against the rulers of the darkness of this world, against wicked spirits in heavenly places. Wherefore take unto you the whole armour of God, that ye may be able to withstand in the evil day, and having done all, to stand."

Heb. 2:14: "Forasmuch then as the children are partakers of flesh and blood, He also Himself likewise took part of the same; that through death He might destroy him that had the power of death, that is, the devil."

Col. 2:15, margin: "And having spoiled principalities and powers, He made a show of them openly, triumphing over them in Himself."

1 Peter 4:1: "Forasmuch then as Christ hath suffered for us in the flesh, arm yourselves likewise with the same mind; for he that hath suffered in the flesh hath ceased from sin."

John 14:27: "Peace I leave with you, My peace I give unto you; not as the world giveth, give I unto you."

1 John 5:4, R.V.: "Whatsoever is begotten of God overcometh the world; and this is the victory that hath overcome the world, even our faith."

DOUBLE FOR SIN

Heb. 1:3: "God ... hath in these last days spoken unto us by His Son ... who ... when He had by Himself purged our sins, sat down on the right hand of the Majesty on high."

Rom. 5:20: "Where sin abounded, grace did much more abound."

John 1:16: "And of His fullness have all we received, and grace for grace."

Isa. 55:7, margin: "Our God ... will multiply to pardon."

Speaking to the Heart

Recall the marginal rendering of the second verse, as given in the study last week, which is literal: "Speak ye to the heart of Jerusalem." When God speaks words of comfort to His people He speaks to the heart. A great many people have an abundance of words at their command, which they can pour into the ears of the afflicted, but which do not really comfort, although they may all be true, and very appropriate to the occasion. Only those who have shared the same experience as the sufferer can speak to the heart; and they may do this without many words.

The Lord's People

Doubtless some one will say, "But I am not one of the Lord's people, and therefore His words of comfort are not addressed to me." Do not allow the devil to cheat you out of your comfort in that way. It may be that you have not acknowledged the Lord, but He has never cast you off; He claims you as His own. The prodigal son is a son nevertheless, no matter how far away he has wandered. The whole of the book of Isaiah shows that it is not merely the good people whom God claims as His own. Read the first chapter, and that alone is sufficient to show that the comfort here offered is for those who are "laden with iniquity."

Comfort for All

"Blessed are they that mourn; for they shall be comforted." Matt. 5:4. There is no exception. Christ does not specify a certain class, and say that they that mourn in a certain way, or for certain things, shall be comforted. His comfort is for all that mourn. Christ was anointed with the Holy Ghost, and sent "to comfort *all* that mourn." Isa. 61:1–2. Doubtless the words from the talk on the mount are generally applied to those who mourn departed friends. Well, they apply there, but they go deeper. Death and pain are but the consequence of sin. It is sin that has caused all the sorrow and mourning in the earth. Therefore the Lord sends comfort to all who mourn because of sin, that is, to all whom sin has in any way caused to mourn. His comfort is as boundless as His life and His love.

Who is the Comforter?

God is the "God of all comfort," and "the only begotten Son, which is in the bosom of the Father, He hath declared Him." John 1:18. So Christ is the Comforter which we have with the Father. Note the close connection of the statement that He is the Comforter with the one that "He is the propitiation for our sins," and for those of the whole world. It is the comfort of pardon, and freedom from the bondage of sin, that He gives. He comforts us by giving us Himself.

The Holy Spirit is Christ's Representative. He is Christ present in the flesh of all men, and not simply in the person of Jesus of Nazareth, He comes in the name of Christ; not merely taking His name, but revealing the living Christ. Therefore He is another Comforter. His comfort is the comfort of Christ. "The comfort of the Holy Ghost" has the effect to multiply believers. Acts 9:31. This is because the Holy Ghost teaches all things that pertain to Christ.

The Comfort of Reproof

Comfort does not always consist merely of smooth words. The surgeon has sometimes to use a knife, and for a time add to the pain, before he can give a sufferer complete relief. So when the Holy Ghost comes to us, He reproves us of sin the first thing. He comes with conviction. In this way He often causes pain where there was before only numbness and insensibility. Shall we complain of this?

Shall we say that we do not wish any such comfort? By no means. Is it not a good thing to rouse the man who is fast becoming insensible through cold? When a man is freezing to death he falls into a condition of insensibility to the cold. He feels as though he were falling into a delicious sleep. But it is the sleep of death. When the rescuer finds him, and begins to restore him to life, he experiences great pain. It may be that he will wildly say that it would have been far better to leave him in his former painless condition; but when he comes to himself, and understand what has been done, he will for ever thank the one who brought him to life at the cost of much suffering. Just as much comfort as there is in life, so much comfort was the rescuer giving the frozen man when he was causing him the pain of experiencing his condition.

Let us never forget, therefore, that the Holy Spirit is always the Comforter. In convicting of sin, He is imparting comfort. If the way of life leads by the cross, then there is just as much comfort in the cross as there is in the life that is gained by it. We must never think that God is angry with us because He makes us know how greatly we have sinned. He is not doing it to taunt us, but to comfort us.

Conviction Not Condemnation

Remember that conviction does not mean condemnation. This is true even in an earthly court. A man may stand convicted of a crime, and still not be under sentence. But this is but a feeble illustration; for we are all condemned already. We are "born under the law." Therefore the conviction of the sin – the bringing home to our consciences the fact that we are sinners – does not make matters any worse than they were. That conviction is but the first and the necessary step towards our freedom from the sin; for we must know and acknowledge the sin before we will accept the remedy for it.

Convicted by the Revelation of Righteousness

It is by the revelation of the righteousness of God, that the Holy Spirit convicts of sin. "By the law is the knowledge of sin." Rom. 3:20. But the law is not sin; on the contrary, it is "holy, and just, and good." Rom. 7:7, 12. No man could ever become convicted of sin by looking at sin. It is by looking at the righteousness of God that we may become conscious of the fact that we are sinners. He who knows nothing of any better state than the one he is in, never desires anything better. Dissatisfaction with one's condition comes only with the knowledge of something better. God produces a feeling of dissatisfaction with our sinful condition, by revealing to us His own perfect righteousness.

No Condemnation From God

This is a most wonderful and blessed thing. That which causes the conviction is that which saves. Therefore we need not be condemned at all. Neither need we go a long time mourning under conviction of sins. If we will but grasp God's way of working, we shall in the very moment of conviction find the comfort of pardon. The righteousness that is revealed for the purpose of taking away the sin, is that which makes it known to us; therefore if we will but believe God's word our suffering for sin may be but as the lightning's flash; the moment of the revelation of sin may be its departure. To be sure the Spirit abides with us as the continual reprover of sin; but since He does this by the revelation of the righteousness of God, we may be in a state of continual justification, although continually conscious of the fact that we are sinners. "There is therefore now no condemnation to them which are in Christ Jesus." Rom. 8:1. "It is God that justifieth. Who is he that comdemneth?" Rom. 8:33–34. Every soul that is condemned is self-condemned; and even wherein our heart condemns us, we may have confidence, and may assure our hearts before Him, because God is greater than our hearts, and knoweth all things, and by His knowledge He justifies. 1 John 3:19–21, R.V.; Isa. 53:11.

"Tribulation worketh patience; and patience, experience." Rom. 5:3–4. Patience means suffering, endurance. No man has patience unless he has something to suffer, for without suffering there is no need of patience. The word is from the Latin word that means, to bear, to suffer. Therefore the possession of patience necessarily imposes suffering. It is not suffering that makes people impatient; it is the lack of faith that does that; suffering works patience, when our faith in Christ makes us suffer with Him.

The Object of Comfort

Patience works experience. If we wish experience, we must not shun suffering, nor refuse to bear burdens. No matter how great the tribulation, God has comfort enough to enable us to endure it. He comforts us in all our affliction and tribulation. Do not forget this; His comfort is inexhaustible. "My grace is sufficient for thee." And why does He comfort us? – In order that we may be able to comfort those who are in any sort of tribulation with the comfort wherewith we ourselves are comforted of God. We are to accept God's comfort, and pass it along. God thus makes us sharers in His own work. The Holy Spirit takes us into copartnership, as it were. He makes us comforters.

Rejecting Comfort

Nobody can give to another that which he himself does not possess. We cannot comfort another unless we have been comforted. And if we never have any tribulation, then we have no need of comfort. There are burdens and tribulations enough in this world for everybody, and we do not need to seek them; but the fault with us is that we often refuse to bear those that naturally and legitimately fall to us; and thus we refuse the comfort that God would bestow upon us. But when we reject the comfort of the Holy Ghost, we reject the possibility of comforting others. Thus we see that by refusing to bear burdens, and by refusing to face tribulation, we are simply refusing to be fitted for the work of helping those who are in trouble. What would be thought of a man who should see people in great distress, perishing before his eyes, and should have the means wherewith to help them, but should turn away, saying, "It is none of my business; I don't care; I shall not lift a finger to help them?" We can scarcely conceive of so heartless a man; and yet that is what we virtually say whenever we refuse to bear some burden that falls to our lot. We are saying, "I do not wish to be a helper of the poor and needy; I do not care to comfort those that mourn."

Invincible Armour

God comforts us by telling us that our warfare is accomplished. We are enjoined to "fight the good fight of faith;" but we do so by laying hold on eternal life. 1 Tim. 6:12. We are to fight only in the armour of God, which is Christ Himself; and He has overcome the world. Note the various pieces of armour. We are to have our loins girt about with truth; and Christ is the truth. John 14:6. Next comes the breastplate of righteousness; and Christ is made unto us righteousness. 1 Cor. 1:30. Our feet are to be shod with the preparation of the Gospel of peace; and Christ is our peace. Eph. 2:14. Most important of all is the shield of faith. Now "faith cometh by hearing, and hearing by the word of God;" and Christ is the Word. It is by the faith of Christ that we are saved. Then we must have the helmet of salvation; and God in Christ is become our salvation. Isa. 12:2. Jesus Christ is the Saviour. "And the sword of the Spirit, which is the Word of God." Christ is the Word. So we see that to put on the whole armour of God is but to put on Christ. That armour has been tested in the fiercest fight, and has been proved invincible.

We have to fight with principalities and powers and wicked spirits; but Christ has "spoiled principalities and powers," and has led them openly in His triumphant procession. He triumphed over them in Himself. He is the Conqueror. He has won the victory. Therefore the foe with whom we wage our warfare is already defeated. What is it then but that our warfare is accomplished? We have but to share in the victory already gained.

We are promised tribulation in this world, but in the midst of it we may be of good cheer. What we have already learned as to the use of tribulation should be enough to make us cheerful; but here we have additional reason: "I have overcome the world." We are in danger of forgetting that all that Jesus did and suffered was for us. He did not need to come to this earth on His own account. It was our sins that He bore, our battle that He fought. Therefore the victory that hath overcome the world is the faith that lays hold of Jesus Christ. He is our peace, because He is our victory. "Thine, O Lord, is the greatest, and the power, and the glory, and the victory, and the majesty." 1 Chron. 29:11.

Because Christ is our peace, in Him we have peace. But peace means a victory won. The fact that in Christ we have peace, shows that the warfare is accomplished. When we fight in the strength of Christ, the battle is won before it is begun. Read the twentieth chapter of 2 Chronicles. See how Israel gained the victory by faith. They began to sing a song of victory, and, lo, the battle was won. There is therefore no need of ever being defeated. Who would run from a defeated foe? Moreover, Christ has disarmed the principalities and powers; for that is the meaning of the statement that He "spoiled them." In some versions it is so rendered. Surely there is no excuse for defeat, when we have invincible armour, and the foe has none at all. Is not this comfort enough for anybody in any tribulation whatsoever?

Our Sins Conquered

Remember that it is through our own sinful disposition that the devil works, and therefore it is our own sins, our sinful nature, that we have to contend with; and it is this that has been overcome. Do you doubt this? Then tell me whose sins it was that Jesus bore. With whose sinful nature did He contend? Was it with His own? Did He have sins of His own, that He must overcome? "Ye know that He was manifested to take away our sins; and in Him is no sin." 1 John 3:5. All that He suffered was altogether for our sakes. It was our sins that He bore, our sinful nature that He took upon Himself. Therefore the victory that He gained was gained over our own personal sins, our own peculiar besetments. So whenever we are tempted by our own lusts, and enticed, we have only to remember that that particular sin has been overcome. What then? – Why, we have only to give thanks to God, who "giveth us the victory through our Lord Jesus Christ." 1 Cor. 15:57. What glorious comfort the Lord gives us!

The Double

"But what about the *double* that we are to receive?" How many people have been troubled over that, and in their trouble they have consulted doctors who did not heal their hurt even slightly. Some translators have even gone to the length of inserting the word "punishment" in the passage. It is not there, and nobody has any right to put it there, or to think of it as being there. Poor souls stand appalled at the thought that they must suffer punishment equal to double the amount of their sins, and of course they see no hope of escape. Strange comfort that! Can anybody extract any comfort from the thought that they are to receive double punishment for their sins? Certainly not. But this is a message of comfort, and therefore there can be in it no such thought.

Even if it were punishment that is referred to, bear in mind that the text does not say that we are to receive double. A good deal is lost by a too hasty reading of the Word. "She *hath received* of the

Lord's hand double for all her sins." Suppose it is punishment; we are alive, and the subjects of the mercy of God; therefore if we have already received double punishment for our sins, we have abundant cause for rejoicing. Surely that is enough, and we are entitled to go free.

There is in this the key to the mystery. God has made to light on Him the iniquity of us all. "He hath borne our griefs, and carried our sorrows; yet we did esteem Him stricken, smitten of God, and afflicted. But He was wounded for our transgressions, He was bruised for our iniquities; the chastisement of our peace was upon Him; and with His stripes we are healed." Isa. 53:4–6. Christ has suffered in His own body all that any unrepentant sinner will ever have to suffer; therefore there is no need that any sinner should suffer for sin. If we but accept the sacrifice of Christ, that is, accept the person of Christ in our own lives, we are freed from all the consequences of sin. We are "dead to the law by the body of Christ." We are counted as having already received our punishment, and therefore are free.

Multiplied Pardon

Thus it is that in Christ grace and peace are multiplied to us. And it is the grace of God that bringeth salvation; therefore we have received of the Lord's hand double salvation. Grace abounds over all sin. God is not niggardly. He gives "good measure, pressed down, and shaken together, and running over." He has enough, and to spare, and of His fullness have all we received. Let us then accept it, and rejoice in the Lord.

That this is not in the least a straining of the text, is provided by the text itself. "Her iniquity is pardoned." Of whom is this spoken? Of a people "laden with iniquity." Has God already pardoned my sins? Certain He has; He says so; can you not believe Him? You never heard of such a thing? Well, then hear it now, and rejoice as you never did before. Let me recall to your mind something that you surely have heard at some time in your life. It has come into your own experience. You have, willfully or otherwise, committed a wrong against somebody. Afterwards you have gone and confessed it, begging pardon, and have been stopped before you could finish your confession, with the words, "Don't mention it; it was forgiven long ago." Perhaps you have yourself used just such language, and have spoken from the fullness of your heart. If you have, then you know the free pardon of God, for it was only His love in your heart that could have made you do so. Can you not admit that God is better than any man, even though that man be a saint? If a man can refuse to hold a grudge, cannot God do the same? Is it so strange a thing that the God who is love should forgive our sins even before we ask forgiveness, and should be longing for us to come and accept the reconciliation? He took all our sins on Himself, and in giving His life for us, He made a purging of sins. Christ "His own self bare our sins in His own body on the tree, that we, being dead to sins, should live unto righteousness; by whose stripes ye were healed." 1 Peter 2:24. "Thanks be unto God for His unspeakable gift." "Now thanks be unto God, which always causeth us to triumph in Christ." 2 Cor. 2:14.

> Christ hath for sin atonement made;
> What a wonderful Saviour!
> We are redeemed! – the price is paid;
> What a wonderful Saviour!
>
> He gives me overcoming power;
> What a wonderful Saviour!
> And triumph in each trying hour;
> What a wonderful Saviour!

CHAPTER 36

PREPARING THE WAY OF THE LORD

(Isa. 40:3–5)

A voice crieth: In the wilderness prepare ye the way of Jehovah! Make straight in the desert a highway for our God!

Every valley shall be exalted, and every mountain and hill be brought low; And the crooked shall become straight, and the rough places a smooth plain;

And the glory of Jehovah shall be revealed; And all flesh shall see together the salvation of our God; For the mouth of Jehovah hath spoken it.

Ps. 119:1–3: "Blessed are the undefiled in the way, who walk in the law of the Lord. Blessed are they that keep His testimonies, and that seek Him with the whole heart. They also do no iniquity; they walk in His ways."

Ps. 125:5: "As for such as turn aside unto their crooked ways, the Lord shall lead them forth with the workers of iniquity; but peace shall be upon Israel."

Ps. 103:7: "He made known His ways unto Moses, His acts unto the children of Israel."

Ps. 25:9: "The meek will He guide in judgment; the meek will He teach His way."

Ps. 18:30: "As for God, His way is perfect."

Ps. 145:17: "The Lord is righteous in all His ways, and holy in all His works."

John 14:6: "Jesus saith unto Him, I am the way, the truth, and the life; no man cometh unto the Father but by Me."

Ps. 77:13: "Thy way, O God, is in the sanctuary; who is so great a God as our God?"

1 Cor. 3:16: "Know ye not that ye are the temple of God, and that the Spirit of God dwelleth in you?"

Luke 1:76–79: "And thou, child, shalt be called the prophet of the Highest; for thou shalt go before the face of the Lord to prepare His ways; to give knowledge of salvation unto His people by the remission of their sins, through the tender mercy of our God; whereby the dayspring from on high hath visited us, to give light to them that sit in darkness and in the shadow of death, to guide our feet into the way of peace."

Luke 1:16–17: "Many of the children of Israel shall he turn to the Lord their God. And he shall go before Him in the Spirit and power of Elias, to turn the hearts of the father to the children, and the disobedient to the wisdom of the just; to make ready a people prepared for the Lord."

Mal 4:5–6: "Behold, I will send you Elijah the prophet before the coming of the great and terrible day of the Lord; and he shall turn the heart of the fathers to the children, and the heart of the children to their fathers, lest I come and smite the earth with a curse," or "utter destruction."

Ps. 85:13: "Righteousness shall go before Him; and shall make His footsteps a way to walk in." Revised Version.

Ps. 19:7–8: "The law of the Lord is perfect, converting the soul; the testimony of the Lord is sure, making wise the simple. The statutes of the Lord are right, rejoicing the heart; the commandment of the Lord is pure, enlightening the eyes."

Let us not forget, in studying this lesson, that while all Scripture is always true, and the Gospel is always applicable, this prophecy of Isaiah has special application in these last days. This message is one to make ready a people prepared for the coming of the Lord in glory, to give reward to His servants, and to give every man according as his work shall be. Do not make the mistake of thinking that because it was written twenty-five hundred years ago, it does not specially concern us. The Word of the Lord is living, and never loses any of its force. Its exhortations are more emphatic "as we see the day approaching."

Remember also what we have learned concerning the message of John the Baptist. It reaches till the coming of the Lord in glory, and all who love the Lord and His coming are commissioned to proclaim it. John the Baptist therefore stood not as a single individual, having a work to do that ended with his death, but as the type of a great movement embracing tens of thousands of people, and reaching till the end of time.

The command to the voice is, "Prepare ye the way of Jehovah!" It is to prepare the way for the Lord's coming. Well, what hinders His coming now? Why could He not have come at any time in the past? Simply because the people were not prepared for His coming. The condition of His professed followers hindered His advent. The way of the Lord is in the sanctuary, and His sanctuary is His people, therefore we see that the way of the Lord is prepared only by the preparation of His people, – by the cleansing of the sanctuary.

The words "straight" and "right" are really the same. The Latin word *rectus*, from which we derive our word "right," as seen in the word "rectitude," the meaning of which everybody knows, means literally, "straight," as can be seen from the word "rectilinear." A "right" line is a straight line, just as a "rectangle" is a right or straight angle. To make the way of the Lord straight is therefore to make it right.

But all the ways of the Lord are right; His way is perfect. Therefore there is nothing about the Lord that needs correcting. Everything with which He has to do is as good as it can be. But we have refused to allow the Lord to have His way, for "we have turned every one to his own way." Isa. 53:6. His rightful way is in us, but we have kept Him back by our unrighteousness. We have made our ways crooked. So the Lord sends His messengers to straighten us out – to make us right before Him, so that there may be nothing to hinder His complete possession of us.

God is light. The characteristic of light is that it proceeds in straight lines. So with God, who is "the Father of lights," there "can be no variation, neither shadow that is cast by turning." James 1:17, R.V. Consequently all in whom He has His way must be sincere, that is, clear and transparent, so that the beams of the Sun of righteousness may not be hindered in their course. The work of this Gospel message is to "give light to them that sit in darkness and in the shadow of death." "Ye were once darkness, but are now light in the Lord; walk as children of light." Eph. 5:8.

"He made known His ways to Moses, His acts unto the children of Israel." Ways and acts are the same. When we say of a person that we do not like his ways, we mean that we do not like his habits, his actions. So the way of the Lord is His manner of life. He made His ways or acts known to Moses and the children of Israel, in revealing to them His law. "Thou camest down also upon Mount Sinai, and spakest with them from heaven, and gavest them right judgments, and true laws, good statutes and commandments; and madest known unto them Thy holy Sabbath, and commanded them precepts, statutes, and laws, by the hand of Moses Thy servant." Neh. 9:13–14. The law of the Lord is His way, as we learn from Ps. 119:1–3. The way of the Lord is prepared, therefore, by putting His law into the hearts of the people.

When the Lord comes in the clouds of heaven, it will be with glory. "The hills melted like wax at the presence of the Lord, at the presence of the Lord of the whole earth. The heavens declare His righteousness, and all the people see His glory." Ps. 97:5–6. Since God is light, and dwells in light, being clothed with light as a garment, it follows that wherever He goes the glory must be revealed. So we read that when the way of the Lord is prepared, the glory of the Lord shall be revealed. This will be because that when His way is prepared He Himself will go in it.

The way of the Lord is in His sanctuary, and His sanctuary is His people. The idea prevails that the coming of the Lord is an arbitrary affair; that He will come when He is ready, regardless of the condition of people on this earth. That is a great mistake. The coming of the Lord is but the consummation, the crowning act, of a great work. It is the natural and inevitable result of what has preceded. Christ came to reveal God to men, so that they might know His will concerning them. It is God's will that men shall be like Him, so as to be fit companions for Him, and to this end Christ was once manifested, to reveal God to men, *in man*; and the possibility of this was secured by His death. His coming to this earth was the empty-ing of Himself, really His death, so that it is only by the death of

Christ that God can be manifest in the flesh. The whole work of the Gospel is to secure this revelation of God in man. It is the work that God began at the creation, when He made man in His own image; and to restore this image is the work of the Gospel. The "new man" is after God "created in righteousness and true holiness." Eph. 4:24. But the heavens must retain Christ "until the times of restoration of all things." Acts 3:20–21. His coming means the restoration of the earth; but this cannot be until the new man is made ready for it, – until it has a ruler, – and so before the coming of the Lord in the clouds of heaven, He must be fully revealed in His people. The shining forth of the Lord from heaven is but the fullness of His revelation. "He shall come to be glorified in His saints." 2 Thess. 1:10. He cannot come, therefore, until in the church the ways of God are seen as perfectly as they were in Jesus of Nazareth.

When the way is prepared, the glory of the Lord will be revealed, and all flesh will see it. This is because as soon as the way is prepared, the Lord goes in it, and wherever He goes the glory must be revealed. But His way is in His people, therefore His glory is to be seen in them. "For God, who commanded the light to shine out of darkness, hath shined in our hearts, to give the light of the knowledge of the glory of God in the face of Jesus Christ." 2 Cor. 4:6. Why has God shined in our hearts? – To give the light of the knowledge of His glory. To give the light of the knowledge of His glory to whom? – To others, of course; for no candle shines for the purpose of giving light to itself. God shines in our hearts in order that others may take knowledge of His glory. "Let your light so shine before men, that they may see your good works, and glorify your Father which is in heaven." Matt. 5:16. Good works are the light, according to these words of Christ. So again we see that God prepares the way by putting His law in our hearts by His Spirit; "for the commandment is a lamp; and the law is light." Prov. 6:23. The preaching of the law of God as revealed in the life and character of Christ, must precede the coming of the Lord. When the last message shall have been completed, these words will be uttered: "Here is the patience of the saints, here are they that keep the commandments of God, and the faith of Jesus." Rev. 19:12.

"And all flesh shall see it together." When the glory is revealed, it will be seen. That will be the testimony to the saving power of our God. In the inanimate things that God has made, His power and Divinity are seen. Rom. 1:20. Although man has proved unfaithful, and has even imposed his evil traits upon the creation that was given into his care, God has not left Himself without witness. "The heavens declare the glory of God and the firmament showeth His handiwork." Ps. 19:1. But that is not enough. Man, the highest creature of God, ought to give the most perfect testimony to His power and goodness, and this will be the case before the Lord comes. Not only must all the works of God praise Him, but His saints must bless Him. When the voice in the wilderness has completed its message, then will the work for which Christ ascended to heaven, namely, "that He might fill all things," be accomplished, and He will come. Then all creatures, animate and inanimate, will unite in saying, "Blessing, and honour, and glory, and power, be unto Him that sitteth on the throne, and unto the Lamb, for ever and ever." Rev. 5:13.

CHAPTER 37

ALL FLESH IS GRASS

(Isa. 40:6–9)

"The voice of one saying, Cry. And one said, What shall I cry? All flesh is grass, and all the goodliness thereof as the flower of the field; the grass withereth, the flower fadeth; because the breath of the Lord bloweth upon it; surely the people is grass. The grass withereth, the flower fadeth; but the Word of our God shall stand forever.

"O thou that tellest good tidings to Zion, get thee up into the high mountain; O thou that tellest good tidings to Jerusalem, lift up thy voice with strength; lift it up, be not afraid; say unto the cities of Judah, Behold your God!" R.V.

Ps. 103:15–17: "As for man, his days are as grass; as a flower of the field so he flourisheth. For the wind passeth over it, and it is gone; and the place thereof shall know it no more. But the mercy of the Lord is from everlasting upon them that fear Him, and His righteousness unto children's children."

Ps. 90:10: "The days of our years are threescore years and ten; and if by reason of strength they be fourscore years, yet is their strength labour and sorrow; for it is soon cut off, and we fly away."

James 1:9–11, R.V. "Let the brother of low degree glory in his high estate; and the rich, in that he is made low; because as the flower of the grass he shall pass away. For the sun ariseth with the scorching wind, and withereth the grass; and the flower thereof falleth, and the grace of the fashion of it perisheth; so also shall the rich man fade away in his goings."

Matt. 6:28–30: "Why are ye anxious concerning raiment? Consider the lilies of the field, how they grow; they toil not, neither do they spin; yet I say unto you, that even Solomon in all his glory was not arrayed like one of these. But if God doth so clothe the grass of the field, which today is, and tomorrow is cast into the oven, shall He not much more clothe you, O ye of little faith?"

Jer. 17:5–7: "Cursed be the man that trusteth in man, and maketh flesh his arm, and whose heart departeth from the Lord. For he shall be like the heath in the desert, and shall not see when good cometh; but shall inhabit the parched places in the wilderness, in a salt land, and not inhabited. Blessed is the man that trusteth in the Lord, and whose hope the Lord is."

Rom. 7:18: "For I know that in me (that is, in my flesh) dwelleth no good thing."

Gal. 5:17: "For the flesh lusteth against the Spirit, and the Spirit against the flesh; and these are contrary the one to the other: so that ye cannot do the things that ye would."

Ps. 33:6: "By the Word of the Lord were the heavens made; and all the host of them by the breath of His mouth."

1 Peter 1:22–25: "Love one another from the heart fervently; having been begotten again, not of corruptible seed, but of incorruptible, through the Word of God, which liveth and abideth for ever,
For all flesh is grass,
And all the glory thereof as the flower of grass.
The grass withereth, and the flower falleth;
But the Word of the Lord abideth for ever.
And this is the Word of good tidings which was preached unto you."

Remember that this is part of the message of comfort. God tells us that our iniquity is pardoned, and we accept the comfort. He tells us that our warfare is accomplished, since He has overcome the world, and we rejoice for the consolation. We ought to be equally glad when He goes on with His comforting words, and says that all flesh is grass, that is, that we have no might nor power nor wisdom in ourselves. That is really what is involved in the announcement that our warfare is accomplished, that Jesus has fought the battle for us; for the only reason why He has fought and overcome for us is that we had no power to fight and overcome for ourselves.

The first impulse one has on reading the Lord's words, "All flesh is grass," is to say, "That does not mean actually that all flesh is grass; I know that I am not grass, for I do not resemble grass at all; there is scarcely any likeness between me and grass." The words are of course used in a figurative sense. It is thus that men make of none effect the words of the Lord, and keep themselves from learning anything. When God tells us something which is entirely new to us, and which we do not understand, the wisest thing for us to do is believe it, and then we shall learn the new thing. He who believes nothing but what he already knows and understands, will have a very limited range of knowledge, and his store of knowledge will continually diminish. It is astonishing what a wide field opens up to us when we accept some statements of the Lord's as actual fact, and proceed on that basis. Things that before were obscure, suddenly become plain. In the statement that "all flesh is grass," we have in a nutshell the whole science of botany and of physiology, as well as the first part of the key to salvation.

From Matt. 6:28–30 we learn that the term "grass" is very comprehensive, including many plants not commonly classed as grass. The lilies of the field are by the Lord called grass. There are, however, very many different kinds of grass, that are so called by botanists. Every species of grain is but a kind of grass. A little thought and observation and comparison will show this fact to any who have not known it before. When this is recognized, it is not difficult to see that all flesh is grass. In fact, the wonder is that anybody should need to be told so simple a thing. Thus, we well know that any animal is composed of what it eats. *Der Mensch ist vas er isst*, says the old German proverb. That is, man is what he eats. Now not only all that we eat, but everything that is on the face of the earth, comes from the ground. Most men eat both vegetables and flesh of animals; but the animals which they eat feed only on vegetables, or grass, so that in every case a man's body is composed only of that which he derives from the vegetable creation. Only in the vegetable world can man find the elements prepared for the sustenance of his body; the ox makes no change whatever in the food elements which he finds in the grass; so that when a man eats the ox he is simply taking his food second hand, after it has done service in another body. He gets nothing that he would not get in a purer form if he took it direct from the plant. Therefore, it is a literal fact that "all flesh is grass."

The stream can rise no higher than its source. Nothing can be any better than the material out of which it is made. A strong garment cannot be made out of rotten cloth. The whole cannot be any greater than the sum of all its parts. Therefore since a man's body is composed only of grass, or the fruit of grass, it is evident that there is in man no more power or wisdom than there is in the grass. How can there be, when man himself is but grass? He is not the grass of the field, but he is grass, nevertheless.

"Well, this is anything but a comforting doctrine, I must say," I hear somebody exclaim. "If I have no more power or wisdom than the grass, there is no use in my trying to do or be anything; there is no hope for anybody." Not so fast, please. You have not heard the whole of the story, or at least have forgotten a part of it. "The Word of God shall stand for ever." It "liveth and abideth." It is almighty and everlasting. The comfort of the fact that all flesh is grass is based on the accompanying fact that God's Word, which is the life of the grass, lives and abides, all-powerful. Do not separate these two facts. Let them always be as closely united as the Lord has made them.

Nevertheless some one will say, "I know that I have power that grass has not. I can move at will, and I can do many things that are impossible for grass." What is the conclusion? – Oh, simply this, that you will prove that the Bible is not true. There is not enough prospect of gain in that to make it worth while trying. But let us examine your statement. You can move, you say. Well, so can the plant. Some plants can even move from place to place, and every plant has certain movements that may be seen by anybody who will take the trouble to look. Did you ever watch a plant growing in the window? You know how it will turn towards the light. Turn it half-way round, so that it leans away from the window, and you will very soon see that it has turned round, and is reaching out to the light again. Plant a tree half-way between a well and a dry sand-bank, and watch how the roots grow. Instead of reaching out in every direction, the most of them will turn towards the water. The roots of a plant always set toward the place where there is nourishment for it in solution, and they always go right the first time, and they go the most direct way. They lose no time in "prospecting," and they do not miss the way. What is the plant doing? Just what the man does – trying to get into the best possible circumstance for living; and it accomplishes its purpose more successfully then the man does.

Watch the plant, and you will also see that it is capable of bearing a great burden. In the first place, the seed must often exert wonderful power, in order to escape from the shell that encases it. Then think how great a weight of earth the tender shoot must push out of its way before it can reach the surface of the ground. Think how great a weight the growing tree lifts up every year. Then above all, remember that the strength of which you are wont to boast is derived from these same despised plants. You have often been hungry and faint. You have often felt so weak that you could not think of working any longer, and have had your strength and courage come back to you after eating a bit of bread. Did you not connect your increased strength with the bread that you ate? Of course you did, for you said, "I cannot do anything more until I have had something to eat." Yet for all that you did not think that all the new strength that you received from eating was formerly in that which you ate. If it had not been, how could you have derived any strength from eating it? "Speak well of the bridge that carries you over." Instead of being so much superior in power to the grass of the field, you are absolutely dependent upon it.

Shall we then worship the grass of the field, as being superior to us? By no means, for you were right in a sense, that the grass has no power. It is used as a symbol of weakness and frailty. Today it is and tomorrow it is not. Whence then comes that wonderful power that is manifested in its growth, and which we derive by eating and assimilating it? – From the word of God, which liveth and abideth. "The word of God is living and active." It is force and energy. It is wisdom. Christ upholds all things by the word of His power. Heb. 1:3. His word in the beginning said, "Let the earth bring forth grass," and in obedience to that word the earth brings forth grass to this day. All the life and energy that is manifested in the growing plant is the life of the word that is in it. The everlasting power and Divinity of God are clearly seen in every living plant. Rom. 1:20. The seeds of the grass, which we eat made into bread, are but the means of conveying to us the life and power of God. Only God is great; only He has life, and wisdom and strength. Worship God.

This is the lesson that we are to learn from the statement that all flesh is grass. It is the simple truth, and there is no comfort in anything but the truth. A lie may deceive us, and make us think that all is right, but it can give no real comfort. The man who tells us that there is no danger, when there is danger, is not a comforter. The comforter is the man who points out the danger and the way of escape. Now as the result of not recognizing the fact that we are grass, we are all engaged in making gods of ourselves. We imagine that we have power in ourselves. The fact is that power belongs to God. Ps. 62:11. Just to the extent that we think that we have any power, do we regard ourselves as God. We propose at the very best to divide honours with God, saying, "I have so little strength," and think that we have made a wonderfully humble confession. In reality we have said, "I am not so great a god as the One in heaven." That is not fearing God, and giving glory to Him. God tells us the plain truth, that we have no strength at all, in order that we may learn to say, "Behold, God is my strength."

"That which thou sowest is not quickened, except it die; and that which thou sowest, thou sowest not that body that shall be, but bare grain, it may chance of wheat or some other grain; but God giveth it a body as it hath pleased Him, and to every seed his own body. All flesh is not the same flesh; but there is one kind of flesh of men, another flesh of beasts, another of fishes, and another of birds. There are also celestial bodies, and bodies terrestrial; but the glory of the celestial is one, and the glory of the terrestrial is another. There is one glory of the sun, and another glory of the moon, and another glory of the stars; for one star differeth from another in glory." 1 Cor. 15:36–41. Even so there is a difference in plants. Indeed, that is what the text says, for God gives to every seed such a body as pleases Him. All plants have not the same purpose. There is infinite variety in the vegetable world, yet the same life is in all plants. The same life in all brings each to the state of perfection which God designs for it. Even so the same life in the human plant will, if given free course, bring the man to the state of perfection designed for him. Nothing is too hard for the Lord, and nothing is too small to escape His attention. The grass of the field is passive in the hands of God, for Him to do with it as He will, and wonderful things are accomplished. If we will but be as passive in God's hands, He will do infinitely greater things for us, inasmuch as He created us for a higher place. But we cannot reach that higher place by striving to lift up ourselves, any more than the ivy could by its own wisdom and power climb to the top of the tower, or split the walls asunder. "It is God that worketh in you, both to will and to do of His good pleasure."

"This is the Word which by the Gospel is preached unto you." The Gospel presents God as Creator, as supreme. It presents an Almighty Saviour, who saves by His power to create, inasmuch as He saves by creating us anew. Therefore we must expect that the nearer we approach the end, the plainer will this Gospel be presented. More and more loudly must the cry be uttered, which shows men that they are in themselves absolutely nothing, but that God is everything. In Him is all fullness, and of His Fullness have all we received. We are nothing, but He gives us everything in giving us Himself.

The Gospel does not tell us to look at ourselves, but at God. It tells us what we are, and then says, "Behold your God." We are to accept God's statement of what we are, and that is not difficult when we have it so patent to our senses. But knowing that we are nothing, we do not need to waste any time looking at ourselves, for it is certainly a waste of time to look at nothing. Our charge is, "Behold your God!" Where shall we look, in order to see Him? Look at everything that He has made, – at the heavens, the seas, the earth, and all that is in them. When we see ourselves, as we must every day, let it be only to recognize the fact that "in Him we live, and move, and have our being." Let no flesh glory in man, but instead, "Fear God, and give glory to Him," "and worship Him that made heaven, and earth, and the sea, and the fountains of waters." Rev. 14:7.

CHAPTER 38

THE LORD GOD WILL COME

(Isa. 40:9–11)

"O thou that tellest good tidings to Zion, get thee up into the high mountain; O thou that tellest good tidings to Jerusalem, lift up thy voice with strength; lift it up, be not afraid; say unto the cities of Judah, Behold your God! Behold, the Lord God will come with strong hand, and His arm shall rule for Him; behold, His reward is with Him, and His work before Him. He shall feed His flock like a shepherd; He shall gather the lambs with His arm, and carry them in His bosom, and shall gently lead those that are with young."

Matt. 2:6, R.V.: "Thou Bethlehem, land of Judah, art in no wise least among the princes of Judah; for out of thee shall come forth a Governor, which shall be shepherd of My people Israel."

John 10:11,27–28: "I am the good Shepherd; the good shepherd giveth His life for the sheep." "My sheep hear My voice, and I know them, and they follow Me; and I give unto them eternal life; and they shall never perish, neither shall any man pluck them out of My hand."

Rev. 22:12: "Behold, I come quickly; and My reward is with Me, to give every man according as his work shall be."

Matt. 16:27: "For the Son of man shall come in the glory of His Father with His angels; and then He shall reward every man according to his works."

2 Thess. 1:6–8: "It is a righteous thing with God to recompense tribulation to them that trouble you; and to you who are troubled rest with us, when the Lord Jesus shall be revealed from heaven with His mighty angels, in flaming fire taking vengeance on them that know not God, and that obey not the Gospel of our Lord Jesus Christ."

Ps. 50:3–5: "Our God shall come, and shall not keep silence; a fire shall devour before Him, and it shall be very tempestuous round about Him. He shall call to the heavens from above, and to the earth, that He may judge His people. Gather My saints together unto Me: those that have made a covenant with Me by sacrifice."

Hab. 3:3–13: "God came from Teman, and the Holy One from Mount Paran. Selah. His glory covered the heavens, and the earth was full of His praise. And His brightness was as the light: He had bright beams coming out of His side [margin]; and there was the hiding of His power. Before Him went the pestilence, and burning coals went forth at His feet. He stood and measured the earth; He beheld and drove asunder the nations; and the everlasting mountains were scattered, the perpetual hills did bow; His ways are everlasting. … The sun and moon stood still in their habitation; at the light of Thine arrows they went, and at the shining of Thy glittering spear. Thou didst march through the land in indignation, Thou didst thresh the heathen in anger. Thou wentest forth for the salvation of Thy people, even for salvation with Thine anointed."

1 Thess. 4:16–18: "The Lord Himself shall descend from heaven with a shout, with the voice of the Archangel, and with the trump of God; and the dead in Christ shall rise first; Then we which are alive and remain shall be caught up with them in the clouds, to meet the Lord in the air; and so shall we ever be with the Lord. Wherefore comfort one another with these words."

1 Cor. 15:51–53: "Behold, I show you a mystery: We shall not all sleep, but we shall all be changed in a moment, in the twinkling of an eye, at the last trump; for the trumpet shall sound, and the dead shall be raised incorruptible, and we shall be changed. For the corruptible must put on incorruption, and this mortal must put on immortality."

Phil. 3:20–21: "Our citizenship is in heaven: from whence also we look for the Saviour, the Lord Jesus Christ; who shall change our vile body, that it may be fashioned like unto His glorious body, according to the working whereby He is able even to subdue all things unto Himself."

Isa. 35:3–4: "Strengthen ye the weak hands, and confirm the feeble knees. Say to them that are of a fearful heart, Be strong, fear not; behold, your God will come with vengeance, even God with a recompense; He will come and save you."

Matt. 15:24: "I am not sent but unto the lost sheep of the house of Israel."

Eze. 34:11–13: "For thus saith the Lord God: Behold I, even I, will both search My sheep, and seek them out. As a shepherd seeketh out his flock in the day he is among the sheep that are scattered; so will I seek out My sheep, and will deliver them out of all places where they have been scattered in the cloudy and dark day. And I will bring them out from the people, and gather them from the countries, and will bring them to their own land, and feed them upon the mountains of Israel by the rivers, and in all the inhabited places of the country."

The preaching of the second coming of Christ, in glory, is as much a part of the preaching of the Gospel – the good news – as is the preaching of the cross of Calvary. In fact, the preaching of the cross is not complete without the preaching of the second advent.

Nothing so awful as the coming of the Lord to judgment has ever taken place on this earth. The earth will quake, and be removed like a cottage, the heavens will depart as a scroll when it is rolled together, every mountain and island will be moved out of their places, and "the kings of the earth, and the great men, and the chief captains, and the mighty men, and every bondman and every freeman" shall hide themselves in the dens and in the caves, and say to the mountains and rocks, "Fall on us, and hide us from the face of Him that sitteth on the throne, and from the wrath of the Lamb; for the great day of His wrath is come; and who shall be able to stand?" Rev. 6:14–17. Yet the announcement of the coming of that great day is part of the message of comfort which God sends to His people. How marvelous is the comfort of God, when even the most terrible judgments are comfort!

The comfort is that Christ is coming to save His people. The prophet Habakkuk, to whom a view of the terrors of the last day were given, said, "Thou wentest forth for the salvation of Thy people." When the hearts of the people grow fearful, and the knees tremble, and the hands hang down, the Lord tell us to strengthen them with the words, "Your God will come with vengeance." The coming of Christ is the "blessed hope" of the Gospel. Titus 2:13. When He shall come, His saints will say, "Lo, this is our God; we have waited for Him, and He will save us; this is the Lord; we have waited for Him; we will be glad and rejoice in His salvation." Isa. 25:9. The announcement of the coming of the Lord is the same comfort as the announcement of the pardon of sins. Whoever preaches the remission of sins, does it only partially if he does not preach the coming of the Lord in glory. The texts quoted in this lesson shows this.

Jesus Christ is the good Shepherd. He is "the Chief Shepherd." 1 Peter 5:4. He came to earth for the purpose of seeking His lost sheep, and He seeks them out, and saves them by giving His life for theirs. On the cross He suffered all the agonies of the lost. Matt. 27:46. He endured everything that men would have been obliged to endure if He had not come, and that the rejecters of Him will have to endure at the last. He took all on Himself, in order to save men. The terrors of the last day, the day of Judgment, were present in full on Calvary. Even so the blessedness and joy of Calvary will be present at the coming of the Lord the second time, in glory.

It is only by the power of the cross that Jesus will come again. He will be seen coming in the clouds of heaven "with power and great glory" (Matt. 24:30), but that will be but the power and glory of the cross. The fire that devours before Him will come from the pierced side. From the side whence flowed the healing stream of life, comes the power to render to the wicked according to their deeds. The power manifested at the coming of the Lord is the power of salvation; it is the power by which Jesus now saves His people from the hand of the enemy.

"His mercy endureth for ever." In wrath He remembers mercy. Hab. 3:2. The waters that will overflow the hiding place of the wicked, will be the waters of salvation that flow from the wounded side of Jesus. "He will swallow up death in victory," and then those who have made a covenant with death, seeking to hide in its shadow, must necessarily be swallowed up with it. Isa. 28:16–18. So although the last day will be the most terrible, it will contain nothing but joy for those who have accepted the redemption that is in Christ Jesus. Do not the righteous joy in the cross of Christ? Is it not the one thing in which to glory? Yet the crucifixion of Christ was a most terrible event, and all the terrors of the wrath of God raged round the cross where Christ died. But for His death on the cross, the Son of man would not have the power to sit in judgment and to execute judgment on the ungodly.

From Bethlehem comes the Governor that is to be the Shepherd of Israel. He rules His people as a shepherd rules his flock. He feeds them, and the food that He gives them is Himself. He gives Himself for the sheep. When the Lord comes, it will be at a time when the wicked will have gathered to make an end of the righteous ones on the earth. A decree will have gone forth that whosoever will not worship the beast or his image, shall be killed. Rev. 13:15. Just at the moment when Satan has stirred up all the forces of evil against the just, and to all human sight it looks as though the righteous were to be cut off from the earth, Christ will appear to save them. It will be but the crowning act in the great drama of the cross. It will be the demonstration to the whole earth that Christ is the saviour. Then those who have rejected Him, and have mocked at His offers of salvation, will be forced to acknowledge that Jesus saves. But the present comfort to the people of God lies in the fact that all that great power to salvation is theirs now. It is all in the cross.

He comes with strong hand, as a Mighty One. "His arm shall rule for Him." But it is that same arm with which He gathers the lambs of the flock. He is gentle, because He is strong. His strength to destroy the wolves and lions that would devour the flock, is His power to feed the flock, and to make the sheep lie down in green pastures. Strange that so many preachers of the Gospel have so little to say about the coming of the Lord, which contains so much comfort for the people of God!

There is in this lesson valuable instruction as to the return of Israel. Jesus is the Shepherd of Israel, and when He comes the second time, "with power and great glory," He comes as a Shepherd. It is then that He will gather together all His people, – the flock that has been scattered and torn, – "and will bring them to their own land, and feed them upon the mountains of Israel by the rivers." When He was here the first time, He said that He had come to seek and to save that which was lost, and He also declared that He was not sent but to the lost sheep of the house of Israel; they were the ones whom he came to seek and to save. But everybody knows that there has not yet been any gathering of Israel. The lost sheep have not yet been gathered together into their own land. Moreover He Himself tells us that it will be when He comes the second time that He will say, "Gather My saints together unto Me." It is then that He will gather out His sheep from all the lands whither they have been scattered. Compare Eze. 34 and Matt. 24:30. Then there shall be one fold and one Shepherd. Eze. 34:22–31; John 10:16. That fold will be the fold of Israel, for all the saved will constitute the Israel of God.

The Apostle Paul describes the coming of the Lord in glory, when the dead shall be raised, and the living caught up together with them in the clouds, to meet the Lord in the air, thus ever to be with Him, and says, "Comfort one another with these words." This is comfort for those who mourn departed friends, who have laid in the dark grave. They need not sorrow as those who have no hope, for "the righteous hath hope in his death." But this is not all the comfort that there is in this announcement. It is the same comfort that the Lord in the fortieth chapter of Isaiah tells His servants to give to His people. It is the comfort of the Gospel of salvation from sin. Notice: When Christ comes with the sound of the trump of God, all the saints of God, both sleeping and waking, will be changed. In the twinkling of an eye the change from mortality, from corruptible to incorruptibility, will take place. All will then be given bodies incapable of disease and decay. What a wonderful change that will be! But mark: This change of our bodies is "according to the working whereby He is able even to subdue all things unto Himself." We are rebellious by nature, and our minds are not subject to the law of God, "neither indeed can be." Rom. 8:7. But He is able to change our minds, giving us a new mind, and a new nature, so that we shall be subject to Him, and shall delight in the law of the Lord; and His power to do this is according to the power by which He will at the last change our bodies from corruption to incorruption. And note that that change will take place in a moment, in the twinkling of an eye; the Lord is able to do marvelous things in a very short time; therefore we may know that if we are but willing, He can in an instant effect this wonderful change in our natures. Is it not worth while to have a belief in the resurrection of the dead? Is there not great comfort in the knowledge of the coming of the Lord? All this shall take place as surely as the mouth of the Lord hath spoken it; therefore, be not afraid.

CHAPTER 39

THE MIGHTY GOD

(Isa. 40:12–24)

12. Who hath measured the waters in the hollow of His hand; and hath meted out the heavens by His span. And hath comprehended the dust of the earth in a tierce; and hath weighed in the scales the mountains and the hills in a balance?

13. Who hath directed the Spirit of Jehovah; and, as one of His council, hath informed Him?

14. Whom hath He consulted, that he should instruct Him, and teach Him the path of judgment; that he should impart to Him science, and inform Him in the way of understanding?

15. Behold, the nations are as a drop from the bucket; as the small dust of the balance shall they be accounted; behold, the islands He taketh up as an atom.

16. And Lebanon is not sufficient for the fire; nor his beasts sufficient for the burnt offering.

17. All the nations are as nothing before Him; they are esteemed by Him as less than naught, and vanity.

18. To whom therefore will ye liken God? And what is the model of resemblance that ye will prepare for Him?

19. The workman casteth an image: and the smith overlayeth it with plates of gold; and forgeth for it chains of silver.

20. He that cannot afford a costly oblation, chooseth a piece of wood that will not rot; he procureth a skillful artist, to erect an image, which shall not be moved.

21. Will ye not know? Will ye not hear? Hath it not been declared to you from the beginning? Have ye not understood from the foundations of the earth?

22. It is He, that sitteth on the circle of the earth; and the inhabitants are to Him as grasshoppers; he extendeth the heavens as a thin veil; and spreadeth them out as a tent to dwell in;

23. That reduceth princes to nothing; that maketh the judges of the earth a mere vanity.

24. Yea, they shall not leave a plant behind them, they shall not be sown, their trunk shall not spread its root in the ground; if He but blow upon them, they instantly wither; and the whirlwind shall bear them away like stubble.

The psalmist sang, "Our help is in the name of the Lord, who made heaven and earth." Ps. 124:8. In contrast with the gods of the heathen, that cannot see nor hear nor smell nor talk nor walk, and must needs be borne, is our God, who is in the heavens, who "hath done whatsoever He hath pleased." Ps. 115:3. King Jehoshaphat said, when he sought help from the Lord in a time of great danger, "Art not Thou God in heaven? and rulest not Thou over all the kingdoms of the heathen? and in Thine hand is there not power and might, so that none is able to withstand Thee?" 2 Chron. 20:6. This was his comfort. God is in the heavens, above all, the Creator and upholder of all. It is this fact that gives us strong confidence in coming to Him for help in time of need. In this lesson we have the utter nothingness and helplessness of man, and the infinite greatness and power of God emphasized. This is the special message for the last days. Man is nothing; God is everything.

He "hath measured the waters in the hollow of His hand." Think of all the waters on the face of the earth, and under the earth, as well as the oceans of waters in the sky, – all held in the hollow of God's hand. In reading this verse we almost always think only of the oceans and seas on this earth. Well, it is a great thing that God holds them in his hand; but when we think of the expanse of waters in the heavens, we shall get a still more comprehensive idea of His power. A rain cloud capable of sending a shower of water to the depth of an inch over the surface of London, would weigh about one million tons. What an inconceivable mass and weight of water is therefore constantly floating about overhead, waiting God's command to fall upon the earth! "He bindeth up the waters in His thick clouds; and the cloud is not rent under them." Job 26:8. All these are gathered in the hollow of His hand. With this in mind, what comfort there is in reading the words of Christ, who comes as a shepherd, gathering the lambs with his arm," My sheep hear My voice, and I know them, and they follow Me; and I give unto them eternal life; and they shall never perish, and no one shall snatch them out of My hand. My Father, which hath given them unto Me, is greater than all; and no one shall snatch them out of the Father's hand. I and My Father are One." John 10:27–30. With what confidence God's people may rest in that mighty hand!

> "That hand which bears creation up,
> Shall guard His children well."

He has also meted out the heavens with His span. Take this in connection with His holding the waters in the hollow of His hand. Were you ever on the ocean in a storm, when the great steamship, the mightiest creation of man's skill and power, is but the plaything of the waves? If you are ever in such a place, and feel any sensation of fear, then comfort yourself by gathering up all the water you can hold in the hollow of your hand, and seeing what an insignificant little drop it is. You can move your hand, and thus agitate the surface of the water, but the movement is but trifling. Well, that represents the size of the ocean, and the extent of the storm in the sight of God. No, it does not represent the size of the ocean, either, for you are on only a small part of the waters which He measures in the hollow of His hand. That thought will give you comfort and peace. And then, even if He should allow the ship with all on board to go to the bottom, you would still be in the hollow of His hand. Nothing can snatch you out of that secure hiding place.

What striking questions are asked in verses 13 and 14. Who is there who could act as counsellor to the Lord? With whom could He consult in making the earth and heavens? When we consider the heavens of God, the moon and stars which His fingers have made, we can only say, "What is man, that Thou art mindful of him? and the son of man, that Thou visitest him?" Ps. 8:3–4. They are not large enough to make any account of, in comparison with the great works of God's hands, much less to be consulted in the making of them. Surely, it would be very becoming in man to be still before the Lord, and listen when He speaks.

But proud man is not willing to do this. On the contrary, he wishes to be heard, and that on the very things of which God has spoken. How many there are who presume to teach God science. "The Bible," say they, "is not an authority in science; its sphere is religion." But religion is the sum of all science. The Gospel includes all the sciences, and only in it can we learn the exact truth of science. Thus: To know God is the sum of all wisdom. "Let not the wise man glory in his wisdom," but only in that he understands and knows God. Jer. 9:23–24. If he does not know God, he has nothing in which to glory, for "the Lord knoweth the thoughts of the wise, that they are vain." 1 Cor. 3:20. Now eternal life, salvation, is but the knowledge of God and Jesus Christ, whom He has sent. John 17:3. So we see that all science is in eternal life. The Bible is preeminently a book of science. To be sure it does not deal in all the unpronounceable names and endless classifications with which so-called scientists delight to puzzle the uninitiated; but it gives the reason and the origin of all things. It takes man into a realm of fact concerning things of which the boasted man of science can only fancy. It gives positive knowledge where books of human science give only theory. Let it be set down as a fact that God's Word is true from the beginning. He has not mingled eternal truths with errors which puny man is to rectify.

In one of our previous lessons we read, "Cease ye from man whose breath is in his nostrils; for wherein is he to be accounted of?" Isa. 2:22. To get a proper idea of the littleness of a man, go to the well or stream and let down a bucket for water. Fill it full, and then draw it up as carefully as you can. Do not spill any. You will notice, however, with all your care, that some drops fall from the bucket as it rises. But what of them? The bucket is full, and no one takes any account of the few drops that dripped from the sides as it came up. Now only one of those unconsidered drops represents, not one man merely, but "the nations"! "All the nations are as nothing before Him; they are esteemed by Him as less than naught, and vanity." What presumption it is for one of these men to think to correct his Maker on a matter of science! Does not the very fact that man can be so presumptuous, show that he is very deficient in true science? that he has no adequate sense of the greatness of the creation of God, and consequently of the greatness of God's wisdom? And how can a man pose as a scientific man if he does not know anything about creation?

Men are wont to speak lightly of the learning of the ancients, especially as regards what is known as "science," although the word "science," really embraces all learning, since it means knowledge. The reason why the learning of the ancients is so lightly esteemed, is that many of their theories concerning nature are now known to have been but nonsense. But men forget that the same thing may be said concerning the theories which scientists held but a few years ago. The theories which men hold today, are only theories, and none know better than the men themselves that in a few years these theories will give place to others. Therefore in that respect the men of old were as well off as are the men of today. But in all matters of practical science, the ancients were the equals, if not the superiors, of the men of the present generation. They were masters in the art of building. In the "fine arts" and in literature, their works serve as models for students today. Thus we see that in keenness of perception, and in range of intellect they were the equals of any. Yet these same men made idols of wood and metal. They well know that these things were not God, but they were made as likenesses of God. Think of the folly of making an image of wood as a likeness of the God who is so great that the forests of Lebanon and all the beasts are not sufficient to make a burnt offering to Him. The princes of the earth are as nothing to Him, and all the wisdom of the judges of earth is but the mutterings of an idiot, compared with the wisdom of God. If He but blows upon them they instantly wither, and the wind will bear them away as the chaff of the summer threshing floor, so that no place is found for them. See Dan. 2:35.

Why does the Lord tell us all these things? Is it to humiliate us, to taunt us with our own littleness in comparison with Him? Not by any means. He does not wish us to become despondent. But these are facts, and cannot be other than they are. Remember that God is not like a man who is puffed up with an undue sense of his own importance, and who looks with contempt on those whom he imagines to be inferior to himself. Far from it. The Lord is great, and cannot be any other than what He is. The relation which is here set forth as existing between God and man is that which actually is, and it cannot be different. He is infinitely greater than man, yet He does not despise man on that account. "Though the Lord be high, yet hath He respect unto the lowly." Ps. 138:6. So much does He regard man, that He gave Himself to redeem him. He gave Himself for us, not for what we are, but for what He is able to make of us. Suppose we are but nothing; God is able to make that which is not bring to naught that which is. 1 Cor. 1:28. He tells us these things that we may know how easily He can do what He will with us. And this is for our comfort. Who is a God like unto our God?

CHAPTER 40

STRENGTH FOR THE HELPLESS

(Isa. 40:25–31)

25. To whom then will ye liken Me? And to whom shall I be equaled? saith the Holy One.

26. Lift up your eyes on high; and see, who hath created these. He draweth forth their armies by number; He calleth them all by name; through the greatness of His strength, and the mightiness of His power, not one of them faileth to appear.

27. Wherefore sayest thou then, O Jacob, and why speakest thou thus, O Israel, my way is hidden from Jehovah, and my cause passesth unregarded by my God.

28. Hast thou not known, hast thou not heard, that Jehovah is the everlasting God, the Creator of the bounds of the earth? That He neither fainteth, nor is wearied; and that His understanding is unsearchable?

29. He giveth strength to the faint, and to the infirm He multiplieth force.

30. The young men shall faint and be wearied; and the chosen youths shall stumble and fall;

31. But they that trust in Jehovah shall gather new strength: they shall put forth fresh feathers like the moulting eagle; they shall run, and not be wearied; they shall march onward, and shall not faint.

In the verses just preceding, in this chapter, we have a vivid presentation of the weakness and insignificance of man. As compared with God, he is less than nothing, and vanity. He is only emptiness. All nations together are but as the fine dust of the balance, which makes no perceptible difference in the weight of any article, and which cannot be seen, to be brushed off. A breath from God would blow away the whole race; and yet these very men presume to make gods for themselves, that is, they presume to make a likeness of the God of heaven. But whatever a man makes must be less than himself; therefore his gods are nothing.

Who can make a likeness of the true God? God manifested Himself to the children of Israel as He never did to any other people (Deut. 4:7), but Moses, speaking of the time when the Lord spoke to them from Sinai, said, "Ye heard the voice of the words, but ye saw no similitude; only ye heard a voice." "Take ye therefore good heed unto yourselves; for ye saw no manner of similitude on the day that the Lord spake unto you in Horeb out of the midst of the fire." Verses 12, 15. Nobody has ever seen God, so that he could make a likeness of His form; whatever image anyone makes, therefore, professing to be a likeness of God, is but his conception of the power and attributes of God. But if men would but use the reason that God has given them, and learn the very first and simplest lesson from creation, they would at once see how impossible it is to make any representation of the living God. How can such a thing be done, when He is in all things? He fills heaven and earth. Every created thing reveals His everlasting power and Divinity; every tint of rose or rainbow exhibits a little of the loveliness of His face. In order to get a representation of God, one would need to bring together every separate phrase of strength and beauty in the entire universe; and even then he would not have a representation of God, because what he would have would be dead, and God is life itself. No one can make an image of life. Therefore there can be no likeness of God. God is, and that is the sum of the matter. Beside Him there is nothing.

"But men need something to keep God in mind," say some, as an excuse for the making of images of the Lord; "something to aid their devotion." Very true; and since that is so, God has provided for it. Do you think that God needed to depend on man to make something as a memento to Himself? Was God so thoughtless that He forgot an important need of mankind? What a libel upon God all such "aids to devotion" are! No; lift up your eyes to the heavens, and see the work of God's fingers, the moon and stars which He has ordained, and there you can always have an aid to devotion. Some one has said that "an undevout astronomer is mad." Why so? Because a man who is continually turning his eyes to the heavens, and exploring their depths, and gazing on their wondrous beauty, beholding the glory of God, which they declare, and yet does not worship their Creator, must be devoid of reason. So it is indeed with anyone who does not worship the God of heaven. Whoever does not recognize and worship the true God, has less sense than his ox or his ass. Isa. 1:2–3. Moreover, God has given us the Sabbath, in which the works of His hands are specially to be remembered. God's created works are the reminders of His power and goodness, and the Sabbath, the last day of every week, is for contemplation of the works of creation, so that none need forget God. Plenty of aids to devotion has God provided. If all kept the Sabbath of the Lord in truth, the knowledge of the glory of God would cover the earth.

"O Lord our Lord, how excellent is Thy name in all the earth! who hast set Thy glory upon the heavens." Ps. 8:1. He "bringeth out their host by number." "He telleth the number of the stars; He calleth them all by their names." Ps. 147:4. How many are there of them? Only God knows. Look up on a clear starry night, and you become lost as you try to count them; yet you see only a few of them. Visit an observatory, and the attendant will turn the huge telescope to some part of the heavens where your eye can discern nothing. Now look, and you will see swarms of suns blazing where it seemed as though there were only empty space. But you have not yet exhausted the possibilities, although such a thought as trying to count them would make you wild. We can see nothing more with the telescope, and now we resort to photography. We make the stars tell their own story. The sensitive plate is exposed for hours, and the light which is too faint, on account of infinite distance, to be taken into account even with the aid of the telescope, gradually accumulates until it makes a tiny speck. Now we have a photograph of that space which appeared to be vacant even when viewed through the most powerful telescope, and lo, there are thousands of spots, each one indicating the presence of a star. The same thing done from any part of the sky would give a similar result.

Thus we see that the stars within man's reach so to speak; that is, the stars of which he is able to detect the existence, are many thousand times more in number than what can be seen with the naked eye. But we have not yet reached the end. We have no more reason for supposing that the limit has been reached by our telescope and camera than the child has for saying that there is nothing beyond the horizon – that his eyes take in the bounds of the universe. The more powerful the instrument through which we look into the heavens, the greater the suggestion of infinite depths beyond. So we may be sure that if we could transport our telescope and photographic apparatus to the farthest star that has yet sent us a glimpse of itself, and should gaze on in the same direction, we should but have the same experience, and so on indefinitely. We are utterly lost in the contemplation of such infinite creation, and can only say, "O Lord, how manifold are Thy works! in wisdom hast Thou made them all."

Now we have some sort of appreciation of the expression, "The host of heaven." "He draweth forth their armies by number; He calleth them all by name." It is said that Caesar knew the names of all the men under his command. That, if true, was a most wonderful accomplishment; few men could retain in memory the names of so many men. Yet there were only a few tens of thousands, whereas God's host is tens of thousands of myriads. We can liken it to a vast flock, of which God is the Shepherd. As the Eastern shepherd, who spends all his life with his flock, becomes so well acquainted with them that he knows each one, so God knows the name of every one of His star flock. And as the shepherd by his faithful watchfulness and his power against the wild beasts, keeps every one of his sheep safe, so God, by His power and wisdom, guards His starry host so that not one of them is ever lacking. Man thinks of his work as great, yet it is at the greatest but a very small part of this earth that it has to do with. Compared with what we can see on this earth, man's work is puny; but what shall we say when we consider the heavens? What an inconceivably vast work God has on His hands!

And God has this work literally on His hands. He metes out the heavens with His span. They are the work of His fingers. What is it that keeps all these vast bodies in their proper places so that there is never any clashing, although all of them are constantly in motion? "Gravitation," they tell us. Take our solar system, for instance. Men leave God out of the question, and speak as though the force exerted was inherent in the heavenly bodies themselves. The sun, say they, keeps the planets in their orbits. Very good, we know that since God's everlasting power and Divinity are seen in everything that He has made, there is force in the sun and all other bodies; but let us think long enough to make sure that it is only God's power. See the earth revolving round the sun. Now it is flying with marvelous rapidity directly away from the sun. The attraction of the other planets is drawing it, they tell us. Very well, why does it not keep on? Why does it stop in its career, and turn back towards the sun? "Oh, the sun draws it!" Yes, but why did not the sun keep it from going? It had just as much power when the earth was flying away from it, as it had when it turned to go back. Why then did it allow it to go so far away? There is no other answer to this question, but the statement – that the hand of God is on the things that He has made. God's own personal presence sustains and controls His works. The fact that astronomers can calculate the relative power manifested through the various heavenly bodies, so that they can tell when to expect any given planet or star at any given place, does not at all destroy the fact that it is God who is personally working. There is no such thing as blind force. There is intelligence directing all power. God has not gone away and left His works to take care of themselves; there would soon be chaos if He should. No, He Himself stays by, "upholding all things by the Word of His power."

What therefore is the conclusion? Is it the common complaint that God has too much to attend to, to be mindful of our little cares? O foolish and blind unbelief! Why will men persistently put comfort away from themselves? "Why sayest thou, O Jacob, and speakest, O Israel, My way is hid from the Lord, and my judgment is passed away from my God? Hast thou not known? Hast thou not heard, that the everlasting God, Jehovah, the Creator of the ends of the earth, fainteth not, neither is weary? There is no searching of His understanding." If you have not heard it, then consider the heavens, and learn it. "Who hath despised the day of small things?" Certainly not God, who warns man against such foolishness. Just because God is so great, He is able to keep the most accurate account of your case. Not a detail escapes His notice of His care. He who numbers the stars, also numbers the very hairs of your head. Matt 10:30. Suppose there is here a great mathematician. He can make the most abstruse calculations. The largest numbers are handled by him with ease. Someone asks, "Can he count? Does he know that two and two are four?" What foolish questions! Of course he can. "Well, I thought that he dealt in such great matters that he would not be able to bother with such small affairs." Know then that the greater includes the less. The power to do great things implies the power to do that which is least. How surprised we are to find a great man of earth to be ignorant of some simple thing. "Is it possible you do not know that?" we exclaim in wonder. But no one can ask any such question concerning God. There is no searching of His understanding. Nobody can ever get to the bounds of it, so as to find something that He does not know. He inhabits eternity, so that infinity, whether it be the infinitely large or the infinitely small, is in Him. All power and wisdom are His, for He is the Creator of all.

"He giveth power to the faint." All this contemplation of the wondrous power of God, as manifested in the heavens, is but a part of the comfort which God says must be proclaimed to His people. A little while ago we read about God's telling the number of the stars, and calling all them by name. Let us now read the connection, and see why that fact is stated. "The Lord doth build up Jerusalem; He gathereth together the outcasts of Israel. He healeth the broken in heart, and bindeth up their wounds. He telleth the number of the stars; He calleth them all by their names. Great is our Lord, and of great power; His understanding is infinite." Ps. 147:2–5. So all this power, that is manifested in numbering and naming and upholding the innumerable stars, is the power with which God binds up the wounds of His people, and heals the brokenhearted. His gentleness in dealing with the wounded is equal to His power in upholding the universe.

The pagan proverb has it that "God helps those who help themselves." That is the way the devil tries to discourage people. All men are helpless, and there are times in every man's life when he feels himself to be absolutely without strength. God would have everybody to feel that way all the time. But when men find themselves in that condition, they think of that heathen proverb, and lose heart. Now the truth is that God helps those who cannot help themselves. "When ye were yet without strength, in due time Christ died for the ungodly." Rom. 5:6. His "strength is made perfect in weakness." 2 Cor. 12:9. He makes men strong out of their weakness. Heb. 11:34. "He giveth power to the faint; and to them that have no might He increaseth strength." He multiplies force to them that are powerless. This He does by giving them Himself. "It is God that worketh in you, both to will and to do of His good pleasure." Think of that! The very same power that is manifested in the heavens, guiding all the planets and stars in their courses, is the power that works in us! All the power that is revealed in the heavens is for us. This is shown by the fact that "He gave Himself for us." He pledged Himself for our salvation. But on Him rests the entire universe. The power that is seen in all creation is His power; it is He Himself at work. Therefore when He gave us Himself, He gave us all the power in the universe. Is it not worthwhile to look up? Do you want an "aid to devotion," and something to put heart into you? Then look up.

Youth is the synonym for strength and endurance. Yet "the youths shall faint and be weary, and the young men shall utterly fall." There is a limit to the endurance of youth. Besides, age comes even to youth, and with age comes weakness and debility. "But they that wait on the Lord shall renew their strength." Mark the implied contrast between youth and age. Youths may fail, but they that wait on the Lord, no matter how old they may be, shall renew their strength. God gives to all who trust in Him eternal life; that is, those who trust in Him get the benefit of it; and the characteristic of eternal life is youth. It renews itself. "Those that be planted in the house of the Lord shall flourish in the courts of our God. They shall still bring forth fruit in old age; they shall be fat and flourishing; to show that the Lord is upright; He is my Rock, and there is no unrighteousness in Him." Ps. 92:13–15. There is in this the miracle of life. Those who *wait* on the Lord, acknowledge Him in all their ways, depending on Him, receive fresh supplies at His hands daily. He shows them the path of life, and directs them in it. He shows them how to live, – how to eat and drink in the right way to renew life. "Godliness is profitable for all things, having promise of the life that now is, and of that which is to come." 1 Tim. 4:8. There are wonderful possibilities in the Christian life, which no man in this generation has yet fathomed. Who will allow God to demonstrate in their bodies what He can do with them that trust Him?

CHAPTER 41

THE GREAT CASE IN COURT

Rev. 14:6: "Fear God, and give glory to Him; for the hour of His judgment is come; and worship Him that made heaven, and earth, and the sea, and fountains of waters."

Isa. 41:1: "Keep silence before Me, O islands; and let the peoples renew their strength; let them come near; then let them speak; let us come near together to Judgment."

Isa. 41:21–23: "Produce your cause, saith the Lord; bring forth your strong reasons, saith the King of Jacob: Let them bring them forth, and show us what shall happen; let them show the former things, what they be, that we may consider them, and know the latter end of them; or declare us things for to come. Show us the things that are to come hereafter, that we may know that ye are gods; yea, do good, or do evil, that we may be dismayed, and behold it together."

Isa. 43:9–12: "Let all the nations be gathered together, and let the people be assembled; who among them can declare this, and show us former things? let them bring forth their witnesses, that they may be justified; or let them hear, and say, it is truth. Ye are My witnesses, saith the Lord, and My servant whom I have chosen; that ye may know, and believe Me, and understand that I am He; before Me there was no god formed, neither shall there be after Me. I, even I, am the Lord, and beside Me there is no Saviour. I have declared, and have saved, and I have showed, when there was no strange god among you; therefore ye are My witnesses, saith the Lord, that I am God."

Ps. 51:3–4: "I acknowledge my transgressions; and my sin is ever before me. Against Thee, Thee only, have I sinned, and done this evil in Thy sight; that Thou mightest be justified when Thou speakest, and be clear when Thou judgest."

Rom. 3:4: "Let God be true, but every man a liar; as it is written, That Thou mightest be justified in Thy sayings, and mightest overcome when Thou art judged."

Isa. 41:28: "I beheld, and there was no man; even among them, and there was no counsellor, that, when I asked of them, could answer a word."

Rom. 3:19: "Now we know that whatsoever the law saith, it saith to them who are under the law; that every mouth may be stopped, and all the world may become guilty before God."

Isa. 1:18: "Come now, and let us reason [literally, "go into court"] together, saith the Lord; though your sins be as scarlet, they shall be as white as snow; though they be red like crimson, they shall be as wool."

1 John 1:9: "If we confess our sins, He is faithful and just to forgive us our sins, and to cleanse us from all unrighteousness."

Isa. 42:21: "The Lord is well pleased for His righteousness sake; He will magnify the law, and make it honourable."

Isa. 43:25–26: "I, even I, am He that blotteth out thy transgressions for Mine own sake, and will not remember thy sins. Put Me in remembrance; let us plead together; declare thou, that thou mayest be justified."

Isa. 45:22–25: "Look unto Me, and be saved, all ye ends of the earth; for I am God, and there is none else. I have sworn by Myself, the word is gone out of My mouth in righteousness, and shall not return, that unto Me every knee shall bow, every tongue shall swear. Surely, shall one say, in the Lord have I righteousness and strength; and all that are incensed against Him shall be ashamed. In the Lord shall all the seed of Israel be justified, and shall glory."

Rom. 14:10–11: "Why dost thou judge thy brother? or why doest thou set at naught thy brother? for we shall all stand before the Judgment seat of Christ. For it is written, As I live, saith the Lord, every knee shall bow to Me, and every tongue shall confess to God."

Before proceeding in our consecutive study of the book of Isaiah, it is necessary to take a general view of the main features of the chapters that follow, since they are so closely connected, and so devoted to one main thought, that we shall not get the full force of them if we go on studying small sections of them without first getting the greater theme in mind.

The whole book of Isaiah is devoted to one great purpose, namely, that of showing who God is. Recall the opening words of the prophecy, where God contrasts His people with the brutes, who know their lord, while His people do not know Him. Since the prophet is sent to those who, through lack of consideration, do not know the Lord, it is self-evident that he must be commissioned to make God known to them in the clearest possible manner, and to bring forward the most striking evidences of His existence and character. Let the student take special notice of the frequent occurrence of the statement, "I am God," and the continual contrasts between the true God and the gods of the heathen.

The book of Isaiah, more than any other in the Bible, is based on the idea of a case in court. When one has learned the fact that the whole universe is a great court, in which a case is continually being tried, and God, the angels both good and bad, and all mankind, are concerned in it, the prophecy of Isaiah, and indeed the whole Bible, can be read with a great deal more pleasure and profit than before.

By most persons the Judgment is doubtless regarded as the time when the Lord determines who are, and who are not, worthy to enter heaven. They imagine all the people of earth gathered about the throne, where an examination is held, and the characters of all men are passed upon. But such an idea as that does very slight justice to the omniscience of God. He does not need to study character in order to discern one's disposition. It is not necessary for Him to study anything. He does not need to make enquiry into a case, and to examine witnesses, as men do, in order to know the facts. "The eyes of the Lord are in every place, beholding the evil and the good." Prov. 15:3. "The word of God is living and active, and sharper than any two-edged sword, and piercing even to the dividing of soul and spirit, of both joints and marrow, and quick to discern the thoughts and intents of the heart." Heb. 4:12. When Jesus was here on earth, "He knew all men, and needed not that any should testify of man; for He knew what was in man." John 2:24–25. The Lord, therefore, does not need, as man does, a time in which to cast up His accounts; for with Him the account is always kept. The exact status of every person living, and every act and every thought of every person who has at any time lived on this earth, could at any moment be set forth by the Lord, who inhabits eternity, and who fills heaven and earth. Therefore it is evidence that the Judgment of the last day is not for the purpose of helping God to a decision as to the worthiness or unworthiness of any person. It will not reveal to the Lord a single thing that He did not know before. Indeed, it will be the Lord Himself who will reveal the hidden things of darkness, and make manifest the counsels of the heart.

Instead of being for the purpose of revealing all the details of the lives of men to God, as so many seem to suppose, the Judgment is for the purpose of revealing to men their own selves, and to make known to them the details of the life of God. Two texts that are quoted in the beginning of this lesson will help to make this appear. Compare Ps. 51:3–4 with Rom. 3:4. In the first instance it is stated that God will be justified when He speaks, and be clear when He judges. In the second, which is a citation of the first, it is stated that He will be justified in His sayings, and will overcome when He is judged. Since the last is but a repetition of the first, and that too by the Spirit, we may be sure that both texts mean exactly the same thing. Therefore we learn that when God judges He Himself is judged. The result will be that He will win the case and be justified.

That last word, "justified," turns our attention to the points in the case. From the very beginning the character of God has been called in question. Satan and his followers have sought to justify their rebellion against God by charging Him with injustice, indifference to the welfare of His subjects, cruelty, and harsh despotism. We see all this set forth in the temptation with which Satan induced Eve to take the forbidden fruit. The Hebrew of the words rendered in Gen. 3:1, "Yea, hath God said, Ye shall not eat of every tree of the garden?" is not by any means fully expressed by that rendering. The serpent's question is accompanied by a covert sneer, a contemptuous sniff, as he says, "Is it so, that God has said, Ye shall not eat of every tree of the garden?" The tempter affects to doubt that even God should be capable of doing so mean a thing as that, thus artfully implanting in the mind of Eve the idea that she has been unjustly dealt with. Then when she repeats the prohibition, the serpent comes out boldly, and says, "Ye shall not surely die; for God knoweth that in the day that ye eat thereof, then your eyes shall be opened, and ye shall be like God, knowing good and evil." He made her believe that God had deceived them in telling them that they should die if they ate of that tree, and that He had told them that story merely to frighten them away from it, because He knew that if they should eat from it they would be equal to Himself, and thus He would lose His prestige and authority over them. By insinuating that God was exalting Himself at their expense, the adversary caused her to feel that she was abused, and to imagine that she had found in the serpent a friend who would help her to secure her rights. From that day to this God has been maligned and willfully misunderstood. Satan's charge of injustice has been repeated by men, and his insinuations have sunk so deeply into the minds of the world, that it does not seem so fearful a thing even for professed followers of the Lord to question His dealings with them. Every doubt is but the echo of the words with which Satan tempted our first parents to sin.

Who has not heard God charged with all the sin and misery in the world? Because God is all-powerful, men say that He is responsible for all the wretchedness; or else, if it be claimed that He is not responsible for it, they say that then He is weak; and in any case they make the presence of sins and misery the fault of God. The spirit of Satan, the prince of the power of the air, works in the children of disobedience (Eph. 2:2), and it is one of the most difficult things in the world to convince anybody that God is love. Absolute trust in God as a tender, loving Father, is a very rare thing, so much so that those who trust Him fully in every detail of life are accounted mildly insane, and unfitted for practical life.

The character of God is therefore on trial. God calls upon men to come into court and prove their charges against Him, and His only defense is the revelation of Himself to them, – the setting forth of

His whole life before them. In Isa. 1:18, where we have, "Come now, and let us reason together," the Hebrew literally rendered is, "Come now, and let us go into court together, saith the Lord." He has been charged with unrighteousness, and His people take up this charge as an excuse for turning away from Him; but God rests His case upon the fact that He forgives sin, and cleanses from all unrighteousness. He is faithful and righteous to forgive us our sins, and this He will do though they be as scarlet. "He was manifested to take away our sins; and in Him is no sin." 1 John 3:5. He never committed a sin, and is not responsible for sin, yet He takes it upon Himself in order that it and all its consequences may for ever be removed. The Judgment is for the purpose of making this clear before every being in the universe; and when that is done, every mouth will be stopped.

The trial is now progressing; the Judgment will be merely the summing up. The Judgment will reveal no new feature that all men may not learn now, or else it would then appear that all men had not had a fair chance. In this present time, while the case is before the jury, which is composed of all creatures, God makes a perfect and complete revelation of Himself and His character, manifesting Himself in all the things that He has made for the benefit of mankind, but chiefly in Jesus Christ whom He has sent. There is no need for anybody to be ignorant of the true character of God. Even the most degraded heathen are "without excuse." Rom. 1:18–20. When in the Judgment men are made to see that to which they have so long willfully shut their eyes; when everything that has been done by men, and by God for men, since the creation, and even God's tender provision for men before the creation of the world, and also the underlying motive of all the acts that have been committed, are set forth before the universe, there will not be found a soul, no matter how malicious and hateful, who can open his mouth to say another word against the love and justice of the Creator and Redeemer. Every one will be compelled by evidence that cannot be evaded, to confess to God, and to bow the knee in token of His right to rule. Even Satan himself will at last be forced by the power of love to acknowledge that "the Lord is righteous in all His ways, and holy in all His works." Ps. 145:17.

Some one will here ask, "Will everybody then be saved?" Not at all; the confession of the wicked will come too late to be counted to them for righteousness. Those who then for the first time confess the love and righteousness of God will not be moved by faith. Although they will acknowledge that God is good, they will have no love for Him. If their probation were continued, they would still go on in the same course of sin. They love sin more than God, or else they would yield to the tender mercy of God while it is now revealed in Christ. Their confession will be only to the effect that the punishment about to be inflicted upon them is just, and but the natural fruit of their own deeds; that they are but receiving the wages for which they have worked all their lives.

We have read that in the Judgment God will be justified in His sayings, that is, in the sentence which He announces. Every word and act of His life will be justified. But we must remember that this Judgment is preceded by a trial, in which there are witnesses. God calls upon all men to be witnesses for Him, and He has a just claim upon their testimony. But Satan is active with his bribes, and he steals away many of God's witnesses. All the world are now taking sides either for or against the Lord. "He that is not with Me is against Me; and he that gathereth not with Me scattereth abroad." Matt. 12:30. Men are now identifying themselves either with the Lord or with the great adversary. It is evident, therefore, that so surely as God is justified will all those be justified who have cast in their lot with Him, and those who have rejected Him, and have challenged His right to rule, declaring that He should not rule over them, must necessarily take themselves out of His dominions when the controversy is ended. But since "His kingdom ruleth over all," it follows that for those who reject God no place in the universe will be found.

This is the time for the friends of God to declare themselves. It is true that in some things *appearances* are against the Lord, but that is only because of our short and distorted vision. We are not wise enough to understand all the workings of God, and we have not exercised ourselves in divine things sufficiently to have our minds toned up to their proper capacity; but enough is made plain to us to enable us to form an opinion. If we declare ourselves on the side of the Lord, even though we cannot explain everything, we are truly

His friends. Enemies may fling their accusations against Him, but we will say, "I do not know all the circumstances, and therefore I cannot give you an explanation of this transaction, but this one thing I do know, that God is just and good, and that if we knew all about this thing of which you accuse Him, you yourself would be compelled to acknowledge that it reveals only the tenderest love and goodness." Such a friend is appreciated by the Lord, and will be acknowledged by Him before the world and angels, at the last day; while those who are ready to doubt the goodness of God at every step, eagerly seizing upon every insinuation which the devil whispers in their ears, thereby shut themselves off from all connection with Him. Character will not be formed, but only declared, in the Judgment.

This is but a brief outline of the case. In the lessons that follow we shall see other features set forth. This court trial is the greatest affair in the universe, and the attention of the student will be called to it in every lesson henceforward. If we all can but realize that we are involved in this case that is now being tried, it would transform our lives. If we but place ourselves close to the throne of grace and view the case as it progresses, it will make clear to us every question that vexes the world.

CHAPTER 42

HE SUMMONS TO THE TRIAL

(Isa. 41:1–13)

"Keep silence before Me, O islands; and let the peoples renew their strength; let them come near; then let them speak; let us come near together to Judgment. Who hath raised up one from the east, whom He calleth in righteousness to His foot? He giveth nations before Him, and maketh Him rule over kings; He giveth them as dust to His sword, and as the driven stubble to his bow. He pursueth them, and passeth on safely; even by a way that He had not gone with His feet. Who hath wrought and done it, calling the generations from the beginning? I the Lord, the first, and with the last, I am He. The isles saw, and feared; the ends of the earth trembled; they drew near, and came. They helped every one his neighbour, and every one said to his brother, Be of good courage. So the carpenter encouraged the goldsmith, and he that smootheth with the hammer him that smiteth the anvil, saying of the soldering, It is good; and he fastened it with nails, that it should not be moved.

"But thou, Israel, My servant, Jacob whom I have chosen, the seed of Abraham My friend; thou whom I have taken hold of from the ends of the earth, and called thee from the corners thereof, and said unto thee, Thou art my servant, I have chosen thee and not cast thee away; fear thou not, for I am with thee; be not dismayed, for I am thy God; I will strengthen thee; yea, I will help thee; yea, I will uphold thee with the right hand of My righteousness. Behold, all they that are incensed against thee shall be ashamed and confounded; they that strive with thee shall be as nothing, and shall perish. Thou shalt seek them, and shalt not find them, even them that contend with thee; they that war against thee shall be as nothing, and as a thing of naught. For I the Lord thy God will hold thy right hand, saying unto thee, Fear not; I will help thee."

Always Comfort

In studying this chapter and all the chapters that follow, do not forget that we are studying the message of comfort which God sends to His people. These last chapters of Isaiah form one connected whole. Right here, in passing, we might notice a fact which may make it more clear to many that this message applies to us in these days. No one who reads these chapters can fail to notice the words of comfort that appear. Promises of God are strewn as thickly as blossoms in spring. These promises have been the support of many Christians, and have helped to bring many sinners to repentance. No believer hesitates to appropriate them to himself. But it is very plain that if this prophecy was given to the Jewish people alone, and applies only to them, then we have no right to the promises that it contains. That is to say, whoever rejects the reproofs which God sends, and the requirements of His law, must also forego the blessings of the Gospel of forgiveness. Men unconsciously appropriate the promises and put aside the law, forgetting that the reproofs of God are comfort. All God's precepts are promises of fulfillment. He gives all that He asks of us. Whenever the law makes sin to abound, it is only for the purpose of driving us to Christ, in whom "the law of the Spirit of Life" super-abounds as grace.

The Whole World Summoned

At every step in our study we shall be reminded of the great trial now on, which was outlined last week. That lesson should be learned so thoroughly that it will be continually in mind without any effort. Those who are using these studies in their Sabbath study should keep the scriptures and the facts set forth in them before them as they study each succeeding lesson. We cannot become too familiar with the fact that a great trial is now taking place, for we have a part in it, and we need to know just what it is. In this chapter we are called to court. The summons is issued to all the world, "the isles," including the utmost bounds of the earth. The heavens are also called upon in this case. Call to mind the opening words of this prophecy (Isa. 1:2), and read also Ps. 50:3–4: "Our God shall come, and shall not keep silence; a fire shall devour before Him, and it shall be very tempestuous round about Him. He shall call to the heavens from above, and to the earth, that He may judge His people." The whole universe is enlisted in this case. It must be so, because the case concerns God Himself, and He upholds the universe.

Keep Silence!

"Silence in the Court!" The case is now being tried, and silence is fitting. What is the case? It is to find out who is God. Men have persuaded themselves that they are gods, and better able to manage the affairs of this world than is the God of the Bible. Now God says, "Be still!" What for? "Be still, and know that I am God; I will be exalted among the heathen; I will be exalted in the earth." Ps. 46:10. If men would only keep still, and not put forth so much of merely human speculation, they would have no difficulty in recognizing God. Being still before the Lord means more than merely refraining from talking. It means to keep silence in the heart, – to let our own thoughts be held in abeyance, that they may be brought into captivity to the obedience of Christ. "The Lord is in His holy temple; let all the earth keep silence before Him." Hab. 2:20. "The Lord's throne is in heaven," and as long as He is able to maintain His place there He has a right to command the silence of all mankind.

In verses 2 and 3 we have undoubted reference to Christ, whom God has raised up, and to whom He has given all power and authority, setting Him over kings. "Also I will make Him My firstborn, higher than the kings of the earth." Ps. 89:27. "Ask of Me, and I will give Thee the heathen for Thine inheritance, and the uttermost parts of the earth for Thy possession. Thou shalt break them with a rod of iron; Thou shalt dash them in pieces like a potter's vessel." Ps. 2:8–9. He is the righteous One, whom God has called in righteousness to do His will.

Some versions of the Bible insert in the margin, as an explanation of verse 2, the word, "Cyrus," meaning that he is the righteous one whom God has called. It is true that later on Cyrus is called by name, and that in his case the foreknowledge of God is displayed, "calling the generations from the beginning," but the text here is sufficient to show that Christ is the One referred to. He is the One upon whom the responsibility of this case rests, for He is the One who declares God to man. God's character is in His keeping. Cyrus was called by name before his birth, but Christ "was foreordained before the foundation of the world." 1 Peter 1:20.

Preparing Their Case

In response to the call the peoples gather. Remember that this case was not called yesterday, but from the very beginning. Every nation under heaven has recognized the fact that a call has been issued to determine who is God, and all have set about the work of making the proof. How do they proceed? They make idols. In the gods that are found in some form in every nation and every tribe on earth, or that has ever existed, there is found proof of the fact that men know that there must be a God, and these idols are their attempts to show who He is. How foolish is their work! The very thing that they depend upon for proof ought to convince them of their folly. They seek to encourage one another, and the carpenter speaks hopefully to the goldsmith, and the founder assures the smith that their work is good and well fastened together. Then to make everything sure, the idol is fastened with nails, so that it may not fall down and be broken to pieces. Note the connection of verses 6 and 7 with verses 18–20 of the preceding chapter.

Self-Justification is Heathenism

The counterpart of this picture is found in the case of every man who seeks to justify himself. The man who will not confess that he is a sinner is putting himself against God. God has said that all men have sinned; and it is certain that there is not a man who is not out of harmony with God. The characters of men are by nature unlike that of God. If therefore men be right, if any man on earth be not a sinner, then it must follow that God is in the wrong. Everybody, therefore, who claims that he has not done wrong in any particular wherein God says that he is a sinner, affirms that God is not the true God, but that he himself is. He is making a god of the works of his own hands. The one who maintains that his course is right, and who is therefore willing to rest his hope on what he himself has done, is in reality just as surely a heathen as is the one who makes images of wood and stone or gold and silver, and worships them. In this picture of the gathering of nations, and their mutual encouragement in their efforts to maintain their cause against the Lord, see a parallel to Ps. 2:1–3.

But now God presents His side of the case. He addresses Himself to Israel. Who is Israel? For an answer turn to Gen. 32:24–28. Jacob wrestled with the Lord, and prevailed when in his helplessness he cast himself on the Lord and asked His blessing. Israel is one who overcomes by faith. Israel represents all who trust the Lord. Israel is the seed of Abraham, who is "the father of all them that believe," and therefore Israel means all who believe.

God's Case

To Israel, that is, to all who will listen to Him, God says, "I have taken thee from the ends of the earth, and called thee from the corners thereof; I have chosen thee, and have not rejected thee." The Lord tells us that He is looking about, seeking to save. The devil as a roaring lion walketh about seeking whom he may devour, while God is searching the world over to find men who will let Him save them. "The Son of man is come to seek and to save that which was lost." Instead of being indifferent to the wants of mankind, God is doing nothing else every moment but watching for chances to save men from the results of their own folly. Go back to the last verses of chapter 40. There is no reason for any to say that God has forgotten them, or that He does not care for their affliction and sorrow. Their way is not hid from the Lord, and their judgment has not passed away from Him. Instead of casting anybody off, God has chosen them, and has gone hunting for them. The Lord says, "Ye have not chosen Me, but I have chosen you." John 15:16. The Apostle Paul addressed the Galatians, who had been rescued from heathenism, as those who had known God, and then he corrected himself by saying that they had rather been known of God. They did not find God by searching, but He revealed Himself to them. "For the Lord will not cast off for ever." Lam. 3:31.

Friendship with God

Abraham is called by God Himself His friend. Just as surely as Abraham was God's friend, God was Abraham's friend. How proud men are to be able to say, "My friend the Duke of ____," or "My friend Lord So-and-So." They feel that a distinction is conferred on them in being acquainted with men of high degree, although those men may be in reality a lie; yet how few esteem it an honour to have God for a friend. Ask a man if he knows Lord This, or Colonel That, and he will be grateful for the compliment, even if he knows nothing of them except their names. He feels honoured to know that you think it possible that he moves in such society. Ask the same man if he knows the Lord, the God of heaven and earth, and nine chances to one he will be offended. Is it not strange?

Just think what a high honour it is to have God say to any man, "My friend." That is what He said of Abraham, and it is what He says of everybody who has the faith of Abraham. Abraham showed his implicit trust in God when he proceeded to offer Isaac on the altar. In that act of faith the scripture was fulfilled which saith, Abraham believed God, and it was imputed to him for righteousness; and he was called the friend of God."

Value of God's Friendship

The Hebrew word rendered "friend" in this scripture before us, is from the verb meaning, to love. It is stronger than the ordinary word for friend or companion. It is used of those who are very intimate, as lovers. When God contracts friendship with men, it is of no ordinary kind. Perfect friendship means the perfection of mutual confidence. Such a thing is really unknown among men, for in the closest intimacies there is always some bar to the complete disclosure of one's self to the other. A feeling that our friend could not understand some things in our own lives, because he has never had any similar experience, and his friendship for us might lessen if he knew of some things in our lives, wherein he himself may never have been tried, causes us to withhold a part of our life from him. We instinctively shrink from making known the secrets of our hearts to anybody, no matter how intimate. But with God the most perfect friendship is possible, for He has experienced everything. He has been tempted in all things like as we are, and so He never despises anybody who has been tempted, but is able to help. If we make Him our confidant, telling Him everything about ourselves, that is confessing our sins and weaknesses, He will in turn show us all of Himself, revealing Himself not merely *to* us, but *in* us, so that we may have righteousness and strength instead of sin and weakness. More than this, He will prove Himself a true friend, and will never betray our confidence. This is the value of confessing to Him. It is not that we tell Him anything about ourselves that He does not already know; but in confessing our sins, we accept His righteousness to cover them. If we do not confess them, then in the Judgment they will be set forth before the whole world; but when we confess them, He takes them away, so that they can never more be found, for they will no more exist, and He Himself will forget them. He will hide the fact that we have sinned from all creation. He will do this by taking away from us every trace of sin. Is not such a friend worth having?

The Comfort of His Presence

"Fear not," God says to the people whom he has chosen, that is, to all who believe and trust Him. Why not fear? – "For I am with thee." He is greater than all, so that none need fear. Read Ps. 27:1–3 and 46 and Isa. 12:2. Read in Matt. 14:22–32 and John 6:16–21 the account of the storm on the sea, when Jesus came to the disciples, walking on the water. When they were afraid, He called out, "I am; be not afraid." It was the same Jesus who said, "Lo, I am with you alway, even to the end of the world." Because He is, there is no cause for fear; for He is everywhere, and is all things that anyone needs. So as soon as the disciples received Him into the boat, immediately they were at the place where they were going. In Him there is the fulfillment of all that we need. Because He is with us, we need not fear though war should rise up and an host encamp against us. In His presence there is fullness of joy. He says that His presence shall go with us, and give us rest. His rod and His staff comfort us, and He prepares a table for us in the presence of our enemies. Do not forget that His rod comforts. We are studying the comfort of the Lord; but too many people think of the rod of the Lord only as an instrument of punishment, an emblem of displeasure. Well, it is true that the Lord does often visit the transgression of His people with the rod, and their iniquity with stripes (Ps. 89:30–32), nevertheless He does not take His loving-kindness from them; the rod of correction is the comfort of the Holy Ghost, who makes known the abounding sin in order to apply the super abounding grace.

The song to be sung in these days is, "Behold, God is my salvation; I will trust, and not be afraid; for the Lord Jehovah is my strength and my song; He also is become my salvation." Isa. 12:2. He strengthens us by His strength. It is interesting to note that the word "taken" in verse 9, "Thou whom I have taken from the ends of the earth," is from the Hebrew word meaning, "to gird," "to make strong." From the ends of the earth God gathers His people, and girds them with strength. He is our strength against the enemy.

Be Not Anxious

Notice the margin in verse 10 in the Revised Version. There we have indicated what is placed in the body of the text in the Danish and Norwegian versions: "Do not look so anxiously around thee." This is very literal and true. The Swedish expresses the same thought, though not so vividly, "Do not seek help from others." God would have His people look straight forward. Time is lost when they look around, and besides they cannot walk straight if they do not look straight ahead. Did you ever notice children when they cross the road? Whoever has driven, or ridden a bicycle, through the streets of a town, cannot fail to have marked it. When a child decides to cross the road, it looks neither to the right nor the left, but goes straight for the opposite side. Surely God has a care for children, else hundreds of them would be killed. They have no thought for themselves. Now whoever would enter the kingdom of heaven must become as a little child. We need not be critical, and say that God does not wish us to be careless. Of course He does not; but He wishes us to be trustful. He tells us to seek the one thing, His kingdom and His righteousness, and everything else will be added to us. We spend too much time calculating probabilities, and discussing possible dangers. God's word to us is, "Go forward." It was when Peter looked around and saw the billows dashing high, that he began to sink. "Looking unto Jesus," is our motto. "Let thine eyes look right on, and let thine eyelids look straight before thee. Ponder the path of thy feet, and let all thy ways be established." Prov. 4:25–26. God will hold our right hand, so that even if we stumble, we shall not utterly fall. "The Lord upholdeth all that fall, and raiseth up all those that be bowed down." Ps. 145:14. So we can say, "Rejoice not against me, O mine enemy; when I fall, I shall arise." Micah 7:8.

CHAPTER 43

FEAR NOT!

(Isa. 41:14–29)

"Fear not, thou worm Jacob, and ye men of Israel. Behold, I will make thee a new sharp threshing instrument having teeth; thou shalt thresh the mountains, and beat them small and shalt make the hills as chaff. Thou shalt fan them, and the wind shall carry them away, and the whirlwind shall scatter them; and thou shalt rejoice in the Lord, thou shalt glory in the Holy One of Israel. The poor and needy seek water and there is none, and their tongue faileth for thirst; I the Lord will answer them, I the God of Israel will not forsake them. I will open rivers on the bare heights, and fountains in the midst of the valleys; I will make the wilderness a pool of water, and the dry land springs of water. I will plant in the wilderness the cedar, the acacia tree, and the myrtle, and the oil tree; I will set in the desert the fir tree, the pine, and the box tree together; that they may see, and know, and consider, and understand together, that the hand of the Lord hath done this, and the Holy One of Israel hath created it.

"Produce your cause, saith the Lord; bring forth your strong reasons saith the King of Jacob. Let them bring them forth, and declare unto us what shall happen; declare ye the former things, what they be, that we may consider them, and know the latter end of them; or show us things for to come. Declare the things that are to come hereafter, that we may know that ye are gods; yea, do good, or do evil, that we may be dismayed, and behold it together. Behold, ye are as nothing, and your work of naught; an abomination is he that chooseth you.

"I have raised up One from the north, and He is come; from the rising of the sun One that calleth upon My name; and He shall come upon rulers as upon mortar, and as the potter treadeth clay. Who hath declared it from the beginning, that we

may know? and beforetime, that we may say, He is righteous? Yea, there is none that declareth, yea there is none that showeth, yea, there is none that heareth your words. I first will say unto Zion, Behold, behold them; and I will give to Jerusalem One that bringeth good tidings. And when I look, there is no man; even among them there is no counsellor, that, when I ask of them, can answer a word. Behold, all of them, their works are vanity and naught; their molten images are wind and confusion."

Another installment of the message of comfort. The title of this entire chapter might well be, "Fear not." This exhortation is parallel to the words so often used by the Saviour, "Be of good cheer." He who says these words is the Creator, the One whose words are things, which contain the very living form and substance of that which they name. Therefore when the Lord says to us, "Fear not;" "Be of good cheer;" He supplies the courage and cheer. "Thou hast put gladness in my heart," says the psalmist. Ps. 4:7. God does not tell us to make ourselves glad, but He Himself makes us glad. "For Thou, Lord, hast made me glad through Thy work; I will triumph in the works of Thy hands." Ps. 92:4. The joy of the Lord is our strength. See Neh. 8:10. God's word is His own life; it is charged with His own personality; when we receive it, we receive Him; therefore when we believe His word implicitly, we have Him and all His joy and peace.

Strength in Weakness

"Thou worm Jacob." Not a very flattering title, is it? But it is the truth. See how the fact is kept before us that the comfort of the Lord does not consist in telling us that we are pretty good, that things are not so bad as they seem, and that if we do not lose confidence in ourselves we shall win. He comforts us by telling us that we are but worms, but grass, nothing at all, and less than nothing. Thus He anticipates every possible doubt on our part. He takes away all ground for saying, "I am so weak and in so desperate a situation that I have no hope; I can surely never overcome." He plucks courage from despair. From the depths He lifts us up to the heights. We often hear some half-hearted professor calling himself a worm as he prays or bears his testimony. We say "half-hearted," advisedly, because in the cases we have in mind they had well-nigh lost heart, and in tones of discouragement they sighed out that they were "but worms of the dust." It was almost a wail of despair, although too feeble to be a wail, and the speaker seemed to think that he ought to grovel before the Lord, and apologize for presuming to come into His presence. But not in any such way does the Lord set the fact before us. When the Lord says, "Thou worm," He does not say it with anything like contempt. He does not despise us. We feel quickened, and breathe in fresh courage, as we hear the words from His lips. There is inspiration in the exclamation. It is a part of the everlasting comfort of the Lord.

Life From the Dead

"And ye men of Israel." This expression is almost meaningless as it stands here, because it does not at all express what the prophet said from the Lord. It is very weak. In the margin of our Bibles a little compensation has been made by inserting the alternative reading, "Ye *few men* of Israel;" But even this does not say what the Lord said. What He plainly said, as it stands in the Hebrew, and as given by Bishop Lowth, is "Ye *mortals* of Israel." Literally, "dying ones." Christ says, "He that believeth in Me, though he were dead, yet shall he live." John 11:25. It is true that God's people are a "little flock" (Luke 12:32), and to them He says, "Fear not;" but they are not only few, they are in a dying condition. They are frail as the grass. They have in themselves no vitality, no principle of life. But what matters that, as long as He is with them, and He is life. Their strength is the Lord Himself. God has chosen us, as we learned from the preceding part of this chapter, but not for what we were worth. He chose us for what He could make of us and do with us.

Instruments in God's Hands

See what He will do with us, weak and frail as we are: He will transform us into a threshing instrument able to thresh even the mountains, and make them small, and to make the hills as chaff. We are nothing, and less than nothing; "but God hath chosen the weak things of the world to confound the things which are mighty; and base things of the world, and things which are despised, hath God chosen, yea, and things which are not, to bring to naught things that are." 1 Cor. 1:27–28. Then let us never again say, "I am so weak, so insignificant, so poor and unknown, so helpless and unworthy, that I cannot do anything." That may all be true, but it does not affect the case. We are not so feeble and despised, so weak and insignificant that the Lord cannot do anything with us. Remember that where the earth and all the starry heavens are now there was nothing until God spoke. Darkness was upon the face of the deep until God said, "Let there be light." Therefore although we be nothing, God can do wonderful things with us. The message of comfort which God sends to His people as a special preparation for His coming makes very prominent the fact that He is the Creator. Whenever we fall into despondency because of our sinfulness and weakness, we lose sight of the fact that God is the Creator, and practically deny it. Let us not do it any more.

Power Over the Nations

Verse 16 says to us poor worms whom the Lord will transform into threshing-machines for threshing mountains to pieces, "Thou shalt fan them, and the wind shall carry them away, and the whirlwind shall scatter them." Now read the prophecy in the second chapter of Daniel, where we read that the stone cut without hands, representing Christ, smote the image which represented all the nations of earth, and broke it to pieces, and it "became like the chaff of the summer threshing-floors; and the wind carried them away, that no place was found for them." Comparing the two texts, we see that the Lord associates His people with Himself in all that He does. He even condescends to acknowledge the help of these poor worms in the work that He does. In a recent Danish translation of Rev. 17:14, where these same kingdoms are spoken of, we find this suggestive reading: "These shall fight against the Lamb, and the Lamb shall overcome them, because it is the Lord of lords and the King of kings and the called and the faithful and the true, who are with Him." In Ps. 2:8–9, we read these words to Christ: "Ask of Me, and I shall give Thee the heathen for Thine inheritance, and the uttermost parts of the earth for Thy possession. Thou shalt break them with a rod of iron; Thou shalt dash them in pieces like a potter's vessel." Now note that in Rev. 2:26–27, the same words are addressed to the saints of God, and the very same power that Jesus Christ Himself receives is given to them: "He that overcometh, and keepeth My works unto the end, to him will I give power over the nations; and he shall rule them with a rod of iron; as the vessels of a potter shall they be broken to shivers; even as I received of My Father." To have the lowest place in the kingdom of God and Christ, is to be exalted to a place higher than that of the kings of the earth; while the weakest soul that can say with full assurance of faith, "Behold, God is my strength," has more power than all the nations.

A Terrible Plague

In verses 17–20 we have undoubted reference to the time of trouble and the glory that shall follow. In Isa. 34 we read of the earth in its desolation. This desolation begins before the coming of the Lord, and continues through the thousand years during which the saints are in heaven with the Lord, sitting in judgment on the wicked. The fourth plague, described in Rev. 16:8–9, dries up everything on the face of the earth. It is such a drought as has never yet been known. By one prophet it is thus vividly described: –

"The barns are broken down; for the corn is withered. How do the beasts groan! the herds of cattle are perplexed, because they have no pasture; yea, the flocks of sheep are made desolate. O Lord, to Thee will I cry; for the fire hath devoured the pastures of the wilderness, and the flame hath burned all the trees of the field. The beasts of the field cry also unto Thee; for the rivers of waters are dried up, and the fire hath devoured the pastures of the wilderness." Joel 1:17–20.

God's People Delivered

But in the midst of this terrible desolation, God's people will not be left to perish. God has not said that they shall not suffer; the disciple is not above his Master, and therefore should not expect to be exempt from suffering with Him. He was hungry and thirsty in the barren wilderness, but He was not forsaken, nor will they be. The promise is, "When the poor and needy seek water, and there is none, and their tongue faileth for thirst, I the Lord will hear them, I the

God of Israel will not forsake them. I will open rivers in high places, and fountains in the midst of the valley; I will make the wilderness a pool of water, and the dry land springs of water." Very forcible is the statement that it is the God of Israel who promises this. That was just what God did for Israel when they came out of Egypt. See Ex. 17:1–6; Ps. 105:41; 114:7–8. God's people will yet have reason to be very grateful for the record of that miracle, for before they are delivered from their sojournings in a strange land to the land of promise, they will need it as a basis for their cry for the same thing to be done for them. Their confidence in that evil day will be the fact that they have drunk from the Fountain of Life, and know that God gives living water. When the "time of trouble such as never was" comes upon the face of the earth, God's people will be delivered, every one whose name is written in the book of life. Dan. 12:1.

A Trial of Strength

The latter part of the forty-first chapter of Isaiah is a call to the nations and their gods to give some proof of their power; to make their case good. "Produce your cause, saith the Lord; bring forth your strong reasons, saith the King of Jacob." State your case, and prove it. Note that the "strong reasons" which the Lord demands are not mere words, but deeds. He backs up His cause by acts. He can point to what He has done in the way of delivering His people. He is the Saviour and Redeemer. What can the false gods show in the way of salvation of a soul? What can any self-righteous man point to in the way of delivering even his own soul from death, to say nothing of helping another? The oppressors who surround God's people,

"Who put their trust in their wealth,
And boast on the extent of their riches,
Yet no one can buy himself off,
None can make payment to God for himself.
The ransom of their soul is too dear, and there is
forever an end of him. Ps. 49:6–9.
(Polychrome edition.)

God tells the end from the beginning. He makes known things to come, by means of the Comforter. John 16:13. Thus His people are able to know what shall come. God inhabits eternity, so that things past, and things present, and things to come are all alike to Him. Therefore whenever anybody either by word or act professes to be God, He has a right to demand that they tell something that is to come, or at the very least tell the whole truth of something that has taken place in the past. Accordingly we find that many false prophets are gone out into the world, attempting to meet this challenge. Spiritualist mediums profess to tell things to come, and create a great sensation by telling people things that have happened in the past. But none of them bear the stamp of Divinity. Compared with the lofty utterances of Inspiration, they are as the peeping of frogs. When God speaks to them, none can answer a word. Thus we have in this chapter an outline of the entire trial, from its call to its conclusion.

CHAPTER 44

THE LORD'S SERVANT

(Isa. 42:1–9)

"Behold My servant, whom I uphold; My chosen, in whom My soul delighteth; I have put My Spirit upon Him; He shall bring forth judgment to the Gentiles. He shall not cry, nor lift up, nor cause His voice to be heard in the street. A bruised reed shall He not break, and the dimly-burning wick shall He not quench; He shall bring forth judgment in truth. He shall not fail nor be discouraged, till He have set judgment in the earth; and the isles shall wait for His law. Thus saith God the Lord, He that created the heavens, and stretched them forth; He that spread abroad the earth, and that which cometh out of it; He that giveth breath unto the people upon it, and spirit to them that walk therein; I the Lord have called thee in righteousness, and will hold Thine hand, and will keep Thee, and give Thee for a covenant of the people, for a light of the Gentiles; to open the blind eyes, to bring out the prisoners from the dungeon, and them that sit in darkness out of the prison house. I am the Lord; that is My name; and My glory will I not give to another, neither My praise unto graven images. Behold, the former things are come to pass, and new things do I declare; before they spring forth I tell you of them."

The student should not fail to note the frequent occurrence of the word "servant," in the book of Isaiah. It would be an interesting and profitable employment to collate all the instances of its use, and compare them. In nothing is there more comfort for us than in the use of this term in the prophecy of Isaiah. By it our relationship to God and Jesus Christ is made very plain.

The reference in this chapter is undoubtedly to Christ. On this there is no possibility for two opinions. Jesus is preeminently the servant of God. In Him the soul of the Father delighteth, for Jesus said, "I came down from heaven, not to do Mine own will, but the will of Him that sent Me" (John 6:38); and, "I do always those things that please Him." John 8:29. He is the only-begotten and well-beloved Son of God, yet He is called God's servant, and this title is given Him as an honour. The servant of God may be a son, and the son can have no higher purpose than faithfully to serve the Father. Note well the fact that Christ is both Servant and Son.

If we obey, we are also servants. Nay, God does not wait to see if we are obedient, before He acknowledges us as His servants; as soon as we yield to Him, we are His. "Know ye not that to whom ye yield yourselves servants to obey, his servants ye are to whom ye obey?" Rom. 6:16. All men are of right the servants of God, in that they owe Him all their service; but so many utterly refuse the service of God that the term is mostly confined to those who are loyal.

Special comfort and encouragement will be derived from the study of Christ as the servant of God, and the words that are spoken of Him in this chapter, if we recall the words addressed to Israel, in the preceding chapter. In verses 8–10 and 13 we read some of the same things that are here said of Christ. "Thou, Israel, My servant, Jacob whom I have chosen, the seed of Abraham My friend; thou whom I have taken hold of from the ends of the earth, and called thee from the corners thereof, and said unto thee, Thou art My servant, I have chosen thee, and not cast thee away; fear thou not, for I am with thee; be not dismayed, for I am thy God; I will strengthen thee; yea, I will help thee; yea, I will uphold thee with the right hand of My righteousness." "I the Lord thy God will hold thy right hand." Israel, it will be remembered, means those who trust the Lord. To those the same terms are applied as to Christ. They are chosen in Him, accepted in the Beloved. Eph. 1:3–6. They are chosen and upheld by the hand, just as is Christ Himself. So in reading this forty-second chapter of Isaiah let us not forget that we are the servants of God equally with Christ, so that the work that is given Him to do is ours also, and all the encouragement that God speaks to Him, He speaks to us also. Jesus calls us to join Him in His service, saying, "Take My yoke upon you, and learn of Me; for I am meek and lowly in heart." Matt. 11:29.

"He shall bring forth judgment to the Gentiles," and He shall set judgment in the earth. To this end the Spirit of God is upon Him. He is the representative of God, charged with the task of carrying on God's case. It is He who conducts God's case at law to a successful issue. He causes judgment to be rendered in God's favour. The Father does not appear in the case at all, except in Christ, who has full authority to speak and act in every matter in the name of the Father. What wonderful confidence the Father has reposed in this Servant! "The Father judgeth no man, but hath committed all judgment unto the Son; that all should honour the Son even as they honour the Father." John 5:22–23. The Father has placed His reputation and even His character in the hands of Jesus Christ. The "faithful and wise servant" of the Lord is made ruler over His household, and set over all His goods. See Matt. 24:45–46. But here again we are brought face to face with the fact that we are servants of the Lord, and that this high place of ruling over the house is entrusted to us. God is not partial. He has no special favourites. What He says to one servant, even though that servant be His only-begotten Son, He says to all. The same love that He has for Christ, He has for us. John 17:23. This places a wonderful responsibility upon us. We see by this, and shall see still more plainly as we proceed, that the Lord has committed His case to us. His character is in our hands. We are to be agents to establish judgment in the earth, and to let the world know who is God.

Jesus, into whose hands so much is committed, is meek and lowly in heart. "He shall not cry, nor lift up, nor cause His voice to be heard in the street." Take notice that this is in the singular, street, and not streets. It does not say that He shall not speak in the open air. As a matter of fact we know that Jesus did most of His teaching in the open air, – in the fields, on the mountain, by the seaside, or sitting by the wayside well. But He was not boisterous and noisy. When speaking in the house, He would not cause His voice to be heard outside. He did not do anything for effect, or seek to attract attention to Himself. See Matt. 12:16–21, where Christ charged the people that they should not make Him known when He had healed a multitude, and it is said to be in fulfillment of this prophecy of Isaiah.

There is undoubtedly much to be learned from Jesus as to the use of the voice, not only in public speaking, but on every occasion. A soft, well-modulated voice, yet clear and distinct, with full tones, marks the master. He who can control his own voice, can control the multitude. A sharp, harsh, rasping voice, pitched in a high key, carries no authority with it. Every servant of the Lord is in duty bound to train his voice as much as the muscles of his arms or legs. It is true that many people in the world do this for gain and applause, and that they become puffed up with pride over the power that it gives them; but this should not deter God's servants from doing so in His name, and for His sake, that they may not misrepresent Him. We can learn of the Lord how to speak properly as well as we can learn anything else; and if we do truly learn of Him, then we shall not become elated over any success that we may have, for He is meek and lowly in heart.

The word rendered "cry," in this instance, is used most frequently of crying out in pain. In this respect it is also true of Christ. "He was oppressed, and He was afflicted, yet He opened not His mouth; He is brought as a lamb to the slaughter, and as a sheep before her shearers is dumb, so He openeth not His mouth." Isa. 53:7. Neither in boasting, nor in anger, nor in pain, did the Lord Jesus cry out. Yet His voice was far-reaching, and many heard. A well-modulated voice is not opposed to the command to lift up the voice with strength and say, "Behold your God!"

Very gentle shall the servant of the Lord be. A reed that is cracked, He will not break off. The candle that is just going out, the wick of which is only a smoking cinder, He will not extinguish. On the contrary, He will breathe upon it, and fan it into a flame again. "For thou wilt light my candle; the Lord God will enlighten my darkness." Ps. 18:28. By this means He will bring forth judgment in truth. This shows that judgment is brought forth by building up that which is weak. God is merciful. He is love. This has been denied by His enemies, and His case is to demonstrate the truth. Therefore those who are charged with the conduct of the Lord's case can win it only by exercising the meekness and gentleness of the Lord. By His care for the poor and needy, the Lord disproves the charges that have been brought against Him.

293

"He shall not fail nor be discouraged till He have set judgment in the earth." It is very interesting to know that the same words are used in this verse as in the preceding. The word rendered "fail" is the same as that rendered "smoking" or "dimly-burning," in verse 3; and "discouraged" is from the word rendered "bruised." He shall not burn dim nor be crushed until His work is accomplished. Of course He will not then; this is an instance of the use of the word "until" where it does not mark the limit. For similar instances, See Gen. 49:10; Ps. 112:8; Gal. 3:19.

A discouraged man is a bruised and crushed man. He is one whose light has almost gone out. Hope is expiring in his breast. Such an one Jesus will restore. He will breathe new life into him. He heals the bruised and crushed one. There is no more difficult task in this world than trying to encourage a despondent person. How many there are who think that they have good reason to be discouraged, because they are so sinful, so easily led astray. They have fallen again and again, until they can scarcely be persuaded that there is any hope of their salvation. The servant of the Lord deals with such cases, whispering words of hope and comfort, and does not himself become discouraged. He receives rebuffs, but will not be crushed by them. His light will not burn dim, but he will gather courage from apparent defeat. What a blessed assurance this is to us when we think of it as applied to Christ! He will not be discouraged until He have set judgment in the earth, that is, in the hearts of men – in our hearts. Then when I am almost discouraged over my many failures, I will think, "The Lord Jesus has the task of making me strong and giving me the victory, and He is not discouraged in spite of my many failures. He knows my weakness and sinfulness better than I do myself. Surely if He is not yet discouraged, I have no cause to be." And thus gathering new courage from the courage of the Lord, we become strong in the Lord, and in the power of His might, and the victory is ours. To us all the Lord says, "Be strong, and of good courage." This was all that He required of Joshua, when He commissioned him to lead Israel into the promised land. Josh 1:6–7,9.

The Lord says that He upholds His servant. The same word is used in the two following instances. "The Lord is the portion of mine inheritance and of my cup; Thou *maintainest* my lot." Ps. 16:5. *"Hold up* my goings in Thy paths, that my footsteps slip not." Ps. 17:5. "I the Lord have called thee in righteousness, and will hold thine hand." "The Lord upholdeth all that fall, and raiseth up all those that be bowed down." Ps. 145:14. Remember that we are the servants of God, if we yield to Him, that is, if we are willing to be His servants; and therefore we have the same promise of being upheld that Jesus Christ Himself had. We have the same power to keep us from falling that He had. Nowhere has the Lord left any ground for discouragement.

The word "hold" in the expression, "hold thine hand," which occurs so frequently in those chapters, is from the Hebrew word meaning *to strengthen*. God promises to strengthen our hand. Everybody knows that one can stand better if he has hold of another's hand, provided, of course, that the other one's hand is stronger than his. Think then what strength comes from having hold of the Lord's hand. He says that He will hold our hand, and uphold us, by the right hand of His righteousness. That is all the encouragement we need. He will not drop our hand, and leave us when danger comes. Remember that the Father is greater than all, and no one can pluck His people out of His hand. John 10:29.

What work has the Lord given His servant? – This, "to open the blind eyes, to bring out the prisoners from the dungeon, and them that sit in darkness out of the prison house." All this we know Christ did; but is anybody else given such work to do? – Most certainly; that is the work of every servant of the Lord, every one whom the Lord chooses. Saul the persecutor was chosen by the Lord to go to the Gentiles, "to open their eyes, and to turn them from darkness to light, and from the power of Satan unto God." Acts. 26:16–18. Now do not straightway say, "Well, I have not the ability of Paul." That has nothing to do with it. Paul was very weak and feeble in body, and had no ability except what the Lord gave him. If the Lord has not given us the ability of Paul, then He does not expect the same work of us; but one thing is certain, namely, that the Lord has sent every one who has accepted Him, every one whom He has chosen in Christ, and made accepted in the Beloved, to do the very same work to which He sent Jesus and Paul. He has not planned for any idle servants. Do not forget that He says, "I the Lord have called thee in righteousness, and will hold thine hand, and will keep thee, and give thee for a covenant of the people, for a light to the Gentiles; to open the blind eyes," etc. If we are connected with an electric battery, all the power of the battery may be felt by anyone who comes in contact with us; so when we have hold of the hand of the Lord, His power becomes ours. Even Paul the Apostle said, "Not that we are sufficient of ourselves to think anything as of ourselves; but our sufficiency is of God, who hath made us able to be ministers of the new covenant." 2 Cor. 3:5.

God will not give His glory to another; that He cannot do, for He cannot deny Himself. He will glorify all who trust in Him, and His glory shall be seen on them; but it will be recognized as His glory. Our light is to shine before men so that they will see our good works and glorify our Father in heaven. God will not divide honours with any creature, much less with a dumb idol, which is nothing in this world. This is not because He wishes to exalt himself at the expense of others, as Satan falsely accused Him of doing, but because He cannot divest Himself of His personality. He *is*; that is His name and His character, and He cannot cease to be. He cannot allow any of the praise due to Him to be given to graven images. He cannot admit that the work of men's hands is right. If He did, that would be the overturning of all righteousness and stability. For the good of all His subjects, and for the maintenance of that which He has created, God must carry the case in which He is concerned to a successful issue. What a blessed assurance it is to know that He will do this. Wrong shall not prevail against God. Though it for a season seems to have the best of the struggle, it is only in appearance, and but for a moment. "In the Lord Jehovah is everlasting strength," and He will gain the victory over all foes. Who will cast in their lot with Him? Who is on the Lord's side?

CHAPTER 45

A NEW SONG

(Isa. 42:10–17)

"Sing unto the Lord a new song, and His praise from the end of the earth; all ye that go down to the sea, and all that is therein, the isles, and the inhabitants thereof. Let the wilderness and the cities thereof lift up their voice, the villages that Kedar doth inhabit; let the inhabitants of Sela sing, let them shout from the top of the mountains. Let them give glory unto the Lord, and declare His praise in the islands. The Lord shall go forth as a mighty man; He shall stir up jealousy like a man of war; He shall cry, yea, He shall shout aloud; He shall do mightily against His enemies. I have long time holden My peace; I have been still, and refrained Myself; now will I cry out like a travailing woman; I will gasp and pant together. I will make waste mountains and hills, and dry up all their herbs; and I will make the rivers islands and will dry up the pools. And I will bring the blind by a way that they know not; in paths that they know not will I lead them; I will make darkness light before them, and crooked places straight. These things will I do, and I will not forsake them. They shall be turned back, they shall be greatly ashamed, that trust in graven images, that say unto molten images, Ye are our gods."

The Song of Deliverance

This new song is the song of deliverance. The thirteenth chapter of Revelation sets before us the exaltation of the Papacy against God, and the influence that it has and will have in all the earth, inducing even the people not nominally under the Papal yoke to do homage to it, and to make an image to it, enacting that all who will not worship either the Papacy or its counterpart shall be killed. But in the midst of that seeming victory of the forces of evil, the prophet saw victory for the people of God. He says: –

"I looked, and lo, a Lamb stood on the Mount Zion, and with Him an hundred, forty and four thousand, having His Father's name written in their foreheads. And I heard a voice from heaven, as the voice of many waters, and as the voice of a great thunder; and I heard the voice of harpers harping with their harps; and they sang as it were a new song before the throne, and before the four beasts, and the elders; and no man could learn that song but the hundred and forty and four thousand which were redeemed from the earth." Rev. 14:1–3.

The Song of Moses

That is to say, none could learn that song except those who had been through the experience. Passing on to the fifteenth chapter, we read: –

"And I saw another sign in heaven, great and marvelous, seven angels having the seven last plagues; for in them is filled up the wrath of God. And I saw as it were a sea of glass mingled with fire; and them that had gotten the victory over the beast, and over the number of his name, stand on the sea of glass, having the harps of God. And they sing the song of Moses the servant of God, and the song of the Lamb, saying, Great and marvelous are Thy works, Lord God Almighty; just and true are Thy ways, Thou King of saints. Who shall not fear Thee, O Lord, and glorify Thy name? for Thou only art holy; for all nations shall come and worship before Thee; for Thy judgments are made manifest." Rev. 15:1–4.

From these texts we see that the new song which the redeemed sing is the song of Moses the servant of God. In the fifteenth chapter of Exodus we find that song recorded. It begins, "I will sing unto the Lord, for He hath triumphed gloriously; the horse and his rider hath He thrown into the sea. The Lord is my strength and song, and He is become my salvation." Then we read, "Who is like unto Thee, O Lord, among the gods? who is like Thee, glorious in holiness, fearful in praises, doing wonders? Thou stretchedest out Thy right hand, the earth swallowed them. Thou in Thy mercy hast led forth the people which Thou hast redeemed; Thou hast guided them in Thy strength unto Thy holy habitation." Verses 11–13. So we see that the new song is a song of exultation at the power of the Lord over all who exalt themselves against Him, professing to be gods. And inasmuch as God triumphs over all false gods, whether it be in the shape of graven or molten images, or in the shape of men who profess to be authorized to speak and act in God's stead, it necessarily follows that all who identify their cause with His must at the same time triumph also. Therefore the new song is a song of thanks to God who giveth us the victory through our Lord Jesus Christ. 1 Cor. 15:57.

The Time of Trouble

Read again the texts cited from the book of Revelation, and note that in each case the new song is mentioned in immediate connection with the time of trouble. When the people of God seem about to be overwhelmed, then the prophet sees them singing a new song on Mount Zion. In this he stands as the representative of all God's people. It is to teach us that the new song, the song of victory, is to be sung in the time of greatest danger. In the portion of Isaiah which we are studying, we see that this is so. The call to sing unto the Lord a new song is immediately followed by a description of the going forth of the Lord as a warrior. It is in connection with the time when mountains and hills are to be laid waste, and rivers and pools are to be dried up. At that time all the earth is called upon to sing a new song. The inhabitants of the desert and the mountain are called upon to give glory unto the Lord, and declare His praise in the islands.

The Reason for Singing

Compare this scripture with the ninety-sixth Psalm: –

"O sing unto the Lord a new song; sing unto the Lord, all the earth. Sing unto the Lord, bless His name; show forth His salvation from day to day. Declare His glory among the heathen, His wonders among all people. For the Lord is great, and greatly to be praised; He is to be feared above all gods. For all the gods of the nations are idols [that is, nothing]; but the Lord made the heavens. Honour and majesty are before Him; strength and beauty are in His sanctuary. Give unto the Lord, O ye kindreds of the people, give unto the Lord glory and strength. Give unto the Lord the glory due unto His name. Bring an offering, and come into His courts. O worship the Lord in the beauty of holiness; fear before Him all the earth. Say among the heathen that the Lord reigneth; the world also shall be established, that it shall not be moved; He shall judge the people righteously. Let the heavens rejoice, and let the earth be glad; let the sea roar, and the fullness thereof. Let the field be joyful, and all that is therein; then shall all the trees of the wood rejoice before the Lord; for He cometh, for He cometh to judge the earth; He shall judge the world with righteousness, and the people with His truth."

This is exactly parallel with the portion of Isaiah which we are studying. It is the triumph of the Lord over all false gods, that is, over every high thing that exalteth itself against the knowledge of God. It is the same thing that is described in Isa. 2, when "the day of the Lord shall be upon every one that is proud and lofty, and upon every one that is lifted up; and he shall be brought low." "And the loftiness of man shall be bowed down, and the haughtiness of men shall be made low, and the Lord alone shall be exalted in that day. And the idols He shall utterly abolish." It is the day when the Lord in "the glory of His majesty" ariseth "to shake terribly the earth." In this time the new song is to be sung by the people of God. God's people are to sing best when the cloud hangs darkest.

This is made still more emphatic in the third chapter of Habakkuk. A terrible time is described by the prophet, so terrible that he trembled at the mere vision of it, and prayed that he might be spared from living through the reality. Yet he says: "Although the fig tree shall not blossom, neither shall fruit be in the vines; the labour of the olive shall fail, and the fields shall yield no meat; the flock shall be cut off from the fold, and there shall be no herd in the stalls [compare Joel 1:10–20]; yet will I rejoice in the Lord, I will joy in the God of my salvation. The Lord God is my strength, and He will make my feet like hinds' feet, and He will make me to walk upon mine high places." Hab. 3:17–19. No trouble can come on the earth that is so great that God's people cannot sing. It is very common for people to sing when they see no trouble; but it is indeed a new song that is sung when trouble is thickest.

The New Song and the Old Story

The last text quoted reminds us of the fortieth Psalm. The prophet says that God has made him sure-footed, so that he can walk safely on high places. So we read: "I waited patiently for the Lord; and He inclined unto me, and heard my cry. He brought me up also out of an horrible pit, out of the miry clay, and set my feet upon a rock, and established my goings. And He hath put a new song into my mouth, even praise unto our God." Ps. 40:1–3. We see therefore that the new song that is to be sung by the saints on Mount Zion is but the song that is sung by them in the wilderness of trial. It is the song of redemption from sin. In the victory over sin, we have the victory over everything.

> "When in scenes of glory,
> I sing the new, new song,
> 'Twill be the old, old story
> That I have loved so long."

The Silent Watcher

The fact that God is silent, and does not at once strike down injustice and those who practice oppression, is no sign that He takes no notice. It is very hasty judgment that declares that God does not care. How can He help caring, when every wrong that is committed is done to Him? He has identified Himself with mankind, so that whosoever does good or evil to one of the least of them, does it to the Lord. Matt. 25:40,45. Do not forget that there is no searching of God's understanding, and nothing too small for His notice. He upholds the heavens and the earth. "But they are great things," you say. True, but they are composed of an infinite number of very small particles; and if God did not have a care over every tiny particle, He could not preserve the whole. God's care for the whole earth is only His care for every atom composing the earth. If he did not look after the fragments, there would be waste. If He did not care for the atoms, because they are small and insignificant, then they would fly off into space, and soon He would have no great things to attend to. So let every soul be assured that the Lord has the same care for him that He has for the whole world.

The Promise Sure

Men are saying, "Where is the promise of His coming?" They are saying that the world is governed by chance, or that God is indifferent to the ills of mankind. Thus they are putting themselves against Him in His great case. They are among His accusers. They forget that "the long-suffering of our God is salvation." 2 Peter 3:15. Mark that word "long-suffering." God suffers when men suffer. He keeps still, not through indifference, but because of infinite patience and forbearance and self-control. This is to teach men patience. It is for the purpose of giving the worst scoffers time for repentance. But He will finally rise up and scatter His enemies. See Ps. 48. "Be patient therefore, brethren, unto the coming of the Lord." James 5:7.

Walking in the Light

What a wonderful promise is in the 16 verse! "I will bring the blind by a way that they know not; in paths that they know not will I lead them; I will make darkness light before them, and crooked places straight." Therefore we may with full confidence pray, "Lead me, O Lord, in Thy righteousness, because of mine enemies; make Thy way straight before my face." Ps. 5:8. That is the day when "the eyes of the blind shall see out of obscurity, and out of darkness." Isa. 29:18. The darkness and the light are both alike to the Lord (Ps. 139:11–12), so that the night shall be light about His people. Remember that all this time God has His people by their right hand. What matter then if they do not know the way? With God leading, a blind man is far better off than a man with eyes who is walking alone, even though it be in the light. Eyes are of no use to those who do not trust the Lord, for the fact that they do not trust Him shows that they do not know Him, and that proves that they cannot see; for He is everywhere plainly revealed. They are like the idols in which they trust, and shall be turned back, and put to confusion, together with the gods in which they trust. The case of the Lord vs. the false gods is as good as settled now, so that whoever puts himself on the Lord's side is taking no risk.

CHAPTER 46

MAGNIFYING THE LAW

(Isa. 42:18–25)

"Hear, ye deaf; and look, ye blind, that ye may see. Who is blind, but My Servant? or deaf, as My Messenger that I send? who is blind as He that is at peace with Me, and blind as the Lord's Servant? Thou seest many things, but Thou observest not; His ears are open, but He heareth not. It pleased the Lord, for His righteousness' sake, to magnify the law, and make it honourable. But this is a people robbed and spoiled; they are all of them snared in holes, and they are hid in prison houses; they are for a prey, and none delivereth; for a spoil, and none sayeth, Restore. Who is there among you who will give ear to this? that will hearken and hear for the time to come? Who gave Jacob for a spoil, and Israel to the robbers? did not the Lord? He against whom we have sinned, and in whose ways they would not walk, neither were they obedient unto His law. Therefore He poured upon him the fury of His anger, and the strength of battle; and it set him on fire round about, yet he knew it not; and it burned him, yet he laid it not to heart."

Always More to Follow

In studying portions of Scripture which are "hard to be understood," we shall save ourselves from falling into error if we adopt the rule, and rigidly adhere to it, never to guess at anything. Another thing we must always bear in mind, and that is, that no one on earth can give any statement as to the teaching of any text, which will be final and authoritative. That is to say, nobody can exhaust any portion of God's Word. When we have stated what we see in any text, that does not hinder somebody else from seeing a great deal more. The trouble with people who read what anyone has written, in whom they may have confidence, is in assuming that he has said all that may be said on that subject. Or, seeing the thing plainly, when it is set before them, they are satisfied, and do not think it worth while to keep on looking, so as to see more. That is wrong. No matter how much we see in any word of the Lord, we may be assured that there is much more that we do not see. A belief in the Divine perfection and fullness of God's Word, would keep any people from ever publishing a "creed," summarizing the teachings of the Bible. Let these things be borne in mind as we study.

Christ's Divine Mission Proved

When Jesus was here on this earth, He proved the Divinity of His mission by causing the blind to see, and the deaf to hear. Matt 11:5. Many miracles did Jesus in the presence of the people, that they might believe that He is the Christ, and that, believing, they might have life through His name. John 20:30. The prophecy of Isaiah shows that the great controversy as to who is God will be continued until the very last day of time, – until the Judgment settles the question for ever. Then since it was necessary that miracles should be performed eighteen hundred years ago, in order to demonstrate the genuineness of the mission of Christ, God's Representative, it cannot be otherwise than that the same things must be repeated as long as there is any doubt over the matter.

Miracles to be Wrought

That miracles of healing will be performed by the servant of the Lord even in the very last days, is evident from the scripture before us. "Hear, ye deaf; and look, ye blind, that ye may see." Someone will say (for there are always people ready to discount the Word of God, and to make out that God has not promised us very much) that this command to the deaf to hear, and to the blind to see, is to be taken in a spiritual sense; that those who do not understand the truth of God, and who are spiritually blind, are to see the Lord, and to understand the truth. Undoubtedly that is true. But the urging of that in order to break the apparent force of the text, shows that they do not appreciate the greatness of the work of conversion. Which is greater, to say, "Thy sins be forgiven thee" or to say to a palsied man, "Rise, take up thy bed, and walk?" Is it easier to make a man behold his God than to cause him to see his fellows? Why should anybody who believes in conversion think it a strange thing that

God should heal any defect in the body? Without doubt all these texts mean that people will understand the Gospel, but that does not show that they will not also receive bodily healing, but the contrary. It may well be, however, that the most of these mighty miracles will be wrought in what are called heathen lands, and that these boasted lands of enlightenment, where the Gospel has been preached so much, and so much slighted, have already had the most of the evidence that will be given them. It is the isles that are waiting for the law of God, and God's servant is commissioned to the Gentiles, to open the blind eyes.

Sight for the Blind

"Who is blind, but My Servant? or deaf, as My Messenger that I send?" "He saved others, Himself He cannot save." This was said of Christ. He Himself suffered all the ills from which He delivered men, yet He did nothing for Himself. And this shows that there is no condition that is hopeless. We are deaf and blind; very well, the Lord says that His Servant whom He upholds, His chosen, in whom His soul has delight, whom He has sent to open the blind eyes, is also blind. He has assumed all our blindness. No one is afflicted as He is, because He has the combined afflictions of all men. No soul of man has so great a weight of sin on him as the Lord Jesus Christ had, for He had the sins of the whole world. But He is "the Holy One and the Just," therefore there is not a soul on earth but may also be just and holy. In Him, all deafness and blindness, all infirmities of whatever kind, both physical and spiritual, are removed. "In Him is no darkness at all." Therefore though we be blind and deaf and dumb and lame and vile, all this is passed from us to Him. "With His stripes we are healed." Even so, with the blindness that He has assumed, we see.

God's Intimate Friends

"Who is blind as He that is perfect?" The Revision has, "as he that is at peace with Me." The Norwegian has it, "as My confidential friend," and this is warranted by the Hebrew fully as much as either of the others. This fits with what has preceded, when we remember that the servant of the Lord is Israel, the seed of Abraham, God's friend. What care we what our condition is, so long as we are God's confidential friends? We may be in prison, but that makes no difference as long as the key is in the hands of our intimate friend. Remember this as you read the last verses of this chapter.

God's Righteousness

The Danish translation of verse 21, "the Lord is well pleased for His righteousness' sake; He will magnify the law, and make it honourable," is, "the Lord has pleasure, for the sake of His righteousness, to make the law great and glorious." This shows that the law of God is His righteousness. The more the law is honoured, the more the righteousness of God is exalted. The greater the law, the greater the righteousness of God. Let us see if there is any comfort in this.

The psalmist says, "If the foundations be destroyed, what can the righteous do?" Ps. 40:3. The foundation of God's throne is righteousness (Ps. 89:14; 97:2); and God's throne upholds the universe. If the foundations were destroyed, therefore, there would be no existence for anybody. If righteousness should cease, of course the righteous would cease to be, as well, since the righteous are the salt of the earth. But there is no danger, for Jesus said, "Think not that I am come to destroy the law, or the prophets; I am not come to destroy, but to fulfill. For verily I say unto you, Till heaven and earth pass, one jot or one tittle shall in no wise pass from the law, till all be fulfilled." Matt. 5:17–18. The Lord will not destroy or alter the law, because that is His righteousness, and He cannot deny Himself.

Fulfilling the Law

A complete answer to anyone who is so perverse that in the face of the plain statement of Christ, that He did not come to destroy the law, he will say that Christ fulfills the law by abolishing it, is found in the words of the text: "He will magnify the law, and make it honourable." What honour can anyone give to Christ, and in what sort of esteem does he hold His work, who says that Christ destroys that which is honourable, and holy, and just and good?

"But He fulfilled the law," says one. That is exactly what He did. What then? "Oh, then we do not need to do it; since He fulfilled it, we can have nothing to do with it." Indeed, that sounds very strange from the lips of one who professes to love the Lord Jesus. It is very easy to understand how one who says, "We will not have this Man to reign over us," can say, "We do not wish to have anything to do with anything that He is connected with." But why should a Christian desire to be separated from that which finds its fullness in Christ?

Not Under the Law

"But we are not under the law." No indeed, thank the Lord for that. And why are we not under it? Because we walk in it. Have you forgotten that the message of comfort prepares the way of the Lord? and that the undefiled in the way are those who walk in the law of the Lord? Ps. 119:1–3. We are delivered from the law, which condemned us to death for our transgression, that we should serve in newness of spirit, and not in the oldness of the letter. Rom. 7:4–6. And this is done by the body of Christ, in whom the law finds its perfect fulfillment. When we are joined to Christ in perfection, then the same fullness of the law will be found in us. The curse of the law is not to them that do it, but upon them that do not continue in all things that are written in it. Gal. 3:10–13. Christ has redeemed us from the curse of the law; that is, He has redeemed us from disobedience, unto perfect obedience.

Sin Abounding, Grace Super-Abounding

"He will magnify the law." "By the law is the knowledge of sin." Rom. 3:20. Therefore the greater the law is made to appear, the greater will sin appear. It was just for this reason that the law entered, "that the offence might abound." Rom. 5:20. "But where sin abounded, grace did much more abound." So we see that in magnifying the law, God is making His grace to abound, in revealing His righteousness, which He puts in and upon us, for the remission of sins. The magnifying of the law, and making it honourable, is but the preaching of the Gospel of Jesus Christ.

The Law of Life and the Law of Death

The law is righteousness, yet righteousness does not come by it. That is, righteousness does not come by any man's works of the law. It is only "the law of the Spirit of life in Christ Jesus" (Rom. 8:2), that makes us free from sin and death. The righteousness which is by the faith of Christ (Phil. 3:9), is the only righteousness that will enable anybody to stand in the day of Christ's coming; for the law is in His heart in perfection. The law in the heart of Christ is the law of which a copy was placed on tables of stone by the finger of God. In Christ we have it upon the Living Stone, and not upon the dead stone. So while on the tables of stone given to Moses, it is only death, on the Living Stone, Christ Jesus, it is life. The magnifying of the law shows us how great is the gift of life which God bestows in Christ.

Precepts and Promises

For it must be known that all the precepts of God are promises. Nobody has ever first given something to the Lord, that it should be recompensed unto him again; "for of Him, and through Him, and to Him, are all things." Rom. 11:35–36. God does not give us life as a reward for something that we have done for Him, but He gives us life which contains the performance of the things which He wishes us to do. When God says, "Thou shalt not," He does not mean that we must keep ourselves from some evil, but that He will provide the means whereby we shall be kept.

By comparing two texts of Scripture we can readily see this. God said to all Israel, "I am the Lord thy God, which have brought thee out of the land of Egypt, out of the house of bondage. Thou shalt have no other gods before Me." Ex. 20:2–3. Again He says: "Hear, O My people, and I will testify unto thee; O Israel, if thou wilt hearken unto Me, there shall no strange god be in thee; neither shalt thou worship any strange god. I am the Lord thy God, which brought thee out of the land of Egypt." Ps. 81:8–10. From this we learn that when God spoke the ten commandments He meant that if the people would but hearken to Him, they should be kept from all evil. The greater the requirement of the law, the greater the gift of

God. The magnifying of the law is the magnifying of the grace of God.

Terrible Manifestations of Mercy

The terrors of Sinai reveal the mercies of Calvary. Men are accustomed to think and speak of the terrors of the law as given on Sinai, but they forget that Calvary is equally terrible. Was it death to touch the mount where the law was proclaimed? even so Calvary meant death. There were thunders and darkness and earthquake at Sinai, and at Calvary there were the same. Yea, even from the throne of grace, to which we are invited to come and obtain mercy and find grace to help in time of need, proceed lightnings and thunderings, and voices which cause the earth to quake. Rev. 4:5; 11:19. The awfulness of Calvary, which wrung from the lips of the Saviour the cry, " My God, My God, why hast Thou forsaken Me?" and which broke His heart, show the greatness of the law which had been broken. On the cross Jesus magnified the law of God. There it was shown that so unchangeable is the law, that it will take the life even of the only begotten Son of God, when He is "numbered among the transgressors." But the greater and more awful it appears, the more may we rejoice, because we know that God has pledged His own existence to the bestowal of all its righteousness upon us. What a blessed promise it is, that God will magnify the law. Let no one speak lightly of that which Christ by His death made honourable.

Time for God to Work

"It is time for Thee, Lord, to work; for they have made void Thy law." Ps. 119:126. Men have despised and rejected the law of God, and in this they have been aided by His professed followers; for there are many who bear the name Christian, who do not hesitate to speak most disparagingly of the law. So it is thought so small a matter, that men have no hesitation in putting their own laws in its stead. In this, they are despising and rejecting Christ, whose life it is. Now as the great controversy is to decide who is God, it follows that in the last days, when the message goes forth, "Behold your God!" the law in Christ must be proclaimed as never before. God will show that He is our Judge, our Lawgiver, and our King, in that He alone can save. Isa. 33:22. But bear in mind that when the Lord works to magnify His law, because men have made it void, He is not working merely to vindicate His own rightful place, but He is working for men. The law of God has been made void in men's hearts, in that they have driven it out, and have turned to their own way. It is time for Him to work, but where? – in men's hearts, to lift up the standard of righteousness. Men by making void the law of God have fallen by their iniquity and God works to restore them by restoring the law in their hearts. And "now is the accepted time, now is the day of salvation."

CHAPTER 47

I AM WITH THEE

(Isa. 43:1–7)

1. "Yet now, thus saith Jehovah; Who created thee, O Jacob; and who formed thee, O Israel: fear thou not, for I have redeemed thee; I have called thee by thy name; thou art Mine.

2. When thou passest through waters, I am with thee; and through rivers, they shall not overwhelm thee; when thou walkest in the fire, thou shalt not be scorched; and the flames shall not take hold of thee.

3. For I am Jehovah, thy God; The Holy One of Israel, thy Redeemer; I have given Egypt for thy ransom; Cush and Seba in thy stead.

4. Because thou hast been precious in My sight, Thou hast been honoured, and I have loved thee; therefore will I give men instead of thee; and peoples instead of thy soul.

5. Fear thou not, for I am with thee; from the east I will bring thy children, and from the west I will gather thee together;

6. I will say to the north, Give up; and to the south, Withhold not; bring My sons from afar; and My daughters from the ends of the earth:

7. Every one that is called by My name, whom for My glory I have created; whom I have formed, yea, whom I have made."

No attention should be paid to the chapter division here, although as a matter of convenience we have made it the division of a lesson. But there is no break in the subject, and we cannot get the full force of the scripture here quoted without reading the last part of chapter 42. "Who gave Jacob for a spoil, and Israel to the robbers? did not the Lord, He against whom we have sinned? for they would not walk in His ways, neither were they obedient unto His law. Therefore He hath poured upon them the fury of His anger, and the strength of battle; and it hath set him on fire round about, yet he

311

knew it not; and it burned him, yet he laid it not to heart. But now thus saith the Lord that created thee, O Jacob, and He that formed thee, O Israel, Fear not; for I have redeemed thee, I have called thee by name; thou art Mine." And then follows the assurance that God is with them even in the fire and the water, and that they shall not be burned or overwhelmed. He who gave Israel into captivity is his Redeemer.

Present Help

Our versions make the mistake of rendering verse 2, "I *will be* with thee." The common version is better than the Revision, in that it places the words "will be" in Italics, indicating that they are not found in the Hebrew, as they are not. There is no verb expressed, as is often the case in the Hebrew, which is very brief. Now it is evident that when the copulative verb is omitted, the simplest form of it is that which should be supplied, which is the present tense, and not the future. Therefore it is correctly given by Lowth, "I *am* with thee." That exactly represents the character of God, whose name is I AM. There can be no doubt that God will be with us, when He is always present. With Him the present contains both the past and the future. He is always I AM; therefore in all the ages to come He will be the hope of His people. But if we read it, "I will be with thee," we are apt to forget the present. The present is all that we are concerned with; if we have God with us as "a very present help in trouble," we can ask for nothing more. With God it is always *now*.

The Secret of Discontent

"Be ye free from the love of money; content with such things as ye have, for Himself hath said, I will in no wise fail thee, neither will I in any wise forsake thee. So that with good courage we may say, "The Lord is my Helper; I will not fear; What shall men do unto me?" Heb. 13:5–6, R.V. Having Him, we have everything. That is true enough, and no one will deny it; and yet we very seldom act as though we believed it. And that shows how rare real Christianity is; for the very fundamental principle of Christianity is the continual presence of the Lord, and that He is everything. He who does not believe that God is always present, always loving, and always all-powerful to carry out His loving designs, does not believe in

God. But whoever believes that must be content, because he knows that with the Lord he has all things. Rom. 8:32. It follows, therefore, that anxiety and worry are marks of heathenism. "Be not therefore anxious, saying, What shall we eat? or, What shall we drink? or, Wherewithal shall we be clothed? For after all these things do the Gentiles seek; for your heavenly Father knoweth that ye have need of these things. But seek ye first His kingdom, and His righteousness; and all these things shall be added unto you." Matt. 6:31–33.

What Constitutes Heathenism

There is more to this than appears on the surface. We are not aware how often we proclaim ourselves heathen. Consider this very apparent distinction between the heathen and the worshiper of the true God: The heathen is not content without a god that he can see; while the Christian trusts the God who dwelleth in the light which no man can approach unto, whom no man hath seen, neither can see. 1 Tim. 6:16. In short, the heathen cannot trust his god out of sight, while the Christian has as much confidence in his God when he cannot see Him as when he can. Now no one would ever complain if he could see all that he desired ready to hand. It is when we cannot see how we are to get on, that we begin to murmur or grow anxious. Yea, it is often a murmur, in that the desponding one says, "God has forsaken me." Because he cannot see God, he thinks that He does not exist. We doubt God, because we cannot see Him. We cannot endure that He should work behind a veil. Thus we proclaim ourselves heathen. People may think that it is not a very great thing to believe in God, but really to believe in God is everything. Real belief in God means freedom from all worry, because God cares for us, and tells us to cast all our care on him. 1 Peter 5:7.

God's Nearness

"I am with thee." Therefore we are not to fear. Jesus came and said, "Lo, I am with you alway, even unto the end of the world," and He had just said, "All power is given unto Me in heaven and in earth." Matt. 28:18,20. He cannot leave us nor forsake us, because He fills heaven and earth. Jer. 23:24. In every sunbeam, in every sparkling drop of water, in every breath of air, the Lord is present, and His presence is with us for the purpose of giving us rest. Ex.

33:14. How near He is, when we can feel His breath upon our cheek, yea, even in our nostrils. "For what nation is there so great, who hath God so nigh unto them, as the Lord our God is in all things that we call upon Him for?" Deut. 4:7.

Christ's Saving Presence

"Fear not!" Why not? "For I am with thee." The Lord has left on record some examples of the saving power of His presence, so that we may learn not to fear. After the miracle of feeding the five thousand with five loaves, when the people were about to take Jesus by force, and make Him king, he constrained His disciples to get into the boat, and to go before Him to the other side of the sea, while He sent the multitudes away. The night came on, and "the sea arose by reason of a great wind that blew," and the ship in which the disciples were "was now in the midst of the sea, tossed with the waves," "and it was now dark, and Jesus had not come to them." Then suddenly they saw a form walking calmly on the angry waters, and they cried out with fear; but Jesus said to them, "It is I;" literally, "I am;" "be not afraid." It is the same word, "Fear not, for I am with thee." They thought that they were alone on the waters, but His eye was upon them all the time. His name is I AM, and He was with them when they could not see Him as well as when He appeared to them.

The Author and Finisher

When the disciples recognized the Lord, "they willingly received Him into the ship." Their fear was past. Then what? "Immediately the ship was at the land whither they went." He is the beginning and the end. With His presence there is the fulfillment of all things. The task that is but just begun is finished if it is begun in Him. They feared no more, after Jesus came to them; yet there was no more reason to fear before they saw Him, than there was afterwards. Would we fear in any circumstances whatever, if we could see Jesus right before us, or at our right hand? You say, "No; not at all." But we do fear, and yet He is present. "I have set the Lord always before me; because He is at my right hand, I shall not be moved." Ps. 16:8. Are our fears due to the fact that we do not have confidence in the saving power of the Lord? or because we do not believe that He is present? In either case, they are a remnant of heathenism that we have not yet shaken off.

In the Fire

There were three Hebrew captives in Babylon, who proved the power of the presence of the Lord. A stern decree had been issued, commanding everybody to bow down before a golden image that the king had set up. The penalty for disregarding the decree was burning in a furnace. They unqualifiedly refused to bow down to the image. Here was a test as to who was God. Was it the king and his idols? or was it the God of Israel? If the three men had bowed down through fear, what would their act have said? It would have said that they did not believe in God; that they could not trust in Him to deliver them from the king and his idols. But their profession of faith was more than a theory. They knew whom they had believed, and that their God was able to deliver them. So into the fiery furnace they went, where the fire was so hot that it slew the men who had to draw near to the outside of it to cast them in. But what of them? God had said, "When you walkest in the fire, thou shalt not be scorched; and the flame shall not take hold on thee;" and so it was. Only their bands were burned off, and the three men rose and walked erect in the midst of the furnace; for God was with them. Then the king commanded them to be brought out, " and the princes, governors, and captains, and the king's counsellors, being gathered together, saw these men, upon whose bodies the fire had no power, nor was an hair of their head singed, neither were their coats changed, nor the smell of fire had passed upon them." Dan. 3:27.

Present Though Invisible

Did you ever think that we hear nothing more about the form of the fourth after the three men were taken from the furnace? He was clearly seen for a few moments, walking to and fro with them in the flames; then the doors were opened and the men were called forth, and their companion disappeared. Did He forsake them? Not at all; He was as near them when they could not see Him as when He appeared. In fact, there is nothing to show that the three men in the fire saw Him at all. His appearance was more for the benefit of the king and his idolatrous court, then for the three men themselves.

They knew that He was present without seeing Him. It was the consciousness of His presence that made them able to stand unmoved in the presence of the threatened punishment. God is unchangeable. Jesus Christ is the same yesterday, and for ever; therefore He is as near when unseen as He is when He is seen. They who believe and trust in His presence when they cannot see Him will at the last have the privilege of seeing His face, and beholding Him for evermore.

Dwelling with Everlasting Burning

There is coming a time when "the heavens being on fire shall be dissolved, and the elements shall melt with fervent heat." 2 Peter 3:12. "The earth also and the works that are therein shall be burned up." Then the inhabitants of the earth shall be burned, and few men will be left. Isa. 24:6. Who will be the few men left? Only those who are able to dwell with the devouring fire, and amidst everlasting burnings. Isa. 33:14–15. Those who make the Most High their habitation, being confident of His presence, even though it may *seem* that He has forsaken them, will be able to dwell in the midst of the fire that devours the earth, for they dwell with God, and "our God is a consuming fire." Heb. 12:29. This promise in Isaiah will be very real to many before very long. But none will be able to trust in it when the great test comes, except those who have lived in the consciousness of God's presence, and the proof of it in the deliverance from sin.

God With Us

What is the practical daily result of having God with us? Well, of course, in the first place it is that we have life, and breath, and all things, for "in Him we live, and move, and have our being." Everybody in the world gets this from the Lord; but those who acknowledge His presence, and who delight in it, get benefits that others do not. Of Christ we read that God anointed Him with the Holy Ghost and with power, and that He "went about doing good, and healing all that were oppressed of the devil; for God was with Him." Acts 10:38. So the benefit that those receive, who love and acknowledge the presence of God with them, is the power to do good to others. Now remember that the name of Jesus is "Emmanuel, which being interpreted is God with us." Matt. 1:28. He is with us all the days until the end, and therefore God is with us, that we, like Him, may do good.

Of the child Samuel we read, "And Samuel grew, and the Lord was with him, and did let none of his words fall to the ground." 1 Sam. 3:19. The result of God's being with him was that he spoke "as the oracles of God," so that his words were too valuable to be lost. If we invite God to stay with us, we must consent to allow Him to manage all our affairs, and us too; but that ought not to be considered a hardship, since His way is perfect.

Perhaps the most instructive case of all, as illustrating the presence of God with a man, is that of Joseph. "The patriarchs, moved with envy, sold Joseph into Egypt; but God was with him, and delivered him out of all his affliction, and gave him favour and wisdom in the sight of Pharaoh." Acts 7:9–10. Note this, that God was with him when he went down to Egypt, although he went as a slave. It was not merely in the prosperity that God was with him, but in his affliction. Indeed, it was God who sent Joseph into Egypt. When Joseph arrived in Egypt, he was sold again, but the Lord did not forsake him. "The Lord was with Joseph, and he was a prosperous man; and he was in the house of his master the Egyptian." Gen. 39:1–2. But it was not all smooth before him, even though God was with him. Joseph was falsely accused, and without being given any chance to clear himself, he was cast into prison. Surely the Lord had forgotten him then. Not at all. "The Lord was with Joseph, and showed him mercy, and gave him favour in the sight of the keeper of the prison. And the keeper of the prison committed to Joseph's hand all the prisoners that were in the prison; and whatsoever they did there, he was the doer of it. And the keeper of the prison looked not to anything that was under his hand; because the Lord was with him, and that which he did, the Lord made it to prosper." Gen. 39:21–23. The Lord is not afraid or ashamed to go to prison, so that the fact that a man is in prison does not prove that the Lord has left him. Indeed, the Lord is often in prison. See Matt. 25:36,43.

After a long time, and much weary waiting, Joseph was taken from prison, and placed over the land of Egypt. He became practically the king of Egypt. He was ruler over all the land, and all that he lacked was a seat on the throne. Joseph did not know what he went to prison for until Pharaoh sent for him; and then he found out that that was the way to the place of power. But Joseph did not spend his time mourning, although he could not see the way out of prison. We can look back to that time, and seeing the end at the same time that we see the experience that he passed through, it seems to us a matter of course that Joseph should do as he did. But we must remember that to Joseph things looked as black and hopeless during those years in prison as they would to us. If we could see our way clear, we should never murmur, nor doubt the presence and goodness of God. Joseph could not see ahead, but he did not mind that; God was with him all the way, and that was sufficient; he did not need to see ahead. If we would but remember that He knows the way that we take, and can see the end from the beginning, it would save us much time and useless despondency. God is with us in the dark as well as in the light, in fire, and water, and prison, as well as in times of ease and prosperity.

CHAPTER 48

GOD'S WITNESSES

(Isa. 43:8–13)

"Bring forth the blind people that have eyes, and the deaf that have ears. Let all the nations be gathered together, and let the peoples be assembled; who among them can declare this, and show us former things? Let them bring their witnesses, that they may be justified; or let them hear, and say, It is truth. Ye are My witnesses, saith the Lord, and My Servant, whom I have chosen; that ye may know and believe Me, and understand that I am He; before Me there was no god formed, neither shall there be after Me. I even I, am the Lord; and beside Me there is no Saviour. I have declared, and I have saved, and I have showed, and there was no strange god among you; therefore ye are My witnesses, saith the Lord, that I am God. Yea, before the day was, I am He; and there is none that can deliver out of My hand; I will work, and who shall let it?"

A New Challenge

This lesson brings us to the very heart of the trial. All nations are challenged to come into court with their witnesses, and justify themselves in their opposition to God. They refuse to submit to His authority. In that case therefore they ought to be able to show themselves superior to Him. This is a repetition of the call made in the forty-first chapter, but the student will notice that the Lord abates something of His demands upon them. In the former instance He called upon them all to come, and to produce their strong reasons, saying, "Let them bring them forth, and show us what shall happen; let them show the former things, what they be, that we may consider them, and know the latter end of them; or declare us things for to come. Show the things that are to come hereafter, that we may know that ye are gods." That was altogether too much, and there was none that could utter a word. Now the Lord says, "Who among them can declare this, and show us former things?" They cannot tell things to come; very well, try something easier: show what has happened. Surely that is the least that could be asked of proud boasters.

The Prophet the Only True Historian

But they cannot do even that. It requires just as much prophetic power to tell correctly what has happened as it does to tell what shall take place in the future. There are thousands of histories written, but after one has read all of them, he does not know the truth of the things concerning which they treat. Even many of the events recorded never took place, but are merely local gossip that grew with the telling, and after the lapse of hundreds of years, is taken as fact. Everybody knows how a rumour will grow, and how in a very few days it will be repeated in all seriousness by the most well-intentioned persons as a veritable fact. It is said that Von Ranke, one of the greatest historians, has an object lesson in this, which made him very careful in his writing. He was absent from home for a few days, and during his absence an accident occurred, by which several persons were injured. On his return he tried to ascertain the facts in the case, but none of his informants, all of whom saw the affair, agreed in their accounts of it. One had one story, and another had another. Of course all could not be correct, and it was quite likely that all were more or less wrong. Then the historian said, "If I cannot get the exact facts about a thing that happened in my own neighbourhood within a few days past, when I can talk with the eyewitnesses, how can I be sure of what happened hundreds of years ago?" We do not need to go abroad for an experience in this respect; who has not had many similar experiences in trying to learn the details of any affair? Carlyle, himself, an historian, says, "Foolish History, ever, more or less, the written epitomized synopsis of Rumour, knows so little that were not as well unknown." Even when we have the exact facts recorded, the human historian cannot tell us the truth of what lay behind the events: the motives of the actors. He draws inferences, but he cannot read the heart; and so the real history remains a sealed book. Only in the Judgment will the exact truth of all things be known. When the hidden things of darkness are brought to light, and the counsels of the heart are made manifest (1 Cor. 4:5), at the coming of the Lord, then we can study the history of the world with certainty.

How to Study History

But can we not know anything of the past? Must we discount everything that we read in history? Is all study of history useless? Yes and no. We may study history profitably or we may study it to no profit whatever. We may *know* some of the things that have happened in the past, if we study in the light of the Word of God, who *was*, and *is*, and *is to come*, and who therefore knows things past and present and future equally well. He can do what He challenges the heathen to do; tell former things and also what shall be. Whoever studies history, and ignores the revelation which God has given, might far better let the study alone. It is to him worse than useless. God, who knows the hearts of men, always tells the exact truth, and He alone can do it. If one will first become acquainted with God's Word, knowing it not merely as a record of facts, but as a living power, he may read history written by men with profit; for being filled with the Spirit of truth, he will be able to discern the truth and error, even of things of which the Bible has not spoken particularly. When we say that the Bible is the place to study history, we do not mean that the Bible contains an account of all that has happened in the past, nor even of all that it may be useful to know; but the Bible does contain an outline of all history, even of what are called "pre-historic times," so that it is a faithful guide, and it enables one to know the truth. This is the promise of Jesus, "If ye continue in My Word, then are ye My disciples indeed; and ye shall know the truth." John 8:31–32. Man cannot tell the truth even of what is passing in his own heart; how foolish then are his assumptions of wisdom in the face of God!

God Alone Speaks Truth

"Let them bring forth their witnesses that they may be justified." If men could tell the truth, the whole truth, then it follows that they would be justified. That is self-evident. If men could substantiate their statements, if they could make their words stand for ever, then there could be no case against them. In that case, God would be disgraced, because their words are against Him. But every day proves how utterly unable man is to tell the truth, even when he does not mean to deceive. On the contrary, the Word of God is settled for ever in heaven, and even the thoughts of His heart endure to all generations. Ps. 119:89; 33:11. Then instead of our seeking to justify ourselves, let us hear the Word of God, and say, "It is truth."

Men to be God's Mouthpieces

Now God speaks to the people whom He has called from the north and the south, and from the ends of the earth, even every one that is called by His name, and says, "Ye are My witnesses." God has spoken, but His word is denied; His character has been impeached; it is evident, therefore, that He must have somebody to testify in His behalf, if He shall win His case. This is not theory, but actual fact. If there could be no one found to testify for God, He would lose His case; for the charge against Him is that He is not able to save. He started out by making man, and placing him over the earth as its lord; man has lost the dominion; he has turned against the One whom he was designed to represent; if therefore God were unable to win anybody back to Him, to be faithful and true witnesses for Him, that would prove that He was not God. So God must have witnesses, and have them He will, even if he should be obliged to make new men out of stones. Although God has spoken, He rests His case on the testimony of men. It is by the lives of men, that the world is to learn the truth of God. John 17:21.

We are associated with Jesus as witnesses in this case. The Lord says, "Ye are My witnesses, and My Servant whom I have chosen." See chapter 42:1–4. From Him we are to learn the kind of witness to be rendered. "No man hath seen God at any time; the only begotten Son, which is in the bosom of the Father, He hath declared Him." John 1:18. Only in Christ can we know who God is, so that we can testify in His behalf, and we can know Him only as He is revealed in us. Let us first then study Christ as a witness for God.

Christ the Faithful and True Witness

His name is the Word of God, and He is also called Faithful and True. Rev. 19:11–13. He is "the faithful and true witness, the beginning of the creation of God." Rev. 3:14. Before Pontius Pilate He "witnessed a good confession" (1 Tim. 6:13), and said to him, "To this end was I born, and for this cause came I into the world, that I should bear witness unto the truth. Every one that is of the truth heareth My voice." John 18:37. He Himself is the truth. John 14:6. In Him all fullness dwells, therefore He tells the whole truth; and there is no unrighteousness in Him, so that He tells nothing but the truth. He is therefore a perfect witness, He does not testify of hearsay, but says, "We speak that we do know, and testify that we have seen." John 52:11.

Jesus was able to render perfect testimony, because "God was with Him." "God was in Christ, reconciling the world unto Himself, not imputing their trespasses unto them." 2 Cor. 5:19. But God is with us, beseeching by us as He was by Christ, and we are ambassadors in the stead of Christ. Therefore if we do not properly represent the Lord it is because we reject His presence.

The Spirit of the True Witness

When God calls our attention to His Servant whom He upholds, He says, "I have put My Spirit upon Him." Isa. 42:1. "It is the Spirit that beareth witness, because the Spirit is truth." 1 John 5:6. Without the Spirit of truth, no one can tell the truth; his very life is a lie. So before Christ sent His disciples forth, He said, "Ye shall receive power, when the Holy Ghost is come upon you, and ye shall be My witnesses both in Jerusalem, and in all Judea and Samaria, and unto the uttermost part of the earth." Acts 1:8. We are therefore placed on an equality with Christ, in the matter of witnessing, since we have the same Spirit given to us that He had.

Reproofs of Instruction

Wisdom cries, and says, "Turn you at My reproof; behold, I will pour out My Spirit upon you, I will make known My words unto you." Prov. 1:23. This is in keeping with the message of comfort. The Holy Spirit, the Comforter, comes with conviction; if we turn at His reproofs, then we receive the fullness of the Spirit, and thus we know the words of God; and then the Spirit dwelling in us will testify of the truth. This testimony will not be merely verbal, but will be the testimony of the life, revealing itself in "love, joy, peace, long-suffering, gentleness, goodness, faith, meekness, temperance" (Gal. 5:22–23); in short, all the attributes of God.

The Witness of Creation

All nature testifies of God. His everlasting power and Divinity are revealed in everything that He has made. Rom. 1:20. Even among heathen peoples, where the Scriptures were never seen, He left not Himself without witness, in that He did good, and gave rain and fruitful seasons, providing food and joy for the people. Acts. 14:17. "The heavens declare the glory of God." From inanimate creation we learn the kind of witness that the Lord desires. It is simply the revealing of His indwelling presence. It is simply to let the world know that *He is*. In that He is, He is in us; therefore if our lives do not reveal the character of God, we are false witnesses; we make Him seem to be other than He is.

God has a claim upon all men; all are rightfully His witnesses. He has summoned all, and has given to all the witness fee, even the blood of Christ – His own life. There is not a soul on earth that does not live solely by the life of God, the life that is secured to us by the death of Jesus Christ whom He has sent. Since all receive life from Him, and it is His own life, it is self-evident that the character of God, and that only, ought to be revealed in all. If any do not reveal the character of God, they say either that it is not the life of God which they have (which is a lie), or else that God is such an one as they are, which is also a lie. Every one who testifies against God is therefore one of God's witnesses who has perjured himself.

God Alone Has Power

In what God has done for us when there was obviously no other helper, He has given evidence that He is God. Verse 2 was specially enacted when Israel came out of Egypt, and crossed the Red Sea. All the idols of Egypt had been overthrown, and the things in which the Egyptians trusted, were shown to be useless, and were destroyed. God saved His people when there was no strange god among them, and they acknowledged that Jehovah was a great King above all gods. By His working among them they were witnesses that He is God. We ourselves are in the same position. Every day are we unconscious witnesses that He is God. Whatever gods men serve besides the only true God, are gods of their own making, and therefore of less power than the men themselves. Every day men breathe, without giving the matter a thought; they even lie down at night and sleep, losing all consciousness, yet they continue breathing. Every breath is therefore a witness to the presence and loving power of God. Then when men speak against God, or speak that which is not truth, they prove themselves to be false witnesses, because their witness is contradictory. With the breath which is evidence of the love and power of God, they deny Him. God's case is sure; there is none but He that can deliver, and there is none that can pluck one of His saved ones out of His hand.

There is the most blessed comfort imaginable in this, that all are of right witnesses. All are "accepted in the Beloved." He has not cast off a single soul. It is on the fact that He in no wise casts any out, but that He receives and pardons and cleanses all, making them new creatures, kings and priests, that God rests His case. God is obliged to receive all who come to Him, or else the charge against Him will stand good. But it is not merely a question of whether or not God will receive a man. He does not leave it uncertain. That is, He does not give anybody cause to wonder if He will receive him. No; God Himself goes out to seek the lost, and whenever He finds one who is dishonouring His name, it may be by lying drunk in the gutter like a beast instead of standing upright like the king that God made man, He says, "You belong to Me; you are one of My witnesses; I have a right to your testimony, for I have given you My life." And by the power of His own life; by the power by which He is from everlasting to everlasting, and by which He upholds all things, He will show His perfect character in that degraded man's life, if the man will surrender to Him. He says, "I will work, and who shall let it?"

CHAPTER 49

THE SIN-BEARER

(Isa. 43:14–28)

"Thus saith the Lord, your Redeemer, the Holy One of Israel: For your sake I have sent to Babylon, and I will bring down all of them as fugitives, even the Chaldeans, in the ships of their rejoicing. I am the Lord, your Holy One, the Creator of Israel, your King. Thus saith the Lord, which maketh a way in the sea, and a path in the mighty waters; which bringeth forth the chariot and horse, the army and the power; they lie down together, they shall not rise; they are extinct, they are quenched as flax: Remember ye not the former things, neither consider the things of old. Behold, I will do a new thing; now shall it spring forth; shall ye not know it? I will even make a way in the wilderness and rivers in the desert. The beasts of the field shall honour Me, the jackals and the ostriches because I give waters in the wilderness, and rivers in the desert, to give drink to My people, My chosen: the people which I formed for Myself, that they might set forth My praise. Yet thou hast not called upon Me, O Jacob; but thou hast been weary of Me, O Israel. Thou hast not brought Me the small cattle of thy burnt offerings; neither hast thou honoured Me with thy sacrifices. I have not made thee to serve with offerings, nor wearied thee with frankincense. Thou hast bought Me no sweet cane with money, neither hast thou filled Me with the fat of thy sacrifices; but thou hast made Me to serve with thy sins, thou hast wearied Me with thine iniquities. I, even I, am He that blotteth out thy transgressions for Mine own sake, and I will not remember thy sins. Put Me in remembrance; let us plead together; set thou forth thy cause, that thou mayest be justified. Thy first father hath sinned, and thine interpreters have transgressed against Me. Therefore I will profane the princes of the sanctuary, and I will make Jacob a curse, and Israel a reviling."

God's Power to Deliver

Again we have a reminder of God's power and His care for His people. We recall from the fortieth chapter that Israel says, "My way is hid from the Lord, and my judgment is passed over from my God." Therefore God tells what He has done for their sake. All the enemies of His people, who put their trust in their war ships, are taken captive by Him. He delivers His people from bondage, even making a way in the sea, and a path in the mighty waters, as when He brought Israel out of Egypt. The chariot and the horse, the army and the power, are as nothing compared with the Lord. "The horse and his rider hath He thrown into the sea." "Pharaoh's chariots and his host hath He cast into the sea; his chosen captains also are drowned in the Red Sea. The depths have covered them; they sank into the bottom as a stone." Ex. 15:1,4–5.

That was a wonderful deliverance; but the Lord will do still more wonderful things. "Behold, the days come, saith the Lord, that they shall no more say, The Lord liveth, which brought up the children of Israel out of the land of Egypt, but the Lord liveth, which brought up and which led the seed of the house of Israel out of the north country, and from all the countries whither I had driven them; and they shall dwell in their own land." Jer. 23:7–8. The things which God will yet do for His people are so great that the marvelous events of the exodus will pale into insignificance by the side of them.

God's Children Delivered from Egypt

The Lord is the God that has brought His people out of the land of Egypt. "Out of Egypt have I called My Son," says the Lord by the prophet, and this is true of every one of His sons. Out of the land of Egypt must we all come; and that wonderful deliverance in the days of Moses, will stand as the evidence of God's power to save, and the quickener of faith, until the future, final deliverance shall have been effected, and then to all eternity the "new thing" that God has done will be the theme of the saved. In the performance of this new thing the Lord will make a way in the wilderness, and rivers in the dessert to give drink to His chosen witnesses, His servants. Now this was written nearly a thousand years after the exodus from Egypt, when God caused the waters to run in the dry places like a river, so that

Israel might drink; and since that time there has never been a similar occurrence, that is, none on a similar scale; therefore it is evident that these things are yet to be fulfilled. That they are to be literally fulfilled, we cannot doubt. If we should deny that we here have statements of what will actually occur, the only reason for it would be the improbability of such things being done, because we are not accustomed to them. But that would be a denial of the Lord. This is a case in which God's power and love are called in question, and He will do such things as will leave no chance for doubt. In the time of trouble of which we have previously read, when the flame devours the pastures of the wilderness, God will cause rivers of water to spring forth from the dry ground to refresh His children.

Power Yet to be Manifested

The wild beasts will also honour God. We remember that Jesus was in the wilderness of temptation forty days, and was with the wild beasts. Mark 1:2,13. They compassed Him about, and gaped upon Him with their mouths, and He was threatened by the lions, and was seemingly about to be tossed by the horns of the wild oxen (Ps. 22:11–13,21); yet not one of them touch Him. They recognized in Him the authority of their Creator. Even so it was with Daniel in the den of lions. Their refusal to harm the prophet of God, although they were hungry, as was shown by their instantly devouring his accusers, was a testimony to the saving power of God. Thus they honoured Him. God's people are yet to be brought into just such close places for their faith, and the wild beasts of the desert will do homage to the power of the righteousness of Jehovah in them. God made man to have dominion over the beasts, and this he had as long as he remained his loyalty to God, and when men become perfect witnesses for God, – when the image of God is perfectly restored in them, and the life of Jesus is manifested in their mortal flesh, – the authority of God in them will be recognized by wild beasts and serpents. When it is thus demonstrated that man has recovered his kingly authority, it will be but a very short time until the first dominion will be restored to him.

God's Glory Revealed In and By Men

"This people have I formed for Myself; they shall show forth My praise." It is of us that the Lord speaks. The Apostle Peter says, "Ye are a chosen generation, a royal priesthood, an holy nation, a peculiar people; that ye should show forth the praises of Him that hath called you out of darkness into His marvelous light." 1 Peter 2:9. That is what God has made us for. He has chosen us as His servants, that He might reveal Himself in us. It is our "high calling in Christ Jesus." Is it not a wonderful thing, that even as the glory of God shone forth of old from the sanctuary, so now He will let His glory shine forth from the men who will acknowledge themselves to be the temples of God? And the glory of God that is seen on them, will be their own glory, shining forth from them. "He will beautify the meek with salvation."

Acceptable Sacrifice

What shall we think of the Lord's complaint against Israel, that they have not brought burnt-offerings to Him, and have not honoured Him with their sacrifices? Does it mean that they had been remiss in their daily and yearly services? Not by any means. Remember what He said to them in the very beginning of the prophecy of Isaiah. "To what purpose is the multitude of your sacrifices unto Me? saith the Lord; I am full of the burnt-offerings of rams and the fat of fed beasts; and I delight not in the blood of bullocks, or of lambs, or of he goats." Isa. 1:11. What does He mean then, by what He says here? He means just what He meant in the beginning, when He said, "Bring no more vain oblations." Their sacrifices were vain, because there was no heart in them. They did not give themselves, and that is all the sacrifice that is acceptable to God. "I beseech you therefore, brethren, by the mercies of God, that ye present your bodies a living sacrifice, holy, acceptable unto God, which is your reasonable service." Rom. 12:1. "The sacrifices of God are a broken spirit; a broken and a contrite heart, O God, Thou wilt not despise." Ps. 51:17. When these are present, God is "pleased with the sacrifices of righteousness." God says, "I have not caused thee to serve with a burnt offering, nor wearied thee with incense." In like manner He said by the prophet Jeremiah: "I spake not unto your fathers, nor commanded them in the day that I brought them out of the land of Egypt, concerning burnt offerings or sacrifices; but this thing commanded I them, saying, Obey My voice, and I will be your God, and ye shall be My people; and walk ye in all the ways that I have commanded you, that it may be well with you." Jer. 7:22–23. Sacrifice was never anything in itself; for God has made the only sacrifice that can be of any value. Sacrifices were never anything more than an expression of trust and thanksgiving.

Making God to Serve

"But thou hast made Me to serve with thy sins; thou hast wearied Me with thine iniquities." This is one of the most striking statements to be found in the Bible. Instead of being the servants of God, we have made Him our servant! The term is the same as that used in Ex. 1:13, where we read that "the Egyptians made the children of Israel to serve with rigour." Also Ex. 6:5: "I have also heard the groaning of the children of Israel, whom the Egyptians *keep in bondage.*" Isn't it shocking? Just as the Egyptians made slaves of the children of Israel, putting them to hard and distasteful service, even so we have done to God, piling upon Him all our sins, and making Him carry the load day after day. Now we begin to get hold of that which will reveal to us the infinite patience of God.

We are all familiar with the words: "Behold the Lamb of God, which taketh away the sin of the world" (John 1:29); but few read the word in the margin, which ought to be in the text, namely, "beareth." If we always thought of Him as the Lamb of God who *bears* the sin of the world, it might make His work mean more to us. "He is the propitiation for our sins; and not for ours only, but also for the sins of the whole world." 1 John 2:2. Mark it; He *is*, not, He makes propitiation for sins. He "His own self bare our sins in His own body on the tree." 1 Peter 2:24. These things we have all heard, and they are so common that they have almost lost their meaning to us. Our lesson brings before us in the most vivid manner the Lord's relation to us and our sins.

All Sin is Upon God's Life

Take the words in the first chapter of Hebrews, that Christ, being the effulgence of the Father's glory, "and the very image of His substance, and upholding all things by the word of His power, when He had made purification of sins, sat down on the right hand of the Majesty on high." He upholds or bears all things. The weight of the universe rests upon Him. Not a thing but is held in place by the power of His life. "In Him all things consist," and "in Him we live, and move, and have our being." He is the Soul of the universe. There is no life anywhere but the life that flows from the heart of God. That is the simple truth, which is easily said, but which we may well think upon for days and years.

The fact that God is in all things, even in sinful man, is scarcely ever thought of; and too often wholly disbelieved. Compare Deut. 30:11–14 with Rom. 10:6–8. In the first passage, together with the context, we learn that Moses was addressing the children of Israel, and exhorting them to obey God. That shows that they were not wholly obedient, and we well know that they were not. Then he tells them that they need have no difficulty in obeying the Lord, for the commandment is not hidden from them, neither is it very far off. They do not need to go across the sea for it, nor ask somebody to go up to heaven, to bring it down for them, that they may hear it and do it. No; the commandment, the Word, is very nigh, in their mouth, and in their heart, that they may do it. It is there whether they do it or not; it is there in order that they may have no excuse for not doing it.

Saved by the Life

Read now the parallel text in Romans. It is quoted from this one, but inasmuch as Christ is the Word, the name "Christ" is substituted for "Word." "The righteousness which is of faith speaketh on this wise, Say not in thine heart, Who shall ascend into heaven? (that is, to bring Christ down from above); or, Who shall descend into the deep? (that is, to bring up Christ again from the dead). But what saith it? The Word is nigh thee, even in thy mouth, and in thy heart, that is, the Word of faith which we preach; that if thou shalt confess with thy mouth the Lord Jesus, and shalt believe in thy heart that God hath raised Him from the dead, thou shalt be saved."

Confessing the Lord Jesus means confessing the truth concerning Him, namely, that He "is come in the flesh," even in our own sinful flesh. Why should He come there? – In order that "the righteousness of the law might be fulfilled in us." Rom. 8:3–4. The theory that would make Christ keep entirely away from sinners until they begin to serve Him, would throw upon them the labour of converting themselves. No; Christ dwells in every man, waiting his permission to reveal Himself. Therefore the wrath of God is justly revealed from heaven against all ungodliness and unrighteousness of men, because they "hold down the truth in unrighteousness." Rom. 1:18. Christ is the truth. John 14:6. That which may be known of God is manifest in wicked men, for God hath showed it unto them; for His everlasting power and Divinity are to be seen in everything that He has made, including man. They are therefore without excuse for their sin. Christ is present in every man to save him from sinning.

It is therefore idle for the sinner to say that the Lord will not receive him. Why, the Lord *has* you; He has been carrying you all your lifetime. There never has been a heart throb, not a pulse beat, not a tingle of a nerve, that did not reveal the presence of the life of God; for all those things reveal the presence of life, and there is no life in the universe but the life of God. If there were, then there would be another God. That is the whole question in controversy – whether creatures can live separate from the Creator. They who think to save God from the disgrace of being in sinful men, do Him no honour. They are conceding all that the devil would claim. If any man can establish his ability to live an hour without the Lord's life, then he can live for ever without Him. But this no man can do, and it is the Lord's mercy that he cannot.

What God Endures for Man

"The Word was made flesh, and dwelt among us." But for that we could not live at all. In our flesh, our life, is the Divine Word, – God Himself. And what is our condition? – "Laden with iniquity, a seed of evil-doers, children that are corrupters;" "the whole head is sick, and the whole heart faint. From the sole of the foot even unto the head there is no soundness in it; but wounds, and bruises, and putrefying sores; they have not been closed, neither bound up, neither mollified with ointment." Isa. 1:4–6. This is the condition of the flesh in which the Divine Word has condescended to dwell. "Himself took our infirmities, and bare our sicknesses." Matt 8:17. All the loathsomeness of sin the Lord who hates sin was pleased to take upon Himself, that we might be freed from it. He has for ever identified Himself with humanity. Every sin that is committed by the vilest transgressor is committed with the life that God has loaned to him. God dwelling in human flesh is made the servant of men's passions. They are corrupters, in that they corrupt the life that God has given them. He is not responsible for a single sin, for "in Him is no sin," yet because it has been committed with His life, He assumes the responsibility. The weight of every sin is upon the Lord, and that it is no small weight is seen from the fact that it crushed the life out of the Son of God. What infinite patience, that He still continues to bear it!

Loathsomeness of Sin

But it is loathsome to Him. With the picture of the body utterly corrupt, full of putrefying ulcers from head to foot, and you have an idea of what God is bearing. Can you wonder then that He says, "I, even I, am He that blotteth out thy transgressions for Mine own sake, and will not remember thy sins?" Ah, we do not need to plead with Him, to make Him willing to cleanse us from all unrighteousness; He is most anxious to do it; it is He who pleads with us to allow Him to do it for us.

Yes, and Christ has by Himself made purification for sins. With all the sins of the world upon Him, He gave up His life; but because He knew no sin He came forth from the grave, and so when we confess that Christ is come in our flesh, we may know that He is risen from the dead, so that He lives in us with the power of the resurrection life. As soon therefore as we make the confession, and yield completely to Him, we are freed from the bondage of sin; for God is not so in love with sin that He will retain it a second after we turn it completely over to Him. He will cast it into the depths of the sea.

The Lord has bought our sins; they belong to Him. He has bought us, and we belong to Him. We therefore have no right to do anything with ourselves. But when we refuse to confess our sins, and at the same time to confess Christ, we are claiming the sins that are upon Him. We are retaining them, because we refuse to acknowledge that they are sins, and we go on putting more sins upon Him. Patiently He abides with us, however, literally suffering long. He has our sins, whether we acknowledge it or not; therefore it does not add one whit to His burden for us to let them rest upon Him alone, and not try to bear any of them ourselves. On the contrary, it relieves Him for us to confess our sins, and cast them entirely upon Him, for then He casts them off, and bears us alone. Before, He bore us and our sins; now He bears us freed from sin. Why not grant the Lord this favour?

He asks us to remind Him of what He has done for us. "Let us plead together," says He. Literally, "Let us go into court together." If we will but declare the truth, we shall be justified, for the truth is that He has all our sins upon Him. All that is required of any man, in order to be saved, is that he tell the simple truth about what he sees. If we admit that God is supporting us, that we live by His life, and that consequently all our sins are upon Him, and that we are in harmony with that arrangement, then we are freed from them. So although our first father sinned, and we as a consequence were born in sin, we are made as free from them as the only begotten Son of God. What a wonderful Saviour!

CHAPTER 50

THE GIFT OF THE SPIRIT

(Isa. 44:1–7)

"But hear now, O Jacob, My servant;
And Israel, whom I have chosen;
Thus saith Jehovah, thy Maker;
And He that formed thee from the womb, and will help thee;
Fear thou not, O My servant Jacob;
And, O Jeshurun, whom I have chosen;
For I will pour out waters on the thirsty;
And flowing streams on the dry ground;
I will pour out My Spirit on thy seed,
And My blessing on thine offspring.
And they shall spring up as grass among the waters;
As the willows beside the aqueducts.
One shall say, I belong to Jehovah;
And another shall be called by the name of Jacob;
And this shall subscribe his hand to Jehovah,
And shall be surnamed by the name of Israel.
Thus saith Jehovah, the King of Israel;
And his Redeemer, Jehovah God of hosts:
I am the first, and I am the last;
And beside Me there is no God.
Who is like unto Me, that he should call forth this event,
And make it known beforehand, and dispose it for Me,
For the time that I appointed the people of the destined age?
The things that are now coming, and are to come hereafter,
let them declare unto us."

The Chosen

How often in these chapters we find the word "chosen." God has chosen Israel. But who are Israel? Israel is the prince of God, the one who overcomes. Does the Lord then choose as His favourites only those who have made a conspicuous success in life? Oh, no: the choice must necessarily be made before the struggle is ended. As we well know, Jacob was chosen before he was born. We are chosen in order that we may overcome. God has blessed us in Christ, "according as He hath chosen us in Him before the foundation of the world, that we should be holy and without blame before Him in love." Eph. 1:3. All are chosen; we have only by submission to His will to make our calling and election sure.

Why God Chooses Us

It is evident that Israel means more than one man. The man Jacob, who was by the Lord named Israel, was dead hundreds of years before the prophet Isaiah wrote these words; they apply to all the children of Israel. And here appears some more of the comfort of God. God has taken away every ground for discouragement, in this promise to Israel. Notice that He uses both names, Jacob and Israel. Jacob is the supplanter, the deceitful schemer, the one whose character is anything but attractive. The Lord indicates that He has chosen Jacob from his birth. That means that He has chosen us from our birth. But we have a bad record. No matter, so had the original Jacob. He has chosen us, that He may make us better. So we need not mourn over our early life; God makes all that pass away in Christ. Every inspired prayer is a promise of what God will do; and in Ps. 25:7 we read: "Remember not the sins of my youth, nor my transgressions." That this is what God promises to do, we have already learned from the preceding chapter, where He says, "I, even I, am He that blotteth out thy transgression for Mine own sake, and will not remember thy "sins." He has chosen us, " that we might be holy and without blame before him." Eph. 1:4.

Little Children

"Fear not, O Jacob, My servant; and thou Jeshurun, whom I have chosen." The word "Jeshurun" occurs only four times in the Bible, the three other times besides this one being in Deut. 32 and 33. It is a diminutive, such as people use as pet names, and is equivalent to "the good little people," or, "the dear little people." It is applied to the whole people, just as a mother uses a term of endearment to her child. It reveals the tender affection of God for His people. It corresponds to the "little children," so frequently used by the Saviour.

The Water of Life

The Spirit of God is the water of life. This is seen from the following texts: "Jesus stood and cried, saying, If any man thirst, let him come unto Me, and drink. He that believeth on Me, as the Scripture hath said, out of his belly shall flow rivers of living water. But this spake He of the Spirit, which they that believed on Him were to receive." John 7:37–39. Remember that this promise in Isaiah is to the same ones who in the preceding chapter are said to be witnesses, and the Spirit is necessary in order that they may bear witness, "and it is the Spirit that beareth witness, because the Spirit is the truth. For there are three who bear witness, the Spirit, and the water, and the blood; and the three agree in one." 1 John 5:7–8, R.V. God, who is the Fountain of living waters, is Spirit. John 4:24. The Spirit "proceedeth from the Father," the stream flowing from the fountain head.

Cooling Streams

Nothing gives a more complete idea of satisfaction than cold water to one who is thirsty. God promises not merely to give the thirsty ones a drink, but to pour water upon them. He giveth liberally. If any one has ever known what it is to be faint from thirst in a dry place on a sultry day, he will appreciate this. He longs not merely for a drink, but to plunge into the water. He does not want simply a cupful of water, but a stream of it; and when he sees the stream in the distance, how he runs to it, and, throwing himself down, buries his head in it, or immerses himself in the refreshing liquid. Even so can the soul who thirsts for the living water find satisfaction.

Thirsting for God

Recall the expressions of longing for God, that appear in the Psalms. "As the hart panteth after the water brooks, so panteth my soul after Thee, O God. My soul thirsteth for God; for the living God." Ps. 42:1–2. "O God, Thou art my God; early will I seek Thee;

my soul thirsteth for Thee; my flesh longest for Thee in a dry and thirsty land, where no water is." Ps. 43:1. All are familiar with the expressions, and yet much of their force is lost because they are considered as only figurative, when as a matter of fact they are very literal. The psalmist does indeed use a figure, but it is only to express his longing for God. The thirsting after God is not the figure; that is the fact. As the hart pants after the water brooks (this is the illustration) so his soul panteth after God. This is the thing illustrated. The thirst which God satisfies is real thirst, and He satisfies it as really as the brook satisfies the panting deer.

Drinking the Life of God

Recall the passage which says that the glorious Lord will be to us a place of broad rivers and streams. Isa. 33:21. Remember that the river of water of life clear as crystal, proceeds from the throne of God and of the Lamb. Rev. 22:1. That the water which proceeds from God and the Lamb is real water, such as will satisfy literal thirst, we are taught by the experience of the children of Israel in the desert. Ex. 17:1–7. Christ is the Rock of Israel, and He stood upon the rock which Moses smote, and we are told that the people "drank of that spiritual Rock which followed them." 1 Cor. 10:4. From the spiritual Rock comes spiritual water; but spiritual water is very real. It was real enough to satisfy the thirst of the whole company of Israel, and also all their cattle. It is of this water that comes from the throne, that God says He will give all the thirsty ones freely. Rev. 22:17. It is from this stream, flowing from the throne of God, that the thirsty land is watered and made fruitful. "Thou visitest the earth, and waterest it; Thou greatly enrichest it with the river of God, which is full of water; Thou preparest them corn, when Thou hast so provided for it. Thou waterest the ridges thereof abundantly; Thou settlest the furrows thereof; Thou makest it soft with showers; Thou blessest the springing thereof. Thou crownest the year with Thy goodness; and Thy paths drop fatness." Ps. 65:9–11. When we remember that two-thirds of the human body is water, it is easy to understand that water is our life; and then when we learn that the water which comes from heaven and gushes forth from the earth in springs comes direct from the throne of God, we can see that we live by the life of God.

God Alone Can Satisfy

It is a fact, therefore, that men may literally thirst after God. Indeed, whenever they thirst for pure, fresh water, it is for God that they are thirsting, although they do not know it. Every desire, every unsatisfied longing, is but an expression of the soul's need of God. He alone satisfies the desire of every living thing. "None but Christ can satisfy," even though the soul does not recognize the fact. Sometimes a man tries to satisfy his thirst with alcoholic liquor, but that never satisfies; it only creates a worse thirst; instead of building up, it tears down. That spirit is not the Spirit of life, but of death. Satan, who tries to make people believe that he is the Lord, and that his work is Divine, has stolen the name of the water of life for his spirit, calling brandy *eau-de vie*. That is what pure water is, while the spirituous liquor is the water of death. The exhortation is "Be not drunk with wine, wherein is excess; but be filled with the Spirit." Eph. 5:18.

Thirsting for Righteousness-Filled

"The Spirit is life because of righteousness." Rom. 8:10. The water and the blood, which agree in one with the Spirit, are also life, and consequently righteousness. We know that the blood of Christ is righteousness, because it cleanses from all sin. Drinking of the water of life is therefore drinking of the blood of Christ which is righteousness and life. "Blessed are they which do hunger and thirst after righteousness; for they shall be filled." Matt. 5:6. Everything that gives us real life is from God. Whenever we take in that which builds up the body, we are receiving of the life of God, the blood of Christ, the water of life. If therefore we recognize God in His gifts, we may actually take in righteousness with every drink of water that we take. All our thirst is but a longing for that which only God can bestow; but we do not, however, always thirst after righteousness. Instead, we try to satisfy the longing with everything except God. It is not popular to acknowledge our dependence upon God. Men have no hesitation in letting it be known that they are thirsty, but they would never think of admitting that they are longing for the life of God. That is why so few become filled with righteousness. Nevertheless God sheds the Spirit upon us abundantly, even though we do not recognize the gift. He gives to the unthankful as well as to the thankful. If we but recognize the gift, and thank Him for every renewal of it, righteousness will be ours as surely as God lives. How easy and plain is the way of righteousness and life!

CHAPTER 51

A STUPID, FALSE WITNESS

(Isa. 44:9–20)

"They that fashion a graven image are all of them vanity; and their delectable things shall not profit; and their own witnesses see not, nor know; that they may be ashamed.

"Who hath fashioned a god, or molten a graven image, that is profitable for nothing? Behold, all his fellows shall be ashamed; and the workmen, they are of men; let them all be gathered together; they shall fear, they shall be ashamed together.

"The smith maketh an axe, and worketh in the coals, and fashioneth it with hammers, and worketh it with his strong arm; yea, he is hungry, and his strength faileth; he drinketh no water, and is faint. The carpenter stretcheth out a line; he marketh it out with a pencil; he shapeth it with planes, and he marketh it out with compasses, and shapeth it after the figure of a man, according to the beauty of a man, to dwell in the house. He heweth him down cedars, and taketh the holm tree and the oak, and strengtheneth for himself one among the trees of the forest; he planteth a fir tree, and the rain doth nourish it, Then shall it be for a man to burn; and he taketh thereof, and warmeth himself; yea, he kindleth it, and baketh bread; yea, he maketh a god, and worshippeth it; he maketh it a graven image, and falleth down thereto. He burneth part thereof in the fire; with part thereof he eateth flesh; he roasteth roast, and is satisfied; yea, he warmeth himself, and saith, Aha, I am warm, I have seen the fire; and the residue thereof he maketh a god, even his graven image; he falleth down unto it; and worshippeth, and prayeth unto it, and saith, Deliver me; for thou art my god.

"They know not, neither do they consider; for He hath shut their eyes, that they cannot see; and their hearts, that they cannot understand. And none calleth to mind, neither is there knowledge nor understanding to say, I have burned part of it in the fire; yea, also I have baked bread upon the coals thereof; I have roasted flesh and eaten it; and shall I make the residue thereof an abomination? shall I fall down to the stock of a tree? He feedeth on ashes; a deceived heart hath turned him aside, that he cannot deliver his soul, nor say, Is there not a lie in my right hand?"

One must search long to find a finer piece of description than this. True to the life, it is at the same time wonderfully cutting and sarcastic; its accuracy, however, is what makes it so. The passage will bear reading many times, and after the reader has done with laughing at the poor, stupid idolater, who makes his own god, he may turn the laugh against himself; for this image-maker's descendants and counterparts are found in every country under heaven, and in every society, and every church.

The careful reader cannot fail to notice that the court is still in session. We ourselves are in the court room. The case will be on until the Judgment day comes. Now the witnesses are being examined, and are giving in their sworn testimony. The trial is to decide who is God, whether the Maker of the heavens and the earth, or the things that man makes, and so, really, man himself.

In the verses preceding the beginning of this lesson, we have the Lord's witnesses again addressed. Indeed, the whole of the preceding chapter concerns them. They are the redeemed of the Lord, those whom He gathers out of every country, who are called by His name, and whom He has created for His glory, and who show it forth. God has blotted out their iniquities, and poured His Spirit upon them in floods, which they have gladly received, so that they may testify to Him. "One shall say I am the Lord's; and another shall call himself by the name of Jacob; and another shall subscribe with his hand unto the Lord, and surname himself by the name of Israel." To them God speaks, and tells them not to be afraid. He is the first and the last, – the only God, – and they, as His witnesses, are not to be afraid to lift up their voices with strength, and to declare His name and fame.

"We know that no idol is anything in the world, and that there is no God but one." 1 Cor. 8:4. There are many that are called gods, but there is only one God, namely the living God, who made all things. No idol is anything, and "they that make them are like unto them; so is every one that trusteth in them." Ps. 115:8. Therefore the maker and worshipper of an idol is nothing. That is what our lesson tells us: "They that make a graven image are all of them vanity." This word "vanity," is from the Hebrew word meaning "emptiness," "confusion," as in Gen. 2:1. "The earth was *without form*." Job 26:7: "He that stretcheth out the north over the *empty place*." Isa. 24:10; 34:11: "The city of *confusion* is broken down;" "He shall stretch upon it the line of *confusion*." Isa. 29:21: "*a thing of naught*." Isa. 41:29: "Their molten images are wind and *confusion*." That is all there is to an idol, and it is all there is to the one who makes and trusts in one. That is, it is all there is to anybody who does not trust in the Lord Jehovah. The Judgment day will prove this, when all who have rejected God will cease to be, so that neither he nor his place will be found. Ps. 37:10.

"Eyes have they, but they will see not." This is spoken of the idols of silver and gold, which are the work of men's hands. These false gods have their witnesses, even as the Lord has His; but on the principle that everybody is like the object of his worship, "their own witnesses see not nor know." The reason for this will soon be made clear, if the reader has not already seen it. But first, let us contrast these witnesses with the "Faithful and True Witness," and with those who range themselves on His side. He says, "We speak that we do know, and testify that we have seen." John 3:11. Peter and John, two of the Lord's witnesses, said, "We cannot but speak the things which we have seen and heard." Acts 4:20. God does not desire that His witnesses shall speak anything else. He says, "Go and tell the things which ye do hear and see." A man who testifies to what he has seen, and what he knows, can answer without fear under any circumstances; but the one who tries to tell what he has not seen, and what he knows nothing about, and what indeed does not exist, will very speedily be put to shame. "If any man willeth to do His will, he shall know of the teaching." John 7:17. There is therefore no need for anybody to be in doubt. The mere curiosity seeker will not find anything; the man who wishes to make an exhibition of his knowledge, will not be able to give any testimony that will bear cross-examination; but whoever wishes to do the will of God, – whoever yields himself to the Lord, – will know. "If ye continue in My Word, then are ye My disciples indeed; and ye shall know the truth, and the truth shall make you free." John 8:31–32.

What constitutes the real difference between the worshippers of the true God and those who trust in the things of naught? – Just this, that the first trust in something, and the others in nothing. Now remember that a man is absolutely nothing of himself. It is only by the Spirit of God that men are made, and by the breath of the Lord that they receive life and understanding. Job 32:8; 33:4. "All nations are before Him as nothing; and they are counted to Him as less than nothing, and vanity." Isa. 40:17. All the substance, the reality, that there is to any man is the presence of God. This is the grand truth that all the world needs to learn. Whoever thinks that he is something, when he is nothing, deceives himself. Gal. 6:3. That is the trouble with the idolater here described as a type of his class. "A deceived heart hath turned him aside." He does not know that there is nothing real but God, and that in Him all things hold together. That is what makes men so proud and boastful. That is the secret of all self-confidence and vain-glory. Now if a man recognizes this truth, and trusts in the Lord wholly, yielding his body as the temple of the Holy Spirit, he will be "filled with all the fullness of God," and there will be substance, reality, to him and his words. He will be able to speak with authority. It is God that worketh in him, and it is the Holy Spirit that speaks in him. But when a man who is nothing to begin with, rejects the source of all life and wisdom, and trusts in that which he himself has made, and which must of necessity be nothing, it follows that the whole thing is emptiness. His words and deeds are wind, and he himself is but chaff. His own testimony carries him away; or, as in Isa. 1:31, the strong is tow, and his work is a spark, so that he has nothing but destruction in himself.

"Let them all be gathered together, let them stand up; yet they shall fear, and they shall be ashamed together." Numbers do not make strength. A thousand million ciphers are of no more value than one alone. A lie does not become the truth because ten thousand men testify to it. Men cannot create anything; and that is the root of the whole matter. People who know that a single lie will be of no avail, imagine that very many of them will stand. But it is folly. "Ye have ploughed wickedness, ye have reaped iniquity; ye have eaten the fruit of lies; because thou didst trust in thy way, in the multitude of thy mighty men." Hosea 10:13. "The hail shall sweep away the refuge of lies, and the waters shall overflow the hiding-place." Isa. 28:17. No man can possibly have any more strength than he has with God in him alone. God's presence in another man will not answer for me; so that I cannot trust even in a good man; how much less, then, in a wicked man. "Thou shalt not follow a multitude to do evil; neither shalt thou bear witness in a cause to turn aside after a multitude to wrest judgment. Ex. 23:2. "Though hand join in hand, the wicked shall not be unpunished." Prov. 11:21. Let no one rest in any way that he is pursuing, confi-dent in the thought that "everybody does so," or that it has been the custom for many years. Find out for yourself what the Lord says, and then you will know that you have the truth, and that your way will stand. His Word is the only real foundation. "Other foundation can no man lay than that is laid, which is Jesus Christ." 1 Cor. 3:11.

Anyone who reads this, anybody who can read the Bible, can see at once the folly of the man who makes a god out of a tree. It would seem that no one could possibly be so foolish as to worship a thing that he himself has made, and could say to it, "Deliver me, for thou art my god." Part of the tree he uses for cooking his dinner, and the remainder he makes into a god. Surely he ought to be able to see that there is no more power to the portion of the tree which he worships than in that which he burns in the fire. Yet the thing is done by men of as good mental ability as any of us. "The deceitfulness of sin" is amazing; and this deceitfulness is in every human heart. See Jer. 17:9.

There is nothing more common in this world than self-justifica-tion – the desire to maintain one's own cause, and to demonstrate that one is in the right, and has done no wrong. We have all had experience in this. The tendency is inherent in human nature. "They all with one consent began to make excuse." Luke 14:18. That is, they all began to show what they regarded as a good reason for not complying with the summons that the king issued. Now if a good reason, a reasonable excuse, can be given for any course, that shows that the course is right. So every excuse that anybody makes for his acts, – for not serving God, – is a claim that he is all right in himself, without heeding the Lord. In what are we trusting, when we do that? – Manifestly in ourselves, – in the works of our own hands. Then we do not differ a particle from the man who is described in this chapter. A deceived heart has turned us aside, and we are feeding on ashes. If we confess our sins, we shall find mercy from God, because in confessing them we are acknowledging that God is, and that He is in the right; and He is mercy. All that is needed therefore, is for us to confess our sins, not because God stands on His dignity, and wishes to humiliate us, but because only by confessing that we are wrong and that He is right will we trust in Him, who is the only source of life and righteousness. "Go and proclaim those words toward the north, and say, Return, thou backsliding Israel, saith the Lord; and I will not cause Mine anger to fall upon you; for I am merciful, saith the Lord, and I will not keep anger for ever. Only acknowledge thine iniquity, and that thou hast transgressed against the Lord thy God." Jer 3:12–13.

"A deceived heart has turned him aside, that he cannot deliver his soul, nor say, Is there not a lie in my right hand." How is there a lie in the right hand of the man who trusts in the works of his hands, that is, in anything that he has done, – the man who will not confess to God, but who maintains that he has life and righteousness in himself? – The answer is very easy. Read the preceding verses. The man who proposes to save himself by his own works, "is hungry, and his strength faileth; he drinketh no water, and is faint." But afterwards he eats and drinks, and is satisfied. But he did not make the food and drink, and he knows it. All the strength that he has comes from what he eats and drinks, that is, from something outside of himself, which he has received. The strength of our right hand is the strength that God has given us, yet we talk and act as if it were our own. Therefore it is evident that there is a lie in our right hands whenever we do so. Yes, we ourselves are lies, for we profess to be something when we are nothing. Every morsel of food that we eat, and upon which we depend for strength to go about our daily work, or which we use in self-gratification, is an evidence that we are wholly dependent on God. The easiest thing in the world to know is God. Anybody who has sense enough to know that eating will give strength, has no excuse for not knowing God. Ah, there are very many stupid people in this world; very many false witnesses. Shall we hearken to the Lord, and be wise, or shall we continue in our folly?

CHAPTER 52

ABOLISHING THE ENMITY

(Isa. 44:21–28)

"Remember these things, O Jacob;
And, Israel; for thou art My servant;
I have formed thee; thou art a servant unto Me;
O Israel, by Me thou shalt not be forgotten.
I have made thy transgressions vanish away like a cloud;
And thy sins like a vapour;
Return unto Me; for I have redeemed thee.
Sing, O ye heavens, for Jehovah hath effected it;
Utter a joyful sound, O ye depths of the earth;
Burst forth into song, O ye mountains;
Thou, forest, and every tree therein!
For Jehovah hath redeemed Jacob;
And will be glorified in Israel.
Thus saith Jehovah, thy redeemer;
Even He that formed thee from the womb;
I am Jehovah, who make all things;
Who stretch out the heavens alone;
Who spread the firm earth by Myself;
I am He who frustrateth the prognostics of the imposters;
And maketh the diviners mad;
Who reverseth the devices of the sages,
And infatuateth their knowledge;
Who establisheth the word of His servant;
And accomplisheth the counsel of His messengers;
Who sayeth to Jerusalem, Thou shalt be inhabited;
And to the cities of Judah, Ye shall be built;
And her desolated places I will restore;
Who sayeth to the deep, Be thou wasted;
And I will make dry thy rivers;

**Who sayeth to Cyrus, Thou art My shepherd!
And he shall fulfill all My pleasure;
Who sayeth to Jerusalem, Thou shalt be built;
And to the temple, Thy foundations shall be laid."**

A Contrast

What a contrast we have here between the true God, and the god made by a man who cannot work a single day without fainting from hunger and thirst, and who takes a portion of the material from which his god is made, and cooks his dinner with it. These things are to be remembered. This was written for us in this nineteenth century. That man who makes his god out of an ash tree is no more of a heathen than is any other man who does not trust in the Lord.

The Blessing of Service

It is a blessed thing for any man to hear the Lord say to him, "Thou art My servant." To whom does He say it? – To every one who will listen to Him. Jesus tasted death for every man, and all have been purchased by the blood of Christ. As soon as anyone yields to the Lord, to serve Him, that moment he is the Lord's servant. Rom. 6:16. Then he has all the privileges of the Lord's house. The Lord's servants are all free men. The loosing of them from bondage is the mark of servitude to Him. Ps. 116:16. The Lord's servants, that is, those who give themselves wholly to His service, are known by their freedom.

In verse 21 we have literally, instead of "I have formed thee; thou art My servant," "I have formed thee My servant." God creates man His servant. When God made man in the beginning, man was God's servant. But he was made a king, with absolute authority over all the earth and everything connected with it. So the Lord's servants are all kings by birth. There are many different grades of servants just as there are different degrees of ability; but the Lord has no one in His service, who is lower in rank than king. Men have lost the dominion. Adam lost control of himself, and therefore all his authority was gone; but Christ came to restore that which was lost; in Him we are created anew, and then the authority is restored. We are given complete dominion over ourselves, and the man who can rule himself can rule anything else under heaven.

God's Watchfulness

Surely there is not a more comforting passage of scripture in the Bible than this. It is full of tender, comforting words. "O Israel, thou shalt not be forgotten of Me." "He that keepeth thee will not slumber. Behold, He that keepeth Israel shall neither slumber nor sleep." Ps. 121:3–4. How often we hear somebody say that God has forgotten him. Why, the very breath that he uses in saying it, is an evidence that God has not forgotten him. A man is not a mere machine. He is not like a clock which the owner winds up, and then leaves to run down when the spring has uncoiled. If that were the case, then everybody would live at least to old age. No man lives of his own power, for "there is no man that has power over the spirit to retain the spirit; neither hath he power in the day of death." Eccl. 8:8. We lie down, and go to sleep, and we awake, simply because the Lord stays awake and watches. In the beginning He breathed the breath of life into man's nostrils, and He has continued doing that every moment since. If He thought only of Himself; if He gathered unto Himself His Spirit and His breath; all flesh would perish together, and man would turn again to dust. Job 34:14–15. But God does not forget a single individual; therefore we live. This does not imply that when a man dies it is because God has forgotten him. Not by any means. No; the God who has so complete a grasp of details that He knows every sparrow, and the number of the hairs upon every head, as well as the names of all the innumerable stars, can never be accused of forgetfulness. Details do not worry Him.

Sin Abolished in Our Flesh

Where are our sins? – They are in us, in our own lives, of course. "From within, out of the heart of men, proceed evil thoughts, adulteries, fornications, murders, thefts, covetousness, wickedness, deceit, lasciviousness, an evil eye, blasphemy, pride, foolishness; all these evil things come from within, and defile the man." Mark 7:21–23. Then when God says, "I have blotted out, as a thick cloud, thy transgressions, and, as a cloud, thy sins," what does He mean? – Simply this, that by His life He cleanses us from all sin – takes it out of us. "If we walk in the light, as He is in the light, we have fellowship one with another, and the blood of Jesus Christ His Son cleanseth us from all sin." 1 John 1:7. The Hebrew word here rendered "blotted out," is the word meaning to wipe off, as one would wipe words from a slate or blackboard. God takes the sins, and obliterates them. Do not make the mistake of saying that there is no such thing as sin, as some people do. There is sin, and it is very real; but it is not in Christ. "He was manifested to take away our sins; and in Him is no sin." 1 John 3:5. He has "condemned sin in the flesh." Rom. 8:4. In His own flesh He has "abolished the enmity" (Eph. 2:15), which is the carnal mind. Although He was in the flesh, the mind of the flesh had no control over Him. But it was our flesh that He took, therefore He has abolished sin in the flesh of every one who will confess Him. It is literally blotted out. He took upon Himself all the sins of the world, yet no person ever saw the slightest trace of a sin in or on Him. In Him the sins were as effectually effaced as if they had never existed.

Come Back! All is Forgiven

When the child plays truant from school, he is afraid to meet the master. The youth gets into bad company, and fears to go home. Conscience – a guilty conscience – makes cowards of us all, ever since Adam and Eve hid themselves from the face of the Lord in the garden of Eden, after they had eaten the forbidden fruit. People judge the Lord by their own hard, unforgiving natures, and think that since they have sinned against Him He must be angry with them; this keeps many away from Him; they do not believe that He will accept them if they come to Him. But He says, "Return unto Me; for I have redeemed thee." He tells us that the sins are blotted out, so that we need have no fear of returning. Nothing is held against us; all is gone in Christ. More blessed than all this is the fact that in this blotting out of our sins their power is destroyed, so that they cannot have dominion over us. God Himself has provided the way so that we need not come back like culprits, cringing and cowering with fear, but like sons, confidently, expecting mercy, and grace to help in time of need.

The Heavens and the Earth Interested

Here is something for the heavens and earth to rejoice over. How often the heavens and earth are called upon, in connection with the work of redemption. In the very first chapter of Isaiah, the heavens and earth are called upon to witness that God has nourished and brought up children, who have rebelled against Him. Now the same heavens and earth are called upon to rejoice, from the utmost heights to the lowest depths, because God has redeemed His people. Why should all nature be called upon to rejoice in this? Ah, there is good reason for it, because all nature was as it were placed in pawn, pledged to man's redemption. God upholds all things: in Christ all things hold together; so when God gave Christ, interposing Himself by an oath, thus pledging His own existence for man's salvation, the whole creation was placed over against the redemption of man. Humanly speaking, all nature was risked by the Lord in the grand enterprise of redeeming man. If the work had failed, if God had broken His word, then His life would have been forfeited, and the universe would have been dissolved. God and all creation, therefore, have a far greater interest in the redemption of man, than any man can have, or than all mankind can have. Their existence depends upon man's salvation. So we can well understand why "heaven and nature" should be called on to sing the grace of God that bringeth salvation, and why they should respond. What a strong ground of faith this gives us. There is not a thing in God's universe that has not an interest in our redemption, and there is nothing that is not calculated to help us in the way of life. Nothing is against us, but everything is for us. "All things are yours; whether Paul, or Apollos, or Cephas, or the world, or life, or death, or things present, or things to come: all are yours; and ye are Christ's, and Christ is God's." 1 Cor. 3:21–23.

God Creates by Himself

God had no helper in the creation of the universe. The Word was with God in the beginning, but the Word was God. He who by Himself created the heavens, and spread out the earth, is competent to redeem His people. Redemption is but creation anew, and the fact that God is Creator, and that without any aid, – when indeed there was no one else to give aid, – He created all things, is sufficient proof that what He has promised concerning man, He is fully able to perform. This is the reason we are called upon in the very last days to give glory to God, and to worship Him as the One who made heaven, and earth, and the sea, and the fountains of waters. Rev. 14:6–7.

The Infallible Word of Men

That which God does by another is as firm as if done without any agency. He confirms the word of His servant. He has reconciled us to Himself, and has put into us the Word of reconciliation. 2 Cor. 5:18–19. "He whom God hath sent, speaketh the words of God." John 3:34. Whoever speaks only the Word of the Lord, need have no fear that one of his words will fail. "If any man speak, let him speak as the oracles of God" (1 Peter 4:11), and he may speak with all boldness. The tokens of liars will be frustrated, and diviners will be seen to be mad, and the worldly-wise will be taken in their own craftiness, and their knowledge shown to be foolishness; but the simple truth uttered by the lowliest follower of God will stand as long as the sun and moon endure.

The last reference in this chapter, concerning Cyrus and his work, will be considered in connection with the first verses of the next chapter, where the subject is continued.

CHAPTER 53

GOD, THE RULER OF NATIONS

(Isa. 45:1–7)

"Thus saith the Lord to His anointed, to Cyrus, whose right hand I have holden, to subdue nations before him, and I will loose the loins of kings, to open before him the two-leaved gates; and the gates shall not be shut; I will go before thee, and make the crooked places straight; I will break in pieces the gates of brass, and cut in sunder the bars of iron; and I will give thee the treasurers of darkness, and hidden riches of secret places, that thou mayest know that I, the Lord, which call thee by thy name, am the God of Israel. For Jacob My servant's sake, and Israel Mine elect, I have even called thee by thy name; I have surnamed thee, though thou hast not known Me. I am the Lord, and there is none else, there is no God beside Me; I girded thee, though thou hast not known Me, that they may know from the rising of the sun, and from the west, that there is none beside Me. I am the Lord, and there is none else. I form the light, and create darkness; I made peace, and create evil; I the Lord do all these things."

When Nebuchadnezzar, king of Babylon, had a dream describing a calamity that was to befall him, he was told that it was to let him "know that the Most High ruleth in the kingdom of men, and giveth it to whomsoever He will." Dan. 4:25. In the scripture before us we have a wonderful example of the truth of this, and also an illustration of the fact that nothing happens by chance, and takes God by surprise, but is provided for long beforehand.

Isaiah prophesied "in the days of Uzziah, Jotham, Ahaz, and Hezekiah, kings of Judah." Isa. 1:1. Hezekiah reigned twenty-nine years (2 Chron. 29:1) and as he lived fifteen years after his great illness (Isa. 38), we know that he had reigned fourteen years at that time. But Isaiah had at that time been prophesying at least forty-six years, for Jotham and Ahaz had each reigned sixteen years. 2 Chron. 27:1; 28:1. We know not certainly how long Isaiah prophesied in the reign of Uzziah, but the sixth chapter seems to indicate that he began in the last year of his reign. The point is that in 714 B.C., which was about the date of Isaiah's special message to Hezekiah, Isaiah had been prophesying between forty-five and fifty years; and that as he did not prophesy later than Hezekiah's reign, he died before the year 698 B.C. We are therefore safe in putting the date of the scripture which we have before us as not later than 712 B.C.

Of what importance is this fact? It shows the minuteness of God's foreknowledge, and the perfection of His plans for the salvation of His people. Babylon was captured by Cyrus in the year 538 B.C., when he was sixty-one years old. We find therefore that Cyrus was named, and his work was described in detail, more than one hundred and thirty years before he was born, and about one hundred and eighty-four years before the work was done. That is to say, more than one hundred years before the children of Israel were carried captive to Babylon, the Lord had not only foretold their release from captivity, but had named the man who should be instrumental in setting them free, and had given a minute description of the incidents of the capture of the city. In view of this, how forcible are the words "I am the Lord, and there is none else, there is no God beside Me."

In order that the exactness of the prophecy may be better appreciated by the reader, we quote the following brief account of the capture of Babylon from Rawlinson's "Great Monarchies." It may be necessary to state, for the aid of some, that Babylon was very large, surrounded by a wall of immense height and thickness, and stored with provisions sufficient to last twenty years. The river Euphrates passed through the city, dividing it into two parts, but there was also a wall on each side of the river, the whole length of its passage through the city, and the twenty-five streets which led across the river were enclosed by huge gates of brass. Having described the progress of Cyrus to Babylon, against which his army began a seemingly hopeless siege, Rawlinson continues: –

"Withdrawing the greater part of his army from the vicinity of the city, and leaving behind him only certain corps of observation, Cyrus marched away up the course of the Euphrates for a certain distance, and there proceeded to make a vigorous use of the spade. His soldiers could now appreciate the value of the experience which they had gained by dispersing the Gyndes, and perceived that the summer and autumn of the preceding year had not been wasted. They dug a channel or channels from the Euphrates, by means of which a great portion of its water would be drawn off, and hoped in this way to render the natural course of the river fordable. When all was prepared, Cyrus determined to wait for the arrival of a certain festival, during which the whole population were wont to engage in drinking and reveling, and then silently in the dead of night to turn the water of the river and make his attack. All fell out as he hoped and wished. The festival was held with even greater pomp and splendour than usual; for Belshazzar, with the natural insolence of youth, to mark his contempt of the besieging army, abandoned himself wholly to the delights of the season, and himself entertained a thousand lords in his palace. Elsewhere the rest of the population was occupied in feasting and dancing. Drunken riot and mad excitement held possession of the town; the siege was forgotten; ordinary precautions were neglected. Following the example of their king, the Babylonians gave themselves up for the night to orgies in which religious frenzy and drunken excess formed a strange and revolting medley.

"Meanwhile, outside the city, in silence and darkness, the Persians watched at the two points where the Euphrates entered and left the walls. Anxiously they noted the gradual sinking of the water in the riverbed; still more anxiously they watched to see if those within the walls would observe the suspicious circumstance and sound an alarm through the town. Should such an alarm be given, all their labours would be lost. If, when they entered the riverbed, they found the river walls manned and the river-gates fast-locked, they would be indeed 'caught in a trap.' Enfiladed on both sides by an enemy whom they could neither see nor reach, they would be overwhelmed and destroyed by his missiles before they could succeed in making their escape. But as they watched, no sounds of alarm reached them – only a confused noise of revel and riot, which showed that the unhappy townsmen were quite unconscious of the approach of danger.

"At last shadowy forms began to emerge from the obscurity of the deep river-bed, and on the landing places opposite the river-gates scattered clusters of men grew into solid columns – the undefended gateways were seized – a war shout was raised – the alarm was taken and spread – and swift runners started off to 'show the king of Babylon that his city was taken at one end.' (Jer. 1:31) In the darkness and confusion of the night a terrible massacre ensued. The drunken revelers could make no resistance. The king, paralyzed with fear, at the awful handwriting upon the wall, which too late had warned him of his peril, could do nothing even to check the progress of his assailants, who carried all before them everywhere. Bursting into the palace, a band of Persians made their way to the presence of the monarch, and slew him on the scene of his impious revelry. Other bands carried fire and sword through the town. When morning came, Cyrus found himself undisputed master of the city, which, if it had not despised his efforts, might with the greatest ease have baffled him."

Note the statements of the prophecy: "I will loose the loins of kings." At the very hour when Cyrus was making his entrance into the city, while Belshazzar was engaged in a wild, idolatrous feast, God caused a writing to appear on the wall of the banqueting hall. "Then the king's countenance was changed, and his thoughts troubled him, so that the joints of his loins were loosed, and his knees smote one against another." Dan. 5:6.

"And the gates shall not be shut." All the skill of Cyrus, and even his stratagem of diverting the course of the river, would have availed nothing, if the gates leading to the river had not been left open. His army might have marched into the city, and out again if it could have got out, but could have inflicted no damage. But in that night of idolatrous revelry, everything was neglected and the way was open. The gods whom the princes praised gave no protection.

This entire prophecy is devoted to showing that there is none but God. He is the Creator and the Redeemer. He can create, and He can destroy. Nothing takes place without His counsel or consent. Everything works out His will. He makes even the wrath of man to praise Him. Ps. 66:10. Kings and nations think that they are controlling, and are doing their own will, when they are simply working out God's plan. We must not make the mistake of thinking that God plans all their wicked practices, but however wicked they are, however opposed to His will, they carry out His purpose even by their opposition.

It was God who said to Jerusalem, "Thou shalt be inhabited; and to the cities of Judah, ye shall be built, and I will raise up the decayed places thereof." He said it, and Cyrus was His agent in carrying it out. God also said to the deep, "Be dry," and it was He who dried up the rivers. So when Cyrus was digging his channels, and turning aside the Euphrates from its bed, he was simply doing God's work. What a marvelous, awe-inspiring thought – that men are factors in the great plan of the Most High God! And how glorious when they yield themselves willingly and understandingly! All the events of this earth's history, are not for the benefit of those who are enacting them, but for the salvation of God's people. Instead of being afraid when wars and rumours of wars and tumults come, thinking they are about to be overwhelmed, the faithful followers of God may be of good courage, knowing that out of these very alarms, and even by means of them, God is working out their deliverance.

God did his work through Cyrus, "that they may know from the rising of the sun, and from the west, that there is none beside Me." And how widely was the name of God known in consequence? – Over all the world. The kingdom of Babylon was world-wide. See Dan. 2:37–38; Jer. 27:4–7. Of course this came under the dominion of Cyrus, and so the decree for the building of the temple ran thus: –

"Now in the first year of Cyrus, king of Persia, that the word of the Lord by the mouth of Jeremiah might be fulfilled; the Lord stirred up the spirit of Cyrus, King of Persia, that he made a proclamation throughout all his kingdom, and put it also into writing, saying, Thus saith Cyrus, King of Persia. The Lord God of heaven hath given me all the kingdoms of the earth; and He hath charged me to build Him an house at Jerusalem, which is in Judah. Who is there among you of all His people? His God be with him, and let him go up to Jerusalem, which is in Judah, and build the house of the Lord God of Israel (He is the God) which is in Jerusalem." Ezra 1:1–3. So we see that the one true God was proclaimed by Cyrus throughout all the world.

"What a wonderful tribute from a heathen king!" some will exclaim. Why do you say, "a heathen king?" True, Cyrus was a Persian. He was brought up in ignorance of the true God: but so was Abraham. Joshua 24:2. God revealed Himself to Abraham, and he believed, and so became the friend of God. Cyrus was surnamed by God while he was yet ignorant of Him, even long before he was born, yet he came at last to know God, and he acknowledged Him before all the world, declaring Him to be God, and confessing that he held his title from Him. What more could anybody do? If there was ever a Christian king in any land, then certainly it was Cyrus, of Persia, as well as Nebuchadnezzar, of Babylon. This man, direct from heathenism, did what the Israelites, with a long ancestry of believers failed to do.

Cyrus was, therefore, an Israelite, even by his own confession. Read his proclamation over again. He declared his belief in the Lord of heaven, who had brought him to the throne, and said, "He is *the God*," and at the same time declared Him to be "the Lord God of Israel." God takes from among the Gentiles a people for His name (Acts 15:14), and Cyrus, the Persian, was one of them. It is not the flesh, but faith, that determines who are Israel. "God is no respecter of persons, but in every nation he that feareth Him, and worketh righteousness, is accepted with Him."

CHAPTER 54

THE UNSEEN GOD

(Isa. 45:8–15)

"Drop down, ye heavens, from above, and let the skies pour down righteousness; let the earth open, that they may bring forth salvation, and let her cause righteousness to spring up together; I the Lord have created it.

"Woe unto him that striveth with his Maker! a potsherd among the potsherds of the earth! Shall the clay say to him that fashioneth it, What makest thou? or thy work, He hath no hands? Woe unto him that saith unto a father, What begettest thou? or to a woman, With what travaillest thou? Thus saith the Lord, the Holy One of Israel, and his Maker. Ask Me of the things that are to come; concerning My sons, and the work of My hands, command ye Me. I have made the earth, and created man upon it: I, even My hands have stretched out the heavens, and all their host have I commanded. I have raised him up in righteousness, and I will make straight all his ways; he shall build My city, and he shall let my exiles go free, not for price nor reward, saith the Lord of hosts.

"Thus saith the Lord, The labour of Egypt, and the merchandise of Ethiopia, and the Sabeans men of stature, shall come over unto thee, and they shall be thine; they shall go over after thee; in chains they shall come over; and they shall fall down unto thee, saying, Surely God is in thee; and there is none else, there is no god. Verily Thou art a God that hidest Thyself, O God of Israel, the Saviour."

We will take the last verse as the key to the whole text, and the basis of our present study. God hides Himself. He is "the King eternal, immortal, invisible," "dwelling in the light which no man can approach unto; whom no man hath seen, nor can see." 1 Tim. 1:17; 6:16. What then is the use of the command, "Behold, your

God!" Why tell people to behold God, when He is invisible, and no man hath seen Him, and no man can see Him? He even hides Himself, so that nobody can see Him, and then sends us a message, saying, "Behold Me, behold Me." Isa. 65:1. Where is the consistency?

This is a fair specimen of the fault that many people find with God and His Word. They make out what seems a very plausible case against Him, and think that they have abundant excuse for their unbelief. Now when it appears that there is not the least inconsistency here, nor shadow of unreasonableness, it ought for ever to put an end to all cavil. When God rests His case on the most inconsistent terms possible, and nevertheless shows Himself perfectly true, it necessarily follows that no case can possibly be made to stand against Him. "The foolishness of God is wiser than men; and the weakness of God is stronger than men." 1 Cor. 1:25.

There is such a thing as seeing the invisible. The things that are impossible to human sight are very easy when the eyes of our understanding are enlightened by the Holy Spirit. Moses "endured as seeing Him who is invisible." Heb. 11:27. Our light afflictions work out for us an eternal weight of glory, "while we look not at the things which are seen, but at the things which are not seen." 2 Cor. 4:18. If we would have pleasure in the place of pain, we must continually look at the things which are invisible, paying no attention to the things which are seen.

Once one of the twelve disciples said to Jesus, "Lord, show us the Father, and it sufficeth us." Jesus replied, "Have I been so long time with you, and yet hast thou not known Me, Philip? he that hath seen Me hath seen the Father; and how sayest thou then, Show us the Father?" John 14:8–9. And then He added, "Believest thou not that I am in the Father, and the Father in Me? the words that I speak unto you I speak not of Myself; but the Father which dwelleth in Me, He doeth the works. Believe Me, that I am in the Father, and the Father in Me; or else believe Me for the very work's sake."

God was in Christ." Jesus was the manifestation of God, and yet there was nothing in His appearance to indicate the fact. It was impossible for anybody to ascertain by His appearance – His flesh and blood – that He was the Son of the living God. Matt. 16:16–17. He was the brightness of the Father's glory, and the very impress of His substance (Heb 1:3), but He veiled His glory with the robe of humanity. Nevertheless "we beheld His glory, the glory as of the only begotten of the Father, full of grace and truth." He was the Saviour, yet He said, "The flesh profiteth nothing." John 6:63. It was not that which could be seen, but that which could not be seen, that profited And the unseen, the hidden life, was made visible; "for the life was manifested, and we have seen it." 1 John 1:2. The visible is nothing; only the invisible is real. This, by the way, should teach all men the folly of trusting to forms and ceremonies for salvation. Ritualism is emptiness.

Where does God hide Himself? – In the light. He dwells in the light. But do we not read that "clouds and darkness are round about Him" (Ps. 97:2), and that "He made darkness His secret place?" Ps. 18:11. Yes; "His pavilion round about Him were dark waters and thick clouds of the skies;" but "the darkness and the light are both alike to Him" (Ps. 139:12); "the night shineth as the day;" so that "at the brightness that was before Him His thick clouds passed." Although He dwells in darkness He covers Himself with light as with a garment (Ps. 104:2.) "and the light shineth in the darkness; and the darkness overcame it not." Light overcomes darkness.

Moreover, "God is light, and in Him is no darkness at all." 1 John 1:5. The case becomes more and more complex, but the very complexity is clearness. God hides Himself, but He hides Himself in light, and He Himself is light, and the light cannot be shut in by any darkness. Why then can we not see Him? – The only reason is that we do not have our eyes adjusted to view the light. If we will but get our eyes anointed with heavenly eye salve, we may see heavenly things. Rev. 3:18. Then "if we walk in the light, as He is in the light, we have fellowship one with another." 1 John 1:7. We become one with Him. He hides Himself in us.

Very few take in the force of this last verse, 1 John 1:7. They seem to think that it is human fellowship that is referred to, whereas it is fellowship with God. If we walk in the light as God is in the light, we have fellowship with Him, and He with us. We and God have fellowship with each other – mutual fellowship. The French of Segond puts it clearly, *nous sommes mutuellement en communion,* we are mutually in communion.

Then where shall we look to find God? Look everywhere. Look within. "The kingdom of God cometh not with observation; neither shall they say, Lo, here! or, lo, there! For, behold, the kingdom of God is within you." Luke 17:20–21. "Every spirit that confesseth that Jesus Christ is come in the flesh is of God." 1 John 4:2. Confess that the Word, which was in the beginning with God, and was God, is come in your flesh, and dwells there, and you are born of God and know God. If haply you feel after Him, you will certainly find Him, for He is not far from every one of us, since "in Him we live, and move, and have our being." Acts 17:27–28. "Know ye that the Lord He is God; it is He that hath made us, and we are His" (Ps. 100:3); and the invisible things of God, even His everlasting power and Divinity, are clearly seen in the things that are made, so that that which may be known of God is manifest in all men. Rom. 1:19–20. Who can charge God with unfairness because He has hidden Himself, when He is light, and hides Himself in the light, and sends the true light into every man that cometh into the world?

God hides Himself in His works. People look at Him, but do not see Him. Have you not often seen hidden faces in pictures? You were told that in a certain picture a face was concealed. You gazed at the picture long and steadily, turning it so as to see it from every possible point, and going away and coming back again, but you could see nothing but what was apparent. At last somebody placed his finger upon a certain spot, or put the picture before you in a certain way, when, lo, the hidden face stood revealed; and then you could not look at the picture without seeing it. In whatever position the picture was placed, you saw the hidden face, and you wondered how you could ever have been so blind as not to see it. It was concealed, yet wonderfully apparent. So God is concealed in His works; most people see nothing of Him; yet as soon as we have eyes for Him, we cannot see a thing without beholding His invisible face plainly revealed.

The skies pour down righteousness, and the earth brings forth truth. In this connection, read Job. 36:24–30: – "Remember that thou magnify His work, whereof men have sung, all men have looked thereon; man beholdeth it afar off. Behold God is great and we know Him not; the number of His years is unsearchable. For He draweth up the drops of water, which distil in rain from His vapour; which the skies pour down and drop upon man abundantly – Yea, can any understand the spreadings of the clouds, the thunderings of His pavilion? Behold, He spreadeth His light around Him; and He covereth the bottom of the sea."

Wondrously does God hide Himself, so that every raindrop, every sunbeam, and every springing flower reveals Him. His doctrine drops as the rain, and His speech distils as the dew, "as the small rain upon the tender herb, and as the showers upon the grass." Deut. 32:2. If we but know where to find Him, we may drink in His righteousness in the rain that falls from heaven, and the light of His countenance will sparkle to us in the drops of dew upon the grass.

When we read verses 9–11 together, it seems evident that the latter verse is a question instead of a direct statement. Thus it is given some translations, "Do you ask Me of things to come concerning My sons, and concerning the work of My hands do you command Me?" "Shall the clay say to Him that fashioneth it, What makest Thou?" "Woe unto him that saith unto his Father, What begettest Thou?" God is our Father; we are but clay, and He is the Maker of all things; who are we that we should presume to question His ways? how dare puny man set himself to criticize God's work? He has made the earth, and created man upon it, and His hands have stretched out the heavens, and He has commanded all their host; yet men criticize and question His actions as though He were the merest apprentice. It would be better to look in quietness, and learn.

There shall come in the last days, the days of which Isaiah prophesized (see chap. 6:11–12), scoffers, walking after their own lusts, and saying, "Where is the promise of His coming? for since the fathers fell asleep all things continue as they were from the beginning of the creation." 2 Peter 3:3–4. But they say falsely, without any thought of what has taken place. In this portion of

Isaiah, together with that which we studied last week, we have one of the proofs that God has given us of the truthfulness of His word, and that, too, with special reference to the coming of Christ to save His people.

Recall the prophecy concerning Cyrus, and how long it was uttered before the event took place, or Cyrus was born. God said, "He shall build My city, and he shall let go My captives, not for price nor reward." God's people had been brought out of Egypt, to dwell in their own land, even the whole earth, which was promised to Abraham. Rom. 4:13. But through lack of faith they never entered into the fullness of their inheritance. At the time of the nation's highest prosperity, the promised inheritance was still future (see 2 Sam. 7:1–10), and King David on the throne, with wealth in abundance, was but a stranger and a sojourner, even as were Abraham, Isaac, and Jacob. 1 Chron. 29:15.

Because the people were no more fit to dwell in the land than the Canaanites had been, God sold them into the hands of their enemies, and they were taken captive to Babylon. But He did not forsake them. Before they were taken away, the exact length of their captivity, seventy years, was foretold. Jer. 29:10–14. By reading the words here referred to, we see that the deliverance from Babylonian captivity was to be the final, complete deliverance of God's people. "Ye shall seek Me, and find Me, when ye shall search for Me with all your heart. And I will be found of you, saith the Lord; and I will turn away your captivity, and I will gather you from all the nations, and from all the places whither I have driven you, saith the Lord; and I will bring you again into the place where I caused you to be carried away captive." If Israel had learned the lesson in captivity, that God designed they should learn, the close of the seventy years would have been the beginning of the time of the promise, even as the deliverance from Egypt was.

Promptly at the time appointed, God sent a man to release the people from Babylon. He fulfilled His word to the letter. But although everybody was free to return to Canaan, and representatives from all the tribes did return, in goodly number, they never really came out of Babylon. Babylon means confusion, departure from the simplicity that is in Christ. From that time even till now God's people have been in Babylon, so that still the call sounds, and still louder will it yet sound, "Come out of her, My people." Rev. 18:4. The coming of the Lord will mark the complete deliverance of God's people from Babylon; and He will come just as surely as Cyrus fulfilled God's word in the decree concerning Jerusalem and the temple.

Then will all the world know that God dwells in His people. They will come, saying, "Surely God is in thee; and there is none else, there is no god." Christ is coming "to be glorified in His saints, and to be admired in all them that believe." 2 Thess. 1:9–10. But before He can come, His way must be prepared, so that He can dwell fully in His saints. Just as God was in Christ, so must He be in His church as a whole, and in each individual member, before Christ can be revealed to the eyes of all the world. It is only as men see God in His people, that they can fully know that there is only one God, the One who created all things. Christ, the fullness of God, must be fully formed in His people, and then will all "See what is the stewardship of the mystery which from all ages hath been hid in God who created all things; to the intent that now unto the principalities and the powers in the heavenly places might be made known through the church the manifold wisdom of God, according to the eternal purpose which He purposed in Christ Jesus our Lord." Eph. 3:9–11, R.V. Then will the world know that God hides Himself in man, in order that man may be glorified by His presence.

CHAPTER 55

OBJECT OF THE EARTH'S CREATION

(Isa. 45:16–19, Lowth's Translation)

They are ashamed, they are even confounded,
His adversaries all of them;
Together they retire in confusion, the fabricators of images.
But Israel shall be saved in the Lord with eternal salvation;
Ye shall not be ashamed, neither shall ye be confounded, to
the ages of eternity.
For thus saith Jehovah,
Who created the heavens; He is God:
Who formed the earth and made it; He hath established it;
He created it not in vain; for He formed it to be inhabited;
I am Jehovah, and none besides;
I have not spoken in secret, in a dark place of the earth;
I have not said to the seed of Jacob, Seek ye Me in vain;
I am Jehovah, who speak truth; who give direct answers.

The Fate of Idols and Their Makers

Long ago we learned in our study of this prophecy that "he that believeth shall not make haste," or be confounded, because he builds up the Sure Foundation, the Rock of Ages, Christ Jesus. "We know that no idol is anything in the world, and that there is no God but one." 1 Cor. 8:4. Therefore those who make and trust in idols must necessarily go to confusion. They literally go to nothing, for the idol is nothing, and "they that make them are like unto them; so is every one that trusteth in them." He who builds up nothing must come to nothing. Thus we read: "For the day of the Lord is near upon all the heathen; as thou hast done, it shall be done unto thee; thy reward shall return unto thine own head. For as ye have drunk upon My holy mountain, so shall all the heathen drink continually, yea, they shall drink, and they shall swallow down, and they shall be as though they had not been." Obadiah 15:16. "The gods that have not made the heavens and the earth, even they shall perish from the earth and from under these heavens." Of course then those who trust in them will perish with them. That is to say, whoever trusts in anything less than the power that made and upholds the heavens and the earth, will go out of existence.

No Want to Those Who Trust God

"But the Lord is the true God, He is the living God, and an everlasting King." Jer. 10:10. He is "from everlasting to everlasting." Ps. 90:2. Therefore "Israel shall be saved in the Lord with an everlasting salvation;" for Israel is the people who depend upon the Lord, and who "have no confidence in the flesh." Jacob's name was changed to Israel when he ceased to wrestle, because unable to stand, and hung on the Lord for support. That was his strength whereby he prevailed. Compare Gen. 32:24–28 with Hosea 12:3–4. It is "in the Lord" that Israel will be saved, not in themselves. "Vain is the help of man." "Cursed be the man that trusteth in man." Jer. 17:5.

Why the Earth Was Created

Why was the earth created? The text tells us that God formed it to be inhabited. This statement immediately follows the statement that "He created it not in vain." That is to say, that if the earth were not inhabited, it would have been formed in vain. There would be no reason for its existence if it had no inhabitants. Note further that the fact that the earth was not formed in vain, but was created to be inhabited, is given as proof that Israel shall be saved in the Lord with an everlasting salvation. Israel shall not be ashamed nor confounded to the ages of eternity, because they will have the earth to dwell on. It is to be the home of the saved, even as in the beginning it was formed to be inhabited by a righteous race.

A Present, Timely Message

This is a message for this time, for the message given to Isaiah was to be proclaimed "until the cities be wasted without inhabitant, and the houses without man, and the land be utterly desolate, and the Lord have removed men far away, and there be a great forsaking in the midst of the land." Isa 6:11–12. Is there any prospect that such a thing will ever take place? There is indeed. God does nothing arbitrarily, and the Lord will not come to take unto Himself His great power, and to reign, "and to destroy the earth" (Rev. 11:17–18), until the earth and its inhabitants are so near total destruction that they would not last any longer, even if His coming were deferred. It is nothing but the coming of the Lord that saves the earth from destruction, which wicked men have brought upon it by their own self-destroying sins. Let us study this matter a little more closely, and we shall see it plainly.

Sin Brings Ruin

Remember that God has placed Himself on trial by the world. The Judgment of the last day will be to determine and demonstrate the righteousness of God's character. He is to be clear when He judges, or, to overcome when He is judged. Ps. 51:4; Rom. 3:4. The judgment will be that God is true, but every man a liar. Thus every sinner will pronounce judgment upon himself. The wicked are now treasuring up unto themselves wrath against the day of wrath and revelation of the righteous judgment of God. Rom. 2:4. In the judgment every sinner will acknowledge that he has brought his fate upon himself, and is simply reaping what he has sown. He that soweth to the flesh shall of the flesh reap corruption, and to be carnally minded is death; it has death in it.

Weigh these texts well. It is made very plain in the Scriptures that the wicked will receive punishment at the hands of God; that they will be burned up with unquenchable fire; but what is here set forth is that the Lord will not administer this punishment until the wicked men and seducers have waxed so bad that if the Lord did not come the race would cease to exist, being self-destroyed. This conclusion necessarily results from the fact that the wicked reap the fruit of their own doings; that "the turning away of the simple shall slay them, and the prosperity of fools shall destroy them." Prov. 1:32. "The strong shall become tow, and his work a spark of fire; and they shall both burn together, and none shall quench them." Isa. 1:31. When the wicked see that the coming of the Lord occurred just as they were about to exterminate themselves, and that He came to save the earth from utter destruction with them, and to make it a place fit for the habitation of those who remain loyal to Him, no tongue can rise up against Him in judgment. The master of the harvest begins His work at the time when the grain would fall of itself if it were not reaped.

The End Approaching

Is there any probability that such a state of things is imminent? There undoubtedly is, although very many people will scoff at the statement. Look at the rapid increase of disease. In the last few years consumption has increased at a most alarming rate, and is carrying off its victims by the hundred thousand. People of middle age can well remember when a consumptive person was a somewhat noted person in a community, lingering along for years; whereas now consumption is one of the most common diseases, and often carries off its victims almost as quickly as the plague. Indeed, it has earned the name of "the great white plague." The same plague is upon the cattle upon which men feed, so that the danger is intensified. If the disease should increase in the next few years at the same rate that it has in the past few years, the human being or the cow that did not have consumption would be an exceptional case.

This is only one of the many causes of death; many others might be named. Vice is increasing by leaps and bounds, and becoming more bold, if not more open. By unnatural practices men and women are "receiving in themselves that recompense of their error which was meet." By wrong habits of eating and drinking, people are undermining their constitutions, and preparing themselves to be a prey to any epidemic that arises; men and women vie with one another to see who can discover something new to eat. The simple things which God gave to man as his food, which are perfectly adapted to the wants of the body, building it up and making it strong, are but little thought of, while more and more abominable things and worse combinations are swallowed, the effect of which is only to fill the body with poisons, and to produce unsound tissues. People flatter themselves that none of these things injure them, even while they are continually dosing themselves with patent nostrums, in order that they may keep their diseased organs from crying out under the strain put upon them, and preserve the *feeling* of health without the reality. Many who have the appearance and the feeling of health are often cut down almost without any warning, because they have been fitting themselves to be a prey to disease. The plagues that come upon the earth are not any "mysterious dispensation of Providence," but are the natural and inevitable result of the gross habits of the people.

Devastating War

Then there is war with all its evils. The thousands that are slaughtered in battle do not by any means mark the sum of the ravages of war. Poverty, disease, and famine naturally follow in the wake of great armies. And when was there ever such preparation for war as at the present time. True there is great talk of peace, but the weapons of war are in hand all the time. No nation will voluntarily talk of peace until it can dictate the terms. Immense armaments are being prepared for use, and who can estimate the slaughter that will take place when all the nations really become angry, and all join in the strife? The most optimistic know that the general struggle cannot be much longer delayed, and none dare contemplate the result. There is nothing more certain than that with all the able-bodied men drawn into the armies, as is fast being the case, and set to killing one another, together with disease eating up the rest, to say nothing of the new ills that are generated by the armies themselves, another hundred years, if the coming of the Lord were delayed so long, would see none left on earth except the few righteous people who keep the truth. This is not speculation, but is exactly what the word of the Lord has foretold. "The land shall be utterly emptied, and utterly spoiled; for the Lord hath spoken this word. The earth mourneth and fadeth away, the world languisheth and fadeth away, the haughty people of the earth do languish. The earth also is defiled under the inhabitants thereof; because they have transgressed the laws, changed the ordinance, broken the everlasting covenant. Therefore hath the curse devoured the earth, and they that dwell therein are desolate; therefore the inhabitants of the earth are burned, and few men left." Isa. 24:3–6.

A Brighter Picture

But this is not to be the end, for the Lord created the earth not in vain, but formed it to be inhabited. When He formed it, He also made man and set him over it, and everything that He had made, including man, was "very good." From this we learn God's purpose in creating the earth. It was to be inhabited. Some one may say, "Well, it is now inhabited." Not by the people for whom God designed it. He did not make the earth to be inhabited by wicked people, those who are in rebellion against His Government. The object of the creation of the earth will not be met until righteousness dwells in it, and sin and sickness are unknown. That time will come just as surely as God lives and is true. The increase of evil, wicked men and seducers waxing worse and worse, deceiving and being deceived, the preparations for war, and the destruction of men by violence, disease, and vice, do not throw any discredit upon God's word, but are in themselves tokens of its truthfulness, and of the near approach of the time when Christ shall come and reign in righteousness.

The Saving Word of God

God has not spoken any word in vain. He is able to save all that put their trust in Him, and His salvation is a perfect salvation. He saves from sin and death, and from every trace of both. He does not deceive. Far more than earthly parents, does He know how to give good gifts, even the gift of His own Spirit, to those who ask Him. The power by which He will keep His people in the time of trouble that is coming on all the world, so that no plague shall come nigh their dwelling even though noisome pestilence walketh in darkness and destruction wasteth at noonday, so that no evil befalls them, neither does any plague come nigh their dwelling, is the selfsame power by which He now keeps them from sin. And He speaks plainly, too. The agents of Satan, wizards and familiar spirits, "peep and mutter," and "whisper out of the dust" (Isa. 8:19; 29:4), but God gives direct answers. There is nothing ambiguous in them, as is the case with heathen oracles. The word "is not hidden from thee, neither is it far off. It is not in heaven, that thou shouldest say, who shall go up for us to heaven, and bring it unto us, that we may hear it, and do it? But the word is very nigh unto thee, in thy mouth, and in thy heart that thou mayest do it." Therefore "If thou shalt confess with thy mouth the Lord Jesus, and shalt believe in thine heart that God hath raised Him from the dead, thou shalt be saved. For with the heart man believeth unto righteousness, and with the mouth confession is made unto salvation." And "behold, now is the accepted time; now is the day of salvation."

CHAPTER 56

THE GOD THAT CAN SAVE

(Isa. 45:20–25)

"Assemble yourselves and come; draw near together, ye that are escaped of the nations; they have no knowledge that set up the wood of their graven image, and pray unto a god that cannot save. Tell ye, and bring them near: yea, let them take counsel together; who hath declared this from ancient time? who hath told it from that time? have not I the Lord? and there is no God else beside Me; a just God and a Saviour; there is none beside Me. Look unto Me, and be ye saved, all the ends of the earth; for I am God, and there is none else. I have sworn by Myself, the word is gone out of My mouth in righteousness, and shall not return, That unto Me every knee shall bow, every tongue shall swear. Surely, shall one say, in the Lord have I righteousness and strength; even to Him shall all men come, and all that are incensed against Him shall be ashamed. In the Lord shall all the seed of Israel be justified, and shall glory."

In order to get the full benefit of these closing words of the forty-fifth chapter of Isaiah, one must have in mind the leading features of all that has preceded, from the fortieth chapter. Remember that in the whole Gospel of Isaiah the prominent feature is the great case in court, where the Government of God is on trial among men, before the whole universe. The question to be decided is, Who is God? The decision of the case depends on who can save: the One who can save is the true God. The witnesses are the men whom God saves. They alone can be true witnesses, telling what they know from personal experience. In these verses we have this court scene vividly presented before us.

"Assemble yourselves and come; draw near together." "Tell ye, and bring them near; yea, let them take counsel together." Here again is the summons to court. God challenges His enemies, those who have brought false charges against Him, to come and establish their case if possible. Let all the strength of all nations be joined together to manufacture a god or multitudes of gods, yet none of them can save; none can deliver those that trust in them. That is to say, no man, nor all men together, can save. Men cannot save themselves. Those who set up a wooden god, or any kind of god that cannot save, have no knowledge. Surely, the least degree of wisdom would teach anybody that when he is in a lost condition he cannot manufacture anything that can save him. This is simply the same thing that we find in the New Testament: "By grace are ye saved through faith; and that not of yourselves; it is the gift of God; not of works, lest any man should boast." Eph. 2:8–9. The Gospel according to Isaiah is identical with that preached by Paul.

Praying for Deliverance

For what purpose does one trust in any god, whether the true God, or one of his own manufacture? – It is for the purpose of support, of salvation. Read again the forty-fourth chapter. The foolish man who makes a god out of the same piece of wood with which he cooks his dinner, falls down before it, and says, "Deliver me; for thou art my god." The fact that he prays this prayer, shows that he feels the need of deliverance. We must not make the mistake of supposing that all the heathen are insincere. There is no doubt as great a proportion of sincerity among the people in openly heathen countries as there is in those that are nominally Christian. It is not every heathen that prays for aid in sin – for the furtherance of his evil designs. True, we learn that among the ancients very many prayed to the gods in order that they might succeed in some proposed plan of robbery or seduction; but then we read that many among professed Christians pray to God, but ask only that they may consume it upon their lusts. James 4:3. So if the heathen have no excuse, the professed Christian has no reason for despising them. Among the heathen who in their blindness bow down to wood and stone, there are very many who are earnestly longing for deliverance from the chains that bind them. Ethiopia is represented as stretching out her hands to God. We are told that when the true light from God shines forth from the people of God, the Gentiles will come to it. Isa. 60:3. So when we hear of men praying, no matter to what they pray, we know that they pray because they desire something.

The heathen pray to a god that cannot save. Yet they continue to pray for year after year. What wonderful perseverance! Praying for deliverance, and continuing to pray, not discouraged by the fact that they never find the thing sought for. There is something in them to admire, even while we pity. Would we be as persevering? It is a question, for very many times we become weary in well-doing, and say that it is a vain thing we serve God. Perhaps we can learn a lesson even from the heathen.

He Who Creates, Saves

Into the midst of this multitude assembled to pray to a god that cannot save, God sends out the message, "Look unto Me, and be ye saved, all the ends of the earth." How is it that He calls to the ends of the earth, to look to Him to be saved? – Because He is "the Creator of the ends of the earth." Isa. 40:28. He can save that which He has made. And He will do it, too, for "all the ends of the earth shall see the salvation of our God." Isa. 52:10. "The heavens are Thine, the earth also is Thine: as for the world, and the fullness thereof, Thou hast founded them. The north and the south, Thou hast created them; Tabor and Hermon shall rejoice in Thy name. Thou hast a mighty arm; strong is Thy hand, and high is Thy right hand." Ps. 89:11–13. In Christ we have redemption, because in Him are all things created, and in Him all things hold together. Col. 1:13–17. The Creator is the Saviour. The cross of Christ saves, because in the cross is the power of a new creation. "If any man be in Christ, he is a new creature." That which reminds us of the fact that God is the Creator of the heavens and the earth, and the sea, and all that is in them is that which presents to us the Gospel of our salvation. It is the Word of truth.

Salvation Natural to God

God is our Father. All the subjects of the King of kings are His children. Yet most people, even professed Christians, think it a surprising thing that God answers prayer. Indeed, it is really a question in the minds of many, whether God does actually hear our prayers. If there were a case reported, of marvelous cure, or deliverance from great danger, or of relief in great distress, many professed Christians would shake their heads, and deplore such fanaticism. Among those who would believe it, it would be reported as a most marvelous thing. Marvelous indeed are all God's mercies, but what we mean is that people would regard it as a strange thing. "This poor man cried," and the Lord actually delivered him out of all his troubles! How strange! We pick up our morning paper, and read the headlines. One says, in startling letters, "Astonishing Occurrence: A rich father actually gives his son a suit of clothes!" Another one says, "Strange Affair: A young man traveling on the Continent telegraphs to his father for money, and receives a check the next day!" You throw down the paper in disgust. "How senseless to publish such commonplace things as those; why, it is the most natural thing in the world for a father to give his son money and clothing, and whatever he needs for his support; that is an everyday occurrence; why take up space to tell what everybody knows?" "If ye then, being evil, know how to give good gifts unto your children, how much more shall your Father which is in heaven give good things to them that ask Him?" Matt. 7:11. We should indeed publish the mercies of the Lord, but not as though it were a rare thing for the Lord to be merciful. Rather should the goodness of the Lord be talked about so much that everybody would know that "He delighteth in mercy," and that it is His nature to give to everyone that asketh. "Every one that asketh receiveth." God saves, and saves immediately. "Shall not God avenge His own elect, which cry to Him day and night, and He is long suffering over them? I say unto you, that He will avenge them speedily." Luke 18:7–8.

Bearing False Witness Against God

Yet thousands professedly pray to God, and receive no definite answers. Indeed, they scarcely expect answers, and would be surprised if any came. How many people are there in Christian lands and in Christian churches who day after day and week after week bow down before the Lord, and pray for deliverance, and yet are not free. They pray for salvation from sin, and yet are not saved; they still go on sinning. How much better off are they than the heathen? The idolater prays to a god that cannot save, and is not saved; the professed Christian prays to the God that can save, and he likewise is not saved. Where is the difference? Not in the men, certainly. The heathen is for all practical purposes as well off as the man who professes to worship the true God. "My brethren, these things ought not so to be," and it is not God's fault that they are so. He hears prayer, and He saves.

Worse than the Heathen

We are God's witnesses, yet we often bear false witness. Every professed Christian who continues to live in sin; every one who prays to God, declaring that he worships only the true and living God, but who does not live in the constant enjoyment of the salvation for which he prays, is a false witness. He is doing God worse service than are the heathen themselves. He is saying that there is no more power in God to save than there is in the gods of the heathen; and inasmuch as he professes to be a servant of God, and is supposed to be intimate with Him, his testimony tells more against God than does the testimony of many heathen. When the heathen looks at such an one, what inducement has he to leave his idols, and worship the God of the Christian? The heathen is indeed without excuse, in that he has all creation before him; but he gets no evidence from this one of the highest of God's creatures. It is well that God has not left Himself without witness, in that He has done all men good, giving them rain from heaven, and fruitful seasons; for the men who have professed His name have too often testified that He could not save, or else that He was indifferent. The only way that we can be true witnesses for God, is by allowing His power to work in us that which is good. It is not enough that we do not indulge in some of the practices of the debased heathen; if we do not take salvation from our God, to whom we pray for deliverance, we are as bad off as are the heathen who set up the wood of their graven image, and pray to a God that cannot save. Let us not libel God any more.

The Secret of Successful Prayer

If men in praying would remember that He is the creator of the ends of the earth, there would not be so many vain prayers. "Ah Lord God! behold, Thou hast made the heaven and the earth by Thy great power and stretched out arm, and there is nothing too hard for Thee." Jer. 32:17. He who made man of the dust of the earth can very easily lift up the poor out of the dust, and set them among the princes of His people, and make them inherit the throne of glory. It is because men have forgotten to worship God as the Creator, that they do not find salvation. The fact that He is the Creator, is the sole difference between Him and the hordes of false gods. Do not forget this essential difference.

Salvation in a Look

God says, "Look unto Me, and be ye saved." Salvation is in a look. "There's life in a look." When the children of Israel were dying in the bites of venomous serpents, "The Lord said unto Moses, Make thee a fiery serpent, and set it upon a pole; and it shall come to pass, that every one that is bitten, when he looketh upon it, shall live. And Moses made a serpent of brass, and put it upon a pole, and it came to pass, that if a serpent had bitten any man, when he beheld the serpent of brass, he lived." Num. 21:8–9. "And as Moses lifted up the serpent in the wilderness, even so must the Son of man be lifted up; that whosoever believe in Him should not perish, but have eternal life." John 3:14–15. Looking in faith saves us. "We all, with open face, beholding as in a glass the glory of the Lord, are changed into the same image from glory to glory." "For our light affliction, which is but for a moment, worketh for us a far more exceeding and eternal weight of glory; while we look not at the things which are seen, but at the things which are not seen." 2 Cor. 3:18; 4:17–18. While we look at the Lord, He looks at us, and the Light of His countenance saves. The light of the knowledge of the glory of God shines in the face of Jesus Christ. When Peter denied the Lord with cursing and swearing, Jesus turned and looked upon Peter, and immediately Peter received repentance and forgiveness. No one can possibly be lost while he is steadfastly looking unto Jesus.

Sworn Testimony

In this great case, all the testimony must be sworn to. God has given testimony in His own behalf, and has sworn to it. He has sworn that none who trust in Him shall be lost. He has sworn to save every one who is willing to be saved, that is, every one who acknowledges himself to be utterly lost, and who therefore cease his vain struggles to save himself, but allows God to do as He will with him. His case rests upon His power and willingness to save the ungodly, and such confidence has He in the outcome, that He has sworn that every knee shall bow before Him, and every tongue confess that He is the Lord. All will do this, constrained by the weight of evidence. The righteous will do it now, even though they cannot see and understand all the dealings of God; the wicked, even the devil himself, will do it at the last, when the hidden things are brought to light, and will thus pronounce their own doom. In the oath of God, He has placed every man under oath. Every man on earth is under obligation to God, to bear witness to His faithfulness and power to save; all are by right God's witnesses; therefore all who do not in their lives bear witness to the fact that God saves, are perjurers. The third commandment is broken by many in their prayers. They take the name of God in vain, because they do not claim the salvation which He has wrought out, and has brought to all mankind.

Our Case God's Case

In the Lord there is righteousness and strength. In the Lord there is justification and glory. When God swore, He swore by Himself. He pledged His life for the salvation of men. He virtually said that if He failed to save anybody, even the humblest person in the remotest part of the earth, who called upon Him for salvation, He would forfeit His own life. Indeed, if righteousness does not come from God, or if it comes from any other source than the Lord Jesus, then His life is already forfeited, for in that case Christ is dead in vain. See Gal. 2:21. But Christ is not dead in vain, and God is from everlasting to everlasting, although He has staked His life. He declares that all men shall yet bear witness, and swear to it, that He is the God that saves. Since He has such confidence in His case, and is willing to stake so much upon it, cannot we put our case along with His? If we join Him, our life is bound up in the bundle of life with His, and we are as sure of everlasting life and happiness as He is. What a great salvation!

CHAPTER 57

THE DOWNFALL OF PRIDE

(Isa. 47:1–15)

"Come down, and sit in the dust, O virgin daughter of Babylon; sit on the ground without a throne, O daughter of the Chaldeans; for thou shalt no more be called tender and delicate. Take the millstones, and grind meal; remove thy veil, strip off the train, uncover the leg, pass through the rivers. Thy nakedness shall be uncovered, yea, thy shame shall be seen; I will take vengeance, and will accept no man. Our Redeemer, the Lord of hosts is His name, the Holy one of Israel. Sit thee silent, and get thee into darkness, O daughter of the Chaldeans; for thou shalt no more be called the Lady of kingdoms. I was wroth with My people, I profaned Mine inheritance, and gave them into thine hand; thou didst show them no mercy; upon the ancients hast thou very heavily laid thy yoke. And thou saidst, I shall be a lady for ever; so thou didst not lay these things to thy heart, neither didst thou remember the latter end thereof.

"Now therefore hear this, thou that art given to pleasures, that dwellest carelessly, that sayest in thine heart, I am, and there is none else beside me; I shall not sit as a widow, neither shall I know the loss of children; but these two things shall come to thee in a moment in one day, the loss of children and widow-hood; in their full measure shall they come upon thee, despite of the multitude of thy sorceries, and the great abundance of thine enchantments. For thou hast trusted in thy wickedness; thou hast said, None seeth Me; thy wisdom and thy knowledge, it hath perverted thee; and thou hast said in thine heart, I am, and there is none else beside me. Therefore shall evil come upon thee, thou shalt not know the dawning thereof; and mischief shall fall upon thee; thou shalt not be able to put it away; and desolation shall come upon thee suddenly, which thou knewest not. Stand thou with thine enchantments, and with the multitude of thy sorceries, wherein thou hast laboured from thy youth; if so be thou shalt be able to profit, if so be thou mayest prevail. Thou art wearied in the multitude of thy counsels; let now the astrologers, and stargazers, the monthly prognosticators, stand up, and save thee from the things that shall come upon thee. Behold, they shall be as stubble; the fire shall burn them; they shall not deliver themselves from the power of the flame; it shall not be a coal to warm at, nor a fire to sit before. Thus shall the things be unto thee wherein thou hast laboured; they that have trafficked with thee from thy youth shall wander every one to his quarter; there shall be none to save thee."

To Whom Is This Spoken

Of what interest is all this to us? How does it concern us to know that such things were prophesized of Babylon, and that they were fulfilled more than twenty-five centuries ago? Is it to us anything more than a mere matter of curiosity such as that with which we read any other record of the past? Or if it be more than a matter of curiosity, has the record any more than an historical interest for us, proving the truthfulness of God's word? Why were these things placed in the Bible for us to read, and why do we read them?

"Whatsoever things were written aforetime were written for our learning, that we through patience and comfort of the Scriptures might have hope." Rom. 15:4. Not unto themselves, but unto us, did the prophets minister the things which are now reported unto us by them that have preached the Gospel by the Holy Ghost sent down from heaven. 1 Peter 1:11–12. The things written in this chapter concern us in this age, at this present time, more than they have ever concerned any other people on this earth. We live very much nearer the fulfillment of these things than did Isaiah or the Jews who were carried captive to Babylon.

Isaiah and Revelation

Compare this chapter with the eighteenth of Revelation, and you cannot fail to see that both prophets are speaking of the very same thing. Indeed, they use exactly the same expressions, so that the higher critic would doubtless say that John copied from Isaiah. But when God has an important message, He is able to send it by more than one messenger, and to give the message to each one of them independently. Rev. 18:7–8, is identical with Isa. 47:8–9. In the last verse of Isa. 47, we have summed up all that is contained in Rev. 18:9–18. In Rev. 17:5–6 we have the parallel to Isa. 47:6–7. Now just as surely as the prophecy concerning Babylon, in the Revelation, has not yet been fulfilled, so surely does the prophecy in Isaiah yet await its fulfillment.

A Rival to God

Note that this Babylon is represented both in Isaiah and Revelation as being opposed to God and His people. She is opposed to them, not as an atheistic power, but as a power professing to be above God. God says, "There is none beside Me" (Isa. 45:6,18,21–22; 46:9); and Babylon says, "I am, and none else beside me." Isa. 47:10. So we see that she sets herself up as the rival of God, claiming to be all that He is.

This was the position of ancient Babylon. In the fourth chapter of Daniel we have an account of a test as to whether Nebuchadnezzar, King of Babylon, or God, was supreme. Although Nebuchadnezzar had learned of the true God, and had been told that "the heavens do rule," and that the God of heaven had given him his kingdom and power and strength and glory, he said, as he walked in the palace of the kingdom of Babylon, "Is not this great Babylon, that I have built for the house of the kingdom by the might of my power, and for the hounour of my majesty?" Dan. 4:30. Then the judgment of God came upon him, until he learned and acknowledged that the God of heaven "liveth for ever, whose dominion is an everlasting dominion, and His kingdom is from generation to generation; and all the inhabitants of the earth are reputed as nothing; and He doeth according to His will in the army of heaven, and among the inhabitants of the earth; and none can stay His hand, or say unto Him, What doest Thou?" "and those that walk in pride He is able to abase." Dan. 4:34–35,37.

Babylon's Blasphemous Pride

But that did not settle the question with Babylon, for although Nebuchadnezzar doubtless went to his grave in the faith of this confession, Belshazzar, who knew all these things did not profit by them, but in his insolent impiety, in the midst of the heathen revel, "brought the golden vessels that were taken out of the temple of the house of God which was at Jerusalem; and the king, and his princes, his wives, and his concubines, drank in them. They drank wine, and praised the gods of gold, and of silver, brass, of iron, of wood, and of stone." Dan. 5:2–4. See also verses 17–23. Daniel recalled to Belshazzar the pride and humiliation of Nebuchadnezzar, and said, "And thou, his son, O Belshazzar, hast not humbled thine heart, though thou knewest all this; but hast lifted up thyself against the Lord of heaven; and they have brought the vessels of His house before thee, and thou, and thy lords, thy wives, and thy concubines, have drunk wine in them; and thou hast praised the gods of silver, and gold, of brass, iron, wood, and stone, which see not, nor hear, nor know; and the God in whose hand thy breath is, and whose are all thy ways, hast thou not glorified."

The Same Spirit Still Active

In 2 Thess. 2:3–8 we have a description of a power identical with this, which is to exist and work even till the coming of the Lord to Judgment. It is called the "man of sin," "the son of perdition, he that opposeth and exalteth himself against all that is called God or that is worshipped; so that he sitteth in the temple of God, setting himself forth as God." Compare this with what we have just been reading about Babylon, and it will appear that the cases are identical. Babylon was the rival of God, yet its greatest king acknowledged God at the last; but the lesson was not learned, and Babylon perished in its proud boasting of supremacy over the God of all the earth.

Transmitted to its Successors

The Medo-Persian kingdom immediately took the place in the world, that had been occupied by Babylon, and although Cyrus publicly acknowledged the true God, the most of the kings of Persia received honours themselves as gods, instead of according the honour to God. They, like Belshazzar of Babylon, were weighed in the balances and found wanting.

The same spirit was prominent throughout the Grecian supremacy; and when Rome took its place as mistress of the world, the spirit of idolatrous pride reached a pitch never before dreamed of. To that power, more than to any other ever known on earth, applies the title, "Mystery, Babylon the Great, the Mother of Harlots and Abominations of the Earth;" and in her are fulfilled these words: "I saw the woman drunken with the blood of the saints, and with the blood of the martyrs of Jesus. "Rev. 17:5–6. Thus we see the very same power described in the prophecy of Isaiah exists unchanged until the coming of the Lord Jesus Christ. It is not that in ancient Babylon we have a type of that which is described in the Revelation, but that it is one and the same power in each case; and the people of God have never been fully out of Babylon since the days of Nebuchadnezzar.

Sudden Destruction

But deliverance is sure. Babylon is to be utterly destroyed, and the call of God is, "Come out of her, My people, that ye be not partakers of her sins, and that ye receive not of her plagues." Rev. 18:4. How quickly utter destruction may follow the greatest seeming prosperity, is seen in the case of Belshazzar. When the kingdom of Babylon had reached the height of its glory, and her kings were most self-complacent, destruction came. That, however, was but the beginning of the end. It was a warning. Just as surely as the ancient city of Babylon fell at the height of its pride and splendour, when she said, "I shall be a lady for ever," so surely will the judgments of God come on the whole earth, when religion, no matter by what name it is called, has reached the place where it is identified with and controls the destinies of the nations. At the time when "the church" is universally acknowledged, so that men begin to say, "Peace, and safety," then will "sudden destruction" come upon them. 1 Thess. 5:3. "For as in the days that were before the flood they were eating and drinking, marrying and giving in marriage, until the day that Noah entered into the ark, and knew not until the flood came, and took them all away; so shall also the coming of the Son of man be." Matt. 24:38–39.

Pride the Religion of Human Nature

It is a sad mistake for anyone to apply all these prophecies to some specific organization, and some special "system of religion." While they undoubtedly have their most complete fulfillment in certain ecclesiastical bodies, the principle is that of human nature, instilled into all men by "the god of this world," the "spirit that now worketh in the children of disobedience," who is himself called the king of Babylon. Isa. 14:4–27. "Thy wisdom and thy knowledge it hath perverted thee." This was what caused the fall of Lucifer. Eze. 28:12–18. Wisdom and knowledge are not to be despised, but the only wisdom and knowledge that are of any real worth, are "the wisdom that comes from above," and the knowledge of God, which is life eternal. The wisdom that puffs one up with pride, that is connected with strife and vainglory, is "earthly, sensual, devilish" (James 3:14–15); but the wisdom from above is "first pure, then peaceable, gentle, and easy to be entreated, full of mercy and good fruits," even the fruits of righteousness, which are by Jesus Christ. Complete renunciation of self, and absolute dependence upon God, deliver souls from Babylon, and from her plagues.

CHAPTER 58

THE PEACE OF RIGHTEOUSNESS

(Isa. 48:12–22)

"Hearken unto Me, O Jacob, and Israel, My called: I am He; I am the first, I also am the last. Mine hand also hath laid the foundation of the earth, and My right hand hath spanned the heavens; when I call unto them, they stand up together. All ye, assemble yourselves, and hear; which among them hath declared these things? The Lord hath loved Him; He will do His pleasure on Babylon, and His arm shall be on the Chaldeans. I, even I, have spoken; yea, I have called Him; I have brought Him, and He shall make His way prosperous.

"Come ye near unto Me, and hear ye this; I have not spoken in secret from the beginning; from the time that it was, there am I; and now the Lord God, and His Spirit, hath sent Me. Thus saith the Lord, thy Redeemer, the Holy One of Israel; I am the Lord thy God which teacheth thee to profit, which leadeth thee by the way that thou shouldst go. O that thou hadst hearkened to My commandments! then had thy peace been as a river, and thy righteousness as the waves of the sea; thy seed also had been as the sand, and the offspring of thy bowels like the gravel thereof; his name should not have been cut off nor destroyed from before Me.

"Go ye forth of Babylon, flee ye from the Chaldeans, with a voice of singing declare ye, tell this, utter it even to the end of the earth; say ye, The Lord hath redeemed His servant Jacob. And they thirsted not when He led them through the deserts; He caused the waters to flow out of the rock for them; He clave the rock also, and the waters gushed out.

"There is no peace, saith the Lord, to the wicked."

Never forget for a moment that the message of Isaiah is to the end of the world; that he was not prophesying merely for those who lived at the time he spoke and wrote, but for everybody who should live until everything of which he prophesized is completed. He foretold the coming of the Lord, and no matter how long that event may seem to be delayed, the message is to all who live until Christ comes.

Come Out of Babylon!

Babylon, the power that thought that the strength received from God was inherent in itself, and that exalted itself above God, is still before us. The houses and walls built by Nebuchadnezzar were long since destroyed, and the kingdom of Babylon has long since ceased to be named among men; nevertheless Babylon is today as really in existence, and is as active, as it was in the days of Isaiah. The message that we are now studying proclaims, "Go ye forth of Babylon, ... say ye, The Lord hath redeemed His servant Jacob." This message is so important that the Lord repeated it several hundred years later, when, as the world reckons, Babylon was out of existence. In the Scriptures called the New Testament, which are not by any professed Christians handed over to the Jews, as their especial property, but which are claimed as the Christian Scriptures, we read, "Come out of her, My people." Rev. 18:4. Isaiah wrote, "Go ye forth of Babylon, flee ye from the Chaldeans, with a voice of singing declare ye, tell this, utter it even to the end of the earth; say ye, The Lord hath redeemed His servant Jacob." John, by the same Spirit, uttered the same message, in almost identical words: "Rejoice over her, thou heaven, and ye holy apostles and prophets; for God hath avenged you on her." The message is no more true or important because it is repeated; but the repetition makes it more emphatic. The fact that it is repeated after the time when men would unthinkingly say that Babylon is a thing of the past, and believers in the fulfillment of prophecy might say that the words of the Lord by Isaiah have been fulfilled, and are now a mere matter of history, to be studied merely as showing that God's Word cannot fail, shows that Babylon still exists, and that Isaiah's prophecy is as live, present truth as any portion of the Bible. Nothing of God's Word has failed, and all that has already come upon Babylon is but a pledge that every prediction will be fulfilled to the letter. Babylon, that proud power that reigns in the hearts of men, leading them to exalt themselves against God, and to ignore Him, and even openly to defy Him, is yet to receive the fullness of her punishment. Come out of her!

Babylon Ancient and Modern

Christ is the one whose arm will accomplish the destruction of Babylon, even as it is He who redeems the people of God. The destruction of Babylon is merely a portion of the work of redemption. "The Lord hath loved Him; He will do His pleasure on Babylon, and His arm shall be on the Chaldeans." He is the Beloved of the Lord. The capture of Babylon by Cyrus was only a foretaste, a pledge, of the final destruction of that "mystery of iniquity," the "man of sin," "the son of perdition," of which Babylon and its king, putting human laws above the law of God, stood as the representative to the end of the world. The spirit of Nebuchadnezzar, when he made a golden image, and commanded all to worship it, thus setting at naught the law of God, and of Belshazzar, who in the pride of his dominion defied God, and thought that he had conquered Him, has been transmitted through all the kingdoms to the present time. And not only is the spirit of Babylon in the kingdoms of the earth, but it is in the professed church of God. When Nebuchadnezzar saw that there was a power above him, and acknowledged it, he presumed to legislate for God, as though God were not able to execute His own laws, and defend His own honour. He began to serve God in the same spirit with which he had just defied Him, and said, "I make a decree, That every people, nation, and language, which speak anything amiss against the God of Shadrach, Meshach, and Abednego, shall be cut in pieces, and their houses shall be made a dunghill; because there is no other God that can deliver after this sort." Dan. 3:29. There speaks religion in Government – the Church working through the State. Nebuchadnezzar was sincere in this supposed service to God, – as sincere as he was when he defied God, and no more, – but his last decree was no more Christian than the first. In both of them he showed that he thought himself at least equal to God. The proclamation recorded in the fourth chapter of Daniel, where Nebuchadnezzar makes his public confession, not as a king, but as a man, is a Christian confession. Although he was king of the mightiest kingdom that ever existed on this earth, he could serve God only as an individual. His example and influence

TREASURES IN ISAIAH

would be more far-reaching than that of any other man; but as a true Christian he could use no other means to make men serve God than his personal confession by faith. But that is not the spirit of Babylon. Babylon did not become imbued with the spirit that possessed Nebuchadnezzar at the last. He died, and the same old spirit of self-exaltation, and of rejection of God, resumed sway. It still exists in the world, in so-called "Christian nations," and even in the professed church of Christ, because it is the spirit of human nature. The call is to forsake it. "Come out of her, My people!"

God's Right and Power to Speak

The Lord speaks. It is He who hath laid the foundation of the earth, who with the span of His hand has measured the heavens. He hath made a memorial for His wonderful works, in order that we may know that He is God. Every week it comes to us, so that we are without excuse if we forget God, and fail to put our whole trust in Him. "In six days the Lord made heaven and earth, the sea, and all that in them is, and rested the seventh day; wherefore the Lord blessed the Sabbath day, and hallowed it." Ex. 20:11. "Hallow My Sabbaths: and they shall be a sign between Me and you, that ye may know that I am the Lord thy God." Eze. 20:20. He is the one who teaches us that which will be of profit to us, and who leads us in the way that we ought to go. We have gone astray; we have turned every one to his own way; and the way of peace we have not known, therefore God cries to us appealingly: "O that thou hadst harkened to My commandments! then had thy peace been as a river, and thy righteousness as the waves of the sea."

What Righteousness Is

Righteousness is right-doing; it is the opposite of unrighteousness, and "all unrighteousness is sin." 1 John 5:17. "Sin is the transgression of the law." 1 John 3:4. Therefore righteousness is the keeping of the law. It is also peace, because it is the way of the Lord (Ps. 119:1–3), and He is "the very God of peace." "Great peace have they which love Thy law; and nothing shall offend them." Ps. 119:165. "They have none occasion of stumbling." "Being justified by faith, we have peace with God, through our Lord Jesus Christ." Rom. 5:1. Thank God, "the chastisement of our peace was upon

390

Him, and with His stripes we are healed." Even though we have sinned, and have departed from the law of peace and righteousness, we may in Christ be brought into the right way, because He is the way, the true way. His name is "the Lord our righteousness." He is of God made unto us wisdom and righteousness. "Christ is the end of the law for righteousness to every one that believeth." Rom. 10:4. Those who forsake their own way, and come to Christ, allowing Him to dwell in their hearts by faith, attain unto righteousness (Rom. 9:30–33), even that righteousness which is witnessed by the law and the prophets. Rom. 3:21–22.

What Peace Means

What is peace? Alas, very few know. Even those who accept the Lord, very often are content with but a fragment of the peace which He bestows. It is wonderfully comprehensive. The Hebrew word here rendered "peace," is a very common one, conveying the idea of wholeness, soundness, health, welfare of every kind. A few instances of its use may be of service to us. In the following texts, the words which are identical with the word "peace" in our lesson, are given in Italic.

Gen. 29:6: Jacob asked the shepherds concerning Laban, "Is he *well*? And they said, He is *well*."

Gen. 43:27–28: Joseph asked his brethren of their *welfare*, and said, "Is your father *well*?" "And they answered, Thy servant our father is in *good health*."

1 Sam. 31:21: "When David came near to the people, he *saluted* them." The margin has it, "He asked them how they did." We ask people how they do; so did the men of old, only instead of saying, "How do you do?" they said, "How is your peace?" meaning the same thing.

2 Sam. 11:7: "And when Uriah was come unto him, David demanded of him *how* Joab *did*, and *how* the people *did*, and *how* the war *prospered*." Literally, he asked after the peace of the people, and after the peace of the war!

2 Sam. 20:9: "And Joab said to Amass, Art thou *in health*, my brother?"

The Hebrew verb from which the noun meaning "peace" is derived, means *finishing, completion, restoration.* It occurs, for example in the following texts: –

Ex. 22:14: "If a man borrow aught of his neighbor, and it be hurt, or die, the owner thereof not being with it, he shall *surely make it good.*"

Lev. 5:16: "He shall *make amends* for the harm that he hath done in the holy thing."

Peace is Health of Soul and Body

These illustrations of the use of the word rendered "peace" are sufficient to show that peace, in the Bible use of the term, is not an abstract thing, a mere sentiment or state of mind. It comprises everything that pertains to man. That which is expressed in Isa. 48:18, as the condition of those who hearken to God's commandments, is identical with what we have in 1 Thess. 5:23, "The very God of peace sanctify you wholly; and I pray God your whole spirit and soul and body be preserved blameless unto the coming of our Lord Jesus Christ." The peace which comes as the result of keeping the commandments, or, rather, the peace which is the keeping of the commandments, means perfect health of body, as well as perfect purity of soul. It is indicated in the words of John: "Beloved, I wish above all things, that thou mayest prosper and be in health, even as thy soul prospereth." 3 John 2. If men had hearkened to the commandments of God, their health of body and of mind would have been as continuous as the current of a river, and as full as the fullness of the sea. We have not hearkened to God's commandments; but there is forgiveness with Him, and the bestowal of righteousness through the Lord Jesus Christ; and in Him we are made complete (Col. 2:10), for "He is our peace." Eph. 2:14. "Of His fullness have all we received." If we will but allow the Holy Spirit to strengthen us according to the riches of the glory of God, so that Christ may dwell in us by the Spirit, we shall "be filled with all the fullness of God." Eph. 3:16–19.

Peace Like a River

God's life flows as a river. From His throne proceeds the river of water of life, clear as crystal (Rev. 22:1), because with Him is the fountain of life. Ps. 36:9. That life flows through the universe, bringing perfect health and righteousness wherever it is allowed to flow unhindered. If we give the Word of life free course in us, then our peace, our righteousness, our physical health, everything that pertains to our welfare, will flow as a river, even as the river of God, because we shall be having the saving health of God's life constantly in us. The stream "flowing, ever flowing," will wash away all impurities, so that no evil of any kind can remain behind to clog the system. He makes the poor sinner, sick in body and mind, "every whit whole." He gives "perfect soundness." The holiness, without which no man shall see the Lord, is but the *wholeness* which the life of God in Christ imparts. The peace of God which passes all understanding will keep our hearts when we trust God for everything. That means that our life will be redeemed from destruction, for out of the heart are the issues of life.

> "Oh, what a salvation this.
> That Christ liveth in me!"

The Fountain Ever Flowing

In proof of the fact that He will make our peace – complete health of spirit, soul, and body – flow as a river, God "caused the waters to flow out of the rock;" "He clave the rock also, and the waters gushed out." And this very thing He continues to do until the present time. Every river that is fed by the rain that descends from heaven, is but one of the branches of the river of life. Ps. 65:9–10. That fountain of water gushing forth from the rock, which so many of us have seen, from which we have slaked our thirst, and the beauty of which we have admired, is caused to flow by the Lord, and comes truly from the Rock Christ Jesus. 1 Cor. 10:4; Ex. 17:6. Every drink and every bath that we take should be a reminder to us that we drink in the life of Christ, which can also cleanse us from all sin; and that that life is perfect peace for us, if we will but take it, – the healing of every wound, every disease, that tends to spoil our peace. Shall we not make it the business of our lives to seek this fountain of peace?

CHAPTER 59

THE DESPISED ONE CHOSEN

(Isa. 49:1–12)

"Listen, O isles, unto Me; and hearken ye peoples, from far; the Lord hath called Me from the womb; from the bowels of My mother hath He made mention of My name; and He hath made My mouth like a sharp sword, in the shadow of His hand hath He hid Me; and He hath made Me a polished shaft, in his quiver hath He kept Me close; and He said unto Me, Thou art My Servant; Israel, in whom I will be glorified.

"But I said, I have laboured in vain, I have spent My strength for naught and vanity; yet surely My judgment is with the Lord, and My recompense with My God.

"And now saith the Lord that formed Me from the womb to be His Servant, to bring Jacob again to Him, and that Israel be gathered unto Him: (for I am honourable in the eyes of the Lord, and My God is become My strength); yea, He saith, It is too light a thing that Thou shouldest be My Servant to raise up the tribes of Jacob, and to restore the preserved of Israel: I will also give Thee for a light to the Gentiles, that Thou mayest be My salvation unto the end of the earth. Thus saith the Lord, the Redeemer of Israel, and His Holy One, to Him whom man despiseth, to Him whom the nation abhorreth, to a servant of rulers; Kings shall see and arise; princes, and they shall worship; because of the Lord that is faithful, even the Holy One of Israel, who hath chosen Thee.

"Thus saith the Lord, In an acceptable time have I answered Thee, and in a day of salvation have I helped Thee; and I will preserve Thee, and give Thee for a covenant of the people, to raise up the land, to make them inherent the desolate heritages; saying to them that are bound, Go forth; to them that are in darkness, Show yourselves. They shall feed in the ways, and on

all bare heights shall be their pasture. They shall not hunger nor thirst; neither shall the heat nor sun smite them; for He that hath mercy on them shall lead them, even by the springs of water shall He guide them. And I will make all My mountains a way, and My highways shall be exalted. Lo, these shall come from far; and, lo, these from the north and from the west; and those from the land of Sinim."

Christ the Speaker

The first thing to be noted in the reading of this lesson is the unmistakable reference to Christ. Called from the womb, to be a light to the Gentiles, and the salvation of God unto the end of the earth; the Chosen of God to restore Israel, and to establish the earth, although despised and rejected of men; His mouth made like a sharp sword (compare Rev. 19:15,21); – there is not the slightest possibility for a doubt that Christ the Redeemer, is the one here speaking. It is doubtful if anybody could read the passage, and get any other idea.

Christ Stands for His People

It would be a great mistake, however, if any should get the idea that the Scripture is fulfilled in the person of Jesus of Nazareth alone. The trouble is that most people rest content with the thought that the language means Christ, and let it pass at that, as though it had no further interest for them. As a matter of fact, we have in this portion of Scripture a good demonstration of the truth that whatever concerns Christ concerns His people, and that He has fully identified Himself with the human race, binding Himself to mankind by cords that can never be broken. Jesus of Nazareth is the Representative Man.

Men Called From Their Birth

Take the first item: "The Lord hath called Me from the womb; from the bowels of My mother hath He made mention of My name." This is, of course pre-eminently true of Jesus; for the angel of the Lord said to Joseph when he was thinking of putting Mary away; "She shall bring forth a Son, and thou shalt call His name Jesus; for He shall save His people from their sins." Matt. 1:21. But our minds involuntarily turn to the great ancestor of Jesus according to the flesh, and we recall the words of the Lord to Abraham: "Sarah thy wife shall bear thee a son indeed; and thou shalt call his name Isaac; and I will establish My covenant with him for an everlasting covenant, and with his seed after him." Gen. 17:19. Read the thirteenth chapter of Judges, and see how the character and work of Samson were described before he was born. John the Baptist is another striking instance. The angel Gabriel said to Zacharias: "Thy wife Elizabeth shall bear thee a son, and thou shalt call his name John. And thou shalt have joy and gladness, and many shall rejoice at his birth. And he shall be great in the sight of the Lord, and shall drink neither wine nor strong drink; and he shall be filled with the Holy Ghost even from his mother's womb. And many of the children of Israel shall he turn to the Lord their God." Luke 1:13–15. We may say that the language in Isaiah applies to John the Baptist as well as to Christ; and the same thing might also be said of Isaac. Indeed, if we should attempt to limit it to any one person, we should have a difficult task; for read these words of the Lord to the prophet Jeremiah: "Before I formed thee in the belly I knew thee; and before thou camest forth out of the womb I sanctified thee, and I ordained thee a prophet unto the nations." "Behold, I have put My words in thy mouth. See, I have this day set thee over the nations and over the kingdoms, to root out, and to pull down, and to destroy, and to throw down, to build, and to plant." Jer. 1:5,9–10. See also Ps. 139:15–16. Then as another striking instance, we have the Apostle Paul, of whom God said, "He is a chosen vessel unto Me, to bear My name before the Gentiles, and kings, and the children of Israel" (Acts 9:15), and Paul himself tells us that he was chosen to this work from his birth. Gal. 1:15–16. To all this list, we have to add the name of Cyrus, who was called by name many years before his birth, and appointed to an important work in the restoration of Israel.

The reader must remember that the Bible does not deal in exceptions. We are not treated to a history of certain, exceptional cases, "freaks of nature," as it were, but to illustrations of God's dealing with all men, and of what is possible for all. The cases just referred to, together with the scripture that we are studying, are to show us that God has a plan for every human being, and calls him to it from his birth, and even before he sees the light. Few ever recognize the voice of God calling them, but they are called nevertheless. God has chosen you, and called you to your work; do you know His voice, and are you doing your work "heartily as unto the Lord," giving diligence to make your calling and election sure? There is marvelous encouragement for us in the fact that God has called us as surely as He called Christ, and has chosen and called us in Him.

Ye are the Light of the World

Another proof that Jesus associates all His people with Himself in the work of the Gospel: Verse 6 says, "I will also give Thee for a light to the Gentiles, that Thou mayest be My salvation unto the end of the earth." Now read the words of Paul and Barnabas, spoken when the Jews rejected their message, contradicting and blaspheming: "It was necessary that the Word of God should first have been spoken to you; but seeing ye put it from you, and judge yourselves unworthy of everlasting life, lo, we turn to the Gentiles. For so hath the Lord commanded us, saying, I have set thee to be a light of the Gentiles, that thou shouldest be for salvation unto the ends of the earth." Acts 13:46–47. They, under the influence of the Holy Spirit, took the words as applying to them personally, and so we may know that they apply equally to all who are chosen and called by the Lord to His service. Jesus says, "As My Father hath sent Me, even so send I you;" and, "God, sent not His Son into the world, to condemn the world; but that the world through Him might be saved." Everybody who receives the Spirit of God is sent forth equally with Christ, to work for the salvation of mankind. Recall 2 Cor. 5:17–20.

Workers Together with God

But there is more yet for us. How often have we heard these words in Gospel talks: "I have heard thee in a time accepted, and in the day of salvation have I succoured thee; behold, now is the accepted time; now is the day of salvation." 2 Cor. 6:2. We have thought that this meant merely that the Lord is willing to accept us when we come to Him. It means that, and much more. It is a light thing for Him to accept and save those for whom He died; but the great wonder of His grace is this, that He accepts us as "workers together with Him." 2 Cor. 6:1. This is most encouraging, because it puts the matter of our own personal salvation entirely beyond all question; inasmuch as we are chosen to be His salvation to the end of the earth, it is self-evident that we ourselves must be saved. We cannot carry salvation to others unless we have it ourselves to carry. So while working with the Master we are relieved from all care as to our own safety. The Lord accepts us, not merely for salvation, but for service.

No Volunteer Rejected

Whom does the Lord accept for service? Is He very particular as to the persons who present themselves for labour in His cause? Must they come with a certificate of good character, and be those who are well spoken of by all men? Listen: "Thus saith the Lord, the Redeemer of Israel, and His Holy One, to him whom man despiseth, to him whom the nation abhorreth, to a servant of rulers, ... In an acceptable time have I heard thee, and in a day of salvation have I helped thee; and I will preserve thee, and give thee for a covenant of the people," etc. The Lord is in need of labourers in His vineyard, and He stands and calls for whosoever will to come. No applicant will be rejected; all will be accepted and set to work.

The Government has called for volunteers to serve in the army; out of thousands who present themselves, only hundreds are accepted; the majority are rejected as unfit for service. Not so with the Lord; He accepts every volunteer, – "whosoever will," – and makes him fit for service – "thoroughly furnished unto all good works." No matter how despised and rejected and cast off by men, – the Lord will receive us, and take us into partnership with Himself. Here is encouragement for the weakest. There is no ground left for anybody to indulge in doubts because of his unworthiness; if you are despised, no matter for what cause, justly or unjustly, the Word of the Lord singles you out, and says, "I have specially chosen you for a very delicate piece of work that I must have done." What wonderful honour God has placed upon fallen man!

Free Agents – Agents of Freedom

What is the work that we are called and chosen to do? – "That thou mayest say to the prisoners, "Go forth; to them that are in darkness, Show yourselves." He calls the bondservants of Satan, the slaves of sin, all who labour, and are heavy laden with iniquities, bound by the cords of their own sins, and not only sets them free, but makes them the agents of releasing others who are in cruel bondage. What more could He say? Come, and enter His service, and taste His power to save, – power not only to save you, but power working in you to save others. "Base things of the world, and things which are despised, hath God chosen, yea, and things which are not, to bring to naught things that are; that no flesh should glory in His presence. But of Him are ye in Christ Jesus, who of God is made unto us wisdom, and righteousness, and sanctification, and redemption; that, according as it is written, he that glorieth, let him glory in the Lord." 1 Cor. 1:28–31. The weaker and more despised you are, the greater will be the glory to God in that which He accomplishes through you. We hear a great deal about man being a "free moral agent." That is only half the truth; he is not only himself free to choose what he will, and in Christ given the freedom of the universe, but is made God's agent in setting at liberty those that are bound.

Courage in Despondency

Yet with all this for our encouragement, feelings of despondency will sometimes oppress us. We say to ourselves, if not to others, "It is no use; my work doesn't amount to anything." Well, the Lord has provided help for just such a time as that; nay, more, He has provided that you should be able to find encouragement even from your despondency. Remember that all the language of this chapter applies to Christ, primarily. Now read again: "But I said, I have laboured in vain, I have spent My strength for naught." What! did Christ ever have such feelings of discouragement? Certainly He did, else it would not be the case that He was in all things "made like unto His brethren," "in all points tempted like as we are." Heb. 2:17; 4:15. The weakness as well the burden of humanity was on Him, and He was tempted many times to give up the struggle. But, thank

God, "without sin." He never gave way to temptation. With the temptation the way of escape is always prepared, and He always took advantage of it. Even in His greatest depression of spirits, He said, "Surely My judgment is with the Lord, and My work with My God." "Himself took our infirmities," so that we may know in every temptation and trial that Christ not only has suffered the same thing, but that He has conquered it by the very same power which He gives to us. If we know that "Christ liveth in me," then whenever the despondency comes, we may know that He is bearing it. The very words of discouragement that come to our mind should be a reminder of these words of Christ, and so should turn to encouragement; and when we have learned this lesson, we shall be reminded of Christ before the words get to our lips. Then that which started as a wail of discouragement will end as a song of triumph. "I can do all things through Christ which strengtheneth me." "When I am weak, then am I strong."

Led to Living Fountains of Water

Verse 10 makes very clear to the thoughtful student what this deliverance from Babylon means, and shows incidentally that as Babylon was a world empire, so Babylon, whether in the Old Testament or the New, is "the present evil world," whether under the garb of Christianity or not. Concerning those who are set free, we read: "They shall not hunger nor thirst; neither shall the heat nor sun smite them; for He that hath mercy on them shall lead them, even by the springs of water shall He guide them."

Now turn to the book of Revelation, which has so much to say about Babylon. John saw in prophetic vision the closing work of redemption, and "after this I beheld, and, lo, a great multitude, which no man could number, of all nations, and kindreds, and people, and tongues, stood before the throne, and before the Lamb, clothed with white robes, and palms in their hands; and cried with a loud voice, saying, "Salvation to our God which sitteth upon the throne, and unto the Lamb." Then one that stood by said to John: "These are they which came out of great tribulation, and have washed their robes, and made them white in the blood of the Lamb. Therefore are they before the throne of God, and serve Him day and night in His temple; and He that sitteth on the throne shall dwell among them. They shall hunger no more, neither thirst any more; neither shall the sun light on them, nor any heat. For the Lamb which is in the midst of the throne shall feed them, and shall lead them unto living fountains of waters; and God shall wipe away all tears from their eyes." Rev. 7:1–17.

We cannot fail to see that the two prophets, Isaiah and John, are describing the same thing, and that deliverance from Babylon is deliverance from sin, and sickness, and sorrow, and death. The scene in the Revelation is undoubtedly in "the heavenly Jerusalem;" but we must know that if we are believers indeed, we even now "do enter into rest" (Heb. 4:3), and that we already "are come unto mount Zion, and unto the city of the living God, the heavenly Jerusalem, … to God the Judge of all, and to the spirits of just men made perfect, and to Jesus the Mediator of the new covenant." Heb. 12:22–24. Not as a mere empty song does the Christian say with David, "The Lord is my Shepherd; I shall not want. He maketh me to lie down in green pastures; He leadeth me beside the still waters. He restoreth my soul; He leadeth me in the paths of righteousness for His name's sake." Ps. 23:1–3. Even now God dwells among His people, and with Him is the fountain of life, for He is indeed "the Fountain of living waters." Jer. 2:13. The water is real, and is as refreshing and life-giving as it is real. It is only for us to appreciate the reality.

Christ Is Israel

In this lesson the question of who constitute Israel is plainly answered. Verse 3 reads: "Thou art My Servant, O Israel, in whom I will be glorified." But it has already been made clear that Christ is the One who is speaking here, and who calls upon the people from far to understand that from birth He has been called to accomplish the work of God. So we learn that Israel is one of the names of Christ. Why should it not be? Rather, How could it be otherwise? For "Israel" means "A Prince of God," or, "He who conquers," and Christ is "the Lion of the tribe of Judah," who "hath prevailed" (Rev. 5:5), – "the great Prince which standeth for the children of Thy people." Dan. 12:1. He is most emphatically Israel, and since we overcome only through the blood of the Lamb, it follows that we become Israel only as we are in Him. "In the Lord shall all the seed of Israel be justified, and shall glory." No person on this earth has, or ever has had, or ever will have, any right to be called Israel unless he has the victory over sin, through faith in Christ. "If ye be Christ's, then are ye Abraham's seed, and heirs according to the promise." Gal. 3:29.

CHAPTER 60

THE EARTH'S INTEREST IN REDEMPTION

(Isa. 49:13–23)

"Sing, O heavens; and be joyful, O earth; and break forth into singing, O mountains; for the Lord hath comforted His people, and will have mercy upon His afflicted.

"But Zion said, The Lord hath forsaken me, and my Lord hath forgotten me. Can a woman forget her sucking child, that she should not have compassion on the son of her womb? yea, they may forget, yet will I not forget thee. Behold I have graven thee upon the palms of My hands; thy walls are continually before Me. Thy children shall make haste; thy destroyers and they that made thee waste shall go forth of thee.

"Lift up thine eyes round about, and behold: all these gather themselves together, and come to thee. As I live, saith the Lord, thou shalt surely clothe thee with them all, as with an ornament, and bind them on thee as a bride doeth. For thy waste and thy desolate places, and the land of thy destruction, shall even now be too narrow by reason of the inhabitants, and they that swallowed thee up shall be far away. The children which thou shalt have, after thou hast lost the other, shall say again in thine ears, The place is too strait for me; give place to me, that I may dwell. Then shalt thou say in thine heart, Who hath begotten me these, seeing I have lost my children, and am desolate, a captive, and removing to and fro? and who hath brought up these? Behold, I was left alone; these, where had they been? Thus saith the Lord God, Behold, I will lift up Mine hand to the Gentiles, and set up My standard to the people; and they shall bring thy sons in their arms, and thy daughters shall be carried upon their shoulders. And kings shall be thy nursing fathers, and queens thy nursing mothers; they shall bow down to thee with their face toward the earth, and lick up the dust of thy feet;

and thou shalt know that I am the Lord; for they shall not be ashamed that wait for Me."

Different Calls to the Earth and Heavens

This is not the first time that earth and heaven have been called upon to take part in something pertaining to men in their relation to God. In the first chapter of Isaiah we read, "Hear, O heavens, and give ear, O earth; for the Lord hath spoken. I have nourished and brought up children, and they have rebelled against Me." The call is very much more emphatic in the second chapter of Jeremiah: "Be astonished, O ye heavens, at this, and be horribly afraid, be ye very desolate, saith the Lord. For My people have committed two evils: They have forsaken Me, the Fountain of living waters, and hewed them out cisterns, broken cisterns, that can hold no water." Jer. 2:12–13. In Deut. 32:1–3 the heavens and earth are called upon to listen to the good doctrine which the Lord imparts to His rebellious children. But in the text before us the heavens are called upon to sing, and the earth to be joyful, and the mountains to break forth into singing, because the Lord hath redeemed His people.

The Earth's Existence Depends on the Gospel

It is easy to see that the heavens and earth are deeply concerned in man's salvation, since they are called in to witness every step in the transgression, and in the progress of redemption. Not only so, but they tremble with terror at the sight of man's causeless rebellion, and sing for joy when he is brought back saved. From these things we can see that the stability of the heavens and the earth depends upon the success of God's work of saving men. "The earnest expectation of the creation waiteth for the revealing of the sons of God. For the creation was subjected to vanity, not of its own will, but by reason of Him who subjected it in hope that the creation itself shall also be delivered from the bondage of corruption into the liberty of the glory of the children of God." Rom. 8:19–21. When God comes to Judgment, the heavens and the earth shall shake, the heavens shall depart as a scroll when it is rolled together (Rev. 6:14), and the earth shall reel to and fro like a drunkard, and shall be removed like a cottage, because of the transgression that is on it (Isa.

24:20); but when God's people come to their own land in peace, the mountains will greet them with songs of rejoicing, and all the trees of the forest will clap their hands in delight. Isa. 55:12.

The Earth Given to Man

Why is all this? – The answer opens to us a fine, large truth, which is full of encouragement to every soul. In the beginning the Lord laid the foundation of the earth, and the heavens are the works of His hands (Heb. 1:10), and at the same time He made man, and crowned him with glory and honour, and set him over the works of His hands, that is, over the heavens and the earth. Heb. 2:6–8. "God created man in His own image, in the image of God created He him; male and female created He them. And God blessed them, and God said unto them, Be fruitful, and multiply, and replenish the earth, and subdue it; and have dominion over the fish of the sea, and over the fowl of the air, and over every living thing that moveth upon the earth." Gen. 1:27–28. But all things are not under him now. Nevertheless, man having been placed in authority in the beginning, as the ruler of the things that God has made, so far as they have intimate connection with this planet, it must needs be that they can of right have no other ruler than man; because "whatsoever God doeth, it shall be for ever; nothing can be put to it, nor anything taken from it." Eccl. 3:14. God never takes back a gift; He never undoes what He has once done; He is never forced to retreat from any position that He has taken. Should such a thing ever be necessary, it would show that He was not supreme and all-wise. Man, therefore, has been placed in authority over this earth, once for all.

The Earth Lost

But behold, what a sad state of things has occurred. Man, the ruler, has lost control of himself; he can no longer control his own body or spirit, much less the heavens and earth. Therefore they are left without a ruler, so far as man is concerned. That is why we see earthquakes, and disturbances in the heavens; and the nearer we approach the end, and as the wickedness of man increases, the greater and more frequent are these disturbances. Creation is groaning in pain because of man's sin. If it should be that "the redemption which is in Christ Jesus" should fail, and men should not be saved, then the earth would have been created in vain, that is, for chaos, for nothingness. See Isa. 45:17–19. We are sometimes told that God could have destroyed man at once, as soon as Adam sinned, and could have peopled the earth with another race of beings. Those who say that, do not understand the works and gifts of God. He could not have destroyed man without destroying the earth also. They both belong together. One was created for the other. In the days of Noah, when the earth was corrupt, because all flesh had corrupted its way upon the earth, God said, "The end of all flesh is come before Me; for the earth is filled with violence through them; and behold, I will destroy them with the earth." Gen. 6:12–13. When man is destroyed, the earth must perish with him. God's word made them both in the beginning, and placed the earth under the dominion of man; the same word destroyed them both together in the flood; and "the heavens and the earth, which are now, by the same word are kept in store, reserved unto fire against the day of Judgment and perdition of ungodly men." 2 Peter 3:7. "Nevertheless, we, according to His promise, look for new heavens and a new earth, wherein dwelleth righteousness." This is the reason why the heavens and earth mourn when man falls, and rejoice when he is redeemed. Their salvation is bound up with man's.

The Universe Pledged for Man's Redemption

But this is not the whole story. "When God made promise to Abraham, because He could swear by no greater, He swore by Himself; ... for men verily swear by the greater; and an oath for confirmation is to them an end of all strife, wherein God, willing more abundantly to show unto the heirs of promise the immutability of His counsel confirmed it by an oath; that by two immutable things, wherein it was impossible for God to lie, we might have a strong consolation, who have fled for refuge to lay hold on the hope set before us." Heb. 4:13–18. God is the One whose great power upholds the earth and heavens. His ability to hold them up is given as the reason why His people need not be discouraged, but always be strong. See Isa. 40:26–31. The word which created the heavens and the earth in the beginning, and which now upholds them, is the same word that brings salvation to man. In swearing by

Himself, God placed the heavens and the earth in the balance against man's salvation. If "the word of truth, the Gospel of salvation," should fail, then the heavens and the earth would fail. Not only would they be deprived of man's sovereignty, but God's word having been broken, they would be no longer under His dominion, and would at once vanish into nothing. But they will not be annihilated, because God's word cannot fail. He "cannot lie. This is our "strong consolation." The weakest and meanest soul on earth has this consolation in fleeing to Christ for refuge. He may know that if God should refuse to pardon him, and give him overcoming grace, the heavens and earth would instantly cease to be. If he asks in faith, and does not instantly hear the wreck of matter and the crush of worlds, he may know that his prayer is answered, and that his sins are forgiven. Then let men join in the song of the starry host, and shout for joy over the fact that God "hath visited and redeemed His people."

God Cannot Forget His People

Who has not heard the complaint, almost in the identical words, "The Lord hath forsaken me, and my Lord hath forgotten me?" Impossible. "Behold, I have graven thee upon the palms of My hands." In the hands of the Lord are the prints of the nails that fixed Him to the cross. But it was our sins that nailed him there. It was our sins that He bore on the tree. Therefore we are crucified with Him, and in the nail prints He sees us. It is not simply a few people who "belong to church," that the Lord remembers; but every sinner on earth is engraved upon His hands, carried in His heart. Zion's walls are continually before Him. What are her walls? – "Salvation will God appoint for walls and bulwarks." Isa. 26:1. Salvation, the salvation of sinners is continually before the Lord, for "with His stripes we are healed." He has reminded Himself of mankind, and of each individual, in such a way that He cannot possibly forget.

The Story of Zion

Zion is here represented as speaking. Where is Zion? – It is the place where the sanctuary of God was built, in Jerusalem. That place is now forsaken, and desolate, given over to strangers. The city of Jerusalem, and its temple, might have stood for ever, if the people had obeyed the Lord; for that was the promise of God. See Jer. 17:24–25. But they disobeyed. They slew those who foretold the coming of the Just One, and when He came they betrayed and murdered Him. So Christ, just before His crucifixion, said, "O Jerusalem, Jerusalem, thou that killest the prophets, and stonest them which are sent unto thee, how often would I have gathered thy children together, even as a hen gathereth her chickens under her wings, and ye would not! Behold, your house is left unto you desolate. For I say unto you, Ye shall not see Me henceforth, till ye shall say, Blessed is He that cometh in the name of the Lord." Matt. 23:37–39. Forsaken it is indeed, but not for ever. Nay, it is not really forsaken at all; because as we have just read, its walls are continually before Him. Christ is anointed upon the holy hill of Zion, in "the city of the living God, the heavenly Jerusalem." That city is yet to come down "from God out of heaven, prepared as a bride adorned for her husband." Rev. 21:1–2. Its adornment will be her inhabitants, "the nations of them that are saved," "for Jerusalem which is above is free, which is the mother of us all." Gal. 4:26.

When the city is restored, and her children "come again to their own border," "from the land of the enemy" (Jer. 31:15–17), there will be so many more inhabitants than old Jerusalem ever had, that they will say, "The place is too strait for me; give place for me that I may dwell." A few hundred thousand people inhabited old Jerusalem at the time of its greatest prosperity, but the New Jerusalem will be peopled by a "great multitude, which no man could number, of all nations, and kindreds, and people, and tongues." Rev. 7:9. Of the enlarging of the place of the city, to make room for its great increase of population, we read in Zech. 14:1–5. When the Lord goes forth to fight against the nations that fight Jerusalem, "His feet shall stand in that day upon the Mount of Olives, which is before Jerusalem on the east, and the Mount of Olives shall cleave in the midst thereof toward the east and toward the west, and there shall be a very great valley."

Of the greatness of the valley thus formed we can get some idea when we read that "the city lieth four square, and the length is as large as the breadth; and he measured the city with a reed, twelve thousand furlongs." Rev. 21:16. Taking this at the smallest, that is, not as the length of each side, but as the distance round the city, we find that it will be three hundred and seventy-five miles square, – a very fair sized city. It is not generally supposed that all of the inhabitants of any country will be able to find room in its capital; but the New Jerusalem will be so large that it could contain every person that has ever been born since the days of Adam; so that none will have been crowded out for lack of room. It will therefore hold all the inhabitants of the new earth, as they come up from one new moon to another, and from one Sabbath to another, to worship before God. Isa. 66:22–23.

The Inhabitants of Zion

Who will inhabit this city? – The answer is, Israel. The city has twelve gates, three on each side, and on these gates are "the names of the twelve tribes of the children of Israel." Rev. 21:12. All who enter that city will have to enter as members of some one of the tribes of Israel. Read verses 21–22 of the lesson, and then read Acts 15:16–17: "After this I will return, and I will build again the tabernacle of David, which is fallen down; and I will build again the ruins thereof, and I will set it up; that the residue of men might seek after the Lord, and all the Gentiles, upon whom My name is called, saith the Lord, who doeth all these things." And this is done by visiting the Gentiles, "to take out of them a people for His name." Verses 13, 15. "Blindness in part is happened to Israel, until the fullness of the Gentiles to come in. And so all Israel shall be saved; as it is written, There shall come out of Sion the Deliverer, and shall turn away ungodliness from Jacob." Rom. 11:25–26. Israel is now scattered amongst all the nations. That is, there are in all nations on earth some who will allow ungodliness to be turned away from them, and that will constitute them Israel, and they will dwell in the New Jerusalem. "Many shall come from the east and west, and shall sit down with Abraham, and Isaac, and Jacob, in the kingdom of heaven. But the children of the kingdom shall be cast out into outer darkness." Matt. 8:11–12. Who will come to the standard which God sets up for the people? All who will, may come, and none who come will ever be put to shame or confusion because of their confidence.

CHAPTER 61

THE TRIUMPH OF SUBMISSION

(Isa. 50:1–11)

"Thus saith the Lord, Where is the bill of your mother's divorcement, wherewith I have put her away? or which of My creditors is it to which I have sold you? Behold, for your iniquities were ye sold, and for your transgressions was your mother put away. Wherefore, when I came, was there no man? when I called, was there none to answer? Is My hand shortened at all, that it cannot redeem? or have I no power to deliver? Behold, at My rebuke I dry up the sea, I make the rivers a wilderness; their fish stinketh, because there is no water, and dieth for thirst. I clothe the heavens with blackness, and I make sackcloth their covering.

"The Lord God hath given Me the tongue of them that are taught, that I should be able to sustain with words him that is weary; He wakeneth morning by morning, He wakeneth Mine ear to hear as they that are taught. The Lord God hath opened Mine ear, and I was not rebellious, neither turned away backward. I gave My back to the smiters, and My cheeks to them that I plucked off the hair; I hid not My face from shame and spitting. For the Lord God will help Me; therefore have I not been confounded; therefore have I set My face like a flint, and I know that I shall not be ashamed. He is near, that justifieth Me; who will contend with Me? let us stand up together; who is Mine adversary? let him come near to Me. Behold, the Lord God will help Me; who is he that shall condemn Me? behold, they all shall wax old as a garment; the moth shall eat them up.

"Who is among you that feareth the Lord, that obeyeth the voice of His Servant? he that walketh in darkness, and hath no light, let him trust in the name of the Lord, and stay upon his God. Behold, all ye that kindle a fire, that gird yourselves about with firebrands; walk ye in the flame of your fire, and among

the brands that ye have kindled. This shall ye have of Mine hand: ye shall lie down in sorrow."

Read Gal. 4:25–26, in order to understand the reference "your mother." Jerusalem which now is, old Jerusalem, answers to the old covenant, and "is in bondage with her children." "But Jerusalem which is above is free, which is the mother of us all," and this answers to the new covenant. Recall what was said concerning Jerusalem, in the last lesson. Although Jerusalem is forsaken, "when the Lord shall build up Zion, He shall appear in His glory" (Ps. 102:16), and the new Jerusalem will come with Him, to take the place of the present city, so that it is considered as a continuation of the Jerusalem that has existed so long. It is the old city rebuilt. So the Lord has not cast off Jerusalem, although the city known on earth as Jerusalem will be destroyed with the rest of "this present evil world." He has not divorced her. Read in this connection Isa. 54, especially verses 4–7, and the first verse of this chapter will be much more easily understood.

God is Not Reduced to Poverty

Among the nations of old it was often the case that a father sold his children into slavery, in order to satisfy a creditor, and this was practiced even among the Jews, as we learn from Ex. 21:7 and Nehemiah 5:1–5; but God never became so poor that He was obliged to resort to that plan. No creditor ever had so great an advantage over the Lord that he could compel Him to sell His children. He had not sold any of His children, even when He allowed them to go into captivity; but they sold themselves. "Ye have sold yourselves for naught; and ye shall be redeemed without money." Isa. 52:3. So far is the Lord from having been obliged to sell His people to satisfy His creditors, that He is able to buy them back, after they have sold themselves.

The Power that Redeems

Who dares doubt God's power to redeem? How can anybody think that He has no power to deliver? We have only to read the account of the deliverance of Israel from the land of Egypt, to see how easy a matter it is for God to save His people. Compare verse 2 with Ex. 14:21 and 7:14–21. That very same power is put forth to save us from our sins, which have been the cause of our being sold into bondage. Don't be afraid of confusing the spiritual and the literal. Every act of God is literal and also spiritual. If God only *told* us of what He can do, we should not have anything tangible to lay hold of; no foundation for our faith; for no matter how much we might be disposed to believe Him, our minds could not grasp the meaning; the reality, of what He said; so He gives us visible examples of His power to save, referring us to all His constant working in nature, and also to special working in the past. That is for the purpose of letting us know that the power which He promises to exert on our behalf is so real that we can perceive it in our own bodies; we may know that He saves us.

Christ is the One "who of God is made unto us wisdom, and righteousness, and sanctification, and redemption." 1 Cor. 1:30. Therefore it is He who speaks here. He is "the everlasting Father;" and the New Jerusalem is "the bride, the Lamb's wife." Rev. 21:9–10. So we see that the prophecy of Isaiah is in perfect accord with that in Revelation. Unmistakable proof that it is Christ who is speaking in this chapter, is found in verse 6: "I gave My back to the smiters, and My cheeks to them that plucked off the hair; I hid not My face from shame and spitting." As we read what He says, we must remember that He suffered in our behalf, as the representative Man; His courage and victory are ours.

The Wisdom of Christ

The learned person is the one who has been taught, and who is still a disciple. So it makes no difference whether we read verse 4 as in the Revision or in the Common version; "the tongue of the learned" is "the tongue of them that have been taught." "I speak that which I have seen with My Father." John 8:38. "The Word which ye hear is not Mine, but the Father's which sent Me." John 14:24. It may be even so with us; for we read, "It is written in the prophets, And they shall be all taught of God." John 6:45. If we come to the Lord to learn, He will give us, as well as Christ, the tongue of the learned. But the learning does not come without labour. Learning of God is not a mere lazy assent to certain doctrines, not a sentimental yielding to Him, and a fancy that because we *say* that God is our

Teacher, we are necessarily taught by Him. Many people have had good teachers, but have not profited by them, because they were too lazy to study.

It is often the case that people think to make their religion a substitute for real knowledge. They have an idea that if God is their teacher, they must never study anything. That is the reason why they should study a great deal more. Here is a man with a thirst for knowledge, but his opportunities are few. At last he has a chance of studying under a celebrated teacher. Ah, it is a rare chance, and he will exert himself in study to the utmost. One must not throw away such an opportunity as that! Even so it ought to be with those who have an opportunity of studying under God's teaching. No moment should be neglected; the Word of God, printed in the Bible, and spread out in all creation, should be studied with zeal and patience. The "royal road to learning" is laid down by the wisest of men in Prov. 2:1–6. No person in the world ought to be content with his present attainments. We cannot exhaust the "treasures of wisdom and knowledge" that are hid in Christ. Dig for them, it is worth while.

What will God's teaching enable us to do? – To speak a word in season to him that is weary; not to speak empty phrases but words that "sustain the weary one." The One of whom we are to learn is "meek and lowly in heart." "The wisdom that is from above is first pure, then peaceable, gentle, and easy to be intreated, full of mercy and good fruits." James 3:17.

Some Words of Comfort

Listen to some of the "words" with which Jesus sustained the weary when He was here on earth. "Son, be of good cheer; thy sins be forgiven thee." Matt. 9:2. "Thy faith hath saved thee; go in peace. Neither do I condemn thee; go, and sin no more." "Daughter, be of good comfort; thy faith hath made thee whole; go in peace." With many such words did Jesus sustain the weary ones; may we speak the same words to sorrowing souls? – Indeed we may, for we are ambassadors on behalf of Christ, as though God were beseeching by us even as by Christ. Sin is the cause of all tribulation, and God "comforteth us in all our tribulation, that we may be able to comfort them which are in any trouble, by the comfort wherewith we ourselves are comforted of God." God sent His Son into the world, "that the world through Him might be saved;" and He says, "As My Father hath sent Me, even so send I you." We are therefore to be able, from personal experience, to speak words that will set at liberty the groaning captives of sin. But we must first receive a tongue from the Lord, and allow Him to control it.

The Lord's Submissive Servant

The secret of success is submission. "The Lord God hath opened Mine ear, and I was not rebellious, neither turned away back." This reminds us of the words of Christ in Ps. 40:6: "Mine ears hast Thou opened." And this also reminds us of what is written in the law. When a servant refused to go away from his master when the year of release came, but said, "I love my master, ... I will not go out free," the order was, "Then his master shall bring him unto the judges; he shall also bring him to the door, or unto the doorpost; and his master shall bore his ear through with an awl; and he shall serve him for ever." Ex. 21:6. That act signified that his ear was his master's, always open to hear his commands. We are the Lord's servants, if we yield ourselves to Him as His servants (Rom. 6:16), and we are to do the will of God on earth as it is done in heaven, where the angels "do His commandments, hearkening unto the voice of His word." Ps. 103:20. Our ears are to be at the service only of God, and what we hear we are to accept as our "reasonable service." If we thus submit to the Lord, we may have the support, and the power to sustain others, that Christ had. "He that hath ears to hear, let him hear."

Christ was not rebellious. He had, as "the Man Christ Jesus," given Himself to be the Lord's servant for ever, and He was not rebellious, and did not draw back, even when the service involved the receiving of blows, and still worse treatment, and also the vilest insults. That was in the contract, when He made the bargain, and He did not back out. So it was with the Apostle Paul. God said, "I will show him how great things he must suffer for My name's sake;" and Paul submitted himself to be the Lord's servant for ever, knowing what it involved; and so when "bonds and afflictions" awaited him in every city, he could calmly say, "None of these things move me." Acts 20:23–24.

Power Gained by Submission

The Master is responsible for the servant, and, knowing this, the Servant says, "The Lord God will help Me; therefore shall I not be confounded; therefore have I set My face like a flint, and I know that I shall not be ashamed." Even so Paul said: "Having therefore obtained help of God, I continue unto this day." Acts 26:22.

"Well, what is the practical use of all this to me?" some one will ask; I "am neither Jesus nor Paul, and cannot expect to do such work as they did, nor to be noticed by the Lord as they were." Why, my dear man, you are losing the benefit of the whole Gospel story. Do you not see that the strength of Jesus and of Paul was their weakness? Jesus said, "I can of Mine own self do nothing." John 5:30. "I do nothing of Myself." John 18:38. "The Father that dwelleth in Me, He doeth the works." John 14:10. It was only when Paul was weak, that he was strong. God said to him, "My grace is sufficient for thee; for My strength is made perfect in weakness;" and Paul exclaimed, "Most gladly therefore will I rather glory in my infirmities, that the power of Christ may rest on me." 2 Cor. 12:9–10. "The power of Christ" that rested on him in weakness, was the same power that rested on Christ in His infirmity. Now here is the comfort for you, whosoever you are: Are you weak, the very weakest of the weak? very good; then you afford the Lord the most excellent opportunity for manifesting the perfection of His strength. Christ's power was His submission to the Father; you certainly are not too weak to allow yourself to rest in the hands of God, that He may do what He will with you. If Christ dwells in your heart, you may, like Him, be "filled with all the fullness of God." Every experience of Christ may be ours. He says that the Lord God will help Him, and that therefore He shall not be confounded nor ashamed; and have we not but recently learned that "Israel shall be saved in the Lord with an everlasting salvation; ye shall not be ashamed nor confounded world without end?" Then let us also set our faces like a flint.

Our Deliverer Near

God is "not far from every one of us." "It is God that justifieth;" therefore we may say with Christ, "He is near that justifieth me." And then we may be as bold as He, in saying, "Who will contend with me? let us stand up together; who is mine adversary? let him come near to me. Behold, the Lord God will help me." "The Lord is my light and my salvation; whom shall I fear? the Lord is the strength of my life; of whom shall I be afraid?" Ps. 27:1. "Though an host should encamp against me, my heart shall not fear;" for "the angel of the Lord encampeth round about them that fear Him, and delivereth them." "Submit yourselves therefore to God. Resist the devil, and he will flee from you." James 4:7.

The True Light

"But the way is so dark!" you exclaim. Very well; "Who is among you that feareth the Lord, that obeyeth the voice of His Servant? although he walketh in darkness, and hath no light, let him trust in the name of the Lord, and stay upon his God." See margin of Isa. 50:10, R.V. So we can say with a humble man of old, "Rejoice not against me, O mine enemy; when I fall, I shall arise; when I sit in darkness, the Lord shall be a light unto me." "He will bring me forth to the light, and I shall behold His righteousness." Micah 7:8–9. None that put their trust in the Lord shall be ashamed.

Take heed, however, not to manufacture a light for yourself. The sparks of your own kindling are a very poor substitute for "the light of the knowledge of the glory of God." "This then is the message which we have heard of Him, and declare unto you, that God is light, and in Him is no darkness at all." "If we walk in the light, as He is in the light, we have fellowship one with another, and the blood of Jesus Christ His Son cleanses us from all sin." Our ideas, our opinions, whatever proceeds from us, is darkness, even though it seems for a moment to flash as light. The word of God is light and with that in our hearts we may successfully resist "the rulers of the darkness of the world." Eph. 6:11–17. "The true light now shineth. Let us therefore give thanks to God, "who hath delivered us from the power of darkness, and hath translated us into the kingdom of His dear Son." Col. 1:12.

CHAPTER 62

EVERLASTING RIGHTEOUSNESS OUR SALVATION

(Isa. 51:1–8, Lowth's Translation)

1. "Hearken unto Me, ye that pursue righteousness, Ye that seek Jehovah. Look unto the rock from whence ye were hewn; and to the hollow of the cave, whence ye were digged.

2. Look unto Abraham your father; and unto Sarah who bore you: for I called him being a single person, and I blessed him, and I multiplied him.

3. Thus therefore shall Jehovah console Sion; He shall console all her desolations; and He shall make her wilderness like Eden; and her desert like the garden of Jehovah; joy and gladness shall be found in her; thanksgiving, and the voice of melody.

4. Attend unto Me, O ye peoples; and give ear unto Me, O ye nations; for the law from Me shall proceed; and My judgments will I cause to break forth for a light to the peoples.

5. My righteousness is at hand; My salvation goeth forth; and Mine arm shall dispense judgment to the peoples; Me the distant lands shall expect; and to Mine arm shall they look with confidence.

6. Lift up unto the heavens your eyes; and look down unto the earth beneath; verily the heavens shall dissolve, like smoke; and the earth shall wax old, like a garment; and its inhabitants shall perish, like the vilest insect; but My salvation shall endure for ever; and My righteousness shall not decay.

7. Hearken unto Me, ye that know righteousness; the people in whose heart is My law; fear not the reproach of wretched man; neither be ye borne down by the revilings.

8. For the moth shall consume them, like a garment; and the worm shall eat them like wool; but My righteousness shall endure for ever; and My salvation to the age of ages."

The reader cannot fail to notice the difference between Lowth's translation and the ordinary rendering of verse 6, and some may wonder what warrant there can be for so much difference, and how we can be sure of anything when translators differ so widely. What similarity can there be between "in like manner" and "like the vilest insect?" The matter is easily explained. It is well known that in our own language there are many instances of words spelled alike, yet having entirely different meanings. We have no difficulty with them, because the connection always tells us which meaning is intended. Even so it is in the Hebrew. The word of "thus" or "so" is spelled the same as that for "gnat" or "fly." All other translations of which the writer has any knowledge, read, "the inhabitants shall die like gnats," and this rendering is suggested in the margin of the Revised Version of the English. A moment's thought is sufficient to show anybody that "like gnats" is much more striking than "as so," which our translators preferred, and that it is evidently what the Lord really says. It is not a vital matter, but is worthy of note.

Abraham an Example of Righteousness

Here we have a call direct to those who would follow the Lord, – to those who seek righteousness. There are many who are seeking it in the wrong way. "Israel, which followed after the law of righteousness, hath not attained to the law of righteousness. Wherefore? Because they sought it not by faith, but as it were by the works of the law." Rom. 9:31–32. We are therefore directed to Abraham, for an example of how righteousness is obtained. "If Abraham were justified by works, he hath whereof to glory; but not before God. For what saith the Scripture? Abraham believed God, and it was counted to him for righteousness. Now to him that worketh is the reward not reckoned of grace, but of debt. But to him that worketh not, but believeth on Him that justifieth the ungodly, his faith is counted for righteousness. Even as David also describeth the blessedness of the man unto whom God imputeth righteousness without works, saying, Blessed are they whose iniquities are forgiven, and whose sins are covered." Rom. 4:2–7.

"The Gentiles, which followed not after righteousness, have attained to righteousness, even the righteousness which is of faith." Abraham was a Gentile, brought up a heathen. See Joshua 24:2–3, where we have almost the exact language as in our lesson in Isaiah. He was but one, yet God gave him a numerous posterity through faith, for "if ye be Christ's then are ye Abraham's seed, and heirs according to the promise." Gal. 3:29. Look to him, and learn the power of faith. Learn how God can work against all human probabilities. Look also to Sarah, who by faith "received power to conceive seed when she was past age, since she counted Him faithful that promised." Heb. 11:11. "Thus therefore shall Jehovah console Sion." In that way, and by that means, will God build up and restore Jerusalem; by the preaching of the Gospel among all nations, will God from among the Gentiles raise up a faithful seed to inherit the land of promise, even as He raised up Abraham in the first place. And herein is comfort for the individual, for it matters not how lonely and weak a man may be, God is able to multiply him and make him great.

The Mercy of God's Justice

It is common for people to look upon the law of God with dread. They regard it as a terrible thing, the instrument only of wrath. That depends wholly upon how they receive it. Out of Christ, it is but an instrument of death, but if we receive it in Christ, it is "the law of the Spirit of life." The throne of grace, to which we are invited to come with boldness, that we may obtain mercy, and find grace to help in time of need (Heb. 4:16), is the very same throne out of which proceed "lightnings, and thunderings, and voices." Rev. 4:5. But we must not forget that it was even so at the cross, where we look for salvation. All the terrors of Sinai were there, yet it is from the cross that all our comfort comes. And the cross was the throne of God, having God's law as its basis, with the stream of life flowing from it. The law is not opposed to the Gospel, and does not even have to be reconciled with it; but the law of God in Christ is the Gospel. Justice does not have to give way to mercy, nor even to be blended with it; but it is the justice of God that justifies the ungodly. Rom. 3:24–26.

> There's a wideness in God's mercy,
> Like the wideness of the sea;
> There's a kindness in His justice,
> That is more than liberty.

> For the love of God is broader
> Than the measure of man's mind;
> And the heart of the Eternal
> Is most wonderfully kind.

But God's heart is just, for God Himself is just. Therefore, because God is just, and His law is His own life, people will learn to trust and hope in it, and will walk in the light of it. God's law is to be loved and delighted in, instead of to be feared and rejected. God's law is salvation to every one who accepts it in Christ.

God says, "My righteousness is near." Yes, for God Himself is "not far from every one of us," and He is our righteousness. Christ is of God made unto us righteousness and sanctification and redemption. His righteousness is near, and His salvation has gone forth. His life is righteousness and salvation, and it has been given freely for all. The gift has been bestowed, and we have not even to ask for it, but only to take it. What a blessed thing it is to know that we may trust on the arm of Jehovah! "The eternal God is thy refuge, and underneath are the everlasting arms."

God's Law Everlasting

Heaven and earth shall pass away, but My words shall not pass away," says Christ. Matt. 24:35. "Think not that I am come to destroy the law, or the prophets; I am not come to destroy, but to fulfill. For verily I say unto you, Till heaven and earth pass, one jot or one tittle shall in no wise pass from the law, till all be fulfilled." Matt. 5:17–18. "It is easier for heaven and earth to pass, than one tittle of the law to fail." Luke 16:17. Everything that can be shaken will be removed; but God's law will stand for ever; it is unchangeable, for it is God's own righteousness, and He is "from everlasting to everlasting." It is the expression of God's will (Rom. 2:17–18), therefore "he that doeth the will of God abideth for ever." 1 John 2:17.

God's Righteousness is the Law

That God's righteousness is His law, is seen from verse 7. God says, "Hearken unto Me, ye that know righteousness, the people in whose heart is My law." That is to say, the people who know righteousness are the people in whose heart God's law is. If this were the only statement of the kind in the Bible, it would be sufficient to show that there can be no righteousness where the law of God is not; but it must be there by faith; for this perfect righteousness of the law is found only in Christ, and He dwells in the heart by faith.

This verse shows another thing also, and that is that no one can know the law except by experience. It is with the heart that man believeth unto righteousness. One may be able to repeat the commandments as glibly as he can the alphabet, he may discourse beautifully about "the plan of salvation," but he knows nothing of God or His righteous law unless he has experienced the power of His salvation. We know what we have lived, and nothing more. All the rest we have merely heard about.

"Thy righteousness is an everlasting righteousness, and Thy law is the truth." Ps. 119:142. It is the law of God, therefore, that is to be the shield and buckler of God's people in the time of trouble. See Ps. 91:4. The law of God will be the defense of His people. It is the one enduring thing, therefore we are exhorted, "fear ye not the reproach of men, neither be ye afraid of their revilings. For the moth shall eat them up like a garment, and the worm shall eat them like wool." Why then should anybody be afraid of the reproaches of men? They have all fallen on Christ, and He has deprived them of all their sting. It is no shame to be reproached with Him. "If ye be reproached for the name of Christ, happy are ye; for the Spirit of glory and of God resteth upon you." 1 Peter 4:14. Ancient Egypt was a wonderfully rich country, and Moses was well acquainted with it; for he had been brought up at the court; yet he esteemed "the reproach of Christ greater riches than the treasures in Egypt." Heb. 11:26. If the reproach of Christ is so wondrously rich in blessing, what must the unveiled glory be?

Review these verses, and note how much stress is laid upon the fact that God's righteousness and salvation are for ever; they cannot be abolished. This constitutes all our hope. Many professed Christians seemed to think that it is their duty as ministers of the Gospel to teach people to disregard the law of God. They forget that in so doing they are ranging themselves with the heathen, who vainly say, "Let us break their bands asunder, and cast away their cords from us." At all such feeble efforts as these God will laugh. And we should laugh also, for in the stability of God's law is our salvation. If God's law could be abolished, that would show that His Government is weak, and that He is not able to protect those who put their trust in Him. Therefore we may say, "Thy statutes have been my songs in the house of my pilgrimage," and also, "O how love I Thy law! it is my meditation all the day." And well it may be, for God's commandment is "exceeding broad," and contains more than the mind of man can fathom even in the ages of eternity. If we long for God's salvation, He will open our eyes, that we may behold wonderful things out of His law.

Salvation that Lasts

"My salvation shall be for ever, and My righteousness shall not be abolished." Remember this; it will help you all your life through. When you are inclined to doubt if you can endure unto the end, and you think that sin and sickness must necessarily overtake you once in a while, recall these words of the Lord. His righteousness is an everlasting righteousness; it cannot be abolished. His salvation, the health and strength of the body and soul, that He gives, is for ever. You are well today; is it an accident? or is your health from God? From God undoubtedly. Well, then, since He has given you health today, can He not continue it indefinitely? You say that He can if He will. Well, do you think that He wishes anything else than that you should be well? The leper said, "Lord, if Thou wilt, Thou canst make me clean;" and Jesus said, "I will." He has said through His beloved disciple, "Beloved, I wish above all things that thou mayest prosper, and be in health." 3 John 2. Be sure, then, that the Lord does not wish that you should be ill. It is no credit to Him to have His children in poor health. If then He wishes you to be well, what can hinder it? You say, and rightly, too, that your ignorance of the laws of health will hinder it. So it is really an accident that you are well today; because you have accidentally come into harmony with the law of your being. But Christ is the law of your being, and for you to say that you do not know the laws of life, is the same as saying that you do not know the Lord. Then get acquainted with Him. Study His life as revealed in all creation, and learn how to come into harmony with it. Then that which happens once in a while accidentally, will be the rule. And likewise with your soul. The life that keeps you from the power of the devil today, will, if yielded to intelligently, keep you every day, even through eternity. "His Divine power hath given unto us all things that pertain unto life and godliness, through the knowledge of Him that hath called us to glory and virtue." 2 Peter 1:3. So "the very God of peace sanctify you wholly; and I pray God your whole spirit and soul and body be preserved blameless unto the coming of our Lord Jesus Christ. Faithful is He that calleth you, who also will do it."

CHAPTER 63

THE POWER THAT SAVES

(Isa. 51:9–16, Lowth's Translation)

9. "Awake, awake, clothe Thyself with strength, O Arm of Jehovah! Awake, as in the days of old, the ancient generations. Art not Thou the same that smote Rahab, that wounded the dragon?

10. Art not Thou the same that dried up the sea, the waters of the great deep? That made the depths of the sea, a path for the redeemed to pass through?

11. Thus shall the ransomed of Jehovah return. And come to Sion with loud acclamations; and everlasting gladness shall crown their heads; joy and gladness shall they obtain, and sorrow and sighing shall flee away.

12. I, even I, am He that comforteth you; Who art thou, that thou shouldst fear wretched man, that dieth? And the son of man, that shall become as the grass?

13. And shouldst forget Jehovah thy Maker, Who Stretched out the heavens, and founded the earth; and shouldst every day be in continued fear, because of the fury of the oppressor, as if he were just ready to destroy? And where now is the fury of the oppressor?

14. He marcheth on with speed, who cometh to set free the captive: that he may not die in the dungeon, and that his bread may not fail.

15. For I am Jehovah thy God; He who at once stilleth the sea, though the waves thereof roar; Jehovah God of hosts is His name.

16. I have put My words in thy mouth; and with the shadow of My hand have I covered thee; to stretch out the heavens, and to lay the foundations of the earth; and to say unto Sion, Thou art My people."

Two words in this lesson, namely, "Rahab" and the "dragon," need a little explanation, in order that the student may read understandingly. But let everybody note that the explanation is given in the Bible itself, so that there is no room for the complaint that "we are not learned, and cannot expect to know all these things." The book of God may be understood by everybody who will study it, no matter though he be not learned; he will become intelligent by the study. True, a previous knowledge of different languages may be a help to him, provided he uses his knowledge in the right way, although those who know the most of language are not the ones who know the most of the Bible; but when a knowledge of languages becomes necessary, then the man who knows the Bible has the advantage of everybody else. "The Lord giveth wisdom; out of His mouth cometh knowledge and understanding."

What "Rahab" Means

Take your Revised Bible (for everybody who studies the Bible ought to have this as well as the so-called "Authorized Version," and should read them both together) and read Isa. 30:7: "For Egypt helpeth in vain, and to no purpose, therefore have I called her Rahab that sitteth still." This is sufficient, and will enable the reader to understand Ps. 139:10: "Thou hast broken Rahab in pieces, as one that is slain; Thou hast scattered Thine enemies with Thy strong arm." Now read Job 26:12 in both versions, comparing them. "He divideth the sea with His power, and by His understanding He smiteth through the proud," or, as in the margin, "through pride." We turn to our Revised Version, and read, "By His understanding He smiteth through Rahab." From this we can learn that the word "Rahab" means "pride." That "Rahab" is a pure Hebrew word, untranslated, we may know from the fact that it is a proper name, the name of one of the ancestors of Christ. When used in other connections, untranslated, it is simply the personification of pride, and is specially applied to Egypt. Egypt is the proud boaster, that does nothing. We are to learn that as God smote through Egypt, so will He bring down the pride of all that rise up against Him. "The day of the Lord of hosts shall be upon every one that is proud and lofty, and

425

upon every one that is lifted up; and he shall be brought low." Isa. 2:12.

The Dragon

And now for the dragon. Read Eze. 29:3: "Thus saith the Lord God: Behold, I am against thee, Pharaoh King of Egypt, the great dragon that lieth in the midst of his rivers, which hath said, My river is mine own, and I have made it for myself." The succeeding verses tell of the judgments to be brought upon Egypt, all of which have been fulfilled, as a token of the still greater fulfillment yet to come. That this judgment which was visited upon Egypt was but the beginning of the great day of judgment, we may learn from Isa. 26:20–21; 27:1; "Come, My people, enter thou into thy chambers, and shut thy doors about thee; hide thyself as it were for a little moment, until the indignation be overpast. For, behold, the Lord cometh out of His place to punish the inhabitants of the earth for their iniquity; the earth also shall disclose her blood, and shall no more cover her slain. In that day the Lord with his sore and great and strong sword shall punish leviathan the piercing serpent, even leviathan that crooked serpent; and He shall slay the dragon that is in the midst of the sea."

Deliverance from "The Pride of Life"

We see, therefore, that both "Rahab" and "the dragon" are terms for Egypt. But that does not exhaust their meaning, since Egypt does not have a monopoly of the pride that is in the earth. The pride of Egypt is but "the pride of life," instilled by "the spirit that now worketh in the children of disobedience." So primarily the dragon is "that old serpent, which is the Devil and Satan," "which deceiveth the whole world." Rev. 20:2, 12:9. It is in heathenism that the characteristics of the devil are fully manifested in the flesh; therefore in prophecy the dragon is sometimes used as a name to indicate the nations that have been openly and completely heathen, opposed to the worship of the one, true God. So we see that the judgments that of old have been visited upon Egypt and Babylon, and other heathen nations that in their pride have boasted against God, are but assurances of the great judgment that is to come upon all pride, in the person of the devil himself. These judgments, indicating the approaching downfall for ever of Satan, the author of pride, are assurances of each individual that God will here and now save him from "the lust of the flesh, and the lust of the eyes, and the pride of life." These two words, therefore, furnish the key to the whole lesson. Verses 9 and 10 show us that we have a right to call upon the Lord to awake and come to our help with the power by which He in ancient times overcame Egypt, and delivered His people from bondage. He delivered them then, in order "that they might observe His statutes, and keep His laws." Ps. 105:45. Therefore we may know that with the same mighty arm, and the same power He will now deliver us from the bondage of sin, "that we being delivered out of the hand of our enemies might serve Him without fear, in holiness and righteousness before Him, all the days of our life." The lesson that we are to learn from the scripture before us is a personal one; it means that every one of us individually has at his disposal all the power by which Israel of old was delivered from Egypt. The same God still lives, and His arm has not lost any of its strength.

Sing the Promises of God

In ancient times the Lord made the depths of the sea a path for the redeemed to pass over, and "thus shall the ransomed of Jehovah return, and come to Sion." They shall come with loud acclamations, with singing and gladness. "But," you say, "there is to be long wandering in the wilderness of sin before that can take place." Not a bit of it. That was not at all God's plan for Israel, but was the result of their unbelief. You see, they stopped singing, and began murmuring. That is the secret of their wandering in the wilderness. Keep on singing, not a forced song, but a song from the heart because God is your strength and your song and your salvation, and you will find that these "songs of deliverance" that compass you about will be a shield that will protect you from every assault of the enemy. This is not theory, but fact that has been demonstrated. The power that divided the Red Sea is the power that is ours every day in our struggle to escape from the bondage of sin. He that believeth shall not be confounded. The "exceeding great and precious promises" of God make us partakers of the Divine nature; therefore sing them.

The Need of These Promises

Verses 12–14 have a peculiar significance in view of what the prophecy tells us will come in the very last days. Revelation 13 brings to view a power, a beast, which is the direct representative of the devil, since it is the devil – the dragon – that gives this beast his power, and his seat, and his great authority. Here we have, therefore, the personification of the arrogant pride of the devil in his fight against God; and this is carried out, as is seen by the reading of the entire chapter. Then later on still another power rises, seeking to enforce the worship of "the beast," that is, to compel men to refuse to worship God, and to substitute the commandments of men for His commandments. He makes an image to the beast, and will "cause that as many as would not worship the image of the beast should be killed." The highest point of proud opposition to God is seen in the attempted changing of the commandments.

The Papacy, which under the name of Christianity, overpasses the deeds of the heathen, having gone farther in opposition to God, in blasphemy against Him, and in persecution of His true followers, than any heathen nation ever did, has presumed to set itself above the law of God, teaching men that, while the commandments teach that the seventh day, commonly called Saturday, is the Sabbath, they need not observe that day, but must instead observe the first day of the week, Sunday. The substitution of this day for that appointed by God is claimed by the Roman Catholic Church as the badge of its authority, and the keeping of it by most of the professed Christians is the only thing by which they all, in spite of their protests against Papal assumptions, acknowledge her power.

Many of those who call themselves Protestants are with all their might seeking to enforce this mark of the Papacy, and so far will they yet go that they will issue a decree authorizing anybody to kill those who do not receive this mark. All the faithful commandment-keepers will be "placed under ban," even as Luther was after the Diet of Worms, and as so many others have been in the past.

That will be a time of sore trial for the people of God. It will be a time to try men's souls, and it will then be determined who has learned to trust in God for salvation. Happy will it then be for everybody who can hear God say to him, "I, even I," the one who divided the sea, and delivered Israel, and who made even the greatest obstacle in their way a path of escape, am He that comforteth you. Why should you be afraid of a puny man that shall die? The One who delivers thee is marching on with speed, and will quickly come, so that you need not die in the pit, and your bread will not fail, even though it run low. It will be well to learn this lesson thoroughly. We shall, if faithful to the Lord, have occasion to remember it before many years have passed.

Present Deliverance

Yes, even now we need to remember it. If we have not learned and applied the lesson in our personal contest with "this present evil world," "the lust of the flesh, the lust of the eyes, and the pride of life," which are seeking to hold us captive, we shall not be able to use it in the coming time of trouble. The promise is, "Because thou hast kept the word of My patience, I also will keep thee from the hour of temptation, which shall come upon all the world, to try them that dwell upon the earth." Rev. 3:10. We cannot afford to lose any time in making a literal, personal application of these lessons to ourselves.

A Wondrous Gift

In the 16 verse we have a most wonderful statement. God says to us, – to every one who follows after righteousness, and seeks the Lord, – "I have put My words in thy mouth." Compare this with 2 Cor. 5:19, margin, where we read that God has put in us – all who are reconciled to Him by Jesus Christ – the word of reconciliation. For what purpose has God put His words in our mouths. The answer is, "To stretch out the heavens, and to lay the foundations of the earth, and to say unto Sion, Thou art My people." That is to say, the word of the Gospel, which God has committed unto us, is the same word that in the beginning made the heavens and all their host (Ps. 28:6), and which will yet make all things new. It is the Word that makes men new creatures, and which will make the earth new for them to dwell in. Here is the climax of all.

Not only does God by the power by which He rules the heaven and earth and sea, deliver us from evil, but He puts the power in us to deliver others who are in bondage. Who with this assurance need ever fear bonds or imprisonment? Every child of God has given him a power greater than that of all the kings of earth. This power he is not to use against those who would do him physical injury, even as Christ did not, but he is to use it in the delivering even his enemies from the bondage of sin. With this word in our mouth, we may bid the devil depart from us, and he will flee. Do you value this gift of the Word of God, and do you use it?

"How firm a foundation, ye saints of the Lord

Is laid for your faith in His excellent word;

What more can He say than to you He hath said,

To you, who to Jesus for refuge have fled?"

CHAPTER 64

BEAUTIFUL PREACHERS OF A GLORIOUS MESSAGE

(Isa. 52:1–12)

"Awake, awake; put on thy strength, O Zion; put on thy beautiful garments, O Jerusalem, the holy city; for thenceforth shall no more come into thee the uncircumcised and the unclean. Shake thyself from the dust; arise, and sit down, O Jerusalem; loose thyself from the bands of thy neck, O captive daughter of Zion. For thus saith the Lord, Ye have sold yourselves for nought; and ye shall be redeemed without money. For thus saith the Lord God, My people went down aforetime into Egypt to sojourn there; and the Assyrian oppressed them without cause. Now therefore what have I here, saith the Lord, that My people is taken away for nought? they that rule over them make them to howl, saith the Lord; and My name continually every day is blasphemed. Therefore My people shall know My name; therefore they shall know in that day that I am He that doth speak; behold, it is I.

"How beautiful upon the mountains are the feet of him that bringeth good tidings, that publisheth peace; that bringeth good tidings of good, that publisheth salvation; that saith unto Zion, Thy God reigneth! Thy watchmen shall lift up the voice; with the voice together shall they sing: for they shall see eye to eye, when the Lord shall bring again Zion.

"Break forth into joy, sing together ye waste places of Jerusalem; for the Lord hath comforted His people, He hath redeemed Zion. The Lord hath made bare His holy arm in the eyes of all the nations; and all the ends of the earth shall see the salvation of our God.

"Depart ye, depart ye, go ye out from thence, touch no unclean thing; go ye out from the midst of her; be ye clean, that

bear the vessels of the Lord. For ye shall not go out with haste, nor go by flight; for the Lord will go before you; and the God of Israel will be your rearward."

Called Out of Babylon

The last paragraph gives us the key to the whole chapter. It is the call to go out of Babylon, the same call that we found in chapter 48 verse 20. God's people are called forth from Babylon, "that ye be not partakers of her sins, and that ye receive not of her plagues" (Rev. 18:4), and so here the call is to come out, and be clean. It is the last call, before the final Judgment at the coming of the Lord. The chapter before us presents the closing of the work "to make ready a people prepared for the Lord." It presents the people prepared, and waiting for His coming. This is seen from the first verse. It takes people to make a city. So all that is said of Zion applies to those who are prepared to dwell in her. The holy city means a holy people. The preceding chapter presents the people in captivity, longing for freedom, and here we have the deliverance complete.

Beautiful Garments

Zion is called upon to put on her beautiful garments. The city itself, the new Jerusalem, is "the bride, the Lamb's wife." Rev. 19:7; 21:9–10. "Jerusalem which is above, is free, which is the mother of us all." But as a mother lives only for her children, so the new Jerusalem exists only for her inhabitants – her children. They are her ornament. Rev. 21:2; Isa. 49:17–18. Therefore the beautiful garments of Zion are the beautiful garments of the inhabitants of Zion. What are they? – "To her it was granted that she should be arrayed in fine linen, clean and white; for the fine linen is the righteousness of saints." Rev. 19:8. The call, "Put on thy beautiful garments," indicate that they are all prepared. We have not to manufacture them; they have been woven in the loom of heaven, by the Master workman; and they are laid up waiting for "whosoever will" take them. "Oh how great is Thy goodness, which Thou hast laid up for them that fear Thee; which Thou hast wrought for them that trust in Thee before the sons of men!" Ps. 31:19.

In this connection read Zech. 3:1–5. Joshua the priest stood before the angel of the Lord, clothed in filthy garments, and Satan stood at his right hand to resist him. The Lord rebuked Satan, and the words are very striking when compared with these in Isaiah. "The Lord rebuke thee, O Satan, even the Lord that hath chosen Jerusalem rebuke thee." Then the Lord said, "Take away the filthy garments from him;" and to Joshua He said: "Behold, I have caused thine iniquity to pass from thee, and I will clothe thee with change of raiment." So there is no possible doubt as to what these beautiful garments are. They are God's salvation, to which the corruption and filth of this present evil world will not stick.

"I will greatly rejoice in the Lord, my soul shall be joyful in my God; for He hath clothed me with the garments of salvation, He hath covered me with the robe of righteousness, as a bridegroom decketh himself with ornaments, and as a bride adorneth herself with her jewels." Isa. 61:10. "For the Lord taketh pleasure in His people; He will beautify the meek with salvation." Ps. 149:4. Clothed with this salvation, we are preserved from "the corruption that is in the world through lust."

Liberty for the Captive

Christ has become partaker of flesh and blood, in order that through death He might destroy him that had the power of death, that is, the devil, "and deliver them who through fear of death were all their lifetime subject to bondage." "He *hath visited and redeemed* His people." Freedom from all bondage is already theirs. It will be remembered that when Jesus saw the woman in the synagogue, who had been bound by Satan with a spirit of infirmity for eighteen years, and who could in nowise lift herself upright, He said to her, "Woman, thou art loosed from thine infirmity." Luke 13:12. She was loosed, even while she was bowed over; Jesus simply proclaimed to her that she was free to rise if she chose; and she did so. Even so Jesus has come to proclaim liberty to the captives. There is not a bond upon a single person on earth, that might not at once be shaken off, if the individual only knew and believed that God had given him his freedom. The captive daughter of Zion is told to loose herself from the bands of her neck. The

433

bands are broken; she has only to throw them off. This is the message that every minister of the Gospel, and every person who has been made one with Christ, is commissioned to proclaim to a world of sinners, – that they have only to assert their liberty in the name of Jesus, and they have it. Christ has broken the bands; it remains only for them to show their desire for freedom, by casting them off. Surely everything has been done that could be done. Let it be proclaimed with a loud voice to the ends of the earth, that there is no soul bound by any sin whatever, except by his own will. He is at liberty, if he wishes to exercise his freedom. Whoever is in bondage to any evil habit, is in bondage because he loves to be, or else he has not yet learned the proclamation of freedom. Then let the sound ring out everywhere, that all who love liberty may have it.

Satan makes great promises, but he never fulfills them. He has nothing to give. His promises are empty. Whoever yields to him, sells himself to be a slave, for nothing. He made Eve believe that by disobeying God she would be like God, but instead she became like him. Instead of life, she found death. "Ye shall be redeemed without money." "Ye were redeemed, not with corruptible things, with silver or gold, from your vain manner of life handed down from your fathers; but with precious blood, as of a lamb without blemish and without spot, even the blood of Christ." 1 Peter 1:18–19. Money is not the most necessary thing in this world. Common things can be bought with it; with money we can buy things that are of no value, and which perish with the using; but the most valuable things cannot be bought with money; there are things so valuable that nothing can buy them, and they must be received as a gift. These are the things that are lasting, things that become more enduring with the using.

Egypt and Babylon

"For thus saith the Lord God, My people went down aforetime into Egypt to sojourn there; and the Assyrian oppressed them without cause." Recall the circumstances under which Israel went into Egypt. It was at the invitation of the king, because he and his whole land and people were under the greatest obligation to the son of Israel. They owed their lives to Joseph. Joseph died, and the people of Israel multiplied exceedingly, and "there arose a new king, which knew not Joseph." There arose another dynasty, a line of kings of Assyrian origin, and they of course had no regard for the sacred traditions of the country, and what Joseph had done for the land was nothing to them. So it was that, going into Egypt, God's people were oppressed by the Assyrian. Babylon was the continuation of Assyria, and Egypt and Babylon are both the personification of pride, and of haughty insolence against God. By both nations have the people of God suffered special hardships, having been in captivity in both countries. The deliverance, therefore, of the people of God is from Egypt and Babylon. Out of both Egypt and Babylon are God's children called. Hosea 11:1.

The Model Preachers

We have already noted the good tidings of peace and freedom that all who know the Lord are to announce to the world. Those who bring these glad tidings are beautiful even to their feet. How beautiful they are, and how they are to give their message, may be learned by comparing a few texts of Scripture. We have to start with this one in Isaiah: "How beautiful upon the mountains are the feet of him that bringeth good tidings, that publisheth peace; that bringeth good tidings of good, that publisheth salvation; that saith unto Zion, Thy God reigneth!" Here are the others: –

"The heavens declare the glory of God; and the firmament showeth His handiwork. Day unto day uttereth speech, and night unto night showeth knowledge. There is no speech nor language where their voice is not heard. Their line is gone out through all the earth, and their words to the end of the world." Ps. 19:1–4.

"Whosoever shall call upon the name of the Lord shall be saved. How then shall they call upon Him in whom they have not believed? and how shall they believe in Him of whom they have not heard? and how shall they hear without a preacher? and how shall they preach except they be sent? as it is written, How beautiful are the feet of them that preach the Gospel of peace, and bring glad tidings of good things! But they have not all obeyed the Gospel. For Esaias saith, Lord, who hath believed our report? So then faith cometh by hearing, and hearing by the word of God. But I say, Have they not heard? Yes, verily, their sound went into all the earth, and their words unto the ends of the world." Rom. 10:13–18.

Notice that in this last portion we have quotations from the first two. The argument is that whoever calls upon the name of the Lord shall be saved; but some might object that many have not had an opportunity to call upon His name, and so the apostle meets this objection, by showing (1) that provision has been made for belief, in that preachers have been sent, and he quotes from Isaiah to prove it; and (2) he shows that everybody has heard the message of peace, and good news of salvation, which these preachers publish, because "their sound went into all the earth, and their words unto the ends of the world." But it is the firmament and the host of heaven, whose words have gone unto the ends of the earth, reaching "every creature which is under heaven." Col. 1:23. Therefore it is the sun, moon, and stars, whose beautiful feet are seen upon the mountains, proclaiming glad tidings of good. They are our models in preaching.

How the Heavens Preach

How do the heavens preach? – Simply by giving out the light that God has given them. That is all, and it is all that He expects of any person on earth. Light is life, and we can give out the light that God has given us, only by allowing the life of Jesus to be manifested in our mortal flesh. "Let your light so shine before men, that they may see your good works, and glorify your Father which is in heaven." Matt. 5:16. Nobody can make known a thing that he himself does not know; and nobody can know the Gospel unless Christ lives in him. Gal. 1:16; Col. 1:27. He who talks that which is not his own life, is giving only empty sound; it is like sounding brass or a tinkling cymbal. Christ is the Word, and the Word is life: so that every word that He uttered was simply the giving out of the fullness of His life. When the Gospel is presented in that way, it beautifies the preacher. So "they that be wise shall shine as the brightness of the firmament; and they that turn many to righteousness as the stars for ever and ever."

The Lord at Work

What an expressive figure is presented in verse 10! We have all seen the farmer or the blacksmith at work. When we see him take off his coat and roll up his sleeves, we know that he intends to work in earnest. He does not wish to be hindered by anything in his way. To "strip for the fight" or for the race, is a well-known term. So the scripture tells us that "the Lord hath made bare His holy arm in the sight of all the nations," and as the result "all the ends of the earth shall see the salvation of our God." Who need fear, with God at work in that manner for his salvation?

The preceding chapter presented to us the view of God's people under ban, captive exiles waiting the coming of Him who is to set them free: here we have it stated that they shall not run from their prisons like goal-breakers: "Ye shall not go out with haste, nor go by flight." Why not? – Because the Lord is before and behind them. Very forcibly is it translated by Lowth: –

"For Jehovah shall march in your front;
And the God of Israel shall bring up your rear."

Therefore "the arrow that flieth by day" will cause no fear. No weapon ever forged or cast in any arsenal of earth can possibly pierce the rampart that the presence of God makes for His people. "The Lord is the strength of my life; of whom shall I be afraid? When the wicked, even mine enemies and my foes, came upon me to eat up my flesh, they stumbled and fell. Though an host should encamp against me, my heart shall not fear; though war should rise up against me, in this will I be confident. One thing I have desired of the Lord, that will I see after: that I may dwell in the house of the Lord all the days of my life, to behold the beauty of the Lord, and to enquire in His temple. For in the time of trouble He shall hide me in His pavilion; in the secret of His tabernacle shall He hide me; He shall set me up upon a rock. And now shall mine head be lifted up above mine enemies round about me; therefore will I offer in His tabernacle sacrifices of joy; I will sing, yea, I will sing praises unto the Lord."

CHAPTER 65

THE ARM OF THE LORD

(Isa. 52:13–15; Isa. 53:1–3)

"Behold, My Servant shall deal wisely, He shall be exalted and lifted up, and shall be very high. Like as many were astonished at Thee, (His visage was so marred more than any man, and His form more than the sons of men,) so shall He startle many nations; kings shall shut their mouths at Him; for that which had not been told them they shall see; and that which they had not heard shall they understand.

"Who hath believed our report? and to whom hath the arm of the Lord been revealed? For He grew up before Him as a tender plant, and as a root out of a dry ground; He hath no form nor comeliness; and when we see Him there is no beauty that we should desire Him. He was despised, and rejected of men; a man of sorrows, and acquainted with grief; and as one from whom men hid their face. He was despised, and we esteemed Him not."

We have quoted these verses from the Revised Version, and have been given the alternative reading found in the margin of verse 15, chapter 52. Right here at the beginning we call attention to the difference, so that we may have the change fixed in our minds once for all.

It is impossible to say how many people have rested the whole case for sprinkling instead of baptism, upon the faulty rendering of verse 15, "So shall He *sprinkle* many nations." Now it is true that the Hebrew word from which this word is translated has the idea of "spouting forth," and this idea is found in leaping, starting, whether for joy or astonishment. It is used of liquids, as to sprinkle blood or water upon a person or thing. But note carefully this distinction, which is strictly observed, that it is not used of things that are not fluid, and which cannot be scattered forth in fine streams. The word is often used in the Bible, where it is rightly translated "sprinkle," but it is the liquid that is sprinkled *upon* the thing. It would be impossible to use it of persons, because men cannot be sprinkled upon anything. We have in the English the accommodated expression, "to sprinkle a man," "to sprinkle clothes," although it is not strictly correct. The washerwoman does not sprinkle the clothes, but sprinkles the water upon the clothes. This distinction is most strictly observed in the Hebrew. See Eze. 36:25. It does not say that the Lord will sprinkle His people, but He says: "Then will I sprinkle clean water upon you, and ye shall be clean." In the passage before us, the rendering "sprinkle" is strained and unnatural, and does violence to the sense; the word "startle" or "astonish" is literal, and consistent. That, or its equivalent is given as the rendering in many translations other than the English.

The Wisdom of God's Servant

Again we have the Servant of the Lord brought before us. In chapters 42, 43 and 49, we have had Him introduced before. Here we are told that He shall deal wisely, or prudently. "He shall be exalted and extolled, and be very high." That this is true of Christ, the whole history of His life shows. So wisely did He deal, that the utmost efforts of all the scribes and Pharisees and doctors of the law failed to entangle Him in His talk. He knew perfectly when to answer a question, and when to hold His peace, and refrain from answering; and when He answered a carping question He always discomfited the questioner, and encouraged the listeners. See Mark 12:34–37. And as to exaltation, He is "by the right hand of God exalted," to the throne of the Majesty in the heavens, "far above all principality, and power, and might, and dominion, and every name that is named." Eph. 1:20–21.

But that is not the whole of the story. It is "Jesus, who was made a little lower than the angels," who is "crowned with glory and honour; that He by the grace of God should taste death for every man." Heb. 2:9. It is "the Man Christ Jesus" who dealt prudently, and who is now exalted. It was all done in the flesh, that He might show His power over all flesh. If we yield to God as completely as He did, then are we the servants of the Lord just as surely as He was, and all that is said of Him as the Servant of the Lord applies to us in Him. What a comforting thought it is to know that the servant of the Lord will deal wisely, because we know that if we are truly His servants we shall also deal wisely. Christ is of God made unto us wisdom, as well as righteousness.

This means, however, that we must indeed serve. We must not be idle, lazy servants. We must be alive to know what the will of the Lord is, and must be so filled with the Spirit that the mind of the Spirit, which is the mind of God, will be our mind. All the treasures of wisdom and knowledge are hidden in Christ, and since we are filled with all the fullness of God when He dwells in our hearts by faith, it follows that all the fullness of God's wisdom may be displayed in us. "Ye have an unction from the Holy One, and know all things." 1 John 2:20. This comes only with the utmost humility, for "the wisdom that is from above is first pure, then peaceable, gentle, and easy to be entreated, full of mercy and good fruits." Then comes the exaltation; for "he that humbleth himself shall be exalted." How highly shall we be exalted as the servants of the Lord? – Even to the right hand of God in the heavenly places. Eph. 2:4–6. "He hath put down the mighty from their seats, and exalted them of low degree." "He raiseth up the poor out of the dust, and lifteth up the beggar from the dunghill, to set them among princes, and to make them inherit the throne of glory." 1 Sam. 2:8. "Hath not God chosen the poor of this world, rich in faith, and heirs of the kingdom which He hath promised to them that love Him?"

Kings Terrified by Christ's Humiliation

We read the account of the mock trial of Jesus. "Herod with his men of war set Him at naught and mocked Him, and arrayed Him in a gorgeous robe, and sent Him again to Pilate." Luke 23:11. "And so Pilate, willing to content the people, released Barabbas unto them, and delivered Jesus, when he had scourged Him, to be crucified. And the soldiers led Him away into the hall, called Praetorium; and they called together the whole band. And they clothed Him with purple, and platted a crown of thorns, and put it upon His head, and began to salute Him, Hail, King of the Jews! And they smote Him on the head with a reed, and did spit upon Him, and bowing their knees, worshipped Him. And when they had mocked Him, they took off the purple from Him, and put His own clothes on Him, and led Him away to crucify Him." Mark 15:16–20. That was rare sport for those rough soldiers. To them he seemed only a half-crazy pretender to the throne, who was about to suffer for His presumption. They would crucify Him today, and forget all about it tomorrow. Nay, so little did they regard the whole affair, that they could calmly sit down at the foot of the cross, and gamble for His clothes. His visage was marred, and His form likewise; but by the power of those very sufferings He will astonish many nations. Then the rabble could mock Him, and set Him at naught; soon kings will crouch in dumb terror at His feet, and will frantically call for the rocks and mountains to fall on them, and hide them from His face. "And they shall go into the holes of the rocks, and into the caves of the earth, for fear of the Lord, and for the glory of His majesty, when He ariseth to shake terribly the earth." Isa. 2:19. And all that power will be only a manifestation of the power by which He "endured the cross, despising the shame."

The Arm of God Mocked

Men did not know it, and they would not have believed it if a man had told it to them, that that poor, silent, despised prisoner was "the arm of the Lord." Often had the Jews who persecuted Jesus chanted in their synagogues, "Thou hast a mighty arm; strong is Thy hand, and high is Thy right hand." Ps. 89:13. And again: "We have heard with our ears, O God, our fathers have told us, that work Thou didst in their days, in the times of old. How Thou didst drive out the heathen with Thy hand, and plantedst them; how Thou didst afflict them, and cast them out. For they got not the land in possession by their own sword, neither did their own arm save them; but Thy right hand, and Thine arm, and the light of Thy countenance, because Thou hadst a favour unto them." Ps. 44:1–3. But never did they think that the humble, despised, and rejected Man before them was the arm of the Lord, by whom all this was done. The prophets were read every Sabbath day; but none of the men who cried for the blood of Jesus to be shed, and were willing to take all the guilt of it upon themselves, had any idea that they were seeing the fulfillment of the prophecy, "The Lord hath made bare His holy arm in the eyes of all the nations; and all the ends of the earth shall see the salvation of our God." Yet so it was. The arm of the Lord, which brings salvation, is Christ the Crucified. The isles shall wait for Him, and on His arm shall they trust (Isa. 51:5), because "He shall gather the lambs with His arm," the very same arm that "shall rule for Him." But although these things have been proclaimed for centuries, even now it may be asked, "Who hath believed our report?"

The Beauty of the Lord

Who would think that a little baby, the child of one of the poorest people, born in a manger, growing up in seclusion and poverty, was the manifestation of the arm of the Lord? What is weaker and more lacking in wisdom than a little babe? "But God hath chosen the foolish things of the world to confound the wise; and God hath chosen the weak things of the world to confound the things which are mighty." A root out of a dry ground!

> "He groweth up in their sight like a tender sucker;
> And like a root from a thirsty soil."

One would not expect any beauty in such a plant. Indeed, one would scarcely expect it to live. It seems not to have enough earth and moisture to supply life to it, yet it supplies life to all the world. A grape vine is one of the barest of things at certain seasons of the year. In some countries the vines are not trained upon supports, but are cut back each year, near to the ground, so that in a few years each vine is a gnarled stump. Such a vineyard looks very much like a field of dry stumps left to rot away in the ground after the timber has been carried away. Yet from that very field, and from those very unsightly stumps, flows a stream of rich wine. Hundreds of huge clusters of the most luscious grapes will be gathered from that root that springs from a dry, rocky soil. And that is the beauty of the plant. It is not what it seems to be, but the fruit that it bears, that determines its beauty. Christ had no beauty that the world could see. His beauty was "the hidden man of the heart, the ornament of the meek and quiet spirit;" the beauty of holiness.

To Whom is the Arm Revealed?

If we read this lesson as a mere historical prophecy, we lose the whole of it. If we think merely of what has taken place in the past, of the rejection of Jesus nineteen hundred years ago, because He did not meet the expectation of the people, we have read to no profit. In that case the arm of the Lord has not been revealed to us. We have not believed the report. What does it mean to us, to you and me? It means that however dry and barren our lives are, God can bring forth from them rich streams of blessing; that tender though we may be, and growing in a dry soil, the mighty power of God may reveal itself in us. "Our circumstances are very unfavourable; we have so many difficulties to contend with; everything is against us; there is no prospect of our ever being able to amount to anything." Ah, yes, we have often mourned in that fashion. We have not believed the report about the root out of the dry ground. That has been the trouble with us, and the only trouble; for when we see the arm of the Lord, there can be no trouble. With God nothing is impossible. Jesus was born and reared under the most unfavourable conditions, in order that nobody might have any cause for discouragement. Nobody was ever any poorer than He was; nobody could ever have any fewer advantages; nobody was ever so despised and ill-treated, and was so little appreciated, as He was. And what was it all for? – To show us that if the life of God is allowed to flow through the deadest root in the driest possible soil, it will not only find nourishment for itself, but will be able to furnish support for all the world. Have you believed the report? Has the arm of the Lord been revealed to you? Whenever you are inclined to grumble over your situation, and your lack of opportunities, or to become discouraged at the prospect, stop and ask yourself these questions. "Examine yourselves, whether ye be in the faith." See if you yet believe the first principles of the Gospel.

CHAPTER 66

THE SILENT SUFFERER

(Isa. 53:4–12)

"Surely He hath borne our sicknesses, and carried our sorrows, yet we did esteem Him stricken, smitten of God, and afflicted. But He was wounded for our transgressions, He was bruised for our iniquities; and the chastisement of our peace was upon Him; and with His stripes we are healed. All we like sheep have gone astray; we have turned every one to his own way; and the Lord hath made to light on Him the iniquity of us all.

"He was oppressed, yet He humbled Himself, and opened not His mouth; as a lamb that is led to the slaughter, and as a sheep that before her shearers is dumb; yea, He opened not His mouth. By oppression and judgment He was taken away; and as for His generation, who among them considered that He was cut off out of the land of the living, for the transgression of My people, to whom the stroke was due? And they made His grave with the wicked, and with the rich in His death; although He had done no violence, neither was any deceit in His mouth.

"Yet it pleased the Lord to bruise Him; He hath put Him to grief; when Thou shalt make His soul an offering for sin, He shall see His seed, He shall prolong His days, and the pleasure of the Lord shall prosper in His hand. He shall see of the travail of His soul, and be satisfied; by His knowledge shall My righteous Servant make many righteous; and He shall bear their iniquities. Therefore will I divide Him a portion with the great, and He shall divide the spoil with the strong; because He poured out His soul unto death, and was numbered with the transgressors; yet He bare the sin of many, and made intercession for the transgressors."

The basis of the foregoing text is the Revised Version, together with the marginal renderings; but in a single instance there has been a slight change from that text, the warrant for which is found in other translations. Do not be content with one reading of it; in every sentence there is food for abundance of meditation.

The central thought of this scripture is Christ the Sin-bearer, but there is a depth in it, which few of those who can so glibly repeat the words of the chapter, have ever thought of. Let us see if we cannot come a little closer to the heart of the matter.

Definition of Prophecy

In the first place, note that although these words were written fully seven hundred years before the crucifixion of Jesus of Nazareth, they are in the past tense. There has been a failure to grasp the breadth of their meaning, owing to a faulty idea of what prophecy is. People have fallen into the idea that a prophet is one who foretells future events, and that all prophecy is merely the statement of something to take place in the future; yet that is not at all the Scripture use of the words. When the woman at the well of Samaria said to Jesus, "Sir, I perceive that Thou art a prophet," it was because He had just told her certain things about her own past life; and when she went into the city to call her friends, she said, "Come, see a man, which told me all things that ever I did; is not this the Christ?" John 4:17–19, 29. Also when the Jews had seized Jesus, and He was being mocked by them in the High Priest's court, "when they had blindfolded Him, they struck Him on the face, and asked Him, saying, "Prophesy, who is it that smote Thee." Luke 22:64. Here we see that to prophesy is to tell things either past or present, which people could not be expected to know of their own wisdom, and that a prophet is one who has the power, the Divine gift, to declare such things.

Again, in the call of Moses we have the Lord's own statement of what a prophet is. When Moses objected to going to Egypt to stand before Pharaoh, on the ground that he was not eloquent, the Lord said, "Is not Aaron the Levite thy brother? I know that he can speak well. And also, behold, he cometh forth to meet thee; and when he seeth thee, he will be glad in his heart. And thou shalt speak unto him, and put the words in his mouth; and I will be with thy mouth, and with his mouth, and will teach you what ye shall do. And he shall be thy spokesman unto the people, and it shall come to pass, that he shall be to thee a mouth, and thou shalt be to him as God." Ex. 4:14–16. "And the Lord said unto Moses, See, I have made thee a god to Pharaoh; and Aaron thy brother, shall be thy prophet." Ex. 7:1. Aaron was the speaker for Moses, acting merely as the mouth of his brother, and therefore he was his prophet. Thus we see that a prophet is one who speaks for another, giving exact utterance to another's thoughts; and so a prophet of God is one who gives exact expression to the thoughts of God, in words which the Holy Ghost teaches. Prophecy therefore is any statement of God's everlasting truth; – not man's statement, take notice, but God's own statement by the mouth of a man.

So this fifty-third chapter of Isaiah is prophecy, but not in the mistaken sense that it is merely a statement of something that was to take place at some time in the future. It is prophecy, because it tells the truth of God, which can never be known without the special enlightenment of the Holy Spirit of God. "No man can say that Jesus is the Lord, but by the Holy Ghost." The things contained in this chapter were as true when Isaiah wrote them as they are today. Prophets are not something out of the ordinary course of God's plan, but are indications of what God would do with all men. God would have all men know Him, and every one able to recognize His truth; but when all go astray, the prophet supplies the lack. It is in God's plan for all to be prophets (See Num. 11:29; 1 Cor. 14:1,5,25); yet this does not indicate that if this blessed state of things existed, no one would have a more full revelation than another, so that he would be able to impart to the rest; for we find that in all times God's acknowledged prophets have learned from one another. Isaiah simply gave utterance in this chapter to that which everybody ought to have known by the Spirit's own revelation to him personally.

How the Lord Knows Men

We do not need to take time or space to recount the things that are stated in the Gospels concerning Jesus and His sufferings. All are familiar with them. This chapter lets us into the secret of those sufferings. "With His stripes we are healed." "By His knowledge shall My righteous Servant make many righteous." Here we have a parallel to the statement, "By the obedience of One shall many be made righteous." Rom. 5:19. How can the obedience of one make many righteous? – Manifestly only by that One's presence in the many, living the obedience. So we have the answer to the question as to how Christ by His knowledge shall make many righteous. How does He know? – Not by laborious search and study, but by personal experience. "The Word of God is living and active, and sharper than any two-edged sword, and piercing even to the dividing of soul and spirit, of both joints and marrow, and quick to discern the thoughts and intents of the heart. And there is no creature that is not manifest in His sight; but all things are naked and laid open before the eyes of Him with whom we have to do." Heb. 4:12–13. And this statement comes in connection with the statement that He is "touched with the feeling of our infirmities." The Lord knows our frame, not simply because He has made us, but because he Himself bears everything that humanity bears. That which was from the beginning, the Word of life, which was in the beginning with God, and was God, and which became flesh, and dwelt among us, penetrates to every fiber of every being, and suffers everything to which human flesh is heir. There is not a sickness, not a pain, not a temptation, not an injustice, that oppresses any of the children of men, that does not press with equal weight upon the Lord; nay, it presses even more strongly upon the Lord than it does upon us, because but for His sensibility to the touch of pain or sorrow, we ourselves should have no consciousness of it. It is only His life in us, that makes us conscious of anything. "He bears the sin of the world." He says, "Thou hast made Me to serve with thy sins, and wearied Me with thine iniquities." He is one with all mankind, and everything that touches humanity touches Him.

The Silent Long-Suffering of God

Yet He keeps silence. Century after century has the human race been piling sin and misery upon the Lord, by their deviation from the truth, the way of life, yet He bears it without a murmur. Here we catch a glimpse of the meaning of the phrase, "the long-suffering of God." We have ignored His life in us, and have not sought to learn its ways, so that we might yield to them, and so allow Him to bear the load in His own way, and to live His own life unhindered and unfettered, and He has borne it all uncomplainingly. It was not simply in the High Priest's palace, and in Pilate's court, and on Calvary, that Jesus bore insult and abuse and pain without murmuring; He has been doing that for the last six thousand years; and the very thing which is to His everlasting honour, has been set down to His reproach. Men have charged the Lord with indifference to human suffering, because He did not rise up in His might, and suddenly put an end to it all. How little they knew! They did not understand that He was literally *suffering* all these evils, allowing them to be heaped upon Him, and that His silence under the burden of sin and oppression and injustice was the only way of salvation from them, to the human race. They did not know that if at any time He had risen up in His might, and cast off the burden, putting a sudden end to all misery, it would at the same time have put an end to the greater part of the human race. "The long-suffering of our God is salvation." Blessed thing that He does keep silence, even though wicked men take advantage of His silence, to accuse Him of being altogether such an one as themselves! "The long-suffering of God waited in the days of Noah," and even yet "the Lord is long-suffering to us-ward, not willing that any should perish, but that all should come to repentance."

But who among the men of His generation consider that He was stricken for the transgression of the people, to whom the stroke was due? Even as nineteen hundred years ago, so today, men do not know the time of their visitation. They do not know that God hath visited His people, even coming into their flesh, and has thereby redeemed them, suffering all things for their sakes. If they did, they would know that "by His stripes we are healed." In the fact that the Lord is personally present with each individual, not merely sharing, but bearing, all his infirmities, his sicknesses, his sorrows, and his sins, is absolute and complete deliverance from all these things. Marvelous Gospel! No wonder that it is called the glorious Gospel.

It makes known to us the fact that our very consciousness of our fallen condition carries with it the remedy. What could God possibly do for men that He has not done?

Let Us Be Still

Shall we stop without learning the lesson of silence for ourselves? Who has not been made to suffer unjust accusation, and even to feel the smart the more keenly in that it came from friends, who ought to have been more charitable. A knowledge of the fact that the Lord has from the beginning borne infinitely more, which He did not deserve, and that He has borne it silently and uncomplainingly, will help us wonderfully to "rejoice, and be exceeding glad." And then when we remember that He bears every ill that comes upon us, and that it comes upon us only through Him, how the sting is removed! Surely we ought to be able to endure our little portion uncomplainingly, when it only comes to us secondarily, and the Lord bears the whole at first hand. This is but a suggestion of the comfort that there is in this Gospel of Isaiah; but whoever receives the Lord Jesus by faith may have daily fresh revelations of His presence and power.

CHAPTER 67

THE BUILDING UP OF JERUSALEM

(Isa. 54:1–17, Lowth's Translation)

1. "Shout for joy, O thou barren, that didst not bear; break forth into joyful shouting, and exult, thou that dist not travail; for more are the children of the desolate, than of the married woman, saith Jehovah.

2. Enlarge the place of thy tent; and let the canopy of thy habitation be extended; spare not: lengthen thy cords, and firmly fix thy stakes;

3. For on the right hand, and on the left, thou shalt burst forth with increase; and thy seed shall inherit the nations; and they shall inhabit the desolate cities.

4. Fear not, for thou shalt not be confounded; and blush not, for thou shalt not be brought to reproach; for thou shalt forget the shame of thy youth; and the reproach of thy widowhood shalt thou remember no more.

5. For thy husband is thy Maker; Jehovah God of Hosts is His name; and thy Redeemer is the Holy One of Israel; the God of the whole earth shall He be called.

6. For as a woman forsaken and deeply afflicted, hath Jehovah recalled thee; and as a wife, wedded in youth, but afterwards rejected, saith thy God.

7. In a little anger have I forsaken thee; but with great mercies will I receive thee again;

8. In a short wrath I hid My face a moment from thee; but with everlasting kindness will I have mercy on thee; saith thy Redeemer Jehovah.

9. The same will I do now, as in the days of Noah, when I swore that the waters of Noah should no more pass over the earth; so have I sworn, that I will not be wroth with thee, nor rebuke thee.

10. For the mountains shall be removed; and the hills shall be overthrown; but My kindness from thee shall not be removed; and the covenant of My peace shall not be overthrown; saith Jehovah, who beareth towards thee the most tender affection.

11. O thou afflicted, beaten with the storm, destitute of consolation! Behold, I lay thy stones with cement of vermilion, and thy foundations with sapphires;

12. And I will make of rubies thy battlements; and thy gates of carbuncles; and the whole circuit of thy walls shall be of precious stones.

13. And all thy children shall be taught by Jehovah; and great shall be the prosperity of thy children.

14. In righteousness shalt thou be established; be thou far from oppression; yea, thou shalt not fear it; and from terror; for it shall not approach thee.

15. Behold, they shall be leagued together, but not by My command; whosoever is leagued against thee, shall come over to thy side.

16. Behold, I have created the smith, who bloweth up the coals into a fire, and produceth instruments according to his work; and I have created the destroyer to lay waste.

17. Whatever weapon is formed against thee, it shall not prosper; and against every tongue that contendeth with thee, thou shalt obtain thy cause. This is the heritage of Jehovah's servants, and their justification from Me, saith Jehovah."

A Key to the Understanding of the Prophecy

We have in the New Testament an inspired comment upon this scripture, which wholly relieves us of any necessity of making conjectures as to its application. In Galatians 4:26–27, we read, "Jerusalem which is above is free, which is the mother of us all. For it is written, Rejoice, thou barren that barest not; break forth and cry, thou that travailest not; for the desolate hath many more children than she which hath an husband." We know, therefore, from God's own word, that "Jerusalem which is above," the New Jerusalem, is the subject of this chapter.

This also serves as a key to many other references to Jerusalem, in the prophecies. From the promises in this chapter, telling of the stability of Jerusalem, and of the return of her children, which plainly refer to the Jerusalem which is above, "which cometh down from God out of heaven," we may understand all the other promises to Jerusalem and its inhabitants. They all apply to the New Jerusalem, which is to take the place of the present city of Jerusalem, and to abide for ever, after the earth has been made new.

The Present Jerusalem and the Old Covenant

"Jerusalem which now is," "is in bondage with her children." Gal. 4:25. Still more; the covenant from mount Sinai, "which gendereth to bondage," is Hagar; "for this Agar [Hagar] is mount Sinai in Arabia, and answereth to Jerusalem which now is, and is in bondage with her children." Every one, therefore, who builds his hopes upon Jerusalem which now exists in the land of Palestine, and who makes every promise of God depend upon the return of the people of God, or any part of them, to that city, is still in the bondage of the old covenant, with the veil still over his face. He is tarrying at mount Sinai, instead of coming to mount Zion, and to the heavenly Jerusalem, the city of the Living God.

Jerusalem Old and New

Many cities on this earth have suffered almost total destruction by fire, and have been rebuilt, yet that fact is not considered as making any break in the continuity of those cities. Rome, for instance, is still said to have been built seven hundred and fifty years before Christ, although there is scarcely a building in the city that was in existence in the days of Christ, and the city was almost wholly destroyed by fire in the reign of Nero, and has suffered from fire many times before and since. Take the city under consideration, namely Jerusalem. It was laid in ruins, its walls demolished, and its chief buildings burned, by Nebuchadnezzar, and afterwards it suffered still greater ravages by the hands of the Romans under Titus, yet it is always thought and spoken of as the city of David and

Solomon. When we speak of Rome and Jerusalem, we do not feel compelled to designate whether we refer to the time before their destruction, or after, since it is Rome and Jerusalem from beginning to end, no matter what vicissitudes they have passed through. Even so it is in the prophecies concerning Jerusalem. The Bible does not always specify, and say that now it refers to the old city, and now to the New Jerusalem, but speaks simply of Jerusalem, leaving the context, and the promises or threatenings, as the case may be, to determine to which state in the history of the city the words apply. The Lord has gone to prepare a place in the heavens, to build up a new city (See John 14:1–3; Ps. 102:16), which is to come down from God out of heaven, to occupy the place now occupied by the city known among men as Jerusalem; and when that city comes down, it will be considered as the old city rebuilt, made new; and so it is always spoken of in the Bible. It may be taken as a fact beyond all contradiction, that there is not a single Bible promise concerning Jerusalem, which applies to Jerusalem in its present condition, or as it has been at any time in its history. Every promise of restoration embraces its being so changed by the Lord as to be incorruptible, imperishable.

The Bride, The Lamb's Wife

From the very beginning, God has considered Himself as occupying the close relation of husband to His people. Read the prophecies of Ezekiel, Jeremiah, and the whole of Hosea. The third chapter of Jeremiah is especially plain. "Turn, O backsliding children, saith the Lord; for I am married unto you." Verse 14. And then the Lord tells what He will do if they will return, using words that can apply only to the redeemed state. Speaking of the making of the new covenant, God says that His people broke the old covenant, "although I was an husband unto them." Jer. 31:32. So, coming to the New Testament, we read that we are to be married to Him that is raised from the dead, that we may bring forth fruit unto God (Rom. 7:4); Paul writes, "I have espoused you to one husband, and I may present you as a chaste virgin to Christ" (2 Cor. 11:2); and in the fifth of Ephesians we read that the same close relation exists between Christ and His people that exists between a man and his wife. See verses 22–32. So by a change in the metaphor, or an enlargement of it, the city of God, Jerusalem, is considered as married to Christ. The very land itself where God's people dwell, is married to Him. This is perfectly in harmony with the fact that Christ, who is "the firstborn among many brethren," is also "the everlasting Father." It is not a mixed metaphor, but the expression of a deeper meaning, a more intimate relation, than human minds have conceived. The chapter before us, therefore, presents Jerusalem as a wife forsaken by her husband, and mourning her widowhood and childlessness, but comforted by the assurance that she has not really been cast off, and is not forgotten, but is still owned by her husband, and will be honoured by Him. The time when these promises will be fulfilled is set forth in Rev. 21; Zech. 14:1–11; and Isa. 49:13–23, all of which should be read in this connection. It is "the Bride, the Lamb's wife," that is addressed.

The Different Phases of Jerusalem's Experience

There was a time when the glory of God was seen resting over the temple in Jerusalem, and filling it. 2 Chron. 7:1–3. God owned that city as His earthly dwelling place, and the promise to its inhabitants was that if they obeyed Him, and refrained from breaking the Sabbath, the city should stand for ever. Jer. 17:24–25. They did not heed His words, and the city was destroyed by Nebuchadnezzar; yet a holy seed was left in it, and the promise of restoration accompanied the threat of its destruction. According to the promise, Christ, "the Desire of all nations," came to the city and temple, but was rejected. Then He wept over it, mourning in bitterness of grief, that the city had so persistently refused His gracious calls, and said, "Behold, your house is left unto you desolate." But this was not to be for ever, for He added, "I say unto you, Ye shall not see Me henceforth, till ye shall say, Blessed is He that cometh in the name of the Lord." Matt. 23:37–39. The centuries that have passed since that time have been only "a little moment" with Him in whose sight a thousand years are but as yesterday when it is past, and as a watch in the night. Not for a moment has the Lord forgotten Zion; its walls are continually before Him, and it is graven upon the palms of His hands. Even though the mountains depart, and the hills be removed, yet His kindness and love will not depart from the city which He has chosen, nor from her children. Consequently even today the faithful worshipers of God direct their prayers to Him, and "look up," thus praying with their faces towards Jerusalem.

The Rebuilding of Jerusalem

No; God has not divorced His spouse (Isa. 1:1), nor cast away His people. Rom. 11:1. He loves them with tender affection. He will return, and will build again the tabernacle of David, which is fallen down, and will build again the ruins thereof, and will set it up; that the residue of men may seek after the Lord; and this He will do by the proclamation of the Gospel to the Gentiles; for it is only from the Gentiles, the nations, that Israel is taken. God chose Abraham from among the Gentiles, for there was no such thing as a Jew or an Israelite, in name, until long after the days of that patriarch. He called Israel out of Egypt, that through them His name might be made known in all the earth. Their business was to be missionaries to the heathen; but instead of performing their mission, they were content to settle down in the land of Palestine, around Jerusalem. Instead of enlarging the place of their habitation, to include all the world, they became conservative, which is another name for selfish, and shut everybody else away from the blessings which they enjoyed, and thereby lost the blessings themselves. Whoever would exclude another from the blessings of the Lord, excludes himself. But God's purpose will be carried out. All who are really born from above, having the New Jerusalem for their mother, will make its glories and its power known, until its fame reaches every part of the earth. As a consequence the place that Jerusalem now occupies will be too small; it "shall break forth and spread abroad on the right hand, and on the left" (See Zech. 14:4), and its seed "shall inherit the Gentiles, and make the desolate cities to be inhabited." Jerusalem, as it will be when the Lord appears in His glory, will be such a city as the world has never yet seen.

Jerusalem's Beautiful Stones

"Thou shalt arise, and have mercy upon Zion; for the time to favour her, yea, the set time, is come. For thy servants take pleasure in her stones, and favour the dust thereof. So shall the heathen fear the name of the Lord, and all the kings of the earth Thy glory." Ps. 102:13–15. What is there in the dust and stones of Jerusalem, in which one can take pleasure? – Nothing whatever, in "Jerusalem which now is." The stones of old Jerusalem are no better than the stones of any other city, and its dust is as disagreeable as that of Constantinople, or any other Eastern city. The stones in which the children of Jerusalem take pleasure as the sapphires and agates and carbuncles, which are laid in "fair colours." Read the list of them in Rev. 21:18–21. The dust of its street is "pure gold, as it were transparent glass." There is something in which to delight; there is a city that will indeed be "the joy of the whole earth." Ps. 48:2.

The Gathering of Armed Forces About Jerusalem

The closing portion of this chapter presents a picture that is drawn out more fully in the book of Revelation. We have already seen that the New Jerusalem, prepared in heaven, comes down to this earth; but nothing that has thus far been noted indicates what condition of things it finds when it comes. This we learn from Rev. 20, and incidentally from other Scriptures. The passage before us says that although the city with its inhabitants will be far from oppression, and will be free from fear, yet "they shall surely gather," and that, too, against the city. In the chapter referred to in the Revelation we learn that after the close of the thousand years, during which Satan will be bound, while all the righteous who have ever lived on earth will be in heaven, sitting on thrones of judgment, deciding the penalty due to the wicked (Rev. 20:3–6; 1 Cor. 6:2–3; Ps. 149:4–9), Satan will be loosed, because all the wicked of earth will be raised, and he will go forth among them, to gather them to battle against the Lord. The statement that all the nations thus gathered "went up on the breadth of the earth, and compassed the camp of the saints about, and the beloved city; and fire came down from God out of heaven, and devoured them," shows that the beloved city will come down to this earth before the earth has been purified by the fires of the last day, and while the wicked are yet here. As Eden remained on the earth a time after the curse came, so it will come back before the curse is removed. But though the wicked, under the leadership of Satan himself, will gather together against the city of God, they cannot prosper, because they are not gathered by the Lord. No weapon that they can forge against the city will have any effect upon it. No cannon ball will ever be able to touch one of its stones. God Himself has created the smith that blows the coals of fire, in order to manufacture the weapon to destroy, and therefore since the man himself is nothing in comparison with God, the weapon that he makes cannot be anything. When the wicked come against the city, fire comes down from God out of heaven, and devours them, and at the same time melts the earth, while the city of God will ride upon the sea of fire as the ark rode safely upon the waters of the flood. Then will the saints "dwell with the devouring fire," and "with everlasting burnings." Isa. 33:15–16. The saints safe in the city will behold, and see the reward of the wicked, but it will not come nigh them.

The Safety of Jerusalem and Its Inhabitants

What will constitute their safety in that terrible time? – The answer is, "In righteousness shalt thou be established." The righteousness in which they will be established is the righteousness of God, that is by the faith of Jesus Christ. But that righteousness is theirs now. Therefore the lesson that is designed for us to learn from the statement of the things to come is the perfect security that we now have against all the assaults of the devil. Just as safe as the people of God will be in the holy city amid the fires that will destroy the wicked, so safe are they now from every sort of evil that Satan would bring upon them, if they but trust in the Lord, and abide in Him. Satan and all his host cannot forge a weapon of any sort, visible or invisible, whether designed to destroy the body or the soul, which can pierce the armour that is provided for the people of God. "The eternal God is Thy refuge, and underneath are the everlasting arms."

> "Not rocks nor hills could guard so well
> Fair Salem's happy ground,
> As those eternal arms of love,
> That every saint surround."

And no one can pluck a saint out of those protecting arms. Blessed be the name of the Lord, into which the righteous run, and are safe!

CHAPTER 68

A GRACIOUS OFFER TO THE POOR

(Isa. 55:1–13, Lowth's Translation)

1. Ho! every one that thirsteth, come ye to the waters! And that hath no silver, come ye, buy, and eat! Yea, come, buy ye without silver; and without price, wine and milk.

2. Wherefore do ye weigh out your silver for that which is not bread? And your riches, for that which will not satisfy? Attend, and hearken unto Me; and eat that which is truly good; and your soul shall feast itself with the richest delicacies.

3. Incline your ear, and come unto Me; attend, and your soul shall live; and I will make with you an everlasting covenant; I will give you the gracious promises made to David, which shall never fail.

4. Behold, for a witness to the peoples I have given Him; a leader, and a lawgiver to the nations.

5. Behold, the nations whom thou knewest not thou shalt call; and the nation who knew not thee shall run unto thee, for the sake of Jehovah thy God; and for the Holy One of Israel, for He hath glorified thee.

6. Seek ye Jehovah, while He may be found; call ye upon Him, while He is near at hand;

7. Let the wicked forsake his way, and the unrighteous man his thoughts; and let him return unto Jehovah, for He will receive him with compassion; and unto our God, for He aboundeth in forgiveness.

8. For My thoughts are not your thoughts; neither are your ways My ways, saith Jehovah.

9. For as the heavens are higher than the earth, so are My ways higher than your ways, and My thoughts than your thoughts.

459

10. Verily, like as the rain descendeth, and the snow, from the heavens; and thither it doth not return, except it moisteneth the earth, and maketh it generate, and put forth its increase; that it may give seed to the sower, and bread to the eater;

11. So shall be the word, which goeth forth from My mouth; it shall not return unto Me fruitless; but it shall effect that which I have willed; and make the purpose succeed, for which I have sent it.

12. Surely with joy shall ye go forth, and with peace shall ye be led onward; the mountains and the hills shall burst forth before you into song; and all the trees of the field shall clap their hands.

13. Instead of the thorny bushes shall grow up the fir tree; and instead of the bramble shall grow up myrtle; and it shall be unto Jehovah for a memorial; for a perpetual sign, which shall not be abolished.

Real, Spiritual Water

In this chapter we have the very same call that is given in John 7:37, and Rev. 22:17. With God is the Fountain of Life. Ps. 36:9. He is "the Fountain of living waters." Jer. 2:13. Jesus Christ is the Rock whence flows the streams of water for the refreshing of the people. 1 Cor. 10:4. This last reference, namely to the giving of the water to the Israelites in the desert, shows that the water which the Lord offers is real water. It is such water as will support life, even animal life; for the beasts as well as the people drank of the water in the wilderness. Nevertheless it was spiritual drink. 1 Cor. 10:4. Thus we are taught that if we recognize the Lord in His gifts day by day, – in our daily food and drink, – we shall find them not only nourishment to our bodies, but to our souls as well. We have nothing whatever, except what the Lord gives us. All things proceed from Him, from His very Being, His life. But God is Spirit, therefore everything that proceeds from Him must be spiritual. He gives nothing to mankind, except that which is spiritual. He "hath blessed us with all spiritual blessings in heavenly things in Christ." Eph. 1:3, margin. If the Israelites in the desert had recognized the Source of that water which they drank every day, and had given Him the glory due to His name, they would not only have experienced the power of an endless life, but they would have been able to impart the same to others wherever they went. See John 7:37–39. God calls us to realities. We have today the same opportunity of drinking from the Living Rock that Israel of old had. May we make better use of it than they did! Let us not fall after the same example of unbelief!

The Best Things to be Had for Nothing

The best things are to be had for nothing, because money cannot be mentioned in connection with them; they are above all price. Men strive for money; they scheme, and plan, and even fight for it, as though it were the chief thing to be desired; yet it will not purchase the things that they most stand in need of: health, life, love. Some one will say that money is necessary in this world, under the present circumstances, since even the necessaries of life, as for instance, water, must be bought of corporations that have gained a monopoly of them. True; but the promise is, "Your heavenly Father knoweth that ye have need of all these things. But seek ye first the kingdom of God, and His righteousness, and all these things shall be added unto you." Matt. 6:32–33. The first thing is not to make a living; indeed, we do not have that to do at all, for God gives us our living, our life, for He is our life. Our first and only business is to glorify God with the life which He has given us so freely. If men would but believe this fact, and would always remember it, there would not be so many compromises and denials of the truth, on the ground that it is necessary in order to live.

No; the Lord says, "Hear, and your soul shall live." Again the objection will be made, "But that means spiritual life!" Well, suppose it does: which is greater and more enduring, physical life or spiritual life? Is not "the life everlasting" greater than the life for a few days? Does not the greater include the less? If God can give us life for eternity, does it not stand to reason that He can keep us in life the short time that we have to spend in this present world? "O ye of little faith!" How can a man persuade himself that he believes in and trusts the Lord for salvation to all eternity, when he is afraid to keep His commandments, lest he should lose his living?

"Hear, and your soul shall live." The God who says this is the God who gives life to the dead. Men will repeat day after day, and year after year, "I believe in the resurrection of the dead," and yet when it comes to trusting the Lord for daily bread wherewith to sustain their life in this present time, they dare not risk it. Do you not see that belief in the power of God to raise the dead involves belief in His power to sustain our present life, and to give us all things necessary thereto? Why will men persist in separating the things of religion from their daily life? The proof that God is "abundantly able to save" is the fact that He saves us and gives us life now.

God's Gifts All Good

God wishes all people to enjoy life and all good things. The trouble with them is that they have a false idea of what good things are. Our taste has been perverted, so that we naturally call evil good, and good evil. We need to accept the exceeding great and precious promises of God, by which we are made partakers of the Divine nature, and then we shall have correct taste and judgment. We shall then like that which is really good, even though to our present, perverted taste it is insipid. That was the lack with Israel of old. They were fed with spiritual food, bread from heaven; but they did not appreciate it, and did not recognize and thank the Giver, and so they were not transformed and made spiritual by it. It was the very best food that anybody on this earth ever had to eat, the food of the angels which excel in strength, "the bread of the mighty," calculated to give inconceivable strength, yet they said, "Our soul is dried away," and, "our soul loatheth this light bread." Num. 11:6; 21:5. Two things are to be taken into consideration in determining whether or not a thing is good. The first is the effect that it has; is it productive of good or ill results? If it is to be followed by good results, then it is good; if evil results follow, then it must be bad, no matter how pleasant it may be to our sight and taste. Then follows the matter of taste. Everything that is really good tastes good, although our perverted senses may not think so at first. But when we know that a certain thing is good, and that it produces only good, then we can educate our taste so that it will recognize the good, and will find it exceedingly pleasant. In due time, if we allow our senses to be educated by the Lord, we shall find that everything that is harmful is disgusting. But it is so only to one who has the Divine nature.

The Sure Mercies of David

"I will make an everlasting covenant with you, even the sure mercies of David." Note that this follows the statement, "Hear, and your soul shall live." That is, the sure mercies of David embrace the resurrection of the dead. God made great promises to David, but none of them could be fulfilled except by the resurrection, and David so understood them. He confessed that he was a stranger and a sojourner as all his fathers – Abraham, Isaac, and Jacob – were. Ps. 39:12. Now all that say such things declare that they seek a better country, that is an heavenly; "wherefore God is not ashamed to be called their God; for He hath prepared for them a city." Heb. 11:13–16. Christ is the Son of David, and He is to sit upon the throne of His father David, and to "reign over the house of Jacob for ever." Luke 1:31–33.

But the fact that the sure mercies of David are performed only through Christ and the resurrection, shows that everybody who believes and accepts Christ has a share in them; for Christ died and rose again for all. Indeed, this is seen from the text before us, for the call is unlimited. The call to drink, and to buy bread and wine and milk without money and without price, is issued to all who need. It is the gracious call of the Gospel to all needy, thirsty, sin-sick souls. Well, to the very same ones is it said, "I will make an everlasting covenant with you, even the sure mercies of David," and this shows that whoever accepts the Gospel becomes a member of the house of David, a subject of the kingdom of Israel. So we find that Israel is not any nation known and recognized on this earth, but is "the righteous nation which keepeth the truth." Isa. 26:2. For such the gates of the heavenly city, the New Jerusalem, will open. Rev. 22:14.

Israel the Banner

Christ is Israel. See Isa. 49:3: "Thou art My Servant; Israel, in whom I will be glorified." Nobody can be saved, except in Christ,

463

and all who are in Christ are Abraham's seed, "and heirs according to the promise." Gal. 3:29. Therefore all who are in Christ are Israel, and none others are. But since Christ is Israel, and Christ is the Banner that is lifted up to the people, it follows that Israel is the ensign to the nations, the banner round which all people are called to rally. From every nation, and kindred, and tongue, and people will men come, and form part of the nation of Israel, and that which will attract them will be the indwelling Christ glorifying His people. He is near to all who call upon Him. Yea, He is near to all, waiting to be called by them. He has not forsaken any man, but has come seeking them, and all who will but turn to Him, instead of running away from Him, will find abundance of pardon, and, being pardoned, they will be enrolled as members of the kingdom of Israel. Not only so, but they will be reckoned as princes, even kings, and priests; for the kingdom of David, over which Christ rules, counts among its subjects none of lower rank than king.

The Thoughts of God

Who can think the thoughts of infinity? – Manifestly none except Him who is infinite. Therefore God must dwell in us, thinking His own high thoughts. Otherwise all our thoughts will be wrong, and to no purpose. In calling upon us to forsake our ways and our thoughts, God does not wish us to be nonentities; He wishes us to think and act, but the spring of all our acts and thoughts must be Himself. He is the Fountain of real life; therefore unless He dwells in us, and His real presence is continually recognized, our life will be but a mirage. What a wonderful truth, that we may have God to think in us, so that our brains will be but the organ of the mind of God! Then will be manifest the miracle of God dwelling and acting in the flesh. This wonderful privilege is offered to all. It is part of the everlasting covenant, the sure mercies of David.

The Word of God Bearing Fruit

We have ventured to change one word in the translation given by Lowth. He has translated the 10 verse the same as it is rendered in the ordinary version, namely, "For as the rain cometh down, and the snow from heaven, and returneth not thither, but watereth the earth," etc. This is not an exact rendering of the Hebrew, and is misleading. The Hebrew expression is the same as in Gen. 32:26. "I will not let Thee go *except* Thou bless me." Therefore the text should read that the rain and the snow return not to the heaven except they water the earth. In the Polychrome Bible the verse is so rendered, and also in the French of Segond, and therefore we have taken the liberty to put it into Lowth's translation, in order that the reader may not overlook it. The scripture does not say that the rain and the snow do not return to heaven at all, but that they do not return thither without having watered the earth, and caused it to bring forth. Then they return laden with the fruit of the earth. Even so shall it be with the Word of the Gospel. It shall not return to the Lord empty, but shall bring forth fruit. To our short sight it may seem as if the Word of God were spoken to no purpose; but God says that it shall accomplish that to which He has sent it. He does not speak in vain. If therefore we will but speak the Word of the Lord, God will see that as in the case of Samuel, none of our words fall to the ground and perish. God's Word is the seed whence everything that grows from the ground comes; it is also the seed that regenerates men, and makes them bring forth fruit unto God.

The Earth Renewed

The closing verses of this chapter present a picture of the earth made new, purified from the curse of thorns and thistles, and bringing forth in perfection, as in the beginning. All this is to be accomplished by the Word of God, the same word which He puts into the mouth of His servants. See Isa. 51:16. This is a still further indication that the sure mercies of David, assured, by the everlasting covenant, to all who heed the gracious call to come to the Lord and to eat and drink from Him, are fulfilled only in the world to come, in the new earth. That is, the new earth is the consummation of them; but they must be accepted and enjoyed here in this present time, or else they will never be realized. It is only as men receive the Word of the Lord, and are transformed by it, – tasting the good word of God, and the powers of the world to come, – that the earth is made new for their habitation.

A Grand Concert

What a blessed concert that will be, when the mountains and the hills break forth into singing, and all the trees of the field clap their hands in applause! Who would not like to be there to hear and see? But, says some wise objector, "that is all figurative; it is not meant to be taken literally, because the mountains and the hills cannot sing, and the trees cannot clap their hands; indeed, they have no hands to clap." Oh, foolish wisdom, which knows so much that it shuts out all knowledge! Even so the disciples of Jesus wondered what He meant when He said that He should rise from the dead. They were sure that His words could not be taken literally, because they thought they knew that He could not die, and rise again. But they were mistaken. If instead of "reasoning" as they did, they had believed His words, they could have been saved much shame and confusion. Suppose that instead of disputing with the Word of the Lord, we allow it to teach us. He says that the mountains and the hills shall break forth into singing, and therefore we believe that they will do so, and that we shall hear them. We shall then learn something about music, which the greatest composers of earth cannot teach us. There is light which human eyes cannot see, and there are many sounds which human ears are too dull to hear; but God both sees and hears. When we become so spiritual that we are worthy to have spiritual bodies, then we shall be able to see and hear things that have never yet come within man's comprehension. These things are made known to us by the Holy Spirit; let us therefore yield ourselves to Him, that we may be made wholly spiritual, and thus be able to attain true wisdom, the wisdom of God. "Eye hath not seen, nor ear heard, neither have entered into the heart of man, the things which God hath prepared for them that love Him. But God hath revealed them unto us by His Spirit."

CHAPTER 69

ISRAEL, THE GENTILES, AND THE SABBATH

(Isa. 56:1–12)

1. "Thus says Jehovah: Keep the law, practice righteousness; for My salvation will soon come, and My righteousness be soon manifested.

2. Happy the man who practices this, the mortal who holds fast thereto, keeping the Sabbath, so as not to profane it, and keeping his hand from any evil.

3. Let not the foreigner, who has joined himself to Jehovah, say: Jehovah will surely separate me from His people; and let not the eunuch say: Behold, I am a dry tree. For thus says Jehovah: As for the eunuchs who keep My Sabbaths, and choose that which I delight in, I will give them, in My house and within My walls, a monument and a memorial better than sons and daughters; I will give them an everlasting memorial which shall not be cut off. And as for the foreigners who join themselves to Jehovah to minister to Him, and to love the name of Jehovah, to be His servants, – every one who so keeps the Sabbath as not to profane it, and who lays hold on My covenant, I will bring to My holy mountain, and gladden in My house of prayer; his burnt offerings and his sacrifices shall be accepted upon My altar; for My house shall be called a house of prayer for all peoples. The oracle of the Lord, Jehovah, who gathers the outcasts of Israel is: Yet will I gather others to Israel, to those of Israel who are already gathered.

9. All ye wild beasts in field and forest, come hither to devour!

10. My watchmen are all blind, and know not how to give heed; they are all dumb dogs which cannot bark, Crouching and lying down, loving to slumber.

11. And the dogs are greedy, they know not how to be satisfied, they all turn to their own way, each for his own lucre.

12. Come, they say let me fetch wine, let us carouse with mead, and tomorrow shall be as today, an exceeding high day."

This is a wonderfully comprehensive chapter, showing the essential unity of the Gospel message in all times, and linking the days of the ancient prophets with ours. Here we have an exhortation to keep the law, based on the fact that the salvation of the Lord is near. This corresponds with the message in Rev. 14:7, "Fear God, and give glory to Him; for the hour of His Judgment is come; and worship Him that made heaven, and earth, and the sea, and the fountains of waters." In this chapter we find that the conditions of salvation were the same in the days of Isaiah that they are today, and that the relation between God and all people, whether called Jews or Gentiles, has not changed in the least in the last four thousand years.

Gentiles Commanded to Keep the Sabbath

We often hear the question asked, "Where in the Bible do you find that the Gentiles were ever commanded to keep the ten commandments or the Sabbath?" The answer is that we find it everywhere in the Bible; for God's commandments are for all mankind; but here in this chapter we have the matter very definitely stated. First, we have the general command, "Keep the law; practice righteousness." Then the foreigner, the Gentile, is especially singled out, and the promise is made to him, if he will keep the Sabbath. Then, as well as in the days of Peter, the promise was unto all that were afar off. Act 2:39. There can be no question as to which day is referred to in this connection. Nobody ever questions the fact that in the times before the first advent of Christ, at least, no other day than that kept by the faithful Jews, the seventh day of the week, was ever called the Sabbath. This is the day that the Gentiles are exhorted to keep. And since the special exhortation is based on the nearness of the salvation of the Lord, it follows that until the coming of the Lord the call to the Gentiles to keep the Sabbath holds good. "The Sabbath was made for man," and every creature that comes under that head is under obligation to God to keep it.

Only One Nation Acknowledged by the Lord

God recognizes only one nation on earth, and it is not one of the nations of earth. That nation is the nation of Israel, of whom it was said by inspiration of God, "The people shall dwell alone, and shall not be reckoned among the nations." It is "the righteous nation which keepeth the truth" (Isa. 26:2), and that does not describe any nation recognized as a nation on this earth. The people of Israel, God's own chosen nation, are on this earth counted as strangers and foreigners (Heb. 11:13), their names and their citizenship being recorded only in heaven. Luke 10:20; Heb. 12:23: Phil. 3:20, R.V. On the other hand, all "Gentiles in the flesh" are "aliens from the commonwealth of Israel, and strangers from the covenants of promise, having no hope, and without God in the world." Eph. 2:11–12. Only when they come to God, being reconciled to Him through the blood of the cross of Christ, are they "no more strangers and foreigners, but fellow-citizens with the saints, and of the household of God, and are built on the foundation of the apostles and prophets, Jesus Christ Himself being the chief corner stone." Eph. 2:19–20. It is God's eternal purpose to "gather together in one all things in Christ" (Eph. 1:10), and the kingdom of which He is the Head is that of Israel. It is a nation of overcomers. Israel means a prince, and every one of the subjects of Christ is a prince, a king. Jesus Christ is King of kings. All His subjects have high rank. There are no "mean persons" in all His dominions.

The God of the Gentiles Also

From this chapter we learn that God was as solicitous for the salvation of the Gentiles in the days of Isaiah as He is today. There was never a time when God was exclusive, shutting Himself up to a particular class, He was the God of the Gentiles then as well as now. Rom. 3:29–30. And He is the God of the Jews today as much as He was then, for He has not cast off His people. The text says, "My house shall be called a house of prayer for all people," and these are the words that Jesus quoted when he cleared the temple of the buyers and sellers. Mark 11:17. Therefore we find that never was the temple designed by the Lord exclusively for the people called Jews. It was never the design of God that any person should be deprived of the privileges of His sanctuary. The wall separating the "court of the Gentiles" from the sanctuary proper, where the Jews were permitted to enter, was the "middle wall of partition" which the Jews themselves, in their selfish pride, had erected.

Gathering the Gentiles to Israel

Jesus said: "And other sheep I have, which are not of this fold; them also I must bring, and they shall hear My voice; and there shall be one fold, and one Shepherd." John 10:16. This is exactly the same thing that is stated in our lesson. "The Lord God which gathereth the outcasts of Israel saith, Yet will I gather others to him, besides those that are gathered to him." And this also is the same thing that was stated by James at the meeting of the apostles and elders in Jerusalem: "Simeon hath declared how God at the first did visit the Gentiles, to take out of them a people for His name. And to this agree the words of the prophets; as it is written, After this I will return, and will build again the tabernacle of David, which is fallen down; and I will build again the ruins thereof, and will set it up; that the residue of men might seek after the Lord, and all the Gentiles, upon whom My name is called, saith the Lord, who doeth all these things. Known unto God are all His works from the beginning of the world." Act 15:14–18. The Lord is the same from the beginning, and His works are always the same. He works no differently in the closing part of the Gospel from what He did in the beginning. He called Abraham when he was but one (Isa. 51:2), and took him from among the heathen. Josh. 24:2–3. All along in the history of Israel He kept adding to them from among the heathen, as in the case of the harlot Rahab, and Ruth the Moabitess, both of whom are among the ancestors of Christ after the flesh. God also sent prophets to the Gentiles, as in the case of Jonah, warning them to repent; and one prophet, Jeremiah, was even before his birth ordained to be a prophet to the Gentiles. See Jer. 1:5, where the word "nations" is exactly the same that is rendered elsewhere "heathen" or "Gentiles." In the Bible, "nations," "heathen," and "Gentiles," are all the same. Israel was begun by the calling of one from among the heathen; it was built up by the calling of others, in spite of the prejudices of those who did not understand the plan of the Lord, and who wished to make Him as exclusive as they were; and the promise still is, "Yet will I gather others to Israel, to those of Israel who are already gathered." And when all have been gathered out, through the preaching of the Gospel, there will then be but one nation in all the earth, for the word of the Lord is, "The nation and kingdom that will not serve thee shall perish." Isa. 60:12. "And the Lord shall be King over all the earth; in that day shall there be one Lord, and His name One." Zech. 14:9.

The people who are thus gathered to Israel will all be Sabbath keepers. The characteristic of that nation will be that every individual will keep the truth, the law of God. It will be established in righteousness. Isa. 54:14. Of those who obey the message, "Fear God, and give glory to Him; for the hour of His Judgment is come; and worship Him that made heaven, and earth, and the sea, and the fountains of waters," which is the message set forth in this chapter, it is said, "Here are they that keep the commandments of God, and the faith of Jesus." Rev. 14:12. There are glorious promises to those Gentiles who keep the Sabbath of the Lord in spirit and in truth, and who by their faith and trust in Christ become members of God's household, the commonwealth of Israel. Who will accept the whole Gospel, and not be content with man's narrow perversion of it?

Perils of the Last Days

The last days are to be perilous, because "men shall be lovers of their own selves, ... lovers of pleasures more than lovers of God; having a form of godliness, but denying the power thereof." 2 Tim. 3:1–5. The prophecy before us, like to many others in the Bible, warns us that in the church of God, among those who have been set to be watchmen, to feed the flock of God, and to give warning of danger, there will be those who will feed themselves rather than the flock, and will feed upon the flock. Acts 20:28–30; Eze. 34:2–6. Men's hearts will be overcharged with surfeiting and drunkenness, and so the day of the Lord will come upon them unawares. Luke 21:34. Eating and drinking will be the snare of the last days. Not that people should not eat and drink; that is a necessity of nature, and is designed by God to be the great means by which He is recognized and glorified; in the preceding chapter God calls men to eat that which is good; but the trouble is that men have perverted the good gifts of God, and as their table has become a snare to them, they have been overcome with a spirit of slumber. "But ye, brethren, are not in darkness, that that day should overtake you as a thief. Ye are all the children of light, and the children of the day; we are not of the night, nor of darkness. Therefore let us not sleep, as do others; but let us watch and be sober." This chapter is given to us as a warning; shall we not heed it?

CHAPTER 70

DWELLERS ON HIGH

(Isa. 57:1–21, Lowth's Translation)

1. The righteous man perisheth, and no one considereth; And pious men are taken away, and no one understandeth that the righteous man is taken away because of the evil.

2. He shall go in peace; he shall rest in his bed; even the perfect man; he that walketh in the straight path.

3. But ye, draw ye near hither, O ye sons of the sorceress; Ye seed of the adulterer, and of the harlot!

4. Of whom do ye make your sport? At whom do ye widen your mouth, and loll the tongue? Are ye not apostate children, a false seed?

5. Burning with the lust of idols under every garden tree; slaying the children in the valleys, under the clefts of the rocks?

6. Among the smooth stones of the valley is thy portion; there, these are thy lot; even to these hast thou poured out thy libation, hast thou presented thine offering. Can I see these things with acquiescence?

7. Upon a high and lofty mountain hast thou set thy bed; even thither hast gone up to offer sacrifice.

8. Behind the door and the doorposts hast thou set thy memorial; thou hast departed from Me, and art gone up; thou hast enlarged thy bed. And thou hast made a covenant with them; thou hast loved their bed; thou hast provided a place for it.

9. And thou hast visited the king with a present of oil; and hast multiplied thy precious ointments; and thou hast sent thine ambassadors afar; and hast debased thyself even to Hades.

10. In the length of thy journeys thou hast wearied thyself; Thou hast said, There is no hope; thou hast found the support of thy life by thy labour; therefore hast thou not utterly fainted.

11. And of whom hast thou been so anxiously afraid, that thou shouldst thus deal falsely? And hast not remembered Me, nor revolved it in thy mind? Is it not because I was silent, and winked; and thou fearest Me not?

12. But I will declare My righteousness; and thy deeds shall not avail thee.

13. When thou criest, let thine associates deliver thee; but the wind shall bear them away; a breath shall take them off. But he that trusteth in Me shall inherit the land, and shall possess My holy mountain.

14. Then will I say: Cast up, cast up the highway; make clear the way; remove every obstacle from the road of My people.

15. For thus saith Jehovah, the High and Lofty; inhabiting eternity; and whose name is the Holy One: the high and holy place will I inhabit; and with the contrite and humble of spirit; to revive the spirit of the humble, and to give life to the heart of the contrite.

16. For I will not always contend; neither for ever will I be wroth; for the spirit from before Me would be overwhelmed; and the living souls which I have made.

17. Because of his iniquity for a short time I was wroth; and I smote him; hiding My face in Mine anger. And he departed, turning back in the way of his own heart.

18. I have seen his ways; and I will heal him, and will be his guide; and I will restore comforts to him, and to his mourners.

19. I create the fruit of the lips: peace, peace, to him that is near, and to him that is afar off, saith Jehovah; and I will heal him.

20. But the wicked are like the troubled sea; for it can never be at rest; but its waters work up filth and mire.

21. There is no peace, saith my God, to the wicked.

A View of the Last Days

In this chapter we have a picture of the last days, – of the time of trouble immediately preceding the coming of the Lord. The student should remember that the destruction of ancient Babylon, and also of Jerusalem, which fell simply because it was dominated by the spirit of Babylon, was but a foretaste of the great destruction at the last day. The characteristic of those times was haughtiness, rejection of God, the exaltation of self above Him, and the persecution of those who were loyal to the truth. Even so will it be, only to a much greater degree, in the days of the coming of the Son of man. "In the last days perilous times shall come. For men shall be lovers of their own selves, covetous, boasters, proud, blasphemers, disobedient to parents, unthankful, unholy, without natural affection, trucebreakers, false accusers, incontinent, fierce, despisers of those that are good, traitors, heady, high-minded, lovers of pleasures more than lovers of God." "Yea, and all that will live godly in Christ Jesus shall suffer persecution. But evil men and seducers shall wax worse and worse, deceiving and being deceived." 2 Tim. 3:1–4,12–13. All this wickedness is to be found in the professed church of Christ, and the professed ministers of God are to be the leaders in the persecution of the despised faithful ones, even as it was in the former days when the Roman Babylon had the ascendancy. It will be remembered that in the fifty-sixth chapter of Isaiah, which was studied last week, where the Sabbath truth is presented as the standard for the rallying of God's people, the watchmen are represented as living only for themselves; and when a man lives only to please himself, he naturally despises those that are good.

Spiritual Adultery and its Fruit

Verse 3 of our present lesson addresses the children of the harlot, the apostate church which is described in Rev. 17:1–6. The church is Christ's lawful bride; for all the true members of it are set free from sin, that they "should be married to another, even to Him who is raised from the dead," that they may bring forth fruit unto God. Rom. 7:4. When the professed church departs from "the simplicity that is in Christ" (2 Cor. 11:3), and forsakes His law, that is adultery of the worst kind. The evil is always opposed to the good, and therefore we have in the fourth and fifth verses of our lesson the statement of the fact that this "false seed," these children of the harlot, are engaged in mocking and persecuting the good, even to death.

This corresponds to the words in Rev. 17:6: "And I saw the woman drunken with the blood of the saints, and with the blood of the martyrs of Jesus." James 5:5–8 shows that feasting and rioting, and persecution of the just, will be the characteristics of the last days; and the verses just referred to in Revelation show from what quarter these persecutions emanate. Compare also verses 7–9 of our lesson with Rev. 18:7–9 and onward, where we have a picture of the church's dalliance with the secular power, by which she obtains exalted position and wealth. These points amply establish the time when our lesson applies, and the events to which it refers. These things being settled, the rest is easy.

The Righteous Taken Away by Wickedness

In order also rightly to understand this chapter, it should be noted that in the Hebrew there is no trace of the words "to come," in the first verse. Accordingly Lowth and many other translators very properly omit them. The Hebrew word, a compound, is the same that is used in Gen. 47:13: "all the land of Canaan fainted *by reason of* the famine;" also in Gen. 36:7: "the land wherein they were strangers could not bear them *because of* their cattle;" and in Gen. 27:46: "I am weary of my life *because of* the daughters of Heth." The same word occurs in verse 16 of this chapter, and is rendered "from before," where the sense plainly indicates that the meaning is "because of." If God were for ever wroth, the spirits of men would be overwhelmed because of Him, or through Him. From this it will be seen that if the rendering placed in the margin of the Revised Version were inserted in the text, we should have the correct statement of the case. Thus: "The righteous perisheth, and no man layeth it to heart; and merciful men are taken away, none considering that *the righteous is taken away through wickedness.*"

The ordinary rendering leads to the supposition that God takes away the righteous to save them from evil that is coming, whereas the true rendering teaches us that in the last days righteous men will be taken away, by the evil. The Hebrew word rendered "taken away," indicates that violence is used. In the very last days, when God's Spirit shall have been fully and finally rejected by the apostate church, and the decree goes forth that anybody is at liberty to kill the righteous, we may be sure that none will be slain, because every one of God's people will in that time of trouble be delivered (Dan. 12:1); their death would not result in bringing anybody to the Lord, and God will not allow righteous blood to be shed uselessly; but before that point shall have been reached, when the blood of martyrs can yet be the seed which shall result in bringing in a harvest of souls, many will be obliged to witness for the truth with their lives.

Why not? Why should anybody shake his head at this statement? The world is always enmity against God, and since evil men and seducers are to wax worse and worse, how can it be supposed that the last days will be more free from persecution than former times have been. Of the little horn of Daniel 7, which represents modern Babylon, the apostate church, we read, "I beheld, and the same horn made war with the saints, and prevailed against them, until the Ancient of Days came, and Judgment was given to the saints of the Most High, and the time came that the saints possessed the kingdom." Those who are counting on an easy time in the service of the Lord, as the end approaches, are preparing themselves for a terrible disappointment.

A Substituted Memorial

Still further: In verse 8, we read, "Behind the door and the door posts hast thou set up *thy memorial*." This is evidently in opposition to God's memorial, which is the Sabbath of the fourth command-ment, the seventh day of the week. The words of this law were commanded to be written "upon the posts of thy house, and on thy gates" (Deut. 6:4–9), a sign that God was the Master of the house, and His law its rule; but in the place of this, "the church" has of its own motion, and without the slightest hint of Divine authority, introduced the observance of the first day of the week, as an indica-tion that it occupies the place of God, setting itself forth as God. This is the crowning act of spiritual adultery and idolatry. It will be over the Sabbath, over the question of whether God or "the church" is to be recognized as sole and supreme authority, that the persecu-tions of the last days will rage.

A Blessing for the Despised and Persecuted

But although the righteous may be slain by the wicked, and none may mark the place where he falls, and he himself, like his Lord, may be reckoned among the transgressors, "he shall rest in peace," while to the wicked who boast in their fancied security and power, there is no peace. Men may cast out the names of the humble ones who fall for the sake of the truth, and may esteem them as lost, but the voice from heaven, speaking especially of the perils and persecutions of the last days, says, "Blessed are the dead which die in the Lord from henceforth; yea, saith the Spirit, that they may rest from their labours; and their works do follow them." Rev. 14:13. For none of those who die in the Lord should we sorrow as do those who have no hope; but for those who fall in the last struggle of the truth against error there is a special blessing pronounced. Those whom the world and the worldly church most despise, are the ones whom the Lord most esteems.

"They shall dwell on high." "For thus saith the High and Lofty One, that inhabiteth eternity, whose name is Holy: I dwell in the high and holy place, with him also that is of a contrite and humble spirit." He dwells in both places at the same time. While dwelling in the high and holy place, God is also in the hearts of the humble and contrite ones. How can that be? It is because the hearts of such ones are His sanctuary, a holy place for the habitation of God through the Spirit, and He has raised them up, made them sit with Christ in the heavenly places, and has given them dominion "far above all principality and power." Eph. 1:19–23; 2:4–6. The promise is, "He that overcometh, and keepeth My works unto the end, to him will I give power over the nations." Rev. 2:27. Those whom the rulers of earth destroy are the real rulers, and never is their power greater than when they yield their bodies that they may not worship any false god. The kings of this world and the "princes of the church" will not know until the Judgment how many kings in the garb of labouring men they have caused to suffer martyrdom. As it was with Christ, even so will it be with His faithful followers. What wonderful riches there are in "the reproach of Christ," and what a privilege to be permitted to share it!

But there is hope held out to all. The Lord has no pleasure in the death of the wicked, but that he should turn from his wicked way, and live; and so He sends Christ, preaching "peace, peace to him that is near, and to him that is afar off." The Lord has healing for all who will turn to Him. His anger endures but for a moment, while His mercy endures for ever. The long-suffering of our God is salvation, and His salvation is very great. Jesus prayed for forgiveness for those who put Him to death, and Peter, filled with the Spirit, said to those who were His betrayers and murders, "Repent ye, therefore, and be converted." Now is the accepted time; now is the day of salvation.

CHAPTER 71

A DELIGHTFUL DAY

(Isa. 58:1–14, Lowth's Translation)

1. Cry aloud; spare not: like a trumpet lift up thy voice, and declare unto My people their transgression, and to the house of Jacob their sin.

2. Yet Me day after day they seek; and to know My ways they take delight; as a nation that doeth righteousness, and hath not forsaken the ordinance of their God. They continually enquire of Me concerning the ordinances of righteousness; they take delight to draw nigh unto God.

3. Wherefore have we fasted, and Thou seest not? Have we afflicted our souls, and Thou dost not regard? Behold, in the day of your fasting ye enjoy your pleasure; and all your demands of labour ye rigorously exact.

4. Behold, ye fast for strife and contention; and to smite with the fist the poor. Wherefore fast ye unto Me in this manner, to make your voice to be heard on high?

5. Is such then the fast which I choose: that a man should afflict his soul for a day? Is it, that he should bow down his head like a bulrush, and spread sackcloth and ashes for his couch? Shall this be called a fast, and a day acceptable to Jehovah?

6. Is not this the fast which I choose? To dissolve the bands of wickedness; to loosen the oppressive burdens; O deliver those that are crushed by violence; and that ye should break asunder every yoke?

7. Is it not to distribute thy bread to the hungry; and to bring the wandering poor into thy house? When thou seest the naked, that thou clothe him; and that thou hide not thyself from thine own flesh?

8. Then shall thy light break forth like the morning; and thy wounds shall speedily be healed over; and thy righteousness

shall go before thee; and the glory of Jehovah shall bring up thy rear.

9. Then shalt thou call, and Jehovah shall answer; thou shalt cry, and He shall say, Lo, I am here! If thou remove from the midst of thee the yoke; the pointing of the finger, and the injurious speech;

10. If thou bring forth thy bread to the hungry, and satisfy the afflicted soul; then shall thy light rise in obscurity, and thy darkness shall be as the noonday.

11. And Jehovah shall lead thee continually, and satisfy thy soul in the severest drought; and He shall renew thy strength; and thou shalt be like a well-watered garden, and like a flowing spring, whose waters never fail.

12. And they that spring forth from thee shall build the ancient ruins; the foundations of old time shall they raise up; and thou shalt be called the repairer of the broken mound; the restorer of paths to be frequented by inhabitants.

13. If thou restrain thy foot from the Sabbath; from doing thy pleasure on My holy day; and shalt call the Sabbath a delight; and the holy feast of Jehovah, honourable; and shalt honour it, by refraining from thy purpose; from pursuing thy pleasure, and from speaking vain words:

14. Then shalt thou delight thyself in Jehovah; and I will make thee ride on the high places of the earth; and I will feed thee on the inheritance of Jacob thy father; for the mouth of Jehovah hath spoken it.

The student surely cannot help noticing that although the entire book of Isaiah is one message, relating to one time, each one of these later chapters is complete in itself. It is as though the prophet himself had made the division, each chapter being the sermon for a certain day. The lesson for this day is one of the richest in the collection, and one day's study will no more than give us an introduction to it.

It will be noticed that in this lesson certain ones are addressed, and are exhorted to give a very definite message to the professed people of God. But a little way back the Lord has declared that His watchmen, – the regular ministers who are set to guard and feed the flock, – "are shepherds that cannot understand;" they "are blind, they are all without knowledge; they are all dumb dogs, they cannot bark; dreaming, lying down, loving to slumber." Therefore He issues a call to whomsoever will hear it, to lift up his voice like a trumpet, to awaken the people from their dangerous slumber. This shows that in the last days God will have men to proclaim His warning message, who are not reckoned among "the clergy," but whose qualification is that they love the Lord, and know His voice, and follow Him.

Tell the Whole Truth

The Lord says, "Spare not." That is, keep nothing back; withhold not. The word is the same as that used in Gen. 39:9, where Joseph says of Potiphar, "Neither hath he *kept back* anything from me." Paul obeyed the injunction, for he said to the elders of Ephesus, "I kept back nothing that was profitable unto you," "for I have not shunned to declare unto you all the counsel of God." Acts 20:20,27. It is true that Jesus said to His disciples, before His crucifixion, "I have yet many things to say unto you, but ye cannot bear them now." John 16:12. But whoever would make this an excuse for withholding from the people any truth that God has revealed unto him, ignores the words of Jesus immediately following, namely, "Howbeit, when He, the Spirit of truth is come, He will guide you into all the truth: for He shall not speak of Himself; but whatsoever He shall hear, that shall He speak: and He will show you things to come." God gives His servants light, in order that they may pass it on to others, and whoever keeps any of it back from the people, is unfaithful to his trust. One must certainly use judgment as to when and how the truth is presented to different persons, but it must not be his own worldly-wise judgment, but that of the Spirit of God. One who is guided by the Spirit of God will discern when a person whom he may meet is in a state of mind to listen to certain phases of truth, or whether or not it is wise to speak to him at all just then; but whoever keeps back truth that has been committed to him, quoting in his own behalf the words of Christ, "I have yet many things to say unto you, but ye cannot hear them now," takes himself out of the ranks of those who are sent, and places himself on a level with the Lord Himself. The Lord has no favourites among men; none whom He takes off in a corner, so to speak, and whispers to them something that He does not wish the others to hear; but what He says to His most intimate disciples, He says to all. Has the Lord revealed Himself to you in a marked manner? Then that is evidence that there is some other soul who is waiting for you to bring the message to him. Do not keep it back, but watch for the fitting opportunity to declare it.

A Warning Against Formality

The message of this chapter relates chiefly to fasting, a thing which is very much misunderstood and perverted. The universal tendency is to make a mere matter of form, an outward show. So it was with the Pharisees of old, against whose example God warns us. "When ye fast, be not, as the hypocrites, of a sad countenance; for they disfigure their faces, that they may appear unto men to fast." Matt. 6:16. "But thou, when thou fastest, anoint thine head, and wash thy face; that thou appear not unto men to fast, but unto thy Father which is in secret; and thy Father, which seeth in secret, shall reward thee openly." In the chapter before us, we find that the people are most active in what they are pleased to term their "religious duties." They go to meeting frequently, they love to listen to preaching, they fast and afflict their souls, and act, to all outward appearances, like a people that do righteousness; but God who looks on the heart and life, knows better. He judges men, not according to their profession, nor to their diligence in going to meeting, nor the length and frequency of their prayers, but "according to their works." Those who "profess that they know God, but in works they deny Him," are counted as the worst sinners. "He that saith he abideth in Him, ought himself also so to walk, even as He walked." 1 John 2:6. How did He walk? – He "went about doing good, and healing all that were oppressed of the devil; for God was with Him." Acts 10:38. The ones to whom this chapter is specially addressed, make their religion consist in fasting on certain days, and in having special seasons of "self-denial," thus confessing that the rest of the time they live to please themselves. The less Christian vitality there is in a people, the more scrupulous will they be in the observance of set forms, and of special religious days. But that will not satisfy the Lord. Read the very beginning of this prophecy. Isa. 1:11–15.

What Fasting Is

The mere act of fasting is in itself a very simple thing. It consists in abstaining entirely from food. Its object is to emphasize to the one fasting, the fact that he lives not by bread alone, but by every word that proceeds out of the mouth of God, and that it is God alone who supports him, and keeps him in life. It is to remind him that nothing that he has belongs to himself, but that, since it comes from "the God and Father of all," that which comes to him belongs to his brother man as well as to him, and that it is given into his hands only to use as the Lord's steward. Therefore the fast in which the Lord delights, is one where the bread is dealt to the hungry, and the poor are taken in and cared for.

What True Fasting Accomplishes for One

While it is impossible for a man to fast all the time, and the Lord would not have it done, because He "giveth us richly all things to enjoy," and tells us to eat that which is good, having made our food one of the chief means of revealing Himself and His Gospel to us, the effects of our fast are to be continual, and not to cease with the day. For one to afflict his soul for a day, does not please the Lord; indeed, doing penance is not what the Lord ever requires. But an acceptable fast to the Lord is one which reaches out beyond the day of abstinence from food, and affects the whole life. To make fasting, or any other religious act, a matter of strife and contention, is most displeasing to the Lord. Instead of contending over forms, the true people of God will be revealing the righteousness of God in their lives. Strife and debate never yet converted a single soul; that is done only by the life of Christ; and since He is in the heavens, hidden from the sight of mortals, it must be manifested in mortal flesh. So the acceptable fast unto the Lord is that which looses the bands of wickedness, and lets those who are oppressed by the devil go free. That means, of course, first of all, that one's own bands are unloosed, and he knows the freedom wherewith Christ makes men free. Fasting, therefore, is for the purpose of bringing the individual into closer relationship with Christ, and giving him a better understanding of His life; and this knowledge and companionship are to be lasting. Their fruits are to be seen in all the days that follow the special season of fasting. Men are to know that a fast has been held, not by any formal announcement of it, but by the results of it. A fast which leaves the faster still in the yoke of bondage, has been to no purpose. In the very time of fasting, one is not to be of a sad countenance, as though he were undergoing torture, for the anointing of the head with oil signifies a cup running over with the goodness of the Lord. See Ps. 23:5. As the body may feel the pangs of hunger, the person is to rejoice in that he is a partaker of Christ's sufferings, because he understands the keeping power of the Lord. He sees that great as is the life and power that are conveyed to us in the visible gifts of God, there is an infinitude of life for us, outside of that which is contained in what our senses can appreciate. This knowledge, which is emphasized by fasting, makes the day of fasting a day of delight.

Deliverance from the Power of Darkness

Wonderful promises are made to those who keep this acceptable fast, using their knowledge of the freedom which God gives, to rescue others from the snare of the devil. They shall walk in the light of the countenance of the Lord all the day, and in His righteousness shall they be exalted. Compare Isa. 58:8 with Ps. 89:15–16. They will be in such complete accord with the Lord, that even the darkness will be light to them. Compare verse 8, 10 and Ps. 139:12. What a marvelous privilege! The soul will be completely delivered from the power of darkness, and translated into the kingdom of the Son of God's love. See Col. 1:12–13.

Health to the True Worshiper

"And thine health shall spring forth speedily." Godliness has promise of the life that now is, as well as that which is to come. How can anybody who believes the Bible, read such passages as this, and still think that it is necessarily the lot of God's people to sufferer from disease? Nothing can be more plain than that the Lord promises health to all those who serve Him intelligently and in truth. Ex. 23:25. This is not an arbitrary thing, but the result of a definite cause. Notice that there is here a close connection between health and food. The rule among men is to consider only their appetite, and to eat whatever pleases it. Most people eat for the mere enjoyment of eating, and not in order that they may have the most perfect life; and thus they defeat themselves; for although they have a momentary enjoyment while the delicate morsels are going down their throats, the suffering which they undergo in consequence of disregarding the laws of life are almost continual; while those who eat only to have life wherewith to glorify God, not only get pleasure in the act of eating, but are continually filled with the joy of the life of the eternal God.

Givers of Life

Christ said of whosoever should believe on Him, that out of him should flow rivers of living water. The life which the believers receive from the Lord, flows out in a stream of blessing to others. Occasional fasting reminds us that we live only by the power of God, and that when we do eat it should be only for the purpose of receiving that life in its fullness and purity. It also reminds us that it is God who supplies the food, and that He can keep us alive just as well when the earth does not bring forth anything as when it yields abundantly. "The Lord shall guide thee continually, and satisfy thy soul in drought," or, as one translation has it, "In times of famine." He who has divided his last crust with the hungry, and still has found that the handful of meal did not fail, will not fear when famine comes over all the land, for he knows whom he trusts. His bones will be as fat in times of scarcity as in times of plenty, for the God who turns the flinty rock into streams of water, can give him abundant drink from the very sands of the desert. The knowledge of all this is indicated in the true fast, which means the distribution of bread to the needy; and such knowledge – the knowledge that he is in touch with the great Creator – cannot fail to make one joyful. Instead of famishing, he himself will be like a watered garden, and like a spring of water, whose waters never fail. That is, although he be poor, he will always be able to distribute something to the needy, because he has the unfailing storehouse of the God of the universe to draw from. "As poor, yet making many rich; as having nothing, and yet possessing all things." 2 Cor. 6:10.

Enveloped in God's Righteousness

"Thy righteousness shall go before thee." This shows that the righteousness will not be from ourselves, but from the Lord. The righteousness which proceeds from a man himself, goes with him, but here we have the picture of a man surrounded by the life of the Lord. His righteousness, the righteousness of God which is by the faith of Jesus Christ, goes before him, and the glory of the Lord is his protection in the rear. He is surrounded by a rampart of righteousness, and the glory of it, through which darkness and sin cannot break.

Sabbath-Keeping

The last message of the Gospel is to fear God, and give glory to Him, and to worship Him as the Creator of the heavens, and the earth, and the sea, and the fountains of waters. Rev. 14:6–7. To give God glory, is to keep His commandments. Compare Eccl. 12:13–14, and Matt. 5:16. So here in giving glory to God as the Creator of the heavens and earth and sea, we have unmistakable reference to the Sabbath, which is the memorial of that work. Ex. 20:8–11. The last proclamation of the Gospel makes the Sabbath of the Lord very prominent, because the Sabbath of the Lord means perfect rest and trust in the Lord, and that must be the condition of those who are prepared for His coming. Keeping the Sabbath of the fourth commandment, does not mean salvation by works, but salvation by resting in the Lord. It is not a grievous thing, but a delight. He who finds the Sabbath a hardship has never kept it, and does not know what it is, for it is a delight. It is the holy of the Lord, and honourable. Therefore let all beware how they despise it.

God's Holy Day

There should be no misunderstanding here as to what day is meant. The Lord says, "My holy day." There is therefore a certain day which He claims as His own above all other days. What day is that? "The seventh day is the Sabbath of the Lord thy God." That is, the seventh day of the week, the day that is commonly known as Saturday, and which follows the sixth day, Friday, which the Mohammedans regard as the prayer day, and which is followed by the first day of the week, known as Sunday, which the Papacy has succeeded in palming off on many Christians instead of the Lord's day. Jesus declared Himself to be the Lord of the Sabbath day, speaking of the day which the Jews professed to observe, and which they falsely accused Him of breaking. So the Lord's day is the seventh day of the week, the day which in the time of Christ, and even now, the Jews kept outwardly, but with no knowledge of the spirituality of it. All who honour the Lord must also honour His day, which He says is honourable.

The Delight Which Sabbath-Keeping Gives

But as with fasting, the results of the Sabbath do not end with the one day of the week which is set apart as the sign of resting in the Lord. The observance of the seventh day, on which God rested from all His work, means constant rest in Him. It is not merely on that day that we are not to do our own pleasure, nor to speak vain words, but every day. At no time have we any right to find our own selfish pleasure, and to speak vanity. We are to be so intimate with the Lord, and so closely conformed to His life, that our religion will not consist in the observance of certain forms and ceremonies at certain times, but in a continual godly life. True Sabbath-keeping means godliness all the week. To limit the prohibition from seeking our own pleasure and doing our own ways and speaking vain words to the day of the Sabbath, is to miss the meaning of this entire chapter, which teaches continual and not occasional service. "Then shalt thou delight thyself in the Lord." The blessing of rest, which the Sabbath brings, will extend throughout the week, and the soul will revel in the deliciousness of it. The true Sabbath-keeper will be a king, set over the highest places of the earth, and his whole life will be one bright glad day. O, accept this glorious message, and delight yourself in the Lord Himself.

CHAPTER 72

A TERRIBLE INDICTMENT AGAINST THE CHURCH

(Isa. 59:1–21, Lowth's Translation)

1. Behold, the hand of Jehovah is not contracted, so that He cannot save; neither is His ear grown dull, so that He cannot hear.

2. But your iniquities have made a separation between you and your God; and your sins have hidden His face from you, that He doth not hear.

3. For your hands are polluted with blood, and your fingers with iniquity; your lips speak falsehood, and your tongue muttereth wickedness.

4. No one preferreth his suit in justice, and no one pleadeth in truth; trusting in vanity, and speaking lies; conceiving mischief, and bringing forth iniquity.

5. They hatch the eggs of the basilisk, and weave the web of the spider; he that eateth of their eggs dieth; and when it is crushed, a viper breaketh forth.

6. Of their webs no garment shall be made; neither shall they cover themselves with their works; their works are works of iniquity, and the deed of violence is in their hands.

7. Their feet run swiftly to evil, and they hasten to shed innocent blood. Their devices are devices of iniquity; destructions and calamity in their paths.

8. The way of peace they know not; neither is their any judgment in their tracks; they have made to themselves crooked paths; whoever goeth in them knoweth not peace.

9. Therefore is judgment far distant from us; neither doth justice overtake us; we look for light, but behold darkness; for brightness, but we walk in obscurity.

10. We grope for the wall, like the blind; and we wander, as those that are deprived of sight. We stumble at midday, as in the twilight; in the midst of delicacies, as among the dead.

11. We groan all of us, like the bears; and like the doves, we make a continued moan. We look for judgment, and there is none; for salvation, and it is far distant from us.

12. For our transgressions are multiplied before Thee; and our sins bring an accusation against us; for our transgressions cleave fast unto us; and our iniquities we acknowledge.

13. By rebelling, and lying against Jehovah; and by turning backward from following our God; by speaking injury and conceiving revolt; and by mediating from the heart lying words,

14. And judgment is turned away backwards; and justice standeth aloof; for truth hath stumbled in the open street; and rectitude hath not been able to enter.

15. And truth is utterly lost; and he that shunneth evil, exposeth himself to be plundered; and Jehovah saw it, and it displeased Him, that there was no judgment.

16. And He saw that there was no man; and He wondered that there was no one to interpose; then His own arm brought salvation for Him; and His righteousness, it supported Him.

17. And He put on righteousness, as a breastplate; and the helmet of salvation was on His head; and He put on the garments of vengeance for His clothing; and He clad Himself with zeal, as with a mantle.

18. He is mighty to recompense; He that is mighty to recompense will requite; wrath to His adversaries, recompense to His enemies; to the distant coasts a recompense will He requite.

19. And they from the west shall revere the name of Jehovah; and they from the rising of the sun His glory; when He shall come, like a river straightened in his course, which a strong wind driveth along.

20. And the Redeemer shall come to Sion; and shall turn away the iniquity from Jacob, saith Jehovah.

21. And this is the covenant, which I make with them, saith Jehovah: My Spirit, which is upon thee, and My words, which I have put in thy mouth; they shall not depart from thy mouth; nor from the mouth of thy seed, nor from the mouth of thy seed's seed, saith Jehovah; from this time forth for ever.

In the fifty-eighth chapter we have the direct word of the Lord to whomsoever will hear, telling them to show His people their transgressions; in this chapter we have evidently the inspired word of the prophet, complying with that injunction. The prophet now, in the name of the Lord, sets before the people who are encased in their self-righteousness the exact state of their case, and it is by no means a pleasant picture to contemplate. A more terrible indictment it would be hard find, and the awfulness is increased by the knowledge of the fact that it states nothing but the truth. Let no one say, "It does not mean me; I am sure that I am not guilty of any of the things here set forth;" the prophet Isaiah classes himself in with the rest and acknowledges himself a sinner. The prophet Daniel, of whom we read nothing but good in the Bible, confessed himself to be guilty of all the sins that had led to the captivity of Israel. See his prayer in Dan. 9:3–20. The best men in the world are they who confess themselves to be the greatest sinners and who trust in the mercy of God.

God's Readiness to Hear

Note carefully the difference in Lowth's rendering of the second verse, from the ordinary version. Our version incorrectly says, that the Lord "*will not* hear;" whereas the text simply states the reason why the Lord does not hear. His ear is not dull, but the sharpest ear cannot hear under certain conditions; and the conditions here are that no sound comes to the ears of the Lord. There is no real prayer for pardon, and therefore nothing for the Lord to hear. The reason why the Lord does not hear is stated in the third verse, and it is but a repetition of what is stated in chapter one, verse fifteen. The hands are polluted with blood and the fingers with iniquity, and the lips speak falsehood. All that the Lord has to give is life, – life that includes everything. Christ came to this world for no other purpose than to give life. See John 10:10. There is no other thing for which

491

we need to pray to the Lord, except for life. But when one professedly prays to the Lord for life, and at the same time destroys life, he shows that there is no sincerity in his prayer; his words are no words at all. The difficulty is not with the Lord's ear, but with the words of the one praying. The actions destroy the words.

The Lord will hear every sincere prayer. He hears every cry, every sigh for deliverance. "For He hath looked down from the height of His sanctuary; from Heaven did the Lord behold the earth; to hear the sighing of the prisoner; to loose the children of death." Ps. 102:19–20, R.V., margin. "For the oppression of the poor, for the sighing of the needy, now will I arise, saith the Lord; I will set him in safety from him that puffeth at him." Ps. 12:5. There is no inarticulate sigh for deliverance, that is too faint for the Lord to hear, for He is listening to hear, and He understands the language of the mute earth; but the loudest prayers, couched in the most polished language, when they proceed from an insincere heart, are in His ears nothing but a confused noise.

All Are Guilty

The hasty reader of this chapter will think that it is addressed to the most degraded people on the earth; but the fact is that it is addressed to the professed Christian church. It is not alone Great Babylon, in which are found "slaves and souls of men" (Rev. 18:13), that is addressed here, but the church which is represented by one of the stars in the right hand of Christ, and which says, "I am rich, and increased with goods," knowing not that it is "wretched, and miserable, and poor, and blind, and naked." Rev. 3:17. The indictment is against the self-righteous, whose ways are outwardly so correct that they think that they have no lack.

The proof of this is found in a comparison of this chapter with the first three chapters of Romans. The first chapter of the book sets forth the sins of the heathen, who in their blindness bow down to wood and stone. The second chapter begins with a home thrust, "Thou art inexcusable, O man, whosoever thou art that judgest; for wherein thou judgest another, thou condemnest thyself; for thou that judgest doest the same things." We pass on through the second chapter and into the third, through a comparison of the heathen with the professed followers of the Lord, until we come to the conversation, which contains a quotation from the chapter of Isaiah which we are studying: "What then? are we better than they? No, in no wise; for we have before proved both Jews and Gentiles, that they are all under sin; as it is written, There is none righteous; no, not one; there is none that understandeth, there is none that seeketh after God. They are all gone out of the way, they are together become unprofitable; there is none that doeth good, no, not one. Their throat is an open sepulcher; with their tongues they have used deceit; the poison of asps is under their lips; whose mouth is full of cursing and bitterness; their feet are swift to shed blood; destruction and misery are in their ways; and the way of peace they have not known; there is no fear of God before their eyes." Rom. 3:9–18. The same fountain cannot send forth at the same time both sweet water and bitter; therefore when we read that their mouth is full of bitterness, we know that no real prayer comes forth for the Lord to hear.

Self-Righteous Ignorance

But some one will say, "I know that I do not do any of the things here charged." A more exact statement would be, "I do not know that I do any of these things." That is why the Lord says, "Show My people their transgressions." If they knew them, there would be no need to show them. But the case is so urgent that the command is, "Cry aloud." The one danger of all mankind is self-righteousness. The one need of all men is to recognize the righteousness of God in Christ as the only real righteousness, and the only thing in which there is everlasting life. The danger of professed Christians, even of those who have known the saving power of the Lord, is of forgetting their absolute dependence upon God, and in thinking that they have attained something by their own goodness, or that they can go on by the power which they acknowledge they received from the Lord, but which they think that they have so made their own that they can dispense with any further gift from Him. Men never put the case to themselves in that way; if they did they would not be deceived; but that is in effect the way in which the professed followers of the Lord fall into grievous sin.

Only One Gospel For All

This chapter, taken in connection with its use in the New Testament, shows us that there is only one Gospel – only one line of preaching – for all men, no matter what their profession, or if they make none. The very same Gospel that saves the man of the world, is that which must be preached continually to the church of Christ, in order not only to reclaim wanderers, but to retain the faithful ones. The first thing to be preached to the sinner who needs salvation from his sins, is Christ the Saviour, and he can never get beyond that need. "He shall save His people from their sins;" and that which saves them from the guilt of their sins, is that which keeps them from falling into them again. Throughout the endless ages of eternity, it will be the cross of Christ, and nothing else, that will keep the redeemed saints in glory. Therefore "God forbid that I should glory, save in the cross of our Lord Jesus Christ." Let no one who calls himself a Christian complain of any minister of the Gospel, that "he preaches to us just as though we were sinners." If he does not do that, he is not a faithful minister of Christ. The Christian who is alive and growing in grace and in the knowledge of Christ, will never make such a complaint. Whoever makes it, and we have often heard it, shows that he is unconsciously in the greatest possible danger.

Vain Confidence: Self-Deception

The people here referred to are those who are "trusting in vanity," instead of in God. They are the self-righteous ones of Romans 2 and 3, who are equally sinful with the heathen. "How?" says one; "I have never murdered anybody, and I never swore in my life, and I never worshipped an idol." To be sure, the self-righteous man never thinks that he has committed the gross sins of the common sinner. If he did, he would not be self-righteous. That is just why the loud cry has to be given, to arouse him from his stupefied condition. Let us examine the case for a minute, and we need not single out any individual, but take the first man we come to. That is, each one may put the questions to himself: –

"Have you always honoured the life that God has given you, and used it to the very best advantage? Have you never wasted it in any way whatever?" We are obliged to plead guilty. Then we are guilty of murder; we have taken life that did not belong to us; we have shed innocent blood. There is no middle ground; he who does not actively love the Lord, hates him; so he who receives the life of the Lord, – the blood of Christ, – and does not use it to His glory, but wastes it, is guilty of the blood of the Lord; and what worse case of murder could there possibly be?

Do we need after this to go into particulars with the other commandments? We need not ask, "Have you never used the name of the Lord unnecessarily?" but only, "Have you as a professed Christian never done or thought a thing that was in the least degree contrary to the perfection of the life of Christ?" Everybody knows that he has done many things that were dishonouring to the Lord. Then he has taken the name of the Lord in vain. And just as surely as we have ever consulted our own pleasure or ease before the glory of God, have we had other gods before Him. And so we might go on through the whole of the commandments, and prove all the world, both sinner and professed saint, guilty before God, – guilty of the grossest crimes.

Christ the Only Hope

"Who then can be saved?" The answer is straight and plain: Nobody can be saved, if he trusts in his own righteousness, but trusting in the righteousness of Christ, there is salvation for all. No man can weave a garment that is anything more than a filthy rag; it cannot cover him. "Of their webs no garment shall be made; neither shall they cover themselves with their works." God has wrought works, and made a garment that is amply sufficient to cover the whole human race; but of this garment we shall speak more particularly when we come to the sixty-first chapter.

Plundering the Righteous: A Severe Test

"He that departeth from evil maketh himself a prey," or, "exposeth himself to be plundered." Space will not permit anything more than a very direct comment upon this. Competition is very keen in this world, especially in these days. It is the case, which every one will recognize, that the man who is conscientious is cut off from many ways of "making money," that are successfully adopted by the unscrupulous.

But this is not all: the strictly honest man in business stands a great chance of having his business taken from him by his unscrupulous neighbours in the same line. There are, in some places, at least, certain lines of business, legitimate enough in themselves, in which corrupt dealing is so prevalent, that the man who does not put his conscience in his pocket, and "do as the rest do," cannot "succeed." Neither is this all. The prophecy that we are studying applies to the last days, and inasmuch as the coming of the Lord is near, the injunction is to cry aloud, and not spare to show God's people their sins, but to declare His whole truth. Accordingly the Sabbath truth, which has been so long forgotten, is presented in chapters fifty-six and fifty-eight. To what does the business man expose himself if he begins to keep God's holy day instead of Satan's counterfeit? – We hear the answer continually: "If I should keep the Sabbath, I should lose my place," or, "I should have to give up my business." Even with regard to the Sunday, we have it constantly reiterated that a law is necessary, to compel all to keep the day, in order that those who wish to keep it may not lose their situations or their business. How much more, then, must it be the case that he who keeps the Sabbath of the Lord, contrary to human law and custom, exposes himself to be plundered? We have no picture of ease and prosperity in this world, as this world counts prosperity, to hold before the one to whom we declare the whole counsel of God. The time will yet come when a decree will go forth, that whoever will keep the Sabbath of the Lord instead of the Sunday of the apostate church, shall be killed (Rev. 13:16–17); and that will be the test: whether men can trust God's promise of life, in the face of man's threat of death.

The Power That Delivers

God is the Saviour of His people. Though He bears long with the ways of men, His long-suffering is salvation. He does not forget. The Deliverer shall turn away ungodliness from Israel. But the salvation of the righteous means the destruction of the ungodly. "He that believeth, and is baptized, shall be saved: and he that believeth not shall be damned." This is the Gospel message, and one part is just as true as the other. Yea, "He that believeth not is condemned already." John 3:18. The cross of Christ, in which alone there is salvation, and which is the revelation of God's love to man, has in it the destruction of sinners; for it was only because Christ was made to be sin for us, and was reckoned among the transgressors, that He hung on the cross. Therefore all who do not die in Christ on the cross, accepting Him as their Saviour, must be slain by that cross in their own person, without any hope of salvation. The salvation of God is like a mighty river, rushing along between narrow banks, and driven by a strong wind. So powerful is the Lord to carry away the ungodly: but His power to destroy the sinners at the last day, is but His power to destroy sin in us at this present time.

So we see that it makes no difference with the facts, whether we read verse 19 as in Lowth and in the Revision, or, as in the common version, "When the enemy shall come in like a flood, the Spirit of the Lord shall lift up a standard against him." The truth set forth is that the Lord will sweep away sin and sinners as with a flood, and that flood is the stream of life from the throne of God. It is, indeed, the Spirit of God, which the new covenant, made with "the house of Israel and the house of Jacob" at the coming of the Lord, insures to every believer as his possession throughout the generations of eternity. In the midst of wrath God remembers mercy (Hab 3:2), because the wrath which destroys the wicked is but the rejected mercy of the Lord, which endureth for ever.

CHAPTER 73

THE RESTORATION OF ZION
GLORY OF THE NEW CREATION

(Isa. 60:1–22)

"Arise, shine; for thy light is come, and the glory of the Lord is risen upon thee. For, behold, darkness shall cover the earth, and gross darkness the peoples: but the Lord shall arise upon thee, and His glory shall be seen upon thee. And nations shall come to thy light, and kings to the brightness of thy rising.

"Lift up thine eyes round about, and see: they all gather themselves together, they come to thee; thy sons shall come from far, and thy daughters shall be carried in the arms. Then thou shalt see and be lightened, and thine heart shall tremble and be enlarged; because the abundance of the sea shall be turned unto thee, and the wealth of the nations shall come unto thee. The multitude of camels shall cover thee, the dromedaries of Midian and Ephah; they all shall come from Sheba; they shall bring gold and frankincense, and shall proclaim the praises of the Lord. All the flocks of Kedar shall be gathered together unto thee, the rams of Nebaioth shall minister unto thee; they shall come up with acceptance on Mine altar, and I will glorify the house of My glory.

"Who are these that fly as a cloud, and as the doves to their windows? Surely the isles shall wait for Me, and the ships of Tarshish first, to bring thy sons from far, their silver and their gold with them, for the name of the Lord thy God, and for the Holy One of Israel, for He hath glorified thee. And strangers shall build up thy walls, and their kings shall minister unto thee; for in My wrath I smote thee, but in My favour have I had mercy on thee.

"Thy gates also shall be open continually; they shall not be shut day nor night; that men may bring unto thee the wealth of the nations, and their kings led with them. For that nation and kingdom that will not serve thee shall perish: yea, those nations shall be utterly wasted. The glory of Lebanon shall come unto thee, the fir tree, the pine, and the box tree together; and I will make the place of My feet glorious.

"And the sons of them that afflicted thee shall come bonding unto thee; and all them that despised thee shall bow themselves down at the soles of thy feet; and they shall call thee The city of the Lord, The Zion of the Holy One of Israel. Whereas thou hast been forsaken and hated, so that no man passed through thee, I will make thee an eternal excellency, a joy of many generations. Thou shalt also suck the milk of the nations, and shalt suck the breast of kings; and thou shalt know that I the Lord am thy Saviour, and thy Redeemer, the Mighty One of Jacob.

"For brass I will bring gold, and for iron I will bring silver, and for wood brass, and for stones iron; I will also make thy officers peace, and all thine exactors righteousness. Violence shall no more be heard in thy land, desolation nor destruction within thy borders; but thou shalt call thy walls salvation, and thy gates praise.

"The sun shall be no more thy light by day; neither for brightness shall the moon give light unto thee; but the Lord shall be unto thee an everlasting light, and thy God thy glory. Thy sun shall no more go down, neither shall thy moon withdraw itself; for the Lord shall be thine everlasting light, and the days of thy mourning shall be ended.

"Thy people also shall be all righteous, they shall inherit the land for ever; the branch of My planting, the work of My hands, that I may be glorified. The little one shall become a thousand, and the small one a great nation; I the Lord will hasten it in his time."

In reading this chapter a few things, to which attention has already been called many times, should be borne in mind.

(1) Whenever reference is unmistakably made to the city of Jerusalem, as in parts of this chapter, it must be remembered that the city is nothing without the inhabitants. When the city is spoken of as rejoicing, we know that it is the people in the city that rejoice. A city is built up only by the accession of inhabitants.

(2) These prophecies were given many years before the Babylonian captivity. At the close of that captivity full liberty was given for every Jew to return to his own land, and no means was withheld, that was necessary to enable them to return; therefore every part of the prophecy that can be thought of as referring merely to temporal things, was fulfilled long ago. That is, it has been fulfilled as far as mere temporal inheritance could do it.

(3) It is most obvious that there are things promised not only in this chapter but also in other places, which have never yet been fulfilled. Moreover, it is plain that these things can be fulfilled only by an everlasting inheritance. This is a prophecy that refers to the last days, and its fulfillment will be accomplished only by the coming of the Lord, and the restoration of all things.

God Fulfills All His Promises

(4) Above all, must one common error be avoided. It is very common to hear expositors say of certain things that have not been fulfilled, that God made them on certain conditions, and that, the conditions not having been met, the fulfillment of the promises could not be expected. Such exposition is a libel upon God. Never in the world has God made a promise that He will not fulfill in good time. "The Lord is not slack concerning His promise." 2 Peter 3:9. "If we are faithless, He abideth faithful; for He cannot deny Himself." 2 Tim. 2:13. Even though every man should be unfaithful, and should reject the promise, His promise would hold good, for He would of the very stones make faithful children, who would accept the offers of mercy. See Matt. 3:9. God is not dependent upon any man for the fulfillment of His promises; and no person either in this world or in the world to come will ever be able to taunt God with having in any instance failed to keep His word, nor will

there ever be the slightest opportunity for doubt to creep into a loyal heart, in view of an unfulfilled promise. Whatever God has promised, He is able also to perform: and whatever God is able to do He will do for the salvation of men.

The Word that Gives Life and Strength

"Arise!" That is, "Stand up!" Compare this with the words in connection with the miracles recorded in Luke 7:14, 8:54; Acts 3:6; 14:10. To the young man who was being carried to burial, and to the little girl just dead, Christ said, "Arise," and they both stood up, alive. Peter said to the lame man at the gate of the temple, who had never walked, "In the name of Jesus Christ of Nazareth, rise up, and walk," and immediately he walked and leaped. In like manner Paul said to the other man, "who never had walked," "Stand upright on thy feet," and he leaped and walked. This is the word which is addressed to us in this lesson. The very first word is the word that raises the dead, and makes the helpless walk. Whoever has faith to be healed, whoever hears this word in faith, will find in the study of this chapter a life that he never before has known. "Awake, thou that sleepest, and arise from the dead, and Christ shall shine upon thee." Eph. 5:14.

Let There be Light

"Shine!" Yes, arise, and shine. Why? Because Christ shall shine upon thee. Nay, more; the light has come, and the glory of the Lord has risen upon thee. Here again we have the word of creation. Although the word used in this instance is not the same as that used in the first chapter of Genesis, that makes no difference; the fact is that here we have the same command as in Gen. 1:3. "God said, Let there be light; and there was light." In the beginning, when there was nothing about this earth but darkness, without a single ray of light, God said, "Be light," and instantly light was. The very darkness sent forth light. "God who commanded the light to shine out of darkness, hath shined in our hearts, to give the light of the knowledge of the glory of God in the face of Jesus Christ." 2 Cor. 4:6. He is the Light, and "the light shineth in the darkness; and the darkness overcame it not." Therefore He can turn our darkness into light. Have we not had the promise? "Then shall thy light break forth as the morning;" "then shall thy light rise in obscurity; and the darkness be as the noonday." It is the God who creates, who is speaking to us here. If we remember Him as the Creator of the heavens and the earth, we shall know the power by which the worlds were made, and by which the dead are raised. This is true Sabbath-keeping.

Lights in the World

When Moses came down from the mountain, after having been in close communion with the Lord, talking with Him face to face, his face shone. It was not merely that it was bright, but it gave off rays of light; light beamed forth from it for the benefit of others, if they were willing to receive it. That was but an illustration of what God wishes all His people to be: Light-bearers. "Ye are the light of the world." Matt. 5:14. The light which His people have is the light of His life, for He says, "He that followeth Me shall not walk in darkness, but shall have the light of life." John 8:12. So we are exhorted to "do all things without murmurings and disputings, that ye may be blameless and harmless, the sons of God, without rebuke, in the midst of a crooked and perverse nation, among whom ye shine as lights in the world; holding forth the Word of life." Phil. 2:14–16. The life is the light of men, and it is a most wonderful thought that this glorious light of God is to be made manifest in mortal flesh (2 Cor. 4:11), so that those who sit enshrouded in the gross darkness of this world are to receive "the light of the knowledge of the glory of God" by seeing it in His humble followers. Surely it is high time to heed the command, "Arise, shine!"

Real Life: The Light of Life the Light of the World

That this is not imaginary light, that shines from the faithful followers of Christ, is evident from what appears later on in the chapter, as well as from other scriptures. Of the city, when it shall be filled with its children, we read that it "had no need of the sun, neither of the moon, to shine in it; for the glory of God did lighten it, and the Lamb is the light thereof." Rev. 21:23. Compare Isa. 60:19–20. The light which shines from God is actual light, far above the shining of the sun, for it is from Him that the sun gets all the light that it has; therefore when His people are as subject to His will as the sun is, they will also shine with real light. "Then shall the righteous shine forth as the sun in the kingdom of their Father." Matt. 13:43. "They that be wise shall shine as the brightness of the firmament; and they that turn many to righteousness as the stars for ever and ever." Daniel 12:3. "Now are we the sons of God, and it doth not yet appear what we shall be." 1 John 3:2. That is, the light that will shine forth from the bodies of the saints, is not yet made manifest, therefore the world knows them not, even as it knew not Christ; nevertheless the life which is manifested in those who are wholly the Lord's is the very same light that shines from the face of the Lord, the same that illuminates the earth. Not all will veil their faces from it; no shining is in vain, no matter how obscure the place in which the life is manifested; for the Gentiles, the heathen, the nations of the earth, will come to the light when it is allowed to shine forth unhindered, and even kings will come to enquire about it. It is true that the coming of the wise men from the east at the birth of Christ was in fulfillment of this prophecy; but we must not imagine that that occurrence exhausted it. That was only a sample of what shall be done when Christ is fully formed in all His people. There are many kings and rulers in so-called heathen lands, who have great power and influence, and many of these will yet be seen enquiring the way of life.

The Building Up of Zion

"Strangers shall build up thy walls." This is but another statement of the fact that the kingdom of Israel is to be built up by the coming in of the people of all the different nations of earth. The calling of the Gentiles is the means by which the ruins of the house of David are to be built up. Acts 15:16–17. Those who were once "aliens from the commonwealth of Israel, and strangers from the covenants of promise, having no hope, and without God in the world," are brought nigh by the blood of Christ, so that they are "no more strangers and foreigners, but fellow-citizens with the saints, and of the household of God; and are built on the foundation of the apostles and prophets, Jesus Christ Himself being the chief corner stone; in whom all the building fitly framed together groweth into an holy temple in the Lord." Eph. 2:11–13,19–21. These, coming to

Christ the Living Stone, are made into living stones, and are built up a spiritual house, an holy priesthood, to offer up spiritual sacrifices acceptable unto God by Jesus Christ. 1 Peter 2:4–5. So it is written, "Him that overcometh will I make a pillar in the temple of My God, and he shall go no more out." Rev. 3:12. Thus will the walls of Jerusalem, the holy city, be built up. The grand work is even now going forward; who will form a part of the grand structure?

Glorifying His House

"I will make the place of My feet glorious." Read again the scripture that has so frequently been referred to in these lessons, namely, Zech. 14:4, which tells us that at the time of the last great battle the Lord shall go forth to fight against the nations that are opposed to Jerusalem, and that His feet shall stand in that day upon the Mount of Olives, and it shall become a great plain, in which the city with its living waters shall stand. Read also verses 6–9 in connection with the chapter we are studying. This, together with Rev. 21, will serve to fix the application of the chapter.

Verse 7 is specially comforting when read in connection with the Scriptures which show that God's people are "builded together for an habitation of God through the Spirit." In Isa. 57:15 we read that God dwells with the lowly, and at the same time "in the high and holy place." His presence in dust animates it; when He dwells with the lowly one, He sets him on high; and when He is allowed to dwell in the meanest and most debased soul, He glorifies it. "I will glorify the house of My glory." Our part is but to be willing and submissive; God's part is to give grace and glory, and strength according to the riches of His glory.

"The Lord God is a sun and shield." Ps. 84:11. This we see from verse 20. The sun of the city of God will never go down, night nor day, because the Lord will be its everlasting light. The sun will shine as it does now, only with greatly increased light, but in the city of God it will not be needed, since the greater light of God Himself will shine there day and night.

A Righteous Nation

"Thy people also shall all be righteous; they shall inherit the land for ever." Thus we see that the consummation of the shining of God's people is the "new heavens and a new earth, wherein dwelleth righteousness." 2 Peter 3:13. That is the consummation, but the beginning must be now, in the midst of the darkness of this present evil world. "The path of the just is as the shining light, that shineth more and more unto the perfect day." Prov. 4:18. The powers of the world to come must be manifested in this present world; the light of the new earth must be seen on the old earth; the salvation and praise that will be the protection of the holy city when the assault is made upon it by the hosts of evil must now be manifested; and the righteousness that will dwell in the new earth must exist here and now in all its fullness. This will be the case by power of Him who can make a little one a strong nation, and who in His faithfulness will do it. 1 Thess. 5:23–24.

CHAPTER 74

THE CLOTHING WHICH GOD GIVES

(Isa. 61:1–11, Lowth's Translation)

1. The Spirit of Jehovah is upon Me, because Jehovah hath anointed Me. To publish glad tidings to the meek hath He sent Me; to bind up the broken-hearted: to proclaim to the captives freedom; and to the bounded perfect liberty:

2. To proclaim the year of acceptance with Jehovah; and the day of vengeance of our God. To comfort all those that mourn.

3. To impart [gladness] to the mourners of Sion; to give them a beautiful crown, instead of ashes; the oil of gladness instead of sorrow; the clothing of praise instead of the spirit of heaviness. That they may be called trees approved; the plantation of Jehovah for His glory.

4. And they that spring from thee shall build up the ruins of old times; they shall restore the ancient desolations; they shall repair the cities laid waste; the desolations of continued ages.

5. And strangers shall stand up and feed your flocks; and the sons of the alien shall be your husbandman and vine-dressers.

6. But ye shall be called the priests of Jehovah; the ministers of our God, shall be your title. The riches of the nations shall ye eat; and in the glory shall ye make your boast.

7. Instead of your shame, ye shall receive a double inheritance; and of your ignominy, ye shall rejoice in their portion; for in their land, a double share shall ye inherit; and everlasting gladness shall ye possess.

8. For I am Jehovah, who love judgment; who hate rapine and iniquity; and I will give them the reward of their work with faithfulness; and an everlasting covenant will I make with them;

9. And their seed shall be illustrious among the nations; and their offspring, in the midst of the peoples. And they that see

them shall acknowledge them, that they are a seed which Jehovah hath blessed.

10. I will greatly rejoice in Jehovah; my soul shall exult in my God. For He hath clothed me with the garments of salvation; he hath covered me with the mantle of righteousness; as the bridegroom decketh himself with a priestly crown; and as a bride adorneth herself with her costly jewels.

11. Surely, as the earth pusheth forth her tender shoots; and as a garden maketh her seed to germinate; so shall the Lord God cause righteousness to spring forth; and praise, in the presence of all the nations.

This is one of the shortest chapters in Isaiah, yet it is one of the fullest in Gospel instruction and comfort. We need not spend any time in noting when it applies, for all that has been said of preceding chapters, and of the entire book, applies here as well; moreover, the fact that Jesus in the synagogue in Nazareth, after reading a portion of this chapter, said, "This day is the scripture fulfilled in your ears," shows that it reached as far as the time of His first advent; and if it was applicable then, how much more now. God has not withdrawn His Spirit of Comfort from the Son, and therefore He is still clothed with the Spirit, "to comfort all that mourn." While there are many things in the chapter that might well claim all our attention, let us spend the most of our time and space in considering the covering which God provides for all people who will receive it.

A Change of Raiment

In two verses of this chapter is this clothing spoken of, namely, the 3 and the 10. The anointed of the Lord is commissioned to proclaim that God has provided "the garment of praise for the spirit of heaviness;" and the prophet breaks forth: "I will greatly rejoice in the Lord, my soul shall be joyful in my God; for He hath clothed me with the garments of salvation, He hath covered me with the robe of righteousness." Suppose we put a few other texts by the side of these, and then see what they teach us.

Ps. 32:1–2: "Blessed is the man whose transgression is forgiven, whose sin is covered. Blessed is the man unto whom the Lord imputeth not iniquity and in whose spirit there is no guile."

Rom. 4:3–8: "What saith the Scripture? Abraham believed God, and it was counted unto him for righteousness. Now to him that worketh is the reward not reckoned of grace, but of debt. But to him that worketh not, but believeth on Him that justifieth the ungodly, his faith is counted for righteousness. Even as David also describeth the blessedness of the man, unto whom God imputeth righteousness without work, saying, Blessed are they whose iniquities are forgiven, and whose sins are covered. Blessed is the man to whom the Lord will not impute sin."

Rom. 3:20–24: "By the deeds of the law there shall no flesh be justified in His sight; for by the law is the knowledge of sin. But now the righteousness of God without the law is manifested, being witnessed by the law and the prophets; even the righteousness of God which is by faith of Jesus Christ, unto all and upon all them that believe; for there is no difference; for all have sinned, and come short of the glory of God; being justified [made righteous] freely by His grace, through the redemption that is in Christ Jesus."

Zech. 3:1–5: "And He showed me Joshua the high priest standing before the angel of the Lord, and Satan standing at his right hand to resist him. And the Lord said unto Satan, "The Lord rebuke thee, O Satan; even the Lord that hath chosen Jerusalem rebuke thee; is not this a brand plucked out of the fire? Now Joshua was clothed with filthy garments, and stood before the angel. And he answered and spake unto those that stood before him, saying, Take away the filthy garments from him. And unto him he said, Behold, I have caused thine iniquity to pass from thee, and I will clothe thee with change of raiment. And I said, Set a fair mitre upon his head, So they set a fair mitre upon his head and clothed him with garments."

Isa. 64:6: "But we are all as an unclean thing, and all our righteousnesses are as filthy rags."

What have we in these texts? – Simply this: that all men are by nature sinful; their nature is sin; they are not only covered with sin, but are filled with it. "Their webs shall not become garments, neither shall they cover themselves with their works." Isa. 59:4. Their best works are full of imperfection, and provide no covering. "Every man at his best state is altogether vanity." But God's works endure for ever, since they are all done in righteousness, and He has wrought a covering for all men, even the garment of His own righteous life, – the garment of salvation, – for we are saved by His life.

God covers Himself with light, as with a garment. Ps. 104:2. In the statement that "all have sinned, and come short of the glory of God" (Rom. 3:23), we learn that the glory of God – the light that surrounds Him – is His own perfect life. Righteousness is glory, even though it is not now so recognized among men; for in the world to come, when everything will appear just as it really is, the righteous will shine forth as the sun. Matt. 13:43. Therefore we know that man's original clothing was the light of the glory of God, and that this was lost and it became necessary to provide manufactured clothing for him only when he sinned. Our clothes are but the mark of the curse; and the fact that we must wear manufactured clothing is a constant sign that our bodies are still unredeemed from the curse. The more gay and pronounced is one's clothing, the more is the shame of the curse emphasized. Our present clothing of the body is nothing to be proud of, but rather something to cause shame. Thank God that it is not to last for ever.

The Clothing of the Life: Clothing that Grows

We have already seen, from the text quoted, that the exchanging of the filthy garment for the clean raiment is the taking away of all iniquity. The "fine linen, clean and white" is "the righteousness of saints." Rev. 19:8. But this righteousness of God through the faith of Jesus Christ, is put into as well as upon all them that believe. And this brings us to the heart of the matter – the way the clothing of the saints is prepared. The covering is the glory – the righteousness – of God, and the glory of God is seen upon His people simply because it is put into them. Remember that God is clothed with light as with a garment, because He Himself is light. His clothing is His life, and that proceeds from within, from the heart. We are clothed with the garment of salvation only when the salvation of God is within us, that is, when we are saved from the sins of our inmost being. Then we have an armour that none of Satan's weapons can pierce. When truth is "in the inward parts" (Ps. 51:6) it is a shield and buckler. Ps. 91:4. The lions did not hurt Daniel, because innocency was found in him; it was impossible that Christ should be held by the grave, because He "knew no sin;" and it was this righteousness in the heart, filling His entire being, that made Him master of the winds and the waves, as well as of wild beasts and men.

Now we can see the intimate connection of verses 10–11, and the force of the word "for," with which the 11 verse begins. "My soul shall be joyful in my God; for He hath clothed me with the garment of salvation, He hath covered me with the robe of righteousness; … for as the earth bringeth forth her bud, and as the garden causeth the things that are sown in it to spring forth, *so* the Lord will cause righteousness and praise to spring forth before all the nations." God's people are clothed with righteousness and salvation just as the earth is clothed with verdure. "So is the kingdom of God, as if a man should cast seed into the ground; … for the earth bringeth forth fruit of herself," that is, automatically. Mark 4:26–28. We have all seen automatons, self-acting machines, and have wondered at the perfection of their movement, but have known that the power to move did not originate in them. So the earth brings forth fruit spontaneously, moved by the indwelling word which was planted in the beginning, when God said, "Let the earth bring forth." So the incorruptible seed, the engrafted Word, abiding in the souls of men, regenerates, produces a new life, which is a covering of glory.

The Garment of Praise

This clothing of salvation and righteousness is at the same time "the garment of praise." Compare verses 3 and 10. There can be no righteousness, no salvation, where there is not praise. The Kingdom of God is "righteousness and peace and joy in the Holy Ghost." Rom. 14:17. The anointing with the Holy Ghost is the anointing with "the oil of gladness." The walls of Zion are Salvation, and her gates are Praise. Isa. 60:18. God compasses His people about with songs of deliverance. Ps. 32:7. Indeed, it is by praise and thanksgiving that we appropriate the salvation that God gives. "In everything by prayer and supplication with thanksgiving let your requests be made known unto God." Phil. 4:6. God says: "Whoso offereth the sacrifice of thanksgiving glorifieth Me, and prepareth a way that I may show him the salvation of God." Ps. 50:23, R.V. margin. The walls of Jerico fell only when Israel shouted victory (Joshua 6:16,20), and it was when Israel, going out to meet the enemy that vastly outnumbered them, began to sing and to "praise the beauty of holiness," that "the Lord set ambushments" against their enemies and utterly destroyed them. It is with singing that the ransomed of the Lord return and come to Zion. They come with "everlasting joy" upon their heads; and this joy is the gladness that springs up in the heart at the knowledge of God's wondrous salvation.

How Real Clothing Grows

It is perfectly in keeping with the thought of the chapter, that God's people should be clothed with the garments of praise and salvation, and covered with the robe of righteousness just as the earth bringeth forth her bud, since they are "trees of righteousness, the planting of the Lord, that He might be glorified." The spring has just come, and the illustration is fresh before our eyes, as we see the bare and seemingly dead trees, and the naked earth suddenly clothed with beautiful garments. Whence came this robe of living green? – It came from within. The life power within manifested itself outwardly. "The life was manifested, and we have seen it" even in animate nature. The tree is clothed with the life that is in it; the life of the good seed – the Word of God – planted in the earth, clothes it with garments of glory and beauty. Even so is Jerusalem to put on her beautiful garments. Isa. 52:1.

Speaking of the lilies, Christ said: "Even Solomon in all his glory was not arrayed like one of these. Wherefore if God so clothe the grass of the field, which today is, and tomorrow is cast into the oven, shall He not much more clothe you?" Matt. 6:29–30. Christ says to us, Why do you worry about something wherewith to clothe the body, when your Heavenly Father, who knows all your needs, not only provides this everyday clothing, that soon wears out, but supplies us with clothing far superior to that of Solomon. Notice: Christ says that God will much more clothe us than the grass of the field; but the clothing of the grass of the field far excels all the glory of Solomon's dress; therefore we learn that God will clothe us even as He does the lily, – with garments that grow from the inner life, – but with a far more glorious dress. The righteous shall shine forth as the sun, even as the stars for ever and ever. The only question is, would we rather be clothed with God's righteousness than to walk naked? See Rev. 3:17–18.

Yet a few words more must be devoted to this wonderful chapter. Note that it is the poor to whom this glad tidings is announced. How fitting that the poor should be clothed! They are set free from prison, and given new clothing, and sent on their way rejoicing.

"He hath sent Me ... to proclaim liberty to the captives, and the opening of the prison to them that are bound." Literally, He hath sent Me to cry to the captives, "Liberty!" and to the bound, "Deliverance!" The Hebrew word rendered "liberty" means, "a swift flight, a wheeling," as of a bird that flies in circles, wheeling in flight through the air, and hence is the term for the swallow. There can be no more perfect picture of absolute freedom than a swallow flying through the air, and this is just the freedom that Christ proclaims to all men. Every one who will, may be as free as a bird; free from sin and everything that is a hindrance to perfect service to God, and this freedom is ours to enjoy now. "Our soul is escaped as a bird out of the snare of the fowler; the snare is broken, and we are escaped." Ps. 124:7.

A Proclamation of Universal Liberty

Remember that this liberty is for all. The Lord sends His servant "to comfort all that mourn." The proclamation of liberty is to all that are bound. Christ has entered into the strong man's prison house and has bound the tyrant that had usurped authority over men, and has taken from him "all his armour wherein he trusted." "Forasmuch then as the children are partakers of flesh and blood, He also Himself likewise took part of the same; that through death He might destroy him that had the power of death, that is, the devil; and deliver them who through fear of death were all their lifetime subject to bondage." Heb. 2:14–15. Every prison door is open; every chain is broken; the captive has only to arise, and loose himself from the bands of his neck. Isa. 52:2. In Christ every soul has been given power to break loose from every sin, every evil habit, every inherited or acquired evil, no matter what its nature. He has given us His own freedom, and when that is said, nothing more can be added. It is yours to claim by faith. If you do not know the way out of the prison, even though the doors be open, – if you cannot find the door, – enquire of Christ, and He will reveal the way to you. He is the Way. Accept Him in His fullness; study the perfection of the manifestation of His life; yield to it; and then stand fast in the liberty wherewith Christ has made you free.

Who May Proclaim this Message?

One thing more, – the greatest of all, – and that is, Who is anointed to proclaim this message of freedom? "Christ," you say. True; but it was a carpenter's son, Himself a journeyman carpenter, who read the message to a company of His neighbors and acquaintances, and said: "This day is this Scripture fulfilled in your ears." He was sent by the Lord God with the message of freedom and comfort, and "He whom God hath sent speaketh the words of God;" and *vice versa*, every one who has received the word of God is sent. God has "reconciled us to Himself through Christ," and has "placed in us the word of reconciliation," so that we are ambassadors on behalf of Christ, as though God were beseeching by us instead of by Christ; so that we pray in Christ's stead, "Be ye reconciled to God." 2 Cor. 5:18–20.

The anointing is by the Spirit of God, and every one who turns at the reproofs of God, which are the way of life, has the Spirit poured out upon him, and the words of God made known to him (Prov. 1:23), and is therefore sent with the message. Remember also that these words were spoken to the Jews by the man Isaiah, nearly eight hundred years before Jesus read them in the synagogue at Nazareth; and they were spoken with burning lips, from a full heart. Isaiah was no actor, but felt every word that he uttered. He was not speaking something that meant nothing to him, and could not mean anything to anybody for hundreds of years. The soul liberty was for the people "in the days of Uzziah, Jotham, Ahaz, and Hezekiah;" and Isaiah, whose soul had been made joyful in God by the clothing of righteousness that he had received (Isa. 61:10) – the purging of his sin, and the taking away of his iniquity (Isa. 6:7), – was commissioned to proclaim it. So is every one who is willing to accept the anointing; for does not the message say to those who will hear, "Ye shall be named the Priests of the Lord: men shall call you the Ministers of our God?" Oh, it is glorious to be free, but that alone is small compared with the freedom to set others at liberty.

CHAPTER 75

GOD'S WATCHFULNESS AND SOLICITUDE FOR HIS PEOPLE

(Isa. 62:1–12, Lowth's Translation)

1. For Sion's sake I will not keep silence; and for the sake of Jerusalem I will not rest; until her righteousness break forth as a strong light; and her salvation, like a blazing torch.

2. And the nations shall see thy righteousness; and all the kings, thy glory; and thou shalt be called by a new name, which the mouth of Jehovah shall fix upon thee.

3. And thou shalt be a beautiful crown in the hand of Jehovah; and a royal diadem in the grasp of thy God.

4. No more shall it be said unto thee, Thou forsaken! Neither to thy land shall it be said any more, Thou desolate! But thou shalt be called, The object of My delight; and thy land, The wedded matron; for Jehovah shall delight in thee; and thy land shall be joined in marriage.

5. For as a young man weddeth a virgin, so shall thy Restorer wed thee; and as the bridegroom rejoiceth in his bride, so shall thy God rejoice in thee.

6. Upon thy walls, O Jerusalem, have I set watchmen all the day; and all the night long they shall not keep silence. O ye that proclaim the name of Jehovah!

7. Keep not silence yourselves, nor let Him rest in silence; until He establish, and until He render Jerusalem a praise in the earth.

8. Jehovah hath sworn by His right hand, and by His powerful arm; I will no more give thy corn for food to thine enemies; nor shall the sons of the stranger drink thy wine, for which thou hast laboured;

9. But they that reap the harvest shall eat it and praise Jehovah; and they that gather the vintage shall eat it in My sacred courts.

10. Pass ye, pass through the gates; prepare the way for the people! Cast ye up, cast up the causeway; clear it from the stones! Lift up on high a standard to the nations!

11. Behold, Jehovah hath thus proclaimed to the end of the earth: Say ye to the daughter of Sion, Lo thy Saviour cometh! Lo, His reward is with Him, and the recompense of His work before Him. And they shall be called, The Holy people, and redeemed of Jehovah;

12. And thou shalt be called, The much desired, the city unforsaken.

It is plainly to be seen that it is God who is speaking in this chapter. It is He who says that He will not hold His peace, nor keep silence until the righteousness of His people – all Jerusalem – breaks forth as a strong light. When we consider this, what comfort we find in the words. God has charged Himself with our case. He is interested in our behalf. Now since God so earnestly desires our righteousness, and has said that He will not relax His efforts to that end, what is there on earth that can keep us from being righteous, if we are but willing? God is almighty, and what He has promised, He is able also to perform. Let no one say that it is impossible to live without sin. With God all things are possible.

God saves us for service. He is not content with merely making us righteous, and so saving us, but He will have the righteousness shine forth for the enlightenment of others, and salvation go forth from His people, even as it does from Himself. What will take place when all the people see the righteousness and the salvation which He brings to us? – "Many shall see it and fear, and turn to the Lord." Ps. 40:1–3.

Compare verse 2 with Rev. 2:17. What intimate relationship and loving companionship this reveals! Two friends, who are much more than mere friends, often know each other by a name that is not known to others. It would be a breach of confidence, almost a sacrilege, if they used the name before others. It is a sign of their mutual love and confidence. So God takes His people into intimate relationship with Himself, and He so takes them not merely as a whole, but individually. He has a special name for each one, which is known only to Him and that one. His love is infinite, and therefore there is enough for each one. There will be no jealousy because another receives the same attention that we do. How precious are His thoughts toward us!

"The Lord taketh pleasure in His people; He will beautify the meek with salvation." Ps. 149:4. He will even make of them a crown of glory, and a royal diadem. Think of the exalted position to which God has determined to elevate His people: He will make them His crown of glory; they will be an adornment even to Him. What an incentive to walk worthy of the calling of God.

How many people there are who are called Forsaken. "Many there be which say of my soul, There is no help for him in God." Ps. 3:2. The devil has told many people that they have committed the unpardonable sin, and that God has forsaken them; and he has, sad to say, agents on earth, who repeat the words. But "the Lord will not cast off for ever." Lam. 3:31. "He that cometh to Me, I will in no wise cast out." John 6:37. "I will never leave thee nor forsake thee." Heb. 13:5. Whoever is oppressed by the thought that God has forsaken him, may know that He has not; because the fact that he feels sad over the supposed casting off, is proof that he does not wish to be separate from God; and it is only man that can effect any such separation. Thank God, the time is soon coming when there will be no possibility for anyone to call another Forsaken, for it will be apparent to all that God is in the midst of His people. But if we are ever to rejoice in God's salvation, we should do it now. God has not forsaken Zion. See Isa. 49:14–16. Therefore "cry out and shout, thou inhabitant of Zion; for great is the Holy One of Israel in the midst of thee." Isa. 12:6.

Watchmen have been set on the walls of Zion by God Himself. This is proof that He has not forsaken His people. It is the devil who would make people believe that God has forsaken them, because he knows that when they feel that they are out of God's care they fall an easy prey to him. But God says of His vineyard, – His people, – "Lest any hurt it I will keep it night and day." Isa. 27:3. So the watchmen whom He appoints, and whose duty it is to sound the alarm of danger, and also to announce glad tidings of good things, are not to hold their peace day nor night. They are the ones who are to "make mention of the Lord," that is, remind people of Him. To them He says: "Keep not silence yourselves, nor let Him rest in silence." "Take no rest, and give Him no rest," until He makes Jerusalem a praise in the whole earth, – until His people are saved, and made to dwell in the New Jerusalem, the capital of the new earth. How different God is from the unjust judge. See Luke 18:1–8. The unjust judge did not wish to be disturbed; he did not wish to have anybody – poor people, at least – come to him with a plea for help. But God, on the contrary, begs us to come to Him, and make known our troubles and needs. "Come any time, come day or night; yea, come both day and night, and do not let there be a minute's intermission, but keep making requests, even demands, of Me," is what God says. What a loving Father! Why will anybody be so distrustful as to go in want?

CHAPTER 76

THE MIGHTY SAVIOUR

(Isa. 63:1–19, Lowth's Translation)

1. *Chorus:* Who is this, that cometh from Edom? With garments deeply dyed from Botsra? This, that is magnificent in His apparel; marching on in the greatness of His strength? *Messiah:* I, who publish righteousness, and am mighty to save.

2. *Chorus:* Wherefore is Thine apparel red? And Thy garments, as of one that treadeth the wine vat?

3. *Messiah:* I have trodden the vat alone: and of the peoples, there was not a man with Me. And I trod them in Mine anger; and I trampled them in Mine indignation: and their life-blood was sprinkled upon My garments; and I have stained all My apparel.

4. For the day of vengeance was in My heart; and the year of My redeemed was come.

5. And I looked, and there was no one to help; and I was astonished, that there was no one to uphold, therefore Mine own arm wrought salvation for Me, and Mine indignation itself sustained Me.

6. And I trod down the peoples in Mine anger; and I crushed them in Mine indignation; and I spilled their life-blood on the ground.

7. The mercies of Jehovah will I record, the praise of Jehovah; according to all that Jehovah hath bestowed upon us: and the greatness of His goodness to the house of Israel! Which He hath bestowed upon them through His tenderness and great kindness.

8. For He said: Surely they are My people, children that will not prove false; and He became their Saviour in all their distress.

9. It was not an envoy, nor an angel of His presence, that saved them; through His love, and His indulgence, He Himself redeemed them; and He took them up, and He bare them, all the days of old.

10. But they rebelled, and grieved His Holy Spirit; so that He became their enemy; and He fought against them.

11. And He remembered the days of old, Moses His servant; how He brought them up from the sea, with the Shepherd of His flock: how He placed in his breast His Holy Spirit.

12. Making His glorious arm to attend Moses on his right hand in his march; cleaving the waters before them, to make Himself a name everlasting.

13. Leading them through the abyss, like a courser in the plain, without obstacle.

14. As the herd descendeth to the valley, the Spirit of Jehovah conducted them; so didst Thou lead Thy people, to make Thyself a name glorious.

15. Look down from heaven, and see, from Thy holy and glorious dwelling: Where is Thy zeal, and Thy mighty power; the yearning of Thy bowels, and Thy tender affections? are they restrained from us?

16. Verily, Thou art our Father; for Abraham knoweth us not, and Israel doth not acknowledge us. Thou, O Jehovah, art our Father: O deliver us for the sake of Thy name!

17. Wherefore, O Jehovah, dost Thou suffer us to err from Thy ways? To harden our hearts with the fear of Thee? Return for the sake of Thy servants; for the sake of the tribes of Thine inheritance.

18. It is little, that they have taken possession of Thy holy mountain; that our enemies have trodden down Thy sanctuary;

19. We have long been as those whom Thou hast ruled; who have not been called by Thy name.

The student certainly cannot fail to be struck with the life and energy of Lowth's translation of this chapter. It will be noticed that the responsive portion is made very clear by the way in which it is presented to the eye. A chorus of voices is represented as asking the questions, and that Christ is the One who answers them there cannot be the slightest doubt.

Verse 9 is translated so entirely different from the ordinary rendering, which is so well known, and which has given so much comfort to so many, that a few words of explanation are demanded. The difference is due simply to the fact that in this instance Lowth has followed the Septuagint, and not the Hebrew. Which is more in harmony with the original text, cannot be decided; but the close student will see that the verse as here translated is no less comforting than in our ordinary English versions, and that the two amount to the same thing in the end. The idea is that it was not to an angel standing in God's presence, no matter how near, that the salvation of Israel was committed, but that God Himself took up their case, and bore them. He Himself was their Saviour. This is of course Gospel truth, in perfect harmony with what is expressed in the words of Paul, spoken to the elders of Ephesus, concerning "the church of God, which He hath purchased with His own blood." Acts 20:28. In support of the thought conveyed by the rendering of the Septuagint, it may be noted that after God had said to Moses, "Behold, I send an angel before thee, to keep thee in the way, to bring thee into the place which I have prepared" (Ex. 23:20), Moses said, "See, Thou sayest unto me, Bring up this people; and Thou hast not let me know whom Thou wilt send with me," and God replied, "My presence [literally, "My face"] shall go with thee, and I will give thee rest." Ex. 33:12,14. The student will find profit and comfort in both translations, and need not trouble his mind as to which is nearest the original.

It seems strange that there ever should have been any mistaken idea as to the time of the application of this chapter; and there could not have been if people had merely held to the text. But a well known song has either impressed a false idea upon the minds of people, or else has given voice to a common idea, to such an extent that attention must be called to it. In the song, "Mighty to Save," the idea is conveyed that this passage describes the crucifixion on Calvary, and in response to the question, "Why is Thine apparel red?" the writer makes the Lord reply,

"With mercy fraught, Mine own arm brought salvation."

Now it is true that "His mercy endureth for ever," but the text says, "Mine own arm brought salvation unto Me; and *My fury*, it upheld Me. And I trod down the peoples in Mine anger, and made them drunk in My fury, and I poured out their life-blood on the ground." How a man could read enough of this chapter to be able to write the song referred to, and yet pass by, or deliberately pervert the words just quoted, so as to write it as he did, is a mystery.

If the student will compare the 34 chapter of Isaiah and Rev. 19:11–21, especially verses 13 and 15, with the verses in our lesson, there cannot be the slightest doubt as to what is referred to. It is nothing less than the Judgment of the last day – the time when the sinners who have persistently and willfully rejected the Lord meet their doom. The land of Idumea, Edom, is set as the representation of the whole earth. "The indignation of the Lord is upon all nations, and His fury upon all their armies:" "for the Lord hath a sacrifice in Bozrah, and a great slaughter in the land of Idumea." Isa. 34:2–6. "It is the day of the Lord's vengeance, and the year of recompenses for the controversy of Zion." Verse. 8; compare Isa. 63:4.

But notwithstanding the fact that this chapter unmistakably represents Christ as returning from the destruction of the wicked, we must not lose sight of the cross. It appears here, although this chapter by no means refers to Calvary. The cross of Christ is not a thing of a day: it covers all time from Paradise lost till Paradise restored, and then its effects continue through eternity. The second coming of Christ, to Judgment, is but the consummation of the crucifixion. He comes to save His people, and it is only by the cross that anybody can be saved. In the third chapter of Habakkuk we have the picture of Christ's triumph over His enemies, when He marches through the land in indignation, and threshes the heathen in anger (verse 12), and it is said, "Thou wentest forth for the salvation of Thy people." Verse 13. But for the second coming of Christ, the cross would have been endured on Calvary in vain; it would be incomplete. Every person may now – "today" – have a complete, full, and perfect salvation; yet salvation is not complete, not merely as regards the whole body of God's people, but as concerns individuals, until Christ comes. For in the first place, it is only by His coming that the saints of all ages can be with Him (John 14:1–3; 1 Thess. 4:13–18), and in the second place the last days are to be so full of peril for God's people, that only His sudden appearance will put a stop to the purpose of a wicked world to put them all to death.

The power of Christ's second coming is the power of the cross. In Hab. 3:4, margin, we read that in His coming to execute vengeance, "He had bright beams coming out of His side; and there was the hiding of His power." That side was pierced by the Roman spear, and from it flowed the blood and water of life; but that is His glory, and the power by which He saves His redeemed from all their foes. "Christ died for the ungodly," because He suffered all that the stubbornly impenitent will at last suffer. He was made to be sin for us, and in the cross of Christ we see the fate of the sinner. The destruction of the wicked as well as the salvation of the righteous, is in the cross, for both are parts of one thing. All the power and glory and awful majesty of the second coming of Christ are in the cross just now, to save whoever will come to it. Read all the references to the last Judgment, that you can find, think of the trump of God and the voice of the archangel, which shakes not only the earth so that the graves open, and the dead hear and come forth, but shakes heaven also, and then instead of trembling in terror at the thought of the future, rejoice in the knowledge that all this inconceivable power is at your disposal in the cross of Christ for present salvation. Those who have knowledge of, and look for, the second coming of the Lord, should be, and must be, the people who, above all other professed Christians on earth, magnify and rejoice in the power of the cross. It must be their constant theme, its grandeur and glory, its infinite and all-comprehensive greatness becoming more and more apparent as they near its consummation, until it alone fills their vision and their being.

It is impossible to go through the chapter, but whoever has read the first verses with the right sense will be able to read the rest more understandingly when he comes to them. Note that the arm of the

Lord, which works so mightily in the destruction of the wicked, is that with which he gathers the lambs, and carries them. Isa. 40:11. God Himself carries His people; even though they be gray-haired with age they are to Him still infants to be borne in His bosom. "Blessed are all they that put their trust in Him."

CHAPTER 77

THE REVELATION OF GOD

(Isa. 64:1–12, Lowth's Translation)

1. O! that Thou wouldst rend the heavens, that Thou wouldst descend; that the mountains might flow down at Thy presence!

2. As the fire kindleth the dry fuel; as the fire causeth the waters to boil; to make known Thy name to Thine enemies; that the nations might tremble at Thy presence.

3. When Thou didst wonderful things, which we expected not; Thou didst descend; at Thy presence the mountains flowed down.

4. For never have men heard, nor perceived by the ear, nor hath eye seen, a God beside Thee, who doeth such things for those that trust in Him.

5. Thou meetest with joy those who work righteousness; who in Thy ways remember Thee. Lo! Thou art angry; for we have sinned: because of our deeds; for we have been rebellious.

6. And we are all of us as a polluted thing; and like a rejected garment are all our righteous deeds; and we are withered way, like a leaf, all of us; and our sins, like the wind, have borne us away.

7. There is no one that invoketh Thy name; that rouseth him up to lay hold on Thee: therefore Thou hast hidden Thy face from us; and hast delivered us up into the hand of our iniquities.

8. But Thou, O Jehovah, Thou art our Father; we are the clay, and Thou hast formed us; we are all of us the work of Thy hands.

9. Be not wroth, O Jehovah, to the uttermost; nor for ever remember iniquity. Behold, look upon us, we beseech Thee; we are all Thy people.

10. Thy holy cities are become a wilderness; Sion is become a wilderness, Jerusalem is desolate.

11. Our glorious and holy temple, wherein our fathers praised Thee, is utterly burnt up with fire; and all the objects of our desire are become a devastation.

12. Wilt Thou contain Thyself at these things, O Jehovah? Wilt Thou keep silence, and still grievously afflict us?

The key-note of this lesson will be found in the fourth verse, a verse often quoted in the form in which it appears in 1 Cor. 2:9, and almost as often misunderstood. The common idea of the text robs it of all present, practical application, and consequently the reader finds no present help and comfort in it. He simply looks forward to the future, as to a time when God will reveal in the New Jerusalem things which nobody has ever had any conception of. It is true enough that God has prepared wondrous things for His people, to be revealed at the coming of Christ, which will infinitely surpass anything that human minds can think, or human tongues speak; but that is not at all what is referred to here.

Let us read 1 Cor. 2:9–10, as given in a most excellent translation. After having said, "We speak the wisdom of God," and then throwing in the observation that none of the princes of this world know it, the apostle repeats the thoughts in other words, saying, "We speak, as it is written, what no eye has seen, and no ear has heard, and what has not been conceived in any man's heart, – that which God has prepared for them that love Him. But God has revealed it to us by His Spirit; for the Spirit searcheth all things, even the depths of God." What is it, then, that the messengers of God make known? – It is God, as revealed in Christ the Wisdom of God. The Spirit searches the depths of God, in order to reveal Him to us in His uttermost perfection.

What about the things that God has prepared for them that love Him? What are they? – They are "the things of God," – "the deep things of God," – "for what man knoweth the things of a man, save the spirit of man which is in him? even so the things of God knoweth no man, but the Spirit of God." And the Spirit searcheth these deep things, to reveal them unto us. These things – God's works – His own character – He hath prepared for those who love

Him. Since the foundation of the world no people have ever seen any god besides Jehovah who "worketh for him that waiteth for Him." He gives to us Himself, and in Him all things consist. But *He is now*; He is from everlasting to everlasting, always the same. Jesus Christ is "the same yesterday, and today, and for ever." His name is I AM. And He has given Himself for us. Therefore all the things that God has prepared for us in Himself, – "above all that we ask or think," – are ours now. The gods of the nations are nothing; they are only the imaginations of men's hearts; and being nothing it is but natural that they should demand human works and human sacrifices. So all idol worship consists in what men can do. But God is everything, and therefore it is but natural that He should give, instead of receiving. No one can give Him anything, but He gives everything, and *He gives it now*. And why not? Now is the time when we need it most, and it is but in keeping with God's character, to give just when the gift is needed.

This revelation of God to man is in everything that He has made. Rom. 1:20: "The invisible things of Him since the creation of the world are clearly seen, being perceived through the things that are made, even His everlasting power and Divinity." There is no excuse for anybody's ignorance of God, "because that which may be known of God [namely His everlasting power and Divinity] is manifest in them; for God manifested it unto them." Verse 19. The true Light – the Word made flesh, the Word of life – "lighteth every man that cometh into the world." If any do not know the Lord, it is because their eyes are blinded to the light, so that they cannot see light in His light, and their ears are deaf to the sounds that mark His presence.

And that is just the case. God is near in every sunbeam, yet men do not perceive Him. His light is not light to them, because they take it as a matter of course. God has been doing wonderful things all our lives, and from the foundation of the world, yet He does them so constantly that men have become dead to all sense that anything at all is being done, and even men called wise discuss with childish gravity the question of whether or not miracles are wrought now. So the prophet, moved by the Spirit, wishes that the power of God might be manifested in a way to startle people out of their drowsy lack of perception, so that they could not help seeing. Let the heavens be rent, and the mountains be melted; let terrible things take place, "that the nations may tremble at Thy presence."

Yet even after the fullest possible revelation of God has been made, no human tongue can express, and no human ear can hear, and no human heart can conceive of or understand the things of God, wrought out in His own life for those who wait for Him. "No man can say that Jesus is the Lord, but by the Holy Ghost." 1 Cor. 12:3. No flesh and blood, not even that of Jesus of Nazareth, but the Spirit of God alone, can make known the truth that Jesus is the Christ, the Son of the living God. Matt. 16:16–17. "Wherefore henceforth know we no man after the flesh; yea, though we had known Christ after the flesh, yet now henceforth know we Him no more." 2 Cor. 5:16. Men may read the words of God, and see nothing in them: other men will read the same words, and by the Spirit will see infinity in them. Moreover, the thoughts of the Lord are great thoughts, "very deep," and no words that human tongues or pens can frame can express their fullness and depth. Yet God's Word reveals God in His fullness. Therefore in every word of God, in every manifestation of His presence, the spiritual man, who "discerneth all things," will discern far more than can possibly be seen by any natural eye, or understood by any ear. But know this, and do not forget it, that this deep meaning lies in the words themselves, and not outside of them. The Spirit is not opposed to the Word, because the Word is the instrument which the Spirit uses. The Holy Spirit is the anointing which makes people know (1 John 2:20), the eye salve that gives sight to the blind. Rev. 3:18. The one who has that Spirit dwelling in him, an abiding Presence, is a seer. He can see what others cannot see, and is often laughed at as a dreamer. But that is of no consequence. Some wonderful things have been made known in dreams. The important thing is to have that Spirit of truth, through the love of the truth, which brings God with all His power and gifts into the heart. The heart is thus cleansed from sin, and its possessor sees and knows God. Therefore give heed to the words, "Receive ye the Holy Ghost."

The prophet, speaking in behalf of all men, said to the Lord, Thou "hast delivered us up into the hand of our iniquities." Isa. 64:7. The Revision has it, Thou "hast consumed us by means of our iniquities," which amounts to the same thing. "His own iniquities shall take the wicked, and he shall be holden with the cords of his sin." Prov. 5:22. Whoever sins is simply laying up for himself "wrath against the day of wrath and revelation of the righteous judgments of God; who will render unto every man according to his deeds." Rom. 2:5–6. The stubbornly impenitent, who at last are "burned up" so that they become "as though they had not been," are consumed by their own sins. Sin is a canker; it is like rust, which eats up iron as surely as fire burns wood. Thus sin eats out the life of men, so that they are nothing but emptiness. The nothingness to which the sinner goes at the last, is only the open manifestation of what he was all the time of his life of sin. Christ, the righteousness of God, whose life cleanses us from all sin, brings into our hearts "all the fullness of God."

In verses 9–12 there is a truth that is very likely to be overlooked. There we read that the "holy cities are a wilderness, Zion is a wilderness, Jerusalem a desolation." But it was many years after the death of Isaiah before Jerusalem was besieged and taken, the temple destroyed, and the land made desolate by the carrying away of the people. Shall we say that the prophet spoke by anticipation? If so, then the same might be said of any other portion of Scripture, which speaks of things as already accomplished. Moreover, in that case, the prophecy would have been utterly meaningless to those to whom it was first spoken or written. No; in these verses we see that whatever is at any time said of the city of Jerusalem, and Zion, applies primarily to the people, since it is always the character of the people that determines the character of the city or country. When the Holy Spirit is not allowed to dwell in the hearts of the people, chaos fills them, even such as the whole earth presented before the Spirit of God hovered over it. And since men are earth's rulers, the land goes to ruin with the people. Moreover human beings are God's temples, and therefore Zion may truthfully be said to be a wilderness when the hearts of men are a wilderness of sin. The earth is under the curse solely on man's account, and it will be made new again only by the same power that makes men new, and by the working of that power in them.

CHAPTER 78

THE GLORIOUS INHERITANCE

(Isa. 65:1–25, Lowth's Translation)

1. I am made known to those that ask not for Me; I am found of those that sought Me not: I have said, Behold Me, here I am, to the nations which never invoked My name;

2. I have stretched out My hands all the day to a rebellious people, who walk in an evil way, after their own devices.

3. A people who provoke Me to My face continually; sacrificing in the gardens, and burning incense on the tiles;

4. Who dwell in the sepulchres, and lodge in the caverns; who eat the flesh of the swine; and the broth of abominable meats is in their vessels:

5. Who say: Keep to thyself; come not near unto me, for I am holier than thou. These kindle a smoke in My nostrils, a fire burning all the day long.

6. Behold, this is recorded in writing before Me: I will not keep silence, but will certainly requite;

7. I will requite unto their bosom their iniquities; and the iniquities of their fathers together, saith Jehovah: Who burnt incense on the mountains, and dishonoured Me on the hill; yea, I will pour into their own bosom the full measure of their former deeds.

8. Thus saith Jehovah: As when one findeth a good grape in the cluster; And sayeth Destroy it not; for a blessing is in it; so will I do for the sake of My servants; I will not destroy the whole.

9. So will I bring forth from Jacob a seed; and from Judah an inheritor of My mountain; and My chosen shall inherit the land; and My servants shall dwell there.

10. And Sharon shall be a fold for the flock, and the valley of Achor a resting for the herd; for My people, who have sought after Me.

11. But ye, who have deserted Jehovah; and have forgotten My holy mountain; who set in order a table for Gad; and fill out a libation to Meni:

12. You will I number out of the sword; and all of you shall bow down to the slaughter. Because I have called, and ye answered not; I spake, and ye would not hear: but ye did that which is evil in My sight; and that in which I delighted not, ye chose.

13. Wherefore thus saith the Lord Jehovah: Behold, My servants shall eat, but ye shall be famished; Behold, My servants shall drink, but ye shall be thirsty; Behold, My servants shall rejoice, but ye shall be confounded;

14. Behold, My servants shall sing aloud, for gladness of heart; but ye shall cry aloud, for grief of heart; and in the anguish of a broken spirit shall ye howl.

15. And ye shall leave your name for a curse to My chosen; and the Lord Jehovah shall slay you; and His servants shall He call by another name.

16. Whoso blesseth himself up the earth shall bless himself in the God of truth. And whoso sweareth upon the earth shall swear by the God of truth. Because the former provocations are forgotten, and because they are hidden from Mine eyes.

17. For, behold, I create new heavens and a new earth; and the former ones shall not be remembered, neither shall they be brought to mind any more.

18. But ye shall rejoice in the age to come, which I create; for lo! I create Jerusalem a subject of joy, and her people of gladness;

19. And I will exult in Jerusalem, and rejoice in My people. And there shall not be found any more therein the voice of weeping, and the voice of a distressful cry;

20. No more shall there be an infant short-lived; nor an old man who hath not fulfilled his days; for he that dieth at an

hundred years, shall die a boy; and the sinner that dieth at an hundred years, shall be deemed accursed.

21. And they shall build houses, and shall inhabit them; and they shall plant vineyards, and shall eat the fruit thereof.

22. They shall not build, and another inhabit; they shall not plant, and another eat; for as the days of a tree shall be the days of My people; and they shall wear out the works of their own hands.

23. My chosen shall not labour in vain; neither shall they generate a short-lived race: for they shall be a seed blessed of Jehovah, they, and their offspring with them.

24. And it shall be, that before they call I will answer; they shall be ye speaking, and I shall have heard.

25. The wolf and the lamb shall feed together; and the lion shall eat straw like the ox; but as for the serpent, dust shall be his food. They shall not hurt, neither shall they destroy, in all My holy mountain, saith Jehovah.

This chapter is naturally divided into two portions, the first sixteen verses showing who are the true Israel, and that no particular race or nation constitute God's people, but that they are gathered out one by one from "all nations, and kindreds and people, and tongues;" while verses 17–25 tell of the new earth, in which "the righteous nation that keepeth the truth" will dwell throughout eternity.

In order to understand the first two verses, we have only to read Rom. 10:19–21. From those verses, taken in connection with what precedes, namely, that the sound of the Gospel has gone to the ends of the earth, we learn that the Gentiles are referred to by the words, "I am inquired of by them that asked not for Me; I am found of them that sought Me not," and that the "rebellious people" to whom God has stretched out His hands all the day is Israel after the flesh. With the inspired comment to guide us, we can have no difficulty in reading the chapter, for in verses 3–7 we have a picture of the Jewish people, who prided themselves upon being God's people, no matter what abominations they committed. The fact that their ancestors had been the objects of special blessings, in the deliverance from Egypt, and subsequently, and that they had the law, was their boast, although they did not keep the law. Rom. 2:17–23. They thought themselves too holy to associate with the uncircumcised heathen; but God has shown that a circumcised heathen is no better than an uncircumcised one, and that it is faith and obedience that distinguishes the true Israelite from the heathen.

Moment by moment the Christian lives. If we gain a victory today, that is no proof that we shall gain another tomorrow. It is a proof of the power and goodness of God, who ever lives to bless; but if we reap the benefit of His mercy in the future, it can only be by continual yielding and consecration. Our breath moment by moment is an evidence that God is with us; but the breath that we breathed yesterday will not profit us today; we need a fresh supply. Much less can we be benefited by that which somebody else has breathed. So for a person to base his confidence on the fact that he belongs to a denomination that at some time in the past had marked evidences of the presence and power of God, is to build his hope for bread today on money that was spent last year. It is a grand thing to have entrusted to us the ark in which are the oracles of God; but we may have this and still be accursed captives of sin. Far better is it to have our own hearts and temples of the Holy Spirit of truth.

Everybody who knows anything about the Bible knows that it forbids the use of swine's flesh: but nothing in the Bible shows so clearly how God regards the filthy beast, and those who take it into the most intimate relation to themselves, than the passing reference in verses 4 and 5. There the eating of swine's flesh is classed by the Lord with the most abominable idolatry. The hog is one of the most filthy and disgusting of animals, gross in its habits, and the imparter of grossness to all who have anything whatever to do with it; yet there is no other animal in the world that is in such demand as food for men. In this we see how God's order has been perverted. Satan has done his best to reverse every design of God, and among the majority of mankind he has succeeded for even thousands of professed Christians, to say nothing of non-professors, seem to be bent on making their religious practices as far different as possible from what God ordained. When Satan induced men to worship devils instead of God, while still professing to serve God, he led them to sacrifice swine upon their altars, in contradistinction to the clean and innocent animals that were sacrificed in the worship of God. It is eminently fitting that the hog should be used by those whose lives are devoted to the service of Satan; but that men and women who profess to worship the God of heaven, and to be guided and controlled by the pure life of Jesus Christ, should take the filthy animal into their bodies is a part of the mystery of iniquity. Everybody is shocked at the impiety of Antiochus Epiphanes, who defiled the temple of God in Jerusalem by offering hogs upon its altar, yet that temple at best was only a figure; think then how much greater sacrilege it is to offer up the swine in our own bodies, which are the real temples of Jehovah.

Concerning the heathen gods mentioned in verse 11, one ancient writer has made the following sensible comment, which may save a great deal of useless speculation: "Why should we be solicitous about it? It appears sufficiently, from the circumstance, that they were false gods, either stars or some other natural object, or a mere fiction. The Holy Scriptures did not deign to explain more clearly what these objects of idolatrous worship were, but chose rather that the memory of the knowledge of them should be utterly abolished. And God be praised that they are so totally abolished that we are now quite at a loss to know what and what sort of things they were."

Just why Lowth has "a good grape" instead of "new wine," in verse 8 it is impossible to tell, for the ordinary Hebrew text most certainly has it as in our common version. The lesson, however, is not materially affected by the difference. As Lowth has it, it shows how God does not take people in bulk, but as individuals. Just as we will pick out a single good grape from a cluster of unripe or decayed fruit, so God selects His people out from the world, or even from among churches and societies that have the name of belonging to Him, until Israel is composed of those in every nation and class in society, who are without guile. This is evidently the lesson to be drawn from verse 8; but there is an incidental lesson in it as rendered in our version, that may be noted. The new wine is found in the cluster, and not in the fermenting vat. And a blessing is in it. When we eat the fruits of the earth in the natural state in which God

534

Himself prepares them for us, or as near it as possible, and recognize God in the gift, we get the blessing of His own life. God's life is most holy and precious, and we should be most careful not to pervert it or misuse it. The stream of life from the throne of God is perfectly pure, but it may become contaminated by the abuse of men; therefore we should be solicitous to go to the fountain head, and take the unperverted life directly from God Himself.

The great lesson from the first section of the chapter is the wondrous love and patience and forbearance of God. He loves those who love Him not. He calls for those who have not inquired for Him, and seeks out those who have never given Him a thought. And more than this, He is not easily offended when slighted and deliberately rejected. He not only seeks out those who are ignorant of Him, but He bears long with the waywardness of those who have known His goodness and have not appreciated it. To Israel He saith, "All day long I have stretched forth My hands unto a disobedient and gain-saying people." Wonderful love! Oh that it may always be ours. It may be; for the Holy Spirit so freely given to us, if received, sheds abroad in our hearts that love that "suffereth long, and is kind," "seeketh not her own, is not easily provoked, thinketh no evil." It is not ours by nature, but grace can give us the Divine nature, of which it is an attribute.

In striking contrast with the sorrow and anguish incident to this present evil world, and the sure destruction that is to be the fate of all who are united to it, is the state of the servants of the Lord. The new heavens and the new earth will obliterate from the mind every thought of the want and the suffering endured in this earth. And as this thought is impressed on our minds in reading this description of the joy and peace of the world to come, let us not forget that God has already placed the world to come in subjection to man, and that we may now taste its power. Just now, in this time of hardship and tribulation, in the midst of all this world's lack, it is ours by the Spirit to know "the riches of the glory of His inheritance in the saints." Eph. 1:18. God has placed eternity in our hearts, so that beginning right now we may be glad and rejoice for ever in that which He creates; for "if any man be in Christ there is a new creation; the old things are passed away; behold, they are become new. But all things are of God." 2 Cor. 5:17–18.

Compare verses 17–19 with Rev. 21:1–5; and there can be no question as to the application. The Lord is not here speaking figuratively of some mere local work to be done in one nation, but is speaking of the real change to come over all the earth, and He uses language as plain and as perfectly adapted to our comprehension as possible.

Life in the world to come will be very real. Strangely enough, the term "real life" conveys to most people a sense of hardness and bitter suffering. How sad it is that so many know of no joy except in imagination, and find no happiness except in dreams. But the real – that which God creates – is infinitely beyond the wildest flights of human imagination. Imagination is not needed by the servants of God, for the real brings to them wonders of joy and happiness and knowledge that have never been conceived of by any human heart. There will be nothing vague or misty or shadowy in the new earth, but people will associate together just as in this world, only with no trace of sin. It is sin that has made this earth what it is, and all the change that is needed to make it new is to remove sin from it. "They shall build houses, and inhabit them; they shall plant vineyards and eat of the fruit of them." There will be possessions in the land, but no buying and selling, for everything will be free as the gift of God. "All mine is thine" will be the motto of every inhabitant. That which socialists vainly dream of, and infinitely more, is assured to men through the Gospel.

"And I heard a great voice out of heaven saying, Behold the tabernacle of God is with men, and He will dwell with them, and they shall be His people, and God Himself shall be with them, and be their God. And God shall wipe away all tears from their eyes; and there shall be no more death, neither sorrow nor crying, neither shall there be any more pain; for the former things are passed away." Rev. 21:3–4. From this we know that verse 20 of our lesson chapter marks the transition stage. Remember that the final destruction of the wicked, and the renewal of the earth, does not take place until a thousand years after the appearing of Christ and the first resurrection (see Rev. 20), during which time the saints have been reigning with Christ in the New Jerusalem in heaven. Consequently the sinner an hundred years old, who dies accursed, is but a boy in comparison with them. Seventy years is considered full age in this life, yet the sinner who goes to destruction at the age of a hundred years is compared with the saints reigning in glory, as one who is cut off in early boyhood. For from the time of Christ's coming there will not be among the saints such a thing as a short-lived infant, but all will live an endless life; yet the thousands of years upon a man's head will not make him old, nor diminish the freshness of youth.

A tree is one of the best representations of continual youthful life, and the tree of life is the model for all trees. Such will be the life of all God's people. They will live for ever, as long as the tree of life, to which they have free access, exists. Their life will be that of God. Do not be misled by the words in Lowth's translation, "they shall wear out the works of their hands." The idea is not that any work of their hands will become so worn as to be thrown aside, like the garments now worn, but that they shall enjoy themselves. They will ever live to enjoy their own work, and will not die and leave it to others. "They shall not labour in vain, nor bring forth for trouble; for they are the seed of the blessed of the Lord, and their offspring with them."

We invite you to view the complete
selection of titles we publish at:

www.TEACHServices.com

or write or email us your praises,
reactions, or thoughts about this
or any other book we publish at:

TEACH Services, Inc.
P.O. Box 954
Ringgold, GA 30736

info@TEACHServices.com

www.ingramcontent.com/pod-product-compliance
Lightning Source LLC
Chambersburg PA
CBHW060316100426
42812CB00003B/791